CENTER FOR ORIGINS RESEARCH

Issues

IN CREATION

A Critical Realist's Theological Method: Returning the Bible and Biblical Theology to be the Framer for Theology and Science

Douglas W. Kennard
Houston Graduate School of Theology

Center for Origins Research Issues in Creation
Number 6

WIPF & STOCK · Eugene, Oregon

A CRITICAL REALIST'S THEOLOGICAL METHOD
Returning the Bible and Biblical Theology to be the Framer for Theology and Science

Wipf & Stock
An imprint of Wipf and Stock Publishers
199 W. 8th Avenue, Suite 3
Eugene OR, 97401
www.wipfandstock.com

ISBN: 978-1-62032-716-6

Manufactured in the U.S.A.

Abstract

A Critical Realist's Theological Method explores a systematic theology method that is grounded in a critical realist epistemology in the wake of Roy Sellars, A. H. Strong, Stuart Hackett, Alister McGrath, Imre Lakatos, and Nancey Murphy that will justify the nesting of science within its methodological branches. Kennard surveys each philosophical and traditional theology approach for their precise contributions and their limitations in order to set out a method for theology and science. Such a critical realist approach has especially become acclaim for working in the field of historical Jesus studies as advocated by N. T. Wright, James Dunn, and Dale Allison. Kennard extends this method to interpretation in a Thiselton-Ricoeur hermeneutic that can fund good exegesis and Biblical theology. This same approach is then extended to a descriptive Biblical theology method in the wake of George Ladd, James Dunn, Geerhardus Vos, and John Goldingay. This Biblical theology method is illustrated by wisdom literature, the traditional reef of the discipline and then developed for the contributions made toward a systematic theology approach as Johann Gabler had originally envisioned funding systematics from Biblical theology. With most of the content for systematic theology coming from inspired Scripture contextualized to the reader's setting, the subtitle for the book identifies the theological goal intended, *Returning the Bible and Biblical Theology to be the Framer for Theology and Science*. This Biblical trajectory through a critical realist method is applied in several ways that fund systematic theology and several disciplines of science. For example, an exegesis of Biblical and second temple creation texts frame the possibilities within which science is able to nest and contribute consistent to this Biblicism. These same insights of Biblical theology frame bio-ethics and an integration of psychology and theology setting out a transactional model for counseling and psychological recovery. This same method explores a framework to fund community and personal work environment, which sets out a communal context for hoping how the discipline of theology can be practiced and cultivated. This *Critical Realist's Theological Method* explains the approach that Kennard has already demonstrated as a theoretician in *The Relationship Between Epistemology, Hermeneutics, Biblical Theology and Contextualization* (Mellen, 1999) and as a practitioner in 1) integrating philosophy, physics, and theology in *The Classical Christian God* (Mellen, 2002), 2) integrating Biblical theology, second temple Jewish literature, and systematic theology in *Messiah*

Jesus: Christology in His Day and Ours (Peter Lang, 2008) and with Marv Pate in *Deliverance Now and Not Yet: The New Testament and the Great Tribulation* (Peter Lang, 2003, 2005), and 3) coursework as Professor of New Testament, Theology, and Philosophy at Houston Graduate School of Theology.

Table of Contents

1. Introduction

This is a book about a critical realist theological method. So this book will discuss exegetical method, theological method, philosophical method and scientific method in an attempt at providing a unified method heavily informed by Biblical theology, in which theology, science and philosophy can work and be integrated.

"Critical Realist Theology" are each terms that need to be defined. By "theology" I mean *the study of God and His relationship to the creation.* By "realism" I mean that *objects have an existence independent of the mind,* so that my mind's task is to try to approximate these objects (God and creation) accurately corresponding to how these objects are in fact. That is, God is a Being which theology is trying to describe. Likewise, the creation includes stars, planets, particles, and animals which science describes. In "Critical realism" our *knowledge of God and the creation is partial but can be true, by using both subjective and objective tools for knowledge.* In this way, theology and science become a map or a model that corresponds to the truth. As such, theology and science are made up of successive paradigms which bring us closer approximations of the real God and truth.

Philosophically, critical realism emerges in the wake of Descartes, Locke and Kant. Descartes argued that the real world and God were objects available as certain knowledge to our own mind, a knowledge built *by deduction upon immovable foundations.* In this, our ideas are distinct from the objects which our ideas approximate. Locke granted simple ideas were known directly *by experience* but more complex ideas like a concept of the Christian God would be *known reasonably* by combining these simple ideas into a complex idea. This Lockian confidence has been championed by a group of evangelicals which could be called commonsense realists. In contrast to them, Immanuel Kant proposed a critical idealism, which claimed that one's knowledge is certain knowledge of the mind, but because the mind functions within transcendental categories and forms, our knowledge can't claim to be of the real world (things in themselves). In reaction to these options in 1916, Roy Sellars proposed the view of critical realism.[1] In chapter two, "The Relationship of Philosophy, Theology and Science" I survey a range of philosophical contributions and construct a positive nuanced critical realist use of philosophy as it contributes to theology and scientific methodology. In that chapter, I argue that philosophy's role in theology

1 Roy Sellars, *Critical Realism* (Chicago: Rand McNally Co., 1916).

should be streamlined to: 1) helping us be precise and coherent in our thought (as a critical realist), within a Renaissance humanism program of "back to the Christian textual roots" which Biblical theology largely provides, 2) helping us think through ramifications of our commitments and the relationships this identifies us with, and 3) providing any additional basic beliefs that are strongly warranted, but do not counter those of Biblical theology. In my version of critical realism, I follow a moderate foundational Lakatos' scientific method[2] which deductively develops some concepts of God and inductively develops theology from Biblical theology and philosophy of religion. The philosophical aspects of this method are described in the next chapter.

This philosophical method can be briefly explained by a model of a tree that identifies that those techniques with greater certainty or plausibility should be given privilege of preferential place in framing worldview, theology, and science. Especially see the next chapter for historical development and evaluation of this briefly stated model. I ground the place of my worldview with moderate foundational roots from: 1) rationalism (e.g., law of identity, law of noncontradiction, "I think therefore I am," and performative language), 2) empiricism (like immediate sensations), and 3) incorrigible (basic beliefs). I allow certain knowledge of mathematical derivation and rationalism (e.g., ontological argument) to frame the trunk of my epistemic tree. The important weight bearing branches are then framed by empiricism which further confirms itself by rational argument (e.g., cosmological argument, teleological argument) and by Charles Peirce's pragmatism.[3] Preferred among this empirically based Peircian pragmatism is a hermeneutical spiral of well attested peer reviewed exegesis of Scripture because it possesses divine authority and the text's interpretive thrust is within the text itself giving it

2 Imre Lakatos, "Falsification and the Methodology of Scientific Research Programs," in *Criticism and the Growth of Knowledge. Proceedings of the International Colloquium in the Philosophy of Science, London, 1965.* edited by Imre Lakatos and Alan Musgrave (Cambridge: Cambridge University Press, 1970), pp. 91–195; "Proofs and Refutations," *British Journal for the Philosophy of Science* 14(1963-64): 1–25, 120–39, 221–43, 296–342; *Problems in the Philosophy of Science* (Amsterdam: North-Holland Pub. Co., 1968); "History of Science and Its Rational Reconstructions," in *Boston Studies in the Philosophy of Science*, vol. 8. edited by R. Buck and R. S. Cohen (Dordrecht: D. Reidel Publishing Co., 1971); R. S. Cohen, P. K. Feyerabend and M. W. Wartofsky, *Essays in Memory of Imre Lakatos. Boston Studies in the Philosophy of Science*, vol. 39 (Dordrecht: D. Reidel Publishing Co., 1976); Paul Feyerabend, "Imre Lakatos," *The British Journal for the Philosophy of Science* 26(1975):1–18; Ian Hacking, "Imre Lakatos's Philosophy of Science," *The British Journal for the Philosophy of Science* 30(1979): 381–402.

3 The Collected Papers of Charles Sanders Peirce, ed. Charles Hartshorne and Paul Weiss (Cambridge: Harvard University Press, 1966); Charles Peirce essays on pragmatism that are particularly helpful include: "The Fixation of Belief," Popular Science Monthly 12(Nov., 1877): 1–15, and "How to Make Our Ideas Clear," Popular Science Monthly 12(Jan., 1878): 286–302.

a distinct edge over empirical observation of other media (cf. chapters 3–7). The peer review aspect of exegesis, theology, and science reflect some of the corporate aspects of critical realism (cf. chapters 8 and 12). This priority of peer reviewed exegesis would insist on theology and science to be nested within Biblicism. So a divinely inspired creation account should be given preferential place in framing issues of origins and a peer reviewed warranted exposition expressing those Biblical sentiments should as well (cf. chapters 9 and 10). Close behind this in credibility is peer reviewed Peircian pragmatically tested empirical science. Of course tentative exegesis and promising but not verified Peircian pragmatic science should be held more tentatively. Thus warranted science can affect the exegesis of texts, such as within a Copernican solar system the Biblical phrases of the "sun rises and sets" should be understood phenomenologically as that of appearance while the earth spins on its axis and revolves around the sun. When tentativeness occurs within theology and science, it should move the research program within its discipline to a more peripheral place of the medium branches of the tree, and should be governed by a Lakatos' method with its sophisticated falsification. Smaller more tentative branches can be governed by William James pragmatism,[4] which should fit within and not contradict the already placed warranted peer reviewed exegesis, theology and science. Even Deweyan pragmatism could be given some place among non-moral twigs of the tree that do not contradict those branches framed by epistemology, exegesis, theology and science. Examples of James and Dewey pragmatism contributing within a Biblically framed integration of psychology and theology are provided in the chapters eleven and twelve. Peripheral place of small twigs and leaves should be given to phenomenological, aesthetic, intuitional, and existential strategies. None of these peripheral options should displace, nor be permitted to overrule the warranted peer reviewed exegesis, theology and science. However, some of the contributions in this peripheral area can be quite significant. For example, my phenomenological commitment to be involved with Boy Scouts with my sons has certainly colored my life in a major way. These peripheral areas of my epistemic tree's canopy also provide a sense of the whole big picture and vitality, which are very important for life.

In a context where evangelical theology tends to be proposed within commonsense realism, there are some critical realist theologians who have proposed a nuanced approach toward God, which admits to subjectivity from one's contexts and point of view. For example, William G. T. Shedd acknowledged progressiveness within the discipline of theology that would be characterized as a discipline-wide critical realism when he wrote, "The first investigator is not so likely to strike upon the

4 William James, *The Will to Believe and Other Essays in Popular Philosophy* (New York: Longmans, Green & Co., 1897), ch. 1 "The Will to Believe."

intrinsic constitution of a thing as the last one, because he has not the light of previous inquiries. Methods of investigation are continually undergoing correction and modification, and are thus brought closer to the organization of the object."[5] With the discipline of theology developing, theology should not be thought of as a static authoritative tradition. My chapter three on "The Role of Tradition in Theology" examines the changing concept and authority of *tradition* through the history of the church to advocate a Biblical theology tradition, which especially respects a scholarly engagement of the Biblical text as the best means of accessing God's revealed authority for theology. The chapter illustrates the changing nature of theology by examining how each traditional shift developed a shifting concept of trinity. Chapters two and three (Philosophical Method and Tradition) are attempts to contribute to history of doctrine, especially on the category of theological methodology.[6] To help sensitize my students in methodological issues, I use these chapters as readings in my courses on history of doctrine, current trends in theology, and theological methods.

Among evangelicals of these earlier days perhaps only A. H. Strong opted for a more nuanced personal critical realist position. Strong affirms that "the laws of our thought are laws of God's thought and that the results are normally conducted thinking with regard to God correspond to the objective reality."[7] At the same time he conceded that "all knowledge is relative to the knowing agent; that is what we know, we know not as it is objectively but only as it is related to our senses and faculties."[8]

Moving to our contemporary day, Alister McGrath presents theology as a critical realist. He identifies his method as an empirically based pragmatic realism and when he adds mathematical derivation to it, he calls this method, "critical realism."[9] In critical realism, "reality is apprehended by the human mind which attempts to express and accommodate that reality as best it can with the tools at its disposal-such as mathematical formulae or mental models."[10] He sees that empirically based pragmatism is the foundation for this realism in the natural

5 William G. T. Shedd, *Dogmatic Theology* (Grand Rapids: Zondervan, n.d.), vol. 1, p.4, Ch. 1, sect. 1.

6 E.g., Louis Berkhof, *The History of Christian Doctrines* (Grand Rapids: Baker, 1937), pp. 37–82; J. N. D. Kelly, *Early Christian Doctrines* (San Francisco: Harper San Francisco, 1978), pp. 3–82.

7 A. H. Strong, *Systematic Theology* (3 vols.: Philadelphia: The Judson Press, 1907), vol. 1, p. 10.

8 A. H. Strong, *Systematic Theology*, 1:10.

9 Alister McGrath, *A Scientific Theology: Reality* (Grand Rapids: Eerdmans, 2002), vol. 2, especially identifying himself as a critical realist, pp. xv-xvi, 123–244, and especially developing his view on p. 188. Bernard Lonergan presents a similar analysis in "Cognitional Structure," *Collection: Papers by Bernard Lonergan* (Toronto: University of Toronto, 1988), pp. 205–21 and *Method in Theology* (London: Darton, Longman and Todd, 1972), p. 238.

10 Alister McGrath, *A Scientific Theology: Reality*, vol. 2, p. 195.

sciences.[11] He illustrates it several times over, especially in physics. He then justifies this realism as against conventionalist approaches, which would be either anti-realist, theory dependent, or indebted to James' pragmatism. He develops a critical realism that engages the world at a variety of levels, each evaluated for its clarity and predictability. He extends this scientific method to theology as an attempt to ground theology as a scientific discipline with a critical realist methodology.

This critical realist approach has been appropriated into contemporary hermeneutics by moderate evangelicals working within historical Jesus studies. These critical realist interpreters wish to express critical realism's *hermeneutical spiral* with precision and find value in allowing epistemic categories to inform hermeneutical ones.[12] That is, the textual data is observed by interpreter, such that they float a proposal for the meaning of a text that is then checked by comparing it to the details present in the text itself. Then the process is repeated drawing closer and closer to what the text actually says in itself. For example, N. T. Wright identifies his form of critical realism.

> This is a way of describing the process of 'knowing' that acknowledges the *reality of the thing known, as other than the knower* (hence 'realism'), while also fully acknowledging that the only access we have to this reality lies along the spiraling path of *appropriate dialog or conversation between the knower and the thing known* (hence 'critical').[13]

James Dunn affirms this approach preferring to call it a *dialog* with the text.[14] Dunn warns us about the parameters of this critical realist dialog with the text.

> The point is that without the interpreter's openness to being addressed by the text, the interpreter can scarcely hope to

11 Alister McGrath, *A Scientific Theology: Reality*, vol. 2, pp. 257, 174–175.

12 Kennard, *The Relationship Between Epistemology, Hermeneutics, Biblical Theology and Contextualization* (Lewiston: Edwin Mellen Press, 1999), pp. 57–58, 124–25, 133–34; other examples regularly occur at the November AAR/SBL meeting.

13 N. T. Wright, *The New Testament and the People of God* (Minneapolis: Fortress Press, 1992), pp. 31–46 and especially p. 35 here with Wright's emphasis. Robert Stewart ("N. T. Wright's Hermeneutic: An Exploration: Part 1 and 2," *Churchman*, 117[2003]:153–175, 235–266, especially p. 154) wrongly identifies Wright as affirming, "one can never have knowledge of the thing-in-itself," which more Jamesian or Kuhnian critical realists do affirm. However, Wright's historical Jesus work identifies him as more Peircian in trying to obtain the real historical Jesus to which the evidence points, when approached with scientific enquiry. Another example is Dale Allison who specifically identifies with Imre Lakatos' version of critical realism (*Constructing Jesus: Memory, Imagination, and History* [Grand Rapids: Baker, 2010], p. 87).

14 James Dunn, *Jesus Remembered* (Grand Rapids: Eerdmans, 2003), pp. 110–111.

> avoid abusing the text. Unless the text is at least in some sense, allowed to set its own agenda, it is questionable whether it is being heard at all.[15]

This critical realist approach to hermeneutics will positively be developed in my chapter "A Thiselton-Ricoeur Hermeneutic," so that we might gain sensitivity to the agenda that the text sets for itself. In this chapter I positively present the contributions from precise hermeneutics of empirically grounded pragmatism, existentialism, and contextualization. At times it is helpful to delineate an approach from alternatives that bear some resemblance. The chapter on "Biblical Authority" examines other close hermeneutical alternatives in our hermeneutical context and clarifies a process of accessing the divine authoritative message among the cacophony of rivals. The guiding strand through the forest in this chapter is in a critical realist's engagement with text as the priority in its context. That is, other approaches that deviate from *text in context Biblical authority* may be interesting but they depart from the divinely authoritative message.

A critical realist theology combines philosophy, historical theology, exegesis and Biblical theology in a particular temporal and cultural context. Each of the chapters of this book focuses on one of these sources and explores issues related to a sensitive warranted inclusion of this area as it contributes to theology. The context within which I operate is provided by chapters two, three, five and eight. I find it helpful to briefly point out the landscape so that my students might better understand the rationale for my path. My positive program is evident in the following chapters: 1) the critical realist section of chapter two, 2) the Biblical theology section of chapter three, 3) chapter four "A Thiselton-Ricoeur Hermeneutic," 4) chapter six "The Reef of Biblical Theology," and 5) chapter seven "Biblical theology Affecting Systematics."

The particular emphasis which I have in my critical realist theology stresses: 1) the Biblical text as supremely, divinely authoritative, and 2) Biblical theology as the main forum to convey that authoritative message into theology. My chapter six "The Reef of Biblical Theology" explains my method for a descriptive Biblical theology. In this, I generalize the content which I construct from inducing exegetical meaning from multiple Biblical texts and Biblical author's works as a whole. I illustrate this methodology in wisdom literature, which tends to be particularly difficult for most attempts of Biblical theology to handle. So my proposal provides a unique resolution for these difficult areas, showing that the easier areas can also be resolved by the same method. Following up on this methodology for doing Biblical theology, I propose a strategy for transforming Systematic theology by these gems. In chapter seven "A

15 Dunn, *Jesus Remembered,* p. 124.

Biblical Theology Affecting Systematics," I explain how such a Biblical theology approach can be incorporated within systematic theology and the gain that this is for systematics in increasingly deep Biblicism. This chapter proposes five methodological assumptions:

1. Use Biblical terms in the Biblical way.
2. Make sure that systematic theology is deeply Biblical in its concerns.
3. Theologically reflect the thrust of the genre utilized.
4. The interpretation of Biblical texts needs to be done from an informed perspective within the possibilities and that which is likely within the historical cultural context of the text under examination.
5. Whatever is Biblical should be reflected within systematic theology.

Using these assumptions, I provide practical suggestions for constructing systematic theology to reflect the Biblical theological thrust, genres and practical concerns of the Biblical text.

Since all theology is done within a context, it is important to explore the contextualization process. Chapter eight analyzes levels of culture and contextual engagement to surface suggestions for community contextualization of theology. This chapter contextualizes this method to that of American evangelicalism early in the twenty-first century. Suggestions from each area sensitize us to issues of contextualizing Biblical theology in a critical realist manner to our setting.

Sometimes examples help. I have included four research programs: 1) Chapter nine "Creation and Fall,", provides a Biblical theology foundation for theology and science from Biblical texts about creation and curse (especially of death). It showcases the Biblical theology agenda being represented by using major passages and their thrust, which I champion as part of my method in chapter seven. 2) Chapter ten "A Biblical Anthropology Funding Bio-Ethics," provides a profoundly integrated approach from Biblical theology that both informs systematics and then spells out progressive practical strategies for the field of bio-ethics. 3) After following my lead through the previous chapter in an earlier form and adding an occasional psychological implication, Paul Holmes of the University of Chicago psychiatry department led his and our integration of psychology in chapter eleven, "A Transactional Model of Human Based on Biblical Theology." These two chapters (10 and 11) serve as a deeply Biblical and profoundly integrative expression of systematic theology and psychology. In an earlier form the combined chapters, minus the bio-ethics material was presented at the Wheaton Theology Conference in 1997 within the topic of the integration of Psychology and Theology. 4) Chapter twelve, "A Theology of Work" takes up a sub-theme from Biblical theology but addresses a rather significant issue from my and my student's contextual situation. Again the agenda is set by Biblical theology but because it is a piece of systematic theology these Biblical theology gems are integrated with contemporary concepts of work and economics. These examples help to show how this critical realist theological method works.

A final chapter, number 13, "Putting the Method Together" integrates the method as a whole, bringing unity after each chapter has focused on its particular aspect, and returning to the issue on how science can nest within this Biblical, theological and philosophical method.

2. The Relationship of Philosophy, Theology and Science

This chapter is structured by a historical survey of grand philosophical programs. Each philosophical program will be expounded enough to identify relationships to theology and science, and to provide a sample of each. More could be said about each philosophy, theology, and science contribution, which if the reader's interest is peaked, I encourage following where the notes lead. One of the purposes of this chapter is to show how philosophy changes theology and science with which it syncretizes. This will provide an opportunity to affirm aspects and to critique other aspects of the philosophies expounded. In the previous chapter I identified briefly my epistemic and theological method as within critical realism. This chapter provides a philosophical rationale for this previous sketched summary. If I provide a critique in this chapter as we travel through each philosophy (such as under Kant) then any following philosophies, theology and science that depend upon such a perspective are also critiqued without further raising the point repetitively.

This survey includes: 1) Stoicism-Tertullian, 2) Plato-Augustine, 3) Aristotle-Aquinas, 4) Renaissance Humanism-Calvin and the Biblical theology movement, 5) Descartes-Rationalists, 6) Locke and Newton-Edwards and Common Sense Realism, with Intelligent Design 7) Kant-Strauss, Ritschl and Crockett, 8) Romanticism-Evolution, Pietism of Schleiermacher and Evangelicalism, 9) Existentialism of Kierkegaard-Barth, Bultmann and Tillich, 10) Marx-Liberation theology, 11) Pragmatisms-Liberation, Evangelicalism, Relativity, and Quantum, 12) Process philosophy of Whitehead and Teilhard de Chardin, 13) Postmodern language games with traditional Christian communities and their theological hermeneutic, and 14) Critical Realism of Shedd, McGrath, Murphy, and Lakatos. I embrace a hybrid view of critical realism in a Lakatos' scientific method. Throughout this survey, I will summarize some of the ways in which philosophy has affected theology and science, and highlight some of how it is affecting evangelical theology now. In the midst of this survey I will assess each view for warrant in a few of its core beliefs. This will provide us with the opportunity to evaluate whether these affects are appropriate and desirable.

I argue for philosophy's role in theology to be streamlined to: 1) helping us be precise and coherent in our thought (as a critical realist), within a Renaissance humanism of program of "back to the Christian textual roots" which Biblical theology largely provides, 2) helping us think through ramifications of our commitments and the relationships this identifies us with, and 3) providing any additional basic beliefs that are strongly warranted, but do not counter those of Biblical theology.[1] This chapter is not addressing the value or limitations of philosophy as a discipline itself; I leave that issue for others at another occasion.

2.1 Stoicism

By the time Christianity arrived, Stoicism had entered its ethical phase and was one of the few highly moral options available in the Roman Empire, along with Judaism and Christianity. When Paul presented the gospel to some stoic philosophers, he resisted the Stoic cyclical metaphysic with its internal idealistic creation and cataclysm,[2] and presented a sovereign personal God, Who creates and draws all history out in a linear arrangement, ultimately heading to judgment and bodily resurrection (Acts 17:18–31).[3] Such a linear view of history is dependent upon the Jewish construct of creation unto Kingdom or more microscopically: exodus to Promised Land as a stage on the way to Kingdom (Ex. 1–19; Deut. 1–4).[4]

However, in a positive direction Christianity utilized Stoic concepts to provide some basic connections in making sense of the concept of the Trinity, as when Tertullian appropriated the concept of *procession* from the Stoic belief system to help Christianity make sense of the Trinity. The Stoic concept of *procession* meant "an extension" as in the economic Divine Being extends Himself from the dominant expression of Father to

---

1 What I have in mind is "A Personal Statement," and chapter on "Faith and Knowledge," in Doug Kennard, *The Relationship Between Epistemology, Hermeneutics, Biblical Theology and Contextualization* (Lewiston: The Mellon Press, 1999), pp. 31–33 and 35–69.

2 Seneca, Nat. quaest. 3.29 in Seneca, Ad Lucilium Epistulae Morales. LCL. trans. R. M. Gummere (Cambridge: Harvard University Press, 1947) 24.4–7; 98.12–14; Silius Italicus, Punica LLC, Trans. J. D. Duff (Cambridge: Harvard, University Press, 1949) 6.531–38; Tacitus, Annals LLC. Trans. J. Jackson (Cambridge: Harvard University Press, 1951); Diogenes Laertius, Lives of the Philosophers (Philosophoi Biol) 8.134; Plutarch, Moral. 1077d.

3 Friedrich Lang, s.v. "πῦρ," *TDNT* (Grand Rapids: Eerdmans, 1968) 6:928–945, claims that such stoic ideas are fused with apocalyptic Jewish cataclysm to fund 2 Peter 3: 7–10, however I think that there is ample source material in the Jewish heritage of the prophets and apocalypses without folding in a philosophical source no where mentioned in the text. Cf. Richard Bauckham, *Jude, 2 Peter* (Waco: Word, 1983), pp. 300–1; 1QH 3.193b; *Sib. Or.* 2.187–213; 3.71–92; 4.171–182; 6.153–161; *1 Enoch* 10.3; Hermas, *Vis.* 4.3.3. Jewish-Christian apocalyptic continued to be rich in descriptions of cataclysm without dependence upon stoicism, e.g., *Apocalypse of Peter*.

4 Thomas Cahill, *The Gifts of the Jews* (New York: Doubleday, 1998), pp. 18–19, 125–131, nicely summarizes the invention of linear history in a context in which all other peoples of the ancient Near East held to cyclical views.

a second and third *persona* of the Son and Holy Spirit.[5] This connection did not impose the Stoic concept of *logos* or *spirit* as a divine impersonal grand metaphysical principle, for Christianity's God concept involved three persons within it. However, the fact that such concepts as *logos* and *spirit* were already in use in Stoic terminology as 'divine' encouraged using other Stoic concepts for describing the Christian's Trinitarian God. Furthermore, the clarity of the revelational "Word" as Christ, resisted being interpreted in a non-personal Stoic manner within the church.

So on the whole, the early church comes out strongly against embracing a Stoic world view,[6] even though a few Stoic concepts contributed to Christian theology.

Stoicism with its idealistic world view resisted the value and development of science. Stoic metaphysics focused on the unseen ultimate, like the fire within everything as a non-personal divine principle that constituted all reality, which would eventually consume all reality in a cataclysm. This distracted the Stoics from the available advances in science such as Pythagoras' mathematical analysis of a spherical earth and Egyptian astronomy, because they did not value the constituents of the universe. Instead, they urged a morality to remain steady within divine determinism.

2.2 Platonism

Plato is a major influence on Western Christian ideas, especially due to a neo-Platonic version of his metaphysic, the theory of forms, and the simplicity of the Good. For example, one does not find in the real world a perfect circle, so Platonism conjectures that there is a realm of the forms which would house these perfect objects. Thus, pure geometrical and mathematical concepts occupy this realm of the forms, which Augustine located for Christianity as in the mind of God.[7] This grounding of geometry and mathematical concepts is the only way in which I can be said to be Platonic.

---

5 Tertullian, Adv. Prax. 4, 5, 7, 8, 11; Against Praxeas. In The Writings of Quintus Sept. Flor. Tertullianus. Edited by Richard Ellmann. (Kila: Kessinger, 1869–70).

6 E.g., Origen, *Contra Celsus* 4.11-13 in *Origen Against Celsus*. Edited by James Bellamy (London: B. Mills, 1660); Irenaeus, *Adv. Haer.* 1.7.1 in *The Ante-Nicene Fathers,* ed. A. Roberts and J. Donaldson, vol. 3 (Grand Rapids: Eerdmans,1995).

7 In this I follow Roger Penrose, *Shadows of the Mind: A Search for the Missing Science of Consciousness* (London: Vintage, 1995). As a theologian, Alister McGrath (in *A Scientific Theology: Reality*, Volume 2 [Grand Rapids: Eerdmans, 2002], pp. 79–83, 170–176) concurs with this assessment and locates this mathematical realism in the mind of God following Augustine. cf. Per Lindstrom "Quasi-realism in Mathematics," *The Monist* 83 (2000): 122–47, but especially pp. 130–132, and p. 138 where he discusses the objective reality of numbers and proposes options including Platonism and Dummett's alternative of a Wittgenstein defined language game that has an intuitional essence beyond the definition, that perhaps accesses real mathematical objects like Putnam proposed.

More extensively, Plato thus provides meaning to the shadows which we see and feel about us in the real world. This level of Platonism is nicely pictured by Plato's myth of the cave.[8] The forms are that which is really true for Plato, in that they are eternal, unchanging, unmoving and indivisible. These forms introduce into all fields a dualism in which the higher realm associated with the forms is the true reality experienced through the lower realm of visible things and the discursive reasoning by which one conjures up the unchanging and indivisible truth of the forms. For Plato, the realm of the forms is only accessible to humans because they have trafficked among the realm of the forms as souls before we were incarnated into our bodies.[9] This pre-embodiment experience funds the Socratic method, so that everybody (even children and slaves) could recollect the truth of the forms with well placed questions to help them recollect this pre-embodiment experience of their souls.

Augustine rejects this preexistence of humans but is confident that the forms illumine our minds to the true reality which informs the sensible shadows.[10] This illumination is a kind of divine inspiration or divine informing about every thought a human thinks, even the pain of bumping one's toe on a stone.

Furthermore, this metaphysical dualism of *form over object* is reflected in a psychological dualism, in which a person *is* a soul held captive within a body until in death she can be set free from her body to the joy of the higher realm. Such a dualistic description of humanity is first noticed in Christian theology through the *Epistle of Diognetus*, but it has remained a very resilient tradition.[11] Plato also maintains a tripartite division of the soul,[12] which serves as the fountainhead of trichotomy in the theology of man, as Justin Martyr expressed it.[13] Such threeness in

8 Plato, *The Republic*, book 6, sections 509–11 in *Great Books of the Western World, #7 Plato* (Chicago: Encyclopaedia Britannica, 1952), pp. 386–88.

9 Plato, *Meno* and *Phaedo* (in *Great Books of the Western World, #7 Plato* [Chicago: Encyclopaedia Britannica, 1952]), this recollection of the soul is discarded by most theologians, except that Origen embraced it with its preexistence and reincarnation, cf. Diogenes Allen, *Philosophy for Understanding Theology* (Atlanta: John Knox Press, 1985), p. 48.

10 Augustine, *Enarrations on the Psalms*, 118 in *A Select Library of the Nicene and Post-Nicene Fathers of the Christian Church*, vol. 8. Edited by Philip Schaff (Edinburgh/Grand Rapids: T & T Clark/Eerdmans, 1994); *De peccatorum meritis et remissione et de baptismo parvulorum* 1.25.38 in *Sanct Aureli Augustini De peccatorum meritis et remissione et de baptismo parvulorum ad Marcellinum libri tres*. Edited by Carl Franz Vrba and Joseph Zycha (Vindobonae, F. Tempsky, 1913); *De civitate Dei* 10.2 or *The City of God* in the *Great Books of the Western World*, vol. 18, edited by William Benton (Chicago:Encyclopaedia Britannica, 1952). The medieval church tends to appreciate platonic illuminationism following Augustine until Aristotelian sensibility wins out in the wake of Aquinas.

11 E.g., *Epistle to Diognetus*. (Leiden: E. J. Brill, 1964).

12 Plato , *The Republic*, book 4, pp. 342–56.

13 Justin Martyr, *Apol.* 1.29 in *Saint Justin Martyr: The First Apology, The Second Apology, Dialogue with Trypho, Exhortation to the Greeks, Discourse to the Greeks,*

the image of man is further justified by the threeness in the One, which for Plato is the True, the Good, and the Beautiful, but in Christianity such Divine threeness is reworked for Biblical reasons to be Father, Son, and Holy Spirit. Each of these three persons of God is combined into a simple, transcending essence for philosophy and theology.[14] Augustine admires this Platonic threefoldness of God further by developing God's roles as to create beings, communicate truth, and cultivate moral goodness through His grace.[15] Of course, Augustine was especially trying to be Biblical so that he embraced a monotheistic concept of God and His creation of things with time, all of which are very foreign to Plantonism's Demiurge and eternal creation. Such models of humanity were significantly reworked by the Biblical theology movement as it redefined Biblical anthropological concepts toward a multifaceted unity rather than these Platonically informed dichotomy or trichotomy.[16]

Under Platonic influence the commitment that all truth is eternal truth frames Trinitarian relations in eternalized ways. For example, as a Platonist, Origen proposed that the three Divine persons were each a distinct *hypostasis* from all eternity. To explain this fact and to combat modalism, he proposed that the Son was eternally generated by the Father.[17] This is reflected at Nicea by Eusebius of Caesarea's suggestion of his own *Creed of Caesarea* with the statement "Son only-begotten ...

The Monarchy; or the Rule of God. Edited by Thomas B. Falls (New York: Christian Heritage, 1949); For discussion of the dichotomy, trichotomy and the descriptive Biblical theology multifaceted unity see the later chapter by "A Biblical Anthropology Funding Bio-Ethics" which grew out of Doug Kennard and Paul Holmes, "The Nature of Man a Biblical theology Approach," earlier presented as a paper at the Wheaton Theology Conference, 1997.

14 Plato, *The Republic*, book 6, sections 509, p. 386 and Augustine, *De Trin.* 5.2.3; 5.16.17; 6.4.6; 6.6.8; 6.7.8; 6.10.11; 15.13.22 in *The Trinity* (Washington: Catholic University of America Press, 1963); *In Joan. Evang.* 99.4 in *Homilies on the Gospel According to St. John, and his First Epistle* (Oxford: J. H. Parker, 1848–49); *De civ. Dei* 11.10.1.3. I have previously critiqued the concept of simplicity as self defeating in Doug Kennard, *The Classical Christian God* (Lewiston: The Mellon Press, 2002), pp. 73–75 after the manner of Alvin Plantinga, *Does God Have a Nature?* (Milwaukee: Marquette University Press, 1980).

15 Augustine, *De civ. Dei* 8.10.2.

16 Doug Kennard, "Biblical Anthropology as a Creation and Revelation Framework for Doing Bio-Ethics," Evangelical Philosophical Society paper 2006 and later chapter of this book; Hans Walter Wolff, Anthropology of the Old Testament (Philadelphia: Fortress Press, 1974); Gerhard Kittel and Gerhard Friedrich, Theological Dictionary of the New Testament (Grand Rapids: Eerdmans, 1964–76); Johannes Botterweck and Helmer Ringgren, Theological Dictionary of the Old Testament (Grand Rapids: Eerdmans, 1974–present); Colin Brown, The New International Dictionary of New Testament Theology (Grand Rapids: Zondervan, 1975); Laird Harris, Gleason Archer, and Bruce Waltke, Theological Wordbook of the Old Testament (Chicago: Moody Press, 1980); Willem VanGemeren, New International Dictionary of Old Testament Theology & Exegesis (Grand Rapids: Zondervan, 1997).

17 Origen, *Comm. Jo.* 2.10.75; 20.22.182f; 32.16.192f. in *The Ante-Nicene Farther. Origen's Commentary on John* (Edinburgh: T & T Clark, 1990).

begotten of the Father before the ages."[18] He reasoned that the Son must be begotten before creation because the Son creates everything, but this language did not make it into the *Nicene Creed*. This *eternal begetting* language finally made it into the Constantinople revision of the *Nicene Creed* (381 A.D.) and more blatantly in the second canon of *The Canons of the Second Council of Constantinople* (553 A.D.). In defense of this view, Victorinus, the Neo-Platonic philosopher took up the defense of the *homoousion* (same essence) view of the persons of the Godhead, against the Arians. He held that God is eternally in motion; His essence is equivalent to that of a perpetual mover. So, eternal generation shows the perpetuity of the movement of the Son and the potentency of the Father to move the Son.[19] This perspective of Victorinus was very influential on Augustine's view as he formulated what became the mature standard view of the Trinity for the Western church in his volume *De trinitate*. Augustine sees that the distinction of the persons is grounded in mutual relations within the Godhead. This concept of relation clarifies that it is not three essences or three accidents in the Aristotelian philosophical categories but three real eternal relations (*aliquid relation*).[20] Therefore, the relations within the Godhead are the Father is eternally begetting, the Son is eternally begotten, and the Spirit is eternally proceeding or being bestowed within the Godhead. Of course, Augustine brings much more to the Trinity than this, but the critical move from conceiving of the persons as extensions of the Divine to conceiving the persons as equal related Ones within the Divine has been made partly under the influence of Platonic commitment to the eternality of truth.

Platonic philosophy also contributed significantly to the theological hermeneutics of patristic and medieval Christianity. Origen set early Christianity upon a Platonic hermeneutic with three levels to reflect a Platonic view of humanity: literal (fleshly), moral (psychic), and spiritual.[21] Origen says that the first level is to attract people to the study of the

---

18 Suggestion from Eusebius shown in his *Epist. Euseb. apund Socrates*; support of this point and the *Creed of Caesarea* shown in Henry Bettenson, *Documents of the Christian Church* (Oxford: Oxford University Press, 1963), pp. 24–25.

19 Victorinus, Adv. Ar. 1.43; 3.7; 4.20–21; De gen. Verb. 2; 29-30; Ib. 1.31; 1.41; 4.20 in Theological Treatises on the Trinity (Washington: Catholic University of America Press, 1981).

20 Augustine, *de trin.* Bks. 5-7; *Ioh. Tract.* 39; *Enar. on the Ps.* 68.1.5; *ep.* 170; 238–41; *de civ. Dei* 11.10. I critique this development of eternal generation in Douglas Kennard, *The Classical Christian God,* (Lewiston: Edwin Mellen Press, 2002), pp. 82–85, and throughout the next chapter, "The Role of Tradition in Theology" earlier presented as a paper at ETS, 2003.

21 R. P. C. Hanson, *Allegory and Event: A Study of the Sources and Significance of Origen's Interpretation of Scripture* (Louisville: Westminster John Knox Press, 2002, originally 1959), especially pp. 62–63, 235–238; Cf. Robert Grant, *The Letter and the Spirit* (New York: Macmillian, 1957), Jean Pipen, *Mythe et Allegorie*: Les origins grecques et les contestations judeo-chretiennes (Paris: Etudes Augustiniennes, 1958, rev. 1976); Manlo Simonetti, *Lettera e/o allegoria: Un contributo alla storia dell'esegesi patristica* (Rome: Institutum Patristicum Augustinianum, 1985); Karen

Bible so that they would transcend it with the allegorical approach.[22] The last level, that of spiritual hermeneutics, was an allegorical approach that would often ignore the previous and allow Platonic philosophical perspectives into Christianity.[23] Hanson concludes that "this openness to non-Christian intellectual influences on the part of Origen meant that he was consciously endeavoring to reconcile the text of the Bible with contemporary philosophy and was under the necessity of finding in the Bible by some means or other his philosophical speculations."[24] Again, the Biblical theology maintains its own voice and hermeneutic with confidence and warrant, such that it does not need to proof text itself or position itself in such philosophical speculations.

Platonic philosophy has left a deep imprint upon Christian theology lived out as well. As Diogenes Allen develops,

> For Plato as for Christianity, this world is not our home. We have a destiny which cannot be fully achieved here, and human life is a journey from this world to ultimate reality. Plato and Christianity differ on the nature of this world, on what our true home is, and on how we get there. But their common insistence that the sensible world depends on a nonsensible reality and that our happiness or well-being is to be found there makes them allies.[25]

Augustine admits indebtedness to this Platonism especially in the formulating of a spiritual being of "unchangeable light" and that evil is a privation in things.[26]

However, because Augustine read Greek poorly he cites only about five of Plato's own works. Instead, Plotinus and at times Porphyry became the conduit carrying Plato's ideas, since they were translated into Latin. Augustine develops that there are two ways to arrive at truth of and reason.[27] In this, Augustine wishes to embrace both faith and reason together.

Torjesen, *Hermeneutical Procedure and Theological Method in Origen's Exegesis* (Berlin: Walter de Gruyter, 1986).

22 Origen, *Contra Celsum* VII.60.

23 Hanson, *Allegory and Event,* p. 238.

24 Hanson, *Allegory and Event,* pp. 361–362.

25 Diogenes Allen, *Philosophy for Understanding Theology*, p. 39.

26 Augustine, *The Confessions* 7.1.1 and 7.10–14 in the *Great Books of the Western World,* vol. 18, edited by William Benton (Chicago: Encyclopaedia Britannica, 1952); Cf. parallel columns in of Plotinus and Augustine in M. Gradgeorge, *Saint Augustin et le neoplatonisme. La possibilité d'une philosophie chrétienne*. Edited by Michele Federico Sciacca (Louvain: Publications universitaires de Louvain, 1956), pp. 70–84, 117–147; also Eugene Portalie, *A Guide to the Thought of Saint Augustine* (Chicago: Henry Regnery Co., 1960), chapter 6, "Neoplatonic Influences," pp. 95–135.

27 Augustine, *Against the Academics.* Edited by John Joseph O'Meara (Westminster: Newman Press, 1950), 3.20.43.

> As regards the matters which are to be investigated by close reasoning, I am of such a mind that I impatiently desire to grasp the truth not only through faith but also by understanding. I am confident that I will find in the Platonists nothing that will be at variance with our sacred literature.[28]

My contention is that Augustine is overconfident of this last opinion and has absorbed some Platonism that also distances him from the Biblical text.[29]

Diogenes Allen highlights another Platonic influence on Augustinian theology as the increase in knowledge of God impacts moral development.

> Another feature of the Augustinians ... describes the ascent of the soul from the sense perception (the cave) to the vision of the Good. Moral improvement or purification of the soul is achieved with increasing knowledge of reality. Thus in theology we have the notion that the increase in knowledge of God goes hand in hand with moral improvement and vice versa. There is no intimate knowledge of God without such a moral change in the knower. This Platonic-Augustinian epistemical tradition goes along with the likeness between knowledge and vision, and the belief that such vision is higher than the knowledge which can be gained discursively with concepts.[30]

Such an emphasis has been reflected in theological diminishment of the human body and ecology, and also the increase of mysticism.[31] The monastic and the mystical lives are in many ways at least as much neo-platonic philosophy as they are Christian.

We need to remind ourselves that Christianity has a deep commitment to reality, rather than the idealism present within Platonism. God created the universe and all that is within it (Gen. 1; John 1:1–3). Our bodies are part of that good creation. The real Christ was incarnated in a real creation (John 1:9–18). The prophets identify that the future Kingdom is on the new earth. Christ identified that his own disciples would have responsibility in this Kingdom on earth everlasting (Matt.

---

28 Augustine, *Against the Academics* 3.20.43.

29 Examples include comments in notes: 10, 13, 17, 25.

30 Allen, *Philosophy for Understanding Theology*, p. 49.

31 An example of this neo-platonic mysticism is in Meister Eckhardt, but Augustine does not embrace such a contemplative aspect of the Christian life, cf. Doug Kennard "Augustine's Concept of the Christian Life" a paper at Dallas Theological Seminary, 1980, pp. 12–15.

19:27–30; Luke 19:17, 19). Even John highlights the ultimate destiny is on earth, as the New Jerusalem descends (Rev. 21). Additionally, the mystical salvation concept championed by Schweitzer does not set up a Platonic mysticism but is better placed upon a foundation of Jewish Merkabah mysticism in which the divine throne room in heaven, and the level of creation we live in (with an earthly tabernacle inhabited by God), are both realities.[32] Likewise, this Platonism never removed the resilient Biblical idea of personal resurrection of body from Christian eschatology,[33] even though the destination moved from the earthly kingdom emphasis (of the prophets, Jesus, synoptics and Revelation 21–22) to heaven as the eternal Kingdom habitation (following Augustine[34]). Could this last shift be a subtle effect of Platonism as well?

Platonism with its idealism resists the development of science because of its focus upon the One and its forms. This orientation distracts and even pities and mocks those who develop astute observation of the visual objects, denigrating these objects as mere shadows of the true reality in the ethereal realm accessible only through mystical recollection, authority and discoursive reasoning.[35] However, this focus aided the grounding of geometrical and mathematical concepts as rooted in the forms but it diminishes scientific examination of objects as real truth, warranting science.

---

32 Often in Hebrews 9:23–28 the better place of heaven is developed through a Platonic framework but this is foreign to the text. In Platonism the heavenly forms are the only reality, with the earthly objects being merely a shadow of this reality imposed upon our senses through the recollection of our souls' preincarnate life among those heavenly forms. In a Platonism, if the truth is present in the heavenly then it is present in the earthly as well, because the earthly is a mere shadow of the heavenly. Here in Hebrews 9:23–25 both the heavenly tabernacle and the earthly copies of the heavenly tabernacle are real as evidenced by the Hebraic pattern of Merkabah mysticism. That is, both the heavenly and earthly tabernacles are real and different things may be occurring in these different realities. For example, the heavenly tabernacle is normally thought to be where God's presence dwells (e.g., Isa. 6:4) but the amazing thing is that with the cleansed tabernacle God dwells on earth, with the ark of the covenant serving as His throne (eg. Ex. 40:34–38). However, the uncleaness of the earthly temple dislodges the divine presence from the earthly temple, while it remains in the heavenly temple (e.g., Ezek. 1:4–28; 11:22–25). The different conditions of the pure heavenly temple and the occasionally unclean earthly temple show that they are both real in this multidimensional Hebraic framework rather than the idealism of the earthly shadows, that a Platonism would portray. Cf. C. Marvin Pate and Douglas Kennard, *Deliverance Now and Not Yet: The New Testament and the Great Tribulation* (New York: Peter Lang, 2003), especially chapters 3–6 and 14–15.

33 Cf. Caroline Walker Bynum, *The Resurrection of the Body* (New York: Columbia University Press, 1995).

34 Augustine, *The City of God*, bk. 20, ch. 6, 9, 10 and bk. 22, ch. 4, 11.

35 Plato, *The Republic*, bk. 7, 514–17 "the cave" in *Plato*, vol. 7, pp. 388–89.

2.3 Aristotle

For centuries Aristotle's works were primarily inaccessible to the West, except for *Categories* and *On Interpretation*, which made major contributions. Aristotle countered Plato with qualities as *present in* primary substances, not their ethereal forms. This approach shifts epistemology to a realism, which accentuates the idea of the *kinds* of substances as absolutely vital for philosophy and theology. One expression of this is apparent in the difference between the meaning of nature as *what* (described by attributes) and person as *who* (described by relations). For example, Gregory of Nyssa makes this point as he corrects Trinity descriptions to be one substance (or what) and three persons (or whos).[36] He points out that *ousia* (what or essence or species) should not be used interchangeably with *hypostasis* (person or who). However, he transcends Aristotle's *Categories* when he develops that God's unity is identical with the unity between the persons. That is, Aristotle had left the unity of persons to be like the species of "humanity;" the kind of understanding that in the Twentieth century would fund social trinity (in which there are three persons within the species of God). However, Gregory points out that the *ousia* of the Father, Son and Holy Spirit is not a secondary substance. That is, they do not *have* the same *ousia,* they *are* the same *ousia*. That is, not that there is a species of God with three occupants but that there is only one God. In Gregory's wake, Augustine looked to primary substance, in particular the mind of a human for an analogy of this unity and diversity within God.[37] Augustine recognized the Trinity in 1) the human mind, 2) its power to know and love, and 3) the object of such knowledge and love. In Augustine, the first usually stands for the Father, while the second Who (the Spirit) as the medium in the expression of knowledge and love to the third Who (the Son).

With new books of Aristotle being discovered in the second half of the twelfth century from among the Muslims of Spain, Aristotle's precision and learning drew a new group who viewed themselves as professional teachers. Among these teachers, Scholasticism (a clear and unifying system of theology) was formed. Scholasticism depended primarily upon logic and the art of organizing truth into rationally intelligible systems of thought. When in 1255 A. D., the faculty of arts of the University of Paris adopted a new syllabus of the study of all Aristotle's works sharp distinctions arose between philosophy and theology (faith and reason, nature and supernature) which had not existed before in

36 Gregory of Nyssa, "Letter 38" in *Nicene and Post-Nicene Fathers,* 2nd ser., ed. Philip Schaff and Henry Wace, trans. Blomfield (Grand Rapids: Eerdmans, 1955), 8:137–38. There is also a nice discussion of this influence of Aristotle on the theologians in Diogenes Allen, *Philosophy for Understanding Theology,* pp. 93–144.

37 Augustine, *de trin.* 5–7.

Christianity, and unfortunately should not exist.[38] In the wake of these distinctions, theology highly depends upon the Bible and tradition, whereas philosophy (under Aristotle) is largely a deductive system from observable principles in the natural world. For example, Aristotle begins with terms (the categories into which terms fall) and then analyzes the meaning of propositions by studying formal terms and syllogisms, which emerge coherently from these categorical presuppositions. In this, a syllogism proves valid conclusions but they do not govern reality unless the premises are shown to be really true as well.

One of the gains of this Aristotelianism is increased precision. For example, this precision is evident in Aristotle's biological writings, which constitute one quarter of all Aristotle's extant manuscripts. In his *History of Animals, On the Parts of Animals,* and *On the Generation of Animals* he categorizes animals into visually distinguishable types. For example, whales are characterized as cetacean, similar to fish but without scales and with air breathing through a blow hole.[39] He includes treatises on the motion and gait of the living animal in its living condition, as well as some sketches and description of animal and human parts from dissection. The precision of the discipline did not remain static, for in the first century A.D., Galen made major advances in the anatomy of humans (which dominated the field for fourteen centuries or longer) with his study of the human skeleton and his dissection, which turned out to be primarily of apes. With this technique of comparative anatomy occasional glitches of human anatomy (funded by ape dissection) were realized by Andreas Vesalius in the sixteenth century. Vesalius' commitment to human dissection made major advances and corrections to the field of human anatomy in his 1543 A.D. of, *On the Structure of the Human Body*.[40] Even though this volume was a magnificent work, Vesalius revised it again in 1555 A.D. with more accurate information and sketches that reflected especially fetal conditions and female reproduction, based on further dissections of human cadavers. When the discipline developed more precision, it was under the commitment that the real, rather than authority, determined the truth of the human body.

38 For example, I show the broad synonymy of faith and knowledge in three ways in Doug Kennard, *The Relationship Between Epistemology, Hermeneutics, Biblical Theology and Contextualization* chapter 3, "Faith and Knowledge," pp. 35–70. The three arguments are: 1) in practice most theologians throughout history use faith as overlapping with knowledge, 2) following John Austin's *How to do things with Words* (Oxford: Oxford University Press, 1962), ordinary use sees these terms as synonyms, and 3) a Biblical theology analysis of faith and knowledge uses the terms synomously.

39 Aristotle, *History of Animals* bk. 8, 1.589b and *On the Parts of Animals* bk. 4, 13. 695b in *The Works of Aristotle: II. Great Books of the Western World* (Chicago: Encyclopaedia Britannica, 1952), pp. 115–6, 227.

40 Jerome Tarshis, *The Father of Modern Anatomy: Andreas Vesalius* (New York: The Deal Press, 1969), pp. 7–17, 30, 45, 60, 73–78, 96–97.

This realist development within the discipline moved beyond Aristotle with further more precise and comprehensive observations.

An additional example of increased precision is in Aristotle's explanation in the *Physics* and *Metaphysics* that there are four levels of cause: 1) material, 2) efficient or movement, 3) essence or form, and 4) final. The heavenly level of contents and causes is seen by him to be immortal and contained an unmoved mover that continuously effects the lower level of generation and decay. For Aristotle, this unmoved mover is not an object of worship, nor a creator, nor really knows anything beyond itself. Aristotle's unmoved mover is a final cause drawing all that exists to itself.

Aristotle's affect upon Aquinas is especially evident with Thomas' five ways to prove the existence of God.[41] Based on the realization that every effect has a cause, he floats four cosmological arguments and a teleological argument. The conclusion of the first way provides the first cause of motion to be a Being which is pure act (in whom there is no potential), which is similar to Aristotle's unmoved mover. The second way goes further than Aristotle in showing a first efficient cause. The third way describes God to be a necessary Being. Aristotle had viewed all heavenly bodies as necessary beings and called them all gods as the other Greeks had done. The fourth way treats God as the exemplar or formal cause of all perfections. The fifth way shows God is the final cause and designer of all things. For Aquinas, on the basis of these arguments and his basic belief in Exodus 3:13–14, God is sheer existence or independent in His aseity.[42] In his argument Aquinas has not philosophically excluded the option of an infinite regress of contingent beings like contemporary Bonaventura tried to do, but he bridges this philosophical gap by dependence on the clarity of the Biblical text.[43] I agree with the basic thrust of Aquinas arguments here, but it is important to notice that he has been more dependent on the Biblical text than is often acknowledged and he modified the God concept which these arguments provide by the Biblical notion of a personal Creator God,[44] allowing the non-Biblical notion of a Necessary Being to be merged with it. That is, the Aristotelianism has been significantly modified by the Biblical model of God, but those aspects of the Aristotelian concept of God that retain external warrant to him are permitted to inform the

41 Aquinas, *Summa Theologica,* First Part, Question 2, article 3 in *Great Books of the Western World.* vols. 19 and 20 (Chicago: Encyclopaedia Britannica, 1952).

42 I disagree with Aquinas interpretation of Exodus 3:13–14 as too philosophical and call us back to a more Hebrew notion evident in the Qal or Hiphil of the "to be" verb, in which God promises to be there for His people; cf. Kennard, *The Classical Christian God,* pp. 106–7.

43 Aquinas, *Summa Theologica,* First Part, Question 2, article 3, "On the Contrary."

44 I also wish to affirm a non-Aristotelian cosmological approach to God, though I also agree that God is a Necessary Being, cf. Kennard, *The Classical Christian God,* pp. 11–61.

real character of God. Because I am here laying out a philosophical and theological framework within which science should operate it is helpful at this point to present a contemporary cosmological argument that defends itself within our modern context, and to explain the God that is defended by such argumentation.

2.3.1. A Cosmological Argument

This argument begins with the experience of existence and floats its argument within the experience of creation. Such a cosmological argument has some evidence of its use within the Bible for purposes of fostering worship, gospel and judgment. For example, Psalm 19:1 testifies to God's grandeur as known from the creation, "The heavens are telling of the glory of God; and their expanse is declaring the work of His hands." Additionally, in a context of gospel proclamation, Paul develops a common ground with the Athenians between the rival Epicurean and Stoic philosophies by appealing to the remembered experience of a plague being averted as pointing to the Creator sovereign God, Who is acknowledged by them but remains largely unknown to them (Acts 17:18–31). Paul develops that this Creator is the One Who has resurrected Christ. This gospel was effective enough for some to come to a saving knowledge of Christ even though most seemed to reject it at the point of Christ's resurrection. For those who reject the gospel or who have never heard the gospel, God is still righteous in judging them with wrath as Paul wrote in Romans 1:19–20, "because that which is known about God is evident within them; for God made it evident to them. For since the creation of the world His invisible attributes, His everlasting power and divine nature, have been clearly seen being understood through what has been made, so that they are without excuse." In Paul's perspective, there is enough evidence in creation to point to God as an everlasting powerful and immortal being. Thus this is a cosmological argument in which this voice from creation is precisely heard.

The particular cosmological argument that is presented here is framed by three mutually exclusive Aristotelian options that cover the whole array of origins contemplated. For example, "uncaused" beings are those which are eternal and through this argument are seen to be actually necessary. In contrast, beings which are "caused by another" in this framework are contingent, with all the changeability and dependence of "happen to be" beings. The third option of "self caused" has in view a range of options like: Stephen Hawking's quantum fluctuation view that within an everlasting universe with imaginary time, the big bang brought about the expanding universe and positive time without outside cause;[45] microscopically Donald Sherburne's naturalistic process view;[46] Fred Hoyle's continuous creation of Hydrogen molecules;[47] and extreme forms of existentialism which see choice involved in creating one's own existence in the first place. From this framework the cosmological argument may be run as follows:

1. If any being exists, then it is either uncaused, caused by another, or self caused.
2. Some contingent beings exist (e.g., I exist).
3. Contingent beings are not uncaused because, they are dependent in their "happen to be existence" (e.g., I had a beginning and need food for growth).
4. Human experience indicates that non-existent contingent beings do not cause themselves to exist (i.e., you can't be prior to yourself).
5. Therefore, contingent beings are caused by another (e.g., I have parents).
6. The cause for these contingent beings existing is either an infinite regress of contingent beings or ultimately a necessary being.
7. An infinite regress of contingent beings is unreasonable because the universe evidences a finite age from observations of its expanding nature.
8. Therefore, it is reasonable to conclude that a necessary being exists, which we call God.

The weakest premise is probably premise 4 because the views of Hawking, Sherburne, Hoyle and extreme existentialists are not stopped by this popular human appeal. However this is not very significant because each option could be diminished. For example, most astronomers do not embrace Hoyle's view of continuous creation because they accept the law of the conservation of energy and explain Hydrogen gas clouds in relation to the forming or exploding of a star. Likewise, most

---

45 Stephen Hawking, *A Brief History of Time From the Big Bang to Black Holes* (New York: Bantam Books, 1988), pp. 46–47, 133, 139, 143.

46 Donald Sherburne, *A Key to Whitehead's Process and Reality* (Chicago: The University of Chicago Press, 1966), process explanation 1–204, atheism is evident in pp. 29–32 and in classroom discussion in class on Whitehead, at Vanderbilt University, Fall, 1985.

47 Simon Mitton, *Conflict in the Cosmos: Fred Hoyle's Life in Science* (Washington D.C.: Joseph Henry Press, 2005), p. 124 discusses the first presentation Hoyle made of this view among friends Hermann Bondi and Thomas Gold in 1948; Cf. G. Burbridge, F. Hoyle, and J. V. Narlikar, "A Different Approach to Cosmology," *Physics Today* 52(1999): 38–44, and A. Albrecht, "Reply to 'A Different Approach to Cosmology,'" *Physics Today* 52(1999): 44–46; G. Burbridge, F. Hoyle, J. V. Narlikar, and A. Albrecht, *A Different Approach to Cosmology* (Cambridge: Cambridge University Press, 2000).

existentialists do not develop these details but recognize that one needs existence in the first place for there to be meaningful choice to frame one's essence and this argument is about explaining where this initial existence comes from. Hawking's basic belief entails that the universe comes into existence through a fluctuation in a quantum field, a condition which we know nearly nothing about. That is, he has the assumption that the rules for our universe are so compelling that they or some aspect from the unknown universe could naturalistically instigate the big bang without any further cause. The expanding universe known to human experience has no observed mechanism to explain the instigation of the big bang. Hawking's basic belief is a claim for which he has no realistic explanation or warrant for the process. Remember, classical and relativity physics still grant the law of the conservation of matter and energy, which would require creations to be done by an agent other than the universe. Hawking's intuition that the universe could simultaneously create our material universe here while an anti-matter universe is formed elsewhere has no basis or warrant. Others like Richard Gott and Li-Xin Li of Princeton join him by mapping a model that permits the universe to become its own mother.[48] Sherburne's naturalistic process denies the God of most process advocates and adds the personal quality of occasions which is extremely foreign to most scientific microscopic analyses. These unusual modifications identify that those who believe the universe to be its own mother is rather small group. So perhaps a popular appeal is not hindered by the few who would side step this argument. For most, the verse sung in the "Sound of Music" still makes sense, "Nothing came from nothing, nothing ever could." Thus premise 4 will hold for most; human experience indicates that non-existent contingent beings do not cause themselves to exist.

Premise 3 has within it the possibility of the cause for contingent being to be a set or nexus of contingent beings, but each set or nexus would then be dependent upon some contingent beings or set of contingent beings. Ultimately this sequence of causes for contingent beings or sets of beings is either an infinite regress of contingency or ultimately begun by a necessary being.

Premise 7 used to be a difficult chasm to close (as evident by Aquinas' appeal to Scripture to bridge this gap) but since the advent of the big bang theory and empirical evidence for the expanding universe this step is significantly easier for those who are scientifically inclined. At the turn of the century, Henriet Levit recognized that the length of time it took to fix the image of a cephied star on a photographic plate indicated the distance this star was from the earth.[49] In 1914 Vesto Slipher observed

48 http://www.sns.ias.edu/~dejan/CCS/of/news/Gott_interview/J.Richard.Gott.III.eng.html#selfcreating%20universe.

49 http://map.gsfc.nasa.gov/m_uni/uni_101exand.html and http://hoa.aavso.org/posterswan.htm

that there was a red shift change in light from distant galaxies, indicating that they were moving away from the earth.[50] In 1917 William de Sitter found that a solution to Einstein's equations of general relativity could be solved, predicting an exploding Universe.[51] Edwin Hubble used these understandings and observations to recognize that the more distant stars had a spectrographic redder Dopler shift of light, and thus an expanding universe.[52] From this awareness, he proposed Hubble's law, which states that distance to stellar objects is proportional to velocity (i.e. twice as far away means twice as great a velocity).[53] In 1963, Arno Penzias and Robert Wilson of the Bell Laboratories discovered cosmic radiation in every direction which corroborated what Ralph Alpher and Robert Herman predicted in 1948 should be expected if there had been a big bang.[54] The Cosmic Background Explorer satellite was launched in 1989 and the summary of COBE's data in April 1992 concluded that it supported a big bang thesis on the basis of cosmic radiation.[55] From these experimental facts the theory of the big bang is constructed and warranted. At least the expanding universe is scientifically observable, whether this means that the big bang occurred where this expanding universe originated or whether creation merely emerged as a later stage of this expanding universe is largely dependent upon one's presupposition for an old or young universe. In the early 1970's the theory of the oscillating universe was floated but it is difficult to maintain today because there is rather broad agreement that the observed masses in the universe are rather small when compared to their high velocities and great distances. The oscillating universe also multiplies inexplicables like: a mechanism for the repeated big bangs, how to turn a black hole of the big crunch into the big bang, how to overwhelm entropy which would decay the oscillations so everlasting oscillations would be impossible, and what is the cause for the believed infusion of energy/matter to overwhelm entropy.[56] A further nail in the coffin for the oscillating model is the study, by both the University of Berkeley astronomer Alex Filippenko and Harvard University team comparing supernovae from one to ten billion light years away from earth, which indicates that the universe is expanding at an increasing rate, rather than slowing down.[57]

50 Robert Jastrow, *God and the Astronomers* (New York: W. W. Norton & Co., 1978), pp. 23–24.

51 Robert Jastrow, *God and the Astronomers*, pp. 24

52 Robert Jastrow, *God and the Astronomers*, pp. 27, 55.

53 http://map.gsfc.nasa.gov/m_uni/uni_101expand.html.

54 Robert Jastrow, *God and the Astronomers*, pp. 14–21.

55 http://aether.lbl.gov/www/projects/cobe/.

56 E.g., Duane Dicus et al., "The Future of the Universe," *Scientific American* (March 1983): 90–101, especially p. 100; "Effects of Proton Decay on the Cosmological Future," *Astrophysical Journal* 252(1982): 1–9.

57 David Pescovitz, "Supernovas Illuminate Dark Energy" *Science Matters@Berkeley* 1:5 available at: http://ofmatters.berkeley.edu/archives/volume1/issue5/story1.php; "Evidence Mounts that the expansion of the Universe is Accelerating" 6 Nov.

With an infinite regress of contingent beings as unlikely then the best explanation for the existence of the expanding universe is an actually necessary being which we call God (premise 8).

2.3.2. The Nature of a Necessary Being

The cosmological argument proposes that an actually necessary being exists which we will call God. This necessary being is always existent immutably and eternally. This level of immutability and eternity means that there is no sequence within God. There is no chronological experience in order for God to not change from non-being to being in a certain way.[58] Furthermore, the knowledge He knows He has always known without variance. God would know all there is to be known for the whole of time as an eternally present experience, without change. However, this does not cause God to be opposed to the knowledge of His creation, for He would always know what every feature of the creation knows from the creation's perspective in space and time while also knowing simultaneously from His unique vantage point. For example, He would eternally know my knowing of the past and my fears of the future from my vantage point and the perspective of every created thing in addition to His unique additional perspectives. So that in an Einsteinian relativistic universe we may have problems defending simultaneity of events but God would know simultaneously because He is not limited by our finite empirical ways of knowing. However, this does not render eternity to be static, for Boethius defines eternity in a more determining manner as the complete possession all at once of illimitable life.[59] The complete possession is an atemporal sourcing that does not change and is not limited but brings about all that has changed in its expressions of finiteness. This God is not only Creator but also Sustainer of the universe. This means that eternity is the source for all power and life. So eternity is not primarily to be known for its static, comprehensive, determining knowledge but for the life revealed to have come from God in His revelational creation.

1998 posted on http://physicsweb.org/articles/news/2/11/3/1; Saul Perlmutter, "Supernovae, Dark Energy, and the Accelerating Universe," *Physics Today* (April 2003): 53–59. Also reported by Doug Duncan, associate professor of astronomy at the University of Chicago, during Odyssey interview on WBEZ Jan. 16, 1999 about 11 a. m.

58 This means that the kenotic view of the divinity of Christ emptying Himself of His divine attributes so that He could become incarnate that Satori proposed in 1831 is excluded as well as the evangelical softened version of a willing nonuse of divine attributes which He continued to possess for both options describe essential change which is impossible for an immutable being. For a further discussion of this see Doug Kennard, *The Classical Christian God,* pp. 78–82.

59 Boethius, *The Consolation of Philosophy,* Book V, Prose 6; and *De trinitate*, chapter 4 in E. K. Rand ed., *Boethius: The Theological Tractates and The Consolation of Philosophy* (Cambridge: Harvard, 1973). For my discussion of issues of eternity and everlasting see: Doug Kennard, *The Classical Christian God*, pp. 43–62.

Because God initiates the whole of the creation (as Creator), including all of its details His knowledge is essentially also determining choice. God's choices are eternal and essential to His nature without variance. To have God as an actually necessary being means His sovereign choice is set, which means that the level of necessity for God includes all of God's thoughts and sovereign choices eternally and immutably. This means that God is not open in growing and gaining more knowledge and choosing in response to this knowledge. God's knowledge and choice would in fact be set within God's essential nature as determinative for the existence, essence, and choices the whole of creation makes.[60] With God's knowledge and choice as essential to His nature, then there is no logical order in God either. This means that all the of options expressing the order of the decree would in fact be contradictory to God's essential nature. There would not be a logical sequence within God Who simultaneously knows and chooses without sequence (i.e. eternally). This should not surprise us, for there are no Biblical texts that talk about any logical or chronological sequence within God of an order of salvation either; all these claimed texts at best indicate that when it comes to the application of God's choice out into the chronologically changing creation that such choice has a sequence of application for the recipient. For example, there is a clear logical and chronological sequence in applying the divine election (*ekletois*) as foreknown, preparative sanctifying the person so that the outcome (*eis*) of this sanctification ushers in obedience and atonement (1 Pet. 1:1–2). At other instances of sequence of the application of salvation there is encouragement for the Christian who has experienced some of the salvation benefits, like justification, who can be reassured that the other benefits, like glorification, will also be his in time (e.g., Rom. 8:29–30). So the whole post-reformation discussion of the order of the decree and the order of salvation within God was an unfortunate exploration that does not apply to this necessary, immutable, and eternal God. Any linkage of logical order or chronological sequence in such works of God is an expression of application order or revelation purpose. Any attempt to communicate eternal truths into a constantly changing environment like the creation will reflect them in sequential ways partly because of the sequential nature of the environment and partly to accommodate to our human understanding. For example, the textual sequences above convey that God graciously applies and guarantees the fullness of salvation to each Christian personally, which is a revelation purpose consistent with God's immutable nature. So that any apparent change in God is actually the refraction of a changeless God through the lens of the changing environment for purposes of applying some benefit to

60 For a further discussion of how the determining sovereignty of God and freedom of man fit in a non contradictory manner that consistently reflect the Biblical text, see Doug Kennard, *The Classical Christian God,* pp. 135–204.

the creation, such as salvation or the communication of certain select truths to a certain group in time. The fact that the truths of God are accommodated to the means of communication does not limit the truths of God, but the context indicates the primary hermeneutical purpose and how the descriptions of God are merely supportive of this purpose.

2.3.3 Aristotelian Science and Ethics

Aristotle contributes to the growth of science by placing great emphasis upon the importance of facts in connection with scientific development.

> Lack of experience diminishes our power of taking a comprehensive view of the admitted facts. Hence those who dwell in intimate association with nature and its phenomena grow more and more able to formulate, as the foundation of their theories, principles such as to admit a wide and coherent development; while those whom devotion to abstract discussions has rendered unobservant of the facts are too ready to dogmatize on the basis of a few observations.[61]

However, with the increase of facts beyond Aristotle, scientific concepts and support move beyond him. The area of causality is a prime example for how Aristotelianism begins to come unraveled.[62] Ptolemy's *Almagest* (late second century A.D.) had better observations than Aristotle's 55 concentric spheres for planetary movement would permit. Medievalists were troubled by the dissonance between Ptolemy's mathematical astronomy and Aristotle's physical theory.

With further precision of Renaissance Humanism, the field of science moved beyond Aristotle. For example, Galileo emphasized that changes did occur in the heavens, immersing the whole universe into change and decay, unraveling Aristotle's immutability of the heavenlies. Copernicus' book *On the Revolutions of the Celestial Spheres* (1543 A.D.) had its conclusions softened to be merely theoretical by a preface added by Osiander that the sun was placed at the center of the universe for the ease of making mathematical calculations. However, Kepler in *Mysterium Cosmographicum* identified the sun as the actual center of the real universe and that the planets were observed to move in elliptical orbits. Newton's *Principia Mathematica* (1687 A.D.) worked out in detail the laws that made sense of Kepler's observations of elliptical orbits, further supporting the Copernican model. Newton and Descartes

---

61 Aristotle, *De Generatione et Corruptione*. Edited by Christopher John Fards Williams (New York: Oxford University Press, 1982), bk. I, Cap. 2.

62 Allen, *Philosophy for Understanding Theology*, pp. 121, 161–69; F. K. Richtmyer, E. H. Kennard, and John N. Cooper, *Introduction to Modern Physics* (New York: McGraw-Hill Book Company, 1969), pp. 1–44.

analyzed the heavenly bodies as local motions which accelerate and slow down due to the effect of gravity upon each of them, further showing that the Aristotelian analysis of motion was destroyed on the reef of the external warrant provided by the experimental method. This method has gone a long way since then, with Faraday, Maxwell, Einstein, Bohr, and Hubble each making course corrections to the previous and showing that in physics Aristotle took merely a first baby step toward real science. Perhaps this development of warrant through rejection of Aristotelian physics by scientific realism should warn us to be careful to limit our commitments to what can be warranted by reality. Additionally, as a discipline grows in precision through critical realism, we should shift our adherence to those commitments which more accurately reflect reality.

In a different direction, Aristotle's view of ethics is a natural teleological framework requiring intrinsic good judgment in our attempt to head towards good (or happiness). The moral virtue is a habit formed by practice of the individual (and especially the state) choosing the particular way that best reaches this end.[63] This disposition to choose avoids the extremes of too much or too little but a mean between them; the virtuous life is neither gluttonous nor ascetic.[64] Aristotle then has a range of virtues including: courage, temperance, liberality, self-respect, gentleness, truthfulness, wittiness, friendliness, modesty and righteous indignation. Philo of Alexandria merged the Stoic theory of natural law with the belief of a divine legislator and the divine natural law theory was born.[65] Aquinas adopts this teleological framework especially for individuals and adds the theological virtues of: faith, hope, and love as infused by grace. So once again he is trying to fuse this Aristotelian philosophical perspective with Biblically affirmed values. Aquinas is also creative in that for him ethics are driven by the beatitude of God.[66] He has diminished Aristotle's ultimacy of the state to be an aid to the individual in achieving temporal goods, while the church becomes the aid to especially achieve supernatural goods. In Aquinas' attempt to

63 Aristotle, *Nicomachean Ethics* in *The Works of Aristotle II*, in the *Great Books of the Western World,* edited by William Benton (Chicago: Encyclopaedia Britannica, 1952), book 1, sect. 1094 or paragraphs 1–3, pp. 339–340.

64 Aristotle, *Nicomachean Ethics*, book 6–7, pp. 387–406.

65 Helmut Koester, "Nomos Physeos: The Concept of Natural Law in Greek thought," in *Religions in Antiquity*. ed. Jacob Neusner (Leiden: Brill, 1968), pp. 521–41; Naomi G. Cohen, *Philo Judaeus: His Universe of Discourse. BEATAJ 24* (Frankfort: Peter Lang, 1995); John W. Martens, "Unwritten Law in Philo: A Response to Naomi G. Cohen," *JJS* 42(1992): 38–45; and for criticism of this view: R. A. Horsley, "The Natural Law in Philo and Cicero," *HTR* 71(1978): 35–59 and Markus Bockmuehl, "Natural Law in Second Temple Judaism," *VT* 45(1995): 38–45. *Wisdom of Solomon* 13:1–15:17 is sometimes claimed to be natural law but the text instead argued that God designed a purposeful creation, so that if Gentiles disregard it or worship features of creation then they are blameworthy, but this is less than natural law because little ethic is available, only condemnation.

66 Aquinas, *Summa Theologica*, Second Part, Question 1.

Biblically ground the natural Law, he divides the Mosaic Law into three separate parts: moral (or natural), civil (judicial), and ceremonial.[67] This division is now broadly recognized by form critical studies of suzerainty treaties to violate the unity of the Mosaic Covenant documents.[68] So perhaps this natural law model helped to impose division on the Biblical text to further a patristic rejection of the Jewishness of the Law for natural law.[69] In this division, the ceremonial law is then justified as diminished on the basis of Hebrews 8–10.

Finally, natural law advocates seem likely to choose their world view preferences and intuitions consistent with their phenomenal perception as Immanuel Kant claims people operate in his *Critique of Practical Reason* and the *Critique of Judgment*?[70] Kant sees such a traditional ethic as deficient communal bias with the flaw proposed by David Hume, namely: what *is* does not necessarily govern what *ought to be*.[71] Furthermore, it is rather difficult to defend *what is* governs what *ought to be*, unless one intuitionally recognizes this connection as so and many do not.

Additionally, within such an Aristotelian natural law appropriation the final cause is the good. As such, one might wonder whether the pursuit of happiness is free of selfishness and sin. Likewise, in an Aristotelian natural law appropriation, does nature so naturally seek the

---

67 Aquinas, *Summa Theologica*, Second Part, Part I, Question 99, Article 3–5.

68 G. E. Mendenhall, "Covenant Forms in Israelite Tradition," *The Biblical Archaeologist*, 17:3 (1954): 50–76; K. Baltzer, *Das Bundesformular. Seine Ursprung und Seine Verwendung im AT*. Wiss. Monograph. 2. A. und N.T. 4 (Neukirchen: Neukirchener Verlag, 1960); Meredith G. Kline, *Treaty of the Great King. The Covenant Structure of Deuteronomy* (Grand Rapids: Eerdmans, 1963).

69 Justin, Dialogue with Trypho 47.2 in Apology. In Saint Justin Martyr: The First Apology, The Second Apology, Dialogue with Trypho, Exhortation to the Greeks, Discourse to the Greeks, The Monarchy; or the Rule of God. Edited by Thomas B. Falls. (New York: Christian Heritage, 1949); Irenaeus, Against Heresies 4.13.1, 4; 15.1; 16.1–5 in The Ante-Nicene Fathers, ed. A. Roberts and J. Donaldson vol. III (Grand Rapids: Grand Rapids, 1995); Tertullian, Virg. 1.1 and Against the Jews 2.7–10 both in The Writings of Quintus Sept. Flor. Tertullianus. Edited by Richard Ellmann. (Kila: Kessinger, 1869–70); Augustine, De spiritu et littera 27.29 edited by William Bright (Oxford: Clarendon, 1914); Wolfhart Pannenberg, Systematic Theology (Grand Rapids: Eerdmans, 2004), 3:70–80; Ernst Troeltsch, The Social Teaching of the Christian Churches (New York: Harper, 1960), pp. 115–7; Philippe Delhaye, Le Décalogue et sa place dans la morale chretienne (Bruxelles: La Pensée, 1963), pp. 66–8.

70 E.g., Immanuel Kant, *Critique of Judgment* in *Great Books of the Western World*, vol. 42, *Kant* (Chicago: Encyclopaedia Britannica, 1952), pp. 459–613, and especially part one, book two, section 26, pp. 500–501 where the concept of the sublime *Weltanschauung* (or worldview) first appeared in 1790. Cf. Werner Betz, "Zur Geschichte des Wortes 'Weltanschauung,'" In *Kursbuch der Weltanschauungen*, Schriften der Carl Friedrich von Siemens Stiftung (Frankfort: Verlag Ullstein, 1980), pp. 18–28, but especially p. 18.

71 David Hume, *A Treatise of Human Nature* (Oxford: Claredon Press, 1978), Bk. 3, part 1, sec. 1; this issue is known as 'Hume's guillotine' by Max Black, "The Gap Between 'Is' and 'Should'," *The Philosophical Review*, 73:2(Apr., 1964): 165–181.

good; can floods, hurricanes and tornadoes all seek the good? Or are they events that happen due to a convergence of influences (*El Niño* and butterfly effects). Furthermore, the good is not a conceptual goal but rather among difficulties in life, the good is a developing Christian character, which God accomplishes, cultivating the Christian to be like the Son (Rom. 8:28–30).

2.4. Renaissance Humanism

In the fourteenth and fifteenth centuries the abstract discourse of Scholastic philosophy seemed irrelevant to the needs of a bustling modern world. The humanists turned more to rhetoric, the way human language worked and the art of persuasion. Such a humanist stance appreciates the classics but especially the classical poets and narratives. For example, Calvin suggests, "Read Demosthenes or Cicero, read Plato, Aristotle, or others of that class: they will, I admit, allure you, delight you, move you, enrapture you in wonderful measure. Then betake yourself to that sacred reading."[72] William Bouwsma identifies the depth of Calvin's allegiance to renaissance humanism.

> His division of the classical authors here into two groups is significant: he mentions first the orators of Greece and Rome; the philosophers come second. His reliance on pagan literature in the *Institutes* and elsewhere is also revealing. He could probably not have avoided treating in places the views of philosophers; they were commonly invoked in theological discourse. But he was under no obligation to cite, as he regularly did, Cicero and Quintilian, Homer and Virgil, Plutarch and Seneca, Horace, Juvenal, and Ovid, the authors most cherished by humanists. He did so not only because the readers whom he chiefly addressed loved these authors but because he loved them himself.[73]

Calvin recognized that the meaning of words was in their use as "the practice of educated men."[74] Thus, he highly valued and cultivated the study of languages so that he might access the meaning of texts. "Since it is almost [the expositor's] only task to unfold the mind of the writer whom he has undertaken to expound, he misses his mark, or at least strays outside his limits, insofar as he leads his readers away from

72 John Calvin, *The Institutes of the Christian Religion,* 1.8.1 (Grand Rapids: Associated Publishers and Authors, n.d.). For Calvin's knowledge of ancient rhetoric see *Calvin's Commentary on Seneca's De Clementia,* tr. And ed. Ford Lewis Battles and Andre Malan Hugo (Leiden: E. J. Brill, 1969), especially the introduction.

73 William Bouwsma, *John Calvin: A Sixteenth Century Portrait* (New York: Oxford University Press, 1988), pp. 114–15.

74 John Calvin, *Com. Sen.,* 91; *Institutes,* oraoria*,* Bk. I, ch. vi, paragraph 45.

the meaning of his author."[75] He was also sensitive to the voices of the Biblical writers in their contexts and commented that Jeremiah had been shaped by the pastoral context that he had come from.[76]

Calvin appreciated the vividness of figures. For example, the darkness at the moment of Christ's death reminded him that "the ancient poets, in their tragedies, imagine that the light of the sun is withdrawn from the earth when any horrible crime is committed, in order to show the portent of divine wrath."[77]

Calvin had a balanced devotion to *eruditio*, as shown in his scholarly precision, and *persuasio*, as shown in his sensitivity to argument. Furthermore the organization of the *Institutes* is not set by a logical agenda but rather a series of overlapping topics generally following the order of the Apostles' Creed. This organization allowed Calvin the flexibility to develop a variety of persuasive strategies. Additionally, the knowledge of God begins with an important persuasive knowledge of oneself as well.[78] However, in the commentaries, he is closer to the text in faithfulness than in soaring persuasion.

Calvin tried to ply closer to Biblical notions on the questions of what is human and how can humans know? He does not embrace the dualism of Plato or Aristotle, but rather maintains a unity of person that probably could be reflected today best as an ontological Biblical functionalism.[79] For example, he saw the Biblical concept of "heart" to be an important wholistic description of a human at times emphasizing within its semantic field concerns about: world view, intellect, emotions, affection, will, and virtues.[80] With such an internal view of knowledge rooted in ones heart, he argues for a middle way of knowing between the dogmatic unthinking of tradition (especially Roman Catholic tradition informed by papacy) and speculation (which explores vain or useless things).[81] So for Calvin, knowledge is especially of the Word of God, personally owned in a manner that brings about real life change.[82] For example, the knowledge of God's benefits inspires in a person a union of reverence

75 John Calvin, *Calvin's Commentaries. Romans* (Grand Rapids: Baker Book House, 1979), v. 19.

76 John Calvin, *Commentaries*, Jer. 50:19, v. 11.

77 John Calvin, *Commentaries*, Matt. 27:45, v. 7.

78 John Calvin, *Institutes*, Bk. I, ch. i.

79 A more fully developed idea in Calvin's wake is the later chapter Biblical Anthropology as a Creation and Revelation Framework for Doing Bio-Ethics.

80 I am aware that "heart" did not make it into *The Institutes* as a subsection, like in bk. 1, ch. 15 but it is a concern there and Calvin is faithful to exposit it in the commentaries and sermons. Cf. John Calvin, *Commentaries*, Deut. 29:4; Isa. 51:7; Matt. 14:24; John 12:40; Rom. 2:15; Eph. 1:16; 1 Thess. 3:13; and Sermon No. 45 on Deut. 4:22.

81 John Calvin, Sermon no. 103 on Job, 521-22; *Commentaries*, 1 Thess. 5:21; cf. Bouwsma, *John Calvin*, p. 159.

82 John Calvin, *Institutes*, Bk. I, ch. v, paragraph 9; Sermon, no. 57 on Job, 711.

and love for God.[83] The primary knowledge available before one would hear the Word of God is the "sense of Deity indelibly engraven on the human heart."[84] With the location of faith being primarily in the heart, Calvin prefers the ear gate as the avenue through which the Word of God becomes the instructor of this real knowledge.[85] In this he is especially diminishing the visual sense of Aristotle (which Locke further develops) and the Catholic tradition of icons. Before such knowledge, flesh was largely seen as designating "men as they are born and as long as they retain their original disposition, for they are wicked so that they neither know nor aspire to anything but what is gross and earthly."[86] That is, "flesh includes our mind and reason" and "all the affections of the heart."[87] As such, he viewed the image of God as including this intellectual and moral aspect of humanity, but in the fall it was a "frightful deformity," "damaged and mutilated" virtually to destruction.[88] Thus sacred knowledge was the practical wisdom retrieving us from these sinful conditions to become a whole person, all experienced through the Word of God.[89]

The offspring of Calvin's renaissance perspective are many but at least two emerge from this approach: Biblical theology, and populous evangelicalism. The descriptive Biblical theology reflects Calvin's epistemic externalism which listens to the Biblical text. Contrasting to this, American Evangelicalism is reflective of Calvin's commitment to communicate to the populous.

Biblical Theology continues this reformation approach emerging in Johann Philip Gabler's lecture at the University of Altdorf in 1787.[90] Gabler's approach offered an optimistic empirical spirit that we could arrive at objective truth about the meaning of the text from a straightforward study of the Biblical text's details. This confidence that a commentator can approach the Biblical text in a descriptive manner is still with us in a more nuanced critical realist way, as in K. Stendahl's article about contemporary Biblical Theology in the *Interpreter's Dictionary of*

83 John Calvin, *Institutes,* Bk. I, ch. ii, and ch. v, paragraph 1.

84 John Calvin, *Institutes,* Bk. I, ch. iii, paragraph 3.

85 John Calvin, *Institutes,* Bk. I, ch. xi, paragraphs 5-7; *Commentaries*, Gen. 15:4; Ps. 19:1; Isa.

86 John Calvin, *Commentaries,* Rom. 7:14, v. 19.

87 John Calvin, *Commentaries*, John 3:6, v. 18.

88 John Calvin, *Institutes,* Bk. I ch. xv, paragraph 4; *Commentaries,* Gen. 1:26, v. 1.

89 John Calvin, *Commentaries*, Ps. 148:3, v. 5; *Institutes* of 1536 "sacred doctrine" is replaced by "our wisdom" in the second edition of the *Institutes*, 1539; cf. Bouwsma, *John Calvin,* p. 160.

90 Gabler's lecture 'On the proper distinction between Biblical and dogmatic theology and specific objectives of each,' is translated and commented on in John Sandys-Wunsch and Laurence Eldredge, 'J. P. Gabler and the Distinction Between Biblical and Dogmatic Theology: Translation, Commentary, and Discussion of his Originality,' *Scottish Journal of Theology* 33 (1980): 133-58 and also in *The Flowering of O. T. Theology,* eds. Ben Ollenburger, Elmer Martens, Gerhard Hasel (Winona Lake: Eisenbrauns, 1992), pp. 492–502.

the Bible, which calls the contemporary commentator to describe the meaning of the Biblical text for the original reader.[91] However, Gabler was aware of some of these subjective aspects in his day as he discussed some who in their Biblical theology occasionally got re-entangled with dogmatic theology, and warned against this.[92] For such a discipline as Biblical theology, that which is most binding is a basic methodology of reflecting the Biblical text wherever it will take you. Or the goal in Biblical theology as I state it is, "to be as clear as the text is clear and to be as ambiguous as the text is ambiguous."

Such an exegetical and theological methodology has a tradition over time that identifies with a heritage of attempts in the past but always goes beyond them to some extent in that each interpreter places his research program within the landscape of those who have gone before him in this discipline. So both the content and the organizing principles try to reflect what the Biblical text says.[93] It would be far better for us Christians to build our model upon the Bible as the descriptive Biblical theology movement proposes it, because such a model demonstratively reflects the Bible itself, even to a deep scholarly level. That is, alternative models which replace the Biblical thought forms run the risk of floating a traditional language game that conceptualizes and values things differently than the Biblical revelation reflection of the truth of the Word of God. If the Bible addresses issues then it establishes a revelational framework of the author's thought forms through which to view these concepts. Such a revelatory framework provides a grid through which theological and scientific proposals can fit or be censured (as incompatible with what the Bible says). A foundational example of this for science is the later chapter evidencing Biblical theology, "Creation and Fall." From this base I then explore a Biblical framework for bio-ethics. Within these, Biblical theologians become nearly unanimous in Biblical anthropology.[94] In such a functional linguistic model the heart (holistic human mental, worldview and emotional nature) is the most emphasized description of humans. That is, anthropology models that do not include heart are simply excluding the Biblical emphasis. Likewise, "image of God" is a holistic description of a human as God's representation and representative. "Soul" is holistically a living, willing individual, whether it is God, human or animal. Furthermore, "body" is holistically humanity with regard to

91 K. Stendahl, 'Biblical Theology, Contemporary,' *Interpreter's Dictionary of the Bible* (Nashville: Abingdon, 1962), 1:418–32.

92 Gabler, in *The Flowering of O.T. Theology*, p. 495.

93 My method for doing descriptive Biblical theology is developed in the chapter "The Reef of the O.T.: A Method for Doing Biblical Theology that Makes Sense for Wisdom Literature." Originally presented at ETS, 2000.

94 Cf. chapter, "Biblical Anthropology as a Creation and Revelation Framework for Doing Bio-ethics" including an earlier paper by: Douglas Kennard and Paul Holmes, "The Nature of Man: A Biblical Theology Approach" presented as a paper at the Wheaton Theology Conference, 1997.

physicality and relationship. Additionally, "spirit" is that aspect in man partaking of the spirit dimension, or that in man relationally orientated to God. If the Bible presents a model like this, then the philosophies that work with other models of humanity to the exclusion of this one are at odds with revelational Christianity, and will likely be valuing things differently than the Biblical thought forms.

American Evangelicalism reflects Calvin's commitment to communicate to the populous. Mark Noll argues that one of the distinctives of American theology is that it tries to be clear populist communication.[95] In fact, the American rejection of the value of class and nobility disconnected the practice of religion from being determined in a region by the preference of kings after which American religion entered a capitalistic marketing-based arena in which each entrepreneur within religion would demonstrate his worth by the extent of a following that he could attract around him. This approach protected religion from its demise as occurred in Europe when the kings were thrown out. That is, American religion was immersed into an arena of pragmatism, in which unpopularity became among the gravest of sins. Alister McGrath and David Wells conclude that American evagelicalism is strongly pragmatic.[96] That is, freedom and religion have been closely linked in America and a populist acceptance or rejection of the novel has told whether the theological innovation amounted to much on the American scene.

> A particular set of American conditions...have opened the door to many opportunities for popular theological innovation. Without a national state church, with few widely revered theological traditions, with no centralized scheme of national education, with all of the denominations compelled to enter into vigorous popular competition for adherents, with innovations in communications implemented by ordinary people, and with significant amounts of wealth widely distributed and available for establishing colleges, publishing houses, newspapers, and other means of disseminating ideas, the United States has been a very fertile medium for popular theologies.[97]

95 Mark Noll, *The Old Religion in a New World* (Grand Rapids: Eerdmans, 2002), e.g., p. 195.

96 Alister McGrath, "Evangelical Theological Method: The State of the Art" in *Evangelical Futures*, edited by John Stackhouse (Grand Rapids: Baker, 2000), p. 16; David F. Wells, *No Place for Truth, or Whatever Happened to Evangelical Theology?* (Grand Rapids: Eerdmans, 1993).

97 Noll, *The Old Religion in a New World*, p. 195.

This independent populism has long characterized the American religious scene as evidenced by the freedom that de Toqueville noticed over a century and a half ago.

> Anglo-American civilization...is the result...of two distinct elements which in other places have been in frequent disagreement, but which the Americans have succeeded in incorporating to some extent one with the other and combining admirably. I allude to the *spirit of religion* and the *spirit of liberty*... On my arrival in the United States the religious aspect of the country was the first thing that struck my attention; and the longer I stayed, the more I perceived the great political consequences resulting from this new state of things. In France, I had always seen the spirit of religion and the spirit of freedom marching in opposite directions. But in America I found they were intimately united and they reigned in common over the same country.[98]

Such American evangelical populism often resists theological depth.[99] However, American evangelicalism tends "to read the Bible as Scripture...in a particular interpretative tradition."[100] For example, Noll explores dispensationalism as a theological movement driven by the popular study and preaching of the English Bible.[101] The dispensational response among the Plymouth Brethren "was to abandon formally organized churches and to place their hope in a dispersed invisible church made up of God's faithful remnant."[102] Noll's conclusion is that of epitomized this populist thrust.

> Dispensational theology never caught on at America's elite universities or seminaries, but it was a huge popular success that drove the activities of conference speakers, lay theological institutes, prophecy conferences, popular magazines, and the publication of thousands of books. Its confidence in both the literal meaning of Scripture and in the ability of lay people to understand the Bible fitted it perfectly to traditional patterns of American Protestant life.[103]

---

98 Alexis de Tocqueville, *Democracy in America,* ed. Thomas Bender (New York: Modern Library, 1981), p. 185.

99 Alister McGrath, "Engaging the Great Tradition," in *Evangelical Futures,* edited by John Stackhouse (Grand Rapids: Baker, 2000), p. 140.

100 Kevin Vanhoozer, *The Cambridge Companion to Postmodern Theology* (Cambridge: The Cambridge University Press, 2003), p. 168.

101 Noll, *The Old Religion in a New World,* pp. 66–67, 196–7.

102 Noll, *The Old Religion in a New World,* p. 197.

103 Noll, *The Old Religion in a New World,* p. 197.

However, after a century of dispensational teaching, there is a deeply lain tradition in this inventive populism as well. The tradition can be clearly seen in the theological statements of dispensational institutions and in the writings of their faculties. This is even more apparent as dispensationalism was challenged by the progressive dispensational movement.

Included among this evangelical populism were those who prided themselves in keeping the faith of a tradition as well, like the offspring of the Reformers who embraced the climax of the reformation confessions. Alister McGrath points out that this is a communal continuity with the past.

> The past generated a tradition to which the present is heir. That tradition involves modes of discourse, ways of conceiving the world, so forth, which it impressed upon the world, and which was perpetuated in a definite historical form, being mediated through both institutions and individuals.[104]

McGrath further points out that "evangelicals have denominational loyalties, which often exercise a subtle influence over the assumptions and agendas that are brought to the theological tasks."[105] For example, Stanley Grenz sees that Christian theology is to "delineate the community's interpretive framework" because "all Christian theology is communitarian."[106] He goes on to point out, "as a result, our respective communities (or traditions) play an indispensable role in shaping our conceptions of rationality, as well as the religious beliefs we deem basic and thus use to test new claims."[107] Their summaries include the dispensationalist communities as well as those who are more intentional about a conventional loyalty, as in a reformed perspective loyal to *The Westminster Confession of Faith,* or Wesleyan with its Quadilatrial (which includes tradition) or other creed of the faith.

Returning to Calvin as our model of Renaissance Humanism, Calvin could choose both to be Biblical and to communicate. However, when Calvin had to choose between the clarity of communication to the populous and Biblicism he chose Biblicism. This is evident in the tightness of his comments to the Biblical text in his commentaries and the growing development of *The Institutes of the Christian Religion* over his life and study.

---

104 Alister McGrath, *The Genesis of Doctrine* (Grand Rapids: Eerdmans, 1990), p. 188.

105 Alister McGrath, "Evangelical Theological Method," p. 27; also *The Genesis of Doctrine*, pp. 178, 183.

106 Stanley Grenz, "Articulating the Christian Belief Mosaic: Theological Method after the Demise of Foundationalism," in *Evangelical Futures,* edited by John Stackhouse (Grand Rapids: Baker, 2000), pp. 123, 130.

107 Grenz, "Articulating the Christian Belief Mosaic," in *Evangelical Futures,* p. 131.

2.4.1 Renaissance Science

There were equally huge advances in science in the Renaissance method that is especially identified with inductionism of Francis Bacon.[108] Scientific inductivism is where scientists see themselves starting with unbiased observations and progressively pile up more facts by means of observations, interpreting them judiciously, and generalizing them into scientific laws. Bacon believed that scientists should model themselves like a bee, to learn the secrets of nature by planned observations and experiments in an organized observation of nature's regularities. Bacon's method begins with tables of instances in which first the positive instances are displayed and then where one might expect to see an observation but that no affirming evidence is provided. These tables would be summarized in a table of comparison, where the natural laws were generalized.

Two examples of such inductionism are: Galileo on astronomy and Vesalius on human anatomy. Both scientists were resisted by the established tradition but in time they were vindicated by those who were committed to allow the real to indicate and warrant truth. So both Galileo and Vesalius champion experiment and observation.

By observation and experiment, Galileo gave credence to the Copernican view of a moving earth around the sun.[109] Additionally, Aristotle had predicted that objects twice as heavy should fall at twice the rate, but Galileo dropped objects of different weights from the top of the Leaning Tower of Pisa and experimentally concluded except for air resistance that the objects fell at the same rate. Galileo likewise concluded that objects without any interference from another object would continue to move in a straight line forever, which denied the Aristotelian view that maintained objects needed a continual agent forcing them for movement to occur. Likewise, Galileo experimented with the newly invented telescope for observation and noticed that the celestial realm was mutable, contrary to Aristotle. Specifically, he discovered four moons revolving around Jupiter. By analogy he reasoned from this observation that the planets revolve around the sun, supporting the Copernican explanation for the solar system.

Similarly, Vesalius' commitment to observations of human dissection made major advances and corrections beyond Galen to the

108 Francis Bacon, *Novum Organum: Aphorisms Concerning the Interpretation of Nature and the Kingdom of Man Great Books of the Western World,* vol. 30 *Francis Bacon,* (Chicago: Encyclopaedia Britannica, 1952), pp. 105–198. J. F. W. Herschel, *Preliminary Discourse on the Study of Natural Philosophy* (London: Longman, 1830) contemporizes this approach through the method of Galileo and Newton as he proposes the first modern account of inductive scientific method.

109 Galileo Galilei, *Dialogues Concerning Two New Sciences.* (New York: Macmillan, 1914); conclusions summarized by Paul Hewitt, *Conceptual Physics* (Boston: Little, Brown and Company, 1981), pp. 9–10.

field of human anatomy in his 1543 A.D. of, *On the Structure of the Human Body*.[110] Vesalius revised his work again in 1555 A.D. with more accurate information from further human dissections, including especially sketches that reflected fetal conditions and female reproduction.

In the Renaissance, commitment that the observable real, rather than authority, began to determine and warrant the truth for all sciences.

2.5. Descartes' Rationalism

Modern philosophy begins with Descartes' publishing of his *Meditations on First Philosophy* (1641).[111] During the Thirty Years War dividing Europe up into the rival church traditions, Descartes sought a rational absolute which is accessible to human reason. Descartes' answer to these rival church traditions is foundational rational analysis. He begins this rational analysis by reflecting the mathematics of projectiles, with their variable velocities and destinations, if its trajectory is modified. This approach requires simplifying objects into their basic descriptions to render them accessible in terms of analysis.[112] Such an approach shows the rejection of the Aristotelian metaphysic, for projectiles continue to change their velocities based on the impetus of their inertia and the forces working on them. He also repudiates the role of syllogism for gaining knowledge but retains the ideal of certainty, which mathematics provides. Descartes provides a derivation of algebra to describe projectile movement, thus initiating the field of dynamics through mathematical derivation.

He then transfers this rationalistic methodology over to philosophy. So he begins by doubting the conjectures and traditions of his predecessors in order to find a certain and clear foundation.[113] He does *not* require that knowledge must begin with self evident starting points, the caricatured classical rational foundationalist. Of course such a straw man does not have a self evident reason for starting with self evident foundations. Instead, Descartes is evaluating what various tools of knowledge can provide and he floats a moderate foundational realization that a self evident foundation would provide a certain and clear starting point. Which is significant because within a world where few epistemic means provide certainty, to begin with such a self evident foundation provides a real gain over the weaker alternative claims. That is, he was seeking a philosophical and theological method that had the certainty of his study

110 Jerome Tarshis, *The Father of Modern Anatomy: Andreas Vesalius* (New York: The Deal Press, 1969), pp. 7–17, 30, 45, 60, 73–78, 96–97.

111 Descartes, *Meditations on First Philosophy, Great Books of the Western World,* vol. 31 *Descartes, Spinoza,* (Chicago: Encyclopaedia Britannica, 1952), pp. 69–103.

112 René Descartes, *Rules for the Direction of the Mind, Great Books of the Western World,* vol. 31 *Descartes, Spinoza,* (Chicago: Encyclopaedia Britannica, 1952), rule 12–13, pp. 18–25.

113 Descartes, *Rules for the Direction of the Mind,* rule 3 and 5, pp. 3, 7–8, and *Meditations on First Philosophy,* especially meditation 1, pp. 75–77.

in geometry and algebra, and he found such certainty in transcendental starting points and rationally tight argumentation from those starting points.[114] He urges his readers to join him in meditations in which they notice in their reflection what he is noticing in his own perspective. His undeniable starting point is that in his doubting his own existence he realized that he was thinking, and such a thought confirmed to him that he exists as a thinking being.[115] Most philosophers grant this insight but most philosophers today do not think that this is very significant, because few people wouldn't already grant that they exist as a thinking being.

The rationalistic strategy is driven by the concept of necessity and logically necessary derivation. Necessity as a concept is used in several ways but these ways can be primarily organized into either logical necessity or actual necessity. Logical necessity normally requires an argument with assumed premises to establish the logically necessary relationship of cogency. In such an instance cogent simply means that the argument is logically tight or logically necessary. Of course, this does not require that a cogent argument is compelling and thereby accepted by the reader, for the assumed premises of the argument may not be granted by the reader. However, with the granting of those premises such logical necessity has implications governing reality.[116] At times, something in the experience of reality logically necessarily requires there to be a particular being in reality. For example, Descartes' maxim of "I think therefore I am" guarantees that for any experience of thinking or doubting that at least this thinker exists in reality as a thinking being. However, sometimes logical necessity governs reality without an experiential ground merely because the concept under consideration logically necessarily requires it to be so. For example, a square circle can never exist in reality for the concept is logically necessarily contradictory, because the concept of square mutually excludes the concept of circle from describing the same object simultaneously. This kind of logical necessity excludes the contradictory concepts from being even possible in reality.

The concept of actual necessity or modal necessity describes a being whose immutable existence is logically necessary and eternal. Such an analysis for the ontological argument extends beyond Descartes' approach to the ontological argument to that of contemporary advocates grounded upon Anselm's second form of the ontological argument.[117]

114 Descartes, *Rules for the Direction of the Mind,* rule 3, p. 3; *Meditations on First Philosophy,* especially meditation 4, pp. 89–93.

115 Descartes, *Discourse on Method of Rightly Conducting the Reason, Great Books of the Western World,* vol. 31 *Descartes, Spinoza,* (Chicago: Encyclopaedia Britannica, 1952), part 4, pp. 51–54.

116 For a defense that the logically necessary is the real cf. Doug Kennard, *The Relationship of Epistemology, Hermeneutics, Biblical Theology, and Contextualization* (Lewiston: Mellen Press, 1999), pp. 42–43.

117 E.g., Alvin Plantinga, *The Nature of Necessity* (Oxford: Clarendon Press, 1974), pp. 197–221; Anselm, *Proslogium* 2 and 3, and *Apologetic Against Gaunilo* in *St.*

That is, such a necessary being must exist in reality if it exists at all. The four Aristotelian categories of modality include: 1) impossibility (which like square circles will never exist in any reality), 2) possibility (might be existence or a potentially dependent being), 3) actuality (happen to be in reality, or an actually dependent being, or a contingent or changing being), and 4) actual necessity (must be immutable eternal existence). Each human has occupied both the category of possibility (as her parents contemplated her conception, birth, and the changes that would make to their family) and actuality (as they exist as a dependent happen to be growing being now). That is, we are dependent upon our parents for our existence and such things as food and circumstances for continued growth in existence. Such categories as possible and actual would most likely have temporal sequence of having possibilities change as events happen, being a particular way then being a different way. If such an actual being continued forever, as in everlasting life, then everlasting (continued temporal existence in which change would continue to occur) would be the appropriate description rather than eternal (existence outside time and sequence, with no essential change). An actually necessary being, if there is such a being, could not merely be a possible or an actual being, for it wouldn't be in the same dependent kind of relationship or happen to be kind of existence or merely everlasting existence as these two categories imply. So, if an actually necessary being exists at all then it must necessarily exist in reality, and if not then it could never exist for it would then be impossible. However, we can not merely assume or illustrate such a necessary being into existence, as though through some sort of a Platonism[118] we were guaranteeing an eternal form from our belief or discursive reasoning. Furthermore, if we maintained such a belief about the existence of God by merely tradition then such a basic belief could probably be strengthened by examining its rationale. Descartes summarizes, "the whole strength of the argument for the existence of God consists in this, that I recognize that it is not possible that my nature should be what it is, and indeed that I should have in myself the idea of a God if He did not truly exist."[119] So for Descartes,

Anselm Basic Writings (LaSalle: Open Court, 1962), pp. 53–54, 311–328.

118 The author acknowledges that the classical model of God as a necessary being emerged as a Platonic and Aristotelian concept among the fathers and scholastics of Christianity but this paper is an attempt to show that the concept should be maintained without dependence upon them. Actually, this author is far more indebted to Locke, Leibniz, Kant, Peirce, Wittgenstein, Hackett, Plantinga, Thiselton, and Ricoeur than these classical influences.

119 Descartes, *Meditations on First Philosophy,* meditation 3 and 5, pp. 81–89, 93–96. Actually when it comes to ontological argumentation Descartes first form is weaker than the second form that Anselm had already developed in his *Proslogium,* 2, but this stronger form of the ontological argument would largely remain lost until the 1950's when Findley and then Alvin Plantinga appropriate the second form expounded here. Stronger cosmological arguments have also been marshaled in recent time under the influence of Bill Craig's *Kalam Cosmological Argument* (New

human knowledge of God's existence is grounded in ontological and cosmological arguments (the latter previously developed within the discussion of Aristotle and Aquinas). This rationalistic section will explore this rationale by examining: an ontological argument, and show a few theological implications for the attributes of God that reflects the nature of a maximally great being defended by these arguments. Elsewhere I corroborate these ideas with a Biblical assessment of whether the God of the Bible is described by these philosophical concepts and arguments, so I won't repeat myself here.[120]

2.5.1. An Ontological Argument

An ontological argument is informed by a powerful concept like that of a maximally great being. For our purposes, a maximally great being will be defined as *that being which has the maximally great set of metaphysical attributes.*[121] One implication from this definition is that such a being is not contradictory, and thus normally considered to be not impossible, for the concept underscores that each of the attributes in the set will mutually limit the other attributes of the set so that no grotesque (a being with one attribute in the extreme) or contradictory being will ensue. For example, omnipotence in such a maximally great being could not mean 'all powerful' because omnipotence limits omnipotence in that he could not make a stone so large that he could not move it. Omnipotence for this maximally great being would mean that this being, if it existed, would have the maximal degree of power it is possible to exemplify including:

1. There are no independent, externally determined constraints on divine power; there are no rival beings who could thwart a maximally great being.
2. All God's internal attributes are fully empowered to perform all that is intrinsically better to have than to lack.
3. God is the sole source and continuous support of all the power there is or could be; all the power of every entity is contained within and derives from God.

Each of these premises is required from the nature of a maximally great being, if it is a being at all. Because we conceive of a matrix of attributes in the set of divine attributes, if there is such a maximally great being then these attributes will be fully empowered (2). Other beings, like

York: Barnes & Noble, 1979); cf. Douglas Kennard, *The Classical Christian God*, pp. 11–42.

120 Doug Kennard, *The Classical Christian God,* pp. 11–42.

121 Thus, contrary to Kant and others, I do have a clear concept of a maximally great being.

ourselves, would be empowered fully from this maximally great being in such a manner that there would be no power which another being has that the maximally great being didn't source without diminishment to His own power (3). Therefore there can be no rival because all other beings are empowered by the power which they have ultimately from this maximally great being, if there is such a being (1). With attributes like this, a maximally great being would be incomparable, in that no other being could be favorably compared to this being. A maximally great being would always be superior. Thus there would only be one maximally great being as a monotheism. Furthermore, such a maximally great being would be a necessary being if he existed. For example, a maximally great being would not change, come into being, go out of being or depend on another being for its existence. If such a necessary being exists, he could not merely "happen to exist" or be "potentially existent" or be a "dependent being." Therefore, a maximally great being is either necessary or impossible. With attributes like these, an ontological argument may be constructed following Plantinga[122] as follows:

4. If a maximally great being exists, his existence is actually necessary.
5. If a maximally great being does not exist, his existence is impossible.
6. Either a maximally great being exists or he does not exist.
7. A maximally great being is either actually necessary or impossible.
8. A maximally great being is not impossible.
9. Therefore a maximally great being exists as an actually necessary being.

Premises 4 and 5 reflect the modal options from the previous discussion of necessity. Premise 6 identifies that there are only two mutually exclusive options available: existence or nonexistence. Premise 7 replaces premise 6 terminology by the implications from premises 4 and 5. Plantinga affirms premise 8 as a basic belief, which is quite natural when we recognize that we do not normally consider a concept to be impossible unless it is shown to be impossible, and a maximally great being has already been shown to be not a contradictory concept. Provided the reader does not approach this issue with the bias of skepticism it is reasonable to assume that a maximally great being is not impossible as a being and not just a concept. Additionally, if any argument for God's existence is compelling for the reader (like the cosmological argument

122 Al Plantinga, *The Nature of Necessity*, pp. 196–221 and slightly modified by Doug Kennard.

developed in section 2.3.1) then such an argument could confirm premise 8. However, premise 8 does not need nearly so strong an argument as this, so I will explore two other arguments for premise 8 to help compel some readers to grant it within this framework.

Within the heritage of William James' *Varieties of Religious Experience,* an inductive argument for the non-impossibility of a maximally great being following Clement Dore[123] could be constructed as follows:

10. It is reasonable to consider that any concept that is internally consistent which is claimed to have been experienced is not impossible.

For example, if you walked into the local police station this Friday night and consistently claimed to have just had the experience of robbing the local convenience store, the police would assume that it is not impossible that you might in fact have robbed this store so they would usher you into the back room for further questioning and probably call that convenience store to check out your story. Depending on how your story checked out with their investigation you would either be prosecuted or sent to a hospital to deal with mental issues. However, the police began to check out the story because they assumed that an internally consistent concept claimed to have been experienced is not impossible. That is, to float this premise all that is needed is the first assumption that anything that is internally consistent that is claimed to have been experienced is not impossible. With this framework the inductive argument for premise 8 would be as follows:

11. A maximally great being is by definition internally consistent.
12. Isaiah 40–48 claims to have experienced a maximally great being under the rubric of incomparability.
13. Therefore, it is reasonable to consider that a maximally great being is not impossible.

This argument does not require Isaiah to be authoritative Scripture but merely a testimony of a claimed experience of an incomparable being. Labuschagne develops the ancient Near East concept of incomparability as essentially the philosophical concept of incomparability in his work *The Incomparability of Yahweh in the Old Testament.*[124] That is, no

123 Clement Dore, "The Possibility of God," *Faith and Philosophy,* 1 (1984): 303–15, and "God, Suffering and Solipism" (Unpublished manuscript, 1986), pp. 3–42, 108–119.

124 C. J. Labuschagne, *The Incomparability of Yahweh in the Old Testament* (Leiden: Brill, 1966).

actual or potential rival can be favorably compared to Yahweh, Who as sovereign is greater than all comers individually and combined (Isaiah 40:18–28; 41:4, 23–24; 42:5; 43:10–13; 44:6–8; 45:5, 21–22; 46:9–10; 48:12–14). It is Yahweh talking with Isaiah, Who is reported to be always present to be able to create, know history from its beginning and predictively reveal the future because He continues to create history bringing about His will, for He has no rival. This incomparable Yahweh is testified to by Isaiah as having talked with him and challenged him and others to take the incomparability of Yahweh seriously, putting away idols and holding to Yahweh alone as their sovereign. Isaiah's experience of such an incomparable being renders such a noncontradictory concept to be not impossible to be experienced. Therefore, an incomparable being is not impossible. Furthermore, the impossibility of such an incomparable being can not be experienced, for with the concept of an incomparable being having freedom from contradiction such a claim would mean that a person is claiming to have experienced the full range of available experiences in the universe and concluded that such a being is not available to be experienced. However, such a claim to have experienced the full range of available experiences is essentially an omniscience claim, which itself is practically impossible for a finite human person to experience. Because the concept of incomparability is championing Yahweh as over all options, real as well as hypothetical ones, the concept of incomparability is essentially identical to a maximally great being. Therefore, premise 8 is affirmed; it is reasonable to consider that a maximally great being is not impossible.

A deductive argument for the non-impossibility of a maximally great being is also available within Plantinga's construction of possible worlds.[125] A possible world is a logically possible state of affairs as indicated by freedom of contradiction both as a concept and with other constituents within that possible world. Non-impossibility is normally defined as that which is logically conceivable without contradiction. However, since it has already been shown that a maximally great being is free of internal contradiction, the issue here is with regard to compossibility (whether this consistent concept of a maximally great being can be instantiated without contradiction with the truths which are conjunctively the case in all possible worlds). Plantinga defined a maximally great being as within each possible world but this is an arbitrarily weaker definition because like a necessary being a maximally great being will be a transworld entity if he exists at all. For example, a necessary being in possible worlds should be defined as *that being, when considered from the standpoint of any possible world, is understood to immutably exist in any and all possible worlds*. Likewise, a maximally great being is defined as *the being when considered from the standpoint of any possible world, is*

125 Plantinga, *The Nature of Necessity*, pp. 218–9.

understood to have maximum metaphysical greatness in any and all possible worlds. Therefore, if a maximally great being exists then any proposed world which contradicts such a maximally great being is not even a possible world. However, Plantinga claimed that a maximally great being in possible worlds terminology does not require one to assume that a maximally great being must exist. He proposed that there are two options besides a maximally great being. However to make those two options in fact mutually exclusive options the definitions of maximally great being must be the same in all these options or they will not in fact exclude a maximally great being from non-impossibility and actual necessary existence. The first alternative is no-maximality defined as the claim that a maximally great being does not exist in any possible world. The second alternative is near-maximality which is defined as a maximally great being exists in some possible worlds but does not exist in other possible worlds including the actual world. Plantinga correctly concludes that all conceptual options are included within these three mutually exclusive options: maximally great being, no-maximality, and near-maximality. This framework permits the following argument:

13. The only available non-impossible option is the one conceptually consistent and compossible option from the following fully inclusive and mutually exclusive options: a maximally great being exists, no-maximality exists, or near-maximality exists.
14. A maximally great being is by definition internally consistent.
15. No-maximality is internally contradictory when the meaning of maximally great being is clarified in the definition of no-maximality as follows: *the being when considered from the standpoint of any possible world, is understood to have maximum metaphysical greatness in any and all possible worlds* does not exist in any possible world.
16. Near-maximality is internally contradictory when the meaning of maximally great being is clarified in the definition of near-maximality as follows: *the being when considered from the standpoint of any possible world, is understood to have maximum metaphysical greatness in any and all possible worlds* exists in some possible worlds but does not exist in other possible worlds including the actual world.
17. Because no-maximality and near-maximality are contradictory concepts they cannot meaningfully exist as states of affairs.

18. With two of the three fully inclusive and mutually exclusive options as contradictory, the only other available option must be that a maximally great being is not impossible.

Therefore, a Maximally Great Being necessarily exists in reality. Premise 8 brought us to that conclusion, whether by basic belief, an argument from testimony or an argument from possible worlds. Because this chapter is developing a philosophical and theological framework within which science should operate there is a need to spell out some of the attributes of this Maximally Great Being.

2.5.2. The Nature of a Maximally Great Being

There necessarily exists a Maximally Great Being, Who is defined by the maximally great set of attributes it is possible to have. Since the kinds of possibility include not just logical possibility but also actual or compossibility as well, then no proposal is credible in which this being entails a contradiction through internal (e.g., claims of contradiction within attributes) or external (e.g., claims of contradiction with the problem of evil) means. All such claims for contradiction with the Maximally Great Being are not even possible because the transworld quality of the Maximally Great Being excludes them from all possible worlds. This means that the Maximally Great Being's attributes are those which when combined in a set are the maximum possible to exemplify as illustrated by omnipotence above (e.g., premises 1–3). The attribute of infinity, which would include transcendence, can describe these attributes by indicating that the Maximally Great Being is not limited by anything other than the necessary relationships among its own maximally great qualities.[126]

Such a Maximally Great Being would be immanently omnipresent and thus immaterial or spiritual as well. That is, the availability and accessibility of objects in the spatial-temporal world is a good trait making them useable to us. Likewise, the availability and accessibility of an immanent omnipresent and everlasting being would be very fitting for the Maximally Great Being as well. However, the Maximally Great Being's omnipresence would be necessarily everywhere without variation or sequence. So such omnipresence would be non-bodily (i.e. spiritual)

126 Such a view would not entail infinite options, for possibilities are limited to that which is not contradictory to the Maximally Great Being, thus excluding the renaissance maximal possibilities suggestion which Leroy Howe suggests in "Existence as a Perfection: A Reconsideration of the Ontological Argument," *Religious Studies* 4(1968): 92–94. Additionally the concept of a process primordial nature would be excluded or severely limited to only those compossible possibilities to a Maximally Great Being.

and immutably (ie. eternal even though such a being might be glimpsed within creation as everlasting). So the spiritual and eternal omnipresence which the Maximally Great Being would instantiate would be exhibited in a non-spatial and non-temporal manner similar to another dimension beyond space and time. Perhaps Tillich's dimensional model for spirit as an immanent causal ground which creates and sustains the whole of creation serves as a paradigm for making sense of omnipresence of this eternal spiritual Being. That is, a person would not expect each location of the universe to contain an instance of the fullness of God but that God's fullness is present to each location in a continuous casual manner creating, determining, sustaining, protecting, relating, knowing from that perspective and recreating the whole of the universe into His kingdom.

Such a Maximally Great Being would be actually necessary, immutable, and eternal. This being could not come into being or go out of being for He would always possess the maximally great set of attributes. Likewise, this being would not grow or degenerate for He would always possess the maximally great set of attributes. Without change in these attributes He is immutable, without chronological sequence and thus eternal.

Since such a Maximally Great Being is defined by His nature, in which the maximally great set of attributes is embracing meaningfully distinct attributes held together in a set, the concept of simplicity embraced within Platonic and Aristotelian Christianity is excluded as contradictory. That is, the following features of the Aquinas/Stump definition of simplicity[127] would be excluded by the divine nature: "there cannot be any real distinction between one essential property and another in God's nature" and "there cannot be a real distinction between essence and existence in God." The meaningfully distinct attributes (such as God's goodness and wrath, or transcendence and immanence) show the impossibility of the Maximally Great Being as this kind of a simple Platonized Christian god because such a simplicity view is contradictory.[128]

The Maximally Great Being is incomparable and thus monotheistic, with no rival individually or corporately. So dualism and polytheism is excluded. No Satan or group of humans could thwart the plan of this Maximally Great Being. That is, a Maximally Great Being could not be a part of a whole which is greater than the former Being alone, so He becomes the sole source and continuous support of all power and all beings who exercise power.

---

127 Thomas Aquinas, *Summa Theologica*, vol. I, Pt. 1, Q3, A7, and Eleonore Stump "Simplicity" in Quinn and Taliaferro, *A Companion to Philosophy of Religion* (Cambridge: Blackwell, 1997) p. 250, and Stump and Kretzmann "Absolute Simplicity," *Faith and Philosophy* 2(1985): 353–81.

128 The author has argued this elsewhere. Cf. Doug Kennard, *A Classical Christian God*, pp. 73–75, following Al Plantinga, *Does God Have a Nature?* (Milwaukee: Marquette University Press, 1980).

Another way to approach maximal greatness is to recognize good traits among humans, and then maximally surpass these good traits to determine maximal greatness. In this process, humans make a good model since they are near the top of any list of naturally known beings that can vie for metaphysical greatness. So the beneficial or great traits that humans have (such as being personal in interacting with those around, knowing what is happening around them, empathizing with others, having a will to act, and doing good) can also be found in the Maximally Great Being or are surpassed by His maximal greatness. This approach excludes non-interactive god concepts such as deism and a fully actualized Aristotelian god who does not feel and interact with those around him. Notice that this technique does not reduce to Ludwig Feuerbach's projected anthropomorphized God concept[129] because there is an argument to support the necessary existence of this Maximally Great Being; He is not merely a wish fulfillment.

Such a maximally Great Being would be personal, communicating to others and receiving prayers as a meaningful communication from them. Since it is advantageous in communication to tell the truth such a Maximally Great Being would be known for only telling the truth without any lie (e.g., Titus 1:2).

Additionally, such a Maximally Great Being would be an empathetic, compassionate merciful God, Who purposes to protect and cultivate those He has chosen (e.g., Jer. 31:20; Hos. 11:8). As a result of protecting His own, there would probably be a place for a Maximally Great Being to express righteous anger against those who attempt to destroy those who are His (e.g., Nah. 1:2). Since this being is omnipresent, He would know everything that happens, feel empathy for all, and sovereignly act for the good of the whole creation.

Such an interactive Maximally Great Being would be multiple persons, for in eternity before the creation the interactive communication, empathy, and love occurring would happen necessarily within Themselves. However, there is not enough here to require that this configuration must be a trinity,[130] though it may need to be more than two persons for the communal value of these attributes to be engaged. This would mean that creating would not be a necessary requirement for the Maximally Great Being but it would be a very natural choice on His part. With the act of creation would come continued involvement, so that the creation would reflect His qualities as it also shows forth the qualities of beings of creation as well.

129 Ludwig Feuerbach, *The Essence of Christianity*. trans. George Eliot (New York: Charles Scribners Sons, 1957).

130 Contra Augustine, Anselm, Swinburne, et. al.

2.5.3. Descartes' Worldview and Science

Such natural theology does not replace science but these philosophical and theological ideas and arguments defend a theological nest within which further philosophizing and science should operate.

Once the existence of the True God is demonstrated, Descartes considers that the likelihood of deceiving demons vanish and the senses can then be trusted from the world view framed by ones own clear and distinct ideas. In this, a representational nature of perception entails, which we call ideas. That is, epistemic dualism maintains a realism that one's ideas are distinct from the objects that the ideas represent. To defend this, Descartes could marshal that, objects have properties (like extension, weight, being eaten) that ideas do not have, therefore ideas are distinct from objects which they approximate. Rationalistic science is built within a recognition that conceptual demonstration describes real objects that our concepts approximate. Such scientific deduction funded Descartes' mathematical description of the dynamics of projectile movement.

Most philosophers think that Descartes is overconfident about the extent of a world view that can be deduced by rationalistic means. For example, he floated a view that the heavenly bodies were in heavenly vortices ("great swirling pools of fine matter which carried the heavenly bodies around like chips of wood floating on a tub of swirling water").[131] Descartes' view of dynamics was replaced by Newton's concept of inertia, forces, and acceleration. Such a Newtonian framework founds the mathematical basis upon which classical physics operates.

While Descartes defends a Christian God, the deists, trying to emulate Descartes' rational confidence, remove God's interactiveness. Alister McGrath nicely critiques this option, so as an aberrant theology, it is unnecessary to critique it here.[132]

2.6. Locke and Newton's Empiricism

In a context of religious wars destroying the credibility of religious authority, the seventeenth century's great triumph was in Isaac Newton's natural science,[133] and John Locke's epistemology and psychology of experience. Both Newton and Locke explored what could be observed by the senses and experience.

---

131 Quoted by Diogenes Allen, *Philosophy for Understanding Theology*, p. 183.

132 Alister McGrath, *A Scientific Theology: Nature*, (Grand Rapids: Eerdmans, 2001), vol. 1, pp. 181–191, 246–248.

133 Imre Lakatos provides a nice summary example of the development of the Newtonian model in "Falsification and Methodology of Scientific Research Programs," in *Criticism and the Growth of Knowledge. Proceedings of the International Colloquium in the Philosophy of Science, London, 1965.* vol. 4 edited by Imre Lakatos and Alan Musgrave (Cambridge: Cambridge University Press, 1970), pp. 135–8.

Newton made substantial contributions in the natural sciences. He began by limiting activity to that which could be learned from experience of scientific inquiry. Newton's Rules of Reasoning in Philosophy describe his scientific method as generalizing observable experiments.[134]

> Rule 1. We are to admit no more causes of natural things than such as are both true and sufficient to explain their appearances.
>
> Rule 2. Therefore to the same natural effects we must, as far as possible, assign the same causes.
>
> Rule 3. The qualities of bodies, which admit neither intensification nor remission of degrees, and which are found to belong to all bodies within the reach of our experiments, are to be esteemed the universal qualities of all bodies whatsoever.
>
> Rule 4. In experimental philosophy we are to look upon propositions inferred by general induction from phenomena as accurately or very nearly true, notwithstanding any contrary hypotheses that may be imagined, till such time as other phenomena occur, by which they may either be made more accurate, or liable to exceptions.

Newton's method was the first fully developed scientific method, and an examination of its application shows he used all these rules to formulate his laws.

Utilizing this method, Newton noticed that white light was made up of spectral colors by using two prisms, improving Descartes' parabolic lenses. From this ray theory of light (a forerunner to the wave theory) he posits that there must be an aetherial medium beyond our atmosphere for light to get from sun and stars to us.[135]

Even greater was Newton's work on mechanics. Positing that every particle in the universe attracts every other particle with a force inversely proportional to the square of the distance between the two particles, he showed that this one universal law governed the motion of

---

134 Isaac Newton, *Mathematical Principles of Natural Philosophy. Great Books of the Western World,* vol. 34 *Newton, Huygens,* (Chicago: Encyclopaedia Britannica, 1952), pp. 270–71.

135 Isaac Newton, "An Hypothesis Explaining the Properties of Light," quoted in F. K. Richtmyer, E. H. Kennard, John Cooper, *Introduction to Modern Physics* (New York: McGraw Hill, 1955), p. 19. Thomas Young in 1801 calculated wave lengths of the colors and showed that the interference patterns were predictable in a Piercian pragmatic manner.

planets around the sun and satellites around their planets. He began to derive the calculus[136] to reflect the relationship between force, velocity, acceleration, mass (a concept he introduced) and distance. Testing this law experimentally by dropping bodies, he laid out his three laws of motion in his *Mathematical Principles of Natural Philosophy,* and then applied them to the bodies of the solar system.

John Locke, the founder of empiricism, likewise based all knowledge on experience; denying innate ideas, he framed an epistemology upon the reality that could be perceived.[137] He was looking for determinate ideas that can be seen and perceived.[138] He agreed with Descartes that we could confirm our own existence as foundationally certain by thinking, but he insisted that such a practice is grounded in the experience of one's thought.[139] This approach positioned itself as passive, allowing nature to imprint upon our mind without active pursuit of the facts.

He valued coherence, in that he insisted that propositions which are contrary to reason cannot have been revealed by God. This commitment to coherence is important because Christianity is built upon such coherent revelation.[140] However, he sees that reason has limitations in that it has been used to float ideas that do not correspond to reality.[141]

Locke agrees with Descartes that sense experience can only provide probability, but he advocates that probability is for the most part good enough.[142] In *An Essay Concerning Human Understanding* he tried to trace all ideas back to their origin in experience. Reflecting a methodology of experimentation similar to that of his friend, the chemist Robert Boyle, who relied on trial and error much of the time, Locke sees experience as the means by which any man can plumb the depths of God's creation, to help us know our duties and to improve our life on earth.[143] From this vantage point of experience, Locke sees that immediate sensation and reflection can provide simple ideas, "which convey themselves into the mind by all the ways of sensation and reflection, viz. pleasure or delight,

---

136 Leibniz concurrently derived calculus from his modal approximations of objects, extending Descartes' rationalistic program further.

137 John Locke, *An Essay Concerning Human Understanding* in *Great Books of the Western World.* vol. 35, *Locke, Berkeley, Hume* (Chicago: Encyclopaedia Britannica, 1952), epistle to the reader and bk. 1 , pp. 89–92 and 95–121.

138 John Locke, *An Essay Concerning Human Understanding,* epistle to the reader, pp. 91–92.

139 John Locke, *An Essay Concerning Human Understanding,* bk. 4, ch. 9.

140 John Locke, *An Essay Concerning Human Understanding,* bk. 4, ch. 7, sect. 11 on the revelational foundation for Christianity and ch. 20, sect. 11, p. 392; he is especially addressing Catholic dogma like transubstantiantion. Jonathan Edwards (*Miscellanies* [New Haven: Yale University Press, 1957], number 1340) agrees with Locke that ideas must be coherent or they are not worthy to be believed.

141 John Locke, *An Essay Concerning Human Understanding,* bk. 4, ch. 17.

142 John Locke, *An Essay Concerning Human Understanding,* introduction, and bk. 4, pp. 94, 307–95.

143 John Locke, *An Essay Concerning Human Understanding,* pp. 385–402.

and its opposite, pain or uneasiness; power; existence; unity."[144] It is a person that maintains a continuity of their identity by consciousness in memory, retaining the recollection of the sensations after they have been experienced.[145]

Complex ideas are built up by combining these simple ideas.[146] This level gets beyond his ideal of knowledge by passive experience for it takes an active intellect to combine such complex models. In this, epistemological dualism is easily defended.[147] That is, two observers can perceive an object simultaneously, wherein the differences of their perceptions identify that neither of the perceptions is identical to the object. Epistemic dualism is also defended from the process of perception; extending Locke into a contemporary physics and neurology, analysis of light as waves or photons and nerves carrying electric charges, there is a causal chain between the object and the perception of the object through sensory organs, neural changes and the synapses of the brain. One of the main ramifications of his representative theory of perception was that truth and falsity was to be measured in how ideas correspond to reality.[148]

For empiricism, philosophy, theology, and science are built up like a layer cake. "The bottom layer is sensory experience, which supports empirical generalizations, topped off by theories."[149] However, there are limits to the generalizing process for a Lockian because empirical facts could not prove universal principles or conclusions, they could merely evidence them. However, this limitation can be overcome by a dependence upon the Biblical text particulars as authoritative statements that occasionally develop universal statements.

Locke maintained primary and secondary qualities as Galileo and Descartes had maintained before him.[150] However, in this form of representative theory of perception there is no means of establishing the distinction between these qualities, which was a point Berkeley and Jonathan Edwards made against Locke.[151]

---

144 John Locke, *An Essay Concerning Human Understanding*, bk. 2, ch. 7, sect. 1; also bk. 1, ch. 1, sect. 17 and bk. 2, ch. 1–8, pp. 121–134.

145 John Locke, *An Essay Concerning Human Understanding*, bk. 2, ch. 10, pp. 141–3.

146 John Locke, *An Essay Concerning Human Understanding*, bk. 2, ch. 12–13, pp. 147–55.

147 John Locke, *An Essay Concerning Human Understanding*, introduction; bk. 2, ch. 7, sect. 7 and ch. 8, sect. 2, p. 95, 132–33.

148 John Locke, *An Essay Concerning Human Understanding*, bk. 2, ch. 32; bk. 4, ch. 4–5, pp. 243–8, 324–31.

149 Nancey Murphy, *Theology in the Age of Scientific Reasoning* (Ithaca: Cornell, 1990), p. 7.

150 Frederick Copleston, *A History of Philosophy* (Garden City: Image Books, 1963), vol. 5, p. 88.

151 YE6: 343–44, 350, cited in Jenson, *America's Theologian*, pp. 31, 200–201.

Jonathan Edwards significantly interacted with Newton's understanding of physics (for personal studies in astronomy and in a general sense of the harmony of the universe)[152] and Locke's concepts for issues epistemology and psychology of humanity. That is, Edwards uses Lockian terms and emphasis for describing the process of understanding and will,[153] and this took him beyond the saving ambiguities of Puritanism. This Lockianism is apparent in Edwards' manuscript notebook *The Mind,* which he returned to and worked over much of his life. In this, Edwards agrees with Locke concerning the mind and personhood; "Well might Mr. Locke say that identity of person consisted in identity of consciousness."[154] That is, a person is a continuing self-identical consciousness, a continuity of memory. However, he rejected Locke's view that human spirit was a separate substance and instead claimed that it is this same consciousness of the mind.[155]

Edwards embraced the representational nature of ideas and epistemic dualism. One implication of this is that a mind could not completely know another mind without a union of personality.

> Clearly, Edwards was on the way to creating a doctrine that consciousnesses are substances by virtue of their self-relatedness, by their metaphysical independence as self-consciousnesses. Just such doctrine was to be created by German idealism of the next century. And indeed, Edwards taught that the "nearer in nature beings are to God, so much the more properly are they beings, and more substantial."[156]

Edwards used these Lockian concepts to primarily talk about God, a different focus than these interlocutors. That is, Newton and Locke's emphasis is to frame the world's beauty, while Edwards' emphasis sees this beauty as reflective of the beauty of God.[157]

---

152 Robert Jenson, *America's Theologian: A Recommendation of Jonathan Edwards* (New York: Oxford University Press, 1988), pp. 23–9.

153 For a discussion on Edwards use of Locke's concept of free-will cf. Douglas Kennard, *The Classical Christian God,* pp. 149–50.

154 Edwards quoted by Robert Jenson, *America's Theologian*, p. 29.

155 YE6: 342–3 and *Miscellanies*, number 267 cited in Jenson, *America's Theologian*, p. 30; this is a point on which I agree based on the overlap of νοός and pneuma, though I use the Tillichian concept of different dimensions to explain this, cf. chapter "A Biblical Anthropology as a Creation and Revelation Framework for Doing Bio-ethics."

156 Robert Jenson, *America's Theologian*, p. 33, with a citation from Edwards, YE6:238.

157 Robert Jenson, *America's Theologian*, pp. 15–17; whereas Locke eventually gets around to running a cosmological argument for God's existence, cf. John Locke, *An Essay Concerning Human Understanding*, bk. 4, ch. 10. Alister McGrath (*A Scientific Theology: Nature*, vol. 1, pp. 231–240) develops the role of beauty and aesthetics as an epistemic method especially in relativity and quantum physics. I think that beauty

In fact, for Edwards, the harmony of the world is ultimately seen through an Augustinian Trinity to be harmony in Himself. This harmony reflects itself by God's dealings with the world as a melody of history (His story).

With this divine interactiveness of God to the world, Edwards also departed from Locke on issues of revivalism, in that Locke specifically wrote against enthusiasm while Edwards channeled it through his grid of religious affections to designate and recognize appropriate expressions fostered by the Spirit as indications of authentic conversion and revival.[158] However, the terminology that Edwards uses in describing the religious affections is that of Locke's description of senses; so religious affections are a *sixth sense* for Edwards. Edwards illustrates this:

> There is a *sense* of the *beauty,* amiableness or sweetness of a thing; so that the *heart* is sensible of pleasure...in the presence of the idea...There is a difference between having a rational judgment that honey is sweet, and having a sense of its sweetness.[159]

That is, notional knowledge can recognize that something is good but only "the *sense* of the heart" grasps its value with will and inclination, and thus transcends the difference between knowing and willing. Since the Spirit provides new light of the idea of God, with affection and inclination to God, this new light provides a certain temper for our mind and spirit. Thus such sanctification is a conversion of the will which "assimilates the soul's nature to the divine nature."[160] In this, "A true *sense* of the divine excellence of the things of God's word doth ...directly ...convince of the truth of them."[161]

However, in 1748, David Hume brought a skeptical turn to empirical confidence.[162] His criticism analyzed the senses and showed that in many ways they could be doubted. As such, *a posteriori* cosmological and teleological arguments are doubted by Hume because they can't provide certainty and one who embraces such an argument assumes an ultimate cause, which he assumes is a condition of which humans are

as an epistemic criteria is overplayed and I would instead substitute warrant (without undue complexity).

158 John Locke, *An Essay Concerning Human Understanding,* bk. 4, ch. 11, sect. 6 and ch. 19, sect. 8; Jonathan Edwards, *Religious Affections*, ed. John Smith (New Haven: Yale University Press, 1957).

159 Edwards, *Miscellanies*, p. 547.

160 Edwards, Sermon, "A Divine and Supernatural Light," Imp., Thirdly, 2 (unpublished sermon).

161 Edwards, Sermon, "A Divine and Supernatural Light," Doc., I, sec. 2.

162 David Hume, *An Enquiry Concerning Human Understanding,* in *Great Books of the Western World* vol. 35, *Locke, Berkeley, Hume* (Chicago: Encyclopaedia Britannica, 1952), pp. 451–509.

ignorant (notice the circular reasoning).[163] Furthermore, if an idea was not grounded in the senses then it is irrelevant; an *a priori* ontological argument is assumed to be an arbitrary assuming of one's conclusion (notice the circular reasoning).[164] He additionally, sharpened deism's arguments against miracles. He argued against Locke, that probabilistic evidence did not support the unlikely (like miracle and prophecy). From all this he concludes in the last lines of his *Enquiry Concerning Human Understanding*:

> If we take in our hand any volume; of divinity or school metaphysics, for instance; let us ask, *Does it contain any experimental quantity or number?* No. *Does it contain any experimental reasoning concerning matter of fact and existence?* No. Commit it then to the flames: for it can contain nothing but sophistry and illusion.[165]

Perhaps such a statement provides a direct lineage for logical positivism of the twentieth century which rendered tradition to be merely conventional language and not describing reality.[166] However, logical positivism became self-stultifying in its inability to justify its own methodology.[167] Anthony Flew attempted to strengthen logical positivism's defenses by positioning its mechanism within the falsifiable. For Flew, only statements that are falsifiable are cognitively meaningful. Flew tells a parable about the unfalsifiable quality and thus the irrelevance of the concept of "God:"

> Once upon a time two explorers came upon a clearing in the jungle. In the clearing were growing many flowers and many weeds. One explorer says, "Some gardener must tend this plot." The other disagrees, "There is no gardener." So they

163 David Hume, *An Enquiry Concerning Human Understanding*, 7.1.55–57, pp. 474–5.

164 David Hume, *An Enquiry Concerning Human Understanding*, 4.1.25–26, p. 460.

165 David Hume, *An Enquiry Concerning Human Understanding*, 12.3, p. 509.

166 E.g., Ludwig Wittgenstein, *Tractatus Logico-Philosophicus* (London: Routledge & Kregan Paul, 1922); A. J. Ayer *Language Truth and Logic* (New York: Dover Publications, 1946). However, the seeds for these views are in Locke's correspondence view of ideas to reality. Likewise, Locke floats the idea of conventionality which Ludwig Wittgenstein does in *Philosophical Investigations* (New York: Macmillan Publishing Co., 1958), cf. John Locke, *An Essay Concerning Human Understanding*, bk. 3, ch. 11, sect. 11, p. 302 and John Locke's constitutional monarchy in *Concerning Civil Government* in *Great Books of the Western World*. vol. 35, *Locke, Berkeley, Hume*. (Chicago: Encyclopaedia Britannica, 1952), pp. 25–84.

167 For example, logical positivism could not verify itself so there was no reason to maintain it. Furthermore, of analysis made universal statements meaningless (requiring an infinite number of verifying experiences) while their denial was meaningful (requiring one particular).

> pitch their tents and set a watch. No gardener is ever seen. "But perhaps he is an invisible gardener." So they set up a barbed-wire fence. They electrify it. They patrol with bloodhounds...But no shrieks ever suggest that some intruder has received a shock. No movements of the wire ever betray an invisible climber. The bloodhounds never give cry. Yet still the Believer is not convinced. "But there is a gardener, invisible, intangible, insensitive to electric shocks, a gardener who comes secretly to look after the garden which he loves." At last the Skeptic despairs, "But what remains of your original assertion? Just how does what you call an invisible, intangible, eternally elusive gardener differ from an imaginary gardener or even from no gardener at all?[168]

This level of challenge of logical positivism did not emerge until into the twentieth century but it attempted to provide a helpful if not skeptical role for correspondence. Locke had tried to answer the seventeenth century side of this issue by defending Christianity as credible because of its record of fulfilled prophecy. Thus Locke thought that God fared rather well against such a falsifiable test as O.T. prophecy realized in Israel's and in Jesus' history.

Many ignored Hume's challenge and took consolation in the Scottish Common Sense Realism whose exponent, Thomas Reid, considered that many of the skeptical elements of Hume could be traced to the epistemological dualism of Descartes and Locke.[169] Reid argued that we have an immediate awareness of objects in a simple (or naive) realism, practically denying epistemic dualism as a harmful over-precision. He also argues for certainty on some matters of belief and morals that also reflect an intentional naiveté. This Scottish Common Sense had considerable influence in the American religious context. The question of religious certainty was resolved for many by an appeal to religious experience, especially the fact of conversion experience at revival meetings,[170] rather than the quality of the conversion life (i.e. religious affections) as Edwards had done.

---

168 Antony Flew in "Theology and Falsification" in *New Essays in Philosophical Theology*. edited by Antony Flew and Alasdair MacIntyre (New York: The Macmillian Co., 1955) as presented by John Hick in *Classical and Contemporary Readings in the Philosophy of Religion* (Englewood Cliffs: Prentice-Hall, 1970), pp. 464–5.

169 S. A. Grave, *The Scottish Philosophy of Common Sense* (Oxford: Claredon Press, 1960); Sydney Ahlstrom, "The Scottish Philosophy and American Theology," *Church History* 24 (1955): 257–272; Douglas Sloan, *The Scottish Enlightenment and the American College Ideal* (New York: Teachers College Press, 1971); Theodore Bozeman, *Protestants in an Age of Science: The Baconian Ideal and Antebellum American Religious Thought* (Chapel Hill: University of North Carolina Press, 1977), pp. 3–31; Mark Noll *The Princeton Theology 1812–1921* (Grand Rapids: Baker, 1983), pp. 30–33.

170 Diogenes Allen, *Philosophy for Understanding Theology*, pp. 192–3.

That is, the Scottish philosophers regarded truth to be a static entity, open equally to all people wherever and whenever they have lived. Resulting from this approach, they proposed 1) an atemporal tradition with little sense of historical development in theology and morality, 2) a defense of Biblical inerrancy and 3) a rationalistic style in apologetics. This philosophical perspective is the chrysalis from which Princeton Theology emerged. It was brought to America by John Witherspoon who became president of Princeton College in 1768. The philosophy and theology teachers following him (William Graham, then Ashbel Green, then Charles and A. A. Hodge, then B.B. Warfield) all continued to embrace the core of this persuasion, modifying only peripheral aspects. The more reformed side of evangelicalism is deeply affected with this perspective from this root. Contemporaries making major contributions to this area of common sense epistemology include Al Plantinga, William Alston, and Nicholas Wolterstorff.[171]

Within this perspective, in 1802 William Paley expressed the design argument on the basis of a part of the creation (namely the eye) which within such common sense realism indicates unusual design, like a machine would, because it is still beyond human ability to replicate.[172] Paley goes on to explain that this teleological argument stands, not within rationalism, but in a kind of aesthetic strategy by which each object (e.g., the eye) conveys the world view take that the observer will understand of it (i.e. created by the Divine Creator).

> Were there no example in the world ...except that of the eye, it would be alone sufficient to support the conclusion which we draw from it, as to the necessity of an intelligent Creator...If there were but one watch in the world, it would not be less certain that it had a maker. If we had never in our lives seen any but one single kind of hydrolic machine; yet, if of that one kind we understood the mechanism and use, we should be as perfectly assured that it proceeded from the hand, and thought, and skill of a workman, as if we visited a museum of the arts, and saw collected there twenty different kinds of

171 E.g., Alvin Plantinga and Nicholas Woltersdorff ed. *Faith and Rationality: Reason and Belief in God* (Notre Dame: University of Notre Dame, 1983; Alvin Plantinga, *Warrant: The Current Debate* (New York: Oxford University Press, 1993); *Warrant and Proper Function* (New York: Oxford University Press, 1993); *Warranted Christian Belief* (New York: Oxford University Press, 2000); William Alston, *A Realist Conception of Truth* (Ithaca: Cornell University Press, 1996).

172 I know that Paley's argument with analogy of body parts to purposeful machines is not original, Aristotle proposed it *In Physics* 2.12.252 (5th century B.C. in *The Works of Aristotle: I. Great Books of the Western World* [Chicago: Encyclopaedia Britannica, 1952]) and Aquinas followed in *Summa Contra Gentiles* 3.3 (13th century A.D. [Romae: Apud Sedem Commisionis Leoninae, 1934]), but Paley's argument became a lightening rod for nineteenth century Christians and opponents so it is worth mentioning in this summary of philosophical theology and science.

> machines for drawing water, or a thousand different kinds for other purposes. Of this point each machine is a proof, independently of all the rest. So it is with the evidences of a divine agency. The proof is not a conclusion which lies at the end of a chain of reasoning, of which chain each instance of contrivance is only a link, and of which, if one link fail, the whole falls; but it is an argument separately supplied by every example. An error in stating an example affects only that example. The argument is cumulative in the fullest sense of that term. The eye proves it without the ear; the ear without the eye. The proof in each example is complete; for when the design of the part, and the conduciveness of its structure to that design, is shown, the mind may set itself at rest: no future consideration can detract any thing from the force of the example.[173]

I think a similar strategy to Paley's is followed by the contemporary approach to Intelligent Design, albeit with more sophistication. This identifies that the contemporary Intelligent Design movement is empirical[174] in its appeals within an intuitional aesthetic inference of design, much like the SETI movement.[175] In both of these movements observations that foster the inference of a sufficiently complex pattern are taken to be design of intelligence, either of God or aliens from another world. This design inference would need to be able to be stated within an argument that makes empirical appeals to the laws of small probabilities with all of the argument's premises being true.[176] For example, the kind of evidence would see DNA as a communication device, like machine code in computer languages.[177]

---

173 William Paley, *Natural Theology: or Evidences of the Existence and Attributes of the Deity, Collected from the Appearances of Nature* (Houston: St. Thomas Press, 1972), pp. 55–56.

174 Phillip Johnson, "The Intelligent Design Movement: Challenging the Modernist Monopoly on Science" in *Signs of Intelligence: Understanding Intelligent Design* ed. William Dembski and James Kushiner (Grand Rapids: Brazos Press, 2001), pp. 29, 31.

175 The Biblical theology is described this intuitional way by advocates: William Dembski, title: *The Design Inference: Eliminating Chance through Small Probabilities* (Cambridge: Cambridge University Press, 1998); "Signs of Intelligence: a Primer on the Discernment of Intelligent Design," Nancy Pearcey, "Design and the Discriminating Public: Gaining a Hearing from Ordinary People," and Bruce Gordon, "Is Intelligent Design Science? The Scientific Status and Future of Design-Theoretic Explanations" in *Signs of Intelligence*, pp. 48, 174–6, 207–9.

176 Bruce Gordon, "Is Intelligent Design Science? The Scientific Status and Future of Design-Theoretic Explanations" in *Signs of Intelligence*, p. 209; William Dembski, *The Design Inference*, pp. 5, 57–58.

177 Stephen Meyer, "Word Games: DNA, Design, and Intelligence" in *Signs of Intelligence*, p. 108.

The 1991 Gallop poll found that 46 percent of Americans believe that humans were created directly from a Creator, which would encourage advocates of Intelligent Design. However, 40 percent believe God guided evolution (only 9 percent believe evolution was guided strictly by natural selection).[178] Which means, 49 percent of the populous believe in evolution, albeit, most with God involved. Such close percentages (46 to 49) make for polarization of alternatives, which diminishes nuanced strategies between them. A number of school boards are wrestling with or are battle grounds for whether Intelligent Design and/or evolution is to be taught in the public schools as fact, law, theory, or at all.

However, there are a growing number of theologians, exegetes, and scientists who would identify themselves in the wake of Locke's empiricism but would advocate a more complex method as critical realists (including William G. T. Shedd, A. H. Strong, Alister McGrath, Nancey Murphy, N. T. Wright, and James Dunn). Within this approach there is usually appreciation for either a sociological or pragmatic role joining with this empiricism, so I will develop this hybrid later under critical realism.

2.7. Kant's Critical Idealism

Historically, Critical philosophy came together in 1781 with Kant's critiques, and especially his *Critique of Pure Reason*.[179] Awakened from his dogmatic slumber by Hume, Kant restricted knowledge to the *phenomena* (appearance) and excluded it from the *noumena* (thing in itself), because the transcendental categories of one's mind inhibited all individuals preventing them from knowing things in themselves. This is an arbitrary opinion that he assumes after briefly dismissing the possibility of an alternative critical realism knowing objects.[180] Additionally, it seems to me that his critical idealism assumption is itself self defeating, in that he is claiming to know something about reality that he claims is unknowable. Thus, Kant assumes that all one knows is experience.

In reaction to these options in 1916, Roy Sellars proposed the view and published *Critical Realism*.[181] If Kant is stopped here, a person could be Kantian and critical realist as the evangelical philosopher Stuart Hackett. In Hackett's transcendental realism, the noumenal reality is recoverable as known because of the foundational strengths of the programs of rationalism, empiricism and empirically grounded pragmatism.[182] If this move is done, it undercuts a rationale for depending

178 Nancy Pearcey, "Design and the Discriminating Public: Gaining a Hearing from Ordinary People" in *Signs of Intelligence*, p. 43.

179 Immanuel Kant, *Critique of Pure Reason*, in *Great Books of the Western World*, vol. 42, *Kant* (Chicago: Encyclopaedia Britannica, 1952), pp. 1–252.

180 Kant, *Critique of Pure Reason*, p. 7.

181 Roy Sellars, *Critical Realism* (Chicago: Rand McNally Co., 1916).

182 Stuart Hackett, *The Resurrection of Theism: Prolegomena to Christian Apology* (Grand Rapids: Baker, 1957) and to a lesser extent *The Reconstruction of the*

on subsequent idealistic (e.g., Kantianism as Kant maintains it, process or Marxism) or aesthetic strategies (e.g., romanticism or existentialism).

However, Kant goes on to analyze classifications of judgment that show him to be a critical idealist. That is, semantic categories for Kant are either: 1) analytic (predicate is contained in the subject [e.g., All mothers are women]) or 2) synthetic (predicate adds something to the subject [e.g., Mary is a mother]). He then combines this with epistemic categories: *a priori* (nonexperiential knowledge) and *a posteriori* (experiential knowledge). He thought that analytic *a piori* statements defined and did not describe reality (e.g., all bachelors are unmarried). Additionally, Kant thought that all empirical statements were synthetic *a posteriori*, and thus the only description of reality. This would mean that there were no analytic *a posteriori* statements, but I think that he is wrong about this. For example, empirically falsifiable statements like "too small to see" and performative statements like "I now pronounce you man and wife" occupy this analytic *a posteriori* domain and describe reality. Likewise, Kant thought that all synthetic *a priori* statements could only describe phenomena and not reality. However, mathematics is framed by synthetic *a priori* statements as a kind of higher order reality.[183] So, if math is noumenally real, mathematical derivation statements are claims to know some of the noumenal realm and not merely the phenomenal. Likewise, exclusionary synthetic *a priori* statements (e.g., nothing green is red) describe reality contrary to Kant's claim. Furthermore, the logically necessary would be synthetic *a priori* statements also governing the real.[184] Additionally, I think that Kant's own categorical imperative is also of this sort, thus describing reality (e.g., It's always wrong to torture for the fun of it). Finally, challenging Kant's criticism, I belief that the ontological argument can prove the existence of God.[185] Likewise, the other arguments for God's existence are also legitimate synthetic *a posteriori* defenses for the existence of God.[186] Instead of getting side tracked here by Kant's criticism concerning these arguments, I have already presented these arguments earlier in ways that answer or side step his criticism.

Christian Revelation Claim: A Philosophical and Critical Apologetic (Grand Rapids: Baker, 1984). Roy Bhaskar also positions himself within transcendental realism of but does not opt for this foundational option since he is more driven by a Durkheimian community of, see section on Critical Realism.

183 See my note # 7 describing numbers as a kind of Platonic form.

184 I defend this point in Doug Kennard, *The Relationship Between Epistemology, Hermeneutics, Biblical Theology and Contextualization*, pp. 41–43.

185 For the popular presentation see earlier in this chapter under the section of "Descartes' Rationalism," or Doug Kennard, *The Classical Christian God*, pp. 11–41, or "An Ontological Argument for God's Existence and Nature," MA Thesis, Trinity Evangelical Divinity School, 1987.

186 For the popular presentation see earlier in this chapter under the section of "Aristotle," or Doug Kennard, *The Classical Christian God*, pp. 11–41

A unified system of knowledge is what Kant means by science.[187] However, natural sciences are "dependent upon the strategy of reflective judgment."[188] That is, natural science is what must be granted to make sense of the phenomena observed. Such Kantian reductionism was defeated in science by non-Euclidean geometry and post Newtonian physics.

In describing the phenomenal, Kant coined a term "worldview" (*Weltanschauung*) to make sublime sense of his unified system.[189] This approach appreciates the coherence of the worldview as a whole, though may also appeal to other forms of warrant. Two expressions of worldview analysis are heavily dependent upon coherentism for their warrant: presuppositionism and idealism. For example, David Naugle traces the history of the Christian worldview concept especially through the presuppositionalist wing of Reformed theology including Gordon Clark,[190] Abraham Kuyper,[191] Herman Dooyeweerd,[192] and Francis Schaeffer.[193] What they include in their worldview may at times be very different from Kant as they depend upon a Calvinistic approach to the Bible to populate much of their world view. Their primary epistemic appeal for apologetics is to the freedom of contradiction that coherentism maintains. However, their approach sets up a community based perception that may limit appreciating data that may challenge or

187 Douglas McGaughey, "Kant on Religion and Science: Independence or Integration?" *Zygon: Journal of Religion and Science* 41:3(Sept. 2006): 727–746, especially pp. 731–2 where he references Immanuel Kant, *Critique of Pure Reason*, B 520–21 and 785; and *Prolegomena zu einer jeden künftigen Metaphysik, die als Wissenschaft wird auftreten können.* (1783) Vol. 3 of *Immanuel Kant: Werke in sechs Bänden,* ed. Wilhelm Weischedel, (Darmstadt: Wissenschaftliche Buchgesellschaft, 1998), p. 173.

188 Douglas McGaughey, "Kant on Religion and Science: Independence or Integration?" *Zygon: Journal of Religion and Science* 41:3(Sept. 2006): 727–746, especially p. 732 where he references Immanuel Kant, *Kritik der Urteilskraft* (Hamburg: Felix Meiner Verlag, 1790, 1974), pp. 221–3.

189 Immanuel Kant, *Critique of Judgment* in *Great Books of the Western World,* vol. 42, *Kant* (Chicago: Encyclopaedia Britannica, 1952), pp. 459–613,and especially part one, book two, section 26, pp. 500–501 where the concept of the sublime *Weltanschauung* (or worldview) first appeared in 1790. Cf. Werner Betz, "Zur Geschichte des Wortes 'Weltanschauung,'" In *Kursbuch der Weltanschauungen,* Schriften der Carl Friedrich von Siemens Stiftung (Frankfort: Verlag Ullstein, 1980), pp. 18–28, but especially p. 18; David Naugle, *Worldview: The History of a Concept* (Grand Rapids: Eerdmans, 2002), p. xix, 58, and 66. On page 58 an extended footnote #14 develops the Kantian origins of worldview.

190 Gordon Clark, *A Christian View of Men and Things: An Introduction to Philosophy* (Grand Rapids: Baker, 1952) and Roland Nash, editor. *The Philosophy of Gordon Clark: A Festschrift* (Philadelphia: The Presbyterian and Reformed Publishing Co., 1968).

191 Abraham Kuyper, *Principles of Sacred Theology* (Grand Rapids: Baker, 1980).

192 Herman Dooyeweerd, *A New Critique of Theoretical Thought,* Vol. I-IV (Ontario: Paideia Press, 1975); *In the Twilight of Western Thought* (Philadelphia: Reformed Publishing Company, 1960).

193 Francis Schaeffer, *A Christian Manifesto* (Westchester: Crossway Books, 1981).

defeat as perceived from a different perspective. Science and theology done within a worldview orientation will be resilient and resistant to change until the evidence is rather overwhelming. Such a privileged traditional approach sets up a Kuhnian construct for world view change. However, change does occur, as is evident in the differences between the theologians: Clark, Kuyper, Dooyeweerd, and Schaeffer. This change occurs more likely by the era, medium, and challenges within which they ply their trade.

Additionally, a range of liberal theologies have followed Kant into a coherent phenomenal unitary belief system. It is as though Kant's critical idealism legitimates the possibility of antirealist or options in their coherence emphasis. However, the imagination wording forth to frame and incite liberal theology usually needs a more passionate intuitive spark than Kant, to fire its liberal flames.

American liberalism is rooted in Unitarianism. Kant set the course for such Unitarianism in his denial of the Trinity, claiming: "absolutely nothing worthwhile for practical life can be made out of the doctrine of the Trinity, taken literally, when one believes that one has understood it adequately, but even less when one perceives that it exceeds all our concepts."[194] Going beyond Kant's rationalism, the torch of such Unitarianism burns brightly in the works of William Ellery Channing.[195] The core commonality between such liberalism and Unitarianism includes the belief in: 1) a monotheistic good God, 2) that Jesus was a good moral teacher, and 3) the Holy Spirit was merely a metaphor for divine activity.

This Unitarian sentiment retains the confidence of a good moral order as defended by Kant's *Critique of Practical Reason.*[196] In such, Kant defends the categorical imperative as a universally binding morality in practice; thus turning a transcendental ethic toward duty. That is, whatever cannot be universalized without detrimental effects should not be done (e.g., cheating) and whatever can be universalized with beneficial effects should be done (e.g., expressing thankfulness to others). Such moralizing tends to reconfigure the human Jesus as an ethical teacher somewhat like Kant presented in *Religion Within the Boundaries of Mere Reason.*[197] However, unlike Kant the early Unitarians retained many of Jesus miracles as evidence of God's favor in Jesus' life and ministry. In time, a higher criticism unraveled the confidence in such

194 Immanuel Kant, *Der Streit der Fäkultaten,* A 50, 57, quoted and translated by Jürgen Moltmann, "The Trinitarian History of God," *Theology* 78(1975): 633.

195 Gary Dorrien, *The Making of American Liberal Theology: Imagining Progressive Religion 1805-1900* (Lousiville: Westminster John Knox Press, 2001), vol. 1, pp. 1–57.

196 Immanuel Kant, *The Critique of Practical Reason* in *Great Books of the Western World,* 42:291–364.

197 Immanuel Kant, *Religion Within the Boundaries of Mere Reason* (Cambridge: Cambridge University Press, 1998).

supernatural manifestations, drawing Unitarianism closer to Kant's root. The miracles were subsequently lost to ethical liberalism throughout the nineteenth century. This Biblical critical explosion began to occur in David Strauss' 1835 incendiary *Life of Jesus: Critically Examined.*[198] However, his presentation was too radical a Hegelian world view for all but the most extreme, so that by his 1863 edition he had conservatized his view of Jesus to a version of ethical worldview that brought it in line with Kant's *Religion Within the Bounds of Mere Reason.* In this, Christianity is reinterpreted to be essentially morality. This approach informed ethical liberalism, upon which Social Gospel was built. For example, Horace Bushell's *God in Christ* showed this ethical liberalism as living truths that could touch reality and spur the imagination for the good of others.[199]

Kant's *The Critique of Judgment* explores an aesthetic and purpose of nature, Kant finds that the assumption of value operates as a bridge between science and concepts like morality, freedom and faith.[200] Kant's judgments of taste inform the evaluation of universal assent. In his analytic of the sublime, he sets up an aesthetic strategy that prepares for existentialism. Tapping this root, Clayton Crockett develops *A Theology of the Sublime* that emerges as a connection is made between the Kantian sublime of the third critique and the transcendental imagination of the first critique.[201] Crockett is trying to stand against John Milbank's post-modern *Radical Orthodoxy*[202] with these critical resources of Kant and the existentialists that work in his wake. For example, drawing upon Vattimo[203] and Heidegger,[204] Crockett highlights the developmental nature of theological tradition.

> A theological investigation does not simply deal with the traditional objects or concepts of theology as they have been already determined and handed down, but in rethinking

198 David Strauss, *Life of Jesus: Critically Examined* (Philadelphia: Fortress Press, 1972).

199 Gary Dorrien, *The Making of American Liberal Theology*, 1:271.

200 Immanuel Kant, *Critique of Judgment,* in *Great Books of the Western World,* 42:461–613.

201 Clayton Crockett, *A Theology of the Sublime* (London: Routledge, 2001).

202 John Milbank, *Theology & Social Theory: Beyond Secular Reason* (Oxford: Backwell, 1990); *Radical Orthodoxy: A New Theology,* edited by John Milbank, Catherine Pickstock and Graham Ward (London: Routledge, 1999).

203 G. Vattimo, *The End of Modernity. Nihilism and Hermeneutics in Post-Modern Culture* (Cambridge: Polity Press, 1988 and 1991).

204 Martin Heidegger, *Being and Time* (New York: Harper,1962); *Kant and the Problem of Metaphysics* (Bloomington: Indiana University Press, 1962); "What is Metaphysics?" in *Existence and Being* edited by W. Brock (Chicago: H. Regnery Co., 1949); "Hölderlin and the Essence of Poetry," in *Existence and Being* edited by W. Brock (Chicago: H. Regney Co., 1949); and *An Introduction to Metaphysics* (New Haven: Yale University Press, 1959).

> theological insights one must deal with the processes of understanding through experience which generate the theological conceptions in the first place. In this way, a theological thinking generates theology itself.[205]

Crockett affirms that philosophy effects theology by presenting philosophical concepts as those through which theologizing will take place.

Kant's critical idealism does not bring about science, but as an epistemic method Kant clears the landscape of the empirical confidence in experiment. Into this void, the Romantic Movement steps, fostering science to be primarily driven by rival intuitional agendas. So while Kant does not himself develop science he remains foundational for all idealistic methods that follow and do contribute to science directly, namely Romanticism, Hegel, Existentialism, Marxism, idealist forms of Pragmatism, Process, and Post-Modernism.

2.8. Romaticism

By the beginning of the nineteenth century, the cold reasoning of Kant was felt to be a good way to know but not a good way to live; life was more organic than analytic; life needed romantic passion. Schelling's romantic influence sparked the liberal flames with subversive intuitions that funded the transcendentalist Unitarianism of Ralph Waldo Emerson and Theodore Parker.[206] For example, Parker reviewed Strauss' *The Life of Jesus: Critically Examined* for the Unitarian *Christian Examiner* and commended the work for its rigorous scholarship but critiqued it for its lack of religious spirit, "It is colder than ice. It is the most melancholy book we ever read."[207] However, Parker added warmth of religious spirit to Strauss' rigor, in Parker's pseudonymously authored[208] pamphlet, "The Previous Question Between Mr. Andrews Norton and His Alumni," making the naturalistic moralizing Jesus more palatable for a liberal populous.

Likewise, the romantic movement of Schelling and Goethe floated an organic view of nature that aesthetically inclined toward evolution and opposed the mechanical ideal stemming from Descartes and Newton. Goethe and Schelling recount that it is an epistemic strategy that moves from the whole to the parts to selectively see evidence that will support the beauty of the whole and is thus dependent on the intuition of the beauty of the whole.[209] Robert Richards, quoting Schelling, recognizes

205 Crockett, *A Theology of the Sublime*, p. 20.

206 Gary Dorrien, *The Making of American Liberal Theology*, 1:58–110.

207 Gary Dorrien, *The Making of American Liberal Theology*, 1:81–82.

208 Theodore Parker's pseudonym was Levi Blodgett.

209 Johann Wolfgang von Goethe, *Zur Morphologie* (1817) as contained in *Goethe: Die Schriften zur Naturwissenschaft,* 21 vols. 1st division, vol. 9: *Morphologische*

that, "Truth would be achieved insofar as the images in our understanding came to adequate 'things as they are performed in the archetypal understanding.'... And beauty would be predicated of archetypes particularly insofar as they united 'the universal and the particular, the species and the individual.'"[210]

Countering Kant, Kielmeyer granted parity to organic and physical laws and proposed that in the same aesthetic strategy that one might grant design by mechanistic laws, one might instead grant organic adaptation by organic laws.[211] Such an organic strategy would make the system and the organ "so united that each becomes mutually cause and effect of the other."[212] Within this organic model nature takes on the role of a quasi-divine ruling principle.[213] Charles Darwin concluded that natural selection altruistically looked out for the welfare of the creatures selected; "man selects only for his own good; Nature only for that of the being which she tends."[214] Thus, natural selection insures the progress of evolution "towards perfection."[215] Furthermore, following Kielmeyer, to some extent Charles Darwin and substantially Ernst Haeckel conceive of evolution as recapitulating forces in embryogenesis and species genesis.[216] Charles Darwin and Ernst Haeckel acknowledge that Goethe

---

Hefte, ed. Dorothea Kuhn (Weimar: Böhlaus Nachfolger, 1954), pp. 79–83; Friedrich Wilhelm Joseph Schelling, *System des transscendentalen Idealismus* and *Ueber den wahren Begriff der Naturphilosophie* in *Schellings Werke,* ed. Manfred Schröter, (Munich: C. H. Beck, 1927–59, 3rd ed.), 2:223 [4:89]; Robert Richards, *The Romantic Conception of Life: Science and Philosophy in the Age of Goethe* (Chicago: The University of Chicago Press, 2002).

210 Robert Richards, *The Romantic Conception of Life,* p. 188, quoting Schelling, *Bruno* in *Schellings Werke,* 3:116 [4:220]; 3:139 [4:243].

211 Kielmeyer, "Verhältnisse der organischen Kräfte," pp. 249–50 as discussed by Robert Richards, *The Romantic Conception of Life,* p. 242. They go on to develop five organic forces: 1) sensibility, 2) irritability, 3) reproduction, 4) secretive, and 5) propulsive forces.

212 Kielmeyer, "Verhältnisse der organischen Kräfte," p. 249 as quoted by Robert Richards, *The Romantic Conception of Life,* p. 241.

213 Friedrich Schlegel, *Gespräch über die Poesie,* in *Kritische Friedrich-Schlegel-Ausgabe,* ed. Ernst Behler 35 vol. to date (Paderborn: Verlag Ferdinand Schöningh, 1958-), 2:285; Friedrich Wilhelm Joseph Schelling, *Abhandlungen zur Erläuterung des Idealismus der Wissenschaftslehre* (1796–67), and *Von der Weltseele, eine Hypothese der höheren Physik zur Erklärung des allegemeinen Organismus,* both in *Schellings Werke,* 1:310 and 419 [2:351]; Robert Richards, *The Romantic Conception of Life,* pp. 111, 138.

214 Charles Darwin, *Origin of the Species* (Philadelphia: University of Pennsylvania Press, 1959), p. 83.

215 Charles Darwin, *Origin of the Species,* p. 489.

216 Kielmeyer, "Verhältnisse der organischen Kräfte," pp. 262 as discussed by Robert Richards, *The Romantic Conception of Life,* p. 244–5; Robert Richards, *The Meaning of Evolution,* p. 113; Peter Bowler, *The Non-Darwinian Rof: Reinterpreting a Historical Myth* (Baltimore: Johns Hopkins University Press, 1988), pp. 11, 13; Ernst Haeckel, *Generelle Morphologie der Organismen* (Berlin: Reimer, 1866), 1:205.

and Alexander Humboldt were romantic predecessors in developing their theories of evolution.[217]

Schelling critiqued Erasmus Darwin's (Charles Darwin's grandfather) evolutionary theory as too difficult to overcome species difference because it started with a single aboriginal form, and Schelling proposed instead several archetypes from which all forms have evolved.[218] When Charles Darwin began his work on species change , he originally proposed that four or more archetypal groups emerged from the Ur-slime (e.g., Vertebrata, articulate, mollusca, and radiate); and then morphological change occurred only within each group.[219]

The find of the *Archaeopteryx* (with its reptilian brain, separate digits, tail and teeth, but also the apparatus for flight) was originally named by Richard Owen because it represented what he took to be an avian archetype.[220] However, under the influence of T. H. Huxley, *Archaeopteryx* became declared a missing link that aided in providing empirical evidence for the theory of evolution.[221] Furthermore, Charles Darwin concluded that evolution also utilized embryonic recapitulation of adult forms (ontogeny recapitulates phylogeny) and Ernst Haeckel gave currency to this "biogenic law."[222]

Critiques have been marshaled from a variety of points of view. For example, some forms of evolution can embrace Divine design, natural law and chance simultaneously, as R. A. Fisher maintained.[223] In contrast, Todd Wood has maintained that "the modern neodarwinian synthesis is inadequate for understanding speciation" and would move from a random selection process to a more nuanced pre-designed, creation process.[224] Wood further maintains that the Biblical and

217 Charles Darwin, "Historical Sketch," introduced in the third edition (1861) *On the Origin of Species by Charles Darwin: A Variorum Text,* ed. Morse Peckham (Philadelphia: University of Pennsylvania Press, 1959), p. 61; Haeckel, *Generelle Morphologie der Organismen,* (Berlin: Reimer, 1866), 2:2, quotes Goethe's poem metamorphysis to open chapter 17; Robert Richards, *The Romantic Conception of Life,* pp. 525–6.

218 Robert Richards, *The Romantic Conception of Life,* p. 301, quoting Schelling, *Erster Entwurf* in *Schellings Werke,* 2:63–64 [3:63–64].

219 Robert Richards, *Meaning of Evolution: The Morphological Construction and Ideological Reconstruction of Darwin's Theory* (Chicago: University of Chicago Press, 1992), pp. 125–26; such a concept could be consistent within creationist baraminology, where God brings about the initial forms.

220 Adrian Desmond, *Archetypes and Ancestors: Palaeontology in Victorian London 1850–1875* (Chicago: The University of Chicago Press, 1982), pp. 42–48, 59.

221 Adrian Desmond, *Archetypes and Ancestors*, pp. 59, 65-66 (Owen had instead used Archegosaurus as a bridge fossil but Archaeopteryx was more sensational for those like T. H. Huxley to champion), 124–135.

222 Charles Darwin, *Origin of the Species,* p. 338; Robert Richards, *The Meaning of Evolution,* pp. 172–3.

223 R. A. Fisher, *The Genetic Theory of Natural Selection* (Oxford: Oxford University Press, 1947), p. 1001.

224 Todd Wood, A Creationist Review and Preliminary Analysis of the History, Geology, Climate, and Biology of the Galápagos Islands. Center for Origins Research *Issues in*

scientific evidence can be embraced within a nuanced creation view that permits change to occur within a series of archetypal groups which God established through creation by His design. Whereas, Dembski of the Intelligent Design movement sees these causalities as "mutually exclusive,"[225] which is no surprise since as an aesthetic strategy based on intuition of design inference,[226] design is mutually exclusive to natural selection in a Kuhnian sense.

In a context in which scientific empiricism and relativizing historicism were tearing away Christianity's foundations, Friedrich Schleiermacher sought to provide a romantic authority as a mediator between religion and its cultured despisers. He is trying to elicit a Christianity to which the Berlin literary idealism could relate.[227] However, there is rigor and criticism that frame his views, as among the best of what Romanticism had to offer. The romantic influence of Schelling can be seen in Schleiermacher through the tendency to define the ultimate as the unity of the antitheses of existence. However, he refused to identify the transcendental unity demanded by thought with being, thus leaving it an epistemic necessity rather than an amorphous metaphysic.[228] He begins by showing that the skeptics have rejected a caricature of religion and that there is a core experience of the feeling of dependence common in humanity that connects us beyond ourselves to the ultimate. For Schleiermacher, romanticism confirmed his belief in the unity of life and joined with his passionate Moravian background in defining the place of the individual as with the relationships of family and community. So the intuition that connects us with the ultimate, beyond mere community, is that feeling of indebtedness and dependence. With this is a sense of unity with all that is real.

> The sum total of religion is to feel that, in its highest unity, all that moves us in feeling is one; to feel that aught single and particular is only possible by means of this unity; to feel...that being and living in and through God.[229]

Creation. 1. (Eugene: Wipf & Stock, 2005), p. 5.

225 W. Dembski, *The Design Inference*, p. 98.

226 The Biblical theology is described this intuitional way by advocates: Nancy Pearcey, "Design and the Discriminating Public: Gaining a Hearing from Ordinary People" and Bruce Gordon, "Is Intelligent Design Science? The Scientific Status and Future of Design-Theoretic Explanations" in *Signs of Intelligence*, edited by William Dembski and James Kushiner (Grand Rapids: Brazos Press, 2001), pp. 48, 207–9.

227 Martin Redeker, *Schleiermacher: Life and Thought,* trans. John Wallhauser (Philadelphia: Fortress Press, 1973), p. 182.

228 Schleiermacher distanced himself from pantheism but not clearly in print until *The Christian Faith,* ed. H. R. Mackintosh and J. S. Stewart (New York: Harper and Row, 1963), especially sec. 8, postscript 2.

229 F. D. E. Schleiermacher, *On Religion: Speeches to its Cultural Despisers* (New York: Harper and Brothers, 1958), pp. 49–50.

Within this muted perspective, and with the passion of pietism, Friedrich Schleiermacher proposes that religion was a "sense and taste for the infinite." Life without this taste is incomplete. Within this taste for the infinite, the essence of religious experience is "a feeling of absolute dependence."[230] Perhaps, echoed by Annie Dillard's metaphor of "holy the firm."[231] With such an internally warranted view for oneself, there is a balancing role provided by the community that one is associated with so that the community feels this dependence together. Only those who are within the community can grasp the inner logic of its faith; "Religion is only comprehensible through itself."[232] However, I wonder if in this post-Kantian phenomenalistic approach we have oversimplified religion and Christianity. It seems to me that my pack of dogs which I keep in my kennel have both an individual sense and a communal sense of absolute dependence upon me, and they grasp within the pack their dependence and the order of the pack. However, I don't think that makes my dogs supremely religious or Christian. It looks like this approach for all its simplicity has lost important Biblical complexity of Christianity.

Evangelicalism also has taken deep drafts of pietism, a religious side to romaticism, though it expressed itself more with passion for the Bible, personal experience with the gospel, sharing of gospel, missions, illumination, and leading of the Spirit. The leading of the Spirit and illumination of the Spirit bleed into each other. Taken together they are similar to the Orthodox and Roman Catholic Spirit enablement of tradition through apostolic succession and the Pope. However, in evangelicalism the illumination of the Spirit is shifted from a divine support of the tradition to usually a work in the individual interpreter to aid him in discerning the message of the Biblical passage.[233] The earliest expressions of this illumination of the Spirit emerged among Lutheran pietism when Phillip Jakob Spener replaced the concept of verbal inspiration of the Scriptures with a personal inspiration or illumination of the believing interpreter, fostering a major controversy with orthodox Lutheranism.[234] Spener

230 F. D. E. Schleiermacher, *The Christian Faith* (Edinburgh: T & T Clark, 1999 originally 1821), especially sections 3 and 4.

231 Annie Dillard, *Holy the Firm* (New York: Harper and Row, 1977).

232 F. D. E. Schleiermacher, *On Religion: Speeches to its Cultural Despisers*, p. 238.

233 An example of this is in *The Chicago Statement on Biblical Hermeneutics* (1978), "Articles of Affirmation and Denial," Article 5, in *Hermeneutics, Inerrancy, & the Bible*. edited by Earl Radmacher and Robert Preus (Grand Rapids: Zondervan, 1984), p. 882.

234 Philipp Jakob Spener, *Consilia Et Judicia Theologia* (Frankfurt A. M., 1709), vol. 3, p. 700; Cf. K. James Stein, "Phillip Jakob Spener (1635–1705)" and Markus Matthias, "August Hermann Franke (1663–1727)" in *The Pietist Theologians: An Introduction to Theology in the Seventeenth Centuries*. edited by Carter Lindberg (Malden: Blackwell, 2005), pp. 88 and 105–6; Johannes Wallmann, *Philipp Jakob Spener und die Aufänge des Pietismus* (Tübigen: Mohr, 1970), pp. 92–96; Emmanuel Hirsch, *Geschichte der neuen Evangelische Theologie in Zusammenhang mit den allgemein Bewegung des Europäischen Denkens* (Gütersloh: Bertelsmann, 1951), vol. 2, p. 114;

agreed with the reformers that the text was clear but viewed humans as so impaired by sin that only "reborn" preachers with the enlightening of the Spirit (like the resurrected Christ provided on the Emmaus road) could rightfully understand the Biblical text. This ushered in one of the most violent controversies which orthodox Reformation thought had against pietism. In 1685 the exhaustive collection of Lutheran theology in *Theologia Didactico-Polemica* by the Johann Quenstedt (nicknamed "the bookkeeper" for his exhaustive cataloging of views) reframed the Spirit's illuminational aid as one of regenerational interpretation and not inspiration.[235] In 1707 David Hollanz embraced this view that the Holy Spirit is promised to every Christian so that they might understand the Biblical text better.[236] Around 1701, August Herman Franke shifted the illumination of the Spirit as *sensus mysticus* when reading the Biblical text, extending John Hus' Spirit regeneration idea to an affective product brought about by the Spirit when studying the Bible.[237] That is, only the person moved by the Spirit can acquire "living" knowledge of the Biblical text that will bring about spiritual affection. Evangelicalism has largely owned Spener and Hollanz's cognitive illumination view, with others in evangelicalism joining Franke's Spirit transformational illumination

---

Volker Jung, *Das Ganze der Heiligen Schrift. Hermeneutik und Schriftauslegung bei Abrham Calov* (Stuttgart: Calwer Verlag, 1999), pp. 100–1.

235 Johann Andreas Quenstedt, *Theologia Didactico-Polemica* (Wittenberg: Johanne Ludolph Quenstedt, 1685). The relevant portion (chapters 1–3) of this is available in English as: *The Nature and Character of Theology: An Introduction to the Thought of J. A. Quenstedt from THEOLOGIA DIDACTIO-POLEMICA SIVE SYSTEMA THEOLOGICUM*. abridged, edited, and translated by Luther Poellot (St. Louis: Concordia, 1986), ch. I "Of Theology in General": question I "Is Theology Given?" paragraph XI, p. 36; ph. XIV, p. 39; ph. XXXI-Observe (1), p. 54; ph. XXXV, p. 57; Section II "Polemic"-"Sources of Rebuttals or Dialysis of Objections": q. I "Is Theology Given?", pp. 64–5; q. II "Is Revealed Theology Necessary in the Church?", pp. 71, 72–3; q. III "Is Theology a God-Given Practical Aptitude?", exposition III & IV, pp. 73–4; rebuttal I, p. 80; ch. III "Of the Sources of Theology", porism IV, pp. 199–200. Stanley Grenz, in *Beyond Foundationalism* (Lousiville: Westminster John Knox Press, 2001), p. 99 claims that this illumination view originated earlier by at least the time of John Hus and cites George Tavard in *Holy Writ or Holy Church: The Crisis of the Protestant Reformation* (New York: Harper & Brothers, 1959), pp. 47–66 which discusses John Hus' view of the soteriological transformation in which the Holy Spirit enables the new believer to be applicationally responsive to the Word of God. From my reading of the Hus material, I agree with Tavard, contrary to Grenz; Hus does not teach this view of the illumination through the Holy Spirit aid to cognitively understand the Bible. I have not found the view any earlier than Spener's, Quenstedt's and Hollanz's pietistic Lutheran systematic theologies.

236 David Hollaz, Examen Theologicum Acroamaticum was published in 1707 and 1725 but is available as Acromaticum Universam Theologiam Thetico-Polemicam Complectens (Lipsiae: B.C. Breitkopfii, 1763).

237 August Hermann Franke introduced his view in 1701, publishing the idea in 1709 and then more fully in 1717 as *Praelectiones Hermeneuticae*, p. 57; cf. Markus Matthias, "August Hermann Franke (1663–1727)" in *The Pietist Theologians: An Introduction to Theology in the Seventeenth Centuries*. edited by Carter Lindberg (Malden: Blackwell, 2005), pp. 106–7.

view. For example, the 1982 evangelical Chicago Statement on Biblical Hermeneutics includes as the fifth article: "WE AFFIRM that the Holy Spirit enables believers to appropriate and apply Scripture to their lives. WE DENY that the natural man is able to discern spiritually the biblical message apart from the Holy Spirit."[238] This statement indicates in its denial a cognitive illuminational element while in its affirmation the transformational illumination is highlighted. This statement reflects the emphasis in evangelicalism that the Holy Spirit aids the individual's use of hermeneutics.

However, some in evangelicalism are advocating a communal illumination. Donald Bloesch is a contemporary advocate of this communal illumination view. He identifies that the Bible's revelatory status "does not reside in its wording as such but in the Spirit of God, who fills the words with meaning and power."[239] This view provides a post textual subjective meaning. Kevin Vanhoozer also wishes to extend this individual illumination into becoming a community illumination of Spirit, "Only a prayerful reading that invokes the Spirit can perceive the true meaning in what is otherwise a dead letter. Such Spirit-led exegesis 'restores the interpretive activity of the spiritual community as the connecting link between text and reader.'"[240] Community textual decisions are essentially saying that the Holy Spirit assures the community that they will interpret correctly as they frame up their tradition. In conservative circles this illumination is often supported through textual appeals to John 14:26; 16:12–15; 1 Cor. 2:6–16; and 1 John 2:27. I argue along with the scholarly commentators that these texts do not teach such an illumination view.[241]

2.9. Hegelian Idealism

Hegel published *The Phenomenology of Spirit* in 1807 as a unique attempt to bridge the Kantian gap with a confidence that transcendentalism provided.[242] This confidence was made even more

---

238 "The Chicago Statement on Biblical Hermeneutics" as contained in *Hermeneutics, Inerrancy, and the Bible*. edited by Earl Radmacher and Robert Preus, p. 891.

239 Donald Bloesch, *Holy Scripture: Revelation, Inspiration & Interpretation* (Downers Grove: InterVarsity, 1994), p. 27.

240 Kevin Vanhoozer, *Is There Meaning in This Text?* (Grand Rapids: Zondervan, 1998), p. 411.

241 Douglas Kennard, "Evangelical Views on Illumination of Scriptures and Critique," Journal of the Evangelical Theological Society 49(Dec. 2006): 797–806; Cf. later chapters: "Thiselton-Ricoeur Hermeneutic" and "Biblical Authority in the Contemporary Hermeneutical Scene" earlier presented at the Wheaton Theology Conference, 2001, The Evangelical Theological Society, 2002, and the American Academy of Religion, 2003, pp. 21–25. Cf. Douglas Kennard, The Relationship Between Epistemology, Hermeneutics, Biblical Theology and Contextualization, pp. 139–42.

242 Georg Wilhelm Friedrich Hegel, *The Phenomenology of Mind,* trans. J. B. Baillie (New York: Harper and Row, 1967).

assured by his intuitive commitment to reflect the transcendental Trinity in the triadic framework of the work. In this idealism the clarity of the overarching transcendental idea, virtually the mind of God, serves as a lens that puts each thing or belief in their place in the progressively revealing tension and resolution of the mind of God. Johann Fichte reappropriates this transcendentalism into a dialecticalism in which the next stage of development draws the preceding into a unified synthesis without the contradictions of the former stages (a similar approach underlies Marxist sociology and much existential philosophy). This tends to set up an evolutionary development, with the advocate as the climax of the model. Hegel shows this evolutionary bias in his *History of Philosophy*,[243] and maybe Darwin does as well, as certainly Haeckel does in his use of evolution.

It is into this idealistic Hegelian methodology that Pannenberg places himself.[244] So for Pannenberg the task of theology following Hegel is to develop "a series of stages in which at any given point, the higher stage is constitutive of the preceding insofar as it synthesizes into a unity the contradictions of the preceding one, and thus contains the provisional whole of the entire dialectical path that had been traversed up to that point."[245] At this point he returns more to Hegel, than Fichte, in that the noncontradictory synthesis is for both (Hegel and Pannenberg) beyond contradictions and thus on that basis evidences especially a picture of the absolute God.[246] From this framework he argues that, "the unity of the tradition can exist despite different dogmatic formulations and in spite of many criticisms of the dogmatic formulations of past times. The unity of the tradition is grounded in the common relation of different theologians of different ages to the norm of the one and the same Christ-event."[247] That is, the historian sees a unity in the "pre-projected unity of history," thus pinning it in relativism, while the theologian finds meaning in the past and present events as it is unified in the future Kingdom of Christ. Or more simply, Jesus' resurrection provides us with a foretaste of our resurrection.

Aristotle, Descartes, or Kant could chime in against Hegel and maybe also Pannenberg at this point and highlight that if the thesis and antithesis were really contradictory (as Hegel claims) then both thesis and antithesis can't be embraced in a noncontradictory synthesis maintaining all of the former two (thesis and antithesis) in one synthesis. That is, either Hegel's triads are not contradictory and can be synthesized (e.g.,

243 Georg Wilhelm Friedrich Hegel, *Lectures on the History of Philosophy*, translated by E. S. Haldane and F. H. Simpson (New York: Humanities Press, 1955).

244 Wolfhart Pannenberg, *Basic Questions in Theology: Collected Essays Volume II* (Philadelphia: Fortress Press, 1971), pp. 21–27.

245 Pannenberg, *Basic Questions*, vol. 2, p. 21.

246 Pannenberg, *Basic Questions*, vol. 2, pp. 21–22.

247 Pannenberg, *Basic Questions*, vol. 1, p. 208.

logic, nature, and mind), or if they are contradictory then no synthesis is possible, without something significant becoming lost if a synthesis is attempted (e.g., being, nonbeing, and becoming; "becoming" has lost much from both "being" and "nonbeing" so it is not a good transcendental synthesis). Furthermore, can Hegel embrace Hume and transcend him as well? Nancey Murphy thinks that Hegel can not coherently maintain the opposites of Hume and his own system within his own synthesis.[248] So Hegel's model is both theoretically and practically self defeating.

Such a form of Hegelian idealism resists engagement or development in science. However, Pannenberg is more amenable to a form of science. For example, Pannenberg embraced a Stoic idea of field or spirit, following Thomas Torrance that permits science to operate on a parallel plain to that of theology.[249] So that theology and science disciplines each operate within the paramenters of their own disciplines but they can dialog with each other, without necessarily resolving the tensions in this dialog.

LeRon Shults refurbished Pannenberg as palatable for some post-moderns in reframing Pannenberg's Hegelianism into a post-foundationalist language game for his followers.[250] Such a post-modern reframing of Pannenberg diminishes the role of Hegel's Transcendentalism for grounding his theology and replaces such a rationale with post-modern community acceptance as that which controls where theology should go. Such a post-modern approach will be developed later.

2.10. Existentialism

Sören Aabye Kierkegaard broke on this scene as "that individual" who strongly reacted against Hegel and stood instead for subjective choice making the difference for a person's life. Through the irony of *Philosophical Fragments, Concluding Unscientific Postscript,* and *Fear*

---

248 Nancey Murphy, *Theology in the Age of Scientific Reasoning*, pp. 42–43; Anthony Thiselton (*The Hermeneutics of Doctrine* [Grand Rapids: Eerdmans, 2007], p. 171 considers Murphy's criticism of Pannenberg's incommensurability to be inappropriate because Hume and Pannenberg's do not have sufficiently shared conceptual grammar, but I side with Murphy because the conceptual grammar that is shared is that of Pannenberg and Hegel by Pannenberg's own claim (Wolfhart Pannenberg, *Basic Questions in Theology: Collected Essays Volume II*, pp. 21–27) and such a Hegelian methodology either embraces contradictions to arrive at synthesis, which is contradictory or their views need to be reinterpreted through a dialecticalism, which I think Thiselton is doing as a progressive development. This is to read Hegel through the Fichtian tradition rather than Hegel in his own context of bridging the Kantian gap.

249 Wolfhart Pannenberg, *Kontingenz und Naturgesetz. Towards a Theology of Nature: Essays on Science and Faith*, ed. Ted Peters (Louisville: Westminster/John Knox, 1970, 1993), pp. 72–122; "Problems Between Science and Theology in Course of Their Modern History," *Zygon* 41:1(March, 2006): 105–12.

250 F. Leron Shults, *The Postfoundationalist Task of Theology* (Grand Rapids: Eerdmans, 1999).

and Trembling[251] he shows that the subjectivity of owning their unique truth is the individual's goal in a unique relationship with God Who does not demand the same thing from everyone. Kierkegaard's goal is that we participate with God as He breaks through to our mundane lives with the truly transcendent and therefore seemingly contradictory demand on our lives. Once such unbridled subjectivity is out of Pandora's box there are few restrictions to those who do not corral it as Kierkegaard does by allowing the synoptic gospels to especially show Christ's narrow way. However, the celebration of life, rather than just the mind, is an important gain that existentialism emphasized.

The existentialist can feel freed from previously granted essences as she positions herself in what seems to authentically fit her life. The essence of human consciousness is freedom itself and thus responsibility is unavoidable, as Sartre said "because freedom is condemned to be free."[252] Laurie Anderson playfully sings this perspective "You were born, so you're free; Happy Birthday." However, freedom is not in the abstract but freedom to change or to do in the situation.[253] "Thus I am absolutely free and absolutely responsible for my situation. But I am never free except *in situation*."[254] So that with this existentialism any new situation has the possibility of birthing a new theological daughter. Existentialism as a theological mother has certainly been prolific. The existentialist may even remind us that any choices or critiques that we make come from our own situation, authentic to ourselves.[255] Might we actually be an existentialist in our own theological clothes? Might our lives be the sum of our choices? What choice do you make? The rock group Rush testifies to choosing free will and reminds us in their song "Freewill" that "if you choose not to decide, that you still have made a choice." I choose in this section to briefly explore a sample of existentialism's family album from the twentieth century.

The twentieth century began with Nietzsche's wildman in the streets crying out "I seek God" and then admitting that we in the modern era had killed Him.[256] This extreme existentialist siren cry called a generation of moderns to live as though there is not a God by willing our power to the extent that we are able. This sort of relativism drew fire in 1926

---

251 Sören Kierkegaard, *Philosophical Fragments* (New York: Princeton, 1958); *Concluding Unscientific Postscript* translated by David Swenson and Walter Lowrie (Princeton: Princeton University Press, 1941) and *Fear and Trembling* Edited and Translated by Howard Hong and Edna Hong (Princeton: Princeton University Press, 1983).

252 Jean-Paul Sartre, *Being and Nothingness* (New York: Washington Square Press, 1956), p. 652.

253 Sartre, *Being and Nothingness,* p. 650.

254 Sartre, *Being and Nothingness,* p. 652.

255 Sartre, *Being and Nothingness*, p. 675.

256 Friedrich Nietzsche, *The Gay Science,* trans. W. Kaufman (New York: Random House, 1974), pp. 180–181.

from Bernard Bell, as the first written theological critique of existential post-modernism, where he argued that there were resources for truth in modern epistemology that warrant our truth claims without reducing things essentially to choice.[257]

However, John Wisdom attempted to express this subjective existential or emotive point of view in the universe by comparing impressions of observers as they return to a long neglected garden. "One says 'A gardener comes unseen and unheard. He is manifested only in his works with which we are all familiar,' the other says, 'There is no gardener' and with this difference in what they say about the gardener goes the difference in how they feel about the garden, in spite of the fact that neither expects anything of it which the other does not expect."[258] J. H. Randall expands this to a communal existential role for emotive language.

> The role of the painter, the musician, the poet, teaches us how to use our eyes, our ears, our minds, and our feelings with greater power and skill.... It shows us how to discern unsuspected qualities in the world encountered, latent powers and possibilities there resident. Still more, it makes us see the new qualities with which the world, in cooperation with the spirit of man, can clothe itself.... Is it otherwise with the prophet and the saint? They too can do something to us, they too can effect changes in us and in our world.... They teach us how to discern what human nature can make out of its natural conditions and materials.... They make us receptive to qualities of the world encountered; and they open our hearts to the new qualities with which that world, in cooperation with the spirit of man, can clothe itself. They enable us to see and feel the religious dimension of our world better, the 'order of splendor,' and of man's experience in and with it. They teach us how to find the Divine; they show us visions of God.[259]

Few of us would be willing to join Randall's naturalism or Nietzsche's a-theology or any of the more recent versions (even to Mark Taylor's[260]), because we believe God exists as a loving Father caring for us and we still seek His kingdom. Of course, Nietzsche fused with evolution and

---

257 Bernard Bell, *Postmodernism and Other Essays* (Milwaukee: Morehouse Publishing Co., 1926).

258 John Wisdom, "Gods," *Proceedings of the Aristotelian Society,* (1944-45): 185–206.

259 J. H. Randall, *The Role of Knowledge in Western Religion.* ch. 4 contained in John Hick *Classical and Contemporary Readings in the Philosophy of Religion*, pp. 424–5.

260 E.g., Mark Taylor, *Erring: A Postmodern A/theology* (Chicago: University of Chicago Press, 1984).

a pride of Germanic superiority was dragged into distasteful contexts as Adolf Hitler's messages advocating National Socialism. However, this message and any abuse like they fostered were definitely inauthentic, so such an existential approach practically violated its own basic code. Additionally, such abuse fostered more existential responses from the abused, tending to produce existential responses to recover from our thrownness to authentic kingdom living.

One such resilient call to theology was neo-orthodoxy's encounter with the Word of God. Perhaps Barth was more blatantly existentialist in his commentaries on Romans, but he seems to retain the existential angle on things even in the *Church Dogmatics*, albeit cloaked under the rubric of God breaking across the Kantian gap to encounter us within our particular crises situations.[261] For Barth, ultimately God is the existentialist but in practice one may wonder whether the mystical intuitional encounter is more than an authentic response to the situation we find ourselves within. Barth reacted existentially against the Nazi threat and called it down as a counterfeit salvation and idolatry. "The Barmen Declaration" and many other reactions exhibited authentic choice within the precarious day in which they lived. Others joined in, like Bonhoeffer who called for costly discipleship and aggressive action because our world has come of age. While he held to a conflicting absolutist ethical strategy he advocated aggressive political action for the Christian smuggling Jews out of Germany and making assassination attempts on the Furer's life. A decade later existential authenticity would reframe such aggressive ethics into the situational ethics of Joseph Fletcher[262] and his ethical offspring. However, Barth's heritage has gone in different directions than these; there remains a hotbed of neo-orthodox thought within evangelical schools, post-liberalism, and liberation theology. For example, when we come to a missions conference and the speaker draws us into Isaiah's call as though it now extends to us, "I heard the voice of the Lord saying, 'Whom shall I send, and who will go for Us?' Then I said, 'Here am I send me!'"(Isa. 6:8). Will we own this call existentially making it our own as from God and be motivated to go to the mission field with confidence that God has an encouraging ministry for us there? If so we have become neo-orthodox in disregarding the details of the Biblical text which calls Isaiah to a ministry of hardening to prepare Israel for blindness and captivity. Do we let a "Word of God" not in the text be the authoritative guide as we disregard details of the text?

---

261 Karl Barth, *The Epistle to the Romans,* trans. Edwyn Hoskyns (London: Oxford University Press, 1933); *Church Dogmatics,* ed. G. W. Bromiley and T. F. Torrance (Edinburg: T. & T. Clark, 1936–69).

262 Joseph Fletcher, *Situation Ethics: The New Morality* (Philadelphia: The Westminster Press, 1966).

Perhaps the most influential existentialist mid-century was Martin Heidegger.[263] For him, everyday existence is inauthentic so the goal is to make my world mine. One should not forfeit life by being distracted by the everyday things or gadgetry that surround me, by becoming merely a member in the crowd, hidden in the rat race of crises and moods. For him, there is only one mood that leads to genuine self-knowledge and away from self-betrayal and that is the mood of dread, especially as it is focused in a life of heading toward death, which we only face alone. This condition of life is not actually pessimistic for those who live it (in spite of most evangelicals claim for it to be), for it ushers into the existentialist an optimistic authentic choice.

Soteriology as authentic choice follows Bultmann's appropriation of Heidegger. For example, Bultmann began with this Heideggerian description of humanity and identifies it with the nonchristian condition. Bultmann's soteriology begins with man willfully misunderstanding himself.[264] Man needs to be totally dependent upon God. Upon hearing the message that God can provide security, man needs to commit himself to this God in order to exist in freedom, openness, love, and authenticity. In our Bible studies do we say, "What does this text mean to you" and let each one in the room paint a different meaning and application that they get from the text? If so we have joined with the existential hermeneutic in a reader response approach while we diminish what the text actually says, for the significance we own largely comes out of our own context.

About 1941 this existential soteriology began to express itself as existential eschatology. Bultmann agreed with Weiss that the kingdom of God transcends the historical order but then de-mythologized it away from the kerygma, leaving each 'now' or 'crises of decision' as always humanity's last time to decide against the world and for God. Norman Perrin extended this existential eschatology into a linguistic eschatology that takes the concept of kingdom of God as a tensive symbol evoking varied meanings of the myth of God's activity as kingship without reference to a present or future.[265] Such a myth existentially would be a complex of stories–some are fact and others are fantasy–which, for various reasons, humans regard as demonstrations of inner meaning of the universe and of human life. This linguistic turn was also within Heidegger, for hermeneutics was how we were to approach all of life interpreting it out of the narrative that is our own story.

---

263 Martin Heidegger, *Being and Time*, trans. J. Macquarrie and E. S. Robinson (New York: Harper, 1962); *An Introduction to Metaphysics*, trans. R. Manheim (New Haven: Yale University Press, 1959).

264 Theses views are more blatant in Rudolf Bultmann, *The Presence of Eternity, History and Eschatology* (New York: Harper & Bros., 1957) and *Jesus Christ and Mythology* (New York: Charles Scribner's Sons, 1958).

265 Norman Perrin, *Jesus and the Language of the Kingdom* (Philadelphia: Fortress, 1976).

Tillich was the leading liberal and existential theologian at mid-century.[266] He reframed Troeltsch's principle of correlation (a forerunner to contextualization)[267] into a method in which of (especially existentialism) would ask questions and theology would provide answers to these questions within a dialog with this philosophy. Questions like "Who am I?" "Why am I here?" and "Does anyone really care about me?" get addressed by an authentic reading of theology and the Bible to help us become oriented in our own existential situations. Since philosophy asked the questions it set the concepts through which theology would respond; philosophy effects theology. Do we try to answer these questions as we go to the Biblical text? All the latest scientific disciplines, like Freudian psychology gave an engaged voice to his theology to keep him on the boundaries of cutting edge theology. For him, the structure and meaning of reality can only be grasped by myths or symbols, which are signs that actually participate in the reality to which they point. The nature of the participation is not clear but it must occur for meaning to be communicated. The only symbol that has any hope of getting beyond mere equivocal analogy is the recognition that God is 'ground of being' and should be known by man as his "ultimate concern."[268] Much is criticized and rejected by him as not being propositions that deal with the object worthy of ultimate concern. This existentially revamps Schleiermacher's essence of religion, popularized by Annie Dillard as "Holy the firm." For Tillich, Jesus showed us the way of ultimate dependence by giving Himself on the cross. In this transparent move He can not be transcended, which is what Tillich meant by the second coming of Christ. This orientation reflects his commitment to expanding the envelope for theological studies, or as he described it, to be the theologian on the boundaries of the discipline. However, theology positions itself within the contents of the Christian faith and correlates it to our existential situation. Thus it is not ignorant of tradition. However, when tradition becomes dogmatics for him, it is "the doctrinal tradition for our present situation."[269] In fact, the way theology warrants itself as *the* theology is to position itself in the tension between the absolutely concrete and the absolutely universal. He criticizes priestly and prophetic theologies (like the reformers, Biblical theologians and evangelicals) as being too concrete. Furthermore, he criticizes mystical and metaphysical theologies (like Orthodoxy, Roman Catholic, and evangelicals) as trying to be too universal, because they lack concreteness. So for him the existentially paradoxical tension in

266 Paul Tillich, *Systematic Theology* (Chicago: University of Chicago Press, 1951–63).

267 Ernst Troeltsch, "Historical and Dogmatic Method in Theology" *GS* 2(1898): 729–753.

268 Paul Tillich, *Systematic Theology* (Chicago: University of Chicago Press, 1951), vol. 1, pp. 11–18.

269 Paul Tillich, *Systematic Theology*, vol. 1, p. 32; cf. Carl Braaten, "The Role of Dogma in Church and Theology" in *The Task of Theology Today*, edited by Victor Pfitzner and Hilary Regan (Grand Rapids: Eerdmans, 1998), pp. 23–54.

theology, yet still held to by a group, is the goal which is universally concrete and absolutely universal. Examples of this kind of tension force us into the trinity issues, like "divine Logos become flesh," or "Being in Christ."

Ricoeur embraced post-structuralism (such as Freud, Marx, and narrative analysis) as a tool of criticism to skeptically keep the inappropriate tradition from being read onto the text.[270] With one's house swept clean sufficiently, he advocates an existential reading of the text which lets the symbol and metaphor in the text vividly impact us so that we would consider our existential condition and the possibilities that could come to us in the midst of this condition. This sensitivity to textual symbolism opens us up to an increased ability to recover the vividness of the story for Hans Frei's narative theology.[271] Though narrative theology has a broad representation, from reader response to Lindbeck's post-liberal neo-orthodoxy to conservative vivid narrative of McClendon's biographical theology,[272] all of narrative theology's advocates participate in some form of the existential approach of reading the of text.

Others, like David Tracy, develop hybrid configurations from existential reading with some other aspect of this correlating existential theology.[273] Tracy extended Tillich's model of correlation and Ricoeur's aesthetic hermeneutic into a new generation of existential hermeneutical thought. So tradition becomes the pre-understanding for textual meaning as it is personally appropriated by the interpreter as he reads the text.[274]

With the emphasis of the twentieth century on framing a theology that authentically fits community in situation, there has been a great rise of liberation theologies and contextually indigenous theologies. Rooted in the liberalizing views of American antislavery movement and the women's rights movement, these existentially connected theologies began to grow. For example, the preaching of Henry Ward Beecher against the ownership or diminishment of any person for: race, color, or gender stirred many in America to see the equality of persons.[275] Of course, many others joined in these causes for equality of: race, color, gender, right to vote, trade unions for safety and a living wage, and

270 Paul Ricoeur, *Interpretation Theory: Discourse and the Surplus of Meaning* (Fort Worth: The Texas Christian University Press, 1976); *Essays on Biblical Interpretation* (Philadelphia: Fortress Press, 1980); *Hermeneutics & the Human Sciences,* trans. John Thompson (Cambridge: Cambridge University Press, 1981).

271 Hans Frei, *The Eclipse of Biblical Narrative* New Haven: Yale University Press, 1974); *Theology & Narrative: Selected Essays,* ed. George Hunsinger and William Placher (New York: Oxford University Press, 1993).

272 E.g., George Lindbeck, *The Nature of Doctrine: Religion and Theology in a Postliberal Age* (Philadelphia: The Westminster Press, 1984); James McClendon, *Doctrine: Systematic Theology,* (Nashville: Abingdon, 1994), vol. 2.

273 David Tracy, *The Analogical Imagination: Christian Theology and the Culture of Pluralism* (New York: Crossroad, 1986).

274 David Tracy, *The Analogical Imagination*, p. 243.

275 Gary Dorrien, *The Making of American Liberal Theology*, 1:179–213.

temperance. In due course, liberation theologies emerged during the 1960's and 70's, which were merely another stage of this sensitizing and taking ownership for their own futures. Liberation theology tries to raise conscious awareness to the plight of those who feel oppressed to help mobilize them to a confident praxis that God is on their side to throw off the oppression.

This existential emphasis fostered an indigenous authenticity. First, the late 1980's saw a more indigenous turn in the spirituality of a number of these liberation theologies. Secondly, the broader thrust within the third world theologies since the 1970's was indigenous theology. Beginning with Minjung of Korea, the African Independent Church Movement and Waterbuffalo theology, the theologies have continued to proliferate fitted to their own situations and concepts. So this new millennium began with a range of post-modern theologies continuing to emerge and fragment Christendom into a Balkanized conglomeration of Christianities. I think that this indigenization tends to Balkanize Christianity and will continue to do so.

I think the primary response that I see each theological camp making tends to draw their own camps into their own confessional traditions and insist that we keep the faith. This is a post-modern strategy which will keep us post-modern, and diminish engagement and understanding with each other. The only resolution to this is creative engagement as we call each other to truth with expressions of love. Such a loving approach takes time and effort. However, we may not love each other enough for that to occur. We may not want to risk our reputations enough to be associated with those we consider to be sinners, even though Jesus did. However, we may just be lazy and unconcerned enough to live as post-moderns while we claim in our communities that we are otherwise. Furthermore, science does not seem to be fostered by this method of choice, but existentialism tends to reduce intuitional approaches to that of aesthetic choice. So in our day, romantic or inferential intuitions of evolution or Intelligent Design may reduce within existentialism to be merely existential choice of whatever the believer would prefer. Such an existentialist process resists nuanced engagement with a scientist who differs in overarching aesthetic, setting up a Kuhnian aesthetic strategy for worldview or paradigm change.

2.11. Marxism

Fusing Fichte's view of Hegel with romanticism and realism begets the revolutionary Marx, a critical rigor to spur these liberation theologies to their hoped future. His statement engraved on his monument in Heidsgate Cemetery sums up his passion, "The philosophers have only interpreted the world in various ways; the point is, to change it."[276] Such change, for him, begins with sensitizing the common man to their condition of alienation, as he wrote in the Paris manuscripts.

> The worker is related to the product of his labor as to an alien object. The object he produces does not belong to him, dominates him, and only serves in the long run to increase his poverty. Alienation appears not only in the result, but also in the process of production and productive activity itself. The worker is not home in his work which he views only as a means of satisfying other needs. It is an activity directed against himself, that is independent of him and does not belong to him. Thirdly, alienated labor succeeds in alienating man from his species. Species life, productive life, life creating life, turns into a mere means of sustaining the worker's individual existence, and man is alienated from his fellow men. Finally, nature itself is alienated from man, who thus loses his own inorganic body.[277]

As a result of this analysis he sees that the world must fall apart into class struggle.

> The worker is degraded to the most miserable sort of commodity; that the misery of the worker is in inverse proportion to the power and size of his production; that the necessary result of competition is the accumulation of capital in a few hands, and thus a more terrible restoration of monopoly; and that between peasant and industrial worker disappears and the whole society must fall apart into the two classes of the property owners and the propertyless workers.[278]

Marx sees that the solution to this pillage of capitalism is the affirmation and protection of communism. This communism is what he envisages as a truly human society.

> Supposing that we had produced in a human manner; each of us would in his production have doubly affirmed himself and his fellow men. I would have: 1) objectified in my production my individuality and its peculiarity and thus both in my activity enjoyed an individual expression of my life and also

276 Initially from Karl Marx, *Writings of the Young Marx on Philosophy and Society*, ed. L. Easton and K. Guddat (Garden City: Doubleday, 1967).

277 Karl Marx, Paris Manuscripts in The Early Texts, ed. D. McLellan (Oxford: Blackwell Publishers, 1971), pp. 137–38.

278 Karl Marx, *The Early Texts*, p. 133.

> in looking at the object have had the pleasure of realizing that my personality was objective, visible to the senses and thus a power raised beyond all doubt. 2) In your enjoyment or use of my product I would have had the direct enjoyment of realizing that I had both satisfied a human need by my work and also objectified the human essence and therefore fashioned for another human being the object that met his need. 3) I would have been for you the mediator between you and the species and thus been acknowledged and felt by you as a completion of your own essence and a necessary part of yourself and have thus realized that I am confirmed both in your thought and in your love. 4) In my expression of my life I would have fashioned your expression of your life, and thus in my activity have realized my own essence, my human, my communal essence.[279]

Such a communal Marxist framework is embraced by some of the Liberationist theologians and then expanded beyond the economic concern to issues of race, ethnicity and gender. For example, Gustavo Gutierrez claims that it is especially Marxist "focusing on praxis and geared to the transformation of the world" that serves as a fruitful confrontation to drive theology to its own sources to begin "to reflect on the meaning of transformation of this world and the action of man in history."[280] Those benefited by this reflection are especially the oppressed who have adapted to the structure of domination in which they are immersed and have become resigned to it. Perhaps the first task is to help the oppressed become motivated for waging the struggle for freedom. James Cone agrees and points out with Marx that part of understanding of freedom is the experience of liberating activity.

> It is not difficult for the oppressed to understand the meaning of freedom. They are forced by the very nature of their condition to interpret their existence in the world contrary to the value-structures of the oppressive society. For the oppressed, to be is to be in revolt against the forces that impede the creation of the new Man. That is what Karl Marx has in mind in his definition of man as praxis which means "directed activity." Praxis expresses man's freedom. "Freedom," writes Marx, "is the essence of man." It "is *not something outside one who freely is, it is the specific mode or structure of being,*" and inherent in it is action. Marx says: "The coincidence of the changing circumstances and of human activity can be

279 Karl Marx, *The Early Texts*, p. 202.

280 Gustavo Gutierrez, *A Theology of Liberation* (Maryknoll: Orbis, 1973), p. 9.

> conceived and rationally understood only as revolutionizing practice (praxis)." Here he shows the inseparable relationship of freedom and liberation activity.[281]

This liberating activity is especially enabled by reminding the oppressed that God is present in history to work for the purposes of liberation. Praxis is the emphasis; whatever one does which transforms the world into the desired goal is a pragmatic approach to theology. In this, action is supreme over reflection. Marxism tries to raise the aspiration of the oppressed and help motivate them to take responsibility for their destiny. Going beyond Marxism, Liberation theology also tries to motivate them from the root of oppression by faith into a communion with God and with all men. Often the role of prophet motivates a pastor to call down the sins that hinder the community and to chart a trajectory toward the kingdom which removes all of these problems. Within the context of Christian theology there can be even greater hope that a new man may be created in salvation. So the goal is not an external fix for economic or racial injustice, but the transformation of oppressor and oppressed alike into a people affirming orientation for each other's edification and welfare.

The fact that a liberation theology has been successful to oust apartheid and work for healing and self-governance in South Africa, shows the kind of Christian sensitivities that liberation theology might wish to work toward.[282] The resolution in the "Truth and Reconciliation Commission" is tantalizing in its ability to honestly hear the stories of abuse and crushed lives, and enable forgiveness to be obtained for the oppressors. With its successful completion after seven years running, they have also recommended reparations to the crushed of about $4000 for each to aid in this reconciliation.[283] The reparations can never repay for the oppression and loss, but no government can pay the actual cost. So part of practicality is to raise up institutions that will not repeat such oppression. Another part of reconciliation is the comfort that the oppressed could achieve by telling their story, but now they need to existentially choose to define themselves by something other than "victim." Hopefully they will choose forgiveness. This reconciliation is still in process but it is one for which to watch. It is certainly negotiating its way through the dicey issues of exclusion better than most others have done. In contrast, most expressions of liberation theology achieve

281 James Cone, *A Black Theology of Liberation* (Philadelphia: J. B. Lippincott Co., 1970), pp. 162–3. Cone quotes Marx here through secondary sources like Jacques Maritain and Norman Bailliey.

282 Desmund M. Tutu, "Forward" in *Forgiveness and Reconciliation,* ed. Raymond Helmick and Rodney Petersen, (Philadelphia: Templeton Foundation Press, 2001), pp. ix–xiii.

283 Reported on "All Things Considered," National Public Radio, April 16, 2003.

more modest goals for localized communities as they continue to wrestle with the tensions of living within a hostile environment.

Marxist history focuses too exclusively on economic and political causation. Likewise, Marxist methods of science focus on how power is wielded to resist paradigm change or to encourage paradigm change. For example, Marxism would analyze whether there are sufficient politicians, judges and populous to permit Intelligent Design to be taught as a rival scientific theory along with evolution in the public schools. While these sociological aspects are part of the corporate transformation process, hopefully each discipline can approach their endeavor honestly questing for where the epistemic evidence provides warrant. I think that it is more helpful to analyze paradigm change by appeals to scientific data rather than through the lens of political and sociological commitments.

2.12. Pragmatism

Pragmatism is associated with truth as determined in so far as it works. However, there are varieties of pragmatism and a range of issues into which it is appropriated. All the levels of pragmatism are revolutionarily activism which believe conceptual frameworks can be developed and replaced by better ones. The approach is conceptually active in that we demolish and create our conceptual frameworks. Within this approach decisions may lead astray but it is the price of the possibility of progress.

The founder of pragmatism, Charles Peirce explains his form of pragmatism as follows: "In order to ascertain the meaning of an intellectual conception one should consider what practical consequences might conceivably result by necessity from the truth of that conception; and the sum of these consequences will constitute the entire meaning of the conception."[284] He is trying to describe a methodology available for modern sciences. He could also be viewed as bridging the Kantian gap by providing a means by which the phenomena provided by empiricism can be checked by reality itself. He is also reacting against the positivist's strictured preoccupation with the process of verification. One aspect of his view could be stated as follows: within one's immediate sense awareness, impressions can be verified by testing proposals with regard to "the thing in itself" beneath the sense awareness. So this approach positions itself against naïve realism on the one hand and idealism on the other. Pierce's pragmatism thwarts Kantian dualism by bridging the Kantian gap by testing the "thing in itself" as the "thing as it appears." According to Peirce, the most rational way to determine beliefs is to test

284 The Collected Papers of Charles Sanders Peirce, ed. Charles Hartshorne and Paul Weiss (Cambridge: Harvard University Press, 1966), vol. 5, paragraph 9; Cf. Charles Peirce essays on of that are particularly helpful include: "The Fixation of Belief," Popular Science Monthly 12(Nov., 1877): 1–15, and "How to Make Our Ideas Clear," Popular Science Monthly 12(Jan., 1878): 286–302.

them fairly but rigorously and repeatedly in an intellectual community, with reference to broadly observable results. Peirce floated this methodology with science directly in view.

One theologian developing this approach at length is Alister McGrath. He often presents his method as an empirically based pragmatic realism or when he adds mathematical derivation to it, he calls this method critical realism.[285] He sees that empirically based pragmatism is the foundation for this realism in the natural sciences.[286] He then justifies this realism as against conventionalist approaches, which would be either anti-realist, theory dependent, or indebted to James' pragmatism. He develops a critical realism that engages the world at a variety of levels, each evaluated for its clarity and predictability. He extends this scientific method to theology as an attempt to ground theology as a scientific discipline with a critical realist methodology. His view will be discussed more fully under the heading of critical realism.

Others like William James and John Dewey expanded Peirce's range of application. Peirce did not approve of James and Dewey's extensions so that Peirce tried to make his theory a little more superficially unattractive by changing the name from "pragmatism" to "pragmaticism."

William James describes his approach as a radical empiricism. Expanding into issues like Pascal's wager, James makes a nice statement of his version of pragmatism in his document, "The Will to Believe."[287] It can be summarized as: after reasonable diligence, when the evidence is inconclusive, one is morally obligated to choose the live and forced option that provides the possibility of the greatest gain. The kind of evidence that he is looking at is largely empirical and testimony, like that available in his *Principles of Psychology* and *Varieties of Religious Experience.*[288] The term 'live' means that the option is *available*. Whereas, the term 'forced' means that the decision renders one *in or out of the option*; like marriage: you are either married or you are not. That is, there is no synthesis of both options. Additionally, the 'greatest gain' is evaluated by James in a communal perspective similar to that of John Stuart Mill's utilitarian principle, "the greatest good for the greatest number." So as a

285 Alister McGrath, *A Scientific Theology: Reality,* vol. 2, pp. especially identifying himself as a critical realist xv-xvi, 123–244, and especially developing his view on p. 188. Bernard Lonergan presents a similar analysis in "Cognitional Structure," *Collection: Papers by Bernard Lonergan* (Toronto: University of Toronto, 1988), pp. 205–21 and *Method in Theology* (London: Darton, Longman and Todd, 1972), p. 238.

286 Alister McGrath, *A Scientific Theology: Reality,* vol. 2, pp. 257, 174–175.

287 William James, *The Will to Believe and Other Essays in Popular Philosophy* (New York: Longmans, Green & Co., 1897), ch. 1.

288 William James, *Principles of Psychology* , in *Great Books of the Western World,* vol. 53 *William James* (Chicago: Encyclopaedia Britannica, 1952), and *Varieties of Religious Experience* (New York: Longmans, 1902).

method it prompts faith to act in these inconclusive areas of life toward the greatest communal gain.

James presented his view as an explanation for why Pascal's wager motivates belief in God and Christ.[289] Presented with the option that if one believes in Christ she has the possibility of everlasting benefit and if one does not believe all one has is this life with its good and bad, the possibility of everlasting benefit should motivate a person to believe in Christ to realize such a greatest gain as Christ's kingdom. Of course, such a perspective might also have a similar draw to woo any adherent from a worldview with inconclusive eschatology to embrace the nearest live exclusive eschatology (even if it is Islam). In such a Jamesian pragmatic approach decisions may lead astray but it is the price of the possibility of progress.

If one would let a conservative Biblical creation account and ethic determine: 1) the evidence permitted and 2) the criteria of evaluating this evidence, then James' pragmatism is a good description of the conservative approach for evangelical decision making floated by Gary Friesen in *Decision Making and the Will of God: A Biblical Alternative to the Traditional View*.[290] However, Friesen shows no evidence of dependence on James for his way of wisdom, he merely expresses a conservative evangelical form of what could be called James' Pragmatism. Rarely is James' pragmatism held to its possibilities by such a thoroughly informed Biblicism.

John Dewey expanded pragmatism into an ethical approach called instrumentalism. Each problem situation is unique and unrepeatable, but the goal is to react in a manner that crafts a resolution to the problem in such a way as to change the environment so that it is no longer hampered by that problem. This removes the spectator from knowledge and places the person who works for change into the knowing position with 'whatever works' becoming the new knowledge.[291] However, Dewey is careful to point out that truth as utility is not intended to identify with "some personal end, some profit upon which a particular individual has set his heart."[292] So, instrumentalism does not deny the objectivity of truth by making it relative to an individual's whims. Rather, all statements, practices and beliefs are revisable. Any revision should be done to resolve problems that emerge, and thus transforming the situation beyond that problem to hopefully a harmonious resolution.

289 William James, *The Will to Believe and Other Essays in Popular Philosophy* (New York: Longmans, Green & Co., 1897), ch. 1.

290 Gary Friesen, *Decision Making and the Will of God: A Biblical Alternative to the Traditional View* (Portland: Multnomah Press, 1980).

291 John Dewey, *Reconstruction in Philosophy* (New York: H. Holt & Co., 1920), p. 156.

292 John Dewey, *Reconstruction in Philosophy*, p. 157.

Within this framework, Quine proposes a belief system as a web or a net.[293]

Nancey Murphy nicely summarizes his model with its ability to bring about pragmatic resolution.

> Beliefs that are most likely to be given up in the face of recalcitrant experience are nearer the center. These latter beliefs less subject to revision not only because they are further from experience, but also because they are interconnected with more elements in the rest of the system. When experience necessitates some change in the meanings of some terms, revising theories, or even, Quine hazards, revising logic. The decision among these possibilities will in the end be pragmatic–how best to restore consistency with the least disturbance to the system as a whole.[294]

Perhaps a theological expression of this Dewey-Quine kind of pragmatism can be seen in liberation theology's attempt to solve the problem of oppression. In the South Africa situation, liberation theology can continue to grow beyond the initial reaction to the condition of oppression. Whereas, other conditions in which this oppressive tension have not been resolved probably will define their base communities by a prolonged inclination against the oppressive power.

The American rejection of the value of class disconnected their practice of religion from the preference of kings to that of a capitalistic marketing based arena in which each entrepreneur within religion would demonstrate his worth by the extent of a following that he could attract around himself. That is, America religion was immersed into an arena of pragmatic populism, in which unpopularity became among the gravest of sins. Robert Bellah's sociological team assessed that Americans are on average especially pragmatic in an individual manner, looking out for the welfare of "me and mine."[295] Within this, Alister McGrath, David Wells, Os Guinness, and Robert E. Webber identify that American evangelicalism is strongly pragmatic.[296] McGrath and Wells bemoan the

293 W. V. O. Quine and J. S. Ullian, *The Web of Belief* (New York: Random House, 1979).

294 Nancey Murphy, Theology in the Age of Scientific Reasoning, p. 8.

295 Robert Bellah, et. al. *Habits of the Heart: Individualism and Commitment in American Life* (Berkley: University of California Press, 1985).

296 Alister McGrath, "Evangelical Theological Method: The State of the Art" in *Evangelical Futures,* edited by John Stackhouse (Grand Rapids: Baker, 2000), p. 16; David F. Wells, *No Place for Truth, or Whatever Happened to Evangelical Theology?* (Grand Rapids: Eerdmans, 1993); Os Guinness, *Fit Bodies, Fat Minds: Why Evangelicals Don't Think and What to do About it* (Grand Rapids: Baker, 1994), pp. 55–59; Robert Webber, *The Younger Evangelicals* (Grand Rapids: Baker, 2002), pp. 16–17, 41–42.

dumbing down of Evangelicalism and the loss of theological thinking that this condition has caused, as evangelicalism continues to proliferate and spread its web to influence decision makers in our country; whereas, Webber especially sees this pragmatism in an era of the leadership of evangelicalism from 1975 to 2000. He describes this leadership style as that of a managerial model with the business emphasis of a C.E.O. He characterizes this era as pragmatic in the market targeting ministry style and need driven social action. The praise choruses that gain popularity on Christian radio wind their way into our church services as an expression of our pragmatic populism. For example, Bruce Wilkinson's *The Prayer of Jabez* has provided a pragmatic rallying cry for our more capitalistic oriented culture.[297] 1 Chronicles 4:9 indicates that Jabez was a righteous man under the Mosaic Covenant and asking for Covenantal blessing of possession of part of the land of Israel, which is appropriate under the Mosaic Covenant (Deut. 28:11). However, when Americans, who are not under such a Mosaic Covenant, pray such a prayer, without reference to Biblical texts promising what we ask in their contexts, it can become a baptized talisman for our capitalistic culture. In this, we abuse the Bible by co-opting it for our capitalistic ends. Such a syncretized version of Evangelicalism shows its indebtedness to pragmatic capitalism. Such an unbridled approach also leaves us wide open to going into adventures that God does not support. For example, Wilkinson's quitting the African AIDS crusade in 2006 shows that some problems are too large and intractable for our efforts and resources, no matter how fervently we evangelicals pray the prayer of Jabez.[298]

I think that these examples show that John Dewey's instrumentalism is a bit too unbounded, except in non-moral issues like how to arrange a cataloging system for a library. That is, whether Houston Graduate School of Theology uses the Library of Congress or Thomas Dewey's Dewey decimal system or some other arrangement seems to be dependent upon which cataloging system serves the best interests of a library and her patrons. Such a non-moral use of John Dewey's pragmatism to me seems perfectly appropriate.

Scientific expressions of Peircian pragmatism (or even better the hybrid of critical realism, with its empiricism, pragmatism and mathematical derivation) can be seen in Einstein's relativity concepts and Bohr's quantum physics. For example, let me paint the picture of Einsteinian relativity and show how the Frisch/Smith experiment

297 Bruce Wilkinson, *The Prayer of Jabez: Breaking Through to the Blessed Life* (Sisters: Multnomah, 2000).

298 Timothy C. Morgan, "Mr Jabez goes to Africa: Bruce Wilkinson expands his borders to include racial reconciliation and HIV/AIDS." *Christianity Today* 47:11(2003): 45–50; "Jabez author quits Africa: disappointments prompt early retirement." *Christianity Today* 50:2(2006):76.

pragmatically verified it and again with contemporary GPS atomic clocks pragmatically verifying Einstein's theories. In 1905 Albert Einstein set forth his theory of relativity, once the speed of light in a vacuum was held to be a constant. Coming through the lens of the 1887 Michelson-Morley derivation and experiment, time is seen as in relationship for any one thing. Time is not an absolute (as in either Augustinian mind of God or Newtonian framework in which everything experiences the same sequence simultaneously) or a Kantian phenomenalogical grid for perception (in which sequence merely becomes a mental category not descriptive of reality) but an Einstinian metaphysical relationship of a thing's experience in relationship to another's experience. For example, Einstein's time dilation is relative to the velocity at which any object moves in relationship to another as expressed through the equation: an object's relativistic time equals observed time divided by the square root of {1-(velocity squared divided by the speed of light squared)}. This makes time a fourth dimension along with the three spatial dimensions. Likewise, an object's experience in these four dimensions and its mass are affected by the velocity of the object in relationship to another to which it is referenced, as expressed by the dilation equations. This special theory of relativity was modified in 1915 into the general theory of relativity, where time is also slowed down by gravity, and the measurement of space is altered by a gravitational field. The theoretical time dilation was experimentally verified by the MIT physicists Frisch and Smith in 1961 when they showed that the mu-mesons (small particles found in the atmosphere and outer space) that were being stopped at sea level had their time slowed down by the longer experience at a velocity near the speed of light as compared to the time of the earth observers or the time of the mu-mesons which were stopped and held relatively stationary in a cloud chamber on the top of Mt. Washington.[299] The mu-mesons which traveled faster for longer then survived longer, verifying the Einstinian expectation that the mathematical derivation of time dilation had predicted. Additionally, the relativistic time dilation was further confirmed experimentally through the time dilation in atomic clocks within GPS satellites, which must be corrected 38 microseconds per day to yield correct GPS data.[300] These verifications indicate that time is in fact a metaphysical reality for anything in relationship to another. In this way time can be thought as a local metaphysical sequence. Anything that has an experience of sequence is then in its own time. Likewise, anything that is related to the experience is then also in its own time as well. This has the theological implication that God experiences time from all locations simultaneously and everlastingly, once He began to experience His creation. I discuss theological implications of this at

299 D. H. Frisch and J. H. Smith, "Measurement of Relativistic Time Dilation Using Mu-Mesons," *American Journal of Physics* 31:5(1963): 342.

300 Phillip Yam, "Time and Time Again," *Scientific American* 291(Sept. 2004): 55.

greater detail elsewhere.[301] However, one consequence for the present relationship of philosophy and science is a further defeating of Kant's dualism by cognitively bridging the "thing as it appears" to the "thing in itself" utilizing Einstein's time dilation equation.

Quantum theory considers that light and electrons are both waves and particles. Let me paint the context of quantum theory and again show how experiments (by Davisson/Germer and Afshar) pragmatically verify it. In the wake of Newton's prism experiments, Huygens and Hooke concluded that light was composed of waves. In 1901 Edington observed the particle nature of light attracted by gravity during an eclipse, showing further that there did not need to be an appeal to an ether medium in space through which light waves travel. Experimental verification of de Broglie's wave nature of an electron was provided in 1926 by Davisson and Germer as they scattered low energy electrons off the surface of a metal crystal. The wave nature of both light and electrons can be compared as they pass through a two slit test showing a similar interference pattern. Plus the particle nature of an electron is indicated by the sensors of microscopic particles. In 2004, the research of Rowan University visiting research professor of Physics and Astronomy, Shaniar Afshar, showed that light is both particle and wave simultaneously.[302] Warranting a more blatant critical realist quantum view, Afshar demonstrated that light remains wavelike in the middle of a test that normally (and does so here as well) shows light to be particle. This experiment by Afshar, showing light to be simultaneously wave and particle in nature, was confirmed by John Cramer of the University of Washington.

The particle nature of electron and quark has raised intriguing issues wrongly appealed to by some moral philosophers to present libertarian free will in philosophy and relativism in ethics. Neither Heisenberg's uncertainty principle, nor Schrödinger's wave equations address libertarianism or ethical relativism. That is, quantum mechanics greater precision required improved instruments. At the edge of instrument sensing ability, Heisenberg's uncertainty principle indicates that there is a limit to testing location and velocity of microscopic particles at the same time. To identify the location of a microscopic particle one must repeatedly bombard it with other microscopic particles and triangulate the ricochet read off the sensors, but each bump changes the tested particle's velocity. To find out the microscopic particle's velocity, one needs to hit the particle once and then compute what the velocity must be based on the starting and ricocheted velocity of the testing particle, but now we don't know where the tested particle is. That is, there are limits to testing both location and velocity of microscopic particles simultaneously. Additionally, the analysis of Schrödinger's wave equations for describing

301 Doug Kennard, *The Classical Christian God*, pp. 43–61.

302 "Quantum Rebel," *New Scientist* 183(July, 2004): 30–35; "Talk of the Nation" interview with Shaniar Afshar, July 30, 2004.

the probable distribution of wave electrons within an electron cloud indicate *probability* of their real locations, not the simultaneity of locations of an electron wave, no matter how odd it might be to illustrate the phenomena by considering multiple locations of a cat, or the oddity of picking up space stranded astronauts in *A Hitchhikers Guide to the Galaxy* with an infinite probability drive. These features of quantum are exploring the limits of testability for microscopic particles, not providing fodder for libertarianian philosophy or relativistic ethics.

2.13. Process

As a mathematician, Alfred North Whitehead became fascinated with the philosophy of science and especially with metaphysics informed by relativity. The Newtonian worldview was superceeded by Einsteinian and quantum when the concept of "ether" in space was abandoned and light was gravitationally attracted to bodies of mass. Whitehead fuses these rival theories permitting relativity to govern the nature of time and perception and quantum to govern the metaphysics of an experiential *occasion*.

In reaction to the Scopes Trial in 1925, Whitehead floated the introductory framework for process of as the Lowell lectures at Harvard,[303] but the full statement was presented as the Gifford lectures in 1929.[304] Whitehead assumes a post-Kantian phenomenalistic idealism so that the only reality is *occasions*, which occur as microscopic experiences in a moment of a Humean occasionalism and with an Einsteinian relativity as to time and space relationships. An "occasion" is a pragmatic (in Dewey's sense) growing together of a momentary microscopic phenomenal concrete experience (concrescence of prehension) and thus the basic building block of everything. However, such a microscopic phenomenalness is largely rejected by relativity and quantum physics, so it is a philosophical imposition not supported by the science. After the moment has its occasion it gives its free will contribution (superject) for the next generation of occasions. Simultaneous to this microscopic phenomenal experience is a Platonic idealism of sorts which is how Whitehead envisions God. The transcendental primordial nature of God houses all possibilities that could be realized and the evolutionary creative thrust to woo toward these pure possibilities. Whereas, in the imminent consequent nature of God, the superject is compared with the next possibility to lure it with an initial impetus toward the subjective aim of God. However, the occasion apprehends itself in a libertarian way, often thwarting God. This experience of the consequential nature of God with the superject has left a lasting legacy in the evolving mind of God. If the creation is considered macroscopically, it is a misplaced

303 Alfred North Whitehead, *Science and the Modern World* (New York: The Free Press, 1925).

304 Alfred North Whitehead, *Process and Reality* (New York: The Free Press, 1978).

concreteness that is phenomenally evolving as the occasions decide. As the universe evolves, so does the consequent nature of God. Such a becoming of God was attractive for some as a Hegelian synthesis to the rival views of "God exists" and "God is dead" being voiced in the early 1960's. Such an evolutionary perspective of God and reality provides an apologetic for religion to evolve as well, and Whitehead said so in reaction to the Scopes Trial.[305] However, in a Whiteheadian process model there is no goal for the universe, just an aimless ramble through the chess moves of all the occasions and the master chessman God playing a trillion games at once. However, the freewill of the occasions decides the outcome, for God can only persuade. Such a framework maintains evil within the creation (as evident by the death of each occasion and the lack of resolution) and within God's consequent nature (as God's omniscient memory of the past), while the consequent nature is claimed to work toward an evolutionary solution, trying to pragmatically remedy the problem of evil. Is the future for the occasions to decide?

This evolutionary process view of reality and God was first made more palatable to some Christians by Marie Joseph Pierre Teilhard de Chardin, who approached the subject from the context of biology and paleontology. He reasoned that if Christianity is to win allegiance of the modern world then it needs to be reconceptualized in line with the most advanced knowledge, namely evolutionary oriented science.[306] Reality, for him, is a temporal process operating under the dynamic and direction of evolution. At critical points reality makes major breakthroughs into phases of pre-life, life, and consciousness. He was encouraged toward this evolution of humanity by his involvement in the discoveries of Peking man and Pithecanthropus. Teilhard considered the final goal of evolution to be Christ, which "omega point" means that all matter and energy is becoming as Christ now is. This pursuit of the next step is necessary because Teilhard felt entropy indicates that we will run out of available energy and if we do not evolve beyond ourselves then the earth will become hostile to us. He sees this goal as realizable because Christ is the evolutionary, immanent God, continuing to create and synthesize everything into his transforming self. Is everything meandering toward being like Christ?

2.14. Conventional Post-Modern

"Post-modern" as a term emerged first in critiquing modern architecture in the 1890's. Then it moved to describe a range of emerging existential views including Fyodor Dostoevsky's voice through

305 Alfred North Whitehead, *Religion in the Making* (New York: Macmillan, 1926).

306 Pierre Teilhard de Chardin, *The Divine Milieu* (New York: Harper and Row, 1965) and *The Phenomenon of Man* (New York: Harper and Row, 1965).

Ivan Karamazov[307] and Friedrich Nietzsche's philosophy. In this view, whatever we choose to authentically fit ourselves is permitted provided you have the will and the power to pull it off. The first philosophical appraisal I have found that critiques this existential post-modernism is that by Bernard Bell, who in 1926 argued that there were resources for truth in modern epistemology that warrant our truth claims without reducing things essentially to choice.[308] However, I have already largely connected the dots for this form of post-modernity under the heading of "existentialism."

The emergence of Ludwig Wittgenstein's functional approach to language in 1947 is hailed as the watershed for the conventional form of post-modernism.

> There are *countless* kinds: countless different kinds of use of what we call "symbols," "words," "sentences." And this multiplicity is not something fixed, given once for all; but new types of language, new language-games, as we may say, come into existence, and others become obsolete and get forgotten.[309]

Each game has its form of life and its rules, which contextualize it so that it makes sense. Like the word "run" that is ambiguous until I identify whether I am describing baseball, or a stocking, or a race, or plumbing, or my car to my mechanic. Likewise, the theological language needs to be contextualized to Mormonism, or Calvinism, or more radically John Milbank's "The Midwinter Sacrifice,"[310] or feminism, or liberation theology, or Mark Taylor's *Erring.*[311]

Karl Popper identified that science has its status not because it is falsifiable but that it sufficiently plays the game of science.[312] Popper's "methodological falsification" is that conventional statements are contextual (not universal) as they are formed by agreement about some of the facts. Popper's basic data report of repeatable experiments and what those in the discipline are willing to grant, rather than the philosopher's

---

307 Fyodor Mikhailovich Dostoevsky, *The Brothers Karamazov* (Chicago: Encyclopedia Britannica, 1952).

308 Bernard Iddings Bell, *Postmodernism and Other Essays* (Milwaukee: Morehouse Publishing Co., 1926).

309 Ludwig Wittgenstein, *Philosophical Investigations* (New York: Macmillan Publishing Co., 1953, 1958), p. 11, #23.

310 John Milbank, "The Midwinter Sacrifice" in *Christian Ethics*, 10(1997) and included in *The Blackwell Companion to Postmodern Theology* edited by Graham Ward (Oxford: Blackwell Publishing, 2001), pp. 107–130. In the rest of this volume are many other varieties of post-modernism as well.

311 Mark Taylor, Erring: A Postmodern A/theology (Chicago: University of Chicago, 1981).

312 Karl Popper, *Logik der Forschung* (Vienna: J. Springer, 1935), trans. Popper et *al.* as *The Logic of Scientific Discovery* (New York: Harper Torchbook, 1965).

sense of data. The logical and empirical data prompt scientists in a context to discard and found theories that obtain some conventional agreement. Popper's metaphor has pilings driven into the swamp to move science forward.

> The empirical basis of objective science has nothing 'absolute' about it. Science does not rest upon solid bedrock. The bold structure of its theories rises, as it were, above the swamp. It is like a building erected on piles. The piles are driven down from above into the swamp, but not down to any natural or 'given' base; and if we stop driving the piles deeper, it is not because we have reached firm ground. We simply stop when we are satisfied that the piles are firm enough to carry the structure, at least for the time being.[313]

Such a subjective swamp metaphor is shocking to an engineer because structures without sufficient support topple in time. However, "pilings in a swamp" does describe the communal subjectivity present within post-modern theology and science. Additionally, in the same manner as a southern Louisiana highway might be really supported for sufficient time by pilings driven into the bayou, Popper reasons that a community's subjective commitments might float an anti-realist theory or worldview. However, the highway is testable through the Peircian pragmatic test of it continuing to stand while the traffic lumbers across it, but Popper's approach diminishes warrant in science such that any presuppositional worldview could be integrated or fused with it, for it functions on the level of existential communal commitments or a communal implementation of Dewey's pragmatism. In this Leonard Brand considers that scientific consensus could be produced by the philosophical and sociological commitments, such as supernaturalism or anti-supernaturalism as a philosophical commitment.[314] In this subjectivity, Popper would want to moderate our shock some by encouraging us that a theory needs to stick its neck out and be testable to some extent. However, in such an approach if scientists attempt to falsify strongly accepted theories they will be written off as kooks and annoyances. In Popper's view decisions may lead astray, which is the price for the possibility of progress. How long will our theologies contribute meaningfully as our communities

313 Karl Popper, *The Logic of Scientific Discovery*, p. 111; At times there is an over confidence that science must be absolutely falsifiable or it is not of (e.g., Judge Jones Dec. 20, 2005 decision in the U.S. District Court for the Middle District of Penn. Tammy Kitzmiller, et.al. Plaintiffs v Dover Area School District, et. al. Defendants), p. 89.

314 Leonard Brand, "A Biblical Perspective on the Philosophy of Science" *Origins* 59(2006): 6–42 but especially 10–11.

change? Is their warrant provided by more than community acceptance? Do our theologies stick their necks out in some form of testability?

Thomas Kuhn explores history and sociology of science for how human factors precipitated fresh disputes and subsequent scientific theories which combine the language game of a paradigm with observations.[315] Kuhn's philosophy replaces foundationalism, and Popper's communal methodological falsification with a holistic view of science. The data are partially determined by the paradigm that they support. The paradigm and the data must be accepted as a whole upon criteria like empirical fit and simplicity. We have seen throughout this chapter that when theological or philosophical observations didn't fit the theory, that this data told against the paradigm. So the data were not completely paradigm dependent but both could be evaluated from either within or beyond the paradigm. When a paradigm was trying to drag sufficient weight that didn't fit toward its goal the paradigm became overwhelmed. As Duhem counseled, a theory would then crumble under the weight of continual repairs and entanglements.[316] After a few failed downs, the community would start to shift its trust to another paradigm which could deliver more effectively in that area of understanding and theology. However, this Kuhnian approach is also critiqued for over-simplistically treating theories as "normal" science which dominate the discipline.[317] There is broad agreement that rival theories vie for a discipline's adherence, even when a community may largely embrace a particular model. In such situations, Lakatos explains that clashes between theories are merely inconsistencies not falsifications.[318] As mentioned before, if scientists attempt to falsify strongly accepted theories they will be written off as kooks and annoyances. Such a condition within Kuhnianism would set up post-modern rival conventional communities that are not heard by the other community, even if they try to communicate. In science this could be seen in the way in which two rival aesthetic programs inoculate adherents in considering alternatives, as in the evolution and Intelligent Design debate.

Stanley Grenz develops that the frame of reference to this post-modern theological approach is the community, especially that of a local

315 Thomas Kuhn, *Structure of Scientific Revolutions* (Chicago: University of Chicago Press, 1970).

316 Pierre Duhem, *The Aim and Structure of Physical Theory* (Princeton: Princeton University Press, 1954).

317 Watkins, Toulmin, Williams, Popper, and Lakatos take Kuhn to task on this point in *Criticism and the Growth of Knowledge*. edited by Imre Lakatos and Alan Musgrave, eg. pp. 101–3, 110.

318 Imre Lakatos, "Falsification and the Methodology of Scientific Research Programs," in *Criticism and the Growth of Knowledge*. edited by Imre Lakatos and Alan Musgrave, pp. 99, 130.

church.[319] Such a community remembers and hopes, thus defining its view between these for now.

> The role of a group as a community of reference is connected with its ability to forge a link to both the past and the future and thereby become what Josiah Royce denotes a "community of memory" and a "community of hope."[320] A community has a history; in fact, it is in an important sense constituted by that history, a history that begins in the past and extends into the future. This "constitutive narrative" does not view time merely as a continuous flow of qualitatively meaningless sensations. Rather, in telling its story, a community punctuates the present–the day, the week, the season, the year–with a sense of the transcendent and thereby presents time as a meaningful whole.[321]

The constitutive narrative begins "with the primal events that called the community into being, and includes the crucial milestones that mark its subsequent trajectory...The act of reciting reconstitutes the community in the present as the contemporary embodiment of a communal of that spans the years."[322] However, the community also hopes for a future that motivates them toward what they consider would fully actualize.

> The community history does not end in the past, but extends into the future. As a result, a community turns the gaze of its members toward the future, anticipating the continuation of, and even the further development of the community. Not only does the community sense that it is moving toward an ideal that lies yet before it, more importantly, it expectantly looks to the ideal or 'eschatological' future, when the purpose and goals–the *telos*–of the community will be fully actualized. This expectation of a glorious future serves as an ongoing admonition to its members to embody the communal vision in the present.[323]

Grunlan and Mayers identify that each community has "rites of intensification" which function to "bring the community together, increase group solidarity, and reinforce commitment to the beliefs of

319 Stanley Grenz, "Ecclesiology" in *The Cambridge Companion to Postmodern Theology*. edited by Kevin Vanhoozer (Cambridge: The Cambridge University Press, 2003), pp. 252–268.

320 Josiah Royce, *The Problem of Christianity*, 2 vols. (New York: Macmillian, 1913), vol. 2, pp. 50–51.

321 Stanley Grenz, "Ecclesiology" in *Postmodern Theology*, p. 255.

322 Stanley Grenz, "Ecclesiology" in *Postmodern Theology*, p. 255.

323 Stanley Grenz, "Ecclesiology" in *Postmodern Theology*, p. 256.

the group."[324] So each community portrays its own distinct form of post-modernism. Within such far flung variety of post-modernism four will be sampled: Lindbeck's cultural-linguistic model, Milbank's radical orthodoxy, Vanhoozer's canonical-linguistic drama, and Webber's millennial generation.

George Lindbeck proposes in post-liberalism a "cultural-linguistic" model of religion.[325] Religion defines a language and practice of a community in their self definition. Hans Frei describes this as "Christian self-description," not correlation with universal "human, cultural quests for ultimate meaning."[326] So the practices and narratives define the communal perspective repeatedly as the community performs them within themselves, and thereby etches on the communal conscience who they are and how they belong to God. For any community, their tradition becomes their own grammar within which the appropriate thought forms function.[327] Such tradition as grammar becomes the necessary condition for cognition and experience to be expressed, interpreted, and understood. Within this perspective faithfulness to tradition is essential; though pioneering beyond what the tradition has expressed is permitted provided the new significance experienced is communally connected within the community's self definition. In this way tradition is both the essential language game and yet it does not make the community become an extinct fossil.

John Milbank calls into question the sociology of religion, and especially that of overrated Marxism, to call the Christian community back to a radical orthodoxy.[328] This radical orthodoxy is possible in the very arena of secularism because of secularism's superficial relationship there. Milbank's team argues that we need to suspend the hold these disciplines have in order to press them into the Christian language game.[329] Radical orthodoxy resituates these areas of secular dominance through a Christian perspective, in terms of Trinity, Christology, the Church and the Eucharist. As these areas are recovered for Christianity, they are recovered phenomenally, for the Wittgensteinian move "refuses to see

---

324 Stephen Grunlan and Marvin Mayers, *Cultural Anthropology: A Christian Perspective* (Grand Rapids: Zondervan, 1988, 2nd edition), p. 222.

325 George Lindbeck, *The Nature of Doctrine: Religion and Theology in a Postliberal Age* (Philadelphia: Westminster, 1984), pp. 32–41.

326 Hans Frei, "Eberhard Busch's Biography of Karl Barth," in H. Martin Rumscheidt, ed. *Karl Barth in Re-View* (Pittsburgh: Pickwick Press, 1981), p. 103.

327 Lindbeck, *The Nature of Doctrine*, pp. 79–88.

328 The critical role of removing the excess is especially seen in John Milbank, *Theology & Social Theory: Beyond Secular Reason* (Oxford: Blackwell, 1990). While the positive project of rebuilding is especially evident in *Radical Orthodoxy: A New Theology*, edited by John Milbank, Catherine Pickstock and Graham Ward (London: Routledge, 1999).

329 John Milbank, Graham Ward and Catherine Pickstock, "Introduction" and Conor Cunningham "LANGUAGE: Wittgenstein after Theology" in *Radical Orthodoxy*, pp. 6–7, 71–87.

them as essences lurking behind phenomena."[330] This Christian x-ray vision reframes the world from the inside out for Christian conceptuality and intimacy. However, it leaves the accessible world vacant except for our corporate experiences. In this, there is no warrant for the unique things thought except the communal agreement of one's own group and any who would existentially choose to join them.

Kevin Vanhoozer reframes theology in this post-modern arena as community tradition theo-drama, prompted by the Spirit.[331] Such an approach views language as vividly dramatic (following Ricoeur and Hans Frei), and performative, especially in communal liturgy and dramatic acts. So the emphasis is post-propositional with the whole life engaging the drama. The parameters of theo-drama are established by the church's communal tradition, through which its participants interpret the Bible. Here Vanhoozer appreciates George Lindbeck's sentiment "that the doctrinally significant aspect of religion resides not in propositional truths or in religious experiences 'but in the story it tells *and in the grammar that informs the way the story is told and used.*'"[332] Vanhoozer concludes, "*What theology now describes is not the 'final form' of the text but the 'form of life' in which the biblical language games function as Scripture.*"[333] In this, tradition's role in theology frees its participants to improvise within it. Here Samuel Wells identifies that, "Improvisation is not about being spontaneous and witty in the moment, but about trusting oneself to do and say the obvious."[334] Vanhoozer appreciates this sentiment and calls for "creative fidelity" or "ruled spontaneity;" "*The directions drawn by Scripture's normative specification of the theo-drama enable the church to improvise, as it were, with a script.*"[335] Thus theology is not so much a system but as Vanhoozer sees Kierkegaard encouraging, that is "faith seeks both theoretical and practical: a knowledge about the *dramatic personae* and the theo-drama; a *lived* knowledge of how to continue the theo-drama *here and now.*"[336] As such, theology is not the individual isolation speech of Descartes ("I think therefore I am") in monologue but to be a participant in dialogical action. "*To be a person is, in this dramatic perspective, to be a communicative agent who can*

330 Cunningham, "LANGUAGE: Wittgenstein after Theology" in *Radical Orthodoxy*, p. 85.

331 Kevin Vanhoozer, *The Drama of Doctrine: A Canonical-Linguistic Approach to Christian Theology* (Louisville: Westminster John Knox Press, 2005).

332 Kevin Vanhoozer (*The Drama of Doctrine*, p. 172) quotes George Lindbeck (*Nature of Doctrine: Religion and Theology in a Postliberal Age* [Philadelphia: Westminster Press, 1984], p. 80) and adds the italics.

333 Kevin Vanhoozer, *The Drama of Doctrine*, p. 172, italics his.

334 Samuel Wells, *Improvisation: The Drama of Christian Ethics* (Grand Rapids: Brazos, 2004), p. 12.

335 Kevin Vanhoozer, *The Drama of Doctrine*, p. 129, italics his.

336 Kevin Vanhoozer, *The Drama of Doctrine*, pp. 307-8, italics his.

enter into dialogical relationships with others."[337] This form of theology works out and converses with others to enable both to enter into a more intimate and growing relationship in Christ. While he protests that this approach does not reduce down to a communal tradition, as did George Lindbeck's *The Nature of Doctrine,* I wonder if it doesn't in fact do that with Vanhoozer's strong commitment to the Reformed tradition and his confidence in "the illumination of the Holy Spirit" to subjectively interpret Scripture through the lens of that tradition.[338] By connecting church tradition and the Divine inspired Bible closely and providing the subjectivity of interpreting the Bible by an illumination of the Spirit, Vanhoozer does not seem to permit a Biblically exegetical interpretive option that can stand outside of one's tradition to critique or call the tradition beyond itself. However, he wishes to critique Lindbeck for this problem and to distance himself from this problem by identifying that the theological map is first "*canonical* before it is *communal.*"[339] That is, he wishes to preserve the authority of the canon and only secondarily allow the postmodern community tradition to inform what the Bible says. Vanhoozer tries to accomplish this through a canon-Linguistic approach which funds "theological plenitude" and "theological diversity" such that competing Christian traditions are each funded provided 1) the "two notions that occupy different conceptual systems are nevertheless *compatible* if neither negates the other," and 2) this "nonreductive evangelical catholic orthodoxy…attempt[s] to preserve both the diversity and the integrity of a theological dialogue *already canonized in Scripture.*"[340] What Vanhoozer has in mind is that each Biblical genre and each Biblical author contributes different compatible voices, and that there is a pastoral advantage to draw on these diverse theological voices to meet the needs of a particular congregation. "*A belief or action is rational, on this view, to the extent that it 'fits' with one or more of the biblical maps.*"[341] For Vanhoozer, "*Good theological judgment is largely, though not exclusively, a matter of being apprenticed to the canon: of having one's capacity for judging (a capacity that involves imagination, reason, emotion, and volition alike) formed and transformed by the ensemble of canonical practices that constitute Scripture.*"[342]

Anthony Thiselton proposes to frame theology as a hermeneutical discipline, maintaining a coherent communal of via Wittgenstein's language games, which set up Lindbeck's socio-linguistic coherence

337 Kevin Vanhoozer, *The Drama of Doctrine,* p. 367, italix his; Vanhoozer clarifies this definition as including fetuses and coma victims.

338 These are my impressions from the following sections of Kevin Vanhoozer, *The Drama of Doctrine,* pp. 117–185, 199–210, 219–237.

339 Kevin Vanhoozer, *The Drama of Doctrine,* p. 294.

340 Kevin Vanhoozer, *The Drama of Doctrine,* pp. 273–6, italix his.

341 Kevin Vanhoozer, *The Drama of Doctrine,* p. 299, italix his.

342 Kevin Vanhoozer, *The Drama of Doctrine,* p. 331, italix his.

with perhaps an appreciation for progressive development which Imre Lakatos and Nancey Murphy advocate.[343] This approach appreciates the contributions from Biblical theology as a base but traditionally ranges from there, rarely returning to check if the language game has changed as the tradition has developed. As such the Bible is authoritative but ultimately understood as significant through a cultural lens of which views a community or church embraces. This is even less an apprenticeship to what the Bible means in its context than Vanhoozer, but both ultimately place the approved community tradition to be more immediately relevant for identifying appropriateness of a community's doctrine. This means Thiselton champions the role of developing polyphonic traditions to show historically where theology is to be valued and to foster the communal experience of the churches to find whatever statement that authentically resonates with their experience. Such a polyphonic approach would fit within post-modernism in that he does not want to submit theology to foundational epistemology, but rather permits the community hermeneutic self-definition to be that which renders the view as appropriate. Thiselton's concern for rationality is primarily to clarify views as non-contradictory and thus coherent though growing traditions. However, the communal experience identifies which view is appropriate to be maintained within whichever community that is being considered. These views are clear rivals and can't be maintained simultaneously by the same communities, but in separate communities they are simultaneously affirmed as appropriate. If however, such views raise epistemic truth (as this chapter develops) then this post-modern strategy is not helpful in affirming traditional views that misunderstand some truth; this post-modern strategy is self-defeating. Rival contradictory views cannot simultaneously be true at the same time and manner. Doctrine does not primarily indicate "look who we are" as Thiselton maintains.[344]

Robert Webber believes that a Younger Evangelical leadership is emerging with a more post-modern congregational approach since around 2000.[345] These Mosaics[346] were raised by a post-modern worldview of "The Simpson's" and reality TV. However, even more influential on them is their music, for it is preferred over all other media.[347] They have replaced Descartes maxim of "I think therefore I am" with their own

343 Anthony Thiselton, *The Hermeneutic of Doctrine*, pp. 62–173, 453, 479–508.

344 Anthony Thiselton, *The Hermeneutics of Doctrine*, p. 127.

345 Robert Webber, *The Younger Evangelicals*, pp. 17–18.

346 Those born between 1984 and 2002 as described by David Kinnaman in *Unchristian: What a New Generation Really Thinks About Christianity...and Why it Matters* (Grand Rapids: Baker, 2007), especially p. 17.

347 Peter Christenson and Donald Roberts, *It's Not Only Rock and Roll: Popular Music in the Lives of Adolescents* (Cresskill, Hampton Press, 1998), pp. 32–34.

"ipod therefore I am."[348] These younger evangelicals find solace in a more community oriented epistemology as evident in their decisions being communally made among the cell phone and txt connected tribe they hang with. Among the younger evangelicals there is an "epistemological shift" from a reason based theology to a more experience based faith "grounded in the whole person, in both body and mind."[349] In this there may be a greater appreciation for ambiguity.[350] Such students are highly visual, appreciating the power of imagination and story that communicates.[351] This fosters a more authentic embodiment in their spirituality. These younger evangelicals yearn to belong to a community and "crave genuine relationships and authentic friendships."[352] So the communal conventions of their friends become a determining feature in defining what they claim to know. There is an attraction to absolutes, not so much because they are demonstrated but because they are "loved and lived."[353] In this, there is an emphasis on "being real and authentic."[354] They consider the previous generation as too sheltered and out of touch with reality.[355] Webber presents these mosaics as in some ways more conservative than their predecessors; these "twenty-somethings desire a stable society, a return to tradition."[356] James Penning and Corwin Smidt in *Evangelicalism: The Next Generation* provide the survey support to delineate such increased conservatism among mosaic evangelical college students over the previous generation.[357] Dale Dirksen and David Taylor concur that there is a more robust consciousness for tradition as a reaction to always living with rapid change and new stuff.[358] However, among this group there is a greater commitment to multiculturalism, multigenerationism in community, and generosity without judgmental attitude or actions to the other around them.[359] For example, "thirty years ago only one in every 100 children born in the United States was of mixed race. Today the number is 1 in 19" and in some areas

348 Chloe Morrison, "I Pod, therefore I am." *Chattanooga Times Free Press* 137:102 (Sunday, March 26, 2006): E2.

349 Wade Roof, *Spiritual Marketplace: Baby Boomers and the Remaking of American Religion* (Princeton: Princeton University, 1999), p. 83.

350 Tom Beaudoin, *Visual Faith: The Irreverent Spiritual Quest of Generation X* (San Francisco: Jossey-Bass Publishers, 1998), p. 178.

351 Webber, *The Younger Evangelicals,* pp. 50–51, 54.

352 Jim Belcher e-mail cited by Robert Webber, *The Younger Evangelicals,* p. 51.

353 Webber, *The Younger Evangelicals,* p. 52.

354 Cherie Harder, "In Defense of Opacity" *Regeneration Quarterly* 4:1 (1998): 9–17.

355 David Kinnaman, *Unchristian*, pp. 28, 30, 34, 121–52.

356 Webber, *The Younger Evangelicals,* p. 46.

357 James Penning and Corwin Smidt, *Evangelicalism: The Next Generation* (Grand Rapids: Baker, 2002), pp. 51, 65, 73, and 76.

358 Webber cites e–mails from both of them, *The Younger Evangelicals,* p. 49.

359 Webber, *The Younger Evangelicals,* p. 52; David Kinnaman, *Unchristian*, pp. 28–30, 34, 41–61, 181–204.

the number is "one in six."[360] This multiculturalism has lessened the mosaic's commitment to a traditional hierarchical family and home, as it shifts toward complementariness.[361] Also in transition is less animosity to homosexuality.[362] Additionally, in reaction to the decades before and after the millennium change, these mosaics consider that the previous generations of evangelicals often sold out the essence of Christianity for political activism placing nationalism and "right to life" over Christ and Kingdom.[363] Instead, the mosaics have a deeper commitment than the previous generation for a transformative communal spirituality following Jesus unto Kingdom.[364] This commitment expresses itself with an increasing consistent commitment to express their faith through service.[365] For example, *US News and World Report* said that "about a quarter of all high school students today regularly perform community service, while an additional 40 percent do so occasionally.[366] Is post-modernism the future of evangelicalism?

2.15. Critical Realism[367]

In reaction to these options in 1916, Roy Wood Sellars proposed the view of "critical realism."[368] The view appreciates the empiricism of Locke and Newton, blending it with the mathematical rationalism of Descartes and Kepler, and the pragmatism of Peirce and James.[369] This locates a critical realist's view of reality within an epistemic dualism.[370] However, standing against idealisms or anti-realisms (like Plato, Berkley,

360 Lynette Clemetson, "Color My World," *Newsweek* (May 8, 2000): 70 and Donna Jackson Nakazawa, "A New Generation is Leading the Way" *Parade Magazine, Chattanooga Times Free Press* (July, 6, 2003), pp. 4–5.

361 James Penning and Corwin Smidt, *Evangelicalism: The Next Generation*, pp. 83–84.

362 James Penning and Corwin Smidt, *Evangelicalism: The Next Generation*, pp. 73 and 76; David Kinnaman, *Unchristian*, pp. 28–29, 34, 91–109, 113–4.

363 David Kinnaman, *Unchristian*, pp. 28, 30, 34, 153–80.

364 David Kinnaman, *Unchristian*, pp. 79–90, 150–2.

365 David Kinnaman, *Unchristian*, pp. 143–4.

366 Angie Cannon and Carolyn Kleiner, "Teens Get Real" *US News and World Report* (Apr. 17, 2000): 50.

367 This section has had a previous life in the peer reviewed academic paper "A Lakatos Philosophy of Science as a Theological Method" presented in the Evangelical Philosophical Society, Nov. 2005, and the other version "A Nuanced Lakatos Philosophy of Theology and Science" presented at the International Creation Conference, Aug. 2008 and published in *Proceedings of The Sixth International Creation Conference: Technical Symposium Sessions* (Pittsburgh: Creation Science Fellowship, 2008), pp. 31–42.

368 Roy Sellars, *Critical Realism* (Chicago: Rand McNally Co., 1916). This would be a sub category "alethic realism" or "truth realism."

369 Sellars, *Critical Realism,* pp. 27, 66, 206.

370 Sellars, *Critical Realism,* pp. 11, 17, 109, 262; Durant Drake, Arthur Lovejoy, James Pratt, Arthur Rogers, George Santayana, Roy Sellars and C. A. Strong, *Essays in Critical Realism: A Co-Operative Study of the Problem of Knowledge* (London: MacMillan and Co., 1920), pp. 18–19, 158, 190.

Kant, and Process) and views dominated by passion (like romanticism, existentialism and other populist approaches), critical realism sees this real world and metaphysical beings as accessible to the human mind through subjective means. Sellars claimed, "Truth is, then, a reflective qualification of those ideas, beliefs, and judgments which we regard as giving us knowledge about some sphere of reality."[371] He acknowledges that in this view, perception is subjective.[372] However, as scientific realism this approach attempts to render the perception more precise.[373] To accomplish this increased precision, pragmatism is utilized to check the perception.[374] "Truth is thus accepted and tested knowledge."[375] Moreland and Craig summarize the core tenets of such a scientific realism:[376]

> SR1: Scientific theories (in mature, developed sciences) are true or approximately true.
>
> SR2: The central observational and theoretical terms of a mature scientific theory genuinely refer to entities in the world. These terms make existence claims.
>
> SR3: Given two rival theories, it is in principle possible to have good reasons for thinking which is more likely to be true or approximately true....conceptual relativism (what is rational for one person or group should not necessarily be so for another person or group since rationality itself is relative to a person, scientific community or theory) is false.
>
> SR4: A scientific theory will embody certain epistemic virtues (simplicity, clarity, an absence of internal and external conceptual problems, predictive success, empirical accuracy, scope of relevance, fruitfulness in guiding new research, utilization of appropriate ways of explaining things...).
>
> SR5: The aim of science is a literally true conception of the theory-independent external world.

371 Sellars, *Critical Realism*, p. 277.

372 Sellars, *Critical Realism*, p. 14; Drake et. al. *Essays in Critical Realism*, p. 3, 206.

373 Sellars, *Critical Realism*, pp. 26, 33, 62.

374 Sellars, *Critical Realism*, pp. 132–4, 164; Drake et. al. *Essays in Critical Realism*, pp. 35–81, 157–160.

375 Sellars, *Critical Realism*, p. 282.

376 J. P. Moreland & William Lane Craig, *Philosophical Foundations for a Christian Worldview* (Downers Grove: InterVarsity, 2003), p. 328.

Thus an outstanding trademark for the critical realist approach is increased precision and warrant for the views articulated in describing the real world.

In the wake of Renaissance Humanism, evangelical theology tends to be proposed within commonsense realism. However, there are some critical realist theologians who have proposed a more nuanced approach toward God, which admits to subjectivity from one's contexts and point of view. These critical realist theologians appreciate renaissance humanism at an even more precise level. For example, William G. T. Shedd acknowledged progressiveness within the discipline of theology that would be characterized as a discipline wide critical realism in his comments that, "The first investigator is not so likely to strike upon the intrinsic constitution of a thing as the last one, because he has not the light of previous inquiries. Methods of investigation are continually undergoing correction and modification, and are thus brought closer to the organization of the object."[377] With the discipline of theology developing, theology should not be thought of as a static authoritative tradition or a Kuhnian "paradigm." Rather, developing theology (as this chapter and the next reflect) should be thought of as Lakatos' "Research Programs" which undergo nuanced revolutionary change as theology proposals develop. This approach is a more accurate description of theological development than viewing such development through a Kuhnian lens because with every new theological development, some advocates of the outmoded positions remain in their earlier less-nuanced positions. For example, the radical shift in paradigms about which Thomas Kuhn wrote about in his *Structure of Scientific Revolutions*[378] are like the change from the view of the Ptolemaic universe (sun and everything revolves around the earth) to a Copernican universe (in the solar system the planets revolve around the sun). Theologically, this would be like the radical shift from one of these philosophical roots to another, such as Platonic to Aristotelian theology. Whereas, a Lakatos theorist would recognize even as the weight of adherence from Platonic to Aristotelian theology shifted, there remained advocates of both approaches. In fact, many philosophical and traditional approaches advocated in the past still have contemporary advocates. Furthermore, many of these theological variants retain aspects of the previous philosophical approach within them as they moved on with a new philosophical base, as is evident by the resilience of such features as Platonic simplicity of God which continues to appear throughout many later theological approaches. So a better paradigm for change than the Copernican model would be the contemporary rivalry among relativistic, quantum, and string theories

377 William G. T. Shedd, *Dogmatic Theology* (Grand Rapids: Zondervan, n.d.), vol. 1, p.4, Ch. 1, sect. 1.

378 Thomas Kuhn, *Structure of Scientific Revolutions* (Chicago: University of Chicago Press, 1962).

in Physics. A critical realist approach of precisely recognizing the differences of these varied approaches, and crafting a nuanced method that reflects this sensitivity.

Among earlier evangelical theologians, perhaps only A. H. Strong opted for a more nuanced personal critical realist position. Strong affirms both [1] that "the laws of our thought are laws of God's thought and [2] that the results are normally conducted thinking with regard to God correspond to the objective reality."[379] At the same time he conceded that "all knowledge is relative to the knowing agent; that is what we know, we know not as it is objectively but only as it is related to our senses and faculties."[380]

The philosopher-theologian Stuart Hackett clearly positioned himself within a critical realist epistemology, with his rational-empiricist Christianity.[381] Hackett saw that moderate foundations provided the starting points for any legitimate world view. These foundations include: rational, empirical and incorrigible contributions. 1) A few rational or self-evident foundations provide the structure of our knowledge, 2) Empirical foundation of a person's immediate awareness of his own states of consciousness largely provides the content of our knowledge. 3) Finally, incorrigibility (that is, whatever a person knows and cannot be convinced otherwise because it would plunge him into paralyzing skepticism if he were consistent with its denial), largely connects a person coherently with the essential basic beliefs of their worldview. The rational foundations which he grants are the laws of identity and contradiction, I think therefore I am, performative statements, and the definitional difference between related terms (like cause and effect, and possible, actual and necessary). Hackett's empirical foundations provide for largely an analytical philosophic approach. From this modest base, he argues for the existence and nature of God and then builds up a theology and metaphysic from there. As a result of these arguments, Hackett grants Biblical authority and informs his worldview from the Bible as part of an incorrigible foundation for his Christianity, philosophy, and theology. He sees God and the world through the lens of epistemological dualism so that there are ways from argument and experience to further warrant the belief system that is being built by the theologian to represent the reality that exists.

379 A. H. Strong, *Systematic Theology* (3 vols.: Philadelphia: The Judson Press, 1907), vol. 1, p. 10, [2] added for clarity.

380 A. H. Strong, *Systematic Theology*, 1:10.

381 Stuart Hackett, *The Resurrection of Theism: Prolegomena to Christian Apology* (Grand Rapids: Baker, 1957), especially pp. 37–175; *The Reconstruction of the Christian Revelation Claim: A Philosophical and Critical Apologetic* (Grand Rapids: Baker, 1984), especially pp. 11–83; a similar approach is argued by philosopher Paul Moser, *Empirical Knowledge* (Savage: Rowman & Littlefield, 1986); *Knowledge and Evidence* (Cambridge: Cambridge University Press, 1989).

Alister McGrath presents theological method as a critical realist. He often presents it as an empirically based pragmatic realism or when he adds mathematical derivation to it, he calls this method, "critical realism."[382] He sees that empirically based pragmatism is the foundation for this realism in the natural sciences, following Roy Bhasker's Scientific Realism.[383] Bhasker's approach is individually Kantian because science is looking for transcendental principles by close analysis but (unlike Kant and idealism's closed system) science utilizes an open system for controlled experiments to surface data which needs to be individually interpreted. Baskher resists both the reduction within: positivism for humans to be viewed as physico-chemical principles, and hermeneutical approaches of social sciences. However, as a realist, Baskher is corporately Durkheimian with a collectivist conception of society which establishes the reality of social facts in an open system which grows.[384] McGrath works within this method where nature is interpreted as a socially mediated construct of science and theology about beings.[385] However, I suspect that McGrath's confidence in mathematical derivation provides a rational underpinning (foundation?) for some aspects of his model that Bhasker does not himself grant within his non-foundational approach. Through the community agreement, Bhasker calls his approach a necessary ontological realism, which for McGrath would preserve a necessary ontological theology.[386] McGrath justifies this unitary approach to science and theology on the basis of

382 Alister McGrath, *A Scientific Theology: Nature,* (Grand Rapids: Eerdmans, 2001), pp. 71–77; *A Scientific Theology: Reality,* (Grand Rapids: Eerdmans, 2002), vol. 2, especially identifying himself as a critical realist pp. xv-xvi, 123–244, and especially developing his view on p. 188. Bernard Lonergan presents a similar analysis in "Cognitional Structure," *Collection: Papers by Bernard Lonergan* (Toronto: University of Toronto, 1988), pp. 205–21 and *Method in Theology* (London: Darton, Longman and Todd, 1972), p. 234; Wentzel van Huyssteen (*Theology and the Justification of Faith: Constructing Theories in Systematic Theology* [Grand Rapids: Eerdmans, 1989], pp. 123–97) also positions his theological method within rational empirical critical realism.

383 Alister McGrath, *A Scientific Theology: Reality,* vol. 2, pp. 257, 174–175; McGrath identifies that he follows Roy Bhaskar in critical realism (Roy Bhaskar, *A Realist Theory of Science* [London: Verso, 1997]; *Scientific Realism and Human Emancipation* [London: Velrso, 1986]; *The Possibility of Naturalism: A Philosophical Critique of the Contemporary Human Sciences* [London: Routledge, 1998]; Andrew Collier, *Critical Realism: An Introduction to Roy Bhasker's Philosophy* [London: Verso, 1994]) and identifies with Thomas Torrance, *Theological Science* (Oxford: Oxford University Press, 1969). I don't think that Bhaskar provides a sufficient framework to explain theory change, but he is good in exposing levels of subjectivity in theory construction.

384 Roy Bhaskar, *The Possibility of Naturalism,* pp. 38-41, 45.

385 Alister McGrath, *A Scientific Theology: Nature,* (Grand Rapids: Eerdmans, 2001), vol. 1, p. 4.

386 Roy Bhaskar, *Scientific Realism and Human Emancipation* (London: Verso, 1986), p. 24.

the Christian doctrine of creation.[387] He illustrates this methodology several times over, especially in physics. He rejects foundationalism for its lack of elegance, but admits that Paul Moser has nicely defended a moderate foundationalism.[388] He then justifies his critical realism as against conventionalist approaches, which would be either anti-realist, theory dependent, or indebted to James pragmatism. McGrath develops a critical engagement of the world at a variety of levels, each evaluated for its clarity and predictability. He extends this scientific method to theology as an attempt to behold reality communally, with theology as a scientific discipline in a critical realist methodology. Theology for him becomes a communal task of the collective wisdom that has won acceptance within the community.[389] "Doctrine may thus be provisionally defined as communally authoritative teachings regarded as essential to the identity of the Christian community, in which the community *tells* itself and outsiders what it has *seen*, and what it has become in response to this vision."[390] However, McGrath admits that when it comes to heresy, there is an individual aspect to doctrine in order for the community to exclude the heretic.[391]

McGrath's strengths take his critical realism in two primary directions of increased precision: 1) issues of science and religion, and 2) church history. With a Ph.D. in molecular biophysics, he repeatedly contributes with precision to the integration of Science and religion.[392] However, with his second Ph.D. in church history, he shows his precision in this area as well.[393]

Alan Padgett contributes significantly toward allowing theology and each science discipline to mutually contribute what they have to give within a critical realism.

> Once we grant that there are different sorts of schemes for explaining the same thing, and they do not reduce to each other, this raises the question of their interrelationship. Since the sort of explanation we have in mind is causal, these schemes postulate certain causal relationships that hold between things. They develop models for the nature and

387 Alister McGrath, *A Scientific Theology: Nature*, vol. 1, p. 21.

388 Alister McGrath, *A Scientific Theology: Reality*, vol. 2, pp. 24, 26–39; Paul Moser, *Empirical Knowledge*; *Knowledge and Evidence*.

389 Alister McGrath, *A Scientific Theology: Theory* (Grand Rapids: Eerdmans, 2003), vol. 3, pp. xiii, 28, 77, 217.

390 Alister McGrath, *A Scientific Theology: Theory*, vol. 3, p. 28.

391 Alister McGrath, *A Scientific Theology: Theory*, vol. 3, p. 223.

392 E.g., Alister McGrath, *Science & Religion: An Introduction* (Oxford: Blackwell, 1999); *The Foundations of Dialogue in Science & Religion* (Oxford: Blackwell, 1998); *A Scientific Theology* in three volumes, which has many examples from physics.

393 E.g., Alister McGrath, *Iustia Dei: A History of the Doctrine of Justification* (Cambridge: Cambridge University Press, 1998).

> powers of things involved, their regular causal relations, laws describing the regularities in these relations, and general theories. What happens, it seems, is that some levels are more fundamental than others in the following sense: the accepted results of the scheme at the more fundamental level is used, and assumed, in the next level up. So particle physics is assumed in thermodynamics, and psychology and sociology are assumed in history.[394]

Alan Padgett continues to develop that there is likely a two way-dialog between these more fundamental and higher order disciplines though he admits that sometimes in social sciences the more fundamental discipline may not be that clear, as may be the case with psychology and sociology.

Nancey Murphy recognizes this sort of higher order and foundational relationship and places theology as the highest order science but able to engage with the other disciplines on down to the foundation.[395] That is, each of these disciplines are commensurable (able to compared to each other) though their focus and scope are different. Within such a framework, theology has the broadest scope as well as distinctive focus. For example, alcoholism can be analyzed: 1) chemically on a level of chemical reactions, 2) biologically, on a level of genetic predisposition, 3) psychologically, as a defense mechanism such as avoidance, 4) sociologically, as a learned trait within families and social groups that destroys them, 5) ethically as a destructive vice, and 6) theologically as rebellious sin, from which one should repent to depend on God (Eph. 5:18). Critical realism would recognize that each of these analyses is accurate and some expressions of this analysis demand volitional change.

Furthermore, Nancey Murphy proposes a critical realist theological method after the pattern of Lakatos philosophy of science.[396] Imre Lakatos articulated a rational model of derivation in the philosophy of mathematics and science that utilized Peircian pragmatism to encourage its productivity and to make sense of paradigm change.[397] Nancey

394 Alan Padgett, "The Mutuality of Theology and science: An Example from Time and Thermodynamics," *Christian Scholars Review* 26(1996): 12–35, especially pp. 18–19; *Science and the Study of God: A Mutuality Model for Theology and science* (Grand Rapids: Eerdmans, 2003).

395 Nancey Murphy, *Religion and Science: God, Evolution, and the Soul* (Scotdale: Herald Press, 2002).

396 Nancey Murphy, *Theology in the Age of Scientific Reasoning,* pp. 51–88; Alan Padgett, *Science and the Study of God: A Mutuality Model for Theology and science* (Grand Rapids: Eerdmans, 2003), pp. 76 follows Murphy and Lakatos. Murphy's proposal is a post-modern theological method but Lakatos method is a moderate foundational rational and Peircian pragmatism.

397 Imre Lakatos, "Falsification and the Methodology of Scientific Research Programs," in *Criticism and the Growth of Knowledge*. edited by Imre Lakatos and Alan

Murphy suggests this method is the best process to explain how change in a theological product can occur while maintaining many of one's other theological commitments. That is, this approach can be seen as a more precise analysis of paradigm change, showing that paradigms are not as monolithic as Kuhn had proposed, nor is data retrievable only from within the paradigm.[398] Each study a person accomplishes in the Biblical text or philosophically or in tradition or in science becomes a "research program" that work along side each other and can be judged as rival programs, whether progressive or degenerative for the whole theological task[399] Lakatos proposes a *sophisticated falsification* view of religious language that encourages development.

> Contrary to naïve falsification [like Kuhn], *no experiment, experimental report, observation statement or well-corroborated low-level falsifying hypothesis alone can lead to falsification. There is no falsification before the emergence of a better theory*...Thus the crucial element in falsification is whether the *new theory* offers any novel, excess information compared with its predecessor and whether some of this excess information is corroborated.[400]

Thus any scientific model needs to focus on crafting better theories or they will never be seriously considered by the academy as a live option. Countering quotes from Popper, Lakatos compares Kuhn's approach to his own.

Musgrave (Cambridge: Cambridge University Press, 1970), pp. 91–195; "Proofs and Refutations," *British Journal for the Philosophy of Science* 14(1963-64): 1–25, 120–39, 221–43, 296–342; *Problems in the Philosophy of Science* (1968); "History of Science and Its Rational Reconstructions," in *Boston Studies in the Philosophy of Science*, vol. 8. edited by R. Buck and R. S. Cohen (Dordrecht: D. Reidel Publishing Co., 1971); R.S. Cohen, P.K. Feyerabend and M.W. Wartofsky, *Essays in Memory of Imre Lakatos. Boston Studies in the Philosophy of Science*, vol. 39 (Dordrecht: D. Reidel Publishing Co., 1976); Paul Feyerabend, "Imre Lakatos," *The British Journal for the Philosophy of Science* 26(1975):1–18; Ian Hacking, "Imre Lakatos's Philosophy of Science," *The British Journal for the Philosophy of Science* 30(1979): 381–402.

398 One of the critiques of Kuhn is that those in one paradigm can not perceive or communicate with those in another paradigm and that is clearly not right. As one paradigm is unraveling the other is building strength of congruity and comprehensiveness.

399 Imre Lakatos, "Falsification and the Methodology of Scientific Research Programs," in *Criticism and the Growth of Knowledge*. edited by Imre Lakatos and Alan Musgrave, pp. 118–9.

400 Imre Lakatos, "Falsification and the Methodology of Scientific Research Programs," in *Criticism and the Growth of Knowledge*. edited by Imre Lakatos and Alan Musgrave, pp. 119–20; Lakatos also cites Popper for this idea, *The Logic of Scientific Discovery* (1959), p. 87 and "Normal Science and its Dangers." in *Criticism and the Growth of Knowledge*. edited by Imre Lakatos and Alan Musgrave, p. 227.

> While naïve falsification stresses 'the urgency of replacing a *falsified* hypothesis by a better one,' sophisticated falsificationism stresses the urgency of replacing *any* hypothesis by a better one. Falsification cannot 'compel the theorist to search for a better theory,' simply because *falsification* cannot precede the better theory.[401]

So the scientist needs to work for better theories or an alternative approach (e.g., evolutionist) will not see falsification of their approach. Likewise, this approach encourages a progressive orientation of a positive theology model to keep theology current with the latest Biblical and philosophically warranted findings rather than static to a tradition. This would encourage a theologian to follow the Bible wherever it leads, provided it is exegeted in a contextually sensitive manner. Likewise, the theologian should follow moderately foundationally grounded logic wherever it leads provided it does not counter clear Biblical statements. That is, Lakatos' approach is not so much a justification for theory choice, as much as a framework for making sense of how one should hold a theory. The justification for the theologian comes from exegesis, grounded philosophizing, and accurately reflecting historical documents.

Implicit in this approach are certain epistemic virtues that aid in formulating accurate knowledge.[402] A tenacity and love for pursuing truth is encouraged by courage to formulate and express what a person thinks they know. This courage to claim to know is tempered with a humility that can always continue to grow and a generosity in reflecting others' point of view. Peer review can especially aid with this balanced accuracy and expression. Certainly this virtue epistemology is driven by a concern to be honest. For exegesis and observational sciences, virtues of sensitive observation in context are imperative.

Lakatos has been criticized by Steve Barnett as not providing prescriptive criteria sufficient to make decisions on whether the programs are progressive or degenerative.[403] That is, Barnett charges that the criterion is too subjective so that whether it is progressive or degenerative is only recognizable after the fact. Trial by error is the risk in pragmatic tests that the observer does not know whether verification or falsification will occur unless he submits his proposal to experiment.

---

401 Imre Lakatos, "Falsification and the Methodology of Scientific Research Programs," in *Criticism and the Growth of Knowledge*. edited by Imre Lakatos and Alan Musgrave, p. 122; quoting Popper, *The Logic of Scientific Discovery*, p. 87, footnote 1; *Logik der Forschung*, section 30.

402 Robert Campbell Roberts and W. Jay Wood, *Intellectual Virtues: An Essay in Regulative Epistemology* (Oxford: Clarendon Press, 2007), especially pp. 151–324; W. Jay Wood, *Epistemology: Becoming Intellectually Virtuous* (Downers Grove: InterVarsity Press, 1998).

403 Steve Barnett is philosopher of science at Bryan College where these criticisms came in conversations.

However, further confirmation by experiments is not a shot in the dark because warranted experiments lay down a trajectory that indicates further confirmation will likely obtain.

Even more, in theology this is not a defeater argument against the Lakatos' method because the method only provides a description for the quest for an epistemically better research program and the sociology for doing this task. That is, biological science's observational data may be available without providing a prescriptive criterion or interpretive thrust,[404] but theology has a different data strain. I think that the prescriptive criteria to choose a superior theological option is provided in the form of data appropriated for a theological project. That is, rational derivation from foundations or transcendental arguments includes criteria of coherence to the rationally foundational and to a lesser degree coherency to the theological project, provided it does not contradict any other strongly warranted feature of the world view. In my *Classical Christian God,* I grounded and framed out my theological program beginning with this approach.[405] However, most of the data appropriated for a theological project will be textual from the Bible. Such textual data has an interpretive thrust within it identifying how the interpreter should understand the data and whether it corresponds appropriately in a Biblical theology to which the Bible contributes. Thus the Bible provides its criteria (of coherence and correspondence with the Biblical text) for warranting theology. That is, we should use Biblical texts to make the points that they are making in their context, rather than imposing upon them our theological agenda. Thus provided theology is congruent with the thrust of the Biblical texts that speak to this issue, a theology warrants itself. In filling out my theology in the *Classical Christian God,* the thrust of the Biblical text dominates the theological content, agenda, and thus provides the criteria for appropriateness within itself.[406] Thus in the analysis of a critical realist theological method, I must supply an analysis of the process of 1) hermeneutics, 2) Biblical theology, and 3) how Biblical theology truths contribute to systematic theology. The rest of this book takes up this process in turn.

In theology, Historical Jesus research especially utilizes critical realist categories and Imre Lakatos method to fund the discipline. In this vein, Dale Allison positions himself identified that specifically the proposal that Jesus is a "millenarian figure" as a "'progressive research programme,' which has led to an ever-enlarging series of new questions

404 I think that the Intelligent Design movement claims that such empirical science does have an interpretive thrust for those observations of sufficient complexity (e.g., Del Ratzsch, *Nature, Design, and Science: The Status of Design in Natural Science* [Albany: State University of New York, 2001]).

405 Douglas Kennard, *The Classical Christian God*, pp. 11–86.

406 Douglas Kennard, *The Classical Christian God,* pp. 87–204.

and useful answers."[407] Allison's Historical Jesus is built up from a congruence of these research programs in his approximation of the real Jesus. This approach permits aspects to be proposed in a tentative fashion reflective of the warrant available in the data. Which means that some aspects of theology have greater demand and hold on one's faith and other aspects might be very tentative.

A number of the authors of *GRUE! The New Riddle of Induction*[408] appeal for a skepticism to the method of science that is caused by the unboundedness of the investigation data (as well as the issue Barnett raised above) and thus the inability to complete a generalization with confidence that removes alternative subjective interpretations. This may at times be a legitimate critique in the empirical scientific condition when rival theories can not exclude the other theory as degenerate. However, theological science can sidestep this criticism for at least two reasons. First, the interpretation thrust is embedded within the Biblical text itself as the thrust of the speech-act, which diminishes rival options as degenerative. Secondly, the Biblical data on any doctrinal point is a self contained body of texts within the canonical bounds of the Bible, so that generalizations can be made with regard to the whole. There is no fear of a larger sample overwhelming the sample studied to date, provided the generalization was made concerning the comprehensive set of Biblical texts (properly understood in their contexts) that address this doctrinal point. Of course, with more information becoming available (like the find of the Dead Sea Scrolls) more can be understood about the context of Biblical texts. However, archaeologically open contexts while influential to inform interpretation possibilities, do not render an interpretation definitive because primarily the context for the Biblical text is provided within the information in the Biblical text itself.[409] Even if there is some development in these background issues, there is no reason for skepticism rather this is a motive to keep current in related disciplines and to be open to subsequent paradigm change as a Lakatos method would encourage.

Likewise, all science is not adrift in a lack of progressive clarity and unboundedness. Those sciences that are mathematically derived and available for nuanced falsification that have marshaled substantial repeated demonstration of their conclusions have also stepped beyond these criticisms. First, mathematical derivation, such as Newton provides for his three laws of motion orient the discipline to an already warranted

407 Dale Allison specifically identifies within Lakatos thought forms and method (*Constructing Jesus: Memory, Imagination, and History* [Grand Rapids: Baker, 2010], p. 87).

408 Douglas Stalker, editor. *GRUE! The New Riddle of Induction* (Chicago: Open Court, 1994).

409 More on this in the chapters of "Thiselton-Ricoeur Hermeneutic" and "Biblical Authority."

option on its rational basis. Then a statistical analysis of repeated testing of these laws shows that they govern reality, provided conditions close to the ideal are met. If additional variables are added (like a thick medium or a resistant wind) then they can be factored in to take them into account as well. So these criticisms do not seem to tell against all forms of science either. This approach of mathematical derivation and empirical testing (Peircian pragmatism) is still being utilized as is apparent by the contribution of Steven Weinberg's derivation and mathematical theory that unifies the weak and electromagnetic forces in an attempt for the unified field theory for the four forces (gravity, electromagnetism, strong and weak forces).

Working within this critical realist approach, each theologian has several research programs. Some of their research programs serve as a personal hard core, which is central to their program. Auxiliary hypotheses that add information that allow the data to be related to the theory are conjoined to the core. Auxiliary hypotheses form a "protective belt" around the hard core because they are modified when falsifying data emerge. Lakatos admits that any theory can be saved from falsification by altering it somewhere (i.e. a *ceteris paribus* clause) and these modifications would occur to this belt of auxiliary hypotheses. However, Lakatos incorporates a simplicity element from Duhem;[410] a progressive, affiliated hypothesis must intimately extend the previous hypothesis rather than merely by conjunction.[411] Lakatos calls this the "tacking paradox" and values a unified solution to problems rather than one that requires multiple contrary tacks like in a sail boat trying to sail close into the wind. In my opinion the remainder of the unified field theory proposed in the esoteric string theory with at least ten dimensions has mired down in huge tacts that have no explainable basis in reality, nor are they able to be tested empirically, so in my opinion this model stands as a real degenerative model, even though the mathematical equations based on conjectures of ten dimensions unify it theoretically. At this point I don't believe that the beauty of a model can save it from the lack of some degree of sophisticated falsification. In this methodolical approach it is better to limit tacks to that which are at least somewhat testable within the reality that the discipline is attempting to describe. Within this method, any individual may be researching several auxiliary hypotheses within a largely resilient world-view, surrounding the individual's hard core theology and science.

Murphy describes such a research program as "a series of complex theories whose core remains the same while auxiliary hypotheses are successively modified, replaced, or amplified in order to account for

410 Pierre Duhem, *The Aim and Structure of Physical Theory*.

411 Imre Lakatos, "Falsification and the Methodology of Scientific Research Programs," in *Criticism and the Growth of Knowledge*. edited by Imre Lakatos and Alan Musgrave, p. 131.

problematic observations."[412] A program is progressive if the internal features are predictive of novel facts, and correspond to the full range of data from the Biblical text in a congruent manner. Contrasting to this, a program is degenerative if it does not take recognized data into account and responds with *ad hoc* face saving devices. Such degenerative techniques become self-stultifying. The relative power of the research program has to do with its ability to increase scientific or theological knowledge.

In science a similar approach can be used within the framework provided by the theological method. Therefore, Biblically grounded theology, with rational and mathematical derivation provides the grid of coherency with which scientific options should be considered. Then scientific Lakatos research programs can be configured within this framework. Progressive programs are those which are empirically coherent and congruent to all the data available to make a responsible proposal. This is similar to the rational criteria that William Bartley provides to eliminate error, with the additional role of Bible and theology added. Bartley's criteria for rational control are:[413]

1. The control of logic: the question whether a given theory is logically consistent.
2. The control of sensory perception: the question whether a theory is empirically falsifiable through sensory perception.
3. The control of the theory of science: the question whether a given theory is in line or in conflict with other scientific hypotheses and with the formulation of problems in philosophy of science as such.
4. The control of the problem: the question of which problem a given theory is supposed to solve, and of whether a given theory is successful in its solution of that problem.

Furthermore, increased confidence in a progressive model is obtained by the most comprehensive pragmatic proposal (without arbitrary complexity) that best predicts and repeatedly demonstrates itself in testing further data. Ernan McMullin, in his presidential address to the American Philosophical Association argued for fruitfulness of epistemic understanding as indicating a better theory, similar to this Lakatos' view.

---

412 Nancey Murphy, *Theology in the Age of Scientific Reasoning*, p. 59.

413 William Bartley, *The Retreat to Commitment* (London: Chatto and Windus, 1964), p. 158; Wentzel van Huyssteen, *Theology and the Justification of Faith: Constructing Theories in Systematic Theology*, p. 42.

> The rationality of science can be philosophically justified. Here I disagree with Kuhn. What philosophers of science have labored so long to show is that such values of fertility are appropriate criterion of theory. Their arguments are in a broad sense logical or epistemological.[414]

Using this approach, repeatable science, as in the making of chemical compounds, shows its progressive hypotheses to be strongly warranted in Peircian pragmatism. Whereas, in non-repeatable science (like historical biology and geology) the fruitfulness of prediction contained in a progressive hypothesis warrants itself until sufficient data challenges this reigning proposal to be considered degenerative. To the extent that equally warranted rival proposals explain the data, the scientist should be tentative about these hypotheses within his discipline. The scientist should resist political moves of arbitrarily excluding rival proposals and their adherents when these proposals have substantial warrant.

Such a Lakatos' approach governs community theology as well. A group's tradition is made up of the commonness of those individuals in this group. This means that what the group agrees upon and considers essential becomes the group's hard core. Any tradition grants that certain affirmations possess an undeniable claim as a hard core of one's world view. So for any group that has defined a hard core doctrinal statement, a denial of such a feature of the hard core could be considered to be heresy, whereas progressive development of this hard core need not be considered to be heresy. Actually, Lakatos would urge us not to identify heresy as denial of communal hard core, for "it still has the right to exist," allowing the weeds to grow among the fruitful theology.[415] However, in theology to challenge a feature of a group's hard core runs the risk of being considered heretical. Such a challenge is not likely to succeed unless the proposed feature, denying an aspect of the hard core, is: 1) grounded elsewhere in the group's hard core or 2) that a clear argument can be marshaled that the group's hard core feature that the proposal is intended to replace is itself contradictory. However, alternative theological proposals should be evaluated by specialists appreciative of nuance who will listen to those who will advocate their views rather than merely the politically connected. Unfortunately, it is often the politically connected that reject proposals that may in some respects challenge a traditional element even though specialists consider these proposals to be productive and helpful.

---

414 Ernan McMullin, "The Goal of Natural Science," *Proceedings of the American Philosophical Association* 58(1984): 37–64, quoting 57.

415 Imre Lakatos, "On Rearing Scholars" in *For and Against Method.* edited by Imre Lakatos and Paul Feyerabend (Chicago: University of Chicago Press, 1999), p. 379; cf. Mt. 13: 29, 38–43.

In physics, such of Lakatos research programs would be the rival theories like that of relativity and quantum, which both excel their Newtonian classical physics predecessor in certain aspects of precision and predictability. Lakatos urges against letting such research programs to become normal science as a worldview.

> One must never allow a research program to become a *Weltanschauung,* or a sort of *scientific rigour,* setting itself up as an arbiter between explanation and non-explanation, as mathematical rigour sets itself up as an arbiter between proof and non-proof. Unfortunately this is the position which Kuhn tends to advocate: indeed, what he calls 'normal science' is nothing but a research programme that has achieved monopoly. But, as a matter of fact, research programmes have achieved complete monopoly only rarely and then only for relatively short periods, in spite of the efforts of some Cartesians, Newtonians and Bohrians. *The history of science has been and should be a history of competing research programmes (or, if you wish 'paradigms'), but it has not been and must not become a succession of periods of normal science: the sooner competition starts, the better for progress.*[416]

Such a Lakatos approach results in the essential ingredient for a living science to be in continuous development. This problem of a worldview is that it has the possibility of blinding the adherent from recognizing challenging and falsifying evidence of his view of the world. Lakatos urges us to continue to recognize these challenges, so that our research programs and worldview will continue to engage these challenges and grow as it meaningfully responds to falsification claims and tacts progressively with nuance and reflection. This issue of 'normal' theology and progressiveness of the discipline will be explored at greater depth within the next chapter. There I argue that rival traditions (Grand Tradition, Orthodox, Roman Catholic, Reformation Founders & Biblical Theology, Critical Theology, majority Evangelicalism with Pietism, and Post-Modern) all claimed this normal status and yet all of them have living advocates. Such a normalcy approach diminishes dialog between these traditions, isolating their advocates to their own traditions. It would be better if these traditions listened to each other, since they often claim to value similar aspects (like Biblical authority) and what any tradition considers appropriate progressiveness could help other traditions think through the implications of its values. I think that Lakatos more precisely

416 Imre Lakatos, "Falsification and the Methodology of Scientific Research Programs," in *Criticism and the Growth of Knowledge*. edited by Imre Lakatos and Alan Musgrave, p. 155.

explains and better encourages how this process is done in theology, than the tendency to normalize one's own tradition.

Unfortunately many in theology view the research programs as more Kuhnian monolithic traditions, either as a grand Christian tradition or as resolving toward the favor of our community's tradition and against all other rival traditions. Such a "normal tradition" view does not help theology as a discipline to progress or keep current with exegetical findings.[417] However, in the next chapter, "The Role of Tradition in Theology" I also show that such a Kuhnian normal tradition view is not accurate to the facts of the history of theology either. For example, with each new traditional framework the older tradition remained with adherents, resulting in several rival traditions continuing as Lakatos had developed that they would. Additionally, the rival traditions sometimes incorporate features at odds with their stated assumptions. A Lakatos method better makes sense of this inconsistency as a degenerative feature rather than as heresy.

In a "normal" theology or Kuhnian approach, any deviation from the tradition becomes heresy. In a Lakatos approach, degenerative and progressive features of the affiliated hypothesis which an individual or group maintains around their hard core would not be heresy. Though, obviously degenerative features would be advantageous to grow beyond even though they are not heretical. Likewise, progressive proposals would be advantageous for a tradition to embrace if it is interested in keeping current with its disciplines or thinking through its implications.

I think that in the science of origins a similar condition occurs between the evangelical populist Creationism and critical Romantic Evolutionism. The Kuhnian approach tends to bifurcate into two camps, ruling out the possibility of a nuanced more accurate way between them. A Lakatosian approach would encourage a more nuanced research program wherever the data stream would lead to truth. One example, is Todd Wood's studies of baraminology, which I briefly identify here in a Lakatosian critical realistic methodology.[418] Todd Wood is a realist in that he starts with taxa and observed characteristics but tries to prevent personal bias by approaching each animal or plant through a multiplicity of frameworks set forward by other researchers and evaluates them all for their similarities and differences (baraminic distance). He is utilizing a strategy pioneered by Robert Sokal and Peter Sneath,[419] but appropriated

417 Reflective of analysis by Imre Lakatos, "Falsification and the Methodology of Scientific Research Programs," in *Criticism and the Growth of Knowledge*. edited by Imre Lakatos and Alan Musgrave, pp. 173–5.

418 This is my conclusion from conversations with Todd Wood and his book, *A Creationist Review and Preliminary Analysis of the History, Geology, Climate, and Biology of the Galápagos Islands. Center for Origins Research Issues in Creation vol. 1.*

419 Robert Sokal and Peter Sneath, *Principles of Taxonomy* (San Francisco: W. H. Freeman and Company, 1963).

and nuanced further by Wood to float a robust method with a progressive research program that reproduces predictable results.

Those who have charted the landscape before Dr. Wood framed this field of baraminology within a critical realist mindset, if not always within a Lakatos approach. However, a brief summary of the development before Wood also indicates that the discipline should be understood to have grown as Lakatos described progressive development to occur. For example, in the 1940s Frank Marsh defined the term *baramin* (off the Hebrew: *bara*/of+*min*/kind) and floated a nuanced theory which permits changes within a kind but not beyond a kind.[420] In 1990, Walter ReMine proposed a discontinuity strategy to exclude baramins from each other. Out of his work came more specific terminology: 1) holobaramin or "a complete set of organisms related by common descent," 2) monobaramin or "a group containing only organisms related by common descent," 3) apobaramin or "a group which contains all ancestors and descendents of any of its members, but contain subgroups that are not related to each other," and 4) polybaramin or "a group of organisms not sharing an ancestor or descendent with any organism outside the group."[421] In 1993, Siegried Scherer also proposed a "basic type" of life for the German Creationist group Wort und Wissen that advanced the classification category into scientific verification.[422] Also in 1990, Kurt Wise fused ReMine's terminology and successive approximations with: 1) Scripture as a source, 2) discontinuity systematics and 3) Basic Type biology, which fusion meant an advance in scientific verification without reference to verifying ancestry.[423] As such, Wise and Wood utilize the following nuanced terminology to distinguish baramins from each other: 1) monobaramin as "a group of organisms which is not completely divided by a phyletic discontinuity, but may or may not be separated from all other organisms by phyletic discontinuities," 2) polybaramin as "a group of organisms divided by at least one discontinuity," and 3) apobaramin

420 E.g., Frank Marsh, *Evolution, Creation, and Science* (Washington D. C.: Review and Herald, 1944), p. 24; Cf. Todd Wood, Kurt Wise, Roger Sanders and Neal Doran, "A Refined Baramin Concept" *Occasional Papers of the Baraminology Study Group # 3* (July 25, 2003): 1–12; Leonard Brand, *Faith, Reason, & Earth History* (Berrin Springs: Andrews University Press, 1997); Todd Wood and Megan Murray *Understanding the Pattern of Life* (Nashville: Broadman & Holman, 2003).

421 Walter ReMine, "Discontinuity Systematics: A New Methodology of Biosystematics Relevant to the Creation Model" in *Proceedings of the Second International Conference on Creationism*. edited by R. E. Walsh and C. L. Brooks (Pittsburg: Creation Science Fellowship, 1990), pp. 207–213; cf. *The Biotic Message: Evolution Versus Message Theory* (St. Paul: St. Paul Science, 1993).

422 S. Scherer, "Basic Types of Life" in *Typen des Lebens* (Berlin: Pascal-Verlag, 1993), pp. 11–30.

423 Kurt Wise, "Baraminology: A Young-earth Creation Biosystematic Method" in *Proceedings of the Second International Conference on Creationism*. pp. 345–58; "Practical Baraminology," *Creation Ex Nihilo Technical Journal* 6(1992): 122–37; *Faith, Form and Time* (Nashville: Broadman & Holman, 2002).

as "separated from all other organisms by phyletic discontinuity, but may not be divided by at least one phyletic discontinuity."

Personally for me in theology, each section of one of my theological papers, chapters or books also becomes a new research program in a Lakatosian sense. Usually, these programs are not rivals in my theology but serve to compliment other studies that deal with similar issues. These complimentary relations are evident in Murphy's phrase, "Philosophy of religion without theology is empty; theology without philosophy of religion is blind."[424] As with Murphy, my philosophy and theology are interpenetrated.[425] However, to this I would add a second phrase, theology is impotent with regard to authority unless it is reflective of Biblical theology, and Biblical theology is impotent with regard to authority unless it is reflective of the Biblical text in its context. I choose a critical realist methodology for my theology for its precise sight and a Biblically theologically driven theology for its retention and clarity of the Biblical message and authority.

Murphy admits "it is conceivable that a theological research program could be built up from the bottom (i.e. 'induction' from data)" [as I am trying to do] but she concludes from her experience "that theologians need an organizing idea before they start."[426] Perhaps my organizing idea is to let contextual Biblical exegesis and grounded philosophizing speak clearly what they have to give. That is, honestly letting the available data speak with its own voice from its context. She suggests that she would start with "a minimal doctrine of God including the Trinitarian nature of God, God's holiness, and God's revelation in Jesus."[427] Furthermore, if she were to produce a systematic theology, she admits that she would find a place for at least two important auxiliary hypotheses: 1) something like Edwards theory regarding the validity of signs of the Holy Spirit, and 2) a doctrine of revelation based on Paul's account of the gifts of the Holy Spirit.[428] These are features I would include as well.

My theological method can be modestly grounded in the philosophical manner of Stuart Hackett but most of the content of my theological method actually is framed by Biblical theology using a Lakatos method to inductively describe the Biblical texts through a hermeneutical spiral. Consistent with Lakatos' mathematical derivation a foundational rational tightness is permitted (as Hackett provides or as I use, as is evident in chapters two and three of *The Classical Christian God,* where I deduce and induce the existence and some attributes of

424 Nancey Murphy, *Theology in the Age of Scientific Reasoning*, p. xii.
425 Cf. Doug Kennard, *The Classical Christian God.*
426 Nancey Murphy, *Theology in the Age of Scientific Reasoning*, p. 184.
427 Nancey Murphy, *Theology in the Age of Scientific Reasoning*, p. 184.
428 Nancey Murphy, *Theology in the Age of Scientific Reasoning*, p. 187.

God philosophically).[429] David Clark advocates a similar moderately foundational Lakatosian theological method.[430]

I recognize that often I do not need to investigate my foundations. I grant Hackett's and Moser's moderate foundations but I don't think that they get you very far theologically. So in many ways my theology primarily rests upon my incorrigible awareness of my basic beliefs. These high priority incorrigible basic beliefs include:

1. A theistic God exists that we can know which we identify with the trinitarian God of the Bible.
2. The Bible itself is God's authoritative revelation and can be understood clearly through normal human means of interpretation.
3. The tools of knowing a reality beyond myself are accessible to us without substantial deception even though they involve subjectivity.
4. Though I allow my perspective to have priority for me, I value others' perspectives in community as corroborating or challenging my own.
5. The Bible portrays a salvation message which I and a historical community of "Christians" may appropriate.
6. This core salvation message for Christians at least includes God graciously providing everlasting life and inheritance in Kingdom on the basis of what God and Christ are and accomplish, which without Their effort would leave humans damned at an eschatological judgment.
7. I have the relationships (wife, family, colleagues, students, and otherwise) that I have.

Some of these beliefs are layered (6 depends upon 5 which depends upon 2, and 7 depends upon 3) but these are helpful to clarify my particular basic orientation for my web of belief. Upon these basic beliefs (and moderate foundations beneath some of them) my subsequent Biblical theology studies are framed as Lakatos research programs that fill out my theological musings. Each of these chapters of this book and the other books which I have written serve as these auxiliary hypotheses in the whole of my theology.

Furthermore, when I am framing a hypothesis, I find that a communal appraisal of my colleagues is helpful to help me to be clear and to balance my subjectivity by their own. But most of these hypotheses begin with individual exegetical studies, which I acknowledge I also approach as a

429 Doug Kennard, *The Classical Christian God*, pp. 11–62.

430 David Clark, *To Know and Love God* (Wheaton: Crossway Books, 2003), pp. 82, 161–3, 304.

critical realist. In these studies, *I try to be as clear as the text is clear and to be as ambiguous as the text is ambiguous.*

This critical realist approach has been appropriated into contemporary hermeneutics by moderate evangelicals working with the historical Jesus. These wish to express critical realism's *hermeneutical spiral* with precision and find value in allowing epistemic categories to inform hermeneutical ones.[431] That is, the textual data is observed by interpreter, such that they float a proposal for the meaning of a text that is then checked by comparing it to the details present in the text itself. Then the process is repeated drawing closer and closer to what the text actually says in itself. This hermeneutical process will be described more fully in the chapter "A Thiselton-Ricoeur Hermeneutic" later in this book.

2.16. Summary

I have obvious allegiances among these philosophical frameworks for the reasons presented in the manuscript. Namely, I am most committed to Biblical theology, which is the Biblical side of the renaissance humanistic root. Beyond this, I also approach things with precision as a critical realist. This means that my philosophy is a conglomeration of a range of philosophers developed and affirmed above.

The features of this critical realist philosophical method can be briefly summarized by a metaphor of a tree that identifies these techniques with greater certainty or plausibility should be given privilege of preferential place in framing a worldview, theology, and science. Returning to this tree metaphor identified in the introduction chapter will help clarify where contributions fit, contributing to my worldview and method for theology and science. I ground the place of my worldview with moderate foundational roots from: 1) rationalism (like law of identity, law of noncontradiction, "I think therefore I am," and performative language), 2) empiricism (like immediate sensations), and 3) incorrigible (basic beliefs). I allow certain knowledge of mathematical derivation and rationalism (e.g., ontological argument) to frame the trunk of my epistemic tree. The important weight bearing branches are then framed by empiricism which further confirms itself by rational argument (e.g., cosmological argument, teleological argument) and by Peircian pragmatism (e.g., exegesis by hermeneutical spiral, testable science, and historical study from evidence). Preferred among this empirically based Peircian pragmatism is a hermeneutical spiral of well attested, peer reviewed exegesis of Scripture because it possesses divine authority and the text's interpretive thrust is within the text itself giving it a distinct edge

431 Kennard, *The Relationship Between Epistemology, Hermeneutics, Biblical Theology and Contextualization*, pp. 57–58, 124–25, 133–34; other examples regularly occur at the November AAR/SBL meeting.

over empirical observation of other media (cf. chapters 3–7). This priority would insist on theology and science to be nested within this Biblicism. So a divinely inspired creation account should be given preferential place in framing issues of origins and a peer reviewed, warranted exposition expressing those Biblical sentiments should as well (cf. chapters 9 and 10). Close behind this in credibility is peer reviewed, Peircian pragmatically tested, empirical science. Of course tentative exegesis and promising but not verified Peircian pragmatic science should be held more tentatively. Thus warranted science can affect the exegesis of texts, such as in a Copernican solar system the Biblical phrases of the "sun rises and sets" should be understood phenomenologically as that of appearance while the earth spins on its axis and revolves around the sun. Such tentativeness within theology and science should move this research program within its discipline to a more peripheral place of the medium branches of the tree, and should be governed by Lakatos' method with its sophisticated falsification. Smaller more tentative branches can be governed by James' pragmatism, which should fit within and not contradict the already placed warranted peer reviewed exegesis, theology and science. Even Dewyian pragmatism could be given some place among non-moral twigs of the tree that do not contradict those branches framed by epistemology, exegesis, theology and science. Examples of James' and Deweyan of contributing within a Biblically framed integration of psychology and theology are provided in the chapters 11 and 12. Peripheral place of small twigs and leaves should be given to phenomenological, aesthetic, intuitional, and existential strategies. None of these peripheral options should displace, nor be permitted to overrule, the warranted, peer reviewed exegesis, theology, and science. However, some of the contributions in this peripheral area can be quite significant. For example, my phenomenological commitment to be involved with Boy Scouts with my sons has certainly colored my life in a major way. These peripheral areas of the tree's canopy also provide a sense of the whole big picture and vitality, which are very important for life. I rarely find existentialism bounded by the concerns of a Biblical world view except in perhaps something like Sören Kierkegaard's reflections from the Synoptics or Abraham or Paul Ricoeur's metaphors reflecting the Biblical text. If such a realist, externalistic epistemology provided limits for existentialism, I would certainly wish to retain existentialism's passion for authentic living. Thus I advocate a passionate quest for truth within these epistemic and methodological means.

3. The Role of Tradition in Theology

(Exampled in Trinity Developments)

This chapter will examine the basic approaches to the role of tradition in theology: Grand Tradition, Orthodox, Catholic, Reformation Founders & Biblical Theology, Critical, Majority Evangelicalism with Pietism, and Post-Modern. One of the points made in this chapter is that theology often reads the Bible through a theological hermeneutic that thinks of itself as Biblical, but is more often dependent upon the tradition for what the theology sees as within the Bible. For example, Kevin Vanhoozer argues that "the best general hermeneutics is a theological hermeneutics"[1] and he is leading evangelicalism into this approach that understands the Bible through the lens of tradition within his *Dictionary for Theological Interpretation of the Bible*.[2] This chapter explores how theological views of the trinity and the interpretation of the Bible changes based on shifting traditions. I argue that if we are trying to be Biblical in a critical realist manner, rather than a post-modern traditional sense then some of these traditional approaches help toward this Biblicism and others lead astray. So this whole book can be seen as opposing the theological hermeneutic movement in an attempt to allow the Biblical text to have its own voice rather than to be dominated by a tradition. This chapter shows allegiance to a tradition can change Biblical interpretations and theological conclusions.

Additionally, this chapter can be considered to be an extended argument for a Lakatos approach to theology since all these rival approaches to tradition have contemporary adherents. That is, to view this chapter through Kuhnian "normal conventions" is to view these contemporary rival traditions as only historical antecedents which lead to one's own model of theology climaxing them all, as Hegel did. That approach is rather egocentric with regard to how theology works. This chapter also demonstrates that any who view their own method as the climax of methodology is an approach that does not represent the historical facts. The fact that rival research programs continue to emerge shows that a Lakatos' framework more precisely describes theology as a discipline with its progressive and degenerative research programs.

---

1 Kevin Vanhoozer, *First Theology: God, Scriptures & Hermeneutics* (Downers Grove: InterVarsity Press, 2002), p. 213.

2 Kevin Vanhoozer, *Dictionary for Theological Interpretation of the Bible* (Grand Rapids: Baker, 2005).

After each view is explained they will be exampled by a study of how they handle the trinity issues of generation of the Son and procession of the Spirit, which as a bit of doctrine showcases the traditions' different rationale and conclusions. The reason for the choice of this doctrine to example the ways these traditions work is grounded in history itself since this is the issue that was the stated reason for the separation of Orthodoxy and Roman Catholic tradition. At this point it is difficult to define the meaning of "generation" and "procession," because it will shift under the different methods of the role of tradition in theology.

These differences in theory and practice will be examined for their epistemic warrant. This warrant will be shown in three ways: 1) Is each tradition coherent in its own methodology? 2) Are there any contradictory conclusions or meaningless concepts from any of the views? and 3) Do the views reflect the Biblical text in its context, when they cite references?

The boundary line of tradition plays out in different ways for each domain. On the individual level tradition is a guide and a cause for reflective examination when it is violated. With regard to a school or an organization, there are written traditions which as a matter of integrity should not be crossed but often the more likely area to be violated is a body of oral tradition that is not usually apparent until a person wanders into the mine field and reactions begin to occur. I will examine some of these, especially the Evangelical Theological Society's controversy with respect to the Open Theism.

The term "tradition" comes from the Latin "*traditio*," meaning simply "a handing over." Stephen Holmes adds that "the English word 'trade' captures another facet of the same idea."[3] So whatever Paul describes *as handed to him* by either Judaism or Christ would be "tradition," and *whatever he then hands over to others* is "tradition." By extension, "tradition is the process whereby one generation inducts its successor into its accumulated wisdom, lore, and values."[4]

Exploring into the Biblical text itself, of (παράδοσιν) is a concept that the scribes and Pharisees honor as identified with the elders of Israel (Matt. 15:2; Mark 7:3, 5). In conversations with them Jesus calls it their tradition and the tradition of men (Matt. 15:3, 6; Mark 7:9, 13). Paul uses this term of the tradition of men to describe the Colossians heresy which he eschews, to point to Christ as the fullness of deity (Col. 2:8–10). Paul identifies that he was advancing in this tradition of the Jewish fathers but that he was called by Christ to His grace, and thus drifted beyond the bounds of this Jewish tradition (Gal. 1:14). Thus tradition and revelation may diverge. If we today are to follow the pattern that Jesus and Paul set

3 Stephen Holmes, "The Authority of the Christian Tradition- An Introductory Essay" in *The Practice of Theology: A Reader*, ed. Colin E. Gunton, Stephen R. Holmes, Murray A. Rae (London: SCM Press, 2001), p. 55.

4 David Wells, *No Place for Truth* (Grand Rapids: Eerdmans, 1993), p. 84.

out, when tradition and divine revelation diverge then we are to follow the more authoritative revelation, even if the departure from the tradition means that traditionalists persecute you, as they did to Jesus and Paul. Hopefully, it will not be Christians persecuting each other.

Paul also uses tradition in an affirming way to refer to that which he has taught his followers, especially when this tradition has to do with the practice of responsible living (2 Thess. 2:15). This serves as the basis for his authoritative exhortation to keep aloof from any brother who leads an unruly and undisciplined life, which is not appropriate to the tradition which Paul has conveyed to them (2 Thess. 3:6–9). Here, Paul's tradition consists especially of his example of hard work and paying his way. Paul's only other instance in mentioning tradition has to do with our being exhorted to follow Paul's example as he follows Christ's example in attempting to edify brethren in contexts where there may be personal disagreement about practices of eating kosher or of food offered to idols or the variance of practice in celebration on certain days (1 Cor. 8:1–11:2). In these areas of disagreement there is liberty, which is restricted by one's own conscience. Paul's and Christ's edifying pattern of hard work in Christian service also provides us with a pattern to emulate. There are few universal practices mandated here except guidelines like not doing anything that would cause a brother to stumble, which means that this brother would somehow be destroyed in damnation (1 Cor. 8:9–13, πρόσκομμα and σκανδαλίσω in Paul's use mean damnation here and elsewhere,[5] cf. Rom. 9:32–33). Such a Pauline sense of tradition would argue against Christians judging the views and practices of a fellow Christian providing it was not actually a sin (e.g., like damning someone as in 1 Cor. 9:3–18 and in the parallel passage especially Rom. 14:4, 13). The Pauline tradition is also sensitive to shaping one's practice to win more to Christ (1 Cor. 10:33 in context with 11:2). This Pauline sense of tradition would argue for responsible living of diligent work and a sensitive tolerance and edification of others, hoping that more may be saved.

3.1. Grand Tradition

Roger Olson argues that there is a Great Tradition that unifies Christiandom.[6] He describes this as "the core of beliefs insisted upon by the majority of early church fathers (as distinct from some of the peripheral notions that individual church fathers developed and promoted as their own)."[7] This strategy could fit itself within Alvin Plantinga's

5 This meaning of damnation is supported also in the gospels and Peter as well.

6 Roger Olson, *The Mosaic of Christian Belief* (Downers Grove: InterVarsity Press, 2002), pp. 30–48; Alister McGrath joins Olson in this great living tradition view (*A Scientific Theology: Nature* [Grand Rapids: Eerdmans, 2001], vol. 1, pp. 35–45).

7 Olson, *The Mosaic of Christian Belief*, p. 32.

epistemic approach of basic belief.[8] That is, beliefs are properly basic if a group normally grants them. These beliefs have a communal context for confirming whether the belief is basic. This could be stated as a goal identified by the Vincentian Canon: "What has been believed by everyone (Christians) everywhere at all times."[9] St. Irenaeus of Lyons lists such a codified "universal rule of faith" that is to be held to in the face of novel teachings.

> The Church, though dispersed through the whole world, even to the ends of the earth, has received from the apostles and their disciples this faith: [she believes] in one God, the Father Almighty, Maker of heaven, and earth, and the sea, and all things that are in them; and in one Christ Jesus, the Son of God, who became incarnate for our salvation; and in the Holy Spirit, who proclaimed through the prophets the dispensations of God, and the advents, and the birth from a virgin, and the passion, and the resurrection from the dead, and the ascension into heaven in the flesh of the beloved Christ Jesus, our Lord, and his manifestation from heaven in the glory of the Father 'to gather all things in one,' and to raise up anew all flesh of the whole human race, in order that to Christ Jesus, our Lord, and God, and Savior, and King, according to the will of the invisible Father, 'every knee should bow, of things in heaven, and things in earth, and things under the earth, and that every tongue should confess' to him, that he should execute just judgment towards all; that he may send 'spiritual wickedness,' and the angels who transgressed and became apostates, together with the ungodly, and unrighteous, and wicked, and profane among men, into everlasting fire; but may in the exercise of his grace, confer immortality on the righteous, and holy, and those who have kept his commandments, and have persevered in his love, some from the beginning, and others from their repentance, and surround them with everlasting glory.[10]

Irenaeus has left us with an impressive list of common belief, especially where it is merely quoting Biblical phrases. I wonder whether all traditions (such as Dispensationalism and Reformed) would agree with the meaning

---

8 Cf. especially Alvin Plantinga, *Warrant and Proper Function* (Oxford: Oxford University Press, 1993).

9 Olson, *The Mosaic of Christian Belief,* p. 34 sums up Vincent of Lerins discussion from *The Commonitorium* especially paragraphs 4–6 and 54–59, taken from *The Nicene and Post-Nicene Fathers*, second series, vol. XI, ed .Phillip Schaff, trans. Edgar C. S. Gibson.

10 St. Irenaeus of Lyons, *Against the Heresies* in *The Ante-Nicene Fathers,* ed. A. Roberts and J. Donaldson vol. III, sect. 1 paragraph 10.

of Irenaeus' terms like "dispensations." I wonder also whether many evangelicals would agree with Irenaeus' view that immortality is granted to those who have certain virtues of character in a relationship with Christ–Irenaeus says for God to "confer immortality on the righteous, and holy, and those who have kept his commandments, and have persevered in his love." This patristic Two Ways soteriology strategy or *imitatio Chrisiti*, which Irenaeus held as part of his recapitulation view,[11] was extremely widely held in his day[12] but it is not very common in American evangelicalism today. Perhaps only those in evangelicalism who appreciate John Bunyan's Two Ways soteriology in *The Pilgrim's Progress*[13] would be open to considering these phrases from Irenaeus with his meaning. Roger Olsen told me that in his opinion he had done justice to this view under his chapter "Salvation: Gift and Task."[14] However, his framework shifts salvation to deal with historical perspectives on the subjective application of God's grace, rather than to let the Two Ways framework proposed by the patristics frame the discussion. C. S. Lewis recommended his own version of the consensus of belief in *Mere Christianity*.[15] In the Wheaton Theology conference held in 1998, it was apparent that even this contemporary hero of evangelicalism held to the Two Ways soteriology, which one would expect from his Anglicanism, even though this is out of vogue in mainline American evangelicalism.[16]

Now Olson does not think that such universality of belief is possible but that the basic approaches that attempt to define Christendom are clear enough. For example, the Eastern Orthodox theologians might identify that the beliefs are those "expressed in the decrees of the first seven ecumenical councils." Roman Catholic theologians might add "as they have been received and authoritatively interpreted by the hierarchy of the church in fellowship with the bishop in Rome." It is often taught that this

11 Irenaeus, *Against the Heresies*, II.2; III.19.1; cf. Louis Bouyer, *The Spirituality of the New Testament and the Fathers*, pp. 227–29.

12 Examples include: *2 Clement*, 1:7; 6:8; 8:4; Ignatius, *Phil.* 5:1-2; *Eph.* 3:1; 5:2; 14:1; *Epistle of Barnabus* 16:7-8; *Shepherd of Hermas* 9:16; 11:5; 30:2; Tertullian, *On Baptism* 1:12; Justin Martyr, *Apology* I.16.8–9; I.61; Tertullian, *Apology* 34; Augustine, *Homilies on the Gospel of John*, pp. 404–5, 450; *Contra Julianum*, 4.3.33; *De Corrept. Et gratia*, 12.38; *City of God* 14.28; *De Spir. Et litt.* 25.42 for many more examples see Doug Kennard, "The Two Ways Christian Life View: A Historical Sketch" a paper present in the Midwest regional ETS meeting, March 1998.

13 John Bunyan, *The Pilgrim's Progress* (Edinburgh: The Banner of Truth Trust, 1977).

14 Roger Olson, *The Mosaic of Christian Belief*, pp. 265–286 and conversation with Roger at the American Academy of Religion meeting Nov. 23, 2003 about 3:50 P.M.

15 C. S. Lewis, *Mere Christianity* (N.Y.: The Macmillan Co. 1960).

16 Doug Kennard, "C. S. Lewis' Narrative Theology Contribution to Two Ways Christian Life View," paper presented at the Wheaton Theology Conference in 1988.

same core of beliefs was rediscovered and embraced by the reformers.[17] Olsen views this historically defined tradition to be a highly regarded secondary authority behind the Bible, much like the Supreme Court is a secondary authority dependent upon the U.S. Constitution. That is, the Bible and the U. S. Constitution do not address contemporary issues. The councils and Supreme Court which *did* address contemporary issues drew heavily upon the principles in these more authoritative sources, but also drew upon other sources as well. His concern for this tradition is to ensure that not just anyone who uses the Bible and claims Jesus can be called Christian; Jehovah's Witnesses and Mormons could still be excluded because of their departure from this common patristic and reformation tradition. While Orthodox, Catholic and Protestants want some way of distinguishing the difference between right and wrong belief, they define tradition differently and allow tradition to function differently for theology. I regret that I am pessimistic about this Olsenian, and especially the Vincentian, over-confidence of a grand tradition, as will become apparent with further examination. However, already the grand tradition would include the Two Ways salvation model with adherents from a range of traditions including: Orthodox, Catholic, Anglican and Episcopalian.

Often those like Olsen who optimistically view a grand tradition do so through the lens of their own tradition. For Olsen, this is the American Methodist and Baptist context, which leaves the Two Way tradition largely excluded. We often do not wish to see the details of the patristics as they are, messy, contradicting, and developing; we often prefer to see them through the filter of our own tradition. However, a critical realist approach to the patristics and to church history will let the historic individuals and manuscripts have their own voice.

This dismissal of a grand tradition does not mean that there are no common beliefs among a proper Christianity. Of course there are common beliefs like: monotheism, and that this personal God created everything, and that Jesus is Lord, and that Jesus Christ provides a gracious salvation, and that Christ's kingdom resolves that which this life lacks. However, when we investigate the details of what these phrases mean we find that believing Christendom has varieties of ways it considers each of these points. Therefore, one who grants the grand tradition view is setting himself up for either a superficial coverage or a neglect of some of the variety within Christianity. Either way does not accurately describe Christianity in such a model, because we bend it to line up with our own tradition (in a Kuhnian approach). In an attempt to be more specific, as a

17 Cf. Thomas Oden, *Systematic Theology* (San Francisco: Harper & Row, 1987–1992); D. H. Williams, *Retrieving the Tradition & Renewing Evangelicalism* (Grand Rapids: Eerdmans, 1999); and James S. Cutsinger, ed. *Reclaiming the Great Tradition: Evangelicals, Catholics & Orthodox in Dialogue* (Downers Grove: InterVarsity Press, 1997).

critical realist, we will now look at different approaches to tradition from a range of Christian branches (reflecting a Lakatos' approach).

3.2. Orthodox

The Orthodox Church emerged with Emperor Licinius' edict of toleration in 313 A.D. and then Constantine's summons from the new capital city Byzantium for the first General Council of the Christian Church to convene at Nicaea in 325 A.D. The seven universal church councils[18] that follow express a church tradition that is claimed to be handed down from the apostles alongside the written Scripture and as the foundational window through which Scripture is accessed. For example, John II, Metropolitan of Russia (1080–89 A.D.) said that "All profess that there are seven holy and Ecumenical Councils, and these are the seven pillars of the faith of the Divine Word on which He erected His holy mansion, the Catholic and Ecumenical Church."[19] The apostolicity of this tradition is as Basil of Caesarea claims "Of the beliefs and practices whether generally accepted or publicly enjoined which are preserved in the Church some we possess from written teaching; others we have received delivered to us 'in a mystery' by the tradition of the apostles."[20] This apostolic tradition had been committed to the Church orally, where it had been handed down from generation to generation, and believed by, as Irenaeus puts it, even those churches which had not received Scriptural manuscripts, and thus it is the apostolic tradition that has kept the Church from error.[21] That is, the faithfulness of this Church tradition is guaranteed by the unbroken succession of bishops in the sees and the councils which go back to the apostles, and that these men are Spirit endowed with "an infallible charism of truth."[22] For example, against the Gnostics, *tradition* rather than Scripture served to be Irenaeus' final court of appeal because: 1) among these "infallible" sources of tradition and Scripture, he considered that tradition had spoken more clearly and 2) the heretics were able to make Scripture say what they desired.[23] So for Irenaeus, the Church is delivered from error in its tradition and the tradition delineates the bounds of salvation. The heretics, who appealed to the Biblical text, were repeatedly charged that they would

---

18 Namely: Nicea 325, Constantinople 381, Ephesus 431, Chalcedon 451, Constantinople 553 and 681, Nicea 787.

19 Quoted by Timothy Ware, *The Orthodox Church* (London: Penguin, 1963), p. 26.

20 St. Basil of Caesarea, *On the Holy Spirit* in *Nicene and Post-Nicene Fathers*, second series, ed. Philip Schaff and Henry Wace, trans. Blomfield Jackson, vol. VIII, paragraph 66.

21 Irenaeus, *Against the Heresies*, 5. praef.; 3.2–5; 3.4.1f in *The Ante-Nicene Fathers*, ed. A. Roberts and J. Donaldson vol. 3. (Grand Rapids: Eerdmans, 1995).

22 Irenaeus, *Against the Heresies*, 3.2.2; 3.3.3; 3.4.1; 3.24.1; 4.26.2; 4.26.5 in *The Ante-Nicene Fathers*, vol. 3.

23 Irenaeus, de praescr. 13, 19; de virg. Vel. 1; adv. Prax. 2 in *The Ante-Nicene Fathers*, vol. 3; these views are echoed by Tertullian for the Latin tradition in the same volume 3:252–57, *On Prescription Against Heretics* especially 21, 27, 30.

The Role of Tradition in Theology =Orthodoxy

not have shipwrecked had they maintained "the church's peculiar and traditionally handed down grasp of the purport of revelation"[24] as their anchor (σκοπὸς ἐκκλησιαστικός).[25] This approach may be encouraging in dispensing with a common enemy like Gnosticism but this same approach and justification was reused against the rise of Calvinism in 1672 in the *Confession of Dositheus*. This Orthodox confession claimed that the Calvinists were in error because the apostolic succession of the bishops (communally enabled by the Holy Spirit) maintained the appropriate truth through which the Church could obtain the infallible interpretation of Scripture.[26] Perhaps their word for us would be that of Alexis Khomiakov, "We are unchanged; we are still the same as we were in the eighth century...Oh that you could only consent to be again what you were once, when we were both united in faith and communion!"[27]

---

24 This phrase was J. N. D. Kelly's description of Athanasius' phrase, *Early Christian Doctrines* (San Francisco: Harper San Francisco, 1978), p. 47.

25 E.g., Athanasius, *C. Ar.* 3.58 in *St. Athanasius Select Works and Letters*. Ed. By Philip Schaff (Grand Rapids: Christian Classics Ethereal Library, 2003).

26 *The Confession of Dositheus,* Decree II and XII In *The Acts and the Decrees of the Synod of Jerusalem* (sometimes called the Council of Bethlehem, under Dositheus, Patriarch of Jerusalem in 1672; translated from the Greek with an appendix containing the confession published with the name of Cyril Lucar condemned by the Synod and with notes by J. N. W. B. Robertson (London: Baker, 1899); small sections are within Gunton et. al. *The Practice of Theology*, pp. 80-82.

27 Quoted in Ware, *The Orthodox Church*, p. 51.

3.2.1. Exampled in Trinity Developments

Of course Alexis refers to the controversy over the *filioque* clause[28] as separating Orthodoxy from the Church of the West. The differences of each of these traditions will be shown in how they handle the issues of procession of Spirit and generation of the Son.

When Tertullian appropriated the concept of procession from the Stoic belief system to help Christianity make sense of Trinity the concept of procession meant "an extension" as in the economic divine extending Himself from the dominant expression of Father to a second and third *persona* of the Son and Holy Spirit.[29] In this budding *Logos* Christology, which Orthodoxy embraced, both the Lord Jesus and the Holy Spirit proceeded from the Divine Father, meaning that both Christ and the Holy Spirit were authentically Divine.

Later, Athanasius would write that "*hypostasis* is the same as *ousia,* signifying nothing other than being itself."[30] Thus, the procession that fosters the *hypostasis* is indicating *the extension of the divine essence*.

Under the influence of neo-platonism's commitment that all truth is eternal truth, Origen proposed that the three persons were distinct *hypostasis* from all eternity. To explain this fact and to combat modalism, he proposed that the Son was *eternally generated* by the Father.[31] This is reflected at Nicea by Eusebius of Caesarea's suggestion of his own *Creed of Caesarea* with the statement "Son only-begotten ... begotten of the Father before the ages." He reasoned that the Son must be begotten before creation because the Son creates everything, but this language did not make it into the *Nicene Creed*. This eternal begetting language finally made it into the second catholic council at Constantinople (381 A.D.) revising the *Nicene Creed* to read (with revision in *italics*):

> We believe...in one Lord Jesus Christ, the Son of God, begotten from the Father, only begotten, *begotten of the Father before all worlds, God of God, Light of Light, very God of very God, begotten, not made*, from the substance of the Father, through Whom all things came into being, things in heaven and things on earth, Who because of our salvation came down and became incarnate, becoming man, suffered and rose again on

28 The Holy Spirit proceeds *from the Son* as well as from the Father.

29 Tertulian, Adv. Prax. 4, 5, 7, 8, 11 in Against Praxeas. In The Writings of Quintus Sept. Flor. Tertullianus. Edited by Richard Ellmann (Kila: Kessinger, 1869–70).

30 Athanasius, *Ep. Ad Afr.* 4; *De decret.* 27; *de syn.* 41 in *St. Athanasius Select Works and Letters*. Ed. By Philip Schaff (Grand Rapids: Christian Classics Ethereal Library, 2003).

31 Origen, *Ioh.* 2.10.75; 20.22.182f; 32.16.192f. in *Commentarii in evangelium Joannis* in *The Ante-Nicene Farthers. Origen's Commentary on John.* (Edinburgh: T & T Clark, 1990).

> the third day, ascended to heaven, and will come to judge the living and the dead.

An even more blatant statement was included within the second canon of *The Canons of the Second Council of Constantinople* (553 A.D.), that is, the fifth catholic council which reads:

> If anyone does not confess that the two begettings of God the Word, one before ages, from the Father, timelessly and incorporeally, the other in the last days, the begetting of the same person, who came down from heaven and was made flesh of the Holy and Glorious God-bearer and ever-virgin Mary, and was born of her, let him be anathema.[32]

Additionally, the procession of the Holy Spirit was included first in the *Creed of Constantinople* (381 A. D., from the second catholic council) as a statement that He was "from the Father."[33] This expression began the development of pneumatology beyond the earlier statements dependent upon the *Apostles Creed,* which merely indicates a belief in the Holy Spirit.

So the statements of extended deity through the "Son's eternal generation" and the "Spirit's procession from the Father" became normative for Orthodoxy because they are incorporated into the seven catholic creeds of Christiandom. Additionally, there appeared to be real development in the ideas of Trinity through Tertullian, Eusebius, and these two catholic creeds. This development would argue against these views being a continuity of the apostolic view. That is, Irenaeus' view of apostolic succession, upon which Orthodoxy has built its dependence of tradition does not stand up to the actual historical facts of the patristic era. The patristics are very diverse and evidence development in their views. That is, Orthodoxy's role of tradition is not sufficiently warranted to indicate that it should be believed, and in such clearly developmental instances the evidence indicates that their confidence in tradition should not be believed. More on the apostolicity question later in the discussion of how Biblical theology takes these concepts.

3.3. Roman Catholic

For Roman Catholicism, tradition is the framework through which the Bible is interpreted as it has been received and authoritatively interpreted by the hierarchy of the church in fellowship with the bishop in Rome, the Pope. This primary honor was given to the bishop of Rome by at least the time of the *Council of Constantinople* of 381 A. D., the second

32 Henry Bettenson *Documents of the Church* (London: Oxford University Press, 1963), p. 92.

33 Bettenson, *Documents of the Church,* p. 25, note # 6.

catholic council.[34] It was at this council that the bishop of Constantinople was given second place to the bishop of Rome because Constantinople was the new Rome.[35] Doesn't this mean that Orthodoxy is further at odds with their own tradition, since the bishop of Constantinople is not in fellowship with the Pope, as Alexis Khomiakov mentioned above and yet the second catholic council, accepted by Orthodoxy, places the Pope in a place of higher authority? How can Orthodoxy maintain that they embrace the seven church councils and yet they violate the second council in their practice? This looks practically contradictory to me.

Returning to Catholicism, the living Pope is granted the role of the maintainer of the tradition, which has the distinct advantage (over historically past councils), in that the Pope can continue to address issues and fold them into the tradition. However, the tradition was closely tied to the councils, which were thought by many to largely be a reflection of Scripture.[36] An exception to this general rule was Basil's reliance upon the liturgy as a compatible tradition that complemented Scripture such as when he tried to demonstrate the deity of the Spirit.[37] Roman Catholic tradition need not be static, but a living and developing expression faithful to the boundaries that the Popes have placed upon it. In defending Augustine's views on free will, Prosper of Aquitaine identifies that Catholics are those who, "profess to follow and to admit only the doctrine sanctioned and taught ...by the Holy See of the Apostle St. Peter through the ministry of its bishops."[38] Prosper appeals to the pronouncements from Pope Innocent, Pope Zosimus and others as settling the issues.[39] Hilary of Poitiers insisted that only those who accepted this church tradition could comprehend what the Bible meant.[40] Augustine considered that the Bible's ambiguous passages could only be cleared up by "the rule of faith" (tradition), and moreover that it was the authority of the church alone that guaranteed the veracity of proper Biblical interpretation.[41] Leo I identified that the authority of the other bishops derived immediately

---

34 Julius, Bishop of Rome in 341 A.D., appeals in a letter, from his position in following the tradition of Peter, to the Council of Antioch urging that they restore Athanasius who was wrongly put out. Cf. Bettenson, *Documents of the Church*, p. 79.

35 Bettenson, *Documents of the Church*, p. 82.

36 E.g., Cyril of Jerusalem, *Cat.* 5:12 in *The Works of Cyril of Jerusalem* (Washington: Catholic University of America Press, 1969–70); Augustine, *Serm. Ad. Cat.* 1; Cassian, *De incarn.* 6.3 in *John Cassian, The Institutes* (New York: Newman Press, 2000).

37 Basil, *De Spir. Sanct.* 16, 66 in *On the Holy Spirit* (Crestwood: St. Vladimir's Seminary Press, 1980).

38 Prosper of Aquitaine: *Defense of St. Augustine* in *Ancient Christian Writers,* series no. 32, trans. P. de Letter (Westminster: The Newman Press, 1963), pp. 178–85, especially the introduction but similar statements also appear in article 7 and 8.

39 E.g., Prosper, *Defense of St. Augustine,* article 1 and 5.

40 Hilary, *In Matt.* 13.1 in *Sur Matthieu* (Paris: Cerf, 1978).

41 Augustine, *De doct. Christ.* 2.12; 3.2; *C. ep. Manich.* 6; *c. Faust. Manich.* 22.79 in *Jésus-Christ mort et ressuscité pour nous*. ed. Suzanne Poque (Paris: Éditions du Cerf, 1986).

from the fellowship that they had with the bishop of Rome. Nicholas I wrote that no higher appeal could be made than to the papal see in Rome and that he could override other councils.[42] The eighth century document *The Donation of Constantine* grants the Pope the right to rule under heaven for the full extent of Constantine's reign, even though in the fifteenth century Lorenzo Valla demonstrated that it was a forgery.[43] Over the next few centuries (eighth to thirteenth centuries) in the struggle over the appointment of officials the Popes Gregory VII and Innocent III excommunicated kings Henry IV and John of England and their subjects until they would repent and resubmit to the Pope. In the midst of this conflict, Pope Gregory VII clarified in *The Dictations of the Pope,*[44] that the Pope is the supreme human of, namely:

1. The Church of Rome is founded by God alone with the universal bishop, and has never erred and never will.
2. The Pope can depose, reinstate, transfer bishops to another see. The Pope can create new sees, make new laws, call general councils. His decrees can be annulled by no one, but he can annul the decrees of anyone.
3. The Pope has the power to depose emperors for he holds the supreme court of appeal.
4. The Pope as emperor requires all, even kings, to do homage to him for he is judged by no one.

The Council of Trent canonized Papal authority as authoritative "unwritten tradition," which was received from Christ and apostles as by the Holy Spirit, along with the Scriptures.[45] When the discussion moved to the mass, then in addition to apostolic tradition, an appeal to the "pious regulations of holy pontiffs" is added.[46]

However, the thirty years war divided up Europe between Rome and the Reformation, thus in bloody fashion ending *the* church in Europe, replacing it by competing church voices. During this same tumultuous time Descartes pioneered the role of reason in criticism as arbiter for all human thought and judgment.

As philosophical and Biblical criticism unraveled the authority of the Church tradition, those loyal to the Roman Catholic Church found

42 Nicholas I, *Preposueramus quidem,* written in 867 A.D. and contained in Bettenson, pp. 94.

43 Bettenson, *Documents of the Church,* pp. 98–101.

44 A number of these *Dictations of the Pope* are contained in Bettenson, *Documents of the Church,* pp. 101–116.

45 *Canons and Decrees of the Council of Trent: Original Text with English Translations,* trans. and ed. by H. J. Schroeder (St. Louis: B. Herder, 1941), Fourth Session, April 8, 1546, Decree Concerning Canonical Scriptures, pp. 17–18.

46 *Council of Trent,* Twenty-Second Session, under the Supreme Pontiff, Pius 4, Sept. 17, 1562, Doctrine Concerning the Sacrifice of the Mass, Chapter 4, pp. 147–8.

papal authority was particularly canonized in the first Vatican Council which identified that when the Pope spoke "*ex cathedra*" (from his throne or chair) that such pronouncements were in fact infallible. So the pronouncements of Mary's immaculate conception pronounced by Pius IX in 1854 and the assumption of Mary, pronounced by Pius XII in 1950 are then official infallible doctrines in Catholic theology. In the Second Vatican Council, from *Dei Verbum*[47] the teaching of the Scriptures is authoritatively restricted to the teaching office of the Church and as such tradition is combined with the sacred Scripture as the authoritative Word of God.

> 9. Hence there exists a close connection and communication between sacred tradition and sacred Scripture. For both of them, flowing from the same divine wellspring, in a certain way merge into a unity and tend toward the same end. For sacred Scripture is the Word of God inasmuch as it is consigned to writing under the inspiration of the divine Spirit, while sacred tradition takes the Word of God entrusted by Christ the Lord and the Holy Spirit to the Apostles, and hands it on to their successors in its full purity, so that led by the light of the Spirit of truth, they may in proclaiming it preserve this Word of God faithfully, explain it, and make it more widely known. Consequently it is not from sacred Scripture alone that the Church draws her certainty about everything which has been revealed. Therefore both sacred tradition and sacred Scripture are to be accepted and venerated with the same sense of loyalty and reverence.[48]
>
> 10. Sacred tradition and sacred Scripture form one sacred deposit of the Word of God, committed to the Church. Holding fast to this deposit the entire holy people united with their shepherds remain always steadfast in the teaching of the Apostles, in the common life, in the breaking of the bread and in prayers (see Acts 8:42), so that holding to, practicing and professing the heritage of the faith, it becomes on the part of the bishops and faithful a single common effort.
>
> But the task of authentically interpreting the word of God, whether written or handed on, has been entrusted exclusively to the living teaching office of the Church, whose authority is exercised in the name of Jesus Christ. This teaching office is not above the Word of God, but serves it, teaching only

47 *The Second Vatican Council, Dei Verbum,* chapter 2 "Handing on Divine Revelation."

48 *The Second Vatican Council, Dei Verbum,* chapter 2 "Handing on Divine Revelation," paragraph 9.

> what has been handed on, listening to it devoutly, guarding it scrupulously and explaining it faithfully in accord with a divine commission and with the help of the Holy Spirit; it draws from this one deposit of faith everything which it presents for belief as divinely revealed.
>
> It is clear, therefore, that sacred tradition, sacred Scripture and the teaching of authority the Church, in accord with God's most wise design, are so linked and joined together that one cannot stand without the others, and that all together and each in its own way under the action of the one Holy Spirit contribute effectively to the salvation of souls.[49]

This authoritative tradition together with the authority of the Pope was ignored by the United States Catholics, when the Pope made his pronouncement against birth control. Average Catholics in America asked. "What does the Pope know about family and birth control?" With repeated "out of touch" pronouncements and the 1960's assailing most authorities in life, tradition as authoritative in the Roman Catholic Church is on the ropes. Now the authority of the Pope is further pummeled under charges of pedophile priests and Episcopal malfeasance.

The Role of Tradition in Theology
Catholic

49 *The Second Vatican Council, Dei Verbum,* chapter 2 "Handing on Divine Revelation," paragraph 10.

3.3.1. Exampled in Trinity Development

In response to the Arian controversy the Cappadocians (Basil the Great, Gregory of Nazianzus, and Gregory of Nyssa) tried to distinguish the mode of origination of the Son and the Spirit. For example, Basil employed the Orthodox framework that the Son's generation and the Spirit's being breathed out of God's mouth are both ineffable but true.[50] He further teaches that the one Spirit "is linked with the one Father through the one Son;" it is through the Son that the divine qualities reach the Spirit from the Father.[51] On the basis of John 15:26 in contrast to John 1:14 and verse 18, Gregory of Nazianzus maintained that the Spirit proceeded from the Father whereas the Son is generated by the Father.[52] However, Gregory of Nyssa provided the definitive statement; the Spirit "is out of God and is of Christ; He proceeds out of the Father and receives from the Son; He cannot be separated from the Word."[53] This Orthodox procession view is a short step from the double procession view which was accepted in the West. That is, the Cappadocians claim that there is one Godhead (*ousia*) and three *hypostasis*.[54] Jerome, who takes *hypostasis* in the orthodox manner as "essence," was alarmed at the way the Cappadocian Fathers were using it in these statements and wrote to Pope Damasus in 376 A.D. admitting he is in the chair of Peter, the Rock upon which the Church is built.[55]

In the West, Victorinus, the Neo-Platonic philosopher took up the defense of the *homoousion* (same essence) view against the Arians. He held that God is eternally in motion, His essence being equivalent to that of a perpetual mover, so that the eternal generation shows the perpetuity of the movement of the Son and the potency of the Father to move the Son.[56]

This perspective of Victorinus was very influential on Augustine, who formulated what became the mature standard view for the West in his volume *De trinitate*. Augustine sees that the distinction of the persons is grounded in mutual relations within the Godhead. This concept of relation clarifies that it is not three essences or three accidents in the Aristotelian philosophical categories but three real eternal relations

50 Basil, *De spir. Sanct.* 46 in *On the Holy Spirit*. ed. David Anderson. (Crestwood: St. Vladimir's Seminary Press, 1980).

51 Basil, *De spir. Sanct.* 45 and 47.

52 Gregory of Nazianzus, *Or.* 31.7–8 in *Select Orations* Washington D.C.: Catholic University of America Press, 2003).

53 J.N.D. Kelly, *Early Christian Doctrines*, p. 262, referring to Gregory's statement in *C. Maced.* 2; 10; 12; 24 and Ib. 2–4.

54 Basil, *Ep.* 8.3; 38.8 in *Letters* (New York: Fathers of the Church, 1951–55); Gregory of Nazianzus, *Or.* 21.14; 42.15 in *Select Orations*; also Didymus, *de trin.* 1.16 (*PG* 39.336).

55 Jerome, Ep. 15, cf. Bettenson, *Documents of the Church*, pp. 80-81.

56 Victorinus, *Adv. Ar.* 1.43; 3.7; 4.20–21; De gen. Verb. 2; 29-30; Ib. 1.31; 1.41; 4.20 in *Theological Treatises on the Trinity* (Washington: Catholic University of America Press, 1981).

(*aliquid relation*).[57] Therefore, *the relations within the Godhead are*: the Father is *eternally begetting*, the Son is *eternally begotten*, and the Spirit is *eternally proceeding* or being bestowed within the Godhead. Of course, Augustine brings much more to the Trinity than this, but the critical move from conceiving of the persons as *extensions of the Divine* (Orthodoxy) to conceiving the persons as *equal related Whos within the Divine* (Western) has been made.

It is this eternal relatedness of equal person within the Trinity that sets up the West for the next move in appreciating the *filioque* clause, that the Spirit proceeds *also from the Son*, and not just from the Father. This clause had been floated at the Council of Toledo (447 A.D.), but it first emerged in a creed of the Church in the rewording of the Creed of Constantinople recited at the third Council of Toledo (589 A.D.).[58] This clause gained popularity in the West as explaining the eternal relationships of Son and Spirit and thus clarifying a distinction from each other. It was inserted in most versions of the creed except when Leo III refused it in 809 A.D.

As political tensions of the Eastern and Western church rose over Papal authority, Photius, patriarch of Constantinople, charged the West and Nicholas I with innovation in an attempt to discredit the Pope. In 867 A.D., as the Latin rites with its "double procession of the Spirit" were introduced into the Church of Bulgaria, Photius attacked them. That same year the Council of Constantinople declared the Roman Church as heretical and excommunicated Pope Nicholas. This breach was patched up for a time around 920 A.D. but as the emperor began to side more closely with the Roman pontif (Pope Leo IX), the metropolitan from Constantinople (Michael Cerularius) decided for schism (the Eastern church left the West over the West's innovative heresy) and anathematized them, making the schism complete.[59]

3.4. Reformation Founders & Biblical Theology

By 1517 A.D., corruption within the Roman Catholic Church was ripe, and Tetzel's selling of forgiveness was a prime expression of it. Luther's 95 Theses confronted this corruption in the church. Called to Worms to defend his teaching, Luther was barraged with learned quotes from patristics and Popes, to which Luther responded,

> Unless I am convicted of error by the testimony of Scriptures or (since I put no trust in the unsupported authority of Pope or of councils, since it is plain that they have often erred and

57 Augustine, *de trin*. Bks. 5-7; *Ioh. Tract*. 39; *enar. In ps*. 68.1.5; *ep*. 170; 238–41; *de civ. Dei* 11.10.

58 Bettenson, *Documents of the Church*, p. 25, note 6.

59 Michael Cerularius, *terra pax hominibus*, in Sept. 1053, cf. Bettenson, *Documents of the Church*, pp. 96–7.

> often contradicted themselves) by manifest reasoning I stand convicted by the Scriptures to which I have appealed, and my conscience is taken captive by God's word, I cannot and will not recant anything, for to act against conscience is neither safe for us, nor open to us. On this I take my stand. I can do no other. God help me. Amen.[60]

Four clear contrasts are made in this statement with what had gone before, namely: 1) The tradition of Popes, fathers, and councils is contradictory and thus not worthy to be trusted on its own merits, 2) the Bible itself is accessible without the filtering of the tradition, and 3) the individual could access this Word of God and understand it, 4) Biblical interpretation provides the definitive authority for theological commitments rather than traditions. Pope Leo X twice excommunicated Luther chronologically before this above statement (in autumn, 1520, and January, 1521) but with this statement Emperor Charles V announced his intent to suppress this "heresy." However, the Reformation was already out of the bag. As such, Luther repeatedly affirmed the authority and accessibility of the Bible, even for the individual interpreter.[61] Melanchthon and his fellow Lutherans followed suit in affirming all four points rather acutely in *The Augsburg Confession* (1530), especially in section 28 on "The Power of Bishops."[62]

Ulrich Zwingli joins this Reformation spirit in which there is confidence in the authority and accessibility of the Word of God. A few citations from *The Sixty-Seven Articles* of (1523) demonstrate this fact.

> I, Ulrich Zwingli, confess that I have preached in the worthy city of Zurich these sixty-seven articles or opinions on the basis of Scripture, which is called *theopneustos* (that is, inspired by God). I offer to defend and vindicate these articles with Scripture. But if I have not understood Scripture correctly, I am ready to be corrected, but only from the same Scripture.[63]

A sample of the articles shows that Zwingli also fights against the vacuousness of tradition and impotence of the Roman Catholic clergy. Notice also his confidence in the clarity and authority of the Word of God, and that the Spirit's role is that of converting the listener to the Word of God by the clarity of the Bible.

---

60 The translation at *The Diet of Worms*, 1521, *Luther's Final Answer,* 18 April *Op. Lat.* vi.8 Kidd, No. 42; also in Bettenson, *Documents of the Church,* pp. 199–201.

61 Dozens of examples of these points are contained in brief in *A Compend of Luther's Theology,* ed. Hugh T. Kerr (Philadelphia: The Westminster Press, 1964), pp. 3–20.

62 Especially in the first four paragraphs of this section.

63 A copy of this is in *Confessions and Catechisms of the Reformation*, ed. Mark Noll, (Grand Rapids: Baker, 1991), p. 39.

> 11. From this we see that so-called ecclesiastical traditions with their pomp, imperiousness, social standing, titles, and laws are a source of all kinds of madness since they do not agree with the head [Christ].
> 12. Therefore, they rage on, but not for the sake of the head. By God's grace, attention has been drawn to this fact in our day. They will not be allowed to rage on forever, but will be brought to listen to the head alone.
> 13. Where people heed the Word of God, they learn the will of God plainly and clearly, they are drawn to him by his Spirit, and they are converted to him.
> 14. Therefore, all Christians should exercise the greatest diligence to see that only the gospel of Christ is preached everywhere.
> 15. For in believing the gospel we are saved, and in believing not we are condemned, for all truth is clearly contained in it.
> 16. In the gospel we learn that the teachings and traditions of men are of no use for salvation.[64]

The document comes to an end with, "But let no one undertake to argue with sophistry or human wisdom, but let Scripture be judge (Scripture breathes the Spirit of God), so that you can either find the truth or, if you have found it, hold on to it. Amen. God grant it!"[65]

Calvin likewise joins in the confidence of the clarity and sufficiency of the Word of God to develop and defend theology and practice. However, He maintains a novel internal view of knowledge rooted in the heart, which sets a trajectory between the dogmatic unthinking of tradition (especially Roman Catholic tradition informed by papacy), and speculation (which explores vain or useless things).[66] So for Calvin, knowledge consists especially of the Word of God, personally owned in a manner that brings about real life change. For example, the first article of *The Geneva Confession* (1536)[67] reads as follows:

> 1. The Word of God
>
> First, we affirm that we desire to follow Scripture alone as the rule of faith and religion, without mixing with it any other thing

64 Noll, *Confessions and Catechisms of the Reformation*, pp. 40–41.

65 Noll, *Confessions and Catechisms of the Reformation*, p. 46.

66 John Calvin, Sermon no. 103 on Job, 521-22; *Commentaries,* 1 Thess. 5:21; cf. William Bouwsma, *John Calvin: A Sixteenth Century Portrait.* (New York: Oxford University Press, 1988), p. 159.

67 A copy of this is present in Noll, *Confessions and Catechisms of the Reformation*, p. 126.

> which might be devised by the opinion of men apart from the Word of God, and without wishing to accept for our spiritual government any other doctrine than what is conveyed to us by the same Word without addition or diminution, according to the command of our Lord.

Calvin emphasizes the authority of the Bible supremely. The Spirit is seen as inspirationally inseparable with this Word of God, and thus there is no rival alternative authority.[68] With regard to councils of the church, Calvin views them as an opportunity to reflect on the issues and opinions conveyed and to consider what the council decided and why.[69] However, the authority remains in the Bible itself.

> Thus councils would come to have the majesty that is their due; yet in the meantime Scripture would stand out in the higher place, with everything subject to its standard. In this way, we willingly embrace and reverence as holy the early councils, such as those of Nicaea, Constantinople, Ephesus I, Chalcedon, and the like, which were concerned with refuting errors- in so far as they relate to the teachings of faith. For they contain nothing but the pure and genuine exposition of the Scripture.[70]

Calvin's opinion is that the church tradition that has developed since these foundational views was not helpful because the church had "degenerated from the purity of that golden age."[71] However, Calvin left his followers with *The Institutes of the Christian Religion* as an interpretive tool to aid in walking between the interpretive anarchy of the heretics and interpretive monarchy of the Pope.

The heritage of these Reformers can be traced in two ways from here. The spirit of the Reformers and their methodology largely extends through the radical reformers into the Biblical theologians, while the product of much of the magisterial Reformers thought is preserved within evangelicalism.

Each step and generation extend this Biblicism to rethink the Western tradition and reframe it in a profoundly Biblical pattern. One example of this development is the absence of a Holy Spirit illumination view which is not proposed until it emerged among Lutheran pietism when Phillip Jakob Spener replaced the concept of verbal inspiration of the Scriptures

---

68 John Calvin, *The Institutes of the Christian Religion* (Grand Rapids: Associated Publishers and Authors, n.d.), ch. 8, paragraph 13.

69 Calvin, *Institutes,* ch. 9, paragraph 8.

70 Calvin, *Institutes,* ch. 9, paragraph 8.

71 Calvin, *Institutes,* ch. 9, paragraph 8.

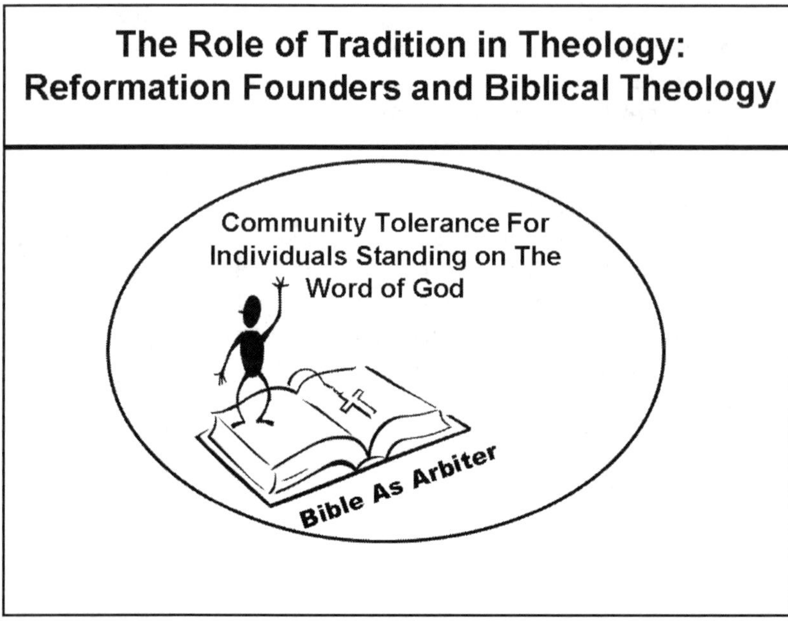

with a personal inspiration or illumination of the believing interpreter.[72] This ushered in one of the most violent controversies which orthodox reformation thought had against pietism. In 1685, Johann Quenstedt reframed the view as one of interpretation and not of inspiration.[73] In

72 Philipp Jakob Spener, *Consilia Et Judicia Theologia* (Frankfurt a.M., 1709), vol. 3, p. 700; Cf. K. James Stein, "Phillip Jakob Spener (1635–1705)" and Markus Matthias, "August Hermann Franke (1663–1727)" in *The Pietist Theologians: An Introduction to Theology in the Seventeenth Centuries*. edited by Carter Lindberg (Malden: Blackwell, 2005), pp. 88 and 105-6; Johannes Wallmann, *Philipp Jakob Spener und die Aufänge des Pietismus* (Tübigen: Mohr, 1970), pp. 92-96; Emmanuel Hirsch, *Geschichte der neuen Evangelische Theologie in Zusammenhang mit den allgemein Bewegung des Europäischen Denkens* (Gütersloh: Bertelsmann, 1951), vol. 2, p. 114; Volker Jung, *Das Ganze der Heiligen Schrift. Hermeneutik und Schriftauslegung bei Abrham Calov* (Stuttgart: Calwer Verlag, 1999), pp. 100–1.

73 Johann Andreas Quenstedt, *Theologia Didactico-Polemica* (Wittenberg: Johanne Ludolph Quenstedt, 1685). The relevant portion (chapters 1–3) of this is available in English as: *The Nature and Character of Theology: An Introduction to the Thought of J. A. Quenstedt from THEOLOGIA DIDACTIO-POLEMICA SIVE SYSTEMA THEOLOGICUM*. abridged, edited, and translated by Luther Poellot (St. Louis: Concordia, 1986), ch. I "Of Theology in General": question I "Is Theology Given?" paragraph XI, p.36; ph. XIV, p. 39; ph. XXXI-Observe (1), p. 54; ph. XXXV, p. 57; Section II "Polemic"-"Sources of Rebuttals or Dialysis of Objections": q. I "Is Theology Given?", pp. 64–5; q. II "Is Revealed Theology Necessary in the Church?", pp. 71, 72–3; q. III "Is Theology a God-Given Practical Aptitude?", exposition III & IV, pp. 73–4; rebuttal I, p. 80; ch. III "Of the Sources of Theology", porism IV, pp. 199–200. Stanley Grenz, in *Beyond Foundationalism* (Lousiville: Westminster John Knox Press, 2001), p. 99 claims that this illumination view originated earlier by at least the time of John Hus and cites George Tavard in *Holy Writ or Holy Church: The Crisis of the Protestant Reformation* (New York: Harper & Brothers, 1959), pp.

1707 David Hollanz embraced the view that the Holy Spirit is promised to every Christian so that they might understand the Biblical text better.[74] August Herman Franke introduced the illumination of the Spirit as *sensus mysticus* around 1701, publishing the idea in 1709 and then more fully in 1717.[75] As such pietism sees the Holy Spirit is promised to every Christian so that he might better understand the Biblical text. So this concept of illumination, so common in evangelicalism is absent from the Reformers. That is, in place of the Spirit leading the councils and the Pope in Orthodoxy and Roman Catholicism, the Reformers identified that the Bible was the accessible arbiter for doctrine.

So the *methodology* of the Reformers, today is carried on by the Biblical theologians, while the *product* (the continuing tradition of the Reformers views), with some novelties (such as illumination) remains within evangelicalism. That is, the product of the Reformers (like descriptions of the Trinity) began to be crystallized and catechized by the creeds that the Reformers expressed. These creeds emerged as a new complimentary tradition through which the concept of tradition is viewed, as will be developed within the section on mainstream Evangelicalism. However, first consider a further look at the spirit of the Reformers as reflected by the Biblical theologians.

In contrast to the confessional reformation and pietism, the descriptive Biblical theology movement emerged and was given expression by Johann Philip Gabler's lecture at the University of Altdorf in 1787.[76] Gabler's approach offered an optimistic empirical spirit that the meaning of the text was accessible to individuals from the straightforward study of the Biblical text's details. The descriptive cataloging of the

---

47-66 which discusses John Hus' view of the soteriological transformation in which the Holy Spirit enables the new believer to be applicationally responsive to the Word of God. From my reading of the Hus material, I agree with Tavard, contrary to Grenz; Hus does not teach this view of the illumination through the Holy Spirit aid to cognitively understand the Bible. I have not found the view any earlier than Spener's pietistic Lutheran systematic theology.

74 David Hollaz, Examen Theologicum Acroamaticum was published in 1707 but is available as Acromaticum Universam Theologiam Thetico-Polemicam Complectens (Lipsiae: B.C. Breitkopfii, 1763).

75 August Hermann Franke, *Praelectiones Hermeneuticae, ad Exponendi Sensvm Scripturae S. Theologiae Stvdiosis Ostendendam Adjiecta est in Fine Brevis et Lvcvlenta Scriptvram S. cvm Frvtv Legendi Institvtio* (Halle: Waisenhaus, 1710) , p. 57; cf. Markus Matthias, "August Hermann Franke (1663-1727)" in *The Pietist Theologians: An Introduction to Theology in the Seventeenth Centuries*. edited by Carter Lindberg (Malden: Blackwell, 2005), pp. 106–7.

76 Gabler's lecture 'On the proper distinction between Biblical and dogmatic theology and specific objectives of each,' is translated and commented on in John Sandys-Wunsch and Laurence Eldredge, 'J. P. Gabler and the Distinction Between Biblical and Dogmatic Theology: Translation, Commentary, and Discussion of his Originality,' *Scottish Journal of Theology* 33(1980): 133–58 and also in *The Flowering of O. T. Theology*, eds. Ben Ollenburger, Elmer Martens, Gerhard Hasel (Winona Lake: Eisenbrauns, 1992), pp. 492–502.

details of the Biblical text would then be used by Gabler to construct a new inductive tradition within Dogmatic theology. The confidence that a commentator can approach the Biblical text in a descriptive manner is still with us in a more nuanced subjective way, as in K. Stendahl's article about contemporary Biblical Theology in the *Interpreter's Dictionary of the Bible,* which calls the contemporary commentator to describe the meaning of the Biblical text in the original context.[77] However, in his day, Gabler was aware of subjective aspects as he discussed some who in their Biblical theology occasionally got re-entangled with dogmatic theology, and warned against this.[78] For such a discipline as Biblical theology, the tradition that is most binding is first to have a basic methodology of reflecting the Biblical text wherever it will lead. Or the goal in Biblical theology as I state it is, "to be as clear as the text is clear and to be as ambiguous as the text is ambiguous." Such a methodology is a progressive tradition that identifies with a heritage of attempts in the past but always goes beyond them to some extent in that each interpreter places his study within the landscape of those who have gone before him in this discipline. So both the content and the organizing principles try to reflect what the text says. This heritage can be reflected by statement of methodology to which I identify, like my own statement in the later chapter, "The Reef of the Old Testament,"[79] or Gerhard Hasel's books on Biblical theology methodology, which I have often used to teach the methodology of this discipline.[80] One's heritage can also be identified by the individual contributors who interpret similarly. For me, that means those major Biblical theology frameworks within which I work, and have my students read, like: Eichrodt,[81] Vos,[82] Smith,[83] Brueggemann,[84]

---

77 K. Stendahl, 'Biblical Theology, Contemporary,' *Interpreter's Dictionary of the Bible*, 1:418-32.

78 Gabler, in *The Flowering of O.T. Theology*, p. 495.

79 Originally presented as an Evangelical Theological Society paper: Doug Kennard, "The Reef of the O.T.: A Method for Doing Biblical Theology that Makes Sense for Wisdom Literature," 2000, included as a later chapter in this book.

80 Gerhard Hasel *Old Testament Theology: Basic Issues in the Current Debate* (Grand Rapids: Eerdmans, 1972, fourth edition 1991) and *New Testament Theology: Basic Issues in the Current Debate* (Grand Rapids: Eerdmans, 1978). A progressive look at the discipline is evident in a volume like *The Flowering of O. T. Theology*.

81 Walther Eichrodt, *Theology of the Old Testament* in two volumes (Philadelphia: The Westminster Press, 1961, 1967).

82 Geerhardus Vos, *Biblical Theology: Old and New Testaments* (Grand Rapids: Eerdmans, 1948).

83 Ralph Smith, *Old Testament Theology: Its History, Method, and Message* (Nashville: Broadman & Holman Publishers, 1993).

84 Walter Brueggemann, *Theology of the Old Testament: Testimony, Dispute, Advocacy* (Minneapolis: Fortress Press, 1997).

House,[85] Goldingay,[86] Merrill,[87] and Waltke[88] for Old Testament, and Schlatter,[89] Ladd,[90] Guthrie,[91] Wright,[92] Strecker,[93] Dunn,[94] Marshall,[95] and Schnelle[96] for the New Testament. This is a helpful way to identify an *interpretive tradition*[97] which frames a trajectory from which future work will be attempted, without requiring the past conclusions to exclude what the Bible actually claims in the text. Likewise, this methodological dimension is a major contribution that Biblical theology brings from the Biblical text as well, in its attempt to reflect the content within progressive revelation.

When in November, 2002, I. H. Marshall addressed the Institute for Biblical Research on developing theology from hermeneutics,[98] his first two points reflected this nature of progressive revelation. For example, he pointed out that Matthew 10 restricts the evangelism of Jesus followers to be among the house of Israel, while Matthew 28 exhorts to go to the

---

85 Paul House, *Old Testament Theology* (Downers Grove: Inter Varsity, 1998).

86 John Goldingay, *Old Testament Theology,* vol. 1 *Israel's Gospel* (Downers Grove: InterVarsity Press, 2003), vol. 2 *Israel's Faith* (Downers Grove: InterVarsity Press, 2006), and vol. 3 *Israel's Life* (Downers Grove: InterVarsity, 2009).

87 Eugene Merrill, *Everlasting Dominion: A Theology of the Old Testament* (Louisville: Broadman and Holman, 2006).

88 Bruce Waltke and Charles Yu, *An Old Testament Theology: An Exegetical, Canonical and Thematic Approach* (Grand Rapids: Zondervan, 2007).

89 Adolf Schlatter, *Die Geschichte des Christus* (Stuttgaart: Calwer Verinsbuchhandlung, 1923) or *The History of the Christ: The Foundation for New Testament Theology* (Grand Rapids: Baker, 1997) and *Die Theologie der Apostel* (Stuttgaart: Calwer Verinsbuchhandlung, 1922) or *The Theology of the Apostles: The Development of New Testament Theology* (Grand Rapids: Baker, 1999).

90 George Eldon Ladd, *A Theology of the New Testament* (Grand Rapids: Eerdmans, 1974, 1993).

91 Donald Guthrie, *New Testament Theology* (Downers Grove: InterVarsity Press, 1981).

92 N.T. Wright, *The New Testament and the People of God* (Minneapolis Press: Fortress Press, 1992), *Jesus and the Victory of God* (Minneapolis: Fortress Press, 1996).

93 Georg Strecker, *Theologie des Neues Testaments* (Berlin: Walter de Gruyter & Co. 1996) or translation: *Theology of the New Testament* Louisville: Westminster John Knox Press, 2000).

94 James Dunn, *The Theology of Paul the Apostle* (Grand Rapids: Eerdmans, 1998).

95 I. Howard Marshall, *New Testament Theology: Many Witnesses, One Gospel* (Downers Grove: InterVarsity, 2004).

96 Udo Schnelle, *Theologie des Neuen Testaments* (Göttingen: Vandenhoeck & Ruprecht GmbH & Co., 2007) or translation by M. Eugene Boring: *Theology of the New Testament* (Grand Rapids: Baker, 2009).

97 Cf. Richard Lints does this same approach with several of the same individuals in *The Fabric of Theology: A Prolegomenon to Evangelical Theology* (Eugene: Wipf and Stock Publishers, 1999), pp. 139–190. I. H. Marshall (in "Developing Theology from Hermeneutics," IBR paper, Nov. 2002) also sees a cross-section tradition, the faith given to the church, as the doctrinal view of the Christian mind, which is used to test prophets and orthodoxy. These papers are now in book form as I. H. Marshall, *Beyond the Bible: Moving from Scripture to Theology* (Grand Rapids: Baker, 2004).

98 I. H. Marshall, "Developing Theology from Hermeneutics," IBR paper, Nov. 2002.

Gentiles. However, when there is a larger gap of time like early O.T. books to the N.T. there may be even a greater revelational development. In such cases, my preference is to develop each text consistent to its contextual revelation stage, and thereby show the real development within the Biblical text. The warrant then comes from the authoritative Biblical text, but there is some corroborative evidencing provided by those scholarly commentators who also are trying to be true to the text. As each one floats their next contribution to the discipline, if the community of scholars resonate with these new ideas then the community provides a sense of reassurance to these new statements of Biblical theology and the discipline moves forward. Other responses from the community of scholars may also come, including attempts to defeat new views and various levels of engagement or disengagement. To the extent that these views become acknowledged to be dissonant to the views of those who are committed to the discipline of Biblical theology, then it should be taken as a warning to hear the replies that the others make and consider them seriously with greater study in the text. But, such dissonance does not necessarily indicate that the views are wrong or else no development would ever be undertaken, and the Reformation Spirit which founds this discipline would be quashed. In the end, the Reformers were right in views, not because others agreed, but because they aligned themselves with the Biblical text.

It is hypothetically possible for some person to discover what the Bible says and not be able to find a living scholar who agrees with him. In such a condition, the scholar should seek out specialists to help him think through each point in his model. The specialists become a community of scholars that transcends our confessional traditions. Provided the community of scholars tolerates his view, it can still be maintained. Provided the community of scholars agrees with the Biblical rationale apparent within a Biblical theology view, then there is reassurance that one's views are likely to be correct. This role of a scholarship community is difficult to maintain today in either our individual oriented society or our local and confessional communities, but it identifies why we need to be in colleges and academic organizations where we share our ideas among colleagues. The community as sounding board helps to clarify and warrant the basic beliefs of both Biblical theologians and exegetes.

3.4.1. Exampled in Trinity Development

This methodology can be sampled by returning to our issue of Trinity. Few of the Reformers deviate from the Western Church tradition on these Trinitarian issues, but Calvin is one who dismisses the Nicene Fathers' speculations. As Warfield summarizes Calvin's view, "It is enough, he says in effect, to believe that the Son derives from the Father, the Spirit from the Father and the Son, without encumbering ourselves with a speculation upon the nature of the eternally generating act to which these hypostases are referred."[99]

However, the Biblical theologians go further; few Biblical theologians think that Trinity is even a Biblical theological concept. One of the minority of Biblical theologians who grants Trinity as Biblical is Donald Guthrie.[100] Following this methodology, we are now entering into a minority position within this discipline. However, I think that the form of epistle used in the first century has been appropriated by at least Peter to accentuate an intentional Trinitarian concept of God in the text, by twice reiterating the threeness of God: in the description of the recipients (1 Pet. 1:2), and again in the longer blessing (1 Pet. 1:3–12).[101] Additionally, it is reassuring that other Biblical theologians like I. H. Marshall concur with this same line of exegesis.[102] I do, therefore grant that a basic concept of a Trinity is being developed in the Biblical text. However, the concept is not so developed as the early church or as most of the Reformers propose.

I am unaware of any Biblical theologian who develops generation and procession as Biblical theology concepts. These are areas of systematic theology. However, there are passages that the church has used to teach the ideas of procession and generation, and scholarly exegetes and Biblical theologians do handle those passages. So there is benefit in exploring what these texts say and comparing it to what the specialists claim that the texts mean, which is the direction we will now take for this study.

The passages to which theological appeals are made to teach eternal generation are: John 1:14, 18; 3:16, 18 and 1 John 4:9. Each of these passages has within it the critical word μονογενὴς. This word μονογενὴς elsewhere in the Bible means "only child" as the case of the only child of a synagogue official that needs Jesus healing or Abraham's only child of promise, whom God has commanded to be sacrificed (Luke 7:12; 8:42; 9:38; Heb. 11:17). However, in John the word is used exclusively of Jesus Christ with reference to His unique historical birth as the revelatory Word, to reveal God through the flesh. For example, John 1:14 describes the unique birthing process as the incarnation of Christ's humanity in flesh so that He as the Word could reveal the divine glory historically through His humanity. The fact that the Word is God (John 1:1) means that the uniquely born God (divine One adding humanity in his birth) is uniquely enabled to explain the Father, which explanation

99 Benjamin B. Warfield, *Calvin and Augustine* (Philadelphia: The Presbyterian and Reformed Publishing Co., 1974), p. 250.

100 Donald Guthrie, *New Testament Theology*, pp. 112–114.

101 Cf. Douglas Kennard, "The Doctrine of God in Petrine Theology" Th. D. Dissertation for Dallas Theological Seminary, 1986, pp. 137, 180–87.

102 I. H. Marshall, First Peter (Downers Grove: InterVarsity Press, 1990), pp. 31–32, 34–48.

took place in the historical incarnation prior to John's writing his gospel (the aorist ἐξηγήσατο; John 1:18). This uniquely born Word (incarnated or born for the purpose of revealing the Father) has revealed God and after the ascension (as John is writing[103]), the divine Word interpenetrated the anthropomorphic breast (κόλπον) of the Father. The Father gives the uniquely born (μονογενὴς) Son of God (in His incarnation coming into the world) for men to believe in Him and thereby obtain everlasting life (John 3:16, 18; 1 John 4:9). Since the Biblical texts used to defend the doctrine of generation emphasize μονογενὴς to be *the historical birthing* of Jesus' humanity in incarnation, it is best to reject the ancient tradition, that Jesus Christ was generated before all ages in eternity. As a historical oddity 'eternal generation' does not reflect the Bible. At this point, the unanimous voice of scholarly commentators agree,[104] further confirming the exegetical view that the generation of the Son should be Biblically

103 ὢν the present tense of εἰμί, indicates a present relationship, but not a continued enwombment that would indicate that the unique birth in this context had not happened because, in fact, with the incarnation the unique birth occurs.

104 E.g., D. Moody, "God's only Son: the translation of John 3:16 in the Revised Standard Version" JBL 72(1953): 213–19; G.R. Beasley-Murray, John (Waco: Word Publishers, 1987), pp. 14–16, 51; Raymond Brown, The Gospel According to John i–xii, vol. 29 (Garden City: Doubleday, 1966), pp. 13-14, 30-34, 129, 134; The Epistles of John. (Garden City: Doubleday, 1982), pp. 516–17; Craig Keener, The Gospel of John: A Commentary (Peabody: Hendrickson, 2003), pp. 412–16, 566–68; Barnabas Lindars, The Gospel of John (Grand Rapids: Eerdmans, 1972), pp. 95–6, 98–99, 159–160; Leon Morris The Gospel according to John (Grand Rapids: Eerdmans, 1971), pp. 105–6, 113–14, 230–4; Stephen Smalley, 1, 2, 3 John (Dallas: Word, 1984), CD disc commentary 1 Jn. 4:9; B. F. Westcott, The Gospel According to St. John, (Grand Rapids: Eerdmans, 1978), pp. 10–14, 55. On rare occasions an individual suggests that the quotes of Psalm 2:7 in the N.T. can be taken in support of eternal generation. Psalm 2:7 "Thou art My Son, today I have begotten Thee" fits into the context of the day in which the Davidic king is installed as king in Jerusalem (Ps. 2:6). In Hebrews 1:5 this statement is already said to the Son and connected with the Davidic covenant (2 Sam. 7:14 also quoted in Heb. 1:5). In Heb. 5:5 the today is identified with the earthly life of Jesus (Who was perfect and did not need a sacrifice [Heb. 5:1–3] and at Gethsemane cried out in effective prayer [Heb. 5:7–8]) in contrast with Psalm 110:4 quoted in Hebrews 5:6 perpetuity of Jesus as a Melchizedekian priest, once He began it in His humanity. Such a priesthood is not eternal because Jesus had to become incarnated before it could begin. In Acts 13:33 Paul's sermon at Pisidian Antioch quote Psalm 2:7 connected with the resurrection of Jesus. Similar affirmations of the beloved Sonship of Jesus are also said in His baptism and transfiguration but none develop eternal generation (Matt. 3:17; 17:5; Mark 1:11; Luke 3:22). When D. A. Carson was asked about these uses of Psalm 2:7 at the Southeast ETS, 2003 meeting, he denied that they had anything to do with eternal generation and denied the concept traditionally attached to μονογενὴς as well. Then he responded with a text in John 6 that he claimed developed aseity, but I think that his text better teaches an economic ministry of sustenance. For example, in John 6:32–33 Jesus (the bread of God) is true bread given by the Father coming out of heaven revelationally for sustenance and thereby life to the world, in a time like manna had been given out in the wilderness (John 6:31). Notice that this is not aseity for it would only be appropriate after creation had occurred, for He came to give life to the world. Additionally, this comment by Jesus would only be appropriate after Jesus' incarnation, for in John 6:38 Jesus identifies that He had come down from

understood as an initiation of an economic ministry of the divine Word incarnating to reveal the Father through His humanity.

Likewise, the procession of the Spirit is best seen as a historical process that occurs after Jesus ascends, rather than an 'eternal procession' as argued by the traditions of the church, as they appeal especially to John 14:25–26, 15:26 and 16:5. However, these Biblical texts indicate that this procession happens historically, when the Holy Spirit is economically sent to continue Jesus' ministry. For example, John 14:17–18 indicates that the disciples with Jesus in the upper room have the Holy Spirit with them but there will be a change as Jesus leaves, for then the Holy Spirit will be in them. After Jesus leaves the Father will send (πέμψει) the Holy Spirit to the disciples to remind these disciples about the things Jesus said to them when He was in fact with them (John 14:25–26). The Holy Spirit will come after Jesus leaves, sent (πέμψω) by Christ and going out (ἐκπορεύεται) from the Father (John 15:26). However, the Son must leave first and return to the Father who sent the Son and thus the disciples will have an advantage as Christ leaves, for the Son will send (πέμψω) the Holy Spirit to them so that the Spirit might convict the world concerning sin, righteousness and judgment (John 16:5, 7–8). The same economic relationship of being sent that the Son had, the Holy Spirit will have, and thus the Holy Spirit is another comforter like Christ. In Acts 1:8 the Holy Spirit had not been received by the disciples yet in this manner, so that they awaited His empowerment in their future. Christ finally ascends in Acts 1:9 leaving His disciples. On the feast of Pentecost the Holy Spirit fills the disciples and they have a dramatic empowerment to proclaim the gospel (Acts 2:2–4). God declares that in the last days He will pour forth (ἐκχεῶ) the Spirit on all mankind (Acts 2:17). Jesus Christ in His exaltation receives (λαβὼν) the promise of the Holy Spirit from the Father and so Christ pours forth (ἐξέχεεν) this Holy Spirit phenomenon which the Jews present can see and hear (Acts 2:33). In the wake of this historical procession which happened at Pentecost, the father sends (ἐξαπέστειλεν) the Spirit into believers' hearts prompting them to intimate prayer by which we cry out, "Daddy, Father" (Gal. 4:6). This condition of the indwelling Spirit who prompts believers to intimate prayer happens for all who belong to Christ, are adopted as sons by the Father and are co-heirs with Christ (Rom. 8:9, 15, 17). Since the Biblical text emphasizes procession to be an economic historical coming of the Spirit at Pentecost with continued economic affect in believers, it is best to reject the ancient traditions that the Spirit is from an eternal procession. Likewise, it is best to see that this procession is economically from the Father and the Son by comparing that the same Greek words describe the Father's sending of the Spirit (πέμψει, ἐκχεῶ) also describe the Son's sending of the Spirit

heaven, sent by the Father to do His Father's will. Therefore, these do not teach aseity, and I agree with Carson that they do not teach eternal generation.

(πέμψω, ἐξέχεεν). The unanimous voice of scholarly commentators[105] at this point agree further confirming the exegetical view that the sending of the Spirit is an economic historical coming to perform certain ministries beginning at Pentecost. At this point, it looks like Orthodoxy and Roman Catholicism have developed a theological methodology that can render them insensitive to what scholarship claims the Biblical text says. How many others will join them?

3.5. Critical Methodology

By critical methodology, I mean primarily the philosophical and theological criticism, though there is also textual criticism happening as well.[106] This critical methodology approach developed here tends to diminish tradition in the normal sense, as too reactionarily conservative, and replaces tradition with some critical intellectual tool like reason.[107] However, there is a kind of tradition even in this approach much like the heritage of individual scholarly approaches that extend the research program of those who have gone before. As David Brown says it, "Traditions of reading continue to maintain their imaginative power not by staying the same but by being open to the transforming power of influences beyond themselves."[108] So tradition can be seen as "the imaginative reappropriation of the past, and not its slavish copying."[109] In the previous chapter, Lakatos' method of research programs explained this process. Such a theological criticism stance emerged with the rise of modern philosophy, which was developed in the previous chapter, so let me here merely summarize a few features sufficient for our purposes.

Modern philosophy begins with Descartes, in 1641, analyzing the role of tradition as able to be brought within the sphere of that which can be doubted.[110] He was seeking a philosophical and theological

105 E.g., G.R. Beasley-Murray, *John* (Waco: Word Publishers, 1987), pp. 261, 286–7; Raymond Brown, *The Gospel According to John xiii-xxi,* vol. 29 (Garden City: Doubleday, 1966), pp. 650–1, 699–700; Craig Keener, *The Gospel of John: A Commentary* (Peabody: Henderickson Publishers, 2003), vol. 2, pp. 951–973, 1022–27, 1035–43; Barnabas Lindars, *The Gospel of John* (Grand Rapids: Eerdmans, 1972), pp. 484, 496; Leon Moris *The Gospel according to John* (Grand Rapids: Eerdmans, 1971), pp. 656–7, 683–4; B. F. Westcott, *The Gospel According to St. John,* (Grand Rapids: Eerdmans, 1978), pp. 208–9, 224–225.

106 Textually, Graph then Welhausen, and then their offspring began to try to recover the historical stages of the biblical text with what they considered certainty, while the text piecemeals in their hands. This form is less helpful for our purposes here since many in literary criticism since the mid 1990's have returned to evaluating text as a whole. This more recent move sets up the strength of Biblical theology all that much more.

107 E.g., David Brown, *Tradition & Imagination: Revelation & Change* (Oxford: Oxford University Press, 1999), p. 61.

108 David Brown, *Tradition & Imagination*, pp. 11–12.

109 David Brown, *Tradition & Imagination*, p. 65.

110 Descartes, *Meditations on First Philosophy,* especially meditation one, *Great Books of the Western World* vol. 31 *Descartes, Spinoza,* (Chicago: Encyclopaedia

method that had the certainty of his study in geometry and algebra. His undeniable starting point is that in his doubting his own existence he realized that he was thinking, and such thought confirmed to him that he was a thinking being. Most philosophers grant this insight but most philosophers today do not think that this is very significant because few people won't already grant that they exist. Likewise, most philosophers think that Descartes is overconfident about the extent of a world view that can be provided by rationalistic means.

Locke jumpstarted British empiricism in 1690 with a confidence in experience as the means by which any man can plumb the depths of God's creation.[111] Locke challenged traditions and tried to remove some of the rubbish that lies in the way to knowledge.[112] He was looking for determinate ideas that can be seen and perceived.[113] He insisted that propositions which are contrary to reason cannot have been revealed by God.[114] However, Locke's empirical confidence is muted in 1748 by David Hume's skepticism within Empiricism.[115] His criticism analyzed the senses and showed that in many ways they could be doubted. Thus Hume becomes profoundly skeptical not grounded by empirical sense as he concludes in the last lines of his *Enquiry Concerning Human Understanding,*

> If we take in our hand any volume; of divinity or school metaphysics, for instance; let us ask, *Does it contain any experimental quantity or number?* No. *Does it contain any experimental reasoning concerning matter of fact and existence?* No. Commit it then to the flames: for it can contain nothing but sophistry and illusion.[116]

Kant's critical philosophy extended Hume's skepticism.[117] Kant restricted knowledge to the phenomena and excluded it from the

---

Britannica, 1952), pp. 75–77.

111 John Locke, *An Essay Concerning Human Understanding,* in *Great Books of the Western World* vol. 35,*Locke, Berkeley, Hume* (Chicago: Encyclopaedia Britannica, 1952), pp. 85–402.

112 John Locke, *An Essay Concerning Human Understanding,* epistle to the reader, p. 89.

113 John Locke, *An Essay Concerning Human Understanding,* epistle to the reader, pp. 91–92.

114 John Locke, *An Essay Concerning Human Understanding,* bk. 4, ch. 20, sect. 11, p. 392; he is especially addressing Catholic dogma like transubstantiantion.

115 David Hume, *An Enquiry Concerning Human Understanding,* in *Great Books of the Western World* vol. 35,*Locke, Berkeley, Hume* (Chicago: Encyclopaedia Britannica, 1952), pp. 451–509.

116 David Hume, *An Enquiry Concerning Human Understanding,* sect. 12, part 3, p. 509.

117 Immanuel Kant, *Critique of Pure Reason,* in *Great Books of the Western World,* vol. 42, *Kant* (Chicago: Encyclopaedia Britannica, 1952), pp. 1–252.

noumena, because the transcendental categories of the mind inhibited all individuals so that they can't know things in themselves. However, Kant finds that the tools of rationalism and empiricism can be employed together, though with muted confidence about things beyond oneself. When Kant's *The Critique of Judgment* explores an aesthetic and purpose of nature, he finds what for him is a bridge between science and concepts like morality, freedom and faith.[118] While not actually using the concept of tradition, it looks to this reader that the concepts of Kant's worldview are in fact traditional concepts available in his day.[119] Such a world view tradition informs the evaluation of universal assent and judgments of taste. In his analytic of the sublime, he sets up an aesthetic strategy that prepares for existentialism. Tapping this root, Clayton Crockett develops *A Theology of the Sublime* that emerges as a connection is made between the Kantian sublime of the third critique and the transcendental imagination of the first critique.[120] Crockett employs the critical resources of Kant and the existentialists who work in Kant's wake. For example, drawing upon Vattimo and Heideggar, Crockett highlights the developmental nature of theological tradition.

> A theological investigation does not simply deal with the traditional objects or concepts of theology as they have been already determined and handed down, but in rethinking theological insights one must deal with the processes of understanding through experience which generate the theological conceptions in the first place. In this way, a theological thinking generates theology itself.[121]

A century before Gerald Smith of the University of Chicago said that what matters in theology is solely whether a belief is practically effective and rationally credible at the present time, not "whether the solutions demanded by present problems do or do not correspond with the doctrine of some former age."[122]

---

118 Immanuel Kant, *Critique of Judgment,* in *Great Books of the Western World,* vol. 42, *Kant* (Chicago: Encyclopaedia Britannica, 1952), pp. 461– 613

119 Immanuel Kant, *Critique of Judgment* in *Great Books of the Western World,* vol. 42, *Kant* (Chicago: Encyclopaedia Britannica, 1952), pp. 459–613, and especially part one, book two, section 26, pp. 500–501 where the concept of the sublime *Weltanschauung* (or of) first appeared in 1790. Cf. Werner Betz, "Zur Geschichte des Wortes 'Weltanschauung,'" In *Kursbuch der Weltanschauungen,* Schriften der Carl Friedrich von Siemens Stiftung (Frankfort: Verlag Ullstein, 1980), pp. 18–28 but especially p.18; cf. David Naugle, *Worldview: The History of a Concept* (Grand Rapids: Eerdmans, 2002), p. xix, 58, and 66. On page 58 an extended footnote #14 develops the Kantian origins of worldview.

120 Clayton Crockett, *A Theology of the Sublime* (London: Routledge, 2001).

121 Crockett, *A Theology of the Sublime*, p. 20.

122 Gerald Birney Smith, "The Task and Method of Systematic Theology," in *A Guide to the Study of the Christian Religion* (Chicago: University of Chicago Press, 1916), p.

Within this muted perspective, and with the passion of pietism, Friedrich Schleiermacher proposes that religion was a "sense and taste for the infinite."[123] Life without this taste is incomplete. Within this taste for the infinite, the essence of religious experience is "a feeling of absolute dependence."[124] With such an internally warranted view for oneself, there is a balancing role provided by the community that one is associated with so that the community feels this dependence together.

Paul Tillich transports this dependence into the existential "ultimate concern."[125] Much of the tradition is criticized and rejected by him as not being propositions that deal with the object worthy of ultimate concern. This orientation reflects his commitment to be expanding the envelope for theological studies. Or as he described it, being the theologian on the boundaries of the discipline. However, theology positions itself within the contents of the Christian faith and correlates it to our existential situation. Thus it is not ignorant of tradition. However, when tradition becomes dogmatics for him, it is "the doctrinal tradition for our present situation."[126] In fact, the way theology warrants itself as *the* theology is to position itself in the tension between the absolutely concrete and the absolutely universal. He criticizes priestly and prophetic theologies (like the Reformers, Biblical theologians and evangelicals) as being too concrete. Furthermore, he criticizes mystical and metaphysical theologies (like Orthodoxy, Roman Catholic, and evangelicals) as being too universal, because they lack concreteness. So for him the existentially paradoxical tension in theology, yet still held to by a group is the goal of that which is universally concrete and absolutely universal. Examples of this kind of tension force us into the trinity issues, like "divine Logos become flesh," or "being in Christ." Tracy extends this model of correlation into a new generation of existential hermeneutical thought. So, tradition becomes the pre-understandings for textual meaning as it is personally appropriated by the interpreter as he reads the text.[127] For Tracy, "the community of theologians either develops or corrects the tradition for the sake of the tradition and in terms of the tradition's own call to constant self-reformation."[128]

226.

123 F. D. E. Schleiermacher, *On Religion: Speeches to its Cultural Despisers* (originally 1799).

124 F. D. E. Schleiermacher, *The Christian Faith* (Edinburgh: T & T Clark, 1999 originally 1821), especially sections 3 and 4.

125 Paul Tillich, *Systematic Theology* (Chicago: University of Chicago Press, 1951), vol. 1, pp. 11–18.

126 Paul Tillich, *Systematic Theology*, 1:32; cf. Carl Braaten, "The Role of Dogma in Church and Theology" in *The Task of Theology Today*, edited by Victor Pfitzner and Hilary Regan (Grand Rapids: Eerdmans, 1998), pp. 23–54.

127 David Tracy, *The Analogical Imagination: Christian Theology and the Culture of Pluralism* (New York: Crossroad, 1986), p. 243.

128 David Tracy, *The Analogical Imagination*, p. 237.

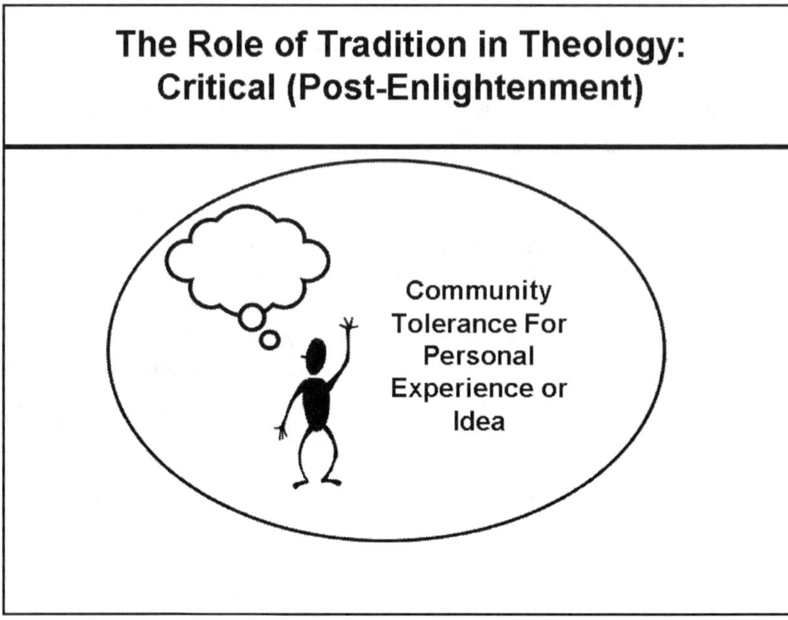

Pannenberg positions himself within Hegel's transcendental idealism and Trinity informed triadic framework.[129] For Hegel, the clarity of the overarching idea, virtually the mind of God, serves as a lens that puts each thing or belief in their place in the progressively revealing tension and resolution of the mind of God. For Pannenberg, the task of theology following Hegel is to develop "a series of stages in which at any given point, the higher stage is constitutive of the preceding insofar as it synthesizes into a unity the contradictions of the preceding one, and thus contains the provisional whole of the entire dialectical path that had been traversed up to that point."[130] At this point he reflects Hegel in a noncontradictory synthesis beyond contradictions and thus on that basis especially pictures the absolute God.[131] From this framework he argues that, "the unity of the tradition can exist despite different dogmatic formulations and in spite of many criticisms of the dogmatic formulations of past times. The unity of the tradition is grounded in the common relation of different theologians of different ages to the norm of the one and the same Christ-event."[132]

129 Georg Wilhelm Friedrich Hegel, *The Phenomenology of Mind*, trans. J. B. Baillie (New York: Harper and Row, 1967); Wolfhart Pannenberg, *Basic Questions in Theology: Collected Essays Volume 2* (Philadelphia: Fortress Press, 1971), pp. 21–27.

130 Pannenberg, *Basic Questions*, vol. 2, p. 21.

131 Pannenberg, *Basic Questions*, vol. 2, pp. 21–22.

132 Pannenberg, *Basic Questions*, vol. 1, p. 208.

3.5.1. Exampled in Trinity Development

The critical perspective contains a wide array of views concerning the Trinity. On the one hand there is Kant who denies the Trinity outright, with his statement that there is "absolutely nothing worthwhile for practical life that can be made out of the doctrine of the Trinity, taken literally, when one believes that one has understood it adequately, but even less when one perceives that it exceeds all our concepts."[133] On the radical opposite side Hegel lets the Trinity dominate his whole metaphysic and epistemology through his triadic structure in *The Phenomenology of Spirit.* There are a range of other options between these.

Few among critical theological diversity explain the idea of generation and procession except as a historical development. Part of this lack of development is as we pointed out above, these concepts are seen as emerging from archaic thought forms such as Stoicism and Platonism. In fact, the Platonic movement to eternalize both procession and generation attempts to preserve these concepts truth value, since in Platonism everything that is really true is eternal as in the realm of the forms. However, the critical orientation deviates from and critiques these philosophical roots as earlier perspectives to grow beyond. For example, Schleiermacher argues that ontological distinction of eternal generation and procession destroys the equality of the persons in the Godhead.[134] Thus for Schleiermacher, theology as a discipline must grow beyond such archaic thought forms. So there is little reason for a critical perspective to dip back into these archaic wells, except to criticize them.

This criticism can be seen as an extension of John Lanshaw Austin's work which investigates the meaning of words.[135] This criticism here includes that these concepts are themselves contradictory and thus not worthy to be believed.[136] For example, in the patristic context eternal means "outside of time, without change, and perpetual" and γεννάω means "birth as a historical instance," so that what would "eternal generation" combining these ideas mean? That is, what would a "perpetual beyond history birth as a historical instance" mean, but a contradiction? Likewise, sending or procession happens historically in time, as we developed under Biblical theology above, so what would "eternal procession" mean? That is, what would a "perpetual beyond history sending as a historical instance" mean, but a contradiction? As contradiction, they are not worthy to be believed.

133 Immanuel Kant, *Der Streit der Fäkultaten,* A 50, 57, translated and quoted by Jürgen Moltmann, "The Trinitarian History of God," *Theology* 78(1975): 633.

134 E.g., F. D. E. Schleiermacher, *The Christian Faith*, pp. 738–751.

135 John Langshaw Austin, *How to do Things With Words* (Oxford: Oxford University Press, 1962) and *Sense and Sensibilia* (Oxford: Oxford University Press, 1962).

136 Doug Kennard, *The Classical Christian God* (Lewiston: The Edwin Mellen Press, 2002), pp. 82–85.

Pannenberg is one critical theologian who still uses these concepts of eternal generation and procession but clarifies that the passages used to teach the view in fact teach an economic generation and procession akin to how I developed them under Biblical theology.[137] For Pannenberg, a form of procession is seen as an eternal description of relationship in the Trinity (following Augustinian tradition and the Western Church without Biblical warrant) while the generation of the Son and the sending of the Spirit happen in time for the economy of salvation (following the Biblical text).[138] This form of synthesis is what one might expect from a Hegelian, however I believe this approach can be critiqued in the spirit of critical methodology. First, the presentation of eternal generation of the Son and eternal procession of the Spirit is maintained by Pannenberg exclusively because the tradition presents them that way. No further evidence is marshaled on their behalf, and all the other evidence (especially the Biblical evidence) normally marshaled on their behalf is reapplied to the economic sendings, like the Biblical theologians did. This shows that while critical methodology protests against tradition, often tradition is smuggled back in to prop up basic beliefs. Secondly, the philosophical contradiction in "eternal generation" itself and "eternal procession" itself renders these concepts in and of themselves not worthy to be believed. This critical philosopher's opinion is that it is not appropriate to believe such contradictories for only traditional reasons; contradictory traditions are to be jettisoned. Furthermore, as I developed in the previous chapter, the Hegelian strategy's third triad does not arrive at transcendental truth that stands above the contradiction between a thesis and its antithesis. Additionally, there is no reason to attempt to transcend the antithesis (of economical sendings) in this case, since all the Biblical evidence lies with this view.

3.6. Mainstream Evangelicalism with Pietism

Mark Noll argues that one of the distinctives of American theology is that it is populist innovation.[139] In fact, the American rejection of the value of class and nobility, disconnected their practice of religion from the preference of kings to a capitalistic marketing based arena in which each entrepreneur within religion would demonstrate his worth by the extent of a following that he could attract around him. This approach protected religion from its demise as occurred in Europe when the kings were thrown out. That is, in America religion was immersed into an arena

137 Wolfhart Pannenberg, *Systematic Theology* (Grand Rapids: Eerdmans, 1988), vol. 1, p. 305.

138 Pannenberg, *Systematic Theology*, vol. 1, pp. 305, 316–319.

139 Mark Noll, *The Old Religion in a New World* (Grand Rapids: Eerdmans, 2002); cf. Os Guinness, *Fit Bodies, Fat Minds: Why Evangelicals Don't Think and What to do About it* (Grand Rapids: Baker, 1994), pp. 44–48. E.g., Jeff Sharlet "Soldiers of Christ, I. Inside America's Most Powerful Megachurch," *Harper's Magazine* 310:1860 (May, 2005): 48.

of pragmatism, in which unpopularity became among the gravest of sins. Alister McGrath and David Wells conclude that American evangelicalism is strongly pragmatic.[140] That is, freedom and religion have been closely linked in America and that populism accepting or rejecting the novel has told whether the theological innovation amounted to much on the American scene.

> A particular set of American conditions ... have opened the door to many opportunities for popular theological innovation. Without a national state church, with few widely revered theological traditions, with no centralized scheme of national education, with all of the denominations compelled to enter into vigorous popular competition for adherents, with innovations in communications implemented by ordinary people, and with significant amounts of wealth widely distributed and available for establishing colleges, publishing houses, newspapers, and other means of disseminating ideas, the United States has been a very fertile medium for popular theologies.[141]

This independent populism has long characterized the American religious scene as evidenced by the freedom that de Toqueville noticed over a century and a half ago.

> Anglo-American civilization ... is the result ... of two distinct elements which in other places have been in frequent disagreement, but which the Americans have succeeded in incorporating to some extent one with the other and combining admirably. I allude to the *spirit of religion* and the *spirit of liberty* ... On my arrival in the United States the religious aspect of the country was the first thing that struck my attention; and the longer I stayed, the more I perceived the great political consequences resulting from this new state of things. In France, I had always seen the spirit of religion and the spirit of freedom marching in opposite directions. But in America I found they were intimately united and they reigned in common over the same country.[142]

---

140 Alister McGrath, "Evangelical Theological Method: The State of the Art" in *Evangelical Futures,* edited by John Stackhouse (Grand Rapids: Baker, 2000), p. 16; David F. Wells, *No Place for Truth, or Whatever Happened to Evangelical Theology?* (Grand Rapids: Eerdmans, 1993).

141 Noll, *The Old Religion in a New World*, p. 195.

142 Alexis de Tocqueville, *Democracy in America,* ed. Thomas Bender (New York: Modern Library, 1981), p. 185.

Such American evangelical populism often resists theological depth.[143] However, American evangelicalism tends "to read the Bible as Scripture...in a particular interpretative tradition."[144] For example, Noll explores dispensationalism as a theological movement driven by the popular study and preaching of the English Bible.[145] The dispensational response among the Plymouth Brethren "was to abandon formally organized churches and to place their hope in a dispersed invisible church made up of God's faithful remnant."[146] Noll's conclusion is that dispensationalism epitomized this populist thrust.

> Dispensational theology never caught on at America's elite universities or seminaries, but it was a huge popular success that drove the activities of conference speakers, lay theological institutes, prophecy conferences, popular magazines, and the publication of thousands of books. Its confidence in both the literal meaning of Scripture and in the ability of lay people to understand the Bible fitted it perfectly to traditional patterns of American Protestant life.[147]

However, after a century of dispensational teaching, there is a deeply lain tradition in this inventive populism as well. The tradition can be clearly seen in the theological statements of dispensational institutions and in the writings of their faculties. This is even more apparent as dispensationalism was challenged by the progressive dispensational movement.

Included among this evangelical populism were those who prided themselves in keeping the faith of a tradition as well, like the offspring of the Reformers who embraced the climax of the reformation confessions. Alister McGrath points out that this is a communal continuity with the past.

> The past generated a tradition to which the present is heir. That tradition involves modes of discourse, ways of conceiving the world, so forth, which it impressed upon the world, and which was perpetuated in a definite historical form, being mediated through both institutions and individuals.[148]

---

143 Alister McGrath, "Engaging the Great Tradition," in *Evangelical Futures,* edited by John Stackhouse (Grand Rapids: Baker, 2000), p. 140.

144 Kevin Vanhoozer, *The Cambridge Companion to Postmodern Theology* (Cambridge: The Cambridge University Press, 2003), p. 168.

145 Noll, *The Old Religion in a New World*, pp. 66–67, 196–7.

146 Noll, *The Old Religion in a New World*, p. 197.

147 Noll, *The Old Religion in a New World*, p. 197.

148 Alister McGrath, *The Genesis of Doctrine* (Grand Rapids: Eerdmans, 1990), p. 188.

McGrath further points out that "evangelicals have denominational loyalties, which often exercise a subtle influence over the assumptions and agendas that are brought to the theological tasks."[149] Stanley Grenz sees that Christian theology is to "delineate the community's interpretive framework" because "all Christian theology is communitarian."[150] He goes on to point out, "as a result, our respective communities (or traditions) play an indispensable role in shaping our conceptions of rationality, as well as the religious beliefs we deem basic and thus use to test new claims."[151] Their summaries include the dispensationalist communities as well as those who are more intentional about a conventional loyalty, as in a reformed perspective loyal to *The Westminster Confession of Faith,* or Wesleyan with its Quadilatrial (which includes tradition) or other creed of the faith.

American evangelicalism has been analyzed as including authoritarian personalities who chart a route through issues with a flock of authoritarian followers following in their paradigms. In such analysis, such authoritarian followers assume that the trusted religious authorities know what is best and submit to their framework more likely than not.[152] Such a psychological orientation tends to maintain theological conventionalism.[153] Within this traditional emphasis a particular Christian worldview encourages such conventionalism. Such authoritarian commitment to conventionalism is intensified when conditions of economic turmoil and left wing threat are perceived to exist.[154] Such authoritarian commitment to conventionalism: 1) limits engagement with novel ideas and 2) limits perception of evidence that would challenge traditional commitments.[155] Within such traditionalism, authoritarian leaders tend to use aggression to stop and harm those who think independently.[156]

Many of these evangelical approaches position themselves within pietism, with its: personal relationship with Christ, passion for Bible and ministry, leading of Spirit and illumination of the Spirit. The leading of the Spirit and illumination of the Spirit bleed into each other. Taken

149 Alister McGrath, "Evangelical Theological Method," p. 27; also *The Genesis of Doctrine*, pp. 178, 183.

150 Stanley Grenz, "Articulating the Christian Belief Mosaic: Theological Method after the Demise of Foundationalism," in *Evangelical Futures,* edited by John Stackhouse (Grand Rapids: Baker, 2000), pp. 123, 130.

151 Grenz, "Articulating the Christian Mosaic," in *Evangelical Futures*, p. 131.

152 Bob Altemeyer, *The Authoritarian Specter* (Cambridge: Harvard University Press, 1996), p. 9.

153 Bob Altemeyer, *The Authoritarian Specter*, pp. 11, 63, 149; cf. Erich Fromm, *Escape from Freedom* (New York: The Hearst Corp., 1965), pp. 208–30.

154 Bob Altemeyer, *The Authoritarian Specter*, p. 91.

155 Bob Altemeyer, *The Authoritarian Specter*, pp. 93–96; cf. Erich Fromm, *Escape from Freedom,* pp. 208–30.

156 Bob Altemeyer, *The Authoritarian Specter*, p. 10; cf. Erich Fromm, *Escape from Freedom*, pp. 184–9.

together they are similar to the Orthodox and Roman Catholic Spirit enablement of tradition through apostolic succession and the Pope. However, in evangelicalism the illumination of the Spirit is shifted from a divine support of the tradition to usually a word in the individual interpreter to aid him in discerning the message of the Biblical passage.[157] The earliest expressions of this illumination of the Spirit emerged among Lutheran pietism when Phillip Jakob Spener replaced the concept of verbal inspiration of the Scriptures with a personal inspiration or illumination of the believing interpreter, fostering a major controversy with orthodox Lutheranism.[158] Spener agreed with the reformers that the text was clear but viewed humans as so impaired by sin so that only "reborn" preachers with the enlightening of the Spirit (like the resurrected Christ provided on the Emmaus road) could rightfully understand the Biblical text. This ushered in one of the most violent controversies which orthodox reformation thought had against pietism. In 1685 the exhaustive collection of Lutheran theology in *Theologia Didactico-Polemica* by the Johann Quenstedt (nicknamed "the bookkeeper" for his exhaustive cataloging of views) reframed the Spirit's illuminational aid as one of regenerational interpretation and not inspiration.[159] In 1707

157 An example of this is in *The Chicago Statement on Biblical Hermeneutics* (1978), "Articles of Affirmation and Denial," Article 5, in *Hermeneutics, Inerrancy, & the Bible*. edited by Earl Radmacher and Robert Preus (Grad Rapids: Zondervan, 1984), p. 882.

158 Philipp Jakob Spener, *Consilia Et Judicia Theologia* (Frankfurt a.M., 1709), vol. 3, p. 700; Cf. K. James Stein, "Phillip Jakob Spener (1635–1705)" and Markus Matthias, "August Hermann Franke (1663–1727)" in *The Pietist Theologians: An Introduction to Theology in the Seventeenth Centuries*. edited by Carter Lindberg (Malden: Blackwell, 2005), pp. 88 and 105–6; Johannes Wallmann, *Philipp Jakob Spener und die Aufänge des Pietismus* (Tübigen: Mohr, 1970), pp. 92–96; Emmanuel Hirsch, *Geschichte der neuen Evangelische Theologie in Zusammenhang mit den allgemein Bewegung des Europäischen Denkens* (Gütersloh: Bertelsmann, 1951), vol. 2, p. 114; Volker Jung, *Das Ganze der Heiligen Schrift. Hermeneutik und Schriftauslegung bei Abrham Calov* (Stuttgart: Calwer Verlag, 1999), pp. 100–1.

159 Johann Andreas Quenstedt, *Theologia Didactico-Polemica* (Wittenberg: Johanne Ludolph Quenstedt, 1685). The relevant portion (chapters 1–3) of this is available in English as: *The Nature and Character of Theology: An Introduction to the Thought of J. A. Quenstedt from THEOLOGIA DIDACTIO-POLEMICA SIVE SYSTEMA THEOLOGICUM*. abridged, edited, and translated by Luther Poellot (St. Louis: Concordia, 1986), ch. I "Of Theology in General": question I "Is Theology Given?" paragraph XI, p. 36; ph. XIV, p. 39; ph. XXXI-Observe (1), p. 54; ph. XXXV, p. 57; Section II "Polemic"-"Sources of Rebuttals or Dialysis of Objections": q. I "Is Theology Given?", pp. 64–5; q. II "Is Revealed Theology Necessary in the Church?", pp. 71, 72–3; q. III "Is Theology a God-Given Practical Aptitude?", exposition III & IV, pp. 73–4; rebuttal I, p. 80; ch. III "Of the Sources of Theology", porism IV, pp. 199–200. Stanley Grenz, in *Beyond Foundationalism* (Lousiville: Westminster John Knox Press, 2001), p. 99 claims that this illumination view originated earlier by at least the time of John Hus and cites George Tavard in *Holy Writ or Holy Church: The Crisis of the Protestant Reformation* (New York: Harper & Brothers, 1959), pp. 47–66 which discusses John Hus' view of the soteriological transformation in which the Holy Spirit enables the new believer to be applicationally responsive to the

David Hollanz embraced this view that the Holy Spirit is promised to every Christian so that they might understand the Biblical text better.[160] Around 1701, August Herman Franke shifted the illumination of the Spirit as *sensus mysticus* when reading the Biblical text, extending John Hus' Spirit regeneration idea to an affective product brought about by the Spirit when studying the Bible.[161] That is, only the person moved by the Spirit can acquire "living" knowledge of the Biblical text that will bring about spiritual affection. Evangelicalism has largely owned Spener and Hollanz's cognitive illumination view, with others in evangelicalism join Franke's Spirit transformational illumination view. For example, the 1982 evangelical Chicago Statement on Biblical Hermeneutics includes as the fifth article: "WE AFFIRM that the Holy Spirit enables believers to appropriate and apply Scripture to their lives. WE DENY that the natural man is able to discern spiritually the biblical message apart from the Holy Spirit."[162] This statement indicates in its denial a cognitive illuminational element while in its affirmation the transformational illumination is highlighted. This statement reflects the emphasis in evangelicalism that the Holy Spirit aids the individual's use of hermeneutics.

However, some in evangelicalism are advocating a communal illumination. A contemporary advocate of this communal illumination view is Donald Bloesch. He identifies that the Bible's revelatory status "does not reside in its wording as such but in the Spirit of God, who fills the words with meaning and power."[163] This view provides a post textual subjective meaning. Kevin Vanhoozer also wishes to extend this individual illumination into becoming a community illumination of Spirit, "Only a prayerful reading that invokes the Spirit can perceive the true meaning in what is otherwise a dead letter. Such Spirit-led exegesis 'restores the interpretive activity of the spiritual community as the connecting link between text and reader.'"[164] Community textual

---

Word of God. From my reading of the Hus material, I agree with Tavard, contrary to Grenz; Hus does not teach this view of the illumination through the Holy Spirit aid to cognitively understand the Bible. I have not found the view any earlier than Spener's, Quenstedt's and Hollanz's pietistic Lutheran systematic theologies.

160 David Hollaz, Examen Theologicum Acroamaticum was published in 1707 and 1725 but is available as Acromaticum Universam Theologiam Thetico-Polemicam Complectens (Lipsiae: B.C. Breitkopfii, 1763).

161 August Hermann Franke introduced his view in 1701, publishing the idea in 1709 and then more fully in 1717 as *Praelectiones Hermeneuticae,* p. 57; cf. *Markus* Matthias, "August Hermann Franke (1663–1727)" in *The Pietist Theologians: An Introduction to Theology in the Seventeenth Centuries.* edited by Carter Lindberg (Malden: Blackwell, 2005), pp. 106–7.

162 The Chicago Statement on Biblical Hermeneutics as contained in *Hermeneutics, Inerrancy, and the Bible.* edited by Earl Radmacher and Robert Preus (Grand Rapids: Zondervan, 1984), p. 891.

163 Donald Bloesch, *Holy Scripture: Revelation, Inspiration & Interpretation* (Downers Grove: InterVarsity, 1994), p. 27.

164 Vanhoozer, *Is There Meaning in This Text* (Grand Rapids: Zondervan, 1998), p. 411.

The Role of Tradition in Theology: Majority Evangelical

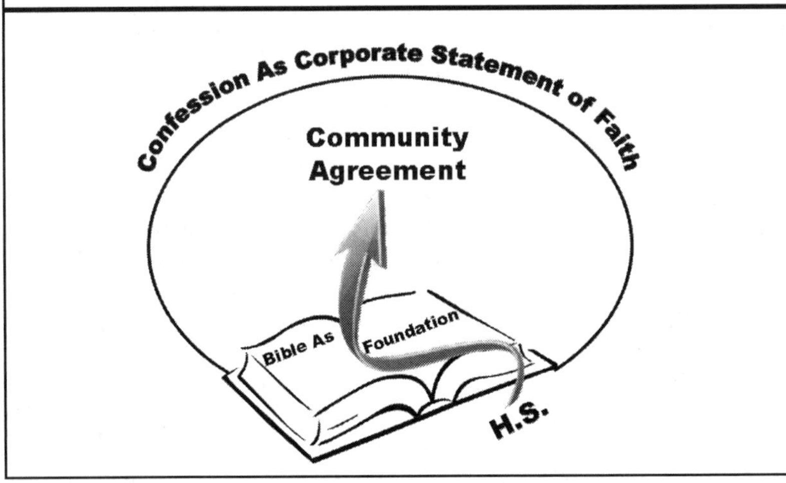

decisions are essentially saying that the Holy Spirit assures the community that they will interpret correctly as they frame up their tradition. In conservative circles this illumination is often supported through textual appeals to John 14:26; 16:12–15; 1 Cor. 2:6–16; and 1 John 2:27. I argue along with the scholarly commentators that these texts do not teach such an illumination view.[165] This argument is briefly contained in the chapters four and five on "Thiselton-Ricoeur Hermeneutic" and "Biblical Authority."

So Evangelicalism often has a confidence that by the aid from the Holy Spirit the community can obtain the correct interpretation of the Biblical text and thereby embrace a corporate agreement to delineate their traditions. This approach functions in church, school and academic societies. However, as evident by the argument in subsequent chapters, I wonder if this basic belief is so well grounded. I think that in fact it is not and if the illumination of the Spirit is not working as they suppose then evangelical reduces to a pragmatic populism[166] that occasionally

165 Douglas Kennard, "Evangelical Views on Illumination of Scripture and Critique," *JETS* 49/4(Dec. 2006): 767–806; cf. later chapters: "Thiselton-Ricoeur Hermeneutic" and "Biblical Authority in the Contemporary Hermeneutical Scene" earlier presented at the Wheaton Theology Conference, 2001, The Evangelical Theological Society, 2002, and the American Academy of Religion, 2003, pp. 21–25. Cf. Douglas Kennard, *The Relationship Between Epistemology, Hermeneutics, Biblical Theology and Contextualization*, pp. 139–42.

166 Alister McGrath, "Evangelical Theological Method: The State of the Art" in *Evangelical Futures*, edited by John Stackhouse, p. 16; David F. Wells, *No Place for Truth, or Whatever Happened to Evangelical Theology?*; Alexis de Tocqueville, *Democracy*

interprets the Biblical text in very traditional ways, which Biblical scholarship does not support.

In evangelicalism, the leading of the Spirit is often seen as a divine personal guidance in the decision making process. This view may not be held by a majority in evangelicalism in the wake of the critique by Gary Friesen, *Decision Making & the Will of God,*[167] but it is still widely held. While this view is usually developed as an individual aid, the individuals that make up a group sometimes appeal to it to support their traditions as a softer version[168] of the Orthodox and Catholic claimed Spirit aid. For example, a church may claim that God is "leading" them into a building program.

How does the Bible use the concept of divine leading? The clear N.T. texts on the leading of the Spirit fit into two basic categories. First, the Spirit lead Jesus into temptation (Matt. 4:1; Mark 1:12; Luke 4:1), which is why Jesus has his disciples pray to the Father, "Do not lead us into temptation" (Matt. 6:13; Luke 11:4). This form of Spirit leading is of little encouragement for the evangelical, since it brought Jesus to temptation rather than gave him success in ministry. The other leading of the Spirit in the N.T. is that developed by Paul as a metaphor for the Spirit's cultivating virtues within the believer like righteousness, the fruit of the Spirit, a sense of belonging in God's family, and intimacy in prayer (Rom. 8:14; Gal. 5:18). Evangelicalism appreciates this ministry of the Spirit but does not let the Biblical terminology of "leading" be restricted to the Biblical uses of the term. That is, evangelicalism has coined the term to mean something else, namely personal guidance. Here, Gary Friesen has ably analyzed the evangelical rationale and concluded that the Biblical texts appealed to do not support the view of personal guidance. Instead, he sees that God has promised to mature us so that we can cultivate the wisdom which is available so that we could make wise decisions.

If Friesen is right about decision making, and Biblical theology excludes "Spirit leading" from normal guidance, and the scholarly Biblical commentators are right about illumination of the Spirit, *then our traditions and statements of faith are in fact community conventions, without any claim to the Spirit as buoying them up.*

With 1976 becoming the year of the Evangelical, according to *Time* magazine, and the rise of evangelical power politics as a power block to be marshaled to get elected, evangelicalism has become a huge

in America, p. 185; cf. Os Guinness (*Fit Bodies, Fat Minds*, pp. 34–39, 44–48, 55–59) argues that pietism, populism and pragmatism in evangelicalism cultivate an anti-intellectual lack of engagement.

167 Gary Friesen, *Decision Making & the Will of God: A Biblical Alternative to the Traditional View* (Portland: Multnomah Press, 1980). Critique of the Spirit leading view explained in pp. 23–150, and the way of wisdom alternative explained in pp. 151–282.

168 I.e. potentially errant version.

gorilla in the jungle throwing its weight around politically. The populous pragmatic power politics is apparent in some schools and academic societies as well. We have infused politics among evangelicalism. This may mean that the image of the "obnoxious American," insensitive to others' concerns may have merged with the "can do" evangelical possibly producing a "kick butt" Christianity. Some authoritarians within evangelicalism operate under a code like: If people are in his way, he helps them turn their cheeks to remove them.

In practice, I think that the varieties of evangelicalism also each have oral traditions salted with land mines that an individual faculty member may only know after the fact, when unfortunately it is too late to do anything and all that can be heard are the sounds leading to his removal. A faculty member may only know where the land mines are by which steps take colleagues out. This leaves a faculty member with an uncomfortable choice between options like: stagnating his research to that which is safe where the trusted people have stepped before (repeating the trusted party line), or expecting that if he follows the Biblical text or where clear historical manuscripts lead him, then he may eventually be among the maimed in this evangelical roulette game. Often the oral tradition develops its rationale in reaction to a perceived excess, too late to save a colleague who stepped on the land mine. Unfortunately, evangelicalism often seems more concerned about excising the "aberrant" than recovering a brother. So when the clear lines are drawn after the fact (clarifying the ambiguous) these lines are still binding, and thus the mine has been stepped on, and the faculty member is gone. Does this approach condemn much of evangelicalism as not very Christian?

When these ideas are expressed in a corporate culture, Adrian Savage describes them as the elements of golf culture, namely: trust, collegiality and patronage.[169] This golf culture is driven by receptivity from the institutional top levels–which means that often these decisions are made by generalists who do not involve themselves in nuanced theology but have a finger on the pulse of their constituency. For a theologian's success in a context as this, scholarship and warranting is largely considered useless unless the message is welcome at the top.[170] For example, an individual pursuing ideas he takes to be Biblical are collegially offered to our evangelical institutions and are critiqued on

169 Adrian Savage, founder and president of PNA Inc., a consulting firm (http://www.nettps.com). I am aware that these issues of privilege and abuse are not limited to evangelical institutions. Unfortunately, they are common in academia. E.g., Scott Smallwood "Tenure Madness: How a Shoe-in at Brooklyn College Almost Got the Boot," *The Chronicle of Higher Education*, vol. 59, no. 37 (May 23, 2003): A10–A12.

170 An example of this is evident in the review of Richard Helms book, *A Look Over My Shoulder* by Joseph Persico, "Company Man," in *New York Times Book Review*, Sunday, May 4, 2003, p. 9.

a continental divide of the conventions and inclinations of institutional leadership, rather than scholarly warrant. Some ideas break one way for a variety of traditions, whereas in other traditions they break another direction. Depending upon where the idea lands in relation to a particular leader and conventional group's tradition, the result will be either: 1) the group will be predisposed to trust the person and be more congenial and benefit them through patronage, *or* 2) suspect the person, isolate the person and put them at risk. Community shunning (being cut out of privileges and responsibilities) is often used to try to motivate this compliance. However, when such shunning doesn't work and we conservatives can't defeat the offending view by reasons or good exegesis, it looks to me like we conservatives often disengage from these individuals, politically abusing them or defaming their reputation.

My concern here is that perceived "normal tradition" often excludes an honest appraisal of the Biblical text as it is. This is especially the case when administrators define the "normal tradition" without nuance and sensitivity to the depth and breadth of a discipline. That is, embracing a Kuhnian *normalcy of tradition* on a popular level rather than a Lakatos' *developmental tradition* reduces scholarly engagement with the Biblical text. In this issue it looks to me that evangelicalism, like any confessional approach runs the risk of domesticating the Bible so that it is turned into a safe pussy cat which provides traditional comfort. We tame the Bible, cage it until it safely sits on our laps and purrs. We propagate this domesticated Bible in the minds of our students and congregations. Instead, the Bible is a wild lion reflecting the character of God. Thus it is not safe but it is good. The Bible will not sit still, for it will continue to prod us and call us to the difficult way of discipleship which is always getting beyond ourselves: to understand it, to apply it, to love others and work for a unified body of Christ and to forgive our abusers. Unfortunately, some evangelicals will stop at very little to defame, exclude and destroy other evangelicals. This abuse isn't right; I hunger and thirst for righteousness among evangelicals.

Darrell Bock also appeals for public square institutions, like our academic societies and publishing houses, within which dialog from a range of opinions can be explored.[171] In this he says, "We need solidly grounded theologian-philosopher-exegetes in evangelicalism. Making too great a dichotomy between these roles will not help the church."[172] To engage and consider issues like Openness of God, a full dialog and exchange in this public forum needs to take place.[173] Additionally, the ground rules are explicit and minimal as tied to the doctrinal statement of the respective society. If the advocates of a position like Openness of

171 Darrell Bock, *Purpose-Directed Theology* (Downers Grove: InterVarsity Press, 2002), pp. 32, 39, 70.

172 Bock, *Purpose-Directed Theology,* p. 33.

173 Bock, *Purpose-Directed Theology,* p. 94.

God embrace the doctrinal position of the society then they should not be evicted by a majority of members present who happen to disagree with their position. Even though I disagree with their view sufficiently to have written a book against their view,[174] I recognize that there is a continuing advantage in having people present in the academic society, with whom I do not always agree, so that when our focus goes to other issues, we might be sensitized by the other.[175] It can help us from becoming isolationist and ignorantly postmodern.

3.6.1. Exampled in Trinity Development

Evangelicalism broadly embraces the Western church's commitment to eternal generation of the Son and the eternal procession of the Spirit as Biblical truths. The confessional expression of evangelicalism can be exampled in the Reformed perspective of *The Westminster Confession of Faith,* chapter II, article 3 which reads, that "the Father is of none, neither begotten, nor proceeding; the Son is eternally begotten of the Father; the Holy Ghost eternally proceeding from the Father and the Son."[176] While this statement did not have Biblical texts cited the rational is often the very same Biblical texts throughout much of the Western church. From the dispensational side of evangelicalism, Lewis Sperry Chafer claims,

> Theologians generally have been emphatic in their insistence that the divine Sonship is from all eternity. Their belief in this matter is based upon clear Scripture evidence. However, if the texts do not support their view, as we developed under the Biblical theology section, this would make this view an unwarranted convention continued because of the resilience of the tradition. He is the *Only Begotten* of the Father from all eternity.[177]

Chafer goes on to cite Richard Watson with approval on the eternal procession of the Spirit from the Father and the Son.[178] The Biblical texts to which Chafer appeals are the same ones previously developed under the Biblical theology section. Many other theologians could be added to these voices, though occasionally, as with Gordon Lewis and Bruce Demarest, the Biblical case for eternal generation also is built off the metaphors of radiance, image, and word as well as the texts mentioned

---

174 Douglas Kennard, *The Classical Christian God.*

175 Cf. John Stackhouse, "Evangelical Theology Should be Evangelical" and Kevin Vanhoozer "The Voice of the Actor" in *Evangelical Futures,* edited by John Stackhouse (Grand Rapids: Baker, 2000), pp. 56–8, 80.

176 *The Westminster Confession of Faith* 2.3; also *Belgic Confession of Faith* art. 11.

177 Lewis Sperry Chafer, *Systematic Theology* (Dallas: Dallas Seminary Press, 1947), vol. 1, p. 314.

178 Chafer, *Systematic Theology,* vol. 1, p. 400.

above.[179] For them the generation and procession is both in eternity and in the redemptive activity. However, aren't "radiance, image and word" revelation metaphors more appropriate for the economy (of revelation and redemption)? Thus I would disconnect these metaphors from supporting generation and procession in eternity.

If the Biblical specialists claim that the Biblical texts teach something other than what our evangelical theology maintains, isn't evangelical theology merely keeping a traditional convention alive? Personally, I do not value tradition highly enough to merely parrot it because it has always been said this way, and as we have seen, it hasn't always been affirmed this way. Likewise, I do not value tradition highly enough to parrot it because it is politically expedient to do so. Truth needs to be driven by other than tradition and power politics. In this, I show myself in my systematic theology method to be identified with Biblical theology methodology as a critical realist. In fact, my appreciation for Lakatos' method of science reflects my desire to grow traditions beyond themselves by progressively following the Biblical text and good reasoning wherever they will lead. If there is no Biblical text reason to maintain a tradition, and no other warranted epistemic reason to grant it, then this bit of theology should be jettisoned as an archaic and degenerative tradition. To not follow this practice leaves us open to being accused of maintaining a post-modern religious convention. For example, Richard Lints describes evangelicalism to be principled pluralism in very modest post-modern ways; each community owns its own belief system with tolerance to other communal perspectives and biases, provided they respect that the Bible is the Word of God.[180] Aren't a number of commitments in evangelicalism essentially post-modern?

3.7. Post-Modern

As a term "post-modern" emerged in the 1890's as a critique of modern architecture but expanded to describe a range of emerging existential views from Fyodor Dostoevsky's voice through Ivan Karamazov[181] and Friedrich Nietzsche's philosophy. This existential post-modernity saw that whatever we choose to authentically fit ourselves is permitted provided you have the will and the power to accomplish it. In 1926, Bernard Bell provided the earliest philosophical critique of this existential post-modernism. Bell argued that there were resources for truth in modern epistemology that warrant our truth claims without reducing

179 Bruce Demarest and Gordon Lewis, *Integrative Theology* (Grand Rapids: Zondervan, 1987), pp. 277–79.

180 Richard Lints, *The Fabric of Theology: A Prolegomenon to Evangelical Theology* (Eugene: Wipf and Stock Publishers, 1999), pp. 97–98.

181 Fyodor Mikhailovich Dostoevsky, *The Brothers Karamazov* (Chicago: Encyclopedia Britannica, 1952).

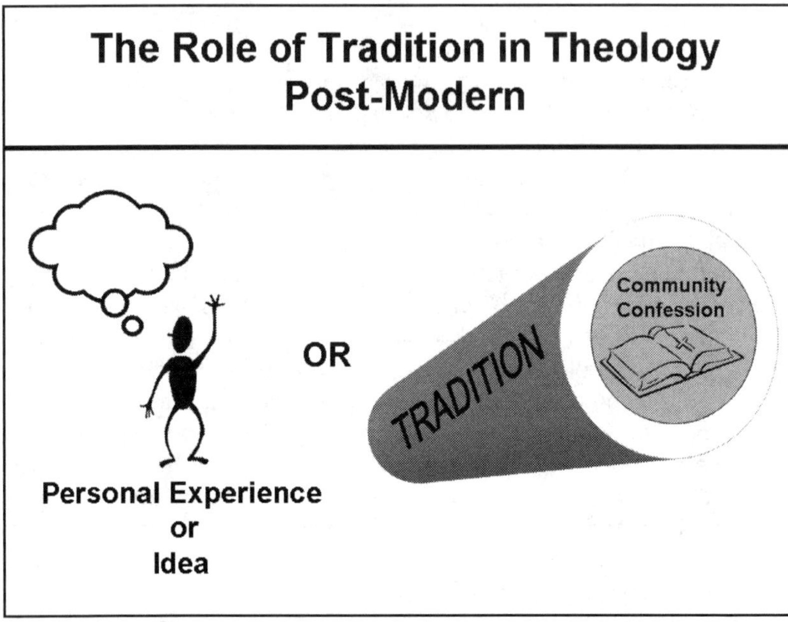

things essentially to choice.[182] This trajectory is already developed somewhat under that of Tillich and Tracy, but there are a host of more radical expressions that pursue this further, to populate the post-modern zoo. I surveyed some of these options in the previous chapter's section on existentialism. However, for our purposes here, this existential post-modern approach commodifies belief in a radically pluralist society. With awareness that social construct is one's reality, there is a decline of the dominant tradition, as Peter Berger explains.

> The religious tradition, which previously could be authoritatively imposed, now has to be *marketed*. It must be "sold" to a clientele that is no longer constrained to "buy." The pluralist situation is, above all, a *market situation*. In it, the religious institutions become marketing agencies and the religious traditions become consumer commodities.[183]

From this perspective of the commodification of tradition, whatever would make a worldview attractive to an individual would be the sort

182 Bernard Iddings Bell, *Postmodernism and Other Essays* (Milwaukee: Morehouse Publishing Co., 1926).

183 Peter Berger, *The Sacred Canopy: Elements of a Sociological Theory of Religion* (Garden City: Doubleday, 1967), p. 138; cf. Reginald Bibby, *Fragmented Gods: The Poverty and Potential of Religion in Canada* (Toronto: Irwin, 1987); David Lyon, *Postmodernity* (Minneapolis: University of Minnesota Press/ Buckingham: Open University Press, 1994), ch. 4.

of thing that would motivate worldview allegiance. This tends to place epistemic skills on the level of an existential aesthetic.

In 1947, Ludwig Wittgenstein pioneered a functional approach to language which is hailed as the watershed for the conventional form post-modernism. Wittgenstein's language games are conventional traditions. These traditions "come into existence, and others become obsolete and get forgotten."[184] Each game has its form of life and it's rules, which contextualize it so that it makes sense.

George Lindbeck's "cultural-linguistic" model of religion proposes that for a community's tradition becomes its own grammar.[185] Such tradition as grammar becomes the necessary condition for cognition and experience to be expressed, interpreted, and understood. Faithfulness to tradition is essential, though pioneering beyond what the tradition has expressed is permitted provided the new significance is communally embraced. In this way tradition is both the essential language game and yet it does not become bondage. So tradition is the linguistic medium that makes possible descriptions of realities and formation of belief; tradition is not a catalog of those beliefs.

Stanley Grenz develops that the frame of reference to his post-modern approach is the local church.[186] Such a community has a history which when it is retold, becomes the church's narrative tradition.[187] The constitutive narrative begins "with the primal events that called the community into being, and includes the crucial milestones that mark its subsequent trajectory...The act of reciting reconstitutes the community in the present as the contemporary embodiment of a communal tradition that spans the years."[188] However, the community tradition includes communal hopes for a future that motivates them toward what they consider would fully actualize the community.

> The community history does not end in the past, but extends into the future. As a result, a community turns the gaze of its members toward the future, anticipating the continuation of, and even the further development of the community. Not only does the community sense that it is moving toward an ideal that lies yet before it, more importantly, it expectantly looks to the ideal or "eschatological" future, when the purpose and goals–the *telos*–of the community will be fully actualized.

---

184 Ludwig Wittgenstein, *Philosophical Investigations* (New York: Macmillan Publishing Co., 1953, 1958), p. 11, #23.

185 George Lindbeck, *The Nature of Doctrine: Religion and Theology in a Postliberal Age* (Philadelphia: Westminster, 1984), pp. 32–41, 79–88.

186 Stanley Grenz, "Ecclesiology" in *The Cambridge Companion to Postmodern Theology*. edited by Kevin Vanhoozer (Cambridge: The Cambridge University Press, 2003), pp. 252–268.

187 Stanley Grenz, "Ecclesiology" in *Postmodern Theology*, p. 255.

188 Stanley Grenz, "Ecclesiology" in *Postmodern Theology*, p. 255.

> This expectation of a glorious future serves as an ongoing admonition to its members to embody the communal vision in the present.[189]

It is in the distinct community tradition that Grunlan and Mayers identify that there are "rites of intensification" which function to "bring the community together, increase group solidarity, and reinforce commitment to the beliefs of the group."[190] So each community portrays its own distinct form of post-modernism.

For example, John Milbank calls the Christian community back to a radical orthodoxy.[191] This radical orthodoxy is a return to tradition with a new twist on the kind and level of questions it asks. This radical orthodoxy is possible by reframing superficial secularism by Christian language games.[192] Radical orthodoxy resituates these areas of secular dominance through a Christian perspective, in phenomenal terms of Trinity, Christology, the Church and the Eucharist.[193] The repeatable tradition is that of our corporate phenomenal experiences. In this, there is no warrant for the unique things thought except the communal agreement of this group and any who would existentially choose to join them.

Kevin Vanhoozer reframes theology in this post-modern arena as community tradition theo-drama, prompted by the Spirit.[194] Church community tradition (through which its participants interpret the Bible) establishes the parameters of theo-drama. Vanhoozer appreciates George Lindbeck's sentiment "that the doctrinally significant aspect of religion resides not in propositional truths or in religious experiences 'but in the story it tells *and in the grammar that informs the way the story is told and used.*'"[195] For Vanhoozer this tradition has more focus on life patterns than propositional doctrine; *"What theology now describes is not the 'final form' of the text but the 'form of life' in which the biblical*

---

189 Stanley Grenz, "Ecclesiology" in *Postmodern Theology*, p. 256.

190 Stephen Grunlan and Marvin Mayers, *Cultural Anthropology: A Christian Perspective* (Grand Rapids: Zondervan, 1988, 2nd edition), p. 222.

191 The critical role of removing the excess is especially seen in John Milbank, *Theology & Social Theory: Beyond Secular Reason* (Oxford: Backwell, 1990). While the positive project of rebuilding is especially evident in *Radical Orthodoxy: A New Theology*, edited by John Milbank, Catherine Pickstock and Graham Ward (London: Routledge, 1999).

192 John Milbank, Graham Ward and Catherine Pickstock, "Introduction" and Conor Cunningham "LANGUAGE: Wittgenstein after Theology" in *Radical Orthodoxy*, pp. 6–7, 71–87.

193 Cunningham, "LANGUAGE: Wittgenstein after Theology" in *Radical Orthodoxy*, p. 85.

194 Kevin Vanhoozer, *The Drama of Doctrine: A Canonical-Linguistic Approach to Christian Theology* (Louisville: Westminster John Knox Press, 2005).

195 Kevin Vanhoozer (*The Drama of Doctrine*, p. 172) quotes and adds the italics to *The Drama of Doctrine*, p. George Lindbeck, *Nature of Doctrine: Religion and Theology in a Postliberal Age* (Philadelphia: Westminster Press, 1984), p. 80.

language games function as Scripture."[196] In this, tradition's role in theology frees its participants to improvise within it. Vanhoozer calls for "creative fidelity" or "ruled spontaneity"; *"The directions drawn by Scripture's normative specification of the theo-drama enable the church to improvise, as it were, with a script."*[197] Within the church's community tradition, theology works out and converses with others to enable all to enter into a more intimate and growing relationship in Christ.

In the previous chapter Robert Webber developed millennial Younger Evangelical leadership as emerging with a more post-modern congregational approach, so I won't repeat myself here. Is postmodernism the future traditional approach of evangelicalism?

3.7.1. Exampled in Trinity Development

Procession and generation are largely irrelevant fossils for the post-moderns, for in this neo-Barthian realm, existential relevance and phenomenal language games dominate. David Cunningham summarizes the post-modern approach to trinity to emphasize: 1) relationality, 2) difference, and 3) rhetoric.[198] In rejecting a modern penchant for division and isolation, he proposes that the post-modern is concerned for relation. "To speak of 'Father' or 'Son' is not to speak of an individual who is potentially isolated from other individuals; rather, the two terms specify *relations* that depend absolutely on *each other* for their meaning."[199] These relations constitute their difference. With regard to rhetoric, Cunningham agrees with Wittgenstein when he says, "*Practice* gives the words their sense."[200] For example, Lindbeck's Yale school tells the narrative of the Son's coming from the Father during the incarnation and the continuance of the salvific struggle when he sends His tag team partner the Spirit to intimately work within us and complete our salvation.

Likewise, Milbank's post-modernism does not even mention procession or generation. Milbank's team explores at greater depth the intimacy in which the phenomenal reality of Mary is impregnated with the Word of God, thus turning the *eros* toward the world through enrapturing bodies into new mystical *agape* love for the infinite.[201] Sensual love woos toward the divine mystical experience which is the only love to continue to enrapture our souls. This wooing is part of the

---

196 Kevin Vanhoozer, *The Drama of Doctrine,* p. 172, italics his.

197 Kevin Vanhoozer, *The Drama of Doctrine,* p. 129, italics his.

198 David Cunningham, "The Trinity" in *The Cambridge Companion to Postmodern Theology*, pp. 186–195.

199 David Cunningham, "The Trinity" in *Postmodern Theology*, p. 189.

200 David Cunningham, "The Trinity" in *Postmodern Theology*, p. 195.

201 Gerard Loughlin, "EROTICS: God's sex" in *Radical Orthodoxy,* pp. 147–50.

superior friendship which the Son provides in His incarnate intimacy with the creation and especially the Christian.[202]

Webber identifies the paradigm theologian for the younger evangelicals to be Stanley Grenz.[203] While the "younger evangelicals" may not have published on Trinity, at least Grenz has identified his commitment to a social Trinity model that reflects the younger evangelicals concern for authentic relationship. Grenz sees the Trinity as "the sine qua non of the Christian faith."[204] He follows Barth's emphasis on the economic Trinity and Frei's narrative theology's 'Revelational Trinitarianism,' appreciating Trinity as developed in the life and experience of the first century.

> The early Christians faced a grave theological problem, namely how to reconcile their inherited commitment to a confession of the one God with the lordship of Jesus Christ and the experience of the Spirit. Far from a philosophical abstraction, therefore, the doctrine of the Trinity was the culmination of an attempt on the part of the church to address the central theological question regarding the content of the Christian faith, a question that arose out of the experience of the earliest followers of Jesus.[205]

He then advocates a social Trinity model pioneered by Leonard Hodgson and developed into academic awareness as a rival model by Jürgen Moltmann.[206] He follows Moltmann and Robert Jenson, who advocate "the idea that God finds his identity in the temporal events of the economy of salvation."[207] In this development, procession and generation are

202 David Moss, "FRIENDSHIP: St. Anselm, *theoria and the convolution of sense,"* in *Radical Orthodoxy,* pp. 147–42.

203 Robert Webber, *The Younger Evangelicals* (Grand Rapids: Baker, 2002), p. 92.

204 Stanley Grenz and John Franke, *Beyond Foundationalism: Shaping Theology in a Postmodern Context* (Louisville: Westminster John Knox Press, 2001), p. 170.

205 Grenz and Franke, *Beyond Foundationalism,* p. 173.

206 Leonard Hodgson, *The Doctrine of the Trinity: Croall Lectures, 1942–1943* (New York: Charles Scribner's Sons, 1944), especially pp. 49–55, 69–77, and 176–194 where Hodgson used social metaphors to express a trinity view that emphasized a Barthian economic model and an adoptionist Christ; Jürgen Moltmann, *The Trinity and the Kingdom* (San Francisco: Harper and Row, 1981) proposed a full scale social trinitarianistic model; cf. Cornelius Plantinga, Jr. "The Hodgson-Welch Debate and the Social Analogy of the Trinity" (Ph. D. dissertation Princeton Theological Seminary, 1982), pp. 49–57, especially p. 51; Royce Gordon Gruenler, *The Trinity in the Gospel of John: A Thematic Commentary on the Fourth Gospel* (Grand Rapids: Baker Book House, 1986); and Cornelius Plantinga, "Social Trinity and Tritheism" in *Trinity, Incarnation and Atonement: Philosophical & Theological* Essays edited by Ronald J. Feenstra and Cornelius Plantinga (Notre Dame: University of Notre Dame, 1989), which are polished presentations from a conference at Marquette University in 1988.

207 Grenz and Franke, *Beyond Foundationalism,* p. 191.

ancient traditional fossils replaced by living relationality. So the core idea of person is Catherine LaCugna's "toward another," which means that the essence of Trinity is "in relation to another.[208] Which implies that the Trinity is essentially a community of love.[209] Furthermore, the Trinity has structural implications for Grenz in defining the image of God as that of relationality in humans.[210] The result of this awareness is that we should strive for fellowship and community.

3.8. Conclusion

Each approach had a role for tradition. Tradition is not neutral but tends to frame one's vision through which the person sees the world and God. I believe that the post-modern's are the most honest about the way terminology works sociologically on a community. However, as a critical realist I believe that truth value of terms should correspond to the essential reality to the extent that it is accessible. I believe that truth is accessible with critical precision upon moderate foundations. I believe that the scholarly precision of the Biblical theologians and scholarly exegetes is the most Biblical in their passionate practice to warrant their views in the Biblical text in its context, as the Word of God. I acknowledge that this commitment to Biblicism is a form of tradition that describes me, but such a tradition does not bind to rigidity when good peer reviewed exegesis lead otherwise. When the other views on tradition lose this Biblical warrant, and they all do at times, then they appear as just another post-modern language game, fitted to a traditional community, but degenerative in that they insulate that community from the truth of the Bible. As a critical realist, that draws me back to the methodology of the Biblical theologian. It is this method that also best exemplifies the spirit of the Reformation, which is also a traditional descriptive for me. However, as a Christian, I am committed to tolerance and love for those who disagree with me.

208 Catherine LaCugna, *God for Us: The Trinity and the Christian Life* (San Francisco: Harper Collins, 1991), pp. 14–15; Grenz and Franke, *Beyond Foundationalism*, pp. 193–194.

209 Grenz and Franke, *Beyond Foundationalism*, p. 195.

210 Grenz and Franke, *Beyond Foundationalism*, pp. 197–202.

4. A Thiselton-Ricoeur Hermeneutic[1]

As we approach the hermeneutical task, one of two questions is often asked. Some ask, "How *do* people interpret?" whereas others ask, "How *should* we interpret?" Those who wish us to explore how people *do* interpret recognize that any text functions on more than a propositional level and that truth can be existentially relational truth. In evangelicalism, as in classical philosophy, there is a recognition that truth is stated through propositions. Wittgenstein has reminded us that words, terms, or metaphors are not themselves the conveyor of information. Information comes in full sentences which contextualize a term to its language game and affirms a complement about this subject. For example, the word "run" may refer variously to stockings, baseball, a track and field event or an automobile. The rest of a sentence provides the language game that provides it with meaning. The metaphor "fleecing the sheep" may refer either to a dutiful farmer who removes the excess wool from his sheep or an abusive pastor; the rest of the proposition identifies the language game and thus provides its meaning.

A univocal proposition such as "God is holy" is defined by the Hebrew word *qadosh* (קָדוֹשׁ)which designates God to be a metaphysically separate being. Biblically, God's holiness is not defined by extrapolating a finite holiness into the infinite, rather that God as holy epitomizes and defines the category of holiness within which we minutely instance the trait, after the pattern: "Be holy as I am holy says the Lord" (1 Pet. 1:16). Likewise, an analogical proposition like, "The Lord is my shepherd" presents a figure that can be generalized as "The Lord is my provider and protector." However, to rephrase a figure in univocal ways loses something of the vividness of the statement. The figure can be sung, has emotional appeal and a clarity that connects the reader personally to the text. Likewise, the relationship of a series of propositions could be generalized into a proposition as a grand figure, such as a literary climax or a narrative turn, but one loses something of its vividness when you restate it in a precise proposition. The quality of vividness includes the

1 An earlier version of this chapter was my presidential address from the Mid-West region of the Evangelical Theological Society and then published in Doug Kennard, *The Relationship Between Epistemology, Hermeneutics, Biblical Theology and Contextualization* (Lewiston: Mellen Press, 1999), pp. 117–152. The names were chosen for their distinct contribution in hermeneutical theory and practice, and their appreciation for the other's contribution. Cf. notes 2 and 3.

experiential roller coaster as you existentially ride the narrative through its dips and turns.

The performative statement, "I now pronounce you man and wife," said by the appropriate person in the appropriate context even creates new propositional truth that was not true of the individuals a moment before. When my wife and I got to our honeymoon hotel our first night we found a hand lettered sign from my Dad. Its message had been communicated to my Dad by his soon-to-be-father-in-law prior to marrying my Mom. It said, "Marriage is like farming. You don't know what you're getting into 'til it's too late." This aphorism has a metaphor followed by a univocal statement. Both univocal statement and metaphor are meaningful to me and warm me as I reflect upon their truth and impact in my own life. Without denying or diminishing anything of these propositional truths, there seems to me to be a vivid existential, relational subjectively contextualized quality of truth which is also not extinguished by such propositional truth. So Jan and I entered into knowing each other intimately, beyond engagement, beyond sexuality, intimately in relationship: rejoicing, weeping, amazed together of the wonder, crying together in the hurt, intuitively, sensitively, promising, repenting, knowing the other even when the other does not speak. So it is also with God and us, with the Biblical text. God communicates with proposition, symbol from within a context and genre. He communicates to us through this process in the text, so that we would understand the text and be drawn into a greater depth of relationship with Him.

My hermeneutical approach could be called a Thiselton-Ricoeur hermeneutic in that this hybrid seems to express significant qualities with which I have also furnished my interpretational model. The foundational hermeneutic spiral within authorial context is deeply indebted to Thiselton or those like Grant Osborne who cross the same terrain.[2] The exegetical aspect to this approach is organized by me through a sophisticated falsification identified with Lakatos scientific method and a linguistic appropriation of Peircian pragmatism. The relational or existential aspects of my hermeneutic are indebted to Ricoeur's understandings in a context of dissatisfaction with existential reader-oriented approaches.[3] My hermeneutic has a third level that recognizes

2 Anthony Thiselton, *The Two Horizons: New Testament Hermeneutics and Philosophical Description* (Grand Rapids: Eerdmans, 1980); cf. Grant Osborne, *The Hermeneutical Spiral* (Downers Grove: InterVarsity, 1991).

3 Paul Ricoeur, *Essays on Biblical Interpretation* (Philadelphia: Fortress Press, 1980; *Interpretation Theory: Discourse and the Surplus of Meaning* (Fort Worth: The Texas Christian University Press, 1976); *The Symbolism of Evil* (Boston: Beacon Press, 1967); *The Conflict of Interpretations* (Evanston: Northwestern University Press, 1974); *Time and Narrative*. volumes 1–3, (Chicago: University of Chicago, 1984, 1985, 1988); *Hermeneutics & the Human Sciences* (Cambridge: Cambridge University Press, 1981); excellent summaries of Ricoeur's hermeneutic are presented by: Kevin Vanhoozer (*Biblical Narrative in the Philosophy of Paul Ricoeur: A*

my context cannot be so easily fused with that of the text as Gadamer presented[4] because we live in a multicultural world and such a simplistic naiveté means that the text is kidnapped by the reader's context into multicultural language games and loses all but a few strands of truth along the way. Contextualization work such as that by Hesselgrave is instrumental in negotiating contextualized truth through contextual mazes in order to retain textual truth in a relevant re-contextualized way.[5] Such contextualized understandings demand our passionate commitment, and deep trust of God in relationship. The hermeneutical process continues as a critical realist process, uniting and drawing together each of these strands into a rope whose combined strength exceeds that of adding together the individual strands. My hermeneutical model has been tested in a wide variety of Biblical text but it also has the unusual advantage of providing real aid in a wide variety of literature, even the contemporary existential literature since T. S. Elliot pioneered this approach in the early nineteen twenties.

My hermeneutical model is a three-level process wherein all three levels operate simultaneously. I find it helpful to academically draw three distinct levels of hermeneutic apart from each other, to clarify major emphases in the process and to preserve us from sloppy and premature fusing of horizons. Such careful precision helps from losing textual truth in the flood of our own context. While it is helpful to explain these as separate levels and at times to focus on certain aspects of these levels within my hermeneutic, I will illustrate them as interpenetrating each other and fleshed out as unified within me, the interpreter.

4.1. Interpretation Level One: Existential

Level One is existential in that it allows me to make varied or vivid existential connections with the text, as the reader feels placed in the story by the juxtapositioning of text close to the reader's context. I feel placed in the story by a wide variety of similarities: familiar relationships, confessional traditions, shared passion, similar experiences and overlapping contexts. Rhetorical devices enliven the text beyond mere proposition such as: space, placement, sequence, motifs, symbols,

---

Study in Hermeneutics and Theology [Cambridge: Cambridge University Press, 1990]) and Dan Stiver (*Theology After Ricoeur: New Directions in Hermeneutical Theology* [Louisville: Westminster John Knox Press, 2001); cf. Anthony Thiselton, *New Horizons in Hermeneutics: The Theory and Practice of Transforming Biblical Reading* (Grand Rapids: Zondervan, 1992).

4 Hans Gadamer, *Truth and Method* (New York: Crossroad, 1984 translated from the second edition which was originally published in German in 1965), especially in the third part, pp. 345–448.

5 David Hesselgrave. "Christian Contextualization and Biblical Theology" in Doug Kennard, *The Relationship of Epistemology, Hermeneutics, Biblical Theology and Contextualization* (Lewiston: Mellon Press, 1999), pp. 153–180; cf. David J. Hesselgrave and Edward Rommen, *Contextualization: Meanings, Methods, and Models* (Grand Rapids: Baker, 1989).

climax, dramatic turns and many more draw the reader through the roller coaster of the narrative account. Additionally, the reader might understand how another could feel placed in the story as they hear how and why the other takes the passage as they do. Perhaps other contemporary contextual perspectives, post-structuralisms, sociological analyses and mythological analysis can be helpful here to sensitize the reader to a host of possibilities but these are not the focus for they can lead away from the text to a host of post-modern reader approaches. James Dunn calls this process a "dialog" with the text, but he warns, "Unless the text is, at least in some sense, allowed to set its own agenda, it is questionable whether it is being heard at all."[6]

Such an existential connection prompts a shared passion and motivation to understand the text and work it out into life. The goal of this level is to surface and retain passion and motivation throughout the dissecting process of the other two levels. The other two levels have a kind of precision that reminds me of my biology lab back in high school. We were issued frogs to dissect so, with scalpel in hand, we went at it, making notes along the way and in the end, what did we have on the table but a lot of notes and dead frog pieces. It is quite normal to bring great precision of the hermeneutical spiral to a text and analyze the text in dissecting detail and when you have done the deed, you have notes and dead text fragments on the table. This existential level surfaces romantic and authentic passion, and motivation that connects authentically with the reader's lives; the search for truth is conducted passionately with a passion for application and relevance.

Such existential connections prompt self-understandings and self-possibilities. There is no need to de-mythologize to find contemporary relevance. There is no need to press the text through a post-structural grid in order to distance traditions by a hermeneutical suspicion. The existential connections which naturally arise as you approach the text with a new naiveté operate usually more in the positive connection, with the text juxtaposed to life, rather than in the shadow of the skeptical. I am confident that my second hermeneutical level of hermeneutic spiral in the text can supply sufficient distancing of traditions without letting such reader oriented suspicion fog the scene. Self-understandings and self-possibilities emerge naturally in the reader's life as she lets the text itself speak to her in her own context. Now at this level these self-understandings and self-possibilities are extremely relevant but may not have textual warrant, which is more supplied by critical realist qualities of the second level.

So, when colleagues claim to find principles in a text, I see them as implications from life which we surmise when our life is juxtaposed closely to a text. Principles we see are statements of our authentic life.

6 James D. G. Dunn, *Jesus Remembered* (Grand Rapids: Eerdmans, 2003), p. 124.

These principles are not divinely authoritative; they are merely existentially relevant to those who propose them. For example, colleagues of mine who preach the book of Nehemiah, claiming to find within it management principles, are not finding divinely authoritative elements in the text; they are instead finding management principles from our twenty first century context which authentically connect with them as they juxtapose the text closely to their own lives. Now I appreciate and read Drucker and other management texts, but level two's hermeneutic spiral will press the Nehemiah text in a different direction than management principles. That is, the book of Nehemiah in its context is a covenant renewal and restoration text, which in reconnecting Israel with their God is a far more significant vertical relationship than the horizontal tidbits we find within our own lives and unfortunately claim as coming from the text.

This existential level of hermeneutics was powerfully brought home to me several years ago as I sat in a colleague's American Literature class. For some reason we read Robert Frost's poem "Out, out" three times during the semester. On a level two analysis the title is seen as alluding to Shakespeare's Macbeth, Act V, lines 23–25, "Out, out brief candle life's but a walking shadow; a poor player that struts and frets his hour upon the stage, and then is heard no more; it is a tale told by an idiot; full of sound and fury signifying nothing." Clearly from such an allusion, Frost's poem is about the vapor of life with its transitoriness and ultimate meaninglessness. I could approach the poem with a hermeneutical spiral noticing: 1) *the details from the author's context*, for instance, that Frost wrote the poem in 1916, in the midst of World War I; 2) *textual details* such as the progressions "little-less-nothing? and that ended it." as life comes to an end, and 3) *the big picture* of the poem as describing a boy who cuts off his hand and dies. However, such analysis can kill the poem if that is all there is. Somewhere in the process it is helpful to let the poem perform its purpose by reading it for all its vividness and voice. So, if you will allow, let us read, "Out, out" by Robert Frost.

The buzz saw snarled and rattled in the yard
And made dust and dropped stove-length sticks of wood,
Sweet-scented stuff when the breeze drew across it.
And from there those that lifted eyes could count
Five mountain ranges one behind the other
Under the sunset far into Vermont.
And the saw snarled and rattled, snarled and rattled,
As it ran light, or had to bear a load.
And nothing happened: day was all but done.
Call it a day, I wish they might have said
To please the boy by giving him the half hour
That a boy counts so much when saved from work.
His sister stood beside them in her apron

To tell them "Supper." At the word, the saw,
As if to prove saws knew what supper meant,
Leaped out at the boy's hand, or seemed to leap—
He must have given the hand. However it was,
Neither refused the meeting. But the hand?
The boy's first outcry was a rueful laugh,
As he swung toward them holding up the hand,
Half in appeal, but half as if to keep
The life from spilling. Then the boy saw all—
Since he was old enough to know, big boy
Doing a man's work, though a child at heart—
He saw all spoiled. "Don't let him cut my hand off—
The doctor, when he comes. Don't let him, sister?"
So. But the hand was gone already.
The doctor put him in the dark of ether.
He lay and puffed his lips out with his breath.
And then–the watcher at his pulse took fright.
No one believed. They listened at his heart.
Little–less–nothing? –and that ended it.
No more to build on there. And they, since they
Were not the one dead, turned to their affairs.

The vividness of the poem draws me in for I use a chain saw to cut my own firewood. I too know what it is to put in a hard day of physical labor and be called for supper. But that semester we read this poem three times and unknown to this colleague of mine I was up a large dead tree four times during that semester, each time precariously wrapped around that large tree, six feet beyond the last rung of my extension ladder, cutting 16" diameter branches with my chain saw snarling at the wood only inches in front of my face. Each time, you know what I was thinking: "Out, Out" with a vividness that screamed out to me from a self-understanding of my own temporality and frailty and self-possibilities, "You better be careful, or you too will be 'Little-less-nothing' with death taking you." The poem "Out, out" was extremely relevant and existentially vivid to me even though Frost probably did not intend for the poem to be a mother's warning when chain sawing is being done. Its siren cry as understood from my context was vivid and relevant and that is part of the hermeneutical process.

4.2. Interpretation Level Two: Textual Critical Realism

Hermeneutics is a spiral within the authorial context, which oscillates between contextual overviews and textual particulars as it tries to clarify the meaning of the text. This is a critical realist approach to text inductively observing the particulars which the text presents. Such induction does not empirically try to get behind the text as one might to bridge Lessing's ugly ditch and apologetically recover the historical Jesus. Instead, such induction is comfortable in recovering the accounts of the witnesses with their theological biases and inductively understanding these texts from the thought forms which these authors portray. These Biblical theological thought forms serve as an epistemic base from which to implement a textually grounded pragmatism (as Charles Peirce located an empirically grounded pragmatism) fueling the hermeneutical spiral. N.T. Wright defends that this is a critical realist's *dialogue* with a text.[7] The dialog begins with a Peircian pragmatic proposal which tries to reflect the details of the Biblical text. That is, such overview generalizations (such as context, narrative themes and Biblical theology) which the interpreter proposes are funded by the textual particulars in the author's context rather than from subjective needs of the interpreter's context and life. In fact, nearly all that is known about the context comes from the text itself. When we take up an excellent commentary and it gives testimony to a book being written to a specific audience (which is wrestling with specific issues), nearly everything that an excellent commentary says about the context is obtained directly from the Biblical book itself. The commentator is answering the question, "What would the original audience need to be like for the Biblical author to say what he says to them?" This means that most of the contextual understanding a modern reader can have for a Biblical text is actually framed inter-textually from the Biblical text.

However, an occasional instance in the O.T. or N.T. of extra-textual contextual information does inform the context of a Biblical text in ways which might effect the interpretation. For example, in Revelation 3:15–16, Jesus accuses the church of Laodicea as being neither hot, nor cold but lukewarm under the metaphor of water since the luke-warm water will be spit out of His mouth. The Laodicean context enjoyed the refreshing hot baths so sought after in the Roman world but more available here, since a hot spring provided their water a mile out of town. Another form of refreshment was that of cool refreshing drinking water. However, the main source of drinking water in Laodicea was the hot spring piped to town, providing a distasteful luke-warm mineral water. The archaeological context helps the reader to recognize that "hot" and "cold" are both metaphors of refreshment.[8] Additionally, the "luke-warm" condition is one that the Laodiceans can relate to on a physical level and may be vivid enough to motivate revulsion. Often when such a contextual fact is known extra-biblically it is known through the testimony of a source somewhat removed from that text and historical instance. However, it is

7 N. T. Wright, *The New Testament and the People of God* (London: SPCK, 1992), pp. 31–46.

8 David Aune (*Revelation. Word Biblical Commentary* vol. 52A [Dallas: Word Books, 1997], p. 257) cites M. J. S. Rudwick and E. M. B. Green, "The Laodicean Lukewarmness," *Expository Times* 69(1957–58): 176–78.

in the thrust of the text that this Laodicean condition is applied to their lack of zealous good deeds. The author develops their poverty into a blindness which only Christ can resolve.

Narrative themes and Biblical theology are also generalizations of individual Biblical author's texts. Such generalizations are cognitive ideas so I see real value in stating them in full sentences rather than one word (e.g., center) so that the communication of a clear idea can be accomplished and concerned that clear truths can be understood, communicated and warranted rather than an ambiguous word or phrase which any reader takes in the way he would like. Interpretations have the possibility of being understood when they are clearly stated. Understanding these as generalization frames Biblical theology as our attempt to understand the text in its original context rather than conjecturing something like Hirsch's authorial intent or post-structuralism's deep structures which in effect claim to know something prior to the text, such as something in the author's mind. Philosophically, I don't think we can obtain an authoritative intention prior to the text, and evangelically, it is the text which has authority and is the means of providing warrant. Clarence Walhout has rehabbed the Hirshian *authorial intent* to be the *textual thrust,* which still closes down the abuses of a reader-response hermeneutic.[9]

To claim to know an authorial intent prior to the text is prideful self-deception. However, if the author tells us in the text why he wrote, as John or Luke does, then we have an authoritative textual statement which can be known to be true but not necessarily the *whole* truth. Luke may have wanted to write his gospel for more reasons than the historically accurate conveying of Jesus' life, death and resurrection but such extra-textual conjectures of authorial intent are unwarranted and therefore unprofitable for understanding the Biblical text even though they help us understand our existential possibilities. If we leave such comments as descriptive generalizations of the text, then they are helpful as we recognize that Luke's text adds a unique valuing of the poor, of women and of Mary over the other synoptic gospels.

For an interpretation to be meaningful, it needs to be coherent, for contradictory statements in the same time and the same way are logically impossible, and cannot be true. Contradictories should not be believed (for one is not properly functioning if he believes such contradictory statements). In this coherence the internal relatedness of the interpretation needs to hang together.

This is not to shave away complexity for an arbitrary simplicity using Ocham's razor or Duhem's theoretical approach. One thing our post-modern age has shown us is that truth is often complex; the truths of relativity or quantum mechanics are complex, and the Biblical text is

9 Roger Ludin, Clarence Walhout, and Anthony Thiselton, *The Promise of Hermeneutics* (Grand Rapids: Eerdmans, 1999), part II.

also often complex, too. This means that an interpretation of a Biblical text should reflect the complexity evident in the text, and of course not be arbitrarily complex. But here the warrant for the interpretation is provided by correspondence to the textual support. This correspondence compares one's interpretation to the text being interpreted. Such a correspondence should not be a naive opinion that one's interpretation is identical to the text as, say, a reader response or Gadamer's fusing horizons. Rather, such correspondence in interpretation needs to be concerned about factors like comprehensiveness (which raises the question, "How well does an interpretation fit with all the particulars of the text") and factors such as congruity (which raises the question of "How appropriate is the interpretation fit with the textual particulars it is trying to describe"). Using these features of correspondence, we can recognize in a critical realist way that our knowledge of the textual data is partial but can be true.

We are aided in this because unlike empirical sense data which is interpreted differently by a plurality of worldviews, a text has its interpretation contained in the grammar, proposition, figure and rhetoric of the text continually attempting to bring our interpretation through successive corresponding paradigms which bring us to closer approximations of the truth of the text. These further comparisons contribute assurances of increasing plausibility, warranting our interpretation as highly plausible in obtaining the author's interpretation and application evident in the text to his intended audience. This application is immediately emerging from and identical to the ethical component of the interpretation, so interpretation and application do not differ, they are consistent expressions of each other. Within this correspondence the hermeneutical spiral involves the interpreter with overview generalizations they have previously made such as contextual features or Biblical theology generalizations from successively removed contexts in the Biblical book, author, genre, progressive revelation phase, and in the testament (O.T. or N.T.).

Notice, systematic theology should not be brought into this spiral, for no systematic theology is a-historically true; they are all colored by their historical context, as I developed in the previous two chapters. For example, Augustine's theology is wonderful but it reflects neo-platonic strands. Aquinas' theology is wonderful but it reflects Aristotelian thought forms throughout. Calvin's theology is wonderful but one may wonder whether his concept of the sovereignty of God is a reaction against the Roman Catholic sovereignty of the Pope. Luther's theology is wonderful but one can see legal concepts perhaps more indebted to his legal training, than which are actually in the texts of some N.T. authors. I obviously don't agree with everything of these four theologians, though I respect them deeply, but at this point systematic theology needs to be kept at bay, for the theological overview appraisal (of Level Two) is the domain of Biblical theology.

To illustrate the features working in my interpretation Level Two, I turn to the Biblical theme of forgiveness and the narrative of Matthew 18:21–35. I go to this passage because it is difficult and requires proper hermeneutical technique to get it right. When I learned to rock climb I learned on at a place where if you did not use the proper technique you would come off the cliff (of course held by a belay rope). So a difficult passage like this helps to accentuate proper hermeneutical technique.

As we approach the concept of forgiveness we realize that there is a passionate attraction to forgiveness among many at an existential level. Ernest Hemingway once told a story about the popularity of the Spanish name Paco. A father put an ad in a Madrid newspaper which read, "Paco, meet me at Hotel Montana noon Wednesday. All is forgiven, Papa." The next day a squadron of Civic Guards was needed to disperse the mob of 800 young men amassed at the Hotel. Forgiveness captures our longing and desire.

Moving to the level of textual study in the authorial context, the concept of forgiveness is developed by the verb ἀφίημι and the noun . Eighty percent (116x) of all instances (144x) of ἀφίημι are in the synoptic gospels and eighty percent (129x) of all instances (163x) of both words are in the synoptic gospels and Acts. So a synoptic Biblical theology will heavily frame the concept, and one needs to be careful not to define the concept by the mere 5% of instances that are Pauline uses or by some larger systematic theology expression like that indebted to Luther or Melanchthon. This non-use by other N. T. authors cannot be attributed to non use elsewhere, for the word is used amply in classical Greek and in the LXX as release and forgiveness. So the word use reflects a theological emphasis that the synoptic gospels especially convey.

The word ἀφίημι has a strong relational sense. In 67% of the N.T. uses it is used of leaving or permitting people to move from something. The word is most used for leaving, as in, the disciples *left* their nets (Matt. 4:20, 22; Mark 1:18, 20) and the disciples *left* everything (Matt. 19:27–29; Mark 10:28–29; Luke 5:11; 18:28-29). Abundant relational examples could be multiplied such as the fever *left* him (Matt. 8:15; Mark 1:31; Luke 4:39; John 4:52), some people will be *left* to go into the eschatological kingdom when others are taken away in judgment (Matt. 24:40–41; Luke 17:34–36). Jesus *left* Judea (John 4:3), the woman *left* her water pot (John 4:28) and all the disciples *left* Jesus and fled (Matt. 26:56; Mark 14:50).

This relational distancing may at times have a more active quality like Jesus' *sending* the multitude away (Matt. 13:36; Mark 4:36). At times the relational sense of the word has to do with permitting something to happen: *to allow* the children *to come* (Matt. 19: 14; Mark 10:14; Luke 18:16), *allow* Mary to anoint Jesus for burial (Mark 14:6; John

12:7), or Jesus would not *allow* people *to follow* him (Mark 5:37; 11:16; Luke 8:51). Such a relational sense could also have a more active sense of exclusion, like the religious leaders who *omit* or *neglect* God's commandments (Matt. 23:23; Mark 7:8; Luke 11:42). With such a strong relational sense ἀφίημι does not really have a reformation legal sense of justification, rather *relational release* is more in view of *letting go* or *permitting an offense to pass from you*. This reflects the LXX use of ἀφίημι, which *lets go* (Judg. 3:1), *leaves* (Judg. 9:9, 11, 13; 2 Sam. 15:16; 20:3; Ps. 17:14) *permits to happen* (2 Sam. 16:10) and *releases* in the year of release (Deut. 15:2). The LXX uses fifty times with 22 instances in Leviticus 25 and 27 (for Hebrew *ywbl*/יוֹבֵל, year of jubilee) and 5 times in Deuteronomy 15:1–9 (for Hebrew *shm'h*/שְׁמִטָּה, release from debt in the year of jubilee). So that, though the concept is used in a legal sense, the meaning has to do with someone relationally releasing the indebtedness of another. Now this meaning does have legal consequences but not in a spiritual, positional level (true for all time) but more on a relational level (no longer obligated in the debt). In general, is used of releasing captives and slaves (Isa. 61:1, quoted in Luke 4:18–19; Jer. 34:8, 15, 17; Ezek. 46:17). Only once does appear in a sense that might be taken as forgiveness (Lev. 16:26 for *'z'zl*/עֲזָאזֵל) but that sense probably is merely the *sending away* of the scapegoat. is used only rarely in the LXX for forgiveness. When it occurs it translates *nś'*/נָשָׂא "to bear away" or "to release from guilt or punishment" (Gen. 13:6; Pss. 25:18; 32:1, 5; 85:2; Isa. 33:24) or *slh*/סָלַח, "to forgive or pardon" (Lev. 4:20; 5:6; Num. 14:19; 15:25; Isa. 55:7) or *kpr*/כִּפֵּר, "to cover or make atonement" (Isa. 22:14). One of the two references of Hebrews use of is the reminder that one may almost say that all things are cleansed with blood and without the shedding of blood there is no forgiveness (Heb. 9:22). While the sacrificial system with its blood atonement is norma1 for atonement, there are exceptions that do not require blood for atonement (Lev. 5:11–13; Num. 16:46; 31:50). The only instance where Paul uses ἀφίημι of forgiveness is a direct quote of the LXX from Ps. 32:1 in Romans 4:7; so that Pauline justification with its positional conventional quality does not inform the relational real forgiveness of allowing the offense to pass from the person, turning to a narrative text and letting it perform its purpose by calling us into its worldview, perhaps changing our perspective.

The relational concept of forgiveness is especially apparent in the kingdom parable Jesus tells in response to Peter asking about the extent it is necessary for him to forgive (Matt. 18:21–35). In the context, church discipline corrects individuals so that they would not be damned but actually gain kingdom. Peter realizes that such perspective of forgiveness requires forgiving a brother. Peter thinks maybe a magnanimous seven times of forgiveness is sufficient and out of interpretation Level One we may think so as well but Jesus virtually says to continue to forgive an indefinite number of times without counting (which is the meaning of the figure of seventy times seven). To press this point home Jesus compares the kingdom to a certain king who wished to settle accounts with his slaves. One slave owed ten thousand talents or virtually the national debt (since a talent was about 58-80 pounds of precious metal, such as gold). This slave did not have the means to repay so the lord commanded that he, his wife, his children and all that he has be sold to recoup a slight part of the loss. The slave fell down, prostrating himself before his lord saying, "Have patience with me, and I will repay you everything." The lord of the slave felt compassion and released him and forgave him the debt. The slave went out and found a fellow slave who owed him a hundred denarii, which from the ancient Near Eastern context is roughly a hundred days' wages for a laborer, and seized him, putting a choke hold on him and saying, "Pay back what you owe." So his fellow slave fell down and began to entreat him saying, "Have patience with me and I will repay you." The first slave was unwilling, however, and instead had him thrown in prison until he should pay back what was owed. Such a debtor's prison in the first century does not pay the debt, it merely removes the person from being able to earn money so that family and friends might step forward to pay the debt. His fellow slaves were deeply grieved over what had happened so they reported it to their lord. The lord summoned the slave saying, "You wicked slave, I forgave you all that debt because you entreated me. Should you not also have had mercy on your fellow slave, even as I had mercy on you?" His lord's forgiveness and the condition of fellow suffering under indebtedness were available motives to forgive. His lord, moved with anger handed him over to the torturers until he should repay all that was owed him, which, of course, is an everlasting torment in debtors' prison since there is no possible way that he could pay the equivalent of the national debt. Described this way, this is obviously a damnation metaphor. From interpretation Level One (such as from our systematic theology) we may think how inappropriate the lord is in forgiving and re-obligating a slave for this debt, but in the ancient Near East context, a master has the right to do this. The really shocking thing about this parable is not what the individuals do in the parable, but it is the next verse, "So shall My heavenly Father also do to you, if each of you does not forgive his brother from your heart." Jesus develops that the everlasting destiny of being relationally forgiven by the Father is contingent upon our having the virtue of forgiveness. That this is salvific forgiveness and not some unrelated family forgiveness is quite clear since in the near context the issue is repeatedly between damnation in everlasting hell fire or gaining the kingdom at whatever cost (Matt. 18:3, 6–10, 14).

Synoptic Biblical theology helps us to see that divine salvific forgiveness is often linked to the extent at which a kingdom participant forgives others. This is not a works salvation but one of virtues such as faith, humility and forgiveness, which identify kingdom participants as those who will be everlastingly benefited in kingdom.

In Jesus teaching about forgiveness ( ) the different levels of divine and human forgiveness are intimately linked. Jesus presents this point at least three other times in a context of prayer and forgiveness: the Sermon on the Mount, when the disciples ask how to pray and when they pass by the cursed fig tree. In each instance, the Father in heaven is the One Who ultimately forgives but each instance connects His ultimate relational forgiveness of others. In the Sermon on the Mount, the disciples are to ask the Father to "Forgive us our debts as ( ) we also have forgiven our debtors" (Matt. 6:12). The request for forgiveness is done in a context where forgiveness is already done toward one's debtors, as evident by the aorist tense. The indicates "in the same manner" or "to the same degree." Divine forgiveness of the kingdom participant is linked in the same manner and degree that they evidence themselves to be forgiving people. To make sure that the disciples understand this point, Jesus emphasizes it by further teaching after the prayer: "For if you forgive men for their transgressions (παραπτώματα), your heavenly Father will also forgive you; but if you do not forgive men, then your Father will not forgive your transgressions (παραπτώματα)" (Matt. 6:14–15). The Father's forgiveness is dependent upon and to the extent that the kingdom participant forgives others. When the disciples ask Jesus to teach them to pray He instructs them in a similar manner. Request from the Father "forgive us our sins ( ) for ( ) we ourselves also forgive everyone who is indebted ( ) to us" (Luke 11:4). Using the same word for "debt" ( ) that Matthew 6:12 used, the meaning now also includes a synonym for "sins" ( ). The linkage to ask for the Father's forgiveness is evident by the ; the reason given for divine forgiveness is that the disciples also forgive others' indebtedness to themselves. In these verses, the Father's forgiveness is dependent upon the Kingdom participant forgiving others. When Jesus passes by the cursed fig tree he urges his disciples to include forgiveness in their prayer lives, "Forgive, if you have anything against anyone; so that ( ) your Father also Who is in heaven may forgive you your transgressions" (παραπτώματα; Mark 11:25).[10] The clause evidences "for the purpose that" or "so that." That is, the Father's forgiveness of the Kingdom participants' transgressions is contingent upon their forgiving anything that they have against anyone.

10 Mark 11:26 is not in the earliest and best manuscripts but it is also redundant with Matthew 6:14–15.

4.3. Interpretation Level Three: Contextual Critical Realism

Hermeneutics is a critical realist spiral from the horizon of the text to the horizon of the reader. This spiral is a textually grounded pragmatic move (like Charles Peirce proposed for warranting empirically grounded pragmatism). Funded by the interpretation of Level Two, the interpreter proposes (in a critical realist manner) about other contexts than the original one and progressively checks these proposals through a correspondence move which compares similarities of these contexts to the original context. The goal is to recover the meaning in the text to the extent that it includes me. This becomes the authoritative textual meaning for me as my interpretation and application. Such an interpretation applied to my context is also often called the significance. The critical realist significance progressively: 1) excludes any of my assumptions, understandings and possibilities which are appropriate to the text, and 2) includes in me those assumptions, understandings and possibilities which are appropriate to the text. This critical realist hermeneutical moves through successive paradigms which try to frame the authorial contextual interpretation and application to my context as its significance. To the extent that this contextualization process enables the interpreter to state his interpretation clearly and coherently, and there are similarities between the original readers and the ones of the interpreter's application, the interpreter can reassure himself with high plausibility that he has obtained the authoritative significance for the ones of the interpreter's application. The clarity of the significance helps to focus and remove ambiguity from the interpretation. Coherence makes the interpretation logically possible. Increased correspondence between the similarities of the original readers and those of the interpreter's significance progressively gain plausibility which further motivates the interpreter to understand and apply.

If we return to Matthew 18 and compare that context with our own we find Matthew and the synoptic gospels expressing a kingdom presently operative in the world. For example, the parable of the wheat and tares includes the Son of Man's interpretation that we are already in the Son of Man's kingdom, which is the world (Matt. 13:38, 41). This present expression of the kingdom will continue into an eschatological expression of the kingdom when eschatological judgment removes the lawless from the world to the furnace of fire (Matt. 13:41–43). The virtuous person following Christ's narrow way of beatitude virtues is the kingdom participant who will enter into the final kingdom expression (Matt. 5:3–12; 7:13–27; Luke 6:20–38). The synoptic gospels contain this kingdom discussion and eschatological warning not merely to inform the first century reader about what Jesus said before the cross to the disciples but so that the kingdom participant in the church ( ) after the cross would benefit by heeding Jesus' message. For example, can you name a tradition within evangelicalism that does not accept that Matthew 18:15–20 church discipline passage as applicable today in the church? The virtual universal acceptance of the applicability of Matthew 18:15–20 for the contemporary church is strong testimony of the need to accept Jesus' teaching for today, especially the next verses (Matt. 18:21–35) which develop the need for forgiveness within church discipline. Because we today are kingdom participants of the church heading towards the eschatological expression of the kingdom this parable is directly applicable to us today, thus informing our systematic theology, which means that you may have been forgiven but to the extent that you forgive others your heavenly Father will salvifically forgive you. Likewise, if you do not forgive others, then your heavenly Father will not salvifically forgive you. Now this is not a works salvation (merely including virtues more than just faith). While in our reformation systematic theology, "the elect" are justified and our forgiving others becomes an evidence of this, like an Edwardsian religious affection. This passage frames it a different way and a proper interpretation of this passage keeps teeth in the insistence of our forgiving others as a virtue in the following linkage: *to the extent that you forgive others your heavenly Father will salvifically forgive you.*

Let us now consider a familiar psalm on forgiveness, Psalm 51. We have all read this psalm and have been existentially drawn into it so let us move to Level Two analysis. We recognize by the superscription that this psalm comes out of David's life as an expression to God for cleansing in the context of his sin with Bathsheba. Furthermore, by form criticism or rhetorical analysis, the distinctive form of the psalm is apparent as a lament. This means that after the introductory petition (Ps. 51:1–2), David develops a lament of his condition (Ps. 51:3–6) followed by petitions (Ps. 51:7–13, 18–19) and his vow to praise God when his petition is answered affirmatively (Ps. 51:14–17). Another aspect of the lament genre is that the psalm utilizes generic language indicating that the design of this prayer within Israel's hymnbook is for any individual who has sin concern to lament his penitential concern to God with this pattern prayer. This lament psalm begins in the standard formal manner containing an introductory petition (Ps. 51:1–2). David asks the compassionate God of loyal love for cleansing (in synonymous parallelism) from his contorted Gollumized perversity in sin. David then laments the depth that this sin has penetrated his being (Ps. 51:3–6). David's sin and consequences are so clear that he cannot escape its presence. Using hypocatasis David expresses his sin against Bathsheba, Uriah, Israel and God as only against God. David's sin is exceptionally blameworthy so that God is then justified to judge him like God had previously judged Saul (1 Sam. 13:13–14). So David's sin though it involved others is especially against God. David expressed that his sin was an expression of his character; as it were, "I have had this bent, 'missing the mark' character since the breading heat of sexual intercourse in which I was conceived" (Ps. 51:5).

This is a deep bent of inner character pursuing 'my precious' perversity which is utterly incongruous to the design of God for me to deeply know and apply wisdom (Ps. 51:6). In such a condition this wisdom calls David and his followers to petition God for forgiveness, cleansing and restoration (Ps. 51:7–12). David asks God for deep internal cleansing after the models of sacrificial cleansing which uses a branch of hyssop dipped in blood to sprinkle the one in need and a baptism that washes uncleanness away (e.g., Lev. 14:4; Num. 18:18). The goal is a cleanness whiter than new fallen snow, as when the sun reflects off it so that the white becomes blindingly reflective of character. Such sin ostracizes the sinner from the congregation so David petitions for the privilege of being able to be united back within the communal joy and gladness (Ps. 51:8). This sin has deeply affected David's own bodily life removing joy under the weight of the divine vise screwed tightly by David's own sin, so David asks God for the ability to join in with the congregational joy. God's presence which destroys sin and sinners, like Saul who became a personal catastrophe divinely rejected from being king and unusable for God's purposes (1 Sam. 13:13–14) becomes a motive for David to ask for the eradication of his sin without being cast off from divine service (Ps. 51:9, 11). Such a cleansing is asked to penetrate to the heart of David's thought life and will so that David would be steadfastly faithful from now on (Ps. 51:10, 12). This transformation from an inclination to that of deep responsive cleanness is brought about by God in the same way as his usability as king is brought about by Spirit enablement. Having seen the Spirit depart from Saul in his disobedience (1 Sam. 16:13–14), David begs for God's mercy to not take the Holy Spirit from himself. We Christians have better promises than this being sealed and indwelt by the Spirit permanently. It is only through such a full remedy as David has petitioned which will restore him joyfully to the usable way of Kingdom.

As a motive to add leverage to David's petition, he vows to praise God with His divine aid (Ps. 51:13–17). This praise includes a pledge to teach sinners God's ways and to recover them to God. If the multiple death sentences ("bloods" for adultery and murder) are removed from hanging over David by the God of salvation, David pledges to sing praise of God's righteousness (Ps. 51:14–15). David would willingly bring a sacrifice but within his highhanded sin no sacrifice pleases God except the crushed brokenness of himself as the sinner (Ps. 51:16–17). David prays for continued prosperity for Jerusalem, for he realizes as sinning king he has put that in jeopardy (Ps. 51:18). David asks for Jerusalem's walls to be built up, perhaps alluding to the construction of the temple walls. In a later day this prayer could have the extended change of significance framed by the physical renewal of Nehemiah's construction of the walls after Israel's sin and captivity. Within the continued favor of God's provision are realized an abundance of sacrifices appropriately given to God (Ps. 51:19). We evangelicals have the altered condition of Christ having died as atonement sacrifice rendering burnt offerings inappropriate (Heb. 10:1–18). So, a Christian's petition for prosperity for Jerusalem so that sacrifices would be appropriately offered to God further changes the significance to a petition for the divine Kingdom to arrive in its eschatological form (Ezek. 40–46), which is an eschatological extension of David's prayer. Now it seems to me that this psalm should be prayed by Christians with the slight modifications of significance noted even though it came out of Israel's prayer book. However, the genre of prayers are performative speech which is not merely to be analyzed, for if one only interprets them without then praying them we rape the text (treating it as merely a testimony) and diminish ourselves (not governing our lives by the genre nature of the Scriptures). So for performative texts, such as psalms, there is a place for folding Level One hermeneutic again within Level Three and praying the psalm, so let's do that.

> Be gracious to me, O God, according to Your loyal love;
> According to your great compassion blot out my transgressions.
> Wash me thoroughly from my iniquity, and cleanse me from my sin.
> For I know my transgressions,
> And my sin is ever before me.
> Against You supremely have I sinned,
> And done what is evil in Your sight,
> So that You are justified when You speak,
> And blameless when You judge.
> Behold, You desire truth in the innermost being,
> And in the hidden part You will make me know wisdom.
> Purify me with hyssop and I shall be clean;
> Wash me, and I shall be whiter than snow.
> Make me to hear joy and gladness,
> Let the bones which You have broken rejoice.
> Hide Your presence from my sins,
> And blot out my iniquities.
> Create in me a clean heart, O God,
> And renew a steadfast spirit within me.
> Do not cast me away from Your Presence and
> Do not reduce the Holy Spirit's enablement for service.
> Restore to me the joy of Your salvation,
> And sustain me with a willing spirit.
> Then I will teach transgressors Your ways
> And sinners will be converted to You.
> Deliver me from divine death sentences, O God of my salvation;

My tongue will joyfully sing of Your righteousness.
O Yahweh, open my lips,
That my mouth may declare Your praise.
For You do not delight in sacrifice, otherwise I would give it;
You are not pleased with burnt offering.
The sacrifices of God are a broken spirit;
A broken and contrite heart, O God, You will not despise.
By Your favor do good to Zion;
Build up the kingdom walls of Jerusalem.
Then You will delight in righteous sacrifices,
In burnt offering and whole burnt offering;
Then young bulls will be offered on Your altar.

Now sometimes the textual meaning of a text may include others and not me because those to whom the text goes are different than me in ways which that text accentuates or other texts clarify. For example, no Christian tradition appropriates the command of 2 Kings 5:10 as for today. The text is quite clear that this is a specific command for Naaman to wash in the Jordan River seven times to be clean from leprosy. This fact does not make that text irrelevant to us for we see in it a dramatic narrative of Yahweh's power to heal and to interactively protect His people Israel through the ministry of His prophet.

Likewise, Jesus' second person statements directly to the disciples in the upper room discourse of John 13–16 appear to have lots of textual particulars indicating that the immediate group of disciples in the upper room are those who are promised and commanded by the second person statements, most of which are plural and will be reflected in English by the American Southern expression "you all." The disciples are the ones who have been with Jesus (John 14:9; 15:27; 16:4, 16–17). The disciples are those to whom Jesus said, "I have spoken to you all" (John 13:19; 14:25, 29; 15:11; 16:1, 4, 12, 15, 25, 33, 17:6). Jesus tells the disciples about His betrayal by one in their midst with words like, "I am telling you all before it comes to pass, so that when it does occur, you all may believe that I am" (John 13:19; 14:29; 16:4). Jesus then said to Judas Iscariot, "What you do, do quickly" (John 13:27). Then Jesus tells Peter, "A cock will not crow until you deny Me three times" (John 13:38). We recognize that these are not promises or commands to the Christian. Then Jesus starts talking about His impending departure from the disciples in the near context in second of says, "Little children I am with you all a little while longer. You all shall seek Me; and as I said to the Jews, I now say to you all also, Where I am going, you all cannot come" (John 13:33, 36; 14:2–3, 18; 16:7, 16–17, 28). All these statements trouble the disciples and the disciples present are those who Jesus comforts with, "Let not your heart be troubled" (John 14:1, 27; 16:20, 22). Now most evangelical traditions recognize that the disciples in the upper room are the audience commanded and that is why most of us do not maintain an ordinance of foot washing when Jesus said, "If I the Lord and Teacher, washed all your feet, you all also ought to wash one another's feet" (John 13:14). However, most of our traditions are sloppy in appropriating for ourselves certain upper room statements which appear to be reserved for the disciples in the upper room in the same manner. For example, Jesus promises the Holy Spirit to aid these disciples with Him in the upper room, "I have spoken to you all, while abiding with you all. But the Helper, the Holy Spirit, whom the Father will send in My name, He will teach all of you all things, and bring to all your remembrance all that I said to you all," and again, "I have many more things to say to you all, but you all cannot bear them now. But when He, the Spirit of truth, comes, He will guide you all into all the truth; for He will not speak on His own initiative but whatever He hears, He will speak; and He will disclose to you all what is to come." (John 4:26; 16:12–15). Immediately following both of these statements Jesus talks about His impending departure, "A little while, and you all will no longer behold Me" (John 14:27–28; 16:16–19).

This means that John 14:26 and 16:12–15 are special promises of Spirit revelation to the eleven disciples present in the upper room so that they might remember Jesus' words in the inspiration of Scriptures and its communication to found Christianity, and they are not promises to the Christian of Holy Spirit enablement to help the Christian properly interpret Bible passages. Now these foundational inspiration promises still have great benefit for we Christians, in that it reassures us that John wrote these statements right by the Spirit's aid. Notice also there are several statements in the upper room discourse in the third person which may include us directly but no statements of a Holy Spirit illumination aid for us (John 14:23–24; 15:6, 23; 16:8–11, 21). It seems to be that there are a few points of our systematic theologies and traditions that need to give way for the warranted truth of the Scripture. Which means that if we embrace a methodology of remaining inter-textual to our tradition as the governing rubric, we then depart from truth and the Bible at certain points. It would be better to exclude any assumptions and doctrinal beliefs inappropriate to the Biblical text and remain inter-textual with the truth as contained in the Biblical text.

Let us now explore an epistle such as Paul's first letter to the Corinthians. In many respects the American church today is the same as Paul and the Corinthian church, we are fairly cosmopolitan, mobile and well traveled. We are like them in preaching Christ crucified and raised as a blatant simple gospel. There are sinners among our churches who need to be connected. There are ignorant among our churches who need compassionate instruction and exhortation.

There are mature Christians among our churches who recognize the gospel as the wisdom of God while some academics in our fields consider this gospel of ours to be utter foolishness (1 Cor. 1:23–24; 2:6–8). Paul instructs and corrects a church like this in 1 Corinthians 2:6–16. In Paul's day rulers had rejected the gospel as demonstrated by their killing Christ (1 Cor. 2:6–8). However, this simple gospel has extensive kingdom benefits prepared for those who love God (1 Cor. 2:9). The Spirit of God knows the mind of God and revealed to Paul and the Corinthians this gospel message which the spirit of the world considers foolishness (1 Cor. 2:10–12). Paul expresses this gospel in spiritual thoughts and words, rather than human wisdom (1 Cor. 2:1–2, 13). A natural ( ) man does not accept this gospel from the Spirit of God (1 Cor. 1:23; 2:6–8, 14) because the gospel is appreciated from spiritual appraisal or examination (, 1 Cor. 2:14). A person who fleshes out this spiritual gospel message is a spiritual or mature person who appreciates this gospel revealed by the Spirit (1 Cor. 2:6, τελείοις; 1 Cor. 2:15,). Such a spiritual person will not be appreciated by natural men because these men do not appreciate the message which the spiritual person fleshes out. However, the spiritual person's gospel perspective enables him to examine or appraise all other things. This gospel perspective is the mind of Christ, which the Spirit revealed (1 Cor. 2:10–13, 16).

Other passages claimed for illumination are like the previous Corinthian example, such as 1 John 2:18–27 anointing with the gospel. John identifies that we are anointed ( ) with truth centering on publicly acknowledging Jesus as the Christ (, anointed), which truth is denied by the antichrists ( ), and their paragon "the eschatological antichrist" (; 1 John 1:3; 2:18, 20, 27). Such a gospel perspective is evident since the anointing is truth heard (; 1 John 2:21, 24) as a message that publicly affirms Jesus as the Christ, without denying Him (1 John 2:22–23), a message that brings about everlasting life (1 John 2:25). This message centered on Christ and gospel teaches about all things (1 John 2:27).

None of these passages promise a work from God for the Holy Spirit to cognitively help us understand and interpret Biblical passages. In fact, the mention of "Holy One" in 1 John 2:20 may not clearly refer to the Holy Spirit at all since John only uses the phrase elsewhere of Christ (1 John 6:69). These passages actually highlight that the gospel has implications such as unity and the Holy Spirit is the guarantor of growth such as the fruit of the Spirit referred to in Galatians 5:22–23 or the spiritual man of Romans 8. These passages promise the Spirit's aid in a kind of application, working virtues into life in conjunction with our choosing these same virtues (e.g., Rom. 6:16–23 with 8:4–17, or Gal. 5:16–26 including 5:22–23). So we reflect the Spirit's qualities, but He does not promise any special aid in cognitively understanding Bible passages. So to me it looks like passages like these call us to exclude the unwarranted assumption of the Holy Spirit as cognitively aiding the believer in understanding Biblical texts because it is not taught in Scripture.

This is an appeal to us to return to the earlier reformation tradition of Luther and Calvin who stood on the Word of God as accessible rather than following the later pietistic subjective intuition tradition of Philipp Jakob Spener[11] as contained in Johann Quenstedt (1685)[12] and David Hollanz,[13] the parents of the contemporary evangelical cognitive illumination view. The related idea of an applicational illumination of the Spirit to move the person to a "living" knowledge of the Biblical text was introduced around 1701 by August Herman Franke, and then published in 1709 and more fully in 1717.[14] Evangelicalism has largely owned the cognitive illumination view of Spener, Quenstedt and Hollanz, with others in evangelicalism joining Franke's spirit transformational illumination view.

Other texts show that interpretation is our responsibility, to be workmen rightly handling the word of truth with the text limiting what should be said to the interpretation contained therein (2 Tim. 2:15; 2 Pet. 1:16–21; 3:16). Now this does not mean we cannot pray, "Lord, help us to understand" when we are in the midst of studying the Bible because of course, God wants us to bring all our concerns to Him, but

---

11 Philipp Jakob Spener, *Consilia Et Judicia Theologia* (Frankfurt a.M., 1709), vol. 3, p. 700; Cf. K. James Stein, "Phillip Jakob Spener (1635–1705)" and Markus Matthias, "August Hermann Franke (1663–1727)" in *The Pietist Theologians: An Introduction to Theology in the Seventeenth Centuries.* edited by Carter Lindberg (Malden: Blackwell, 2005), pp. 88 and 105–6; Johannes Wallmann, *Philipp Jakob Spener und die Aufänge des Pietismus* (Tübigen: Mohr, 1970), pp. 92–96; Emmanuel Hirsch, *Geschichte der neuen Evangelische Theologie in Zusammenhang mit den allgemein Bewegung des Europäischen Denkens* (Gütersloh: Bertelsmann, 1951), vol. 2, p. 114; Volker Jung, *Das Ganze der Heiligen Schrift. Hermeneutik und Schriftauslegung bei Abrham Calov* (Stuttgart: Calwer Verlag, 1999), pp. 100–1.

12 Johann Andreas Quenstedt, *Theologia Didactico-Polemica* (Wittenberg: Johanne Ludolph Quenstedt, 1685). The relevant portion (chapters 1–3) of this is available in English as: *The Nature and Character of Theology: An Introduction to the Thought of J. A. Quenstedt from THEOLOGIA DIDACTIO-POLEMICA SIVE SYSTEMA THEOLOGICUM.* abridged, edited, and translated by Luther Poellot (St. Louis: Concordia, 1986), ch. I "Of Theology in General": question I "Is Theology Given?" paragraph XI, p. 36; ph. XIV, p. 39; ph. XXXI-Observe (1), p. 54; ph. XXXV, p. 57; Section II "Polemic"-"Sources of Rebuttals or Dialysis of Objections": q. I "Is Theology Given?", pp. 64–5; q. II "Is Revealed Theology Necessary in the Church?", pp. 71–3; q. III "Is Theology a God-Given Practical Aptitude?", exposition III & IV, pp. 73–4; rebuttal I, p. 80; ch. III "Of the Sources of Theology", porism IV, pp. 199–200; cf. Douglas Kennard, "Evangelical Views on Illumination of Scripture and Critique," *JETS* 49:4(Dec. 2006): 797–806.

13 David Hollaz, Examen Theologicum Acroamaticum published in 1707 is available as Acromaticum Universam Theologiam Thetico-Polemicam Complectens (Lipsiae: B.C. Breitkopfii, 1763).

14 August Hermann Franke, *Praelectiones Hermeneuticae,* p. 57; cf. *Markus* Matthias, "August Hermann Franke (1663–1727)" in *The Pietist Theologians: An Introduction to Theology in the Seventeenth Centuries.* edited by Carter Lindberg (Malden: Blackwell, 2005), pp. 106–7.

He nowhere promises to provide this aid and I consider it presumptuous of us to expect that He will help us to cognitively understand Bible passages when God has nowhere promised this aid. Doesn't this view have a better correspondence in life, too? When godly men differ in their interpretations, the issue is not that someone is not listening to the Spirit's illumination, rather the issue is What are the particulars of the Bible saying and warranting? Doesn't this also help explain why non-Christian scholars in some of our fields can accurately tell you the interpretation of the passage without personally appropriating it for themselves? So interpretation is our responsibility to accomplish in a warranted fashion and the authoritative application directly flows from that warranted interpretation. This biblical material which we have cognitively understood within our abilities is then worked out in our life as virtues guaranteed by the Holy Spirit and chosen by our will (e.g., Rom. 6:11–23 with Rom. 8:5; Gal. 5:16, 22–26). Doesn't this also show that remaining inter-textual with our traditions is at times a flawed theological method flying headlong into post-modernism and losing truths. Instead warranted epistemology and hermeneutics are the answer with the text of the Bible being our anchor. I recognize that I have stepped on a number of traditional toes in the use of my hermeneutical method in these passages. I hope my hermeneutical method is not written off because of this, and I hope my interpretations are not written off because of this.

These are difficult passages yet they nicely showcase sensitivities and decisions we need to make in the hermeneutical process for us to get warranted truth from the Biblical text. In many passages the contemporary evangelical person may obtain truth without doing all these steps because the passage is easy to understand and lines up with the tradition, but the best way of warranting your interpretation is to be precise in your use of proper hermeneutical method even in easier passages. Furthermore, difficult passages such as these require proper hermeneutical method for the truth to be obtained from the passage.

Let us look at one more difficult passage that accentuates contextualization decisions evident in the transposition of the original context's interpretation and application into our context to the extent that its significance includes us. The passage is 1 Corinthians 11:2–16. Let us read the passage to allow for hermeneutical Level One to contribute. The passage follows an appeal to edify one another, imitating Paul as he imitates Christ.

> 2 Now I praise you because you remember me in everything,
> and hold firmly to the traditions, just as I delivered them to
> you. 3 But I want you to understand that Christ is the head
> of every man, and the man is the head of a woman, and God
> is the head of Christ. 4 Every man who has something on his

> head while praying or prophesying, disgraces his head. 5 But
> every woman who has her head uncovered while praying or
> prophesying, disgraces her head; for she is one and the same
> with her whose head is shaved. 6 For if a woman does not
> cover her head, let her also have her hair cut off; but if it is
> disgraceful for a woman to have her hair cut off or her head
> shaved, let her cover her head. 7 For a man ought not to have
> his head covered, since he is the image and glory of God; but
> the woman is the glory of man. 8 For man does not originate
> from woman, but woman from man; 9 for indeed man was not
> created for the woman's sake, but woman for the man's sake.
> 10 Therefore the woman ought to have a symbol of authority
> on her head, because of the angels. 11 However, in the Lord,
> neither is woman independent of man, nor is man independent
> of woman. 12 For as the woman originates from the man, so
> also the man has his birth through the woman, and all things
> originate from God. 13 Judge for yourselves: is it proper for
> a woman to pray to God with head uncovered. 14 Does not
> even nature itself teach you that if a man has long hair, it is a
> dishonor to him. 15 but if a woman has long hair, it is a glory
> to her? For her hair is given to her for a covering. 16 But if one
> is inclined to be contentious, we have no other practice, nor
> have the churches of God.

To many of us the passage may sound strange. Some may wonder about the woman's ministry role, the foreign-to-us nature of prophecy, or ask the question "Does nature really tell us much about the length of hair?" Now let us enter into Level Two's hermeneutical spiral within the authorial context.

The Corinthian church had remembered aspects of the Christian traditions but it seems that there are aspects which Paul needs to correct and this passage leads off these connections which extend to improprieties in the Lord's Supper and the use of gifts (1 Cor. 11:2). The concept of head (   ) is used by Paul 35% of the time and in this passage in a univocal way as the physical head uncovered or with hair, veil or something on it (1 Cor. 11:4 at least the first one, 5 at least first and third, 6, 7, 10). The concept of head is also used analogically as a metaphor (1 Cor. 1:3, perhaps the second reference in 4 and 5). Some traditions will see the essence of this metaphoric meaning of   as source by appealing to classical Greek usage which permits it and the explanation of origination in verses 8 and 9. Other traditions see the essence of this metaphoric meaning of   as authority by appealing to Pauline theology. That is, sixty-five percent of Paul's use of   and the near context authority (ἐξουσίαν) issue in verse 10 and the issue of disgrace (καταισχύνει in verses 4 and 5) prefer the second view. In

Colossians must be authority and not source because Christ is viewed as the head of the church sourced by another. Christ is head over every man as authority over all things (Eph. 1:27), and all powers (Col. 2:10). In Ephesians 5:23 the headship of Christ over the church parallels the husband's headship over his wife. So in Paul's thought when is head of it probably means not all men over all women in the church but rather a particular role of authority in marriage that the husband is to fulfill in loving, nourishing and cherishing his wife (Eph. 5:23, 25, 28–29). In this sort of relationship the wife is to be submissive ( ) as all Christians are to be to each other in the Church in the fear of Christ (since the verb of Eph. 5:22 is implied from 5:21). Such a role of wives submitting to caring husbands should not be odious, but it has implications. In 1 Corinthians 11:3 is best seen as the husband is the head of his wife after the parallel from Ephesians 5:23 . In both places Christ's authority over the Church serves as a model of care and submissiveness. Additionally, Christ submits to God as His head, showing us a model of edification which we are to imitate as Paul does as well (1 Cor. 11:3). The Christian man shows he submits to Christ by not covering his head when he prays or prophesies, for it he has something on his head at those select times he disgraces his head (1 Cor. 11:4).

Now prophecy is not preaching, for every time a message of a prophecy is contained in the Bible the message includes predictive statements or foretelling amid the forth-telling statements. Prophecy is not teaching since they are two separate gifts (1 Cor. 12:20; Rom. 12:6–7), though Christians learn from prophecy (1 Cor. 14:31). Prophecy is not exhortation since they are two separate gifts (Rom. 12:6, 8), though prophecy can exhort (1 Cor. 14:31). preaching is gospel proclamation and not to be seen as identical to prophecy though prophecy can preach the gospel (e.g., Acts 2). The pastor-teacher is not a prophet since they are two separate gifts (Eph. 4:11). Prophets foretold the future in the authorial context, so through Level Three the command in 1 Corinthians 4 may be slightly irrelevant to a contemporary situation, if prophecy is not the public speech one expresses.

While prophecy may be restricted to only those so gifted by the Spirit, the inclusion of public prayer in this discussion opens the relevancy for this text to include all who pray publicly.

If a Christian man led public prayer then in the first century he should not wear a head covering or he would shame Christ. However, in the first century there is almost no evidence of men wearing a hat or prayer shawl from Roman, Greek or Jewish culture, though in Goodenough's *Jewish Symbols in the Greco-Roman Period,* volume 9, paintings from a temple in Pompeii depict a priest with a winged hat (fig. 98), and a prophet with the *himation* part of his tunic covering his head (fig. 99).[15] Such a command to not wear a head covering contextualized to contemporary North America is no trouble since the first world society encourages men to remove their hats (if they are wearing them at all) when they come inside or when they pray as a matter of propriety. How does this transfer to a context like an American Indian or African tribe where a clan leader identifies his role in the clan by his headdress? Perhaps such clan authority indicators are to be removed to submit ultimately to Christ's authority when they pray publicly.

Back in the first century, Greek women used nets, hair bags, kerchiefs and a body shawl (*himation*) which could be thrown over their head, especially at weddings and funerals. Paul addresses that when a woman who ministers through public prayer or prophecy, she must be properly attired or her husband is disgraced (1 Cor. 11:5). In my critical realist perspective the testimony of Gordon Fee, *The First Epistle to the Corinthians*, p. 509, note 71 shows many first century women of Pompeii with or without head coverings and no established pattern; this means I moved my trust from the testimony of F. W. Grosheide (*Commentary on the First Epistle to the Corinthians*), to the closer empirically based testimony of Lucian, whom Fee follows.[16] The views presented by Fee of these first century Pompeii sources are further corroborated by Anthony Thiselton, and the contemporary and classical sources he cites.[17] The role of corroboration among careful scholarship helps to reassure the interpreter that his view is likely to be correct. So that, if a woman prayed or prophesied publicly without an appropriate head covering there was a confusion of gender roles. As such she has entered the disgraceful role of mannishness illustrated by Lucian in *The Runaways* as a fugitive wife with hair clipped, hiding among the slaves[18] and a lesbian who had shaved her head like an athlete.[19] Either *clipped* or shaved hair indicates

15 Erwin Ramsdell Goodenough, *Jewish Symbols in the Greco-Roman Period* (New York: Pantheon Books, 1964), volume 9, figures 98 and 99.

16 For Lucian cf. notes 14 and 15; Gordon Fee, *The First Epistle to the Corinthians. NICNT* (Grand Rapids: Eerdmans, 1987) as a later stage from F. W. Grosheide, *Commentary on the First Epistle to the Corinthians. NICNT* (Grand Rapids: Eerdmans, 1954).

17 Anthony Thiselton, *The First Epistle to the Corinthians. The New International Greek Testament Commentary* (Grand Rapids: Eerdmans, 2000), pp. 832–833; Thiselton includes contemporary sources like C. S. Keener, *Paul, Women, Wives: Marriage and Women's Ministry in the Letters of Paul* (Peabody: Hendrickson, 1992), pp. 32–36; Thiselton also cites classical source like Dio Cassius, *History of Rome* 15.10.5.

18 Lucian, *fug.* 27 in *Loeb Classical Library Volume V. The Passsing of Peregrinus, The Runaways, Toxaris or Friendship, The Dance, Lexiphanes, The Eunich, Astrology, The Mistaken Critic, The Parliament of the Gods, The Tyrannicide, Disowned* (Cambridge: Harvard University Press, 1987), p. 85.

19 Lucian, *dial. het.*_5.3 in *Loeb Classical Library Volume VII. Dialogues of the Dead, Dialogues of the Sea-Gods, Dialogs of the Gods, Dialogs of the Courtesans* (Cambridge: Harvard University Press, 1961), p. 383.

shame of rebellion to the submissiveness a wife should manifest to her husband (1 Cor. 11:6). Her submissiveness honors the man since she is his glory (1 Cor. 11:7). This issue of submissiveness is rooted beyond culture in the order and purpose of the original creation of Adam and Eve and observed by transcultural beings, namely angels (1 Cor. 11:8–10), so the submissiveness issue is not to be written off or reduced to a cultural issue though Paul does reflect the cultural propriety of the first century. This view explained here from first century sources was affirmed and mandated as the appropriate way to take this passage in 325 A.D. at the *Council of Gangra*, canon 17.[20]

The first century Christian wife evidences this submissiveness by a culturally meaningful head covering as a symbol of recognition of authority when she ministers in certain ways. Such living within the submissive roles unto Christ or husband retains both husband and wife as interdependently interrelated. That is, the husband and wife are unable to be independent as is graphically illustrated from Eve's coming from Adam and all other males being birthed by their mothers (1 Cor. 11:11–12). Paul recognizes that the natural order or the way things are from the first century perspective requires Christian wives to cover their heads when they pray in public and that the gender roles are evidenced by shortness of men's hair and length of women's hair (1 Cor. 1:13–15). This natural perspective is also the first century traditional perspective for the churches (1 Cor. 11:16). Since the whole argument for reflecting the submissiveness of a wife to her husband has been expressed by description, tradition, propriety and shame, rather than outright command, it may indicate this discussion is not as important as the Lord's Supper discussion that follows, but the inclusion of this teaching in the Biblical text shows this teaching to be important in its own right. Since women's head coverings and hair have lost meaning in our American first world culture, perhaps a way of manifesting the everlasting truth of submission of a Christian wife to her husband may be shown today by culturally meaningful expressions which present the wife in ways that do not confuse gender roles or display rebellion. This rule of thumb would still provide guidance as to a range of styles, which of course, would change from culture to culture. In South African public prayer, for instance, a wife is required to wear a skirt whereas at my Chicago church some expression of femininity amidst the jeans would be required of a woman who prays publicly; "butch" appearance is excluded as inappropriate.

---

20 *Council of Gangra*, canon 17 in *The Nicene and Post-Nicene Fathers*, ed. Philip Schaff and Henry Wace (Edinburgh: T & T Clark, 1991), 2nd series, vol. 14, p. 99; Gration, *Corpus Juris Canonici*, (Graz: Akademische druck u. verlagsanstalt, 1959 following Coloniae Munatianae Impensis E. & J. R. Thurnisiorum, 1717and Leipzig: Tauchnitz, 1928), volume 1, *Decretum Gratiani*, Pars. 1, Dist. 30, c.ij.

My hermeneutical method maintains three levels: 1) existential, 2) hermeneutical spiral within authorial context, and 3) hermeneutical spiral between contexts. Unless your hermeneutic has these components you are probably cutting the passage short for what it has to say or you are reducing the interpretation or contextualization process to too naive a level. Proper hermeneutics is our responsibility; do not try to do the task with too simplistic a methodology.

INTERPRETATION
is a three level process
in which all three levels operate simultaneously

LEVEL ONE: EXISTENTIAL

The reader feels placed in the story by:
familiar relationships, confessional traditions, shared passion, similar experiences, overlapping contexts and rhetorical devices (space, placement, motifs, symbols, climax...)

Authorial Context

Reader's Context

Which all prompt:

1 and 2: Shared passion and motivation to understand and work it out into life. (The goal of this level is to surface and retain passion and motivation throughout the dissecting process of the other two levels).

3 and 4: Self understanding and self possibilities (i.e. Principles are implications for our life which we surmise when our life is juxtaposed closely to a text. These principles are not divinely authoritative; they are merely existentially relevant to those who propose them).

INTERPRETATION LEVEL TWO: Hermeneutical Spiral Within Authorial Context

Hermeneutics is a spiral within the authorial context from contextual overviews to textual particulars which clarifies the meaning in the text. The goal is to understand the meaning in the text for the author and readers of the original context. To the extent that the meaning is clear and coherent, and has textual support, I can reassure myself with high plausibility that I have obtained the author's interpretation and application for them.

INTERPRETATION LEVEL THREE: Spiral Between Contexts

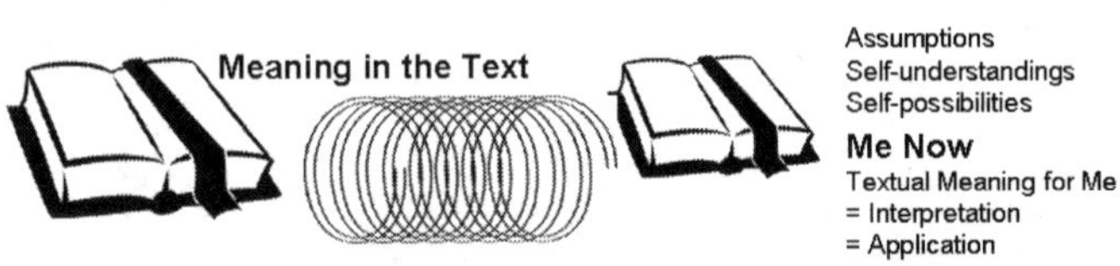

Hermeneutics is a spiral from the horizon of the text to the horizon of the reader which progressively:

1. excludes any of my assumptions, understandings and possibilities which are inappropriate to the text and
2. includes in me those assumptions, understandings and possibilities which are appropriate to the text. The goal is to recover the meaning in the text to the extent that it includes me. This becomes the authoritative textual meaning may actually include others and not me. Then my textual meaning is my interpretation which these others should apply, and not me. To the extent that I can state this interpretation clearly, coherently, and these are similarities between the original readers and the ones of my application. I can reassure myself with high plausibility that I have obtained the authoritative interpretation and application for now. This sense of high plausibility adds motivation to understand and apply.

5. Biblical Authority in the Contemporary Hermeneutical Scene

Authority as a philosophical concept is the recognized power to influence the opinion, belief or action of another. We tend to grant authority to a variety of sources in our lives. For example, an informed speaker is seen as an authority on a subject. However, when the speaker veers off into topics less well known by him we tend to remove what he says from the realm of authority, taking it with a great deal of salt. This skepticism may recede as he returns to some topic upon which we are more confident that he is informed. Additionally, when more than one authority is addressing a subject, there is the opportunity that they will differ with each other. The disagreement between these authorities provides an opportunity to evaluate what the authority says. You may conclude that both are right if their statements are nuanced more precisely, or that one is right and the other wrong, or that neither are right and the truth lies elsewhere. Such a concept of authority does not place such statements beyond the bounds of evaluation. For example, as children, our parents were a dominant authority in our lives, because they wielded the specter of consequences over our behavior. In such an arrangement, rewards encourage behavior and removal of privileges discourages behavior. Both parental responses help to retain parents as an authority in our lives provided they are not pushing their will too far beyond what we consider appropriate. As we mature they may lose their status as prominent authority. Each of our spouses may emerge as a major authority in our life, not because they are specialists in a field of study, perhaps because she wields consequences in your life but even more because she cares about you and has demonstrated this concern over the long haul. We accept statements that she makes about us because these statements have a demonstrated fit, authentically describing us. Such an authority may reflect a certain existential authenticity in our lives.

Some may wonder at the subjective post-enlightenment way that I have taken "authority" here. Is there not an objective quality of authority? Well certainly God, Who is our creator, is the authority for all His creation over which He rules. This same God has communicated His Word, which is authoritative for humans to understand the divinely revealed perspective and to submit to it. We should submit to God and

His Word, thus treating them as authoritative in our life, because they speak the truth, and God is in the unique position as sovereign, Who mandates His will with everlasting consequences. Thus the objective authority of God and His Word become subjective authorities to us as we submit to them. However, often our distinctive communities understand and reflect their concept of God and the Biblical text in ways that reflect a community or traditional emphasis. However, not only is the text often taken in a community oriented way as an authority but individuals are also taken as an authority within a communal tradition.

Many of the "authorities" of life are authorities for their distinctive communities, and not really an authority beyond this community. For example, the Pope is an authority for the Roman Catholic Church or a president for a school or a nation. These kinds of authorities are authoritative for their community with regard to the orientation and practice of that community, to the extent that they do not exceed the role which these communities or its trustees have granted to them. For example, a president of a school who violates academic freedom has on that point become rogue, and indicates to the faculty member it is time for the faculty member to leave the school, no longer treating the president as an authority in his life, as he had previously done. So there is a Lockian[1] subjective authority by virtue of the community relationship. This Lockian subjective authority is grounded in a social contract as binding to the extent that the written or understood parameters which the community grants as governing them. If an authority violates these parameters for the community, then it is for the community to take action or they pragmatically cede that level of abuse as acceptable to their authority.

If an individual no longer grants the parameters that the community grants for that "authority" then he should depart from that community. I think that this is a matter of integrity and also an attempt at being a peacemaker to enable the community to be unified.

Often authorities for one community would like to be treated as an authority beyond their community. For example, the Pope is clearly an authority for his denomination but he seems to make claims for authority over the whole Body of Christ. This issue of authority is however probably the most resilient issue keeping the divide between Roman Catholicism and protestant denominations. We can recognize that he is an authority for Roman Catholic teaching and practice, so that if we wish to characterize the Roman Catholic views we would need to include the Pope's views within our discussion. For example, the Roman Catholic teachings on birth control and abortion would need

---

1 This is an allusion to John Locke's political theory of social contract that is expressed in governing documents and community attitude. Cf. John Locke, "The second treatise" in *The Two Treatises of Government*, edited by Peter Laslett (Cambridge: Cambridge Press, 1960).

to include the Pope's views as a major authoritative voice. However, Roman Catholics in the United States largely disregard the Pope's views on birth control and abortion. A major segment of that denomination disregards the Pope as an authority in their life for these issues because they find him to be out of touch with their own existential condition and values. Maybe we do the same for the Pope, or a president, or a pastor who we find disconnected from our existential situation and value. For example, pedophile priests and Episcopal malfeasance has certainly lost moral authority for the Roman Catholic Church. Furthermore, to the extent that one authority is devalued it will probably effect the way our society will consider other authorities; a domino effect. Do we diminish the authority of God, the Bible, or our traditions from our lives?

Within Christendom, authority as a defining way of knowing has been granted to a range of avenues of knowing, including God's revelation, testimony about God's revelation, tradition, an intuitive sense that the Holy Spirit is speaking and authenticity within one's existential situation. These levels of influence will be analyzed to explore their warrant and limitations for providing authority. A critical realist theological methodology will be advocated as the best route through these authority issues, utilizing a Thiselton-Ricoeur hermeneutic correlated through a descriptive Biblical theology approach.[2] My presuppositions for this study include that we should let the Bible (in its nearer textual and historical-cultural context) be the primary authority for faith and practice. This near context hermeneutic is followed by the secondary authority of a respective descriptive Biblical theology (which integrates the interpretation of multiple texts in the ancient Near Eastern context). This Biblical theology is followed by a third level of authority framed by a critical realist method of systematic theology (which permits tradition to be worked into our own contemporary context to reflect the significance of this Biblical theology). Each of these levels of authority evidence a commitment to Biblical authority. This commitment to Biblical authority motivates me on a practical level to maintain an interpretive rule *to be as clear as the text is clear and to be as ambiguous as the text is ambiguous.* This paper will be an exposé and evaluation of the contemporary hermeneutical options, including my own hermeneutical view, under the lens of the primary authority being that of Biblical authority as seen through the lens of the priority of the nearer context surrounding the text.

---

2 The latest edition of this paper is the previous chapter. These concepts are developed in Douglas Kennard, The Relationship Between Epistemology, Hermeneutics, Biblical Theology and Contextualization (Lewiston: The Edwin Mellen Press, 1999), pp. 1–70, 117–84; and the next chapter, "The Reef of the O.T.: A Method for Doing Biblical Theology that Makes Sense for Wisdom Literature" which was initially a paper presented at the Mid-West regional Evangelical Theological Society, March, 2000.

In evangelicalism we affirm that the divine Holy Spirit inspires the autographs and superintends translation (of at least LXX)[3] so that what is written is God breathed to be there in the text (2 Tim. 3:16–17; 2 Pet. 1:20–21). Though centuries removed from the time of writing, the texts are preserved as the divine authority for later days as well. So Jesus presents the Law as preserved by God and still in effect even to minute letters and parts of letters because heaven and earth have not passed away and nor has all the Law been fulfilled (Matt. 5:18–20). Also, Paul urges Timothy to see the inspirational profitability of the O.T. Greek LXX texts[4] (that he had been trained from his youth) for a range of practical purposes such as reproof, correction, and training in righteousness (2 Tim. 3:15–17). Likewise, Peter sees real encouragement in hoping for kingdom salvation because the prophets are quite explicit in developing this eschatological salvation and Peter's own transfiguration experience confirms the reality of the kingdom through the lens of Christ's powerful coming. Such prophecy is not available to be interpreted any way we might want, for the damned false teachers are known for such Scripture twisting (2 Pet. 1:20–21; 3:16–17). Thus Scripture retains the divine authority through the preservation process until centuries after the composition and revelation of the text. God's revelation retains a place for divine authority in our life. So, the Law and the prophets come with a 'Thus says the Lord.' They bring consequences of blessing or curse for Israel and others based on how they respond to the command of God. The N.T. extends these consequences to kingdom or wrath based on our response to Christ and His kingdom. We evangelicals recognize that the Biblical text is the primary authority for our theology and our lives.

The remainder of this chapter I will explore close alternatives to Biblical authority from several options which exegetes, including evangelical exegetes, propose to substitute for Biblical authority.

---

3 This position was broadly affirmed by the LXX specialists who presented papers (from 2 Tim. 3:14–16 and that the LXX was the O.T. text of the dispersion) at the Institute for Biblical Research meeting Nov. 19-20, 2004, namely: Karen Jobes, "When God Spoke Greek: The Place of the Greek Bible in Evangelical Scholarship," *IBR Bulletin for Biblical Research* 16(2006): 219–236 especially pp. 219–221; Peter Gentry, "The Septuagint and the Text of the Old Testament" *IBR Bulletin for Biblical Research* 16(2006): 193–218 and Tim McLay's oral response; cf. Martin Hengel, *The Septuagint as Christian Scripture: Its Prehistory and the Problem of Its Canon* (New York: T. & T. Clark, 2002), p. 22; Johan Lust, *Messianism and the Septuagint: Collected Essays by J. Lust*, ed. Katrin Hauspie (Leuven: Leuven University Press, 2004), p. 153; Sidney Jellicoe, "Septuagint Studies in the Current Century," *JBL* 88(1969): 191–99; Natalio F. Marcos, *The Septuagint in Context: Introduction to the Greek Versions of the Bible* (Leiden: Brill, 2000), p. 322.

4 Remember that the texts have not been bound together as yet so that the LXX Greek OT identifies that this inspiration extends through translation of separate scrolls of OT books without raising the issue of canonicity, since most Jews did not consider the sectarian acceptance of the apocrypha to be authoritative Scripture.

5.1. Textual Realism or Internal Coherentism

When we enter into the pulpit or classroom to teach or write commentaries we recognize that we have moved from the primary authority of the Biblical text itself to a secondary authority of our informed opinion or testimony of how the text is to be understood. These forms of testimony can be expressions of post-modernism like Bruggemann[5] develops or deeply rooted pre-modern traditions like in orthodoxy's seven church councils or the confessional traditions of modern theology. How are we to evaluate such expressions of testimony? Thomas Reid urged us to believe the credible in such testimony. However, David Hume was more skeptical in his admonition to believe the reliable. An alternative coherentist strategy is to believe your own worldview or tradition. I treat testimony about texts through the same lens in which I approach testimony about empirical data.[6] I am a realist (and an externalist), so I let the reality of the data inform my view. So the trust that I have in my own faculties can be extended to others in so far as I think that others' faculties are similar to how I would want to confidently function if I were in their environment. Each of these responses to testimony utilizes subjective means to translate the meaning of the Biblical text for an interpreter and a context.

Within the context of testimony there is a range of approaches vying for our adherence. Some of them use conherence as the grid through which the commentator is evaluated. One aspect of this could be coherence within the interpreter's own point of view. For certainly if an interpreter is contradicting himself then there is something in his view not to be believed.

However, usually the coherentist's granting of authority to the commentator has to do with the commentator's coherence within a doctrinal tradition, like *The Westminster Confession of Faith* or a doctrinal statement of one's church or school. So provided the commentator utilizes a theological hermeneutic or a meta-narrative granted by the community, his comments are accepted as authoritative. Usually it is the reader's tradition that serves as the grid by which the commentator is evaluated. For example, Hans-Georg Gadamer proposed that we interpret through our preunderstanding, which from his Kantian anti-realist vantage point allows for the tradition to naively fuse with the text and essentially define the meaning of the text by what the person's tradition says.[7] Some might also make a proposal utilizing the tools of reformed epistemology that their of provides an internalist strategy of

5 Walter Bruggemann, *Theology of the Old Testament* (Minneapolis: Fortress Press, 1997), especially pp. 61–114.

6 Douglas Kennard, *The Relationship Between Epistemology, Hermeneutics, Biblical Theology and Contextualization, pp.* 32, 43–51, 62–65.

7 Hans-Georg Gadamer, *Truth and Method* (New York: Crossroad, 1984).

basic belief through which texts take on meaning.[8] This was essentially the option that Grant Osborne and Harold Netland advocated in the discussion time at the Mid-West regional ETS meeting in 1997.[9] Such a view was countered by David Hesselgrave and myself (the other plenary speakers) as we advocated an externalist strategy, which appreciated the clarity and authority of the Biblical text and the field of Biblical theology. Another coherentist, Brevard Childs also advocates an internalist strategy of a traditional lens as his form of canonical criticism through which interpretation and Biblical theology is to be accomplished and evaluated.[10] Further examples of this approach can be seen in Stephen Fowl's collection of a range of theological interpretations within his edited volume *The Theological Interpretation of Scripture* or Kevin Vanhoozer's collection in his edited volume *Dictionary for Theological Interpretation of the Bible.*[11] Theological hermeneutical approaches have been nicely critiqued by Charlie Trimm.[12] These traditional parameters have emerged in every era since the early church. For our context of Christendom, the Reformation was extremely fruitful for delineating rival traditions, which excluded the alternative Reformation options. Within a decade of the beginning of the Reformation, Zwingli had his *Sixty-Seven Articles* (1523), Anabaptism had the *Schleitheim Confession* (1527), and Luther had his *Smaller Confession* (1529) and *The Augsburg Confession* (1530).[13] Within another six years the Reformed tradition had also added *The Geneva Confession* (1536) and Calvin's *The Institutes of the Christian Religion* (1st edition 1536).[14] Each of these confessions and the many more to follow divide up Christianity into competing authoritative church voices. The fact that the princes chose up sides during the Thirty Years War pressed these confessional voices into practice that tended to harden the confessional sides in their communities, further isolating each

---

8 Usually such a strategy is not this simple as to utilize a hermeneutic like Alvin Plantinga's epistemology but features of this approach can be seen within Woltersdorf's more complex hermeneutic. Cf. Alvin Plantinga, *Warrant and Proper Function* (N.Y.: Oxford University Press, 1993), and Nicholas Woltersdorff, *Divine Discourse: Philosophical Reflections on the Claim That God Speaks* (Cambridge: Cambridge University Press, 1995).

9 This interchange is developed in Douglas Kennard, *The Relationship Between Epistemology, Hermeneutics, Biblical Theology and Contextualization,* p. 2.

10 Brevard Childs, *Old Testament Theology in a Canonical Context* (Philadelphia: Fortress, 1985).

11 Stephen Fowl, *The Theological Interpretation of Scripture* (Cambridge: Blackwell Publishers, 1997); Kevin Vanhoozer, *Dictionary for Theological Interpretation of the Bible* (Grand Rapids: Baker, 2005).

12 Charlie Trimm, "Evangelicals, Theology, and Biblical Interpretation: Reflections on the Theological Interpretation of Scripture," *BBR* 20:3(2010): 311–30.

13 For succinct statements of these creeds see: *Confessions and Catechisms of the Reformation.* edited by Mark Noll (Grand Rapids: Baker, 1991).

14 The slim six chapters of the original were revised by John Calvin five times to expand to the more substantial: *The Institutes of the Christian Religion* (Grand Rapids: Associated Publishers and Author's Inc., n.d.).

tradition from the other. It is as though each tradition is guarding its own family jewels. However, all these varied traditions can't each be right, because they contradict each other's claims in some points concerning the Biblical text.

The Biblical text itself is the arbiter (as an accessible externalism maintains)[15] between these traditions to call these traditions back to whatever the divine authority of the Biblical text articulates and warrants. Likewise, on the issues of historical facticity, it is the historical documents produced by individuals in a respective context that should be used to govern whether something should be viewed as a fact. So, if the issue is what did second Temple Judaisms believe then the documents which Jews produced in that context are most definitive in designating and warranting such beliefs.

Centuries later and on other soil it is still somewhat difficult to enable these voices to cross-pollinate or to break beyond the church traditions that bind us so that we might appreciate the other's sensitivities to text. For example, if an interpreter is too dispensational or Arminian for a good fit within one's own tradition, say *The Westminster Confession of Faith*, then the interpreter's comments are devalued. Such traditions also float orally or from certain accepted books that never went through a canonization process. An example of this is the way some in dispensationalism (as defined by Charles Ryrie) accuse some others as heretics, who may teach what might be called progressive dispensationalism. If the commentator doesn't fit the valued tradition, the commentator can be dropped from a reading list, fired from his job or shunned within his context as aberrant. In such a conventional hermeneutical framework, the convention has in fact become the primary conceptual authority for the person's or community's theology. Often those with this approach do not even wish to consider whether an interpretation should be more nuanced or altered because their commitment to the tradition insulates them from even considering alternatives, which may claim to be more precisely Biblical than the tradition. Christian worldviews, theological hermeneutics or meta-narratives have the danger of blinding their adherents from the Biblical data if the Biblical text diverges from the traditional worldview.

Shouldn't the Biblical text provide a role as arbitrator between traditions? That is, traditions can be evaluated by how well they approximate the primary authority of the Biblical text? For example, a commentator may be trying to reflect the Biblical text and not any set tradition at that moment. And it is hypothetically possible that any tradition might be a bit simplistic in its attempt to represent all the texts that come to bear on an issue. For example, George Lindbeck advocates an internalistic strategy for defining the rationality of faith

15 Kennard, *The Relationship Between Epistemology, Hermeneutics, Biblical Theology and Contextualization,* pp. 40–68, 116–48 develops and defends his accessible realistic externalism in epistemology and hermeneutics.

wholly internal to the tradition, which could be simply described as confessional keeping the faith.[16] Lindbeck grants that the Biblical text is itself to be the primary first level authority, encouraging the reading of the Bible. However, once the thought of the Bible is conceptualized theologically (or hermeneutically beyond the reading of the text itself) it looks as though this second order authority dominates, which in Lindbeck is the only way texts are accessible to us, through the pre-understanding of the confessional tradition. If internalistic strategies of a tradition serve to insulate one from taking the Bible as one's primary authority in formulating theological thought forms then the product will be traditional and not primarily Biblical. So I see Lindbeck's strategy as self-defeating, in that it insulates the interpreter using such a method from getting beyond the second order tradition to the Biblical text itself.

Contrasting to this, externalist strategies draw the commentator to expand the conceptual envelope dependent upon the greater authority of the Biblical text, making one Biblical rather than merely traditional. The primary divine authority of the Biblical text is to be preferred over the secondary authority of a tradition. In one's quest to be Biblical one may find that a new composite view may emerge that will incorporate many nuanced features within which a variety of traditions allow themselves to be each dominated by one or a few of those features as its ruling paradigm. However, the situation is not as simple as this. For the commentator is not himself the divine authority, and his attempt to know the text has filtered the text through his subjectivity which makes him a secondary authority as well. The commentator might be like Calvin who uses a simple humanist framework to understand the Bible straightforwardly as one might any human communication and then proclaims the understood message of the Bible as from God. This Biblical message departs from and expands Calvin's humanism significantly. Calvin shows his commitment to the text by over his life allowing his traditional grid of his *Institutes* to grow and undergo change under the influence of his commentaries.

5.2. Textual Realism or Contextual Realism

Within critical realist externalisms, Sailhamer explored a few aspects of this textual versus traditional issue in a paper he presented at the Evangelical Theological Society Hermeneutics study group that was later published in *JETS* as "Johann August Ernesti: The Role of History in Biblical Interpretation."[17] The views he highlights in this article raise

16 George Lindbeck, *The Nature of Doctrine* (Philadelphia: The Westminster Press, 1984) describes a methodology which articulates the handling of a confessional tradition in the manner to which Gadamer and Childs appeal. Evangelical historians like Mark Noll commend the same strategy of keeping the confessional faith.

17 John Sailhamer, "Johann August Ernesti: The Role of History in Biblical Interpretation," *JETS* 44:2 (June 2001): 193–206.

different externalist places of emphasis for grounding authority in the contemporary hermeneutical options, which I intend to evaluate for how they relate to the issue of authority. Sailhamer aligns himself with Ernesti's approach, which developed that the inspiration and meaning was to be known by the *words* of the text (and in philological study which compares words among other texts from the same context) not the *things* to which these words refer.[18] Ernesti's approach was "hailed as the definite statement of what was to be known as the 'grammatical-historical method'"[19] and as such was seen as a "safe haven from the 'historical critical method.'"[20] The phrase "grammatical-historical" was coined by Karl Keil, as he followed Ernesti in studying the Bible like any book, but his method added a distinctive historical approach to the grammatical (thus the hyphen) to follow Johann Semler a student of Sigmund Jakob Baumgarten.[21]

Sailhamer quotes historian Emanuel Hirsch as developing a contrasting confessional historical view of Baumgarten, where 'Biblical history' came to mean events referred to in the Bible, "Hence divine revelation was to be found in the events referred to in Scripture, rather than in the Scriptures themselves."[22] Sailhamer then follows Hans-Joachim Kraus in tracing the route of Baumgarten's thought appropriated by Coccejus and Buddeus. For example, Kraus claims Johannes Coccejus understood history as an actual flow of events, changing with time leading to a definite conclusion, which means that "the things to which the Biblical *words* referred were forever changed into dynamic, unrepeatable events."[23]

Coccejus' approach means that Biblical teaching is that teaching about the people and events of the Bible, rather than the textual agenda which the descriptive Biblical theology movement tries to surface. Kraus later identifies Franz Buddeus as the first Biblical scholar to approach the

18 Johann Augus Ernesti, *Institutio Interpretis Novi Testamenti* (Leipzig, 1761; edito altera 1765), p. 13; Sailhamer, "Johann August Ernesti: The Role of History in Biblical Interpretation," *JETS* 44:2 (June 2001): 199, 201, 206.

19 Sailhamer, "Johann August Ernesti: The Role of History in Biblical Interpretation," *JETS* 44:2 (June 2001): 194.

20 Sailhamer, "Johann August Ernesti: The Role of History in Biblical Interpretation," *JETS* 44:2 (June 2001): 195.

21 Karl Augustus Theophilos Keil, *Elementa Hermeneutices* (translated into Latin by Christoph August Emmerling; Leipzig, 1811); Karl Keil edited by J. D. Goldhorn, *Keilii opuscula academica ad N.T. interpretationem grammatico-historicam et theologiae christianae origins pertinentia* (Leipzig, 1820); Sailhamer, "Johann August Ernesti: The Role of History in Biblical Interpretation," *JETS* 44:2 (June 2001): 195–6.

22 Sailhamer, "Johann August Ernesti: The Role of History in Biblical Interpretation," JETS 44:2 (June 2001): 196, 199; Emanuel Hirsch, Geschichte der neuern Evangelischen Theologie vol. 2 (Gütersloh: C. Bertelsmann, 1951), p. 373.

23 Sailhamer, "Johann August Ernesti: The Role of History in Biblical Interpretation," *JETS* 44:2 (June 2001): 200; Hans-Joachim Kraus, *Geshichte der historisch-kritischen Erforschung des Alten Testaments* (Neukirchen: Neukirchener, 1969), p. 21.

events and meaning of Biblical "history" as independent of the *words* of Scripture.[24] However, Karl Keil wished to combine these views of *words* for the grammatical meaning and *things* which provide a better grasp of the world view of the author including the meaning of the *words*.[25] In contrast, Ernesti had argued that the meaning was in the *words* not the *things*, except in the rare instances in which words are ambiguous and then contextual options of the meaning are then provided by the *things*.[26] Sailhamer agreed with Ernesti's view.

This historical discussion continued in miniature when at the ETS meeting John Walton was called for the official response. Walton raised the value of cultural objects behind the text for deciphering the meaning of text, much like Keil had done, and much like Walton does in his Bible backgrounds commentaries.[27] The Sailhamer/Walton dialog reduced down to a discussion of the sin at the tower of Babel, which played to the subject of John Walton's dissertation, an analysis of the tower of Babel. Walton reminds us that Babylonian ziggurats' highest platform was thought of culturally as heaven, the place of the gods which means that Walton identifies the sin of Genesis 11:4 to be the construction of a tower accessing this high level of the heavens; meaning determined by the object behind the text. Sailhamer replied that a divine command was implied in the blessing for man to fill the earth (Genesis 1:28 and 9:1). So for Sailhamer, the sin in Genesis 11:4 was humanity's attempt to keep themselves from being scattered over the face of the earth in rebellion to this "fill the earth" command. In this solution, Sailhamer is proposing a text-based solution to the meaning of the text. While I agree with Walton's insight concerning Babylonian culture, I think that the text describes this aspect of the Babylonians intent for their tower as simply a description of their aspiration, thus not the sin. In this situation, if one grants that the genre of blessing has ethical relevance, then Sailhamer does have an authoritative text based explanation for the sin of Genesis 11:4, which would be preferred over the Walton option because *the authoritative revelation is the Biblical text and the text itself is the locus for the meaning communicated by text.*

24 Sailhamer, "Johann August Ernesti: The Role of History in Biblical Interpretation," *JETS* 44:2 (June 2001): 200; Hans-Joachim Kraus, *Die Biblische Theologie* (Neukircheniuer-Vluyn: Neukirchener, 1983), p. 24.

25 Karl Keil, *Keilii Opuscula,* p. 14; Sailhamer, "Johann August Ernesti: The Role of History in Biblical Interpretation," *JETS* 44:2 (June 2001): 202.

26 Ernesti, *Institutio,* p.13; Sailhamer, "Johann August Ernesti: The Role of History in Biblical Interpretation," *JETS* 44:2 (June 2001): 203.

27 John Walton, Victor Matthews & Mark Chavalas, *The IVP Bible Background Commentary: Old Testament* (Downers Grove: InterVarsity Press, 2000) also the 1997 version of Genesis-Deuteronomy included within it.

5.3. Pre-Text Tradition History or Textual Realism

Another facet of a traditional approach was pioneered by W. Wrede in 1897 A.D. as the *Traditionsgeschichte* or the "tradition history" movement. Wrede argued that the community created a tradition which circulated orally for a period of time and then was written down. During this period, the traditions were shaped by the historical situation (*Sitz im Leben)* of the communities in which they circulated. By studying the differences in the various traditions, it was concluded that a commentator could determine which tradition goes back to the historical Jesus, and what was the situation of the early church when the tradition arose.[28] Likewise, in O.T. studies, pioneers like Sigmund Mowinckel appropriated a tradition approach to O.T. texts like the Psalms, conjecturing that Jews in the Diaspora setting of Babylon were inclined to appropriate standardized lament and hymn forms which are identifiable through form criticism as reflecting the Babylonian settings like the Akitu (New Year's) festival.[29]

While I have evaluated each of these approaches in more detail elsewhere, a few points of critique can be raised here. First, these approaches are creative and trying to make sense of texts in light of significant ancient Near Eastern contexts. However, these contexts are largely conjectured to apply to these Biblical texts in such a manner as to radically alter the meaning of these texts. For example, the synoptic orientation ignores the author's theological agenda expressed in the text in order to seek a "behind the text" meaning of the conjectured event of the historical Jesus and the community concerns that are conjectured to source the available text. Likewise, the canonical reconfiguration diminishes the nature of the known *Sitz im Leben* (where superscriptions in the psalms are known) by placing more profound authority on the conjectured *Sitz im Leben* in which the psalm is seen as being produced or arranged in the canon. While we know some facts of the ancient Near Eastern context, this model is substantially dependent upon a re-appropriation of those contexts conjectured to develop the Biblical texts, an event behind text method. Furthermore, there is not a lot of evidence to support these conjectured scenarios and there is substantial evidence for the described *Sitz im Leben* mentioned in the text. For example, Biblical examples of prayer and psalm superscriptions argue for a deep and widespread Jewish prayer life, with a special emphasis around the Temple, not mimicking pagan rituals. Additionally, the abundance of

---

28 For a more detailed discussion of the quests of the historical Jesus see C. Marvin Pate and Doug Kennard, *Deliverance Now and Not Yet* (New York: Peter Lang, 2002, 2005), ch. 16, where we evaluate which criteria enable and which criteria hinder these kinds of decisions.

29 For a more detailed discussion of the merits and unwarranted assumptions of such tradition criticism see Doug Kennard, "Theology of the Lament Psalms" a paper completed for a doctoral class at Dallas Theological Seminary on the Theology of the Psalms, 1982.

Lament and Hymn documents throughout the ancient Near East identify a common textual informed mindset rather than a growing oral tradition out of which the Biblical psalms evolve.

Likewise, the intentional claims of an author like Luke show that Luke is selective in the telling of the story of Jesus for his purposes. This point can be seen in Luke's use of sources and eyewitnesses, writing to a particular audience (Theophilus) with a particular agenda, including the historical credibility of this testimony about Jesus within Luke's agenda (Luke 1:1–4). The fact that Luke utilized eyewitnesses indicates that not much time for oral transmission has taken place. With little time for oral transmission and an indebtedness to written sources, many would consider that the hermeneutical task is thereby moved out of the realm of tradition and into redaction. Furthermore, to the extent that this view is dependent upon a conjectured tradition and *Sitz im Leben,* one's interpretation moves from the authority and warranting which the text provides into the realm of subjectivity and opinion evident by the conjectured tradition. Only if such conjectured options are substantially warranted in the text should we retain these views, and then we do so not as traditions before the text but as features of the text which we can pragmatically check after the pattern of Charles Peirce, which moves this study to a level of critical realism.

5.4. Redaction Criticism and the Hardcopy Textual Versions Available

At this point "redaction criticism" often replaces the "tradition history" approach. G. Bornkamm pioneered such a view when he wrote his 1948 article "The Stilling of the Storm in Matthew," in which he argued that Matthew had reinterpreted Mark's miracle story into a paradigm for discipleship of the little ship of the church. In his wake, redaction criticism reached a high water mark in the Hans Conzelmann's *The Theology of St. Luke* (1954), in which he argued that Luke was a theologian (rather than a historian) who developed that the delay of the *Parousia* led Luke to replace the immanent eschatology of Mark with a salvation history perspective. The term *Redaktionsgeschichte* (redaction criticism) was first used by W. Marxsen in his *Mark the Evangelist* (1956) where he criticizes the tradition history approach with missing the significant *Sitz im Leben* of the author of the work itself. This approach of redaction criticism has the possibility of strongly valuing the Biblical text as a whole or in individual passages with a descriptive Biblical theology orientation. However, when this sort of analysis is done with regards to the text's structure and persuasion techniques, this approach would more appropriately be referred to as rhetorical criticism.

J. Muilenburg originated the use of rhetorical criticism for Biblical studies in his 1968 presidential address to the Society of Biblical Literature. Rhetorical criticism more readily appreciates genre and the artistry of each pericope of the text, rather than an archaeology of conjectured editors behind the text. An example of the use of Muilenburg's approach is J. Dewey's study of Mark 2:1–3:6 where she makes a case for the text being composed with an intentional concentric literary pattern.[30] A different emphasis surfaces in the work of W. Kurz as he draws on the rhetorical handbooks available from the ancient Greco-Roman world, namely those of Aristotle, Cicero and Quintilian. He argued that the author of Luke-Acts was likely trained in rhetoric as part of his secondary education.[31] Extending this approach further, the classicist G. Kennedy proposed a five step process for using Greco-Roman rhetorical handbooks in analysis:[32]

1. Determine the rhetorical unit.
2. Analyze the rhetorical situation.
3. Determine the kind of rhetoric and what it is trying to accomplish.
4. Analyze arrangement and style for accomplishing these ends.
5. Evaluate the rhetorical effectiveness of the text towards accomplishing these ends.

The strength of these approaches can be their sensitivity to the text under analysis. The weakness of these approaches is the occasional imposition of foreign rhetorical devices upon the text, which may not always be in the Biblical text. So the issue of Biblical authority is especially spotlighted by rhetorical criticism in the hands of these critics. Within a balanced evangelical approach, as say Craig Blomberg utilizes it, the authority of text is valued and determines meaning.[33] Using this approach in my book *Messiah Jesus: Christology in His Day and Ours* I evaluate the questions asked by the religious leaders during Jesus final week before his death to be the standard rhetorical questions asked to assess the quality of a scribe.[34] Thus the sections of the synoptic gospels working these questions warrants Jesus' authority to teach as a superior scribe, while He also shames the religious leaders with their lack of authority. However, in some of the other rhetorical approaches already mentioned, a foreign rhetoric is imported into the Biblical text laying such approaches open to the charge of eisegesis.

---

30 J. Dewey, *Markan Public Debate: Literary Technique, Concentric Structure, and Theology in Mark 2:1–3:6* (SBLDS 48; Ann Arbor: Scholars Press, 1980).

31 W. S. Kurz, "Hellenistic Rhetoric in the Christological Proof of Luke–Acts," *CBQ* 42(1980): 171–95.

32 G. A. Kennedy, *New Testament Interpretation through Rhetorical Criticism* (Chapel Hill: University of North Carolina, 1984).

33 Craig Blomberg, *Jesus and the Gospels* (Nashville: Broadman & Holman Publishers, 1997).

34 Douglas W. Kennard, *Messiah Jesus: Christology in His Day and Ours* (New York: Peter Lang, 2008), pp. 133–7.

In an idiosyncratic critical realist approach of redaction and rhetorical criticism (which he calls canonical criticism), Sailhamer proposed a novel solution of later editors adding material, from even later than the Babylonian captivity in the process of arranging the final form of the canon.[35] The influence of the canonicaler's redactions can only be discerned by an intra-textual comparison of the composition of the final form of the *TaNaK* (i.e. O.T. Hebrew) text. For example, Deuteronomy 34:9–12 and Joshua 1:1–9 are compared to Malachi 3:22–24 and Psalm 1, which he claims are at the seams of the divisions of this *TaNaK* text between covenant and prophets and writings. This process also involves inter-textual comparisons as well to especially recognize macrocompositional seams, which he takes to be indicators of a canonicaler's context and not the original author's. Part of the nature of Sailhamer's canonical hermeneutical approach is that the canonicaler's authorial and context take precedence over the original author's intent and context when the hermeneutical meaning is to be understood. That is, meaning of the text is to be understood through the full final form of the text. An example is by looking at the poetic texts of the Pentateuch: Genesis 49; Numbers 24; and Deuteronomy 32. Sailhamer concludes, "In each, the central of figure (Jacob, Balaam, Moses) calls together God's people (imperatives) and proclaims (cohortatives) 'what will happen' 'in the last days,'" which he connects with eschatological prophets.[36] Sailhamer recognizes that in Numbers 24:7 'Agag' is read by some early textual variants as 'Gog,' which incline him to connect it with Ezekiel 38:16 and at least would indicate that the Pentateuch was being read eschatologically even in identical terms of Daniel 11 and Ezekiel 38–39.[37] One of the consequences of this approach is that the theology of the O.T. is not developed nearly so progressively with incipient forms eventually becoming extensive presentations after further revelational development, for the so-called incipient places are often seen by Sailhamer to be canonicaler insertions of a more developed theological era raising the theological complexity of the earlier textual material to be the elaborate theology of the later era, during the Babylonian captivity. This theological flattening of the canonical text shows the transposition of authority from the original author to that of the canonicaler. Few follow Sailhamer in this textually complex strategy. Such creatively textually warranted options at least would admit that many of Sailhamer's proposals are possible. However, I often think that the original author's context and textual message, which is the major portion of the material

35 E.g., John Sailhamer, *Introduction to O.T. Theology* (Grand Rapids: Zondervan, 1995), p. 240.

36 John Sailhamer, "Creation, Genesis 1–11, and the Canon," *Bulletin for Biblical Research* 10(2000): 92.

37 Sailhamer, "Creation, Genesis 1–11, and the Canon," *BBR* 10(2000): 97–100.

of these texts is in fact being diminished by Sailhamer in its contribution, replaced by the conjectured later material from the canonicaler.

It is better to let the textual emphasis and use determine meaning. So, following descriptive Biblical theology, I let the earlier texts surface incipient comments with some ambiguity authentic to that earlier context. The later texts build upon this earlier Biblical theology with some increased complexity that reflect the later stages which progressive revelation brings. So there is real progression of Biblical theological development within the Biblical authors.

5.5. Extra-Biblical Context and Textual Realism

An offshoot of this progression is the tendency to use extra-Biblical sources to inform one's interpretation of the Biblical text. My opinion is that the extra-Biblical material is suggestive and can be both insightful and complementarily warranting for an interpretation, but the interpretation of a text needs to be substantially warranted within the text itself. For example, the similarities of *The Proclamation of Telepinu* and the *Apology of Hattusilis* to the book of Samuel is reassuring that one of the main purposes of this book of Samuel is a justification of David's legitimacy as king, grounded in the Davidic Covenant.[38] However, David's case stands in the book of Samuel rather than primarily these extra-Biblical texts. By drawing into even closer parallels like the similarities of the *Instruction of Amenemope*[39] and Proverbs 22:17–24:22, which are nearly identical, thus probably indicates some common appropriation of the material. However, the genre of wisdom still requires reflective thinking in the exegetical context, and in our own context as well, for wisdom to perform its function in our lives today. Furthermore, Marv Pate and I folded in many second Temple sources in our book: *Deliverance Now and Not Yet*,[40] because they were highly suggestive of the possibilities with which the Biblical authors work. I contend that the higher authority stands with the Biblical text in its context than these second Temple suggestions of possibilities. For example, we recognize that *1 Enoch* 70–71 presents Israel with a mystical participation in heavenly glory that can serve as a developing concept that Paul in Ephesians 1 develops further. When we develop the Ephesians eschatology, the meaning of the text must be warranted within the Biblical text of Ephesians, for this is where the authority lies.

---

38 See these ancient documents in Herbert Wolf, *The Apology of Hattusilis compared with other Political Self-justifications of the Ancient New East* (Waltham, Mass.: Brandeis University, 1967); William McNeal and Jean Sedlar, *The Ancient Near East* (New York: Oxford Press, 1968) and Louis Cohn-Haft, *Source Readings in Ancient History: the Ancient Near East and Greece* (New York: Thomas Crowell, 1965).

39 James Roger Black, *The Instruction of Amenemope: A Critical Edition and Commentary Prolegomenon and Prologue* (Internet material OCLC, 2002).

40 C. Marvin Pate and Douglas W. Kennard, *Deliverance Now and Not Yet: The New Testament and the Great Tribulation* (New York: Peter Lang, 2003, 2005).

John Sailhamer takes these textual/confessional issues in another direction as he wished to disagree with the descriptive Biblical theology movement. That is, Sailhamer explores an intentional canonical approach to hermeneutics that moves to a critical realist epistemology but is intentionally confessional.[41]

In contrast to this confessional reformation and pietism the descriptive Biblical theology movement emerged in Johann Philip Gabler's lecture at the University of Altdorf in 1787 to call for a Biblical theology being reframed by the thrust of the Biblical text itself.[42] Gabler was optimistic that we could arrive at objective truth about the meaning of the text from the straightforward study of the Biblical text's details. This confidence that a commentator can approach the Biblical text in a descriptive manner is still with us in a more nuanced subjective way, as in K. Stendahl's article about contemporary Biblical theology in the *Interpreter's Dictionary of the Bible,* which calls the contemporary commentator to describe the meaning of the Biblical text for the original reader.[43]

Sailhamer admits that this descriptive approach freed the interpreter from having to handle the Biblical text in dogmatic categories and that it freed us from always seeking contemporary relevance.[44] However, Sailhamer claims that this descriptive approach is too confident that it can objectively approach a Biblical text from a neutral framework, without bias.[45] I think that Stendahl has already answered this charge through his nuanced subjective epistemology. Furthermore, the Biblical texts are written as truth to believers, who are not neutral. He also claims that this descriptive approach too readily separates what the texts meant from what they mean in the contemporary context. A final reason for his rejecting the descriptive approach is found among those who do not see its unique voice against the landscape of the ancient Near Eastern context.

---

41 John Sailhamer, *Introduction to Old Testament Theology: A Canonical Approach,* especially pp. 115–83. A similar confessional orientation was argued by Grant Osborne and Harold Netland at the 1997 Midwest regional meeting of the Evangelical Theological Society meeting as shown in my book. David Hesselgrave and I countered this confessional orientation with a communal critical realism informed through the methodology of the descriptive Biblical theology movement. Cf. Douglas Kennard, *The Relationship Between Epistemology, Hermeneutics, Biblical Theology and Contextualization,* p. 2.

42 Gabler's lecture 'On the proper distinction between Biblical and dogmatic theology and specific objectives of each,' is translated and commented on in John Sandys-Wunsch and Laurence Eldredge, 'J. P. Gabler and the Distinction Between Biblical and Dogmatic Theology: Translation, Commentary, and Discussion of his Originality,' *Scottish Journal of Theology* 33 (1980): 133-58 and also in *The Flowering of O. T. Theology,* eds. Ben Ollenburger, Elmer Martens, Gerhard Hasel (Winona Lake: Eisenbrauns, 1992), pp. 492–502.

43 K. Stendahl, 'Biblical Theology, Contemporary,' *Interpreter's Dictionary of the Bible* (Nashville: Abingdon, 1962), 1:418–32.

44 Sailhamer, *Introduction to O.T. Theology,* pp. 167–8.

45 Sailhamer, *Introduction to O.T. Theology,* pp. 168–9.

These criticisms may be accurate against some exegetes but in this commentator's opinion they are not accurate against all working in the field, and do not constitute sufficient reason for rejecting the descriptive accessibility of the text. God accommodated Himself through the revelational means to craft the Biblical text as accessible to us so that we can understand the Biblical text and recognize that it is claiming divine authority for itself. So that whether we approach the Biblical text in a straight forwardly humanist approach like Calvin or with a more critical realist approach like myself, we may say part of the efficacious nature of God's revelation is that it is accessible to us. My critical realist approach admits that objectivity from a neutral vantage point isn't the goal. Rather the goal of hermeneutics includes the recovery of the truthful meaning of the Biblical text in its original context to the extent that it is accessible to us today. We all approach the text with biases but there are available means to access the meaning of the text and to check the meaning of the text so that our biases do not have to hinder us from obtaining that textual meaning.[46] For example, a text of Leviticus can be understood by us Christians even though we are not embracing the Judaism of the original readers as our own. We can recognize that these Jews needed to bring sacrificial animals as the Biblical text describes to recover them individually and nationally at the Day of Atonement. This does not reduce the Old Testament's meaning of atonement sacrifices to be a common ancient Near Eastern meaning of sacrifices as merely placating God so that we might be able to have our way with Him. That is, the text is clear enough for a good exegete to recognize and distinguish the difference between the meaning of the Biblical text and the cultural practices of the peoples surrounding ancient Israel.

I agree with Sailhamer in that hermeneutics is ultimately textually dependent and not oriented to event behind or around the text.[47] However, within the meaning of the Leviticus text, Jews at Sinai are mandated to be involved with sacrifice and Day of Atonement. Such texts stand as within an everlasting covenant between Yahweh and the nation Israel (Ex. 31:16–17), so that Jews since should follow these patterns of sacrifice as well. However, there is no requirement that a Gentile Christian needs to do these practices. It looks to me that the text itself separates its meaning (Jews must be involved) from the significances for many of us today. That is, the Mosaic Covenant texts on sacrifices do have meaningful significance to us Gentiles today; however Exodus-Leviticus does not have the same significance for me that it did for Moses and the Jews of the Exodus. In my opinion, this is not 'too readily separating what the text meant from what it means' because I believe that the Jews

46 I explained and defended this approach at length in: Doug Kennard, *The Relationship Between Epistemology, Hermeneutics, Biblical Theology and Contextualization,* pp. 1–70, 117–152, 181–5.

47 Sailhamer, *Introduction to O.T. Theology,* pp. 36–86.

should still be sacrificing and celebrating the Day of Atonement as an expression of Yahweh's suzerainty treaty with them and will be doing these practices eschatologically (Jer. 31:33; 33:18, 21; Ezek. 45–46). So unlike Sailhamer, who is guilty of his own criticism, for he too readily separates what this Leviticus text meant from what it means, I do not. That is, the continuing legacy of Israel is still to be obedient to the suzerainty treaty Exodus-Leviticus, and eschatologically they will be obedient in offering the sacrifices commanded of them.

Furthermore, by comparing the final paragraphs of this chapter, which applies Genesis 2:24 to an evangelical context, the reader can see that I am committed to keeping the authoritative textual meaning together with its contemporary significance when the context groups are similar in respect to the issues of the passage. In such a situation, the issue transfers directly the textual meaning is the significance. So there is no good reason for embracing a confessional tradition as a primary authority to inform conceptuality, over the primacy of the Biblical text itself. So Calvin's practice of exegesis growing theology has given us a good model in allowing his *Institutes* to grow throughout his life under the influence of the primacy of the Biblical text as the primary authority for our thinking and living.

5.6. Critical Realism Critiqued?

Roger Ludin offers a metaphor of critique that the traditionalists might make against critical realist approaches but answers it largely by the resources of Wittgenstein.[48] The traditional critique considers that Descartes' rejection of tradition as a weak foundation for knowledge and a shift to the "individual thinking being" renders one "fatherless" and thus "orphans." This approach is sometimes caricatured by the deconstructionist as alienated from others and our past however that is too great a disconnect for me. That is, I advocate the same movement upon which Martin Luther grounded the reformation in his rejection of some church traditions for the claim to be able to stand on the Word of God.

This reformation approach shows a confidence that the Biblical text is accessible by individuals and groups of Christians. Luther and this approach do not reject everything about Christian tradition to date while they call for specifics to be evaluated under the spotlight of the Word of God. In this approach, the group's traditional heritage might be rethought by individuals persuading the community in a way that preserved the Biblical text as having primary authority to call the tradition into submission, with the tradition being reworked wherever the Biblical text might take the interpreter. The resources to make sense

48 Roger Ludin, Clarence Walhout, and Anthony Thiselton, *The Promise of Hermeneutics* (Grand Rapids: Eerdmans, 1999), part I.

of this hermeneutic approach of a growing traditional language game, within a Lakatos' progressive research program, are especially available in Wittgenstein and others of his ilk, as will be developed in a few pages as critical realism's hermeneutic and theological method.

With regard to this theological method, I consider that it is helpful to view tradition within the lens that a Lakatos' philosophy of science. That is, I do not view tradition as monolithic. Nor is theological tradition viewed as Kuhnian "paradigms" that replace each other through revolution. That is, theologically, this would be like the radical shift from the classical Christian God to that of a process God concept. Development of theology is more subtle and nuanced as was developed in the first three chapters.

Lakatos suggests that a more modest proposal of potential change better reflects the findings of exegetical work in the Biblical text as "research programs." These exegetical research programs work along side each other and can be judged as rival programs whether progressive or degenerative for the whole theological task a program is progressive if the internal features are predictive of novel facts, and correspond to the full range of data from the Biblical text in a congruent manner. Contrasting to this, a program is degenerative if it does not take recognized data into account. Each research program has a hard core surrounded by auxiliary hypotheses, which are surrounded by data. Any individual could have pliable features (of auxiliary hypotheses) within a largely resilient world-view, surrounding the individual's hard core theology. A group's tradition is made up of the commonness of those individuals in this group. This means that what the group agrees upon becomes the group's hard core. Any tradition grants that certain affirmations possess an undeniable claim as a hard core of one's world view. In physics, such progressive Lakatos' research programs would be the rival theories of relativity and quantum mechanics, which both excel their Newtonian classical physics predecessor in certain aspects of precision and predictability.

In theology, there is a need to engage the issues and evaluate the rival theological research proposals, as for example: 1) a relational classical Christian eternal God,[49] or 2) a relational temporal sovereign God,[50] or 3) open theism.[51] For each group, the hard core is so well grounded and warranted for the individual or group, with repeated textual evidence, that it becomes a resilient systematic theological framework to place new data within.

49 Examples include: Millard Erickson, *God the Father Almighty* (Grand Rapids: Baker, 1998) and Doug Kennard, *The Classical Christian God* (Lewiston: The Edwin Mellen Press, 2002).

50 E.g., John Feinberg, *No One Like Him* (Wheaton: Crossway Books, 2001).

51 E.g., Clark Pinnock, Richard Rice, John Sanders, William Hasker, David Basinger, *The Openness of God* (Downers Grove: InterVarsity, 1994).

The theological commitments that surround this traditional hard core (the affiliated hypotheses) are more pliable and more likely to be challenged or rethought than the hard core. Though Alister McGrath describes that for some "the decision to accept one theory rather than another rests not so much on experimental evidence, as on various social values, vested interests, and institutional concerns. This has raised the very significant question of whether religious doctrines correspond to anything that is 'real,' or whether they can be seen as determined by social factors."[52] In my opinion, the data surrounds these levels of tradition and theology, and is incorporated within the theological levels best in a critical realist model. That is, we are still trying to reflect the Biblical text in our theology. So hermeneutics and theology should not be socially determined, for that is in fact post-modernism in its conventional practice. That is, the truth of the Bible critiques such community views.

By appealing to Lakatos' framework of research programs, I have not moved the problem of confessional tradition to a new level (which would be the case if McGrath's post-modern scenario ensued) because the hard core still attempts to model the Biblical textual data in a critical realist perspective.[53] That is, the whole framework (even including the hard core) is dependent upon and reflects the Biblical textual data in its context. Therefore, even the hard core is challenged by the Biblical text, but the overwhelming Biblical evidence already marshaled for the hard core renders the hard core unlikely to change, except in nuanced statements of the same thing. However, the affiliated hypotheses reflect their dependency on the data by continuing to be challenged and changed by additional hermeneutical studies of the Biblical text. I welcome this development of theology, for in our love relation with God we do not have exhaustive knowledge of our Lover and Loved One. The relation with God continues and the growth of such knowledge of God does as well.

Unfortunately, most evangelicals operate generally or occasionally with a naïve Gadamerian[54] ideological hermeneutic while claiming to be Biblical. Most of these evangelicals will probably be annoyed by someone or a group operating theologically in a more critical realist approach with this Lakatos philosophy of science. The pliability of the auxiliary hypotheses may unnerve them into an uneasy feeling that the family jewels are being tampered with or that the hard core is as vulnerable to change as auxiliary hypotheses happen to be. Remember

52 Alister McGrath, *Science & Religion* (Oxford: Blackwell, 1999), p. 83.

53 For more extensive development see Kennard, *The Relationship Between Epistemology, Hermeneutics, Biblical Theology and Contextualization*, pp. 31–33, 35–65.

54 This is an allusion to the method advocated by Hans-Georg Gadamer in *Truth and Method* (New York: Crossroad Publishing Co., 1984), especially the third part pp. 345–447.

that this approach does not put the hard core at risk. I grieve about some of evangelicalism's critical reactions from their respective traditions against what I consider the clear teaching of the Word of God. However, I think that it is preferable to be methodologically precise and Biblically grounded even if we need to run the risk of being misunderstood (and even persecuted) by evangelical theologians, rather than to dull down one's theological method to not engage the Biblical text itself or to remain isolated from engaging contemporary theological options fairly.

5.7. Calvin's Spirit Witness

Another level of authority, which can serve as an example of Biblical text challenging tradition, is Calvin's view of the Holy Spirit's witness to the Biblical text as divine authority.[55] For Calvin, this internal witness of Spirit does not indicate meaning of the text but it does encourage the believer to take the Biblical text seriously as from God with full divine authority.

Astute readers will recognize that such a view has been emulated within Mormonism's claim to take *The Book of Mormon* in hand and pray for the witness of the Spirit. The warm assurance that Mormons have when they do this is taken to be sufficient indication that *The Book of Mormon* is of primary divine authority.

This is a very subjective approach to determining authority. I wonder whether such witnesses of the Spirit are in fact warranting and warranted since rival traditions of cults utilize the same method. Both rival intuitions can't be true. So how do we choose between them? Do we merely allow our tradition to settle which "witness of the Spirit" we accept? If so, we have set ourselves up for post-modernism; each tradition having its own tacit claim to truth from the Spirit.

Such an intuition might be a purveyor of tacit knowledge but if the Biblical text does not promise the Holy Spirit's witness to function in this way it would be presumptuous of the reader to claim that such an intuitive witness was in fact available and regularly occurring. Calvin proof-texts his view from Ephesians and Isaiah, but these texts do not address the issue. Kevin Vanhoozer continues to maintain a witness of the Spirit in this Calvinistic sense, but does not develop a rationale for the view either Biblically or philosophically.[56]

The Biblical concept of the "witness of the Spirit" is not an internal testimony to the authority of the Word of God but rather an internal witness to the authentic salvation experience enlivening our human spirits and utilizing religious affections fostered by the Spirit in our life to encourage our enlivened spirit that we are in fact children of God

55 John Calvin, *Institutes of the Christian Religion* (Grand Rapids: Associated Publishers and Authors, n.d.), Bk. 1, Chapter 7; cf. *The Westminster Confession of Faith* 1.5.

56 Kevin Vanhoozer, *Is There Meaning in this Text?* (Grand Rapids: Zondervan, 1998), p. 413.

(Rom. 8:4–16; 1 John 5:1–13). That is, Biblically the witness of Spirit is soteriological and not supporting the authority of the Bible. Such a Biblically taught divine witness utilizes the external evidence of Spirit transforming our life so that as a divinely authoritative witness it can be warranted and confirmed. However, Calvin's witness of Spirit has no definitive warranting evidence or Biblical promise so that it should be rejected as a degenerative traditional oddity. The Bible itself is self-authenticating as it claims divine authority, and nowhere claims an additional witness of the Spirit to prop up the authority of the Bible.

5.8. Spirit Illumination?

A similar major avenue of claimed authority is that funded through Lutheran pietism as the illumination of the Holy Spirit. Phillip Jakob Spener replaced the concept of verbal inspiration of the Scriptures with a personal inspiration or illumination of the believing interpreter, fostering a major controversy with orthodox Lutheranism.[57] In 1685 Johann Quenstedt reframed the view as a hermeneutic.[58] In 1707 David Hollanz echoed the view that the Holy Spirit is promised to every

57 Philipp Jakob Spener, *Consilia Et Judicia Theologia* (Frankfurt a.M., 1709), vol. 3, p. 700; Cf. K. James Stein, "Phillip Jakob Spener (1635–1705)" and Markus Matthias, "August Hermann Franke (1663–1727)" in *The Pietist Theologians: An Introduction to Theology in the Seventeenth Centuries*. edited by Carter Lindberg (Malden: Blackwell, 2005), pp. 88 and 105–6; Johannes Wallmann, *Philipp Jakob Spener und die Aufänge des Pietismus* (Tübigen: Mohr, 1970), pp. 92–96; Emmanuel Hirsch, *Geschichte der neuen Evangelische Theologie in Zusammenhang mit den allgemein Bewegung des Europäischen Denkens* (Gütersloh: Bertelsmann, 1951), vol. 2, p. 114; Volker Jung, *Das Ganze der Heiligen Schrift. Hermeneutik und Schriftauslegung bei Abrham Calov* (Stuttgart: Calwer Verlag, 1999), pp. 100–1; cf. Douglas Kennard, "Evangelical Views of Illumination of Scripture and Critique," *JETS* 49(Dec. 2006): 797–806.

58 Johann Andreas Quenstedt, *Theologia Didactico-Polemica* (Wittenberg: Johanne Ludolph Quenstedt, 1685). The relevant portion (chapters 1–3) of this is available in English as: *The Nature and Character of Theology: An Introduction to the Thought of J. A. Quenstedt from THEOLOGIA DIDACTIO-POLEMICA SIVE SYSTEMA THEOLOGICUM*. abridged, edited, and translated by Luther Poellot (St. Louis: Concordia, 1986), ch. I "Of Theology in General": question I "Is Theology Given?" paragraph XI, p. 36; ph. XIV, p. 39; ph. XXXI-Observe (1), p. 54; ph. XXXV, p. 57; Section II "Polemic"-"Sources of Rebuttals or Dialysis of Objections": q. I "Is Theology Given?", pp. 64–5; q. II "Is Revealed Theology Necessary in the Church?", pp. 71, 72–3; q. III "Is Theology a God-Given Practical Aptitude?", exposition III & IV, pp. 73–4; rebuttal I, p. 80; ch. III "Of the Sources of Theology", porism IV, pp. 199–200. Stanley Grenz, in *Beyond Foundationalism* (Lousiville: Westminster John Knox Press, 2001), p. 99 claims that this illumination view originated earlier by at least the time of John Hus and cites George Tavard in *Holy Writ or Holy Church: The Crisis of the Protestant Reformation* (New York: Harper & Brothers, 1959), pp. 47–66 which discusses John Hus' view of the soteriological transformation in which the Holy Spirit enables the new believer to be applicationally responsive to the Word of God. From my reading of the Hus material, I agree with Tavard, contrary to Grenz; Hus does not teach this view of the illumination through the Holy Spirit aid to cognitively understand the Bible. I have not found the view any earlier than Spener's, Quenstedt's and Hollanz's pietistic Lutheran systematic theologies.

Christian so that they might understand the Biblical text better.[59] Around 1701, August Herman Franke introduced the illumination of the Spirit as a "living" knowledge of the Biblical text that will bring about spiritual affection.[60] Evangelicalism has largely owned Spener, Quenstedt, and Hollanz's cognitive illumination view, with others in evangelicalism joining Franke's spirit transformational illumination view. This raises the possibility of an internalist authority on the level of a divine intuition. Unlike Spener and Schlieirmacher, this pietistic evangelical view attempts to remain orthodox in claiming a legitimate verbal inspirational view for the production of the Biblical text. However, Schleiermacher develops a psychological side of the hermeneutical process, echoing Spener's personal inspirational view, including this illumination which motivates the reader to depend deeply upon God.

This liberal interpretation view of illumination (as inspiration) was championed by Cardinal John Henry Newman through his "illative" (or confident intuitive) sense.[61] Some these days may view this illumination through Michael Polanyi's tacit intuitional way of knowing. That is, whether conservative or liberal, the illumination from the Holy Spirit is seen as rendering clear the authoritative message of the Word of God.

Such an illuminative aid would be hermeneutical. Usually evangelicalism sees this hermeneutical aid functioning individually. For example, the 1982 evangelical Chicago Statement on Biblical Hermeneutics includes as the fifth article: "WE AFFIRM that the Holy Spirit enables believers to appropriate and apply Scripture to their lives. WE DENY that the natural man is able to discern spiritually the biblical message apart from the Holy Spirit."[62] This statement indicates in its denial a cognitive illuminational element while in its affirmation the transformational illumination is highlighted. This statement reflects the emphasis in evangelicalism that the Holy Spirit aids the individual's use of hermeneutics.

However, occasionally in contemporary evangelicalism this illumination is taken as communal. A contemporary advocate of this communal conservative illumination view is Donald Bloesch. He

59 David Hollaz, Examen Theologicum Acroamaticum published in 1707 is available as Acromaticum Universam Theologiam Thetico-Polemicam Complectens (Lipsiae: B.C. Breitkopfii, 1763).

60 August Hermann Franke, *Praelectiones Hermeneuticae, ad Exponendi Sensvm Scripturae S. Theologiae Stvdiosis Ostendendam Adjiecta est in Fine Brevis et Lvcvlenta Scriptvram S. cvm Frvtv Legendi Institvtio* (Halle: Waisenhaus, 1710) , p. 57; cf. *Markus* Matthias, "August Hermann Franke (1663–1727)" in *The Pietist Theologians: An Introduction to Theology in the Seventeenth Centuries.* edited by Carter Lindberg (Malden: Blackwell, 2005), pp. 106–7.

61 Cardinal John Henry Newman, *An Essay in Aid of A Grammar of Assent* (London: Longmans, Green & Co., 1870, 1903).

62 The Chicago Statement on Biblical Hermeneutics as contained in *Hermeneutics, Inerrancy, and the Bible.* edited by Earl Radmacher and Robert Preus (Grand Rapids: Zondervan, 1984), p. 891.

identifies that the Bible's revelatory status 'does not reside in its wording as such but in the Spirit of God, who fills the words with meaning and power.'[63] This view provides a post textual subjective meaning. Kevin Vanhoozer also wishes to extend this individual illumination into becoming a community illumination of Spirit, "Only a prayerful reading that invokes the Spirit can perceive the true meaning in what is otherwise a dead letter. Such Spirit-led exegesis 'restores the interpretive activity of the spiritual community as the connecting link between text and reader.'"[64] Within this view, the authority is the Holy Spirit within the corporate communal intuitive process of illumination. Even with the community quality that draws a present tradition into the mix, like Gadamer above, the primary authority is the Holy Spirit who illumines. Vanhoozer develops the gain and need for this illumination as follows:

> The Spirit illumines the letter by impressing its illocution force on the reader. Thanks to the illumination of the Spirit, we see and hear speech acts for what they are - warnings, promises, commands, assertions - together with their implicit claim in our minds and hearts. In so doing, the Spirit does not alter but ministers the meaning: 'The spiritual sense is the literal sense correctly understood.' The distinction between 'letter' and 'spirit' is precisely that between reading the words and grasping what one reads. Likewise, the difference between a 'natural' and 'an illuminated' understanding is that between holding an opinion and having a deep sense of its profundity.[65]

It is my contention that such speech-acts as commands and promises are clearly indicated in the divinely accommodated Biblical text itself without the need of an intuitive work of the Spirit to render the meaning of the text clear. Most speech-act theorists would agree that the meaning of the statement is apparent in the contextualized textual statement, rather than through this sort of evangelical appeal to illumination. For example, God promising aid to rescue Israel from Egypt is clear in the statement of God's promise, without needing the Spirit to vivify the promise to Christian minds. Moses shows this clarity by counting on this promise from God through the exodus experience.

---

63 Donald Bloesch, *Holy Scripture: Revelation, Inspiration & Interpretation* (Downers Grove: InterVarsity, 1994), p. 27.

64 Vanhoozer, *Is There Meaning in this Text?* p. 411.

65 Vanhoozer, *Is There Meaning in this Text?* p. 413. In contrast to Vanhoozer's illumination view of Spirit verses letter, I defended that the contrast here is instead the Spirit's applying the His qualities and fruit home deeply into the life of a believer, like Johnathan Edward's religious affections, rather than external doing of the ritual mandates of the Mosaic Law. Cf. Doug Kennard, 'Paul and the Law,' a paper presented to the Evangelical Theological Society, March, 1996.

In conservative circles this illumination view is often supported through textual appeals to John 14:26; 16:12–15; 1 Cor. 2:6–16; and 1 John 2:27. In chapter four on "Thiselton-Ricoeur Hermeneutic," I argued that these texts do not in fact teach such an illumination view.[66]

The two gospel of John texts are deeply contextually developed as promises of inspiration to the disciples, so that as Jesus leaves these disciples, they would be reminded of what Jesus said to them when He was here, and that the Spirit would also instruct them about prophetic things that these disciples could not handle in that night, but these prophecies were yet to be revealed through the Spirit to them. These promises took place to these disciples and we have the results of these promises in documents like the Biblical gospels and the book of Revelation.

Likewise, the issue in 1 Corinthians 1–2 is not that the Holy Spirit aids in interpreting Bible passages but that the gospel focusing on Christ is revealed by the Spirit, and unfortunately some reject this gospel as foolishness. This gospel was supernaturally revealed (, 1 Cor. 2:10) from the Spirit but the soulish person (, 1 Cor. 2:14) rejects this wisdom of God as foolishness (compare with 1 Cor. 1:18–24). Furthermore, the Spirit's work to make believer's in the gospel to be spiritual is a transformation of the Christian to think out through the Spirit's world-view. This is not a hermeneutical promise for understanding the Biblical text but rather a transformed life that can serve as the basis for evaluating everything in life. For example, the eternal perspective of the gospel serves as a grid for evaluating whether the results of activities will last. Likewise, the non-Christian who rejects the gospel as foolishness won't be able to appreciate a Christian who personifies the gospel's eternal perspective.

Furthermore, the text of 1 John 2:18–23 discusses the gospel message that affirms a relationship to the Father and the Son. Such a gospel message anoints or christicizes the believer from the Holy One (1 John 2:20, 27). In fact, the Holy Spirit isn't even in this text in any clear way for John only uses this expression 'Holy One' elsewhere of Christ (the anointed One; John 6:69). Likewise, the antichrists (those opposed to the anointed One) reject this message of the gospel which speaks of the relationship of the Father and Son. In contrast, the Christians have heard this message from the beginning and have received everlasting life through this same gospel message (1 John 2:24–5). It is through this gospel message that these Christians are taught; the Holy Spirit and illumination are not even in this passage.

One way to help some reassure themselves that this broadly evangelical illumination view is foreign to the Scripture is to recognize

66 Douglas Kennard, *The Relationship Between Epistemology, Hermeneutics, Biblical Theology and Contextualization*, pp. 139–42; this is contained within the chapter "Thiselton-Ricoeur Hermeneutic" and "Evangelical Views on Illumination of Scripture and Critique," *JETS* 49:4(Dec. 2006): 797–806.

that my brief summaries of these passages are right in line with the scholarly commentaries on these passages.[67] Thus, if the Spirit did illumine so many well-informed and godly commentators, then the doctrine of illumination is not a Biblical teaching that anyone can count upon, because these commentators deny such an illumination teaching is Biblical.

Additionally, the absence of such an illumination aid makes more sense of two hermeneutical conditions. The first is that rather repeatedly *godly commentators disagree* with features which other godly commentators may say are within the meaning of a text. If godly Christians were given this illumination aid, then it would unify Christian commentaries but we find that the Arminian ones repeatedly disagree with the Reformed ones, and *vice versa*. The reason for this disagreement is not that some of these commentators are not listening to the illumination of the Spirit but rather each commentator has his own sensitivities to context, grammar, authorial thought forms and theological construct. Perhaps they are fusing the text to a theological model that allows the secondary authority of tradition to be primarily determinative over the primary authority of the Biblical text. They allow tradition to determine meaning rather than textual meaning challenging and modifying a growing and developing tradition. However, even within the same tradition there is still disagreement. Here their sensitivity to these textual features identifies why their interpretations differ.

Secondly, if such an illumination aid occurred for Christians then they would always be able to produce superior commentaries, *but sometimes non-Christians in fact have produced the best commentaries on a book of the Bible*. For example, the best commentary on Leviticus

67 For example, the following sample of commentators support my view: Raymond Brown, *The Gospel According to John 13–21* (Garden City: Doubleday & Co., 1983); Leon Morris, *The Gospel According to John* (Grand rapids: Eerdmans,1971), Frederic Godet, *Commentary on John's Gospel* (Grand Rapids: Kregel Publications, 1978), Craig Keener, *The Gospel of John: A Commentary* (Peabody: Hendenckson Publishers, 2003); Barnabus Lindars, *The Gospel of John* (Grand Rapids: Eerdmans, 1972); R.V.G. Tasker, *The Gospel According to St. John* (Grand Rapids: Eerdmans, 1960); B. F. Westcott *The Gospel According to St. John* (Grand Rapids: Eerdmans, 1978); James Dunn, *The Theology of Paul the Apostle* (Grand Rapids: Eerdmans, 1998); C. K. Barrett *The First Epistle to the Corinthians* (New York: Harper and Row, 1968); F. F. Bruce, *1 and 2 Corinthians* (Grand Rapids: Eerdmans, 1971); Gordon Fee, *The First Epistle to the Corinthians* (Grand Rapids: Eerdmans, 1987); F. W. Grosheide, *Commentary on the First Epistle to the Corinthians* (Grand Rapids: Eerdmans, 1953); Leon Morris, *The First Epistle of Paul to the Corinthians* (Grand Rapids: Eerdmans, 1958); William Orr and James Walther, *1 Corinthians* (Garden City: Doubleday & Co., 1976); Archibald Robertson and Alfred Plummer, *First Epistle of St. Paul to the Corinthians* (Edinburgh: T. & T. Clark, 1911); Anthony Thiselton, *The First Epistle to the Corinthians* Grand Rapids: Eerdmans, 2000); Raymond Brown, *The Epistles of John* (Garden City: Doubleday & Co., 1982); W. Robert Cook, *The Theology of John* (Chicago: Moody Press, 1979); Robert Law, *The Tests of Life* (Grand Rapids: Baker, 1968).

1–16 is by Jacob Milgrom,[68] who as a Jew is very sensitive to the textual and contextual features within that book. Milgrom accurately and passionately embraces his interpretation; he is not merely working on the level of intellectual assent. Thus, such illumination is an impotent aid or no aid at all if merely attention to text in context produces a superior product of understanding. Anything that God does not promise to give and is not effective in demonstrating its ability to provide superior interpretation, accuracy, and unity should not be depended upon as coming from God. Thus claims from illumination as authority are not properly warranted.

Furthermore, reading the Law through the Spirit rather than by mere letter in Paul is not an illumination aid but the Holy Spirit's New Covenant ministry within the believer which transforms them to serve with righteousness and fruit of Spirit (Jer. 31:33–34; Rom. 2:14–15, 29; 7:6; 8:2, 4–17; 14:17–18; 2 Cor. 3:3, 6, 9, 17–18; Gal. 5:13–26). This is not a ministry for understanding the Biblical text, nor is it actually a ministry of the Spirit to apply the Biblical text into our lives. No Biblical text actually talks about the Spirit applying the Biblical text into a Christian's life. These Biblical texts, just cited, underscore that the Holy Spirit is the guarantor of growth and that He would transform the Christian to think and do the things of the Spirit. Because the Christian as she matures will distinctly reflect the Spirit's qualities out through her life, then the Spirit will witness to the Christian that she is in fact a child of God and a co-heir with Christ. We can thank the Spirit for transforming us but the responsibility Paul places us under when it comes to interpretation is that we should study to show ourselves approved as a workman rightly handling the Word of God (2 Tim. 2:15). Interpretation is our responsibility. Likewise abuse of the Biblical text is also our responsibility (e.g., 2 Pet. 3:16). The Holy Spirit neither takes the credit nor the blame for our interpretations.

The Holy Spirit nowhere claims to be providing an illumination ministry to help understand Biblical passages and it is presumptuous of us to claim that He will in fact do this claimed ministry. The claimed ministry does not do any better than an unbeliever who has finely honed skills and is sensitive to the text and in some instances (as above) the Christian may actually fare worse than a skilled non-Christian in interpreting the Biblical text. Therefore there is no legitimate warranting for this illumination view and the Spirit cannot be claimed as the authority for our interpretations. Furthermore, interpretations claimed to come through this means of illumination are often just wrongfully abusing the text.

---

68 Jacob Milgrom, *Leviticus 1–16* (New York: Doubleday, 1991). Of course with the completion of Milgrom's third volume this case could be expanded for Milgrom has the best commentary on the whole of Leviticus.

Clearly, the Holy Spirit should not be claimed to be illuminating us if in fact when the text is checked it becomes apparent that the interpreter arrives at falsehood. For example, many years at school missions conferences there were missions appeals from a text like Isaiah 6 to go for God to a mission field. Such approaches can give a lofty view of God as holy. We are seen with Isaiah as benefiting from His forgiveness. Then the call goes out from God to all of us "Who shall I send and who will go for us?" to which the speaker wishes we will all emulate Isaiah as a divinely authoritative call "Here am I, send me!" However, in this move of supposed "illumination" we have become neo-orthodox, disregarding the text for the existential crisis moment in our own reader response hermeneutic. What does the text go on to say in the context?

> And He said, 'Go and tell this people:
> Keep on listening, but do not perceive;
> Keep on looking, but do not understand.
> Render the hearts of this people insensitive,
> Their ears dull, and their eyes dim,
> Lest they see with eyes,
> Hear with their ears,
> Understand with their hearts,
> And return and be healed.'
> Then I said, 'Lord, how long?
> And He answered,
> Until cities are devastated without inhabitant,
> Houses are without people,
> And the land is utterly desolate...(Isa. 6:9–11).

How many of you desire this to be your ministry? This text has clear meaning in Isaiah's context in which he has been offering Israel the opportunity to be healed if they would repent, but no longer after Isaiah 6 for Israel is heading for captivity because they have gone too far in their sin. If the "illumination of the Spirit" regularly takes this text as a call to ministry then it is working cross-purposes to the clarity of the text, which the Holy Spirit inspires. The Holy Spirit does not contradict Himself. The "illumination of the Spirit" is not warranted; it is merely cover for a sloppy or reader-response hermeneutic.[69] Furthermore, if there is a text

69 An example of the sloppiness of hermeneutic or misappropriation of significance is how Vanhoozer, *Is There Meaning in this Text?* p. 414 uses Isaiah 55:11 in the midst of his discussion of illumination as an example of the Spirit convicting, illuming and sanctifying the reader in order to accomplish the divine purpose. However, this is not what is going on in this context. Rather, there is a repeated theme in Isaiah in which God's Word goes out to judge the nations (and Israel) in order to eventually regather Israel through a new exodus into the land in a new covenant blessed condition (e.g., Isa. 40:3–8; 55:6–13). To disregard textual features and to co-opt a text for one's own theologically traditional agenda can not be rectified by

elsewhere to support your appeal, then you need to present your appeal from a text that actually supports the point rather than a Biblical text that does not. The issue is reflecting the Bible's meaning and authority in our teaching and life not imposing our views upon a text.

5.9. Critical Realism Champions Text in Context

The deep appreciation of the text in its context is especially championed these days through a critical realist approach. Schleiermacher pioneered a critical realist approach in hermeneutics especially on the grammatical side of the process.

> For the enterprise of interpretation there are from the start two functions - the divinatory and the comparative - which reflect back on one another and should not be isolated from one another. The divinatory is the function by which one as it were transforms himself into the author, seeking directly what is individual. The comparative function regards what is to be understood first as something general, and then finds out what is unique by comparing it with other things subsumed under the same general idea.[70]

The divinatory step is an author-oriented proposal, which tries to make sense of what an author might mean given the available textual features in this context. This proposal is then checked and warranted by the comparative move. Then the process is repeated. This same critical realist pose I proposed to be more precisely stated as a version of Charles Peirce's empirically grounded pragmatism.[71] Simply put, hermeneutics involves moving from the details of the text to making a proposal within the authorial context in which the reader tries to make sense of the context, narrative themes and Biblical theology. Within this Peircian idea we move beyond the hermeneutical circle of Schleiermacher to a hermeneutical spiral within the authorial context from contextual overviews to textual particulars which clarify the meaning in the text. The goal is to understand the meaning in the text for the author and readers of the original context. This approach requires repeatedly comparing the latest proposal to the text and then proposing a more finely nuanced proposal that reflects the text in its context a little more

---

appeals to illumination of the Spirit. The Spirit is not at odds with His inspired clear text.

70 Friedrich D. E. Schleiermacher, *Hermeneutik*. (Heidelberg: Carl Winter, 1959), p. 109.

71 Kennard, *The Relationship Between Epistemology, Hermeneutics, Biblical Theology and Contextualization*, pp. 57–58, 124–25, 133–34; Charles Peirce explains these views in his essays 'The Fixation of Belief' *Popular Science Monthly* 12(Nov., 1877): 1–15 and 'How to Make Our Ideas Clear' *Popular Science Monthly* 12(Jan., 1878): 286–302.

closely. To the extent that the meaning is clear and coherent, and has textual support, I can reassure myself with high plausibility that I have obtained the author's interpretation and application for them. This critical realist proposal comes with divine authority to the extent that one can reassure oneself that he has in fact captured the meaning in the text. A post-enlightenment subjectivity is admitted but not to such an extent as to render truth inaccessible. The textual truth is warranted to the reader by comparing the details of the text to the latest proposal through which the reader has to make sense of this text. In this approach any text is viewed as a series of interconnected propositions that make sense in how they are used in this nearer context primarily and only secondarily in broader contexts.[72] This delineation and prioritizing of the near context tends to set up a role for a descriptive Biblical theology as a secondary authority by which we may evaluate the meaning of a text. This Biblical theology is the correlation of multiple texts that address these themes, especially as they showcase distinctive authorial thought forms. Whatever the text is determined to mean then is granted to have primary authority over Biblical theology; the Biblical text can always challenge one's interpretation of said text. The two interpretive moves serve in a tension in which the text in context provides the precise details to take into account and to warrant the view, and the authorial view in Biblical theology provides a range of possibilities within which the near text's view becomes more likely. The authority of Biblical theology should be granted this second tier level over such other levels of authority like tradition of systematic theology and existential authenticity.

John Austin argued that knowledge is a state of assurance which is not stronger than the most assured belief.[73] An outstanding example is in his work to develop performative language for it simultaneously involves testimony, a domain of faith, a linguistic expression of the law of identity (which is self-evident knowledge), and pragmatically accomplishes the truth it claims. Performative utterances use verbs in the first person to present the doing of things rather than merely describing what is being done. So performative speech is a form of foundational pragmatism. For example, the extremely meaningful statement of, "I now pronounce you man and wife" renders what had not been true to be true in the licensed

72 I argued for this near context in Kennard, *The Relationship Between Epistemology, Hermeneutics, Biblical Theology and Contextualization*, pp. 134–48, 83–84.

73 John Austin, *How to Do Things with Words* (Cambridge: Harvard University Press, 1975); I further discusses Austin's contribution to my own epistemology in Kennard, *The Relationship Between Epistemology, Hermeneutics, Biblical Theology and Contextualization*, p. 56 and I illustrate this Austinian methodology for defining faith and knowledge as largely synonyms, Kennard, *The Relationship Between Epistemology, Hermeneutics, Biblical Theology and Contextualization*, p. 62–65; A. C. Thiselton explores the genres of promise, blessing and curse as performative (*Thiselton on Hermeneutics: Collected Work with New Essays* [Grand Rapids: Eerdmans, 2006], pp. 61–64, 117–29).

persons saying of it. The speaker believes the statement to be true and so he says it; and in the saying of it all who hear now know it to be true as well. Other verbs of this type include theologically significant words such as: I promise, I covenant, I worship, I pray, I ask, I forgive, I curse, I honor, I reward, I explain, I declare, and I reveal. All of these, said by the speaker, render them true in the performance of the words. For example, "I declare to you..." renders a pronouncement to be declared in the saying of it.

Ludwig Wittgenstein expands the variety of language games to nearly all communication levels.

> But how many different kinds of sentence are there? Say, assertion, question, and command? There are *countless* kinds: countless different kinds of use of what we call 'symbols,' 'words,' 'sentences.' And this multiplicity is not something fixed, given once for all, but new types of language, new language-games, as we say, come into existence, and others become obsolete and get forgotten.[74]

Wittgenstein's language games are often a form of Peircian pragmatism in that these language games have empirical connectedness to settings out of which they emerge and bring the truth of their statement about with the completion of the statement. Wittgenstein reviews their multiplicity of language-games as including the following:

> Giving orders, and obeying them-
> Describing the appearance of an object, or giving its measurements-
> Constructing an object from a description (a drawing)-
> Reporting an event-
> Forming and testing a hypothesis-
> Presenting the results of an experiment in tables and diagrams-
> Making up a story; and reading it-
> Play-acting-
> Singing catches-
> Guessing riddles-
> Making a joke; telling it-
> Solving a problem in practical arithmetic-
> Translating from one language into another-
> Asking, thanking, cursing, greeting, praying.-

74 Ludwig Wittgenstein, *Philosophical Investigations* (New York: Macmillan Publishing Co., 1958), p. 11.

> It is interesting to compare the multiplicity of the tools in language and all the ways they are used.[75]

Anthony Thiselton positions himself in the wake of Wittgenstein in that the way a text uses the language game determines the textual meaning for the words.[76] Thiselton's approach clarifies that it does not obtain certainty but with the emphasis on the use of words it also distances itself from idiosyncratic novelty as well.[77] This is the same contribution made from the linguistics side by James Barr who called down the etymological fallacy and strongly argued that meaning of words was derived from use.[78]

E. D. Hirsch used this insight of authorial use of words determines meaning to establish that the hermeneutical task is to retrieve the authorial intent of the author, in reaction against an existentialist aesthetic response. Stated this way (as authorial intent) it places Hirsch's goal behind the text in the mind of the author but Hirsch insists on a textually realized intent as a public accomplishment and not merely a private wish.[79] Clarence Walhout presents this speech-act theory in a constructive alternative, more precisely nuancing Hirsch's view as authorial stance, rather than authorial intent.[80] Such an approach places the hermeneutic in the intersubjective world of human interaction in a manner that preserves the role of author as the one who gives meaning to text. Which means that Hirsch and Thiselton are in agreement on reflecting textually purposeful language games. Of course, the intentionality of the text is given the text by the author but it is only accessed through the text which is the only continuing expression reflective of that author's intent. This approach places the emphasis for determining meaning upon the particular text in its authorial context, or that of the textual thrust. Hirsch reminds us that it is not preexistent thought forms before the author writes which are determinative but rather the actual meaning with which the author writes to float a text of a particular sort into that context.[81]

Kevin Vanhoozer develops this as a hermeneutical realism with an authorial trajectory.

---

75 Wittgenstein, *Philosophical Investigations,* pp. 11–12.

76 Anthony Thiselton, *The Two Horizons* (Grand Rapids: Eerdmans, 1980).

77 This point is especially apparent in Roger Ludin, Clarence Walhout, and Anthony Thiselton, *The Promise of Hermeneutics* (Grand Rapids: Eerdmans, 1999), part III.

78 James Barr, *The Semantics of Biblical Language* (Oxford: Oxford University Press, 1961).

79 E. D. Hirsch, *Validity in Interpretation* (New Haven: Yale University Press, 1967), p. 11.

80 Roger Ludin, Clarence Walhout, and Anthony Thiselton, *The Promise of Hermeneutics* (Grand Rapids: Eerdmans, 1999), part II.

81 E. D. Hirsch, *Validity in Interpretation,* p. 47.

> Hermeneutic realism claims that the author's intended meaning is 'there' enacted in the text. Hermeneutic rationality maintains that the form and content of a communicative act- what it is and what it is about- can be known with adequacy. The author is a communicative agent and the text a communicative act with matter (propositional comment) and energy (illocutionary force). Texts also have, like arrows, a certain trajectory and direction (perlocutionary aim). With respect to this third aspect, however, everything hinges on the readers response.[82]

The propositional aspects of the text are accessible through the grammar and use of the words in the text. The illocutionary force can be analyzed as the figures of speech and rhetorical devices are analyzed. However, sometimes the force of these techniques is lost in the analysis, so I will also recommend (in a few pages) a contribution indebted to Ricoeur's reading of metaphors. For example, "the Lord is my shepherd" can be analyzed for its picture of protecting, providing, directing and caring, but with this precision some of the impact of the metaphor is lost, and Ricoeur has insights that will help retain that existential impact to compliment this precision analyzed here. The perlocutionary aim is the particular expression and style of a particular author for his readers to undertake a particular action. To a great extent this concern is taken up in the field of Biblical theology with its distinctive authorial thought forms.[83] Part of this is genre study which I develop as an extension of the performative language of Austin and Wittgensteinian language games. These can be applied to genre analysis to accomplish particular tasks in the reading and understanding of the text.[84]

Practical hermeneutical guides[85] even for the English bound to develop such genre analysis as an important textual feature to be taken into account for such interpretation of the text. Thus the hymn or lament forms of the psalms divinely call for participational reading to pray these psalms, when appropriate, as one is reading or attempting to understand them, or the reader is in fact aborting the textual design of the psalm apparent in its generic language. Likewise, wisdom forms are generic for all people including the modern reader to position herself within the creation for blessing. If a reader of wisdom texts doesn't reflect on how they might need to reposition themselves in light of the generic truth

82 Kevin Vanhoozer, *Is There Meaning in this Text?* p. 367.

83 Kennard and David Hesselgrave develop the value of this Biblical theology contribution in Kennard, *The Relationship Between Epistemology, Hermeneutics, Biblical Theology and Contextualization,* pp. 157–8, 167–9, 182–5.

84 Kennard, *The Relationship Between Epistemology, Hermeneutics, Biblical Theology and Contextualization,* pp. 122, 130, 137, 182.

85 Outstanding examples include: Grant Osborne, *The Hermeneutical Spiral* (Downers Grove: InterVarsity Press, 1991) and D. Brent Sandy and Ronald L. Giese, *Cracking Old Testament Codes* (Nashville: Broadman & Holman Publishers, 1995).

they read in the proverb then they also thwart the formal divine design and authority of the text. Contrasting to this, covenant forms rehearse the divinely authoritative binding of a particular people, like Israel, to another in a distinctive relationship that is not to be artificially extended to other groups. The study of covenant texts, like Deuteronomy, explores the grand sovereignty of the great King Yahweh and the distinctive covenant relationship that Israel has with this God. Narrative and prophetic texts built upon this covenant relationship reflect the distinctive obligation Israel has to continue the blessing while disobedience brings curse from Yahweh. These texts reveal the distinctive covenant relationship that Israel has with their God and thus paints the landscape of their hope. The gospels portray their authoritatively distinctive narrow way as Jews (Matthew) and Gentiles (Mark, Luke and John) follow their Messiah on to kingdom. The reader needs to emulate the strictured way of following Christ or they cut themselves off from the aspirations of the kingdom that Christ will bring. Acts takes the intentional Lukan pattern and then extrapolates it for the continuing definition of Christ's way for the next couple of generations of church and church leadership. The epistles are occasional letters to select churches but broadly applicable with divine authority to churches in similar settings. The reader needs to reflect on their similarity of setting and apply that which still fits them as they follow Christ unto kingdom, abstaining from implementing that which does not fit her context today.

This genre approach to hermeneutics can be seen as hosting a variety of testimonies each with their distinctive textual ways to understand the texts. Each approach within this text-in-context approach is committed to the divine authority being communicated through the text to the original reader and then being extrapolated on to the twenty first century reader if their context happens to fit within that textual genre's purpose.[86] In this step, hermeneutics is a spiral from the horizon of the text to the horizon of the reader which progressively excludes any of my assumptions, understandings and possibilities which are inappropriate to the text, and includes in me those assumptions, understandings and possibilities which are appropriate to the text. The goal is to recover the meaning in the text to the extent that it includes me. This becomes the authoritative textual meaning for me as my interpretation and application. I follow E. D. Hirsch in calling this the significance.[87]

86 Kennard implements a critical realist technique to contextualize and apply the meaningful text into contemporary life; cf. Kennard, *The Relationship Between Epistemology, Hermeneutics, Biblical Theology and Contextualization*, pp. 133–48.

87 Kennard, *The Relationship Between Epistemology, Hermeneutics, Biblical Theology and Contextualization*, p. 184.

> Meaning is the stable object of knowledge in interpretation, without which wider humanistic knowledge would be impossible. The chief significance on the other hand, is in the unstable realm of value. The significance of meaning in a particular context determines its value in that context.[88]

This significance retains divine of secondarily behind the primary authority of the Biblical text into a particular context.

I propose the significance to be another critical realist strategy in which a Peircian pragmatic proposal is made from the meaning of the text in its original context to its new significance context. The proposal attempts to reflect all that is applicable from the meaning and application of the text into the new contemporary context for the people to whom the significance is trying to be applied. The significance would be checked by the similarities of the original readers to our own contemporary readers. Consideration would be engaged on the level of whether the similarities between the readers are within the landscape of meaning or beyond the things being considered for meaning. Then a sharpened proposal would be made again. To the extent that I can state this interpretation and significance clearly and coherently, and there are similarities between the original readers and the ones of my significance, I can reassure myself with high plausibility that I have obtained the authoritative significance for that group now. If possible this critical realistic process would be undertaken among a community[89] where text and the new context of the contextualization are both highly valued and dialogued about. Though this process is able to be accomplished by sensitive individuals, a sensitive interactive community usually brings a real gain in sensitivity concerning textual and contextual features. In the church (as in life), few people are really self-sufficient; the goal is instead to be inter-dependently growing together as a unified community. The community grows as it embraces or reflects upon the interpretations that each of its members brings to it for its communal consideration. Inter-dependent growth is especially realized as each member of the community helps the others to apply these interpretations in their communal and individual life.

5.10. Post-Textual Testimony or Textual Realism

In a different direction, it has become popular in some circles (like the Society of Biblical Literature) to extend these testimonies beyond their textual genre to a communal conventional tradition or even individual conventions. Brueggemann is a good example of an intentional post-

88 E. D. Hirsch, *The Aims of Interpretation* (Chicago: University of Chicago, 1976), p. 146.

89 Cf. chapter later in this volume on Contextualization. Also, David Hesselgrave helps to explain this process in Kennard, *The Relationship Between Epistemology, Hermeneutics, Biblical Theology and Contextualization*, pp. 163–80.

modern approach to testimony that wishes to retain the Biblical testimonies but add additional testimonies from our contemporary day and personal distinctives.[90] This can foster the communal post-modern conventions[91] or those post-modern strategies, which are more existentialist.[92] The post-modern conventional patterns might return to the concern of coherence within an oral tradition that we have already covered. However, there is a valuable role of a community of scholars who can help a critical realist exegete keep from reading texts in a biased manner that does not take into account all the data. So as a sounding board such a community is invaluable if they will engage with the exegete and text to help sharpen each other based on the details of the Biblical text. Likewise, a community of mature practitioners of the text, who are deeply aware of the culture and preferably native to the culture, is invaluable in formulating how the significance of a text is to be applied into a particular setting in their own culture.[93] It is not that the group overrules the individual but that the group pools their communal wisdom which helps sensitize each of the individuals to a fuller range of the situation details and thereby serves as a level of persuasion, which is a third level of authority after the primacy of the Biblical text and the secondary level of appropriate Biblical hermeneutic authority relevant to the text under consideration. Hopefully this third level of community grounds itself in empirical sensitivities to the text and relevant contexts. Features like systmatic theology and tradition will inform them, but hopefully that remains a fourth level of authority challenged by and answerable to the Biblical text, their interpretation of the text within the Biblical author's thought forms and context, and the communal sensitivities they bring concerning said text. Thus traditions as language games might grow and modify over time under the influence of good scholarship of the Biblical text and the Biblical theology and contextualization that result from this exegesis.

90 Walter Bruggemann, *Theology of the Old Testament,* especially pp. 61–114.

91 John Webster and George Schner have edited *Theology After Liberalism* (Oxford: Blackwell, 2000) to especially champion the conventionality of theology and the hermeneutical process in chapters 1–3, 8 and 15. The Afterword by George Lindbeck, "Toward a Postliberal Theology," pp. 361–86 is the most explicit on this point. However, the chapter by James Buckley "Beyond the Hermeneutical Deadlock," pp. 187–203 begins (pp. 187–8) with an attack on engaging hermeneutics in an epistemological manner. I admit that my approach has recognized that the hermeneutical process is a complex venture, but I think that there is a real gain in my approach for precision and textual warrant. Thus my approach reflects the authorial stance of the text and is not held captive to the conventional inclination of the group whether it be feminist (chapter 12) or post-modern (chapter 13) or whatever.

92 Existential post-modernism is present in Bernard Bell's outstanding critique of it in *Postmodernism and Other Essays* (Milwaukee: Morehouse Publishing Co., 1926).

93 David Hesselgrave makes this point in Kennard, *The Relationship Between Epistemology, Hermeneutics, Biblical Theology and Contextualization,* pp. 163–80.

5.11. Existentialism and Text

Existentialism brought into the level of authority the concept of authenticity or fit to one's own life. If this existential context and choice is the basis of value then whatever is vivid enough to woo one's own creativity and imagination in the desired direction is what is to be valued. So while the existentialists don't have to neglect argument, imagination and compelling metaphor are often valued more highly. That which is considered to be truth is shown to be truth subjectively in the choices made by the reader. It is in this way that Kierkegaard held to truth as subjectivity; only that which you apply is practically truth for you.[94] If you do not apply some point in your life, then you show that you are not in fact committed to that point as truth. Moving into post-modernity, the twentieth century began with Friedrich Nietzsche calling the modern man to be an authentic person who will own the truths and relationships that he chooses to own. This can be exemplified in Nietzsche's definition of truth.

> What then is truth? A mobile army of metaphors, metonyms, and anthropomorphisms-in short, a sum of human relations, which have been enhanced, transposed, and embellished poetically and rhetorically, which after long use seem firm, canonical and obligatory to a people: truths are illusions about which one has forgotten that this is what they are: metaphors which are worn out and without sensuous power; coins which have lost their pictures and now matter only as metal, no longer as coins.[95]

This phenomenological assessment of the existentially changing nature of truth and an existentialist means of operating within such truth are brought to the critical issue by Lewis Carroll in *Through the Looking Glass*, "'The question is' said Alice, 'whether you can make words mean so many different things.' 'The question is,' said Humpty Dumpty, 'which is to be master - that's all.'"[96] Authority as existential authenticity makes the reader supremely the master. Derrida epitomizes this commitment that it is the individual who chooses his own meaning so that the task of interpretation is to de-center oneself enough to discern one's own aesthetic choice. While this is a radical postmodern strategy it does revel in a truth, that we do know subjectively, and is honest enough to admit that we will never have truth without viewing it through our

---

94 Sören Kierkegaard, *Concluding Unscientific Postscript* (Princeton: Princeton University Press, 1968), pp. 169–224.

95 Friedrich Nietzsche, 'On Truth and Lie in an Extra-Moral Sense,' *The Portable Nietzsche* (New York: Viking Press, 1954), pp. 46–7.

96 Lewis Carroll, Sir John Tenniel, *The Complete Works of Lewis Carroll [pseudo.]* (New York: Modern Library, 1936).

own subjectivity. This means that we can never strip the subjectivity off the truth to compare the essence of the truth to which one holds to the essence of the truth held by another. Derrida leaves us an island even if such deconstruction is seen as applicable to only some genres. Of course, if deconstructionism is held to govern all genres and relationships, then it is self-defeating. However, I think that it is better to view some media like lecture and description as not primarily in the deconstructionist sights, as they call each of us through said lecture to posses our own different meaning in the narrative or poetry we read. Notice, that if deconstructionists didn't set aside these genres of lecture and description as beyond their deconstructionism then they would in fact be self-defeating. That is, if their authorial stance does not in fact communicate their deconstructional message then a reader could deconstruct them to be saying anything, even as advocating my own conservative post-critical views. In radical deconstruction communication simply would not happen. This realization may make the milder form of existential hermeneutics popularly known as reader-response more attractive. Such a view considers a book to be a modern artistic piece that like modern art, once it leaves the hands of the painter, the painting is open to being interpreted for its meaning anyway that anyone so wishes. This existential post-modern approach has been critiqued all century long for its personal relativistic construct of truth.[97] Such deconstructionist and reader-response devalue a heritage of hermeneutics as the authority because the present authenticity to one's life is seen as the primary reason for embracing one's view.

This view also devalues the textual details as authoritative and replaces the hermeneutic authority to be one's own authentic existential condition, with secondary authority becoming those textual or traditional features that help one to see one's own condition authentically being addressed. Thus, my previous appeal for authorial stance as accessible from the Biblical text (as evident in Austin's performative speech, Wittgenstein's language games, Barr's use of words and genres in their context) strongly argues against such a reader response view. That is, reader response as a method obtains existential authenticity as authoritative to the neglect of the Biblical text as authoritative. However, we evangelicals tend to proliferate the view of a reader-response hermeneutic as we ask in our Bible studies the question "What did the text mean to you?" and we nod acceptingly to a range of answers that have little to do with the text. Provided that the text authentically connects with our life we see ourselves in the characters of the novel or movie. Perhaps we define ourselves as a theological Dirty Hairy or Gandalf, whatever movie speaks to me.

97 Critiques of existential post-modernism began at least by 1926 by Bernard Iddings Bell, *Postmodernism and Other Essays* (Milwaukee: Morehouse Publishing Co., 1926).

In this vein, Jean Baudrillard develops a radically post-modern existentialist strategy which considers that the new history or fact is that which has been experienced through DVD viewing.[98] Such a hyper-real world erodes any distinction between the real and that of merely persuasive media. And this has Biblical hermeneutic implications because in my lectures, which explore theology from Matthew or John or Acts, in class we read texts from these three books by viewing them from *The Visual Bible*.[99] This means that my students are viewing the Bible through existential DVD viewing skills and developing a sense of the historical context commented upon by the Biblical author through the lens that the DVD viewer provides. That is, my students think of Jesus, Peter, and Paul in the ways that the contemporary DVD presents them, rather than seeing this DVD as merely another second tier commentary being viewed. That is, it is important to preserve a historical Jesus that these commentary media merely approximate rather than replace. Additionally, when we read or view texts through this existential reader response, we are more directly connected to the metaphor or character in our existential way of seeing ourselves. What happens to these characters prompts us to self-reflection about who we are and what our future possibilities might be. Such compelling accounts might motivate us to choose as authentic within ourselves characteristics we see in the hero or heroine. If this is the case then there is something in the text that is actually transferring to us the readers in the process of reading; the whole of the text, or the events behind it, is not ours to remake after our image.

Here is where Ricoeur calls for the existentialist to value that texts have meaning available from within the text itself. Ricoeur begins with a critical move (of post-structural critiques like Descartes, or Marx, or Nietzsche, or Freud, or feminism or ethnic criticism) to distance ourselves from naively reading our tradition as fused to the text. Such a move may be helpful if we are prone to read ideologically or straightforwardly in a reader-response manner because it helps to slow down the process and surface alternatives. The gain in this technique is especially apparent if you start to recognize the differing levels of authority vying for your allegiance. To see a naïve tradition as an ideology that it is so that you might be able to evaluate whether such an ideology in fact fits with this text is invaluable. To see your attraction to this text as on a level of existential authenticity may be invaluable provided the text itself is allowed to speak and challenge one's own reader-response reading.

98 Jean Baudrillard, *Simulations* (N.Y.: Semiotext, 1983). A populous expression of this perspective is played with in the movie 'Matrix.' In fact, the main character of the movie, Neo early on hides money and computer disks in a cut away copy of this book.

99 *The Visual Bible* is a dramatized version of the New International Version of the Biblical text in which the Biblical text is the only audible statement. For further information see: www.visualbible.com.

Personally I don't employ such criticisms very often for I find that this critical move in my hermeneutic is often more accomplished by an awareness of how a range of rival traditions have taken or could take the text that I am reading. For me this multi-traditional awareness provides sufficient distancing so that I don't naively read ideologically. However, my commitment to the details of the text in their context and the possibility of Biblical theology (which correlates these texts) also draws me beyond ideological or authentic reading to value what the Biblical text says as with divine authority. With regard to the precision of a textual argument, other textual approaches, which utilize the critical realist strategies mentioned above, may excel Ricoeur, but for capturing and transferring the vividness of compelling metaphor and story, Ricoeur's existentialism gives the imagination a powerful place. As a theologian, imagination or other human roles of interpretation do not threaten the divine role of the Spirit applying the religious affections in our life because elsewhere I have defended that divine and human causalities are compatible in a redundant compatibilist way.[100] So the value of including Ricoeur's positive approach is that it allows the reader to make varied and vivid existential connections with the text as she feels placed in the story by the juxtaposition of text close to the reader's own context.[101] I feel placed in the story by a wide variety of similarities familiar relationships, confessional traditions, shared passion, similar experiences and overlapping contexts. Rhetorical devices enliven the text beyond mere proposition such as space, placement, sequence, motifs, symbols, climax, dramatic turns and many more. Often the vividness of symbol operates on a more existential level than that of the critical realist analysis. Such an existentialist connection prompts a shared passion and motivation to understand the text and work it out into life. The goal of this level of hermeneutic is to surface and retain passion and motivation throughout the dissecting process of the critical realist levels of hermeneutics. However, a critical realist contextualization still calls us to evaluate the appropriateness of this reflection for whether and to what extent this reflection fits with the text under consideration. If such self understandings or self possibilities do not fit with Biblical text under consideration then they need to be discarded as interesting postmodern reflection but irrelevant meaning or significances of the Biblical text.

100 Doug Kennard, 'Sovereignty of God and Human Freewill,' Paper presented at the Evangelical Theological Society meeting Nov. 2000; also in Douglas Kennard. *The Classical Christian God*, pp. 135–166.

101 The previous chapter and Doug Kennard, *The Relationship Between Epistemology, Hermeneutics, Biblical Theology and Contextualization*, pp. 120–4 develops the positive process and value of this Ricoeurian approach in hermeneutics.

5.12. Conclusion

I consider that Clarence Walhout's approach is an ally to my own Thiselton-Ricoeur approach. As developed above, Walhout especially unpacks hermeneutics in a speech-act theory but along side this Hirschian approach there is a role of "mimesis" that is similar to Ricoeur's approach to narrative metaphors.[102] The descriptive reference of the text identifies a state of affairs, which the text projects. Mimesis describes the relationship of the perceived state of affairs projected by the text to that of the actual world. Thus this is a changing significance because the state of affairs of our lives continues to change. However, this form of surfacing and applying significance operates on a more straightforward existential level of authenticity and provoking the imagination by vividness of the textual projection. However, I see real value in having a more critical realist contextualization process as developed above. So that the existential avenue (championed by post-moderns) is rehabilitated to help the interpreter arrive at vivid Biblical theological truth that is really there in a particular text and resonates our lives in deeply authentic ways. This is a real gain over just the critical realist's approach on its own, thus warranting my description of this hermeneutic as a Thiselton-Ricoeur hermeneutic.

Summing up, Christianity has always desired to maintain and claim divine authority in some facet of informing our hermeneutics and theology. However, post-enlightenment views recognize that the human process in hermeneutics and theology includes subjectivity. This subjectivity often unfortunately imports features that limit the accessibility of this divine authority. I prefer a modern critical realist strategy to access reality providing a range of rational, empirical, pragmatic and existentialist tools that attempt to diminish distracting subjectivity while funding warranting means through one's subjectivity. This critical realist strategy is incorporated in a hermeneutical process to likewise provide substantial warrant for attempts at recovering meaning in text with accessible divine warrant.[103] A hybrid hermeneutic, which I call a Thiselton-Ricoeur hermeneutic[104] has been proposed which incorporates the warranted strengths of each of the avenues of warranted truth and tries to diminish distracting and excessive claims and criticism.

---

102 Roger Ludin, Clarence Walhout, and Anthony Thiselton, *The Promise of Hermeneutics* (Grand Rapids: Eerdmans, 1999), part II.

103 For an epistemological look at some of the features in this critical realist view see Kennard, *The Relationship of Epistemology, Hermeneutics, Biblical Theology and Contextualization,* chapters 2 and 3.

104 An overall glimpse of this hybrid is evident in the previous chapter and Kennard, *The Relationship of Epistemology, Hermeneutics, Biblical Theology and Contextualization*, chapter 6.

5.12.1. Biblical Textual Example: Genesis 2:24

A practical example of an exposition from a Biblical text is helpful to showcase this hybrid hermeneutic with its nuances for authority. For simplicity sake, let's take a brief but concentrated text, like Genesis 2:24, to elucidate these issues. A common North American evangelical traditional perspective often sees this text as informing directly the dating and marriage situation. Often the meaning is seen as when you get married you must leave home and stand on your own two feet economically, separate from your parents so that the groom and bride might be able to work toward becoming one in Christ within their new marriage. However, if we hold to this meaning or significance for this passage then we have disregarded both the text and the original context out of and into which this text comes. Such a hermeneutic allows the reader-response of our existential context and tradition to dominate and silences the divine authority of the Biblical text. However, in said silencing of text we are turned to our own deaf inauthentic wanderings.

This verse with its "leave his father and mother," which Adam does not have, helps us from jumping to the other extreme by which we largely teach these Genesis passages as comment on the historical context behind the text to inform us what really happened with God and Adam and Eve in relationship. Assuming Mosaic authorship for Genesis 2:24 which Jesus affirms (Mark 10:4, 8), the Biblical text, in its compositional context of exodus and wilderness wandering,[105] is the divine authority, not the historical context which the narrative describes, nor our contemporary context. In the Israel context of revelational composition and reception of this text, marriages were arranged. When a marriage was arranged in this exodus context by a couple's parents, and especially the fathers, then the newly married couple would move into the camel haired tent with the husband's parents. At best the tent was enlarged a little. Even when Israel moved into the Promised Land many families only had a one-room house and the newly married wife would add her mat to the mats of her husband's family in the one room. So "leave" does not mean leave home; it must mean disconnect from parents in a more subjective way of defining oneself in relationship. That is, parents diminish as the primary

105 The Pentateuch is traditionally seen as Mosaic in conservative circles, even if this means that Moses utilized previous materials to frame the compositional *toledot* structure of Genesis. Additionally, when Jesus asks about Moses command in Mark 10:3 and the Pharisees quote Deuteronomy 24:1 and 3, Jesus calls them back from this Mosaic permission for hardened Jews to focus instead on the beginning design (Mark 10:6–9) evident in Genesis 1:27 and 2:24 (our verse here). It looks like in this Markan context that Genesis 2:24 settles the divorce issue with no divorce, unless you wish to disobey and become hardened in disobedience. Which would mean that the right answer to Jesus question of Mark 10:3 was what Jesus said in Mark 10:6–9, implying that Genesis 1:27 and 2:24 is correctly viewed by Jesus as Mosaic, and thus addressing Moses' exodus context. The early church also follows suit (e.g., Chrysostom, *Homilies on Genesis* 2.5, in *Fathers of the Church* 46.83; 21.379 in *Patrologia Graeca* edited by J. P. Migne (Paris: Migne, 1857-86).

defining relationship of oneself in family, and the spouse is to take on that primary defining relationship in family; "leave" is replaced by "cleave." Likewise, this text can't mean economic independence either, because a boy was raised in the family business and when marriage began he would continue in this family business with the same family tools and location of carpentry or farming or fishing. So that in the exodus context there is a great deal of interdependence and multigenerational communal living and occupation. Any meaning that we claim that this text possesses must especially make sense within this authorial context.

A look at the textual unit which begins in Genesis 2:4 reflects this Semitic context but the text has its own textual agenda. The creation account in Genesis 2 emphasizes God in the role as Father creating the environment for His son Adam with the provision for place, resources, occupation, blessings and an arranged marriage. Man should recognize that the resources lovingly enable the occupation which God has for man. The occupation itself has man expressing his care for the orchard (which is what an ancient Near Eastern garden was).

Normally an ancient Near Eastern garden was surrounded by a hedge or a wall, setting it off from the outside world (Gen. 2:8; 3:23). The fact that God is met in the garden hints that the garden is sacred space (Gen. 2:8; 3:8–9).[106] In the ancient Near East the meeting place of heaven and earth was on a mountain where a sacred stream ushers forth, which similar description further hints that the garden is sacred space (Gen. 2:10; 3:23–24). When humans are finally excluded from the garden, the garden is then seen as holy in comparison to the surrounding area, which is common. At that point they are met by cherubim at the gate back to the garden, which creatures are associated in the ancient Near East with royalty and temples, thus further hinting that the garden is sacred space (Gen. 3:24). However, at this point the sacredness of the space is subsumed to the purposes of God as Father preparing and caring for His son.

The words of the care of the garden focus man toward the sacredness of his task as serving God. For example, "cultivate" (*'bdh*/עֲבֹדָה) elsewhere in the Pentateuch expresses the idea of servant to God, which is the highest role a man can have (Gen. 2:15; Ex. 3:12; 10:3, 8, 11, 24, 26). Likewise, the word "keep" (*lšmrh*/לְשָׁמְרָה) is used elsewhere in the Pentateuch as obeying God's commands (Gen. 2:15; Ex. 15:26;

106 For development of this theme see Gordon Wenham, "Sanctuary Symbolism in the Garden of Eden Story" in *Proceedings of the Ninth World Congress of Jewish Studies* (Jerusalem: World Union of Jewish Studies, 1986). Additionally, Jon D. Levenson, "The Temple and the World," *Journal of Religion* 64(1984): 275–98 develops the creation narratives as viewing the cosmos as a temple. Furthermore, Kathryn Gleason, "Gardens in Preclassical Times" *Oxford Encyclopedia of Archaeology in the Near East*, ed. E. Meyers (New York: Oxford, 1997), 2:383 develops the close relationship that temples tend to have with gardens in the ancient Near East.

16:28; 19:5; 20:6, 8). These words hint that man's responsibility in chapter two may be priestly and show allegiance to the Great King of the Mosaic covenant, to balance the creative and regal thrust of chapter one, but all these roles can be subsumed within the role of man being the son of God. Humans reflect God in miniature as creative and ruling. Ancient near East father roles include getting a son, creating an environment to live within, providing for the son's benefit, providing the son with a vocation, and arranging the son's marriage. All these fatherly roles Yahweh does for Adam in Genesis 2.

To enable these roles, God arranges a marriage for Adam. In fact, the only thing of the two creation accounts that is declared to not be good is that man is alone. The Hebrew for alone (*lbd*/לְבַדּוֹ) means without aid or helpless; it does not mean psychologically lonely, as our psychologically sensitive evangelical culture so often teaches. The point is not man's need for a companion but that he can't do the tasks given him by his Father Yahweh, like procreate without the women's aid. The woman becomes a helper (*'zr*/עֵזֶר), like God who assists in these tasks (Gen. 2:18, 20; Ps. 121:1–2). So helper (*'zr*/עֵזֶר) does not demean her, since God describes Himself in the same manner. Her suitability for this role does not raise class, race, culture, or ethnic issues. No other humans are available and the animals are not suitable. Because she is a helper corresponding (*kngd*/כְּנֶגְדּוֹ) to man she is to be seen as a duplicate or corresponding copy of himself. The descriptions of the woman further develop this similarity. "One of his ribs" (*wyyšz wyqḥ 'ḥt mṣl'tyw*/וַיִּישָׁן וַיִּקַּח אַחַת מִצַּלְעֹתָיו) actually means a side portion as in barbequed ribs that have meat and bone together. No evangelical cultural point is being made about companionship from this side reference, which is not from Adam's head so that she would rule him or from the feet that Adam would rule her.[107] Such a teaching as is common in evangelicalism is again existential reader response, neglecting biblical text for our culture. In the ancient Near Eastern context, a wife would be essentially ruled by her husband. This Biblical text still reflects Adam's right to rule as he names his wife; the naming role reserved for sovereigns in the ancient Near East, but that is not the point of this passage. Rather, the point being made about the side is that she is made of the same stuff as he is. Adam recognizes that they are made of the same flesh and bone, so that he poetically names her *woman* (*'šh*/אִשָּׁה), which contains the name man (*'yš*/אִישׁ) within it (Gen. 2:23). In fact, this poetic point of the mutual

107 Likewise, there is no *midrash* in the Biblical text as in *Deuteronomy Rabbah* on Deuteronomy 16:5. That is, not from the eye that she not be haughty when she saw like in Genesis 3:6. Not from the ear that she not be an eves dropper, but Sarah heard (Gen. 18:6). Not from the mouth that she not be talkative, but Miriam spoke (Deut. 16:5). Not from the hand that she not be a thief, but Rachel stole the teraphim (Gen. 31:19). And not from the foot that she not be a gad about, but Leah went out to meet him (Gen. 30:16).

definition of these two (woman and man) is accentuated by these words appearing immediately next to each other (*'šh kî m'š*/אִשָּׁה כִּי מֵאִישׁ). These poetic images within the narrative account have the vivid impact of a Ricoeurian symbol with the import of: "WOW! She's like me." Much is made in this text of the physical similarity of the husband and the wife so that they might be able to function physically as a pair in union. In the divine commentary (Genesis 2:24) explaining this narrative for Israelite readers, arranged marriages enable the man to leave or forsake a physical oneness with one's parents (as in the infantile hugging which defines us with them) in order to cleave or physically join to each other in loyal love, ushering in sexual intercourse and progeny. The "one flesh" would either be the sexual union of the marriage partners or the one flesh who would crawl and walk around as the progeny of this sexual union. This drive for marriage can be seen as an outworking of the original union of one flesh of man and woman in the creation. So the union in sex within marriage fits within the original design harmony and material unity from which humans were made.

The contemporary significance for an evangelical is to retain this authoritative meaning of this text as the authoritative significance into our somewhat different context. In North America we don't tend to have marriages arranged and we don't tend to live multi-generationally in the same house and business. We also tend to have multi-room houses. Though the context is different, the issue is the same: a man and a woman define themselves as married through sexual intercourse in marriage. Which means that the authoritative significance of Genesis 2:24 for today is the same as its meaning: when a man gets married today he is to forsake a physical oneness with his parents in order to cleave or physically join to his wife through sexual intercourse, with the possibility of a baby that unifies their flesh as the result. This is not merely an academic matter so as I married Jan nearly three decades ago we intimately followed this pattern as one that helped to define our marriage. We have two boys evidencing the commitment to carrying this out in the one flesh - ones who walk but mostly run around or drive now. Yet the significance of this expression of one flesh for those who adopt may still be an extension of their commitment to married sexual unity even though their kids are not the biological product of their sexual relationship. However, many of my students and friends are not married, so this remains instruction which they should implement in their lives only if and when they get married. This is teaching which we can not merely abstractly inform our world view, for it requires authentic embodiment in our involvement with our spouse in intimate bodily expression of sexual union in marriage. There is nothing more profound in hermeneutics than to apply a text into ones life in the manner which the Biblical text authoritatively indicates that it should be; the reader's response shows whether the reader is deeply committed to the truth of the text with profound subjectivity of sexual intercourse in marriage. We should apply everything of all the Biblical texts which include us within the text's significance for us.

6. The Reef of Biblical Theology: A Method for Doing Biblical Theology that Makes Sense for Wisdom Literature

Biblical theology may be defined *as that branch of theological science which organizes in respect to proposition, form, symbol and emphasis the historically conditioned progress of the Divine revelation about God and His creation as deposited in the Bible.* The reef for Biblical theology is the wisdom literature of the Bible because it does not fit in the broad frameworks of the rest of the Bible.

This chapter places wisdom in its ancient Near East perspective and then unpacks several features of this Biblical theology methodology by illustrating them through this Old Testament wisdom. Ultimately, the chapter places a Biblical theology of Old Testament wisdom within the overarching Old Testament Biblical theology strategy. It is at this point, if not before, that most of the Old Testament Biblical theologies hit the reef of wisdom literature. There are many Titanics and lesser yawls strewn on the ocean floor around this reef. However, there is one clear passage through this reef and that is with critical realism surfacing creation theology, so this creation theology will be developed to position the wisdom program within. Examples of the theological contribution will be developed within this framework.

6.1. O.T. Wisdom Within its Ancient Near Eastern Perspective

The wisdom books do not seem to fit within the dominant Old Testament covenant strategy for Israel, as do the Law and the prophets. W. G. Lambert reminds us that the piety of wisdom "is completely detached from the law and ritual, which gives it a distinctive place in the Hebrew Bible."[1] As the covenant strategy moves from the covenant grants of Noahic and Abrahamic to the suzerainty treaty of the Mosaic covenant, much more than simply revealing God is at stake for Biblical theology. The covenant grants champion reassuring blessings which set the mindset, hopes and destinies of those so blessed. These covenants also surface obligation as Abraham circumcises his family (Gen. 17). However, the suzerainty treaty of the Mosaic covenant is laden with stipulation as tied to blessing or curse (especially in Deut. 28–30).

1 W. G. Lambert, *Babylonian Wisdom Literature* (Oxford: Clarendon Press, 1967), p. 1.

However, this suzerainty covenant strategy is very foreign to the focus of Old Testament wisdom. While the wisdom psalms and second Temple Jewish religious texts refer to the Mosaic covenant strategy as *torah* to inform them and direct the meditation of the wise people (e.g., Pss. 1:2; 37:31),[2] there is no indication that the Old Testament wisdom books themselves are positioned conceptually within the Mosaic covenant. For example, the use of *berit* or covenant within wisdom is best seen as referring to other kinds of relationships, like the marriage covenant that an adulteress spurns even though it is from God (Prov. 2:17). Eliphaz uses *berit* as a metaphor of peace in a synonymous parallel relationship to *shalom* (Job 5:23). Job confesses that he has covenanted with his eyes not to gaze on a virgin in lust (Job 31:1). God also barrages Job with questions like "Will you covenant with Leviathan to make him your servant?" (Job 41:4). Furthermore, *torah* in Job is a reference from Eliphaz that his own instruction is viewed by him as God's (Job 22:22). However, the dominant pattern of *torah* in Proverbs is that of parental instruction, that especially a boy's father tells his son, and the son must obey (Prov. 1:8; 3:1; 4:2; 6:20, 23; 7:2; 23:14; 28:4, 7, 9; 29:18; 31:26).[3] This of course positions Proverbs as within the emphasis of ancient Near East wisdom as it communicates broadly known instruction of how creation works communicated from father to son.[4] Attempts (like Eichrodt's *Theology of the Old Testament* and others) to capture the whole theology of the Old Testament under the rubric of covenant are doomed to fail by the reef of wisdom literature, at least in regard to wisdom's place and contribution.

The strategy of ancient Near Eastern wisdom draws upon the common wisdom available from observing the way creation works. For

---

2 E.g., *Ben Sirach* and the *Wisdom of Solomon*.

3 Hassell Bullock has produced a nice volume in *An Introduction to the Old Testament Poetic Books* (Chicago: Moody Press, 1988) but in this volume p. 31 he alludes to overlapping and borrowing of wisdom from Law and in two Evangelical Theological Society papers he defends this view. He seems to follow Gerhard von Rad, *Old Testament Theology* (N.Y.: Harper and Row, 1962), I:433–34 and R. B. Y. Scott, "Priesthood, Prophecy, Wisdom, and the Knowledge of God," *JBL* 80 (1961): 1–15 in this view. However, the evidence of these terms in the wisdom books contexts seems to go otherwise than to connect wisdom with Law. Wisdom and Law only seem to get connected in Psalms 1, 19, 111, and 119, and the second Temple works of *Ben Sirach* and the *Wisdom of Solomon*, showing that wisdom and Law are not opposed to each other, even though neither seems to show evidence of being dependent on the other. Within the New Testament wisdom and Law are intimately connected in the ministries of Jesus as sage and new Moses, and echoed in wisdom books like James. All this shows that wisdom and Law are harmonious but are grounded in different strategies.

4 The forum of wisdom being communicated in the ancient near East as from father to son is broadly exampled by the following few samples: Sumerian *Instructions of Suruppak,* Babylonian *Counsels of Wisdom,* Ugaritic *Counsels of Shubeawilum,* Egyptian *Instruction of Merikare, Instruction of Ptahhotep,* and *Instruction of Any.*

example, the Egyptian *Instruction of Amenemope*[5] gives thirty chapters for well-being with many close parallels with Proverbs 22:17–24:22. Additionally, Westermann in *Roots of Wisdom* makes nice comparisons with this broad wisdom tradition.[6] Michael Fox summarizes this ancient Near East wisdom context as follows:

> The similarities in form and content between Israelite and Egyptian didactic wisdom literature have been so well established that there can be no doubt that Israelite Wisdom is part of an international genre (which includes Mesopotamian wisdom) and cannot be properly studied in isolation.[7]

However, the similarities penetrate deeper than structure to the fundamental concepts. For example, Crenshaw develops the foundational role for justice in wisdom literature.

> The fundamental concept which underlies these instructions is *ma'at*, which may be translated as justice, order, truth. No distinction exists between secular and religious truth for this literature. God's will can be read from the natural order, social relations and political events. Life in accordance with the principle of order paid off in tangible blessings, just as conduct at variance with *ma'at* brought adversity.[8]

Some of the characteristics of the wise individual are good skills, manners and speech coupled with the discretion of when to be silent and listen.

Similarities extend to narrative wisdom as well. For example Job has slight similarities to the Indian legend of Haris-candra in *The Mārkaṇḍeya Purāṇa* though Haris-candra brings his sufferings upon himself by giving his wealth away, while Job is struck down by the sovereignty of God and the adversary in His court.[9] The Ugaritic *Story of Keret* affirms the retribution principle[10] by following the placating of the gods through ritual prayers which Job's counselors encourage (e.g., Job 11). The use of

5 James Roger Black, *The Instruction of Amenemope: A Critical Edition and Commentary Prolegomenon and Prologue* (Internet material OCLC, 2002).

6 Claus Westermann, *Roots of Wisdom* (Louisville: Westminster/ John Knox Press, 1990), especially pp. 140–164.

7 Michael Fox, "Two Decades of Research in Egyptian *Wisdom Literature*," *ZAS* 107(1980): 120.

8 James Crenshaw, *Old Testament Wisdom* (Atlanta: John Knox Press, 1981), p. 214.

9 F. E. Pargiter, *The Mārkandeya Purāna* (Delhi: Indological Book House, 1969).

10 A nice discussion of the retribution principle and its corollaries is carried on by my previous colleague John Walton, in *Ancient Israelite Literature in its Cultural Context* (Grand Rapids: Zondervan, 1989), pp. 179–89; document is contained in Wilfred G. E. Watson and N. Wyatt, *Handbook of Ugaritic Studies* (Boston: Brill, 1999).

speeches and appeals in the course of narrative wisdom is common in Job, *The Babylonian Theodicy,*[11] and the Egyptian *The Protest of the Eloquent Peasant.*[12] Even Qoheleth has a high degree of similarity to Babylonian *Dialogue of Pessimism*[13] and Egyptian works, like *The Harper's Song* and *The Dispute Between a Man and His Ba* (soul).[14] This does not require that everything is the same in these expressions of wisdom. K. van der Torn reminds us that the antithetic mode of expression between wise and fool is most emphasized within Hebrew wisdom and largely absent from Mesopotamian and Ugaritic wisdom.[15]

Even Song of Songs has some parallels in the ancient Near Eastern love poetry. There are six songs that describe the Sumerian love song of the shepherd-king Dumuzi and five of them describe the marriage and love play as it attempts to insure the fertility of the land. This narrative approach to love songs is loosely parallel to the narrative approach of the Song of Songs as it works up to the joys of procession, celebration and love making of marriage in chapters 3–4. The descriptive song form with its praise of the beloved in anatomical praise, admiration of beauty and in admiration of common in Egyptian psalms 31 and 54 sensitize the interpreter of Songs of Songs to the value of the lovers' praise of each other.[16] Perhaps the Egyptian patterns of *Paraclusithyron* in which the lover is at his mistress's door is loosely parallel to Song of Songs chapter 5. John Walton reminds us that like other wisdom literature this genre also fits into the broad wisdom pattern.

> It will be recalled that in every other genre the greatest differences have been seen when Israelite beliefs about YHWH and her monotheistic faith enter the picture. In a work like Song of Songs, that never happens. Fox insists with good reason that this is secular literature (as opposed to the literature of the Sacred Marriage Rite that was used in cultic performances). Without the element of monotheism or the perception of deity being involved, we would expect that Israelite literature

---

11 W. G. Lambert, *Babylonian Wisdom Literature* (Oxford: Clarendon Press, 1960), pp. 68–69; James Pritchard, *Ancient Near Eastern Texts: Relating to the Old Testament* (Princeton: Princeton University Press, 1969), pp. 438–40, 601–4.

12 John Foster, *Ancient Egyptian Literature: An Anthology* (Austin: University of Texas Press, 2001).

13 Lambert, *Babylonian Wisdom Literature*, p. 142; James Pritchard, *Ancient Near Eastern Texts*, pp. 437–8.

14 John Foster, *Ancient Egyptian Literature: An Anthology*.

15 K. van der Toorn, *Sin and Sanction in Israel and Mesopotamia* (Assen: Van Gorcum, 1986), p. 101.

16 Michael Fox, *The Song of Songs and the Ancient Egyptian Love Songs* (Madison: U. of Wisconsin, 1985), p. 271. Fox also translates the Egyptian love songs alluded to in the manuscript above; cf. Louis Cohn-Haft, *Source Readings in Ancient History: The Ancient Near East and Greece* (New York: Thomas Crowell Co., 1965), pp. 140–48.

> would look like any other literature in the ancient Near East, and indeed, that seems to be the case here.[17]

Thus the import of the Song of Songs as contained in the canon is to affirm that the believer can engage in intimate love making with all its joys as the unbeliever can, especially if Song of Songs 5:1c is God's voice, "Eat, friends; drink and imbibe deeply, O lovers."

There are however clear differences with the Biblical wisdom when compared to the broader ancient Near Eastern wisdom. A clear example of the difference is seen in the absence from Song of Songs of those things so common among other ancient Near Eastern love poetry like cultic practices, gods, personified nature, drunkenness, lust, seduction, faithlessness, and jealousy. Unlike other ancient Near Eastern wisdom, Qoheleth incorporates occasional vertical refrains of God's generosity (Eccl. 2:24–26; 3:12–15, 22; 7:14; 8:15; 12:9–14) amid the common cynical human perspective "under the sun." In the eighties the upbeat refrains were emphasized in Biblical theology but as post-modernism continues to develop, the pessimism of the vanity of vanities tends to predominate contemporary Biblical theology of Qoheleth.[18] Likewise in the book of Job, *El Shadday*'s dominance of the created order to overwhelm the retribution principle sets the book of Job apart as superior to other ancient Near Eastern theodicy texts. Of all the Old Testament wisdom texts Proverbs is actually the closest parallel but even here there is a greater emphasis of an orientation toward God than other ancient Near Eastern wisdom's nearly exclusive social orientation. This means that if we are to do a Biblical theology of Old Testament wisdom then we must see a clear difference that the Biblical canonical context brings rather than identifying Biblical wisdom as identical to ancient Near Eastern wisdom.[19] That which is distinctive of Biblical wisdom needs to shine through in a Biblical theology.

6.2 Biblical

Biblical theology must first be Biblical. Its source material is God's revelation as contained in the Christian canon. It is not the beliefs and practices of men described in or built upon the Bible, though it fully envisions the Bible as within its historical and cultural context. It is then a text-based theology inductively reflective of the Christian canonical

17 Walton, *Ancient Israelite Literature in its Cultural Context*, pp. 191–2.

18 This point is illustrated in some of the recent works that show increasing effect of post-modernism such as Michael Fox, *A Time to Tear Down & A Time to Build Up* (Grand Rapids: Eerdmans, 1999) in contrast to Michael Fox *Qohelet and His Contradictions* (Sheffield: Almond Press, 1989). Cf. William Anderson *Qoheleth and Its Pessimistic Theology: Hermeneutical Struggles in Wisdom Literature* (Lampeter: Edwin Mellen Press, 1997).

19 Contrary to Claus Westermann, *Roots of Wisdom*.

text. It is the correlation of the exegesis of the Biblical text, not that which may predate or grow from the text.

6.2.1. Tradition versus Scripture

One of the major debates still raging is whether the primary theological emphasis should be placed on the tradition *process* or on the final *result* of this process.[20]

Tradition history has been one avenue in which Biblical theology has been attempted. Von Rad's Biblical theology had to do with the history of the transmission of traditions antedating the Biblical texts in their final form. His point was that at whatever level of tradition was chosen, Biblical theology was characteristically descriptive, "retelling" the story. For him, "event has priority over logos."[21] Traditio-historical theologians go even further than von Rad by emphasizing in the process of the transmission of traditions. In this process people in a community on the move cope with the needs of their life situation, by searching for understanding of their identity and the identity of God.[22] Claus Westermann endeavors to penetrate behind the Biblical texts in order to perceive the lively process through which the community's wisdom statements develop.[23] This entire heritage is then related to contemporary experience to help a person understand where he fits in this same unfolding process today.[24] Under this view the Biblical text becomes merely one snapshot among the myriads of slices of the history of theological views. Depending on how the text gets into its finished authorial form, this snapshot is either in Solomon's day or during the Babylonian captivity, if approached from a critical perspective. After becoming aware of the critical issues, there is a place for becoming post critical and approaching the text with a new naivete that appreciates claims for authorship that the text actually makes of itself, like the text substantially coming from Solomon's hand (Prov. 1:1; 10:1; 25:1; Eccl. 1:1, 12; maybe 12:9; Song 1:1; 1 Kgs. 4:32). This orientation of authorship also connects Biblical theology to a historical-cultural context that now surrounds the narrative or other genre so that the interpreter does not allow the text to float freely in an a-historical manner.

---

20 Bernard Anderson, "Tradition and Scripture in the Community of Faith," *JBL* 100(1981): 7; Westermann's *Roots of Wisdom* provides a good example of exploring the process which is valuable but not really Biblical theology.

21 von Rad. *Old Testament Theology,* 1:116.

22 James Sanders, 'Adaptable for Life: The Nature and Function of the Canon,' in *Tradition and Theology in the Old Testament,* edited by Douglas A. Knight, pp. 531–60 and 'Biblical Criticism and the Bible as Canon,' *USQR* 32 (1977): 157–65.

23 Westermann, *Roots of Wisdom*.

24 R. E. Clements, *Wisdom in Theology* (Grand Rapids: Eerdmans, 1992) which is a publication of the Didsbury Lectures delivered at the British Isles Nazarene College, Manchester. This volume is a nice presentation of Hebrew wisdom heritage particularly slanted for applicability today.

Brevard Childs points out that one of the crises for the Biblical theology movement was "its failure to take the Biblical text seriously in its canonical form."[25] Sailhamer argued at length for finding the meaning in the text and not in the historical events behind the text.[26] Even though there is development which lies behind the formation of canon, the focus of Biblical theology must be on the Bible if it is to be properly termed Biblical. Thus, the primary source for Biblical theology is resident *in* the words of the text, not *behind* the words in some event or "original meaning" antedating the text. Only when the Bible is valued as the source for Biblical theology is there proper recognition of the inspiration of Scripture. As such each of the wisdom books as a whole will be explored as unified authorial projects available for literary criticism and genre study together rather than in fragmented ways. Part of the important contribution to the Biblical theology has then to identify what each part is doing within the whole. For example the counselors of Job can not be accepted as saying the truth of the matter in the whole account which has their counsel changing and God finally pointing out that they spoke in error. However, we know that Childs takes this canonical perspective to the completion of the canon, including the New Testament. This later perspective radically shifts the context from the authorial context to another author's context, like Paul or John's. A number of authors extend this even further to reading the Biblical text and its theology out of a Christian traditional systematic theology perspective.[27] These approaches distance the text under consideration from its own context (in which its genre makes a great deal of sense) and reframe it within a much later context that has no parallels within its genre. Better to let each of these books make their contribution in the context out of which they emerge. That is, this approach preserves within which these texts emerge rather than loose or confuse the distinctive of each text in its own context.

---

25 Brevard Childs, *Biblical Theology in Crises* (Philadelphia: The Westminster Press, 1970), pp. 52, 102. However, Childs *Biblical Theology of the Old and New Testaments* (Minneapolis: Augsburg/Fortress, 1992) develops a Christian canonical strategy which opens the O.T. texts up to unhelpful significant influence by reading N.T. texts back into them.

26 John Sailhamer, *Introduction to Old Testament Theology: A Canonical Approach* (Grand Rapids: Zondervan, 1995), pp. 36–85. Unfortunately, Sailhamer's canonical strategy flattens the progression of O.T. texts by allowing for continuing textual development of early Mosaic texts until the Babylonian captivity.

27 A example of this approach are a number of authors in *Between Two Horizons* ed. Joel Green and Max Turner (Grand Rapids: Eerdmans, 2000) especially Robert Wall, "Canonical Context and Canonical Conversations," pp. 165–82, and Trevor Hart "Tradition, Authority and a Christian Approach to the Bible as Scripture," pp. 183–204.

6.2.2. Historical-cultural Context

The Bible when properly viewed is within a historical context of author and recipients. Krister Stendahl calls us to the historical-cultural context.

> The task of biblical studies, even of biblical theology, is to *describe*, to relive and relate in the terms and the presuppositions of the period of the texts what they meant to their authors and their contemporaries. To furnish the original.[28]

Biblical texts were written to address historical-cultural issues through the use of genres which made sense in their context. Brevard Childs summarizes the Biblical theology movement's view of the relation of the Bible to its environment as follows:

> The Bible reflects the influence of its environment both in terms of its form and content, and therefore cannot be understood apart from the study of its common Near Eastern background. Yet in spite of its appropriations the Bible has used these common elements in a way that is totally distinct and unique from its environment.[29]

The Bible utilizes concept and writing style to communicate with the people who were familiar with them. So in an ancient Near Eastern context the Song of Songs is seen as love poetry celebrating love within marriage and the cultivation of this love in spite of the difficulties. It should not be ripped from its context to be reinterpreted as a metaphor of God's love for Israel or the church, even if such ideas were helpful to get this steamy text accepted as within the canon in the first place. It is not as though all pagan thought or worldviews are brought within the framework of the Bible by our recognition that familiar genres are utilized. In fact, I previously acknowledged the absence from Song of Songs of those things so common among other ancient Near Eastern love poetry like cultic practices, gods, personified nature, drunkenness, lust, seduction, faithlessness, and jealousy. These changes show that the Biblical books are appropriating contextual thought forms selectively for their author's purposes, not merely being reflective of their ancient Near Eastern context. Biblical theology must describe these authorial purposes as communicated within the text.

After the meaning is understood in its historical-cultural of then this meaning must be explicated for modern man. The goal of Biblical theology here is to explain clearly the meaning of the text with its

28 Krister Stendahl, "Implications of Form-Criticism and Tradition-Criticism for Biblical Interpretation," *JBL* 77(1958): 38.

29 Childs, *Biblical Theology in Crises,* p. 48.

authorial application as evident in the text. Issues addressed by the text need to carry their full ethical weight calling the continuation of the original audience to faith and repentance. The Bible does not describe sins and warnings to merely inform; it describes such things to change lives. However, if understanding has actually been obtained then it can and must be communicated across the historical-cultural barriers to modern man. Increased correspondence between the similarities of the original readers and the modern ones indicate an increased likelihood of the applicability of these ethical demands on the particular modern audience in question.[30] So that part of Biblical theology is to retain the same level of authoritative exhortation for the corresponding audience being addressed by the text. Which audience for wisdom is the broad range of humanity within the creation order, so there is no exclusive group like Israel or the church singled out for special instruction. Thus application is merely developing equivalence of the practice in the contemporary situation. For example, though there are few kings in today's context most of the proverbs concerning kings still carry applicational weight for those in authority. Like with all wisdom, if one finds a wise saying that informs one's context, it is not good enough to know it, one must think through how to implement this wisdom into life in a thoughtful manner.

6.2.3. Linguistic context

Within this historical-cultural of one needs to approach Biblical theology with exegesis utilizing the full linguistic context. This linguistic context is first the grammatical arrangement of words within the propositions of the text. Exegesis is not a series of loosely knit words, which serve to set up word studies but rather the utilization of these words in relation to one another in the text. When a normal hermeneutic is applied to these propositions the messages of the respective segments can be obtained. In this, hermeneutics is a spiral within the authorial context, which oscillates between contextual overviews and textual particulars as it tries to clarify the meaning of the text.[31] This is a critical realist approach to the text, inductively observing the particulars which the text presents. Such induction does not try to get behind the text as one might to bridge Lessing's ugly ditch and apologetically recover the historic Solomon. Instead, such induction is committed to recovering the accounts of wisdom themselves with their theological biases, and inductively understanding these texts from the thought forms which these authors portray. These Biblical thought forms serve as an inductive

30 This process is explained and exampled by Doug Kennard in *The Relationship Between Epistemology, Hermeneutics, Biblical Theology and Contextualization* (Lewiston: Mellen, 1999), pp. 133–48, 184.

31 Cf. Kennard, *The Relationship Between Epistemology, Hermeneutics, Biblical Theology and Contextualization*, pp. 124–33.

base from which to implement a textually grounded pragmatism (as Charles Peirce located an empirically grounded pragmatism) fueling the hermeneutic spiral. That is, the overview generalizations such as context, narrative themes and Biblical theology which the interpreter proposes are funded by the textual particulars in the author's context and life. The fact that Biblical theology is a generalization and correlation of multiple texts means that it is our best attempt at representing what these texts say in their thought forms. We are not trying to get behind the text to something like Hirsch's authorial intent or post-structuralism's deep structures. These, in effect, are claiming to know something prior to the text, such as something in the author's mind. Philosophically, I don't think we can obtain anything authoritative prior to the text, and for Biblical theology, it is the Biblical text which has authority and is the means of providing warrant. This warrant begins with coherent statements of the Biblical theology to be represented, for one is not properly functioning if he believes contradictory statements. The warrant for the interpretation and Biblical theology is provided by correspondence to the textual support. This correspondence compares one's interpretation to the text being interpreted. Such a correspondence should not be a naïve opinion that one's interpretation is identical to the text as, say a reader response or Gadamer's fusing horizons or postmodern Biblical theology[32] from each of our human existential contexts. The plausibility of this correspondence is increased by the interpretation's comprehensiveness and congruity to the textual data. The correlation of these messages together is the major ingredient for Biblical theology, which is a kind of Peircian pragmatic proposal that should be revisited for warranting and sharpening whenever appropriate textual information is found.

These propositions are united making up a larger order in the text. This order includes a logical order of argument through the book and matters of form. Matters of form are significant in two ways. First, propositions are arranged in ways meaningful within the historical-cultural context. These matters of form serve as the main arrangement of some books, such as the various forms of wisdom and love poetry. Secondly, literary style highlights certain features in the book. The logical order conveys meaning through the propositions but other vivid meaning is also conveyed through the metaphors and symbols.[33] The compelling vivid

32 Walter Brueggemann in his *Theology of the Old Testament: Testimony, Dispute, Advocacy* (Minneapolis: Fortress, 1997) intentionally positions himself as developing a postmodern Biblical theology and legitimating the variety of voices form within the text and from the contemporary context as expressing intriguing testimonials of what is significant in Biblical theology. However, I think that many of the sage voices have been silenced by him to largely limit wisdom's contribution to theodicy and as a reminder of the role of human partner with God.

33 Leo. G. Perdue in *Wisdom and Creation: The Theology of Wisdom Literature* (Nashville: Abingdon, 1994), pp. 59–63 seems to appreciate Ricoeur's aesthetic hermeneutic process for interpreting symbol and metaphorical language.

presentation of descriptions of the beloved in Song of Songs expresses the passion involved in the love making process which clearly goes beyond trying to inform an artist's description. Such symbol legitimates the passionate love speak that motivates lovers to give themselves to each other in ravishing feast. Here, textually vivid metaphors existentially connect with the reader as urged by Ricoeur's aesthetic hermeneutic, surfacing vivid existential connections with the text to enable the reader to appreciate how to read this genre.[34] Such an existential connection prompts a shared passion and motivation to understand the text and work it out into life. The goal of this kind of engagement is to surface and to retain this passion and motivation throughout the dissecting process of the levels of correspondence. Additionally, such existential connections prompt self-understandings and self-possibilities which naturally arise from a new naïve reading of the text without tools of hermeneutical suspicion. Those self-understandings and self-possibilities which survive the process of warranting through correspondence need to be folded into the Biblical theology statement as well. The other self-understandings and self-possibilities which find warrant in our context but not really from the context of the Biblical author are relevant significances for our context to reflect upon but are inappropriate to be seen as material for Biblical theology or to grant it divine authority for life.[35]

The concept of context also includes the authorial perspective and emphasis, which is evident in the text. This is necessary so that the full body of material is dealt with and applied appropriately. This is not to say that major elements which are clear need excess pages of unnecessary description. It is to say that minor elements should not take over with excessive description or become the organizing principle. Additionally, the way a concept is used in the passage needs to be reflected in Biblical theology statement. Biblical theology must consist both of clear tight logic, coherence and rhetorical elements aimed at motivating the reader to partake of the ethic and passion of the book, where appropriate. Some descriptions by their nature may be highly technical and as dry as dust but hopefully gold dust. This is not where such an explanation should stop. Biblical theology reflects a living faith, not a dead orthodoxy. Biblical concepts of knowledge extend to include the appropriation of this knowledge into proper action and feeling. A good example of this is the narrative parallel in proverbs between the enticing adulteress in the square and lady wisdom as a compelling rival metaphor to motivate young men to choose to live wisely.[36] Which option will they choose? We

34 Cf. Kennard, *The Relationship Between Epistemology, Hermeneutics, Biblical Theology and Contextualization*, pp. 120–24.

35 Cf. Kennard, *The Relationship Between Epistemology, Hermeneutics, Biblical Theology and Contextualization*, pp. 133–48, 184.

36 At this point Perdue (*Wisdom and Creation*, pp. 88–100) is too oversensitive to the extra-biblical context as he sees lady wisdom through goddess imagery, for

will only know by the life choice our students make. Perhaps metaphors like this are to best be sampled by more intimate exposition of these texts in the classroom so that the challenge with its outcomes comes alive to these students where they live.

The aim is to discover what the text meant in the context of its original author for his intended audience. The author is no longer present, nor the authorial intent, except as it is contained in the body of the text. In this, one is limited to what the text has to say about itself within its context (as best as it can be recaptured). Thus, we have a critical realism spiral process of interpreting particulars and correlating them as Biblical theology. Exegesis provides the building blocks of Biblical theology; Biblical theology is regulative of exegesis. The message can be obtained by the cooperative effort of the two. Biblical theology is not exegesis but it is wholly intertwined with it. Biblical theology must be Biblical.

6.2.4. Canonically Christian

Biblical theology should be based on the Christian canon. F. Watson argues that, "Biblical theology is *Biblical,* that is, concerned with the whole Christian Bible; it is more than the sum of Old Testament theology and New Testament theology, understood as separate disciplines."[37] This is not to diminish Old Testament theology and New Testament theology, for they are valid Biblical theology disciplines in their own right. That is, specialists in Hebrew scholarship and others in Greek scholarship mine the gems that each testament has to offer. However, Biblical theology hopefully interacts with both of these realms of legitimate Biblical theology disciplines to formulate a whole Biblical theology. There is significant gain in doing a whole Biblical theology. As P. Stuhlmacher said, "the Old and New Testaments have belonged together in a most intimate way since the beginning of the Christian Church. They belong together to such a degree that the testimony of the statement cannot be adequately understood without the Old and the exegesis of the Old Testament remains incomplete without taking the New into view."[38]

Few New Testament theologians would take issue with this stance since the Old Testament becomes part of the historical-cultural-linguistic context within which the New Testament is revealed. However, some Old Testament theologians do take issue with this stance since they do

---

the Biblical texts monotheism limits the range of acceptable options, excluding any queen of heaven as not properly Biblical. Also Leo Perdue *Wisdom in Revolt: Creation Theology in the Book of Job. JSOT 121* (Sheffield: JSOT/Almond, 1991) reflects a polytheistic post Babylonian context for its metaphors of theology.

37 F. Watson, *Text and Truth: Redefining Biblical Theology* (Grand Rapids: Eerdmans, 1997), p. 8.

38 P. Stuhlmacher, *How to Do Biblical Theology* (Allison: Pickwick, 1995), p. 2; Cf. Gerhard Hasel, "Biblical Theology: Then, Now, and Tomorrow," *HBT* 4(1982): 74; Charles Scobie, *The Ways of Our God: An Approach to Biblical Theology* (Grand Rapids: Eerdmans, 2003), pp. 58–60.

not wish to import later revelational material into a passage framed by an earlier stage of progressive revelation.[39] I resonate with this concern and have taught Old Testament theology as a course in its own right as a descriptive discipline to explain these earlier stages of revelation in their own context. Even when I trace an idea through the whole Biblical canon, I wish to handle the earlier material faithfully within its own context, so that the greater perspective is added as the idea matures within the canon (say in the prophets or the New Testament).

Another canonical concern has to do with the format of each canon and the relationship of the books to each other. For the New Testament, this concern is simple as evident by the broad agreement across Christiandom for the contents of the New Testament. Occasional challenges are levied against a book, like Luther's challenge against James, but they have never been generally accepted. So this issue reduces to merely a matter of textual criticism. Since I hold to a critical text philosophy with regard to textual criticism, the issue of the canon is mainly a matter of exclusion of later scribal additions like Mark 16:9–20 and John 7:53–8:11.

The Old Testament presents additional concerns for a Christian canon since both the Hebrew Masoretic text (MT) and the Septuagint (LXX) were used as authoritative Jewish and Christian canons. Early these two different formats of the O.T. were merely scrolls of separate books or groups of books (like the Twelve prophets). There are slight differences between the *Samaritan Pentateuch* and the MT that are worth checking but these differences are primarily reassuring concerning the care of both copying traditions and the fixity of the canon since they are both independent traditions from probably the ninth century B.C. when the northern tribes split from Judah. However, with the third to fifth century A.D. the independent scroll texts begin to be bound together into books, which began to raise the issue of canonicity in practical ways. The MT and LXX present a different order but in mainstream Judaism the contents were the same. While in Christian traditions that become Catholic or Anglican or Orthodox some additional books only accepted by sectarian Judaism were added to the LXX bound additions. The LXX includes as part of this continuing sectarian Jewish tradition the following books that are not part of the Hebrew canon: *1 Esdras, Tobit, Judith, Additions to Esther, The Wisdom of Solomon, Ecclesisticus* (=*Ben Sirach*), *Baruch, Letter of Jeremiah, Additions to Daniel* (*The Prayer of Azariah and the Song of the Three Young Men, Susanna, Bel and the Dragon*), *Prayer of Manasses, 1* and *2 Maccabees*. The Old Latin and editions of the Vulgate also included *2 Esdras*. These additions, except for *The Prayer*

39 E.g., J. L. McKenzie, *Theology of the Old Testament* (Garden City: Doubleday, 1974), p. 319; R. P. Knierim, "The Task of Old Testament Theology." *HBT* 6(1984): 52; R. Rendtorff, "Must 'Biblical Theology' Be Christian Theology?" *BRev* 4(1988): 42.

of Manasses, *1* and *2 Esdras*, were accepted as the Catholic canon at the Council of Trent.[40] *The New English Bible* printed the *Apocrypha* with the downgraded books interspersed among the others. The Eastern Orthodox churches included within their canon all of the above and: *Psalm 151*, and *3* and *4 Maccabees*. As Judaism worked its way into a Mishnaic and Talmudic traditional orientation, the *Apocrypha* was excluded as less authoritative from the Hebrew Scriptures that became the Masoretic text.[41] That is, the *Apocrypha* "does not defile the hands" of the reader as the Hebrew MT does. The Protestant churches followed the Hebrew Scriptural contents and placed them in the LXX order. The Protestants excluded the *Apocrypha* following some patristic documentation such as Athanasius' Easter letter and the *Synod of Laodicea* (343 AD), and in reaction to Catholic acceptance and its use to teach purgatory (e.g., *2 Macc.* 12:43–45).[42] I exclude the *Apocrypha* from my Christian canon partly because my tradition has but more because I don't see that these books make claim to inspiration. Remember that inspiration and authority is the issue in canonicity. For example, *2 Maccabees* concludes, "I will

40 Council of Trent (1545-1563), Fourth Session celebrated on the eighth day of April, 1546, Decree Concerning the Canonical Scriptures similar to earliest official indication in Canon 87 Council of Carthage A.D. 397 except *Esdras* was included. The Syriac canon is close to that of the Orthodox Church, especially the Slavonic Orthodox except that for them *2 Esdras* only contains chapters 3–14, which is referred to as *4 Ezra*. The Ethiopian canon adds *3 Maccabees* and splits Proverbs into two books as compared to the Roman Catholic pattern.

41 *Babylonian Talmud, Baba Bathra* 14b; Augustine admits Jews did not accept Apocrypha, especially *Judith* into their canon even though they helpfully record history (*The City of God* 18.26 in *Augustine* vol. 18 of *Great Books of the Western World*, edited by Mortimer Adler [Chicago: Encyclopaedia Britannica, 1952], p. 485).

42 E.g., *The French Confession* (1559) art. 3–5 in *Creeds and Confessions of Faith in the Christian Tradition: Reformation Era*, edited by Jaroslav Pelikan and Valerie Hotchkiss (New Haven: Yale University Press, 2003), vol. 2, p. 376; *Belgic Confession of Faith* (1561) art. 4 and 6; *Second Helvetic Confession* (1566) 1.9; *The Concept of Cologne* (1591) art. 18; *The Irish Articles* (1615) art. 2–3; *The Westminster Confession of Faith* (1647) ch. 1.1.2–3 in Pelikan and Hotchkiss, *Creeds and Confessions* and *Reformed Confessions Harmonized: With an Annotated Bibliography of Reformed Doctrinal Works* edited by Joel Beeke & Sinclair Ferguson (Grand Rapids: Baker, 1999) and *The Westminster Confession of Faith for Study Classes* edited by G. I. Williamson (Phillipsburg: Presbyterian and Reformed Publishing Co., 1964), p. 4; *The Thirty-Nine Articles of the Church of England* (1571) article 6 in *Confessions and Catechisms of the Reformation*. Ed. Mark Noll (Grand Rapids: Baker, 1991), pp. 215–6; Athanasius "Easter Letter" in *A Select Library of Nicene and Post-Nicene Fathers of the Christian Church*. Ed. Philip Schaff and Henry Wade (Edinburgh: T & T Clark, 1991), 2nd series, vol. 4, p. 552, letter 39, sect. 4 and 5; *Synod of Laodicea* 343 AD, canon 59–60 in *A Select Library of Nicene and Post-Nicene Fathers of the Christian Church*. 2nd series, vol. 14, p. 159; Augustine admits Jews did not accept Apocrypha, especially *Judith* into their canon even though they helpfully record history (*The City of God* 18.26 in *Augustine* vol. 18 of *Great Books of the Western World*, edited by Mortimer Adler [Chicago: Encyclopaedia Britannica, 1952], p. 485).

bring my work to an end. If it is found well written and aptly composed, that is what I myself hoped for; if cheap and mediocre, I could only do my best."[43] Such a claim falls far short of the prophetic "Thus says the Lord." Likewise, the New Testament does not quote the *Apocrypha* with divine authority, though allusions probably influence some texts. Additionally, pseudepigraphal texts (like *1* and *2 Enoch*) that do claim inspiration, were not accepted by either the broader Jewish community or the broader Christian community, so I do not accept them as well.[44]

This dissonance of MT and LXX is made more acute because both these Old Testament versions are affirmed in the New Testament as Scripture. The continued authoritative nature of the Hebrew Scriptures is affirmed by Christ's statement that the smallest letter (*yod*) or stroke as part of a consonant letter will not pass away until all is accomplished, that is, until Kingdom is fully realized (Matt. 5:18; Luke 16:17). Additionally, the MT consonantal text is more authoritative than the vowel pointing added millennia later, reflecting Jewish rabbinic interpretation. However, Paul writes to Timothy and reminds him that the sacred writings in which he has been instructed from his youth (which in the dispersion for Jews would be the LXX) are God breathed or inspired (; 1 Tim. 3:15–17).[45] This means that inspiration needs to be redefined to fit the Biblical concept as: *God's superintending of human authors so that, using their own individual personalities, they composed and recorded*

43 *2 Macc.* 15:38.

44 Though I acknowledge Tertullian makes a case for the acceptance of *1 Enoch* into the canon on the basis of its edification and because Jude quotes it, even though he acknowledges that neither the Jews nor the church accept it among the canon (*On the Apparel of Women* 3).

45 Second Temple Judaism supported the view that translations were viewed as Divinely inspired Scripture, such as: LXX (Philo, *Vita Mos.* 2.7; *Letter of Aristeas* 305–317) and an Aramaic O.T. (*Meg.* 3a). This position was broadly affirmed by the LXX specialists who presented papers at the Institute for Biblical Research Nov. 19-20, 2004, namely: Karen Jobes, "When God Spoke Greek: The Place of the Greek Bible in Evangelical Scholarship," *IBR Bulletin for Biblical Research* 16(2006): 219–236 especially pp. 219–221, Peter Gentry, "The Septuagint and the Text of the Old Testament" *IBR Bulletin for Biblical Research* 16(2006): 193-218 and Tim McLay's oral response; cf. Martin Hengel, *The Septuagint as Christian Scripture: Its Prehistory and the Problem of Its Canon* (New York: T. & T. Clark, 2002), p. 22; Johan Lust, *Messianism and the Septuagint: Collected Essays by J. Lust*, ed. Katrin Hauspie (Leuven: Leuven University Press, 2004), p. 153; Sidney Jellicoe, "Septuagint Studies in the Current Century," *JBL* 88(1969): 191-99; Natalio F. Marcos, *The Septuagint in Context: Introduction to the Greek Versions of the Bible* (Leiden: Brill, 2000), p. 322. Additionally, patristics presented the LXX as authoritative Scripture (e.g., Irenaeus, *Ag. Her.* 3.21.3 in *Ante-Nicene Fathers,* ed. Alexander Roberts and James Donaldson [Edinburgh: T & T Clark, 1989], 1:452). Some patristics even preferred the LXX over the Hebrew, such as when Augustine takes Jerome to task for not translating the Latin *Vulgate* closer to the LXX (Augustine letter 56 to Jerome in *A Select Library of Nicene and Post-Nicene Fathers of the Christian Church.* edited by Phillip Schaff and Henry Wace (Edinburgh: T & T Clark, 1991), series 2, vol. 6, p. 112.

without error in the words of the original autographs His revelation to man, and that this revelation is preserved with divine authority and benefit through accurate translations and copies. Many evangelical theologians frame inspiration just to autograph in contrast to the liberal definition of inspiration for reader. Notice the Biblical use of inspiration does both in a particular way. Also notice that the evangelical definition of inspiration as restricted to the autograph does not reflect the issue of the continuing authority of the Biblical text. The Biblical text retains continuing authority as part of its definition of inspiration. This continuing authority of the inspiration of the LXX is how the N.T. and the apostolic fathers treat the LXX. About 80% of the New Testament quotes of the Old Testament evidence dependency upon LXX as the authoritative text quoted. Most of the patristics continued to quote from the LXX as the authoritative text or a translation of it into their own language. This also has the ramification that our English Bibles can be seen as inspired by God and thus continuing with divine authority. Thus our English Bibles, LXX and MT are "profitable for teaching, for reproof, for correction, for training in righteousness; that God's person may be fully equipped for every good work" (2 Tim. 3:16–17).

In the field of textual criticism, Septuagint specialists still need to do considerable work but I would approach it through a critical text orientation as well. So differences in versions of the texts may well be handled as scribal emendations. However, some texts such as Jeremiah evidence multiple copies, some of which were destroyed. So that it may be possible to consider both MT and LXX versions of this book as accurate to stages of autograph.

The recent interest on the final form of canonical text also raises interesting issues since the Hebrew canon has a different structure to that of the Christian Old Testament (and LXX).

Tanakh	**Old Testament (i.e. LXX excluding Apocrypha)**
Law (*Torah*)	
Genesis	Genesis
Exodus	Exodus
Leviticus	Leviticus
Numbers	Numbers
Deuteronomy	Deuteronomy
Prophets (*Nebhi'im*)	
Former	
Joshua	Joshua
Judges	Judges
	Ruth
Samuel	1 & 2 Samuel
Kings	1 & 2 Kings
	1 & 2 Chronicles

	Ezra
	Nehemiah
	Esther
	Job
	Psalms
	Proverbs
	Ecclesiastes
	Song of Songs
Latter	
Isaiah	Isaiah
Jeremiah	Jeremiah
	Lamentations
Ezekiel	Ezekiel
	Daniel
Book of Twelve	Hosea through Malachi

Writings (*Kethubhim*)
Psalms
Job
Proverbs
Ruth
Song of Songs
Ecclesiastes
Lamentations
Esther
Daniel
Ezra-Nehemiah
Chronicles

In both structures the core of the Old Testament is the *Torah* or Pentateuch. The Christian LXX order emphasizes that from this Covenantal base, the narrative unfolds with God's continued interaction with His people, and thus some popularity of narrative as of late. However, the Hebrew categorizing and order emphasizes that the prophetic program echoes and answers and calls the people Israel back to the Mosaic Covenant. Both features are helpful to recognize in these texts. That is, God actively responds to His people but the agenda is that of His Mosaic Covenant.

Wisdom and the Psalms serve as an alternative program to that of the Mosaic Covenant, as was developed earlier in this chapter. This is indicated in the *Tanakh* by including them within the less authoritative *Kethubhim* or "Writings." In this configuration, the sequence of Proverbs 31, Ruth and Song of Songs contributes a focused unit on the ideal wife and the enjoyment of sex. So Ruth's different place in the *Tanakh* examples the ideal wife, while in the LXX Ruth contributes toward the historical justification of David as king. Also, in the English and LXX Old Testament order, Psalms and Wisdom texts occupy a barrier category between the history and the prophets. Many of the wisdom texts would be seen as placed in this category as coming out from the history of Solomon the wise. Perhaps conceptually, the history tells where Israel had been and wisdom calls the faithful to live for God now, while the prophet especially includes the future hope of Israel. Either way wisdom is arranged, it serves as a helpful guide for contemporary living. However, in the Christian order, the Psalms enmeshed in wisdom are framed more as instruction, whereas in the *Tanakh* they are more patterned prayers to perform (thus encouraging liturgy). Joining the Writings, Ruth is handled more like wisdom emphasizing generosity and Lamentations extends the psalm laments in light of life and captivity issues.

The *Tanakh* diminishes the place of narrative theology mainstreaming Joshua-Kings as prophets in the dominant Covenant-Prophets program. Here narrative theology is carried by the narrative Babylonian exile and resolution texts (Esther, Daniel, Ezra-Nehemiah, and Chronicles). Notice that Daniel and Lamentations are framed for their prophetic emphasis in the English and LXX order, while in the Writings, Daniel is valued as a narrative that provides guidance for how the Jew is to live. Esther, a narrative book in both configurations is shocking in the absence of God from the text, both in the Hebrew and in the lack of LXX expansion so common in Daniel and Ezra-Nehemiah. This lack of God in the varieties of Esther underscores the depth of God's rejection of Israel during the Babylonian captivity. Placing Ezra-Nehemiah and Chronicles at the end of the Writings provides a conclusion and climax to the entire canon that underscores the restoration of Israel and Temple with the establishment of the *Torah* as the norm of the community. Embedded within this establishment is a more ultimate Messianic hope after the pattern of the Davidic Covenant whereas the LXX order diffuses the Messianic hope to that of the continuing narrative saga, leaving the last statement of the prophet Malachi hoping for an Elijah who will bring about New Covenant restoration of hearts multi-generationally with God.

The Writings section sets up Jewish festival traditional readings and Temple functioning. Psalms leads out the Writings as the main contributor to Temple worship in providing pattern prayers, in contrast to the LXX and English pattern of Psalms as instruction, being surrounded by wisdom. Ruth among the History grounds the Davidic Kingship in a line of blessing while among the Writings calls Israel to generous living. It is little wonder why Jewish tradition reads Ruth to celebrate the harvest festival of the Feast of Weeks for harvest is a theme in the book which provides the context for generosity and recovery. Furthermore, Passover utilizes Song of Songs as an allegorical love for Yahweh, a view imposed on the genre by tradition. The reflective feast of Tabernacles utilizes Qoheleth to remind that value comes through the vertical relationship with God (consistent with its refrain: Eccl. 2:24–26; 3:12–15, 22; 7:14; 8:15; 12:9–14). Lamentations is the fitting choice for the Ninth of Ab fast that commemorates the destruction of Jerusalem and Temple. Likewise, the book of Esther comes to a close explaining the historical roots for the Feast of Purim, during which it is read traditionally.

The addition of the New Testament shifts the focus away from *Torah* to underscore the Kingdom (to which the covenants pointed) and the King, Lord Jesus Christ. Both arrangements of the Old Testament set this up in different ways as was mentioned above.

6.3. Theology

Biblical theology must be theology. It is a message that communicates the unity and diversity. The unity is evident in the organizing principle; the diversity in the particulars and progress of the organization.

6.3.1. Organizing principle

The Bible is a collection of various manuscripts, which address a multitude of issues. Most Biblical theologies are organized under a concept of center, which is a one- or few-word concept which is supposed to permeate the whole passage or section of Scripture. It is to be the focal point around which all else revolves, encompassing the particulars. However, the concept of center fails to do justice to Biblical theology in four main areas. This author advocates its replacement by the message. The message is a concise complex unity, which accurately reflects the particulars of the text and the order inherent between these particulars. Ken Barker develops this concept of message as a "center" but still retains the complex unity, which accurately reflects the particulars of the text.[46] The critical feature is not the name as much as it is the methodology and for our purposes here the names "center" and "message" help to distinguish the basic methodologies. In the four areas in which the concept of center fails, the concept of message demonstrates sufficiency.

First, center does not communicate clearly as does the message. The idea of a center as a one- or few-word concept is supposed to permeate the whole passage of Scripture. Examples of center include: covenant, kingdom, salvation history, and Jesus Christ. These terms are virtually meaningless as a center because whoever utilizes them imports his own meaning to them; the terms do not convey this meaning in and of themselves. To convey meaning with any clarity one needs to have a propositional statement expressing this meaning. Both the subject and the complement need to be included as the message of the passage rather than merely stating the subject and allowing others to import their own complement and thereby import their own meanings to it.

Secondly, the center is a philosophical impossibility, while the concept of message is philosophically possible. For Gerhard Hasel, the

46 This was developed by Ken Barker in doctoral classes like the theology of Isaiah and conversations at Dallas Theological Seminary in 1982.

idea of center permeates and controls the author's writing of the passage.[47] A center is in a certain sense in the author's mind (as an authorial intent), while the concept of message is the reader's summarization of the correlation of content expressed in the passage. E. D. Hirsch proposed authorial intent as the way to obtain validity in interpretation as opposed to reader response.[48] However, the text itself provides a significant guide and warrant as the alternative to these existential and Hirschian conjectures. The center (and authorial intent) is behind and controlling the text; the message is expressed in the authorial thrust of the text. No one today can get behind the text with any warrant. C. S. Lewis was once asked about what he thought about literary critics who claimed that things were written because of a variety of authorial reasons. He thought rather poorly of them because they were almost always wrong when they claimed he wrote from a certain source for a particular intent, and they could have asked him.[49] We do not have the author to tell us what his center is or intent. Those who say that the author is God and He illuminates one to the center of specific passages do not settle the issue, they merely push it back one step into a mystical sphere. God does not tell one exegete a clear statement of what the center is.[50] He allows exegetes to understand the message of a passage as expressed in the words of the text. All that one has today is the text and thus it is only possible to arrive at meaning that can be found in the text: that is the message.

The concept of center does not reflect the text as does the message. Any center is an attempt at conveying that which the book says in a simplicity; the message conveys what the book says in a complex unified whole. Any book of the Bible has complexity and divergent themes within its unity. There is none that is a simplicity; the concept of center is simplistic. Much of the Old Testament has been viewed under the centers like covenant and much of the New Testament has been viewed under the center of Christ. However, the wisdom literature of the Bible is the reef of both Old and New Testament theology. For example Proverbs does not develop covenant but rather clearly identifies the *torah* as familial instruction rather than Law or Mosaic. Likewise, in the New Testament, James (a wisdom epistle) has virtually no Christology,

47 Gerhard Hasel, *New Testament Theology: Basic Issues in the Current Debate* (Grand Rapids: Eerdmans, 1978), p. 142. Such a philosophical impossibility exist in trying to decipher any meaning which tries to get behind the text, as Hirsch's authorial intent, or post-structualism, or text as apologetic of history.

48 E. D. Hirsch, *Validity in Interpretation* (New Haven: Yale University Press, 1967).

49 C. S. Lewis, *Christian Reflection* (Grand Rapids: Eerdmans, 1967), pp. 158–60.

50 God nowhere promises to illume the meaning of passages to interpreters so that they would cognitively know what the passage means. For a further development and defense of this claim cf. chapters on "Thiselton-Ricoeur Hermeneutic" and " Biblical Authority;" cf. Kennard, *The Relationship Between Epistemology, Hermeneutics, Biblical Theology and Contextualization*, pp. 139–42.

while it does develop some monotheism. Even von Rad's center of God hits the reef in such Old Testament books as Proverbs, which clearly emphasize the horizontal social relationships within the creation. There is no kingdom or salvation history development in Proverbs either. To see them there is to abuse the text and land your scheme on the reef.

Finally, an accepted concept of center cannot be found. There is no center on which exegetes agree. A brief survey of twentieth-century centers shows the problem: holiness (Hänel, 1931),[51] God as Lord (Köhler, 1958),[52] Israel's election (Wildberger, 1959),[53] of (Eichrodt, 1961, 1967),[54] Yahweh (von Rad, 1963),[55] the Kingdom of God (Klein, 1970),[56] communion with God (Vriezen, 1970),[57] the blessing/promise plan (Kaiser, 1978),[58] and of testimony (Brueggmann, 1997).[59] If there ever could be agreement then these arguments could be muted a bit, but these arguments are the very reasons for why no center will ever capture the field. On the other hand, a message is easily arrived at and checked because it is ultimately tied to the text.

The messages of wisdom books can be summarized in the following inductive generalizations for your consideration and sharpening. Old Testament wisdom as a whole is summarized as: the wise man will hear, fear and obey Yahweh and live life well according to the framework of how creation works (including the joys of love), understanding that apparent futility and suffering should not dissuade from faithfulness to God. The various components of Old Testament wisdom's message are seen as coming from respective books. For example, Proverbs can be summarized as: the wise man will hear, fear and obey Yahweh, and live life well according to the framework of how creation works, whereas many others will be destroyed in their wicked plans. Additionally, the Song of Songs narratively and poetically illustrates the joys and pains of love while affirming erotic expressions of physical beauty. Furthermore, the message of Job is that the righteous sometimes suffer for sin, sometimes for purification and sometimes for reasons which they may never know under God's sovereignty, so that they need to remain faithful to God in

51 J. Hänel, *Die Religion der Heiligkeit* (Gütersloh: C. Bertelsmann, 1931).

52 Ludwig Köhler, *Old Testament Theology* (Philadelphia: Westminster,1958).

53 H. Wildberger, "to choose" in *Theological Lexicon of the Old Testament*. edited by Ernst Jenni and Claus Westermann. Translated by Mark E. Biddle. Peabody: Hendrickson Publishers, 1997).

54 Walter Eichrodt, *Theology of the Old Testament* (Philadelphia: Westminster, 1961 and 1967).

55 Gerhard von Rad, *Old Testament Theology*.

56 Günther Klein, "The Biblical Understanding of 'The Kingdom of God'," *Interpretation* 26(1972): 393.

57 Theodorus Christian Vriezen, *An Outline of Old Testament Theology* (Oxford: Basil Blackwell, 1970).

58 Walter C. Kaiser, *Toward an Old Testament Theology* (Grand Rapids: Zondervan, 1978).

59 Walter Brueggemann, *Theology of the Old Testament*.

whatever circumstances they find themselves. Likewise, in Qoheleth life appears to be futile in its aimless wanderings and problems under the sun, but life is a gift from God to be enjoyed to the fullest and God is to be obeyed, since He will eventually judge all men. Furthermore, in the New Testament, James exhorts Jewish believers in dispersion to maintain a consistent allegiance to God, as maturity, through the endurance of purifying trials, by readily receiving and applying the Law, by properly controlling oneself (especially one's tongue) and by humbly submitting to God's wisdom.

6.3.2. Organization

The content and organization developed in a Biblical theology is limited to the Biblical source material utilized. For example, when one investigates a theology of Job one does not actually obtain all or only what Job knew and believed. All we know is what the text actually reveals in its theologically constructed narrative conversational format. It is the text that surfaces the categories and warrants the generalizations of Biblical theology.

Biblical theology needs to draw its categories, themes, motifs, and concepts from the Biblical texts themselves. In the past it has drawn too often on the concepts of systematic theology or other concepts of doctrine such as God, man, salvation. The recent situation of Biblical theology seems to maintain the same problem but only under the categories of contemporary philosophy. Such categories and presuppositions tend to bias a work. It is possible to cross examine a Biblical text on the basis of modern philosophy or theology, as say Bultmann did, and to obtain answers about subjects that the contemporary reader desires of which the Biblical authors show no evidence that they ever thought in those ways.[60] For example, in the epistle of James there is so little material about Jesus Christ that at best it should be a minute sub-category. The issue is even made more obvious when the Old Testament is considered with its Hebraic concepts and lack of Western philosophical categories.[61] Biblical theology needs to distinguish the concepts utilized within the text by observing the various components that make up the message of the books utilized within the scope of this study. Once this is done Biblical theology needs to utilize these same concepts as the components of its content and organization.

One category to be discussed in each section of Scripture that is significant for Biblical theology is the concept of God.[62] The word

60 J. Munck, "Pauline Research Since Schweitzer," in *The Bible in Modern Scholarship*, pp. 175–6.

61 Gerhard Ebeling, "The Meaning of 'Biblical Theology,'" *JThSt* 6(1955): 222.

62 This is also the case in books like Esther which do not mention the name of God. A major ingredient to a theology of Esther should be the shocking absence of God from covenantly cursed Israel. Cf. Kennard notes in 'A Biblical Theology of Esther' for this

"theology" suggests that God and His activity are in view. The primary interest of the Bible is not man's experience and thought; it is what God declares, demands and does. A vital study of Biblical theology cannot proceed as though God does not exist.[63] In fact, the Biblical wisdom makes significant advances in theology. Perhaps the most dramatic is the use of *shadday* in Job. This name is only used 48 times in the Old Testament but 31 of these times come from the book of Job and from nearly every speaker as well. So that when it comes to developing the meaning of *shadday,* the text of Job should predominate by indicating through its use a meaning of *shadday* as the powerful sovereign God who generously gives, creates and destroys. Such a meaning excludes the idea of an Akkadian localized god of mountains or the narrowness of Hebrew etymology from *shadod* 'to destroy.' Additionally, Proverbs distinguishes itself from common ancient Near Eastern wisdom by being significantly more oriented toward God than the predominant social orientation. In fact, for Qoheleth the role of God is so significant as to change the futile perspective of experience under the sun to an encouraging refrain of God providing the simple joys of life like work, food, and drink (Eccl. 2:24–26; 3:12–15, 22; 7:14; 8:15; 12:9–14). These repeated choruses serve as providing a positive vertical direction for the theology through the book, which elevates above the futile horizontal or social perspective. Additionally, in the love poetry of Song of Songs perhaps God has a speaking part (Song 5:1b) but there is a stark contrast to other ancient love poetry in the removal of the entwining cult practices and pagan gods.

The relationship between Biblical concepts should be reflected in Biblical theology. The tensions and variant emphases within and between these concepts should be maintained. One must resist the tendency to develop an artificial consistency.[64] For example, in Proverbs the concept of wisdom dominates the range of issues that are developed in the book. This predominance of wisdom is indicated by the emphasis in the introduction, the repetition of these themes, the strength of exhortation from the parents, and the vividness of metaphor like lady wisdom. With this much emphasis, the theme of wisdom should be developed early and positioned prominently. The theme of the fear of Yahweh as the beginning of wisdom (Prov. 1:7) extends this theme as a rider on the predominant wisdom theme. In Proverbs, the repeated contrasts between wisdom and foolishness elevate the theme of foolishness to the basic framework from the range of issues that follow. In these contrasts, the creation-based retribution principle of reaping what you sow is

point and the textual critical resistance to soften this point in multiple generations of Esther texts.

63 Floyd Filson, "A New Testament Students' Approach to Biblical Theology," *JBR* 14(1946): 23.

64 Wayne Ward, "Towards a Biblical Theology," *RExpos* 74(1977): 373.

developed. The greatest example of this foolish lifestyle is that of the adulteress, so that theme seems to come best next in the exposition. Beyond the development of wisdom or fool there is no clear pattern of categories that should dominate. In fact, the long section of individual proverbs accentuate a style that breaks up any overarching structure. The significant social and life issues that illustrate the wise and foolish lives require that these other topics be developed. However, the lack of a textual order leaves me to choose an alphabetical order to communicate a sense of completeness and to mirror the occasional strategy of acrostic that Proverbs chooses when it communicates a sense of completeness on a particular topic (e.g., Pr. 31:10–31).

When narrative genres develop their material, Biblical theology should not simply reconfigure the theology into an a-historical descriptive method but draw the reader into the essence of the drama to help accentuate the critical issues. Perhaps when these are developed orally in class, a sample of the vivid of can enable the student to enter into the poetic and nuanced issues even further. Often of Biblical texts have a video version (like *Prince of Egypt* for Exodus or *The Visual Bible* for Matthew, John and Acts) to render the narrative vividly for the student. Within the accounting of the narrative overarching issues should not be lost. An example in Song of Songs is the drawing out the comparison between the love poetry of description of physical beauty, which seems to bring a wholesome balance, legitimacy and encouragement to verbal love making as said by both male and female[65] in relationship. Though this is a significant and healthy issue in the book the narrative also serves as more than vivid glue that connects these descriptive love poems. In fact the joys, tensions and pains in relationship are only really seen as the twists and turns of the narrative plays out. With other wisdom literature one requires a wise sensitivity to discern how to take each part of the narrative. Additional wisdom is required to develop the self-understandings and self-possibilities that our lives might engage in juxtaposed closely to this text.

In the midst of narrative and counseling conversation, Job presents unique issues of practical theodicy as it is worked out through suffering. However, the issues are much more varied than merely theodicy. As mentioned earlier, the most significant development of *shadday* in all the Old Testament comes from this book. Since Biblical theology is especially about God, and the narrative begins with God in His throne room and the answer God eventually gives to Job is Himself, my Biblical theology of Job begins with God. The second topic is set up in the contrast of the narrative with the adversary (*hasatan*). Development of *hasatan* is rather minimal in the Old Testament (elsewhere only in 1 Chr. 21:1; Ps.109:6;

65 The inclusion of so much love description or physical beauty from the female perspective contrasts with ancient Near Eastern texts.

Zech. 3:1–2) but with thirteen references in Job 1–2 this is clearly the only context to develop the possibility of this descriptive raising to the status of a name. It is also the best place to develop the limitation of *hasatan* as merely one of many small emisaries in the court of the sovereign God. The narrative introduction brings a profound tension for the reader because he knows that the counsel is askew as he hears Job's friends urge him to placate Yahweh as one would for an ancient Near East god to remove the suffering within a mechanistic exposition of the retribution principle. The repeated interchanges which the narrative supplies helps to remind the reader that resisting this simplistic strategy is part of what a sufferer is to do without going to the other extreme of pridefully demanding God to answer (Elihu's counsel paints Job as falling prey here). The nature of the narrative and sheer volume of the interchanges sets Yahweh up in stark contrast, for the answer to suffering is not an answer to why Job suffers; it is that we must all know our humble place before a extremely sovereign God who gets to do whatever He desires including the initiation and overseeing the suffering in our lives. In Biblical theology I try to retain this gem of narrative theology, and in class it is helpful to develop by sampling selective counsel and then polemicizing it by the divine blast from the whirlwind concerning creation and Behemoth-Leviathan.

6.3.3. Progressive

Biblical theology reflects the history and progressive nature of divine revelation. To properly understand the meaning of a passage one needs to see and understand it within its historical and conceptual context. Where several passages are concerned the historical progression should be reflected but this returns us to the point previously developed concerning the gems of narrative theology which don't need to be developed again. Where there is conceptual development like the wisdom program provides, the wisdom program should be nested within the conceptual framework in which it fits. Since the wisdom program has already been developed to be in the era of Solomon with subsequent sages for final arrangement, features like the Mosaic and Davidic covenants are in the context but they just don't seem to be developed conceptually within the wisdom texts.

The nesting of the wisdom program seems to best fit conceptually within creation theology. That is, the sovereign God has effortlessly brought the universe into existence out of the waters of chaos (Gen. 1:2–26; 8). The order that God brought to the chaos (as indicated by separation Gen. 1:4–7, 10, and by designed purposefulness *tob*, and the governance of time by the heavenly objects Gen. 1:14–18; 8:22) serves to provide man with obligation to fit within this order as a player within creation. The role for man as image of God serves to set man as God's representative on the scene as we minutely picture God's creating and sovereignty at work. Some of this obligation comes with the blessing of

God to be fruitful, multiply, fill, subdue and rule the earth (Gen. 1:28; 9:1–7). Other obligation comes by God's fiat framing specific obligations within this purposeful order (Gen. 1:26; 2:15–17, 24; 9:2–6). There are significant benefits to be obtained in living rightly to this order (e.g., Gen. 6:8–9; 8:1). However, so often mankind departs from this righteousness and plunges the creation order into a chaos of his own doing, which God responds with curse or a return to chaos within the created order, fighting chaos with chaos (Gen. 3:6–21; 4:8–15; 6:2–7:24; 9:21–25; 11:1–9). The order of the creation that remains after these judgments is a frustrating, with futility among the order.

This application of creation theology is made more vivid by the wisdom texts. If man is to negotiate his way around the creation staying within those ways that bring success and staying clear of the pits of futility then this person needs wisdom. The retribution principle of "you reap what you sow" is part of this wise perspective. Proverbs joins in at this point to provide a variety of specific wise stepping stones, which strengthen both mind and will. For example, with regard to the specific issue of love and marriage there are many practical guidelines within the book of Proverbs ranging from the adulteress to avoid, to the ideal wife praised by all her family, and a host of scattered comments between. None of these quite has the same poetic passion of Adam's recognition of the fleshness of Eve and the implications to become one flesh for mankind (Gen. 2:23–24). However, Proverbs develops further counsel within this context of marriage that helps complement the Genesis pattern. Here is where the Song of Songs encourages the love passion (which Adam briefly expressed) but it comes within a context that is also tainted by tension, conflict and pain (Gen. 3:16). So the Song of Songs reflects these elements of relationship with frustrating futility as well. This futility within the divine order is acutely driven home by the experimental nature of Qoheleth with periodic reminders that the divine order is still there when one takes into account the vertical blessings that come from God. The recognition of these blessings should motivate the wise person to enjoy the blessings and limit the range of one's own futile experimentation. However, sometimes the futility overwhelms the servant of God in excruciating suffering. Here, Job displays God's sovereignty because the whole process of extreme suffering is in the crucible of futility. While many judgments are brought on by our reaping the consequences of sin and foolishness, there are times when no explanation is given and we must still worship God and serve Him righteously; Job reminds us of this struggle. Wisdom nests in creation theology and conceptually develops an alternative universal revelatory program for the whole of humankind, which continues to stand as applicable to all humankind. As such, it provides a complementary voice to the profoundly Jewish program of Law and prophets. With these issues in mind, my course of Old Testament Biblical theology develops this wisdom theology after the creation theology and before the Jewish covenant program (which is so central to the Old Testament). Throughout the course this wisdom program is not forgotten, for the Law and the prophets do draw upon it. With so much of the revelatory program being God revealing Himself to us, I find it helpful to conclude the course with the theology of the psalms which provides an opportunity to review wisdom theology again among a review of many of the other features of Old Testament Biblical theology. However, the psalms provide a different orientation as affirmation and outcry from the congregation draws the students into a deeper commitment of performing these prayers and to possibly even affirm to live by wisdom's guiding light.

6.4. Conclusion

Briefly put, Biblical theology should be Biblically accurate and complete, and theologically sensitive. This descriptive method traversing wisdom shows how Biblical theology can consistently be accomplished in a critical realist method without destroying itself on the reef for Biblical theology, wisdom literature.

7. Biblical Theology Affecting Systematics:

What would a systematic theology be like, if it listened to the thought forms and gems of Biblical theology?

Systematic theology has been variously arranged to reflect the logical structure and thought forms of its belief system somewhat reactive to the issues faced in that day. However, the systematics approach has reflected substantial indebtedness to a slowly developing theological tradition and its epistemic orientation.[1] In contrast, the field of Biblical theology has arisen with an alternative orientation to try to reflect the thought forms and agenda of the Biblical text from their contexts. In recent time the Biblical theology movement has shown some evidence of occasionally being co-opted by issues of tradition and underlying epistemic concerns even within its discipline.[2] This chapter is not an attempt to show what Biblical theology would be in its own right, I have done that elsewhere.[3] This chapter begins by some recognition of the problem from the vantage point of Biblical theologians. It is followed by a personal statement of some of the more fruitful methodological results of Biblical theology that can be incorporated into a systemic theology to help reframe some of its concepts and structure so that systematics might be more Biblical. These are factors that I incorporate into my systematic theology. To unpack this approach, I will first highlight the basic orientation and then I will suggest briefly some ways in which these approaches can be realized.

7.1. Biblical Theology Method at Odds with Systematics

In contrast to the confessional reformation and pietism, the descriptive Biblical theology movement emerged and was given

1 Cf. chapters: 1) "The Relationship of Philosophy, Theology, and Science" (originally two papers presented at the Evangelical Philosophical Society: "Philosophy Effects Theology," Nov. 2003 and "A Lakatos' Philosophy of Theology," Nov. 2005) and 2) "The Role of Tradition" (originally a Paper presented at the Evangelical Theological Society, Nov. 2003).

2 For example a postmodern approach has been championed by Walter Brueggemann, *Theology of the Old Testament* (Minneapolis: Fortress, 1997). Likewise, when the Wheaton Theology Conference met to discuss Biblical theology and Justification in April 2000 and 2004, they approached the subject from the vantage point of individual Christian traditions.

3 Cf. chapter 6: "The Reef of Biblical Theology" (originally a paper presented to the Evangelical Theological Society, March, 2000).

expression by Johann Philip Gabler's lecture at the University of Altdorf in 1787.[4] Gabler's approach offered an optimistic empirical spirit that we could arrive at objective truth about the meaning of the text from the straightforward study of the Biblical text's details. So for Gabler, the first task of Biblical theology was to catalog the variety of ideas. However, the second task of Biblical theology that Gabler articulated was to sift through this catalog to recognize the important ideas of structure (*dicta classica*), which would then provide empirically and inductively the content and structure for dogmatic (or systematic) theology. So that, in the initial articulation, Biblical theology had as a major part of its agenda, to affect systematic theology with its gems.

Gabler floated both tasks of Biblical theology from within a critical realist perspective. For example, in his day, Gabler discussed subjective aspects of the discipline, because some in the field of Biblical theology occasionally got re-entangled with dogmatic theology, and warned against this.[5]

Charles Scobie and other Biblical theologians have returned to including this affecting of systematics as part of Biblical theology's goals. Scobie sees "Biblical theology as a bridge discipline, situated between the historical study of Scripture on the one hand and its use by the church in its faith and life on the other."[6]

For such a discipline as Biblical theology, the tradition that is most binding is first to have a basic methodology of reflecting the Biblical text in its authorial context wherever it will lead. Or the goal in Biblical theology as I state it is: *to be as clear as the text is clear and to be as ambiguous as the text is ambiguous.*

Such a methodology is a progressive theology that identifies with a heritage of attempts of Biblical description in the past but always goes beyond them to some extent in that each interpreter places his study within the landscape of those who have gone before him in this discipline. In this manner, both the content and the organizing principles try to reflect what the text says. This heritage can be reflected

4 Gabler's lecture 'On the proper distinction between Biblical and dogmatic theology and specific objectives of each,' is translated and commented on in John Sandys-Wunsch and Laurence Eldredge, 'J. P. Gabler and the Distinction Between Biblical and Dogmatic Theology: Translation, Commentary, and Discussion of his Originality,' *Scottish Journal of Theology* 33 (1980): 133–58 and also in *The Flowering of O. T. Theology*, eds. Ben Ollenburger, Elmer Martens, Gerhard Hasel (Winona Lake: Eisenbrauns, 1992), pp. 492–502.

5 Gabler, in *The Flowering of O.T. Theology*, p. 495.

6 Charles Scobie, *The Ways of Our God: An Approach to Biblical Theology* (Grand Rapids: Eerdmans, 2003), p. 46. There are other Biblical theologians who make the same point. Cf. G. Goldsworthy, *Gospel and Kingdom: A Christian Interpretation of the Old Testament* (Exeter: Paternoster, 1981), p. 43; Brevard Childs, *Biblical Theology of the Old and New Testaments: Theological Reflection on the Christian Bible* (Minneapolis: Fortress, 1992), p. 481; R. P. Knierim, "The Task of Old Testament Theology" *HBT* 6(1984): 47.

by a statement of methodology to which I identify, like my own statement,[7] or by positioning oneself within Gerhard Hasel's books on Biblical theology methodology, which I have often used to teach the methodology of this discipline.[8] One's heritage can also be identified by the individual contributors who interpret similarly. For me, that means those major Biblical theology frameworks within which I work, and have my students read, like Eichrodt,[9] Vos,[10] Smith,[11] Brueggemann,[12] House,[13] Goldingay,[14] Merrill,[15] and Waltke[16] for Old Testament, and for the New Testament: Schlatter,[17] Ladd,[18] Gutherie,[19] Wright,[20] Strecker,[21] Dunn,[22] Marshall,[23] and Schnelle.[24] This is a helpful way to identify an

7 Cf. previous chapter, "The Reef of the O.T.: A Method for Doing Biblical Theology that Makes Sense for Wisdom Literature" earlier presented as a paper at ETS, 2000.

8 Gerhard Hasel *Old Testament Theology: Basic Issues in the Current Debate* (Grand Rapids: Eerdmans, 1972, fourth edition 1991) and *New Testament Theology: Basic Issues in the Current Debate* (Grand Rapids: Eerdmans, 1978). A progressive look at the discipline is evident in a volume like *The Flowering of O. T. Theology*.

9 Walther Eichrodt, *Theology of the Old Testament* in two volumes (Philadelphia: The Westminster Press, 1961, 1967).

10 Geerhardus Vos, *Biblical Theology: Old and New Testaments* (Grand Rapids: Eerdmans, 1948).

11 Ralph Smith, *Old Testament Theology: Its History, Method, and Message* (Nashville: Broadman & Holman Publishers, 1993).

12 Walter Brueggemann, *Theology of the Old Testament: Testimony, Dispute, Advocacy* (Minneapolis: Fortress Press, 1997).

13 Paul House, *Old Testament Theology* (Downers Grove: Inter Varsity, 1998).

14 John Goldingay, *Old Testament Theology*, vol. 1 *Israel's Gospel* (Downers Grove: InterVarsity Press, 2003), vol. 2 *Israel's Faith* (Downers Grove: InterVarsity Press, 2006), and vol. 3 *Israel's Life* (Downers Grove: InterVarsity, 2009).

15 Eugene Merrill, *Everlasting Dominion: A Theology of the Old Testament* (Louisville: Broadman and Holman, 2006).

16 Bruce Waltke and Charles Yu, *An Old Testament Theology: An Exegetical, Canonical and Thematic Approach* (Grand Rapids: Zondervan, 2007).

17 Adolf Schlatter, *Die Geschichte des Christus* (Stuttgaart: Calwer Verinsbuchhandlung, 1923) or *The History of the Christ: The Foundation for New Testament Theology* (Grand Rapids: Baker, 1997) and *Die Theologie der Apostel* (Stuttgaart: Calwer Verinsbuchhandlung, 1922) or *The Theology of the Apostles: The Development of New Testament Theology* (Grand Rapids: Baker, 1999).

18 George Eldon Ladd, *A Theology of the New Testament* (Grand Rapids: Eerdmans, 1974, 1993).

19 Donald Gutherie, *New Testament Theology* (Downers Grove: InterVarsity Press, 1981).

20 N.T. Wright, *The New Testament and the People of God* (Minneapolis Press: Fortress Press, 1992), *Jesus and the Victory of God* (Minneapolis: Fortress Press, 1996).

21 Georg Strecker, *Theologie des Neues Testaments* (Berlin: Walter de Gruyter & Co. 1996) or translation: *Theology of the New Testament* Louisville: Westminster John Knox Press, 2000).

22 James Dunn, *The Theology of Paul the Apostle* (Grand Rapids: Eerdmans, 1998).

23 I. Howard Marshall, *New Testament Theology: Many Witnesses, One Gospel* (Downers Grove: InterVarsity, 2004).

24 Udo Schnelle, *Theologie des Neuen Testaments* (Göttingen: Vandenhoeck & Ruprecht GmbH & Co., 2007) or translation by M. Eugene Boring: *Theology of the New Testament* (Grand Rapids: Baker, 2009).

interpretive tradition[25] which frames a trajectory from which future work will be attempted, without requiring the past conclusions to exclude what the Biblical text actually claims in its authorial context. Likewise, this methodological dimension is a major contribution that Biblical theology brings from the Biblical text as well, in its attempt to reflect the content within progressive revelation. It is in this way that the gems of this Biblical theology tradition surface significant differences with systematic theology traditions.

Contemporary Biblical theologians notice that the church and its' systematic theology is askew from the thrust and many of the particulars of the Bible. John Goldingay calls attention to this fact.

> There is a virtually unacknowledged conflict between the church's metanarrative and that of the Old Testament (and the New Testament, actually, but that is another story). I refer not to churches that do not claim to stick too close to Scripture, but to churches that do so claim. The point is well illustrated by the nature of the creeds, which may (or may not) have been appropriate situational responses to the contexts in which they arose but do not form a reliable guide to the contents of biblical faith.[26]

I agree with Goldigay's assessment. We are not alone in making these claims. One additional example is provided by Walter Brueggemann.

> *Old Testament theological articulation does not conform to established church faith,* either in its official declaration or in its more popular propensities. There is much that is wild and untamed about the theological witness of the Old Testament that church theology does not face.[27]

In response to this condition, Goldingay suggests that we should frame our theology by the Bible rather than limit our framework by the community conventions or the community confidence in the Spirit's guidance. What he is here proposing especially for Biblical theology includes systematic theology. I join Goldingay in underscoring that this approach should be extended to systematics as well.

---

25 Cf. Richard Lints does this same approach with several of the same individuals in *The Fabric of Theology: A Prolegomenon to Evangelical Theology* (Eugene: Wipf and Stock Publishers, 1999), pp. 139–190. I. H. Marshall (in "Developing Theology from Hermeneutics," IBR paper, Nov. 2002) also sees a cross-section tradition, the faith given to the church, as the doctrinal view of the Christian mind, which is used to test prophets and orthodoxy.

26 John Goldingay, *Old Testament Theology: Volume One: Israel's Gospel* (Downers Grove: InterVarsity Press, 2003), p. 22.

27 Walter Brueggemann, *Theology of the Old Testament*, p. 107.

> I therefore resist the principle that interpretation must recognize the limits set by the church's creed, "within which it must work and beyond which it must not stray."[28] The church's faith may function as a preliminary understanding, a way into theological study of Scripture, not least in the conviction that the Holy Spirit has been guiding the church in its understanding of Scripture over the centuries. But we know that in general the Holy Spirit's success in conforming the church to God's will and vision is somewhat partial. One would expect this also to apply to the church's interaction with Scripture, and a look at the relationship between the Scriptures and the church's faith and life makes it clear that this is indeed so.[29]

Goldingay's approach is helpful to recover a full-orbed Biblical theology of the Old Testament, however the gems of such Biblical theology study should not stop there. If this approach is of benefit for Biblical theology, then it should be continued into a Systematic theology that is trying to carry this truth over to affect the church's doctrine. As a bridge discipline, Scobie advocates this role for Biblical theology.[30] This chapter proposes a strategy to do exactly that. Namely, I intend to propose a Biblical theology orientation with suggestions for their implementation, to enable systematics to become more Biblical.

7.2. Biblical Theology Orientation

Certain basic assumptions of methodological orientation are helpful for reclaiming a theology for Biblicism. I suggest five basic assumptions.

First, theological concepts lifted from the Bible should reflect the Biblical theology thrust and world-view that they are immersed within in their authorial Biblical context. Or briefly put, *use Biblical terms in the Biblical way*. The reverse of this principle is to be avoided, namely try not to read traditions or contemporary agendas onto or "from" the Biblical text, when it is not what the text is trying to accomplish in its context. One way of insuring this careful handling of the Biblical text is to resist inventing new terms. Instead use the terms and concepts which the Biblical text itself surfaces. One aspect of this is to recognize that different Biblical authors use the same term in unique ways. We should describe these distinctions to maintain the unique authorial

28 Francis Watson, *Text, Church and World* (Edinburgh: T & T Clark/ Grand Rapids: Eerdmans, 1994), p. 6.

29 John Goldingay, *Old Testament Theology,* vol. 1, p. 22.

30 Charles Scobie, *The Ways of Our God*, p. 46. There are other Biblical theologians who make the same point. Cf. G. Goldsworthy, *Gospel and Kingdom: A Christian Interpretation of the Old Testament* (Exeter: Paternoster, 1981), p. 43; Brevard Childs, *Biblical Theology of the Old and New Testaments*, p. 481; R. P. Knierim, "The Task of Old Testament Theology" *HBT* 6(1984): 47.

contributions made from each Biblical perspective. A familiar example of this is the relationship between justification and faith. Simply put, in James 2, justification is *a demonstratable vindication that is best evident to God and man by a person showing his faith by his works*. Whereas, in Paul (say Romans 4), justification is *a condition of being acceptable to God that had normally been associated in second Temple Judaism as being within the Mosaic covenant, but to include Gentiles, such justification is accomplished by faith in Jesus as Lord after the pattern of father Abraham*. As you might know, this Pauline view of justification is undergoing review today, reconsidering whether its emphasis is more legal, or covenantal or mystical.[31] However one resolves this Pauline authorial meaning, it needs to be understood from the authorial context, which for Paul includes second Temple Judaism, rather than reformation reactions to Roman Catholicism.

Another way to maintain this authorial Biblicism is to *not* connect texts with terms not found in those contexts. For example, much of the contemporary debate about "imputation" violates this. To discuss imputation from Romans 3–8, Galatians 1–5, and Ephesians 1–2 so misses what those texts are actually saying because they are twisted to the agenda of the terms one brings to these texts. Instead each text surfaces its unique contributions to salvation, of which only one verse (Rom. 5:13 or two if you include Philemon 18) addresses the issue of imputation. So a doctrine of Christian imputation should be developed exclusively from Romans 5:13 and Philemon and their contexts. Theologians should teach such concepts from the texts that actually mention them and let other texts have their own voice contributing toward other metaphors.

Second, Biblical theology, reflecting the Bible's emphasis, raises concepts and issues of life that are frequently neglected by systematics but should be addressed because they *reflect God's Biblical concerns*. These concepts and structure show the Biblical emphasis and the Biblical thought forms. Or briefly put, *make sure that your theology is deeply Biblical in its concerns*. That is, systematics should not merely address traditional issues or philosophical issues but also Biblical ones as well. One way to do this is to discuss the issues that are raised in the Biblical context in which they present themselves, rather than abstractly. My chapter on the "Creation and Fall" is an example of this sort of contextual approach as I present primarily the perspective from Genesis 1-3 and Psalms 8, 19 and 104. A side benefit of this approach will be that the practicality of the Bible connects theology to life issues thereby keeping one's theology deeply practical with Biblical exhortation calling our readers to practical life decisions.

---

31 One brief discussion of these possibilities is within N. T. Wright, *What Saint Paul Really Said: Was Paul of Tarsus the Real Founder of Christianity?* (Grand Rapids: Eerdmanns, 1997), pp. 12–20, 77–133.

An example of this is that often eschatological prophecy comes with exhortation to be watchful, faithful and in some cases more specific instructions. When such prophecy is discussed in our systematics we should make sure that this ethical and spiritual exhortation is heard by our students. Thus we should resist systematizing that either silences or diminishes this textual voice. Marv Pate and I tried to retain the different authorial voices with their exhortative elements as we did our volume on eschatology, *Deliverance Now and Not Yet.*[32]

Third, the Bible approaches its subjects and events with different genres. My assumption is that *theologically we should reflect the thrust of the genre utilized.* These different genres attempt to accomplish differing goals within the reader. Evangelical Systematics has mined mostly the genre of epistle. The narrative theology movement has championed the genre of narrative, which may at most occupy a third of the Biblical text. Joining with narrative are other important genres (covenant, wisdom, psalm, prophetic, apocalyptic) which each contribute significantly in their own right. Systematic theology would be enriched if it cultivated each of the genres of the Biblical text for what they have to give. But we need to be careful here, for if a genre (like a psalm) is logically analyzed to describe the concepts of this genre, the impact of the genre (which calls the reader to performative prayer) may be lost as it is reframed into a different genre, that of theological description. So perhaps selections of the more important of passages can be sampled within their own genre carefully to maintain the thrust that these Biblical texts have to contribute as well as their concepts. Or briefly put, *make sure that your theology is deeply Biblical.* This also has the ramification that if you go to a Biblical text to support a theological point, then also one should use this same text to address its thrust in its context. This approach will also tend to bring practical exhortations and promises into systematic theology that are usually left for the exegete and Biblical theologian. For example, if you are unpacking the Olivet discourse, also include its ethic and soteriology, not merely its eschatology for the text is repeatedly punctuated with exhortation for the disciples' lives.

A fourth assumption is that *the interpretation of Biblical texts reflect the possibilities and that which is likely within the historical cultural context of the text under examination.* This is such a common evangelical assumption for exegetes some may wonder why I feel the need to mention it. I am particularly concerned that as a field, we theologians keep up with the discoveries of the Biblical specialists so that when we use the Old Testament we need to be informed and interacting with ancient Near Eastern thought forms. Likewise, when we approach the New Testament, we need to do so aware of and interacting with second

32 C. Marvin Pate & Douglas W. Kennard, *Deliverance Now and Not Yet: The New Testament and the Great Tribulation. Studies in Biblical Literature 54* (New York: Peter Lang, 2003, 2005).

Temple Jewish concepts. This is not to say that the Biblical text does not alter these concepts. It does at times. However, this historical-cultural contextual approach sensitizes us to the possibilities and that which is likely from the text's original context so that we are a little less likely to read our traditional approach on to a text.

Fifth, *whatever is Biblical should be reflected within systematic theology*. It is through this assumption that these previous assumptions will now be applied to systematic theology for the enrichment that they will bring.

7.4. Biblical Theology Suggestions for Systematics' Gain

These suggestions are made from the vantage point of encouraging American evangelicalism to include or shift in particular ways. Some traditions may already be sensitive in these ways. However, what is driving this presentation here is the contribution from Biblical theology, not a traditional sensitivity.

Biblical theology sensitizes the exegete to the authorial thought forms and the progressive development of where its concepts emerged and grew. An outstanding example of the benefit which Biblical theology provides concerning concepts is in the area of Biblical anthropology. There is nearly a unanimous agreement among Biblical theology in the framing and meaning of Biblical anthropology terms. This is evident in the broad agreement among Biblical theology wordbooks on the meaning of these terms. However, most systematics, Christian philosophy, and Christian psychology persist in appropriating some of the same terms with alternative traditional meanings in their discipline, a meaning foreign to the way Biblical theology takes them. My suggestion is that for the cause of integration there would be a significant gain if these disciplines embraced the Biblical meaning and nuance within such concepts as soul, image of God, spirit, body, heart, mind and the like. In the chapter "A Biblical Anthropology Funding Bio-Ethics" I attempt to show how this is done.[33] Other concepts could also undergo a shift in meaning. For example, the contribution of Isaiah proposes a new attribute for God under ancient Near Eastern terms of *incomparability*, which argue for the supremacy of monotheistic Yahweh and our need to be loyal to Him. It is important for an approach that is trying to be Biblical to surface these Biblical attributes rather than be governed by traditional categories. I folded a discussion of Yahweh's incomparability into my volume of *The Classical Christian God* in two places. First it was helpful to focus on it

33 Cf. subsequent chapter "The Nature of Humanity: A Biblical Theology Approach" which was presented for EPS, Nov. 2004; earlier versions of this paper were presented with Paul Holmes of the University of Chicago, at the Wheaton Theology Conference, Apr. 1997; and my initial paper was strongly received by O.T. scholars at ETS, Nov. 1990.

squarely to foster understanding and worship of God within the reader.[34] Secondly, the concept actually had some apologetic value as a bridge to a defensible philosophical concept of God in the ontological argument.[35] Likewise, concepts may shift their meaning under the lens of Biblical theology. For example, Oscar Cullmann and more recently John Feinberg argued that the Biblical concept expressed by or *'lm/* should be understood as temporally everlasting rather than eternal.[36] This is a more accurate handling of the Biblical text as it relates to these concepts. Such an embrace of using the Biblical terms in the Biblical way does not mean that theology has to loose traditional nuances that are not seen to be Biblically justified, provided that there is a sufficient reason for advocating it by some other means. For example, I still maintain that God is atemporally eternal for philosophical reasons rather than trying to defend it from Biblical texts that in my opinion do not teach the view.[37]

A corollary application to these Biblical concepts is that we should let the Biblical contexts within which these concepts appear be that to which is appealed for defining and defending the meaning of these concepts. For example, the concept of the "image of God" needs to make sense within a context of Genesis chapters 1, 5, 9 and the ancient Near East environment which these texts address.[38] Traditional, philosophical, and psychological definitions have no place in defining these Biblical terms. Such reworked definitions deny the voice of the text as they impose a different system into their disciplines.

The evolution of concepts over time within the Biblical text is another feature that Biblical theology provides from its commitment to the progressiveness of revelation. Again, Biblical anthropology provides a good example of the development of concepts in progressive revelation. For example, the development of personal eschatology is one that has very little evidence for resurrection in the O.T. It seems to be just emerging with a source like Daniel 12:2. Prior to that, concepts like "gathered to forefathers" and "embodied in *sheol*" describe personal afterlife. When

34 Douglas Kennard, *The Classical Christian God. Toronto Studies in Theology 86* (Lewiston: Mellen Press, 2002), pp. 121–134.

35 Kennard, *The Classical Christian God.* pp. 16–17.

36 Oscar Cullmann, *Christus und die Zeit. Die urchristliche Zeit- und Geschichtsauffassung* (Zollikon-Zürich: Evangelischer Verlag, 1946) translated as *Christ and Time* (London: SCM Publishers, 1962); John Feinberg, *No One Like Him: Foundations of Evangelical Theology: The Doctrine of God* (Wheaton: Crossway Books, 2001), pp. 255–264; I argued the same in: Kennard, *The Classical Christian God,* pp. 52–61.

37 Kennard, *The Classical Christian God,* pp. 20, 27–32, 43–61.

38 Hans Walter Wolff, *Anthropology of the Old Testament* (Philadelphia: Fortress Press, 1974), pp. 160–161; Doug Kennard, "The Nature of Humanity: A Biblical Theology Approach " A paper presented for EPS, Nov. 2004, p. 3; earlier versions of this paper were presented with Paul Holmes of the University of Chicago, at the Wheaton Theology Conference, Apr. 1997; and my initial paper was strongly received by O.T. scholars at ETS, Nov. 1990.

this first concern is wedded to my fourth concern, that of extra-Biblical context, the evolution of the concepts continues through second Temple Jewish sources. It is in this framework that the concept of personal resurrection develops full blown.[39] So that when the New Testament theologian notices the fully developed concept of personal resurrection in the N.T. it is significantly reflective of this contextual second Temple development. In elucidating these progressive developments, few excel as ably as James Dunn's works.[40] Of course, I am not as skeptical as Dunn is but on the whole he does help sensitize us to real historical texts and to the conceptual development within them.[41] When a theologian traces the concept through these texts, a progression of the development of the concept surfaces and should be developed in our systematic theology, as well as in our Biblical theology. Within this framework the N.T. presents personal resurrection of the body and an everlasting destiny of meaningful service to God on the new earth. That is, traditional theology that views our afterlife as souls in heaven has departed from the Biblical emphasis, probably under the influence of platonizing philosophy.

39 E.g., *1 En.* 58.3; 91.10; 92.2; 108.11–14; *2 Mac.* 7.9–14, 22–23; 14.43–46; *4 Macc.* 7.19; 16.25; *4 Ezra 7.32*; *Sib. Or.* 4.180; *T. of Ben. 10.6–8*; *T. of Hos*. 6:2 interprets this text to be resurrection whereas the text speaks of the reviving of Israel on the third day; *Tg. Jon.* on Isa. 27:12f describes salvation as being accomplished on the third day; *bSanh.* 90b where Gamaliel claims that God would give the resurrected patriarchs land, not merely their descendants and Johanan Numbers 18:28 the portion of YHWH given to Aaron is taken that he will be alive again, likewise Num. 15:31 is claimed that the remaining guilt of the offender will be accountable in the world to come; 91b–92a; *mSanh.* 10.1, 3; *T. Mos.* 10.8–10; *Genesis Rabbah* 14.5; *Leviticus Rabbah* 14.9; *Messianic Apocalypse* adds resurrection to a modification of Psalm 146:5–9 as a Messianic expectation to be done to others; *T. Jud.* 25.4 claims this Messianic resurrection would begin with Abraham, Isaac, and Jacob; *T. Benj.* claims that after these are raised the whole of Israel will be raised; *Psalms of Solomon* 3.11–12; *4Q521* frag. 2, col. 2.1–13; frags. 7 and 5, col. 2.1–7; *1QH* 14.29–35; 19.10–14; the benediction in the *Amidah*, the *Shemoneh Esre*. However, *Wis. of Sol.* 3.1; 8.19–20; 9.15 and Josephus' description of the Pharisees (*Ant.* 17.152–154; 18.1.3–5; *Jew. Wars* 2.151–153; 2.8.14; *Ap.* 2.217–8) follow more a Platonic immortality of the soul view, but even here the soul eventually is given a body to match (*Wis. of Sol.* 9.15; Josephus, *Jew. Wars* 2.163). Also the Biblical authors (Mt. 22:23–33; Mk. 12:18–27; Acts 23:6–7) and the *Eighteen Benedictions* present the Pharisees as believing the resurrection of the dead; cf. Neil Gillman, *The Death of Death: Resurrection and Immortality in Jewish Thought* (Woodstock: Jewish Lights Publishing, 2000), pp. 101–142; N. T. Wright, *The Resurrection of the Son of God* (Minneapolis: Fortress Press, 2003), pp. 129–206 for the post-Biblical Jewish view. The early church from patristic through medieval eras embraced bodily resurrection instead of Platonic immortality of the soul with regard to personal eschatology (cf. Caroline Walker Bynum, *The Resurrection the Body in Western Christianity, 200-1336* [New York: Columbia University Press, 1995]; N.T. Wright, *Resurrection*, pp. 480–552).

40 E.g., James Dunn, *Jesus Remembered* (Grand Rapids: Eerdmans, 2003).

41 I have tried to implement this strategy in Christology in Douglas Kennard, *Messiah Jesus: Christology in His Day and Ours* (New York: Peter Lang, 2007) and in eschatology in Marv Pate and Douglas Kennard, *Deliverance Now and Not Yet: The New Testament and the Great Tribulation* (New York: Peter Lang, 2003, 2005).

Extending the Biblical concepts further, Richard Lints argues that "the structure of systematic theology ought to mirror in some important way the structure of biblical theology. The dominant themes of redemptive revelation ought to be the dominant themes of systematic theology."[42] One expression of such a structural issue is seen in his suggestion that the Biblical theology of Geerhardus Vos tried to develop a pattern closely following the structure of the Biblical text.

When the Biblical theology life concerns (#2 above) are combined with Biblical genres (#3 above) in this context (#1 and #4 above) a number of suggestions for enriching systematic theology follow. The different genres contribute in unique ways.

First, the O.T. begins by laying a framework describing God and humans within the creation and fallen order. Several genres are used. The narrative (and genealogy) contribute that the earth has a real historical heritage reflected in the Biblical texts. This would argue for a young earth that has real purposefulness. Such design and purposefulness is best seen within a narrative showing the matrix of relationships. For example, in my book, *The Classical Christian God,* I included a chapter on creation theology entitled "Elohim the Creator,"[43] which has been rewritten and expanded for this volume as the chapter "Creation and Fall." In such a creation theology narrative, the grandeur of God is portrayed above the design of the creation. Such design order sets the parameters within which we should think of the players, whether it is God or ourselves, or whoever. Against this backdrop the vulnerability and propensity of man to sin is shown in the progressive choices individuals and groups make within the narrative. Secondly, within this creation theology framework the genre of covenant obligates and privileges the lives of the creation under the blessings and obligations of the Noahic Covenant. The level of certainty supplied by God vowing to do something by an oath should be reflected in the emphasis and confidence of a theological statement. For example, I have my students read a short paper on the Noahic Covenant to be framed by this covenantal authoritative system.[44]

Biblical covenants provide structure for understanding God's governance. Both a reformed and dispensationalist approach has folded this sentiment that "covenant is significant" into their theology. However, the two or three covenants of reformed Covenantal thought have no Biblical text basis. Likewise, developments in form-criticism have substantially concluded that the whole of the book of Deuteronomy is

---

42 Richard Lints, *The Fabric of Theology* (Eugene: Wipf and Stock Publishers, 1999), pp. 270–1.

43 Doug Kennard, *The Classical Christian God*, pp. 87–104.

44 Doug Kennard, "Noahic Covenant," a chapter in a manuscript entitled *Biblical Covenantalism*.

a suzerainty treaty.[45] This could redirect Covenant theology to actual Biblical covenants. It would also have ramifications for dispensational theology for such a Deuteronomy as suzerainty treaty shows that the "Palestinian Covenant" (Deuteronomy 29–30) is an arbitrary human construct which has no textual basis. That is, both the "witnesses" and the "curse and blessing" section continue over this arbitrary break dispensationalists make in the Deuteronomy text conjecturing a Palestinian Covenant (Deut. 4:26; 27:1–8; 28–30; 31:19–28; 32). This means that the dispensationalist confidence for Israel's future based on Deuteronomy 29–30 is really an expression of the everlasting applicability of the Mosaic Covenant as both the prophets and second Temple Judaism express.[46] However one understands these Biblical covenants, it would be significant for framing one's understanding of Israel, the church, eschatological hopes and ethics. So I have my students interact with a series of papers on the Mosaic Covenant, Davidic Covenant, and New Covenant so that they will think these issues through from a Biblical theology framework.[47]

Furthermore, other genres work in the wake of this creation theology. For example, wisdom literature is usually recognized in Biblical theology to provide sage statements that a maturing person can reflect on concerning how the creation order works so that they might apply their reflections into practical living. The insights obtained from these human reflections do not have the same level of authority as does the Noahic Covenant but they have important contributions to be made to the development of the person's mind and to a range of practical issues. They also interact with "a theology of work" that I put together incorporating wisdom texts so that they might reflect upon a framework for their pursuit of vocation.[48]

Fourth, narrative theology could make significant contributions, especially from those narratives that are emphasized. The most emphasized narrative of the O.T. is the exodus story, and from the N.T. the life of Jesus is repeatedly emphasized. Theology would then be enriched with the drama and power of God miraculously creating His people Israel, and God's responsiveness to recover and discipline the people as they wandered. For example, John Goldingay's *Old Testament Theology: Volume One, Israel's Gospel* provides a nice summary of the

45 G. E. Mendenhall, "Covenant Forms in Israelite Tradition," The Biblical Archaeologist, 17:3 (1954): 50–76; K. Baltzer, Das Bundesformular. Seine Ursprung und Seine Verwendung im AT. Wiss. Monograph. 2. A. und N.T. 4 (Neukirchen: Neukirchener Verlag, 1960); Meredith G. Kline, Treaty of the Great King. The Covenant Structure of Deuteronomy (Grand Rapids: Eerdmans, 1963).

46 cf. Doug Kennard, "Jesus as Mosaic Teacher of the Law," *Messiah Jesus: Christology in His Day and Ours* (New York: Peter Lang, 2008), pp. 107–51.

47 Doug Kennard, each paper is a chapter in a manuscript entitled "Biblical Covenantalism."

48 Cf. chapter "Theology of Work."

narrative gems of the Old Testament. Likewise, I have tried to enrich a systematic theology presentation concerning God with a few of these gems. In my book, *The Classical Christian God,* I included chapters on the exodus as illustrative of Yahweh's dramatic interactive approach with the founding and establishment of Israel.[49] In my visual presentation I interact with sections of the movie *The Prince of Egypt* to illustrate the power, compassion, interactiveness and severity of God. Some attributes show forth the real life and interactiveness of our God when seen only through the lens of narrative. If systematic theology mentions these attributes in a logical list they lay flat, lacking the vibrance the narrative genre provides within its context.

Likewise, the gospels provide pictures of Jesus doing the same miraculous creation of the Kingdom people. This gospels-informed Christology would develop fleshed out roles of Christ that have Him exampling His Christology, providing a Kingdom framework for ecclesiology, ethics and soteriology (as gaining Kingdom). The synoptic gospels provide a Christology from below that is very helpful and balanced by the Johannine Christology from above. Both of these narrative voices for Christology also balance the evangelical dominance in Christology from Paul and Hebrews. For example, my Christology volume, *Messiah Jesus: Christology in His Day and Ours* incorporates major Biblical theology and second Temple Jewish contributions to the presentation of Christ. When it comes to unpacking Jesus as sage, I explore Jesus' proverbs and parables.[50] When it comes to exampling Jesus as prophet, the Olivet discourse is an important inclusion.[51] When it comes to unpacking Jesus as scribe rhetorical critical analysis of second Temple scribal questions spotlight the competency and honor of the level of Jesus as a Jewish scribe. Theological statements which merely itemize His titles, ignoring His wisdom and prophecy, practically rape Jesus of these terms that they are mentioned about Him. That is, Jesus as sage identifies Jesus as a teacher of wisdom, and likewise the role of prophet identifies Jesus as a conduit of prophecy, and finally, Jesus as scribe identifies Jesus as the definitive interpreter of the Law.[52] Unless we theologians learn and heed His wisdom, teaching, and prophecy, we can not claim to be disciples of Jesus. The Biblical pattern is not merely to learn about Jesus, especially in the gospels it is to learn from Him.

Each avenue of narrative reframes its material into a dramatic linear thrust going from somewhere (like creation, exodus, announcement of kingly birth) to somewhere (like the Promised Land and eschatological Kingdom). Such a narrative draws a person in to be defined not primarily

49 Doug Kennard, *The Classical Christian God*, pp. 105–114.

50 Doug Kennard, "Jesus as Sage" in *Messiah Jesus*, pp. 211–42.

51 Doug Kennard, "Jesus as Prophet" in *Messiah Jesus*, pp. 243–68.

52 Doug Kennard, "Jesus as the Superior Jewish Scribe" in *Messiah Jesus,* pp. 133–37.

by the boundaries of Christian tradition. Rather, the defining feature in such a narrative approach is the continuity of traveling the journey toward the goal. The way towards Kingdom becomes a major definition for oneself and community, and thus surfaces a more prominent place for a two-way soteriology.

Fifth, a more prominent place should be made for a two-way soteriology in our systematic theology since it is strongly emphasized from several genres. For example, the framework set up by narrative has been briefly mentioned. Furthermore, the Mosaic covenant sets up a way of blessing and a way of curse dependent upon the covenant community's loyalty to God's gracious Covenant. The narrative portions of the O.T. likewise show God's responsiveness to bless the faithful and curse the rebellious. The *Tanakh* pattern places considerable portions of the Christian Old Testament within the former Prophets as a reminder that it echos and calls Israel back to Covenant. The prophets call Israel back from their unfaithfulness to a faithfulness to the God of the Covenant. So the prophets should inform an ethic for those who are within the Covenant framework that the prophets work within. Additionally, wisdom genres provide guidance concerning the way of the wise who is blessed because he fits within how creation works and keeps clear of the way of the fool. This same two-ways framework is extended beyond this life into an afterlife soteriology strategy by Pharisaic and sectarian second Temple Judaism. Sectarian Judaism demanded a greater internal purity and obedience in its attempt to purify Judaism, consistent with the Mosaic Covenant (a Deuteronomist perspective). For example, Israel is already blessed in a covenant relationship with Yahweh. This relationship is expressed as coming from exodus and heading toward the Promised Land and the Kingdom. Furthermore, if Israel were to obey all the Law then they would be wonderfully blessed, enabling the Kingdom to come (Deut. 28:1–14; 30:8–20). However, if Israel disobeys then they will be horribly cursed (Deut. 28:15–30:20). This sets up a narrow way of blessing and a broad way of wrath. The prophets call Israel back from their wandering ways to the narrow way of covenant faithfulness (e.g., 1 Kgs. 19:10; Jer. 21:8; Ezek. 9:8–10). However, these two ways (one of blessing and the other of curse) are also evident in the wisdom program, for wisdom calls the wise to follow in a narrow way, fitting into the patterns of creation, in contrast to the many broad ways of the fool that lead to destruction. In this program, wisdom is vindicated in showing a consistency to the narrow way of the wise, in contrast to the broad way of the fool (Pr. 28:6; Matt. 7:24–27; 11:19: Luke 7:35). These programs, covenant and wisdom, have come together through a two-ways expression in the wisdom and torah psalms (e.g., Pss. 1:6; 119:29–32; 139:24) and even more in sectarian purifying Judaism of the second Temple period.[53] The continuation of the domination of Israel by Gentile powers indicated in this Deuteronomist approach that Israel had repeatedly chosen the way of disobedience (Deut. 9:7; 28:15–30:20; 2 Kgs. 17:23; Neh. 9:32; Isa. 9:1–2; Ezek. 21:3; 20:31; Mic. 5:3–4).[54] Their precarious condition was confessed by *Baruch* 1.18–19.

> We have disobeyed Him, and have not heeded the voice of the Lord our God, to walk in the statutes of the Lord that he set before us. From the time when the Lord brought our ancestors out of the land of Egypt to this day.

So while Judaism hoped for the Kingdom, their disobedience reminded them that they were dominated by Gentiles because they repeatedly chose the broad way of rebellion.

Jesus and the early church especially continue this strategy through the synoptics' narrow way to Kingdom, Acts' Christian way, Hebrews exodus way unto rest, and Revelation's overcoming way. Perhaps the evangelical emphasis upon the initial soteriology has led to the neglect among us that our life matters now and for Kingdom.

Sixth, wisdom as a genre calls for a reflective reading and evaluation that requires the reader to also develop his ability to evaluate a text's applicability from the Biblical situations to one's own day. When wisdom texts are cited we need to maintain this feature for our handling of the Biblical text. We do a disservice to our readers if we give them pabulum or dogmaticism from such wisdom texts. Wisdom exercises and trains the person. A systematic theology use of wisdom needs to maintain this active reading and evaluation component that this genre requires.

Seventh, likewise, for the little love poetry that is contained within the Biblical text. The poetic descriptions of the beloved should encourage the freedom of verbal love play with one's own beloved, after the celebrated pattern of love poetry (Gen. 2:23; Song. 1:9–2:5; 4:1–15; 5:10–15; 6:4–10; 7:1–9). And the narrative of the love poetry perhaps provides a forum to learn how different aspects of a love relationship work or get diminished. This could be a helpful corrective to our culture

---

53 E.g., *Ecclus* 2.12; 15.11–17; 21:10–14; *Wisd.* 5.6–7 *2 Esd.* 7:6–14; 30.15; 42.10; *Pss. Sol.* 9.5; 14.10; *3 Macc.* 5.51; *2 Bar.* 59.10; 85.13; *4 Ezra* 7.3–9, 48, 82, 129, 137; *Sib. Or.* 2.150*b*. *Ber.* 28b; *m'Abot* 2.9; Philo, *Sacr. AC* 2; *Agric.* 103–104; *ARN* 14, 18, 25; *T. Asher* 1:3, 5; 6.3; *T. Jacob* 2.17; *Pesq. R.* 179b; *t. Sota* 7.11; *t Sanh.* 14.4; *b. Ber.* 28b;_*b. Hag.* 3b; *b. 'Erub.* 19a; *Mek.* on Ex. 14:28; *Sipre* on Deut. 11:26; *1QS* 3:13–4.26; *Apoc. Zeph.* 3.9. The early church continued in this two ways teaching: *Did.* 1–6; *Barn.* 18–20; *Herm. m.* 6, *s.* 9.12.5; *Ps.-Clem. Hom.* 3.52.2; 5.7; *T. Abr.* 10–11; *Apos. Const.* 1–5; cf. Doug Kennard, "The Two Ways Christian Life View: A Historical Sketch" a paper presented at ETS, March, 1998; N. T. Wright, *Jesus and the Victory of God*, pp. 313–314.

54 *1 Esdr.* 8.73–74; *2 Esdr.* 9.7; *Bar.* 1.13, 18–19; 2.6.

with its lust-based personal gratification focus, that love is other focused, encouraging one's beloved in her love.

Eighth, when the psalm genre is appropriated to inform theology, then it is important to pray these performative prayers lest we rape them of their role as pattern prayers. While this issue is quite explicit from form criticism, it is also accentuated by the Psalms placement in the *Tanakh* as leading off the Writings. This revelational contribution to doxastic and petitionary theology is not merely that which accepts the descending theology from God, but also as theology it should ascend to God with petition and praise following these pattern prayers. For example, in my *Classical Christian God,* I develop Psalm 139 as a praise and lament to God as an attempt to call ourselves beyond passive reading of theology, to a more active praying of theology.[55]

Ninth, the genre of prophecy includes prediction with exhortation. As prophecy looks back to the covenant framework, it often calls the community of God to repent from their sin. This is a good framework with which to teach about sin. For example, the range of different terminology for sin is profoundly colorful as I lead my students through the covenant lawsuit of Isaiah 1. However, more than being colorful, the text is ethically blunt mentioning specific sins for which God destroyed Israel in judgment. There is a real advantage in seeing sin handled in a context like this for it blatantly makes the point that sin always has consequences, and these are usually in judgment. Sin should not be taught in the abstract for as sin is placed in the context of judgment there is strong warning to depart from these sins and return to God. This is especially the case in a covenant lawsuit like Isaiah 1, which calls Israel to repent before they had gone too far. However, once the student sees Isaiah 6 in its context, God's holiness has consequences of forgiveness for repentant Isaiah but hardening to destruction for unrepentant Israel. To not develop these issues out of the strengths of this genre leaves these issues too abstract and disconnected to their consequences. The *Nebhi'im* Former Prophets remind us that prophecy comes from narrative context and connects with life through the lens of context.

Likewise in prophecy, the salvation oracle comes with prediction and exhortation. The twentieth century saw a lot of development in minutely analyzing the aspects of prophecy but with these approaches often the ethical exhortations were left out. When prophecy is proof-texted to develop a system the exhortations are often ignored. This is a travesty because usually it was the exhortation which the prophecy was trying to support, showing why the disciple needed to be faithful or watchful. So it is important to handle prophetic texts in their genre and context. When this is done as say in the Olivet Discourse, the warnings

55 Doug Kennard, *The Classical Christian God*, pp. 115–120.

and guidance unto salvation is extremely rich and practical for the disciple of Jesus.

Finally, in apocalyptic literature we should recognize that its primary purpose is not the extensive unpacking of identifiable stages. The main emphasis that apocalyptic contributes is that of the final resolution that God and Christ wins with Kingdom. Thus we should resist tendencies to either allegorize these figurative texts or through a literal reading of apocalyptic identify all the players and expectations of the future. The emphasis of such apocalyptic texts is to emphasize the goal of Kingdom and to foster a hope and deep hunger within our being for realizing this goal. Systematics should utilize apocalyptic to foster this hope. That is, our teaching from this genre should make our students yearn for the coming Kingdom.

These have been a few suggestions that help maintain the Biblical thrust and the interests of Biblical theology within our systematics. My agenda here has been to modify systematic theology in this direction of deep Biblicism and Biblical theology.

8. Contextualization

We are all immersed within a culture. Clyde Kluckholn says, "Culture is a way of thinking, feeling, believing. It is the group's knowledge stored up for future use."[1] Louis Luzbetak describes culture as that growing environment through which people perceive the world around them.

> Culture is a design for living. It is *a plan according to which society adapts itself to its physical, social, and ideational environment.* A plan for coping with the physical environment would include such matters as food production and all technical knowledge and skill. Political systems, kinships and family organization, and law are examples of social adaptation, a plan according to which one is to interact with his fellows. Man copes with his ideational environment through knowledge, art, magic, science, philosophy, and religion. Cultures are but different answers to essentially the same human problems.[2]

Linwood Barney indicates that culture at its fundamental level can be described in three ways: 1) technological (artifacts and activities), 2) sociological (relationships and behavior), and 3) ideological (knowledge, beliefs, worldview, and values).[3] This would mean that there are no a-cultural persons, nor a-cultural theology. Theology is always contextualized. The question is: has one's context been thought through to foster reflective sensitive contextualization.

Such theology needs to be appraised on each of these levels. Theologians tend to emphasize the thought and worldview descriptions, and we should not neglect this area. This tends to bleed into a commitment on our part to prompt consistent belief within this worldview analysis. Theologians, who keep employed at a set location tend also to understand and reflect the sociology of their community, as I developed especially in chapter three, "The Role of Tradition in Theology." However, in that chapter I developed that, this social sensitivity tends to foster theological hermeneutics which at times isolates and insulates from the Biblical text.

1 Clyde Kluckholn, *Mirror for Man* (New York: Whittlesey, 1949), p. 23.

2 Louis Luzbetak, *The Church and Cultures* (Techny: Divine Word, 1963), pp. 60–61.

3 G. Linwood Barney, "Supracultural and the Cultural: Implications for Frontier Missions," in *The Gospel and Frontier Peoples,* ed. R. Pierce Beaver (Pasadena: William Carey, 1973), pp. 48–55.

I have made a prolonged argument over several chapters that such a theological hermeneutic is not a good way to obtain or retain Biblicism, even though it has begun the contextualization process.

Clemens Sedmak argues that the process of contextualization of theology can be compared to local cooking and food.[4]

- We eat because we are hungry (we do theology out of hunger and thirst).
- Food is served (theology has a service function).
- Food is necessary but always found within a cultural context (doing theology is natural but always takes a particular cultural shape).
- Food nourishes and energizes (theology empowers).
- Sharing food can be a purpose in itself (like sharing theological discussions).
- Sharing food ties a community together (theology is community-building).
- Food is, next to language, *the* local cultural product par excellence; there is Thai food and Filipino food and Kenyan food and a cuisine française and a cucina Italiana and so forth. Each family has its favorite recipes (local theologies have particular nuances and particular flavors).

Such sensitivity would argue that a theology contextualized to evangelicalism would need to sensitively reflect the flavors of its context while maintaining the Biblicism that is the core of evangelicalism. This chapter attempts to explore these flavors of our evangelical context so that ideas are understood.

However, theology needs to go further, into affect, value, virtue and action. To try to do this I try to marshal a range of tools. In my book, *The Classical Christian God*,[5] I tried to ask and show theological solutions from several sides, including affective or emotional angles. In my book, *Messiah Jesus: Christology in His Day and Ours*[6] I set out Old Testament and second Temple Jewish expectations, which raise the readers' sensitivity to hope in Jesus as some of the people of Jesus' day did. Such an orientation is shockingly Jewish and eschatological. When I present the Biblical material identifying which aspects Jesus in the first century fulfilled of these hopes, and which aspects have hope deferred so that we should join them with this hope. Then in electronic form,

---

4 Clemens Sedmak, *Doing Local Theology: A Guide for Artisans of a New Humanity* (Maryknoll: Orbis Books, 2002, p. 19.

5 Douglas Kennard, *The Classical Christian God* (Lewiston: Edwin Mellen Press, 2002).

6 Douglas Kennard, *Messiah Jesus: Christology in His Day and Ours* (New York: Peter Lang, 2008).

each of my chapters in this volume finish with a second look at these issues of Jesus' roles, life, and teaching, from the angle of classical and contemporary art, literature, and movies. I am trying in this strategy to help my students to see the issues afresh and to feel it in new ways. This continues in the assignments for my classes, in that the student can opt to complete a theological artistic project (of any medium) instead of writing a paper, with my view that such an approach will likely embed some theological nugget on the student's soul as they express it through painting, poetry, or dance of their composition and implementation. Plus, such an educational strategy shows the student and her classmates that theology is fun and vital, as my theology classes have their art exhibit and performance. Theology is also practical, for some of my students still have these theological pieces of art still hanging in their rooms, as do I. I think it is an educational strategy that draws the visual and tactile learner into the joys and affections of theology. I think that the auditory learner also can enter into a richness as she sees and hears theology in a different tune.

To engage the theological student in ethics makes theology acute. So in my theological presentation I try to raise the ethical and applicational questions and possibilities, to try to prompt value, choice, action, and virtue. This requires a sensitivity to who the students are and to what aspects of their ethical lives could use some encouragement and direction. That is part of what this contextualization chapter is about, to show where my students are, so that needful, as well as felt issues, can be addressed, and be addressed on a deep level drawing on aspects of our common heritage as well as the Bible to drive these points home into our worldviews, affections, and lives.

Culture continues to develop as aspects change. David Hesselgrave identifies that culture is: 1) *learned* (and not biologically determined), 2) culture is *shared* in common by a society, 3) culture is an *integrated whole* in which all parts affect each other, and 4) "culture constantly *changes* as a result of innovations, internal pressures, and cross-cultural borrowing." [7] Theology needs to continue to remain sensitive to these changes, even if it says the same things. Theology needs to preserve the timeless truth in ways that are heard and felt in our changing world. The faculty at Houston Graduate School of Theology explores these developments within us individually and corporately, especially through our regular lunches. The dialog continues percolating beyond this time but the focused discussion is fertile to explore our development and consider their implications as well as incite the others to reflective thought. The small class sizes as well as the discipleship times which

7 David Hesselgrave, *Communicating Christ Cross-Culturally: An Introduction to Missionary Communication* (Grand Rapids: Zondervan, 1991), pp. 100–101.

we as a faculty engage in with our disciples are productive for eliciting theological reflection and change.

H. Richard Niebuhr identified some basic patterns of how Christians respond to culture.

1. Christ *against* of–i.e., Christ is the sole authority, the claims of culture are rejected.
2. Christ *of* culture–i.e., the Christian worldview and culture have a lot in common so we should select the best of culture to inform our Christianity.
3. Christ *above* culture–i.e., there is a continuity from the observable order into the divinely revealed, with the aspects of Christianity taking precedence over those of culture.
4. Christ and culture in *paradox*–i.e., both authorities are to be obeyed and the Christian lives in both worlds, thus living in tension.
5. Christ as *Transformer* of culture–i.e., culture reflects fallen humanity and Christ redeems humans and culture on to Kingdom.[8]

I have previously analyzed part of this issue in the attempt to show the relationship of faith and knowledge,[9] so I won't do the same here except to remind us that I thought that these categories seem arbitrarily presented by Niebuhr, and they did not describe the practice of his theoretical examples accurately. Often the individuals were much more complex in practice than these simple models would indicate. For our purposes here, if we use these as models of contextualization there would be remarkable differences in response. For example, the Christ *against* culture and the Christ *above* culture models tend to resist contextualization and thus will prompt an indigenous people to reject such a foreign model of Christ to their context. Whereas on the other hand, the Christ *of* culture model and the model of Christ and culture in *paradox* will set up syncretism in which important aspects of Christ are lost because the culture will overrule them. In this situation it is likely that forms of idolatry and imperialism will replace God and Christ. Niebuhr argues for the last option, or that culture is to be transformed by our understanding of Christ. Such an option would require high commitment to Christ from those in that culture to permit Christ to have precedence. Often real life is more complex than this, in that we wish to transform some aspects of culture by Christ (say the red colors of culture),

8 H, Richard Niebuhr, *Christ and Culture* (New York: Harper & Row, 1951).

9 Doug Kennard, "Faith and Knowledge" in *The Relationship Between Epistemology, Hermeneutics, Biblical Theology and Contextualization* (Lewiston: Mellen Press, 1999), pp. 35–70.

but there are other aspects of any culture that can be appealed to in order to clarify theological meaning as well (perhaps the blue coloring of culture). Furthermore, any culture which has had some history of interacting with Christ has developed a complex of nuanced positive and negative engagement (perhaps like a plaid complex). In this, Niebuhr has not provided the kind of lens through which we can evaluate what of culture or what of Christianity is to be preserved. Niebuhr has only provided an argument for the priority of Christ. However, Christ is not so apparently walking and visibly challenging aspects of our culture today. So the mechanism to evaluate the contextualization process needs to be practically explained if there is any hope that such a practice will be realized or applied. Real life is complex, so the process needs to be able to handle the range of issues faced in real examples of such complex lives. We need to go deeper than this.

The term "contextualization" was coined in the early 1970's by more or less liberal theologians who primarily wished to express the indigenization process.[10] Such a model appreciated that all religions and cultures conveyed truth and thus set up syncretism as the operating strategy, urging tolerance. In the indigenization process, the thought forms from one's context frame their theological thought, much like Thai thought forms gave rise to *Waterbuffalo Theology*.[11] With the rise of neo-orthodox and existential approaches, the truth that grabbed one became the kerygmatic Word or the authentic message which would be embraced and communicated. Such a process felt the context of oppression deeply and called the community to conscientization in a manner that would help the community within that context.[12] Such approaches are indebted to what adherents might call either a divine intuition, or existentialism motivated by an ideology to meet needs (such as Marxism) with the hope that a goal of improved life could be realized (pragmatically) through theological speech and reflection unto consistent practice (praxis). In chapter two "The Relationship of Philosophy, Theology and Science" several of these epistemic aspects have been analyzed. Each of these approaches would distract us from the task at hand because they give the contextual issues from our lives priority over the Biblical, and what we need is to give Biblical authority the priority. However, one issue is

---

10 E.g., "Dialogue Between Men of Living Faiths," a WCC sponsored consultation in Ajaltoun, Lebanon, March 1970 which brought together Christians, Budhists, Hindus, and Muslims for ten days of conversation and voluntary corporate worship. Presentations were published in S. J. Samartha, ed. *Dialogue Between Men of Living Faiths* (Geneva: World Council of Churches, 1971); also *Ministry in Context: The Third Mandate Programme of the Theological Education Fund (1970–77)* (Bromily: Theological Education Fund, 1972).

11 Kosuke Koyama, *Waterbuffalo Theology* (Maryknoll: Orbis Books, 1987, originally published in 1974 by SCM Press).

12 E.g., Gustavo Gutierrez, *A Theology of Liberation. History, Politics and Salvation* (Maryknoll: Orbis, 1973).

probably critical, since contextualization done in this original manner sets up a post-modern strategy in which a community expects to hear and read theology in its convention. This means that if evangelicals only do theology in a manner that repeats and reassures their own community, then they too have gone post-modern. There is a place for at least an occasional jeremiad, calling evangelicalism beyond itself, to the Bible and to truth. Good theology is forceful and fitting to a community, or as Darrel Whiteman indicates, "Good contextualization offends people for the right reasons. Bad contextualization, or the lack of it altogether, offends for the wrong reasons."[13] Hopefully the community will appreciate the theologian's contribution here and not use tools of power. That is, contextualization does not determine the truth. However, the difficult task is to say the truth in a sensitive manner, so that the community and its power brokers do not reject the messenger but grow with the truth. As such, we need to conceive and proclaim Biblical theology sensitive to our context.[14] So we will continue to develop the positive issue of what Hesselgrave calls "Christian contextualization"[15] or "apostolic contextualization."[16] Byang Kato says, "We understand the term to mean making concepts or ideals relevant in a given situation."[17] Hesselgrave clarifies that if theology is to be understood, "contextualization must be true to the complete authority and unadulterated message of the Bible on the one hand, and it must be related to the cultural, linguistic, and religious background of the respondents on the other."[18]

Hesselgrave summarizes that there are a range of seven dimensions of cross–cultural communication, to which I have added the third, including:[19]

1. Worldviews – ways of perceiving the world.
2. Cognitive Processes – ways of thinking.
3. Values – Subconsciously learned through culture.
4. Linguistic Forms – ways of expressing ideas.
5. Behavioral Patterns – ways of acting.

---

13 Darrel Whiteman, "Contextualization: The Theory, the Gap, the Challenge," *International Bulletin of Missionary Research* 21(1997): 2.

14 David Hesselgrave, *Scripture and Strategy: The Use of the Bible in Postmodern Church and Mission* (Pasadena: William Carey Library, 1994), pp. 71–72.

15 David Hesselgrave, "Christian Contextualization and Biblical Theology" in *The Relationship Between Epistemology, Hermeneutics, Biblical Theology and Contextualization*, edited by Douglas Kennard, pp. 153–180.

16 David Hesselgrave, *Communicating Christ Cross-Culturally*, pp. 139–140.

17 Byang H. Kato, "The Gospel, Cultural Context, and Religious Syncretism," in *Let the Earth Hear His Voice*, edited by J. D. Douglas (Minneapolis:World Wide, 1975), p. 1217.

18 David Hesselgrave & Edward Rommen, *Contextualization: Meaning, Methods, and Models* (Grand Rapids: Baker, 1989), p. xi.

19 David Hesselgrave, *Communicating Christ Cross-Culturally*, pp. 193–638; Lloyd Milligan of Wycliffe Bible Translators suggested the third item.

6. Social Structures – ways of interacting.
7. Media Influence – ways of channeling the message.
8. Motivational Resources – ways of deciding.

Theology (along with several other disciplines) addresses each of these concerns. However, critically contextualized theology engages people on all of these areas, prodding and wooing them to be formed and transformed by Scripture's trajectory. For example, theology at many evangelical colleges benefits from the concept of a holistic Christian worldview, which concept could be rooted back to individuals like Kant.[20] However, while not embracing Kant's worldview or its limits, worldview courses flesh out a Christian worldview. They explore such theological worldview issues as ultimate Being, creation and our being in it, epistemology of the creation and divine revelation, meaningfulness of history, ethics and afterlife. This orientation can provide helpful direction but it also can insulate the advocate of a Christian worldview from sensitively perceiving the facts as they are beyond one's worldview.[21] Critical realism equips a student with epistemic means to think through a worldview, rather than providing it in a predigested tradition.

Paul Hiebert defends that proper contextualization entails a critical realist epiestemology that gives us real but partial understanding of reality, providing the theologian with models that complement each other.[22] At Houston Graduate School of Theology, this epistemic area is particularly examined by the students in two courses. Epistemic analysis is preliminarily explored by all MDiv students in our research and writings course. Then within a Philosophy of Religion course, an in-depth examination of religious epiestemology, genre hermeneutics, and theological method is engaged in to assess epistemic and methodological concerns. The other chapters in this volume explore aspects of these. The dimensions of linguistic forms, behavioral patterns and media influence are engaged through the manner these courses are taught so that the students might relate to them and be encouraged to use them where

20 William Brown and Gary Phillips, *Making Sense of Your World: From a Biblical Viewpoint* (Chicago: Moody Press, 1991); Immanuel Kant, *Critique of Judgment* in *Great Books of the Western World,* vol. 42, *Kant* (Chicago: Encyclopaedia Britannica, 1952), pp. 459–613, and especially part one, book two, section 26, pp. 500–501 where the concept of the sublime *Weltanschauung* (or worldview) first appeared in 1790. Cf. David Naugle, *Worldview: The History of a Concept* (Grand Rapids: Eerdmans, 2002), p. xix, 58, and 66. On page 58 an extended footnote #14 develops the Kantian origins of worldview; Werner Betz, "Zur Geschichte des Wortes 'Weltanschauung,'" In *Kursbuch der Weltanschauungen,* Schriften der Carl Friedrich von Siemens Stiftung (Frankfort: Verlag Ullstein, 1980) pp. 18–28 but especially p. 18.

21 Bob Altemeyer, *The Authoritarian Specter* (Cambridge: Harvard University Press, 1996), pp. 93–96.

22 Paul Hiebert, "Critical Contextualization," *International Bulletin of Missionary Research* 11:3(1987): 109.

appropriate. Behavioral patterns and the motivation to do them are also examined, especially as the Biblical text addresses our context so that we should obey as we ought. Additionally I addressed how my students engage the affective aspects of theology a few pages ago.

David Hesselgrave addressed the process of contextualization of theology through a series of five propositions.[23]

> 1. Christian contextualization is concerned not alone with the nature of Scripture, but also with its function as God's Word.
> 2. Christian contextualization recognizes that it is the Bible itself, not its messages, or even its central message, that constitutes the most needful and effective contextualization of the Christian gospel. [That is, the Bible takes precedence and greater authority than theology which is built upon the Bible].
> 3. As is the case with all truly Christian theologizing, the *arche* or starting point of Christian contextualizing is the Bible and Biblical theology.
> 4. In Christian contextualization the Bible must be allowed to determine its own priorities, set its own agenda, and unfold its own plan.
> 5. The whole of Scripture–the Bible in its entirety–must be communicated in Christian contextualization.

In the previous chapters, I have already shown a great degree of loyalty to Hesselgrave's process of contextualization, as I addressed the contextualization process entailing a sensitive critical realist hermeneutic which appreciates the function of the text, in contexts of thrust, genre and Biblical theology. I affirm what I said before, which resonates with Hesselgrave's commitment here. In fact, when Hesselgrave presented these points and I presented my "Thiselton-Ricoeur Hermeneutic" at the March 1997 Midwest regional meeting of the Evangelical Theological Society there was a closing forum in which Hesselgrave and I joined to further underscore the need to allow Biblical theology to have the priority in setting the agenda for hermeneutics and theology. Opposing us were the other plenary speakers (Grant Osborne and Harold Netland), who instead conjectured that the interpreter's own tradition does and should frame their interpretation and theology. The content of theology should be determined by the Bible and warranted epistemic commitments (like historical facts). Several of the chapters here have shown in different ways that I believe that tradition-dependent approaches (like theological

23 David Hesselgrave, "Christian Contextualization and Biblical Theology" in *The Relationship Between Epistemology, Hermeneutics, Biblical Theology and Contextualization*. edited by Douglas Kennard, pp. 163–172.

hermeneutics) do not maintain the appropriate sense of Biblical authority. I have argued this issue at length especially in chapters 5 and 7 on "Biblical Authority" and how "Biblical Theology Affects Systematics."

However, traditions are part of the contextualization process because they provide language, technical resolution to problems, focus, emphasis, parameters and heritage. These areas have the ability to control a theology. So part of a critical realist Biblically driven theology is to reeducate our traditions by how the Bible and warranted facts would redirect these concepts. That is, instead of letting our theological terms be dominated by our traditional take on things, let the Bible's terms be the avenue through which we refer to theological ideas. Take the Biblical terms in the Biblical way. Instead of following a logical order through the details of theology, allow major Bible passages to raise and resolve the important theological problems. It is through this Biblical theology approach, that the Biblical parameters of concepts are then challenging our traditions to emulate the Bible. Likewise, the Bible then sets the agenda on what our theology would then focus on and what emphasis we would bring in our presentation of the discipline. Of course, such Biblicity needs to be sensitively communicated to our heritage, so it is important that the theologian become acutely aware of his heritages by becoming a student of his contexts.

All the areas of theology are implemented and maintained on a corporate level so that it is likewise important to cultivate a team that can be both a sounding board as well as a corporate change agent, if there is something theologically in which your setting should grow.

Hesselgrave's second point sets up two side issues: 1) the Bible has priority over its message, and 2) Bible translation is needed. First, the issue of the Bible over its message, I have already worked at length in the chapter on Biblical Authority. Second, the process of Bible translation is important.

Let us get really practical; contextualization entails: 1) conscientization of a group of individuals, and 2) corporate commitment to resolve ensuing dissonance toward the group's values. Contextualization is best done when an individual recognizes the similarity between us and the Biblical author's readers, and reflects upon what significances the author's application for his readers would entail for us. Then this individual also needs to reflect these conjectured significances within a group of reflective mature Christians deeply familiar with their context and with similar felt values. Likewise, this individual also needs to be available for the rest of the group as they raise the issues that they are concerned about. Contextualization thus often has an *individual component* as a person prompted by the study of a text and aware of the tensions between the text and our context. However, contextualization is also a *corporate process* among reflective friends who value each other enough to corporately think, pray, listen, share, work and serve with each other. When this level of friendship is engaged in, it is a rich jewel of fellowship. Out of this sort of corporate life together a balanced contextualization can be realized and lived. Having been involved with such groups four times in my life, I consider them to be the richest of all experiences. The most continuous is my life with Jan, my wife, and especially our Saturday morning and Sunday afternoon coffee times which go for hours as we discuss what the other has been reading and the implications that we make from these. Another of these times was as a graduate student and manager of a construction company of other graduate students that thought through our Christianity on the job. While I was at Moody Bible Institute, I repeatedly initiated an open discussion about hermeneutics and how genre mattered. Currently at Houston Graduate School issues like these emerge during our regular lunches. In the contextualization process we need a corporate community of reflective thinkers sensitive to our context to both foster meaningful contextualization and to keep oddities of personality from becoming presented as universally applicable for all. Hopefully, such a group functions to give the theologian sensitivity to their context so that they can engage ideas and float proposals in a more protected arena, before they stick their necks out and either alienate an audience or be diminished by tools of power by more conservative administrations.

To implement change requires some sensitivity and often certain individual's involvement. For example, Stephen Grunlan and Marvin Mayers ask a series of questions to sensitize us to Biblical absolutism and cultural relativism.[24]

1. What is the norm in this culture?
2. Is the behavior that of a responsible member of this culture?
3. Does the cultural norm need changing or is it another way that the absolute Biblical authority could be reflected?
4. Who is responsible for changing the norm?

It is often easier to see contextualization in a foreign context first. To enable this, Lloyd Milligan tells of contextualization in his ministry in Papua New Guinea.[25] He was invited to bring Wycliffe translation and the Bible into a village by a Christian who was reaching his village for Christ. Often at the end of a translation day the group of Christians would ask a question that had surfaced in the translation that day, and it would usher into a chance for these elders to *study the Bible* on a particular topic. Sometimes beliefs and practices would be decided on the basis of the Bible, as in granting the freedom to come to church in a variety of

24 Stephen Grunlan and Marvin Mayers, *Cultural Anthropology: A Christian Perspective* (Grand Rapids: Zondervan, 1979), pp. 30–31.

25 Various conversations with Lloyd Milligan but especially Sept. 1, 2004.

clothes styles. The traditional white shirts of the United Church of Papua New Guinea and Solomon Islands had been insisted upon as against the colorful patterns of the Catholic but upon studying they recognized that God looks on the heart not on the outward appearance. From this the community embraced a freedom of worship patterns.

Other times *practical reason* dominated as the rationale for change in theology and practice. For example, this village used to not be able to afford beer. However, with increased wealth beer came in ample supply. When drunkenness became rampant Lloyd tried to shame those who staggered and fell into a stupor. Such shaming did not work; they felt no shame. However, when two brothers almost killed each other the elders called a council, then after a lengthy community discussion a consensus was obtained and then reported to the village that alcohol was banned from the *Mangsang* village *Lavege*. Their rationale was that: 1) it hurt people relationally which violated a major value, 2) it hurt people physically and 3) it was too costly a waste of resources. The village complied because it took too much effort and took the fun out of it to leave the village to go drink in seclusion. Additionally, with generosity as a high virtue in the culture, social drinking and sharing beer had worked toward a prestige-gaining activity but with it censored from the village, drinking in seclusion would be a prestige-lowering practice, so it demotivated the practice.

Sometimes practices would bubble up from the community and be *officially blessed*. One example was that the dancing that had been in the festivals entered the church services and was blessed by the pastor so it became a regular practice to accompany their congregational singing. However, when a Wycliffe musicologist analyzed their singing that had accompanied this dancing and composed hymns in the same style, they were not accepted for they reminded them of the old animistic ways.

The *Mangsang* village is very community minded and major decisions (like whether they would pursue a cash crop like oil palm) might take six months or longer for the community to decide whether to pursue it. In such issues, everyone would have his say, though some were more influential for the group. They would talk until there was consensus. Then the elders would pronounce the decision. The community would follow the decision, applying a little social pressure to help the community comply. Little community pressure was needed because they had owned the new direction through the process.

Now that we have seen contextualization issues from a distance, it is time to bring these concerns closer to home. The need for contextualization work is crucial or alienation or rejection will occur.[26] I have done these

26 Robert Penn Warren tells of his personal sense of appreciation and alienation in moving from Tennessee culture and considering a return to it in Marshall Walker, "Robert Penn Warren: An Interview," *Journal of American Studies,* 8(August, 1974): 230; "The South: Distance and Change. A Conversation with Robert Penn Warren,

kinds of studies for each of the areas in which I have ministered: Dallas; Memphis; Chicago; Dayton, Tennessee; and now Houston. The pleasant surprise for me in Houston was that an organization, Mission Houston, already did a lot of the leg work for such contextualization by employing professional sociologists from Baylor University to undertake this study and make it publically available on the web as the "Houston Profile Project."[27] This sort of analysis empowers the theologian to be missional in his contextualization of theology. Hopefully, those who live beyond our region can benefit from this exercise as it shows them how they might also gain sensitivity to context and contextualize theology in their setting.

Often contextualization issues appear as a surprise that provides dissonance with the host culture. That is, the host culture includes assumptions and practices that do not always reflect the Biblical text. So that when a claim is made that the host culture does not fit with the Biblical text, there is an opportunity to see which authority is stronger for the community. Those in the host culture may find that a cultural barrier to receptivity is invisible until the Bible challenges it. Usually those of the host culture are not aware that their worldview and practice do not fit with the Bible until the Bible is carefully expounded into the host culture and the dissonance occurs. In the *Mangsang* context there was a commitment to the Bible over tradition, to community discussion and to consensus of thought and practice. In such a first generation Christian context, there was an expectation that there would be an occasional instance in which their culture would be challenged by the Bible. So they were predisposed toward encouraging Biblical theology as the governing framework. It is a challenge to call a Western individualistic culture steeped in traditional Christian thought forms to such a contextualization process. We do not naturally have the frameworks for community discussion or communal acceptance. We do not expect to be challenged by the Bible very often, since the thought forms of our host culture are framed with Biblical language already. Our individualism, however, is among the values and practices in our host culture that is most unbiblical. So evangelicalism should look for communal, consensus-building formats to empower contextualization of theology. This is partly why school lunch discussions, chapels, and campus colloquium are so valuable in developing a campus wide engagement of these issues.

However, a broader assessment is also helpful as we try to live within and contextualize our theology within evangelicalism. This next

---

William Styron and Louis D. Rubin, Jr.," in *The American South: A Portrait of a Culture*. edited by Louis D. Rubin Jr. (Baton Rouge: Louisiana State University Press, 1979), p. 307; Richard Slade, "An Interview in New Haven with Robert Penn Warren," *Studies in the Novel* 2(Fall, 1970): 325.

27 http://www.missionhouston.org/hpp.html. "Houston Profile Project"

section tries to contextualize a few of the recent discussions within evangelicalism as a whole.

8.2 Evangelicalism[28]

During 1910–1915, Christian fundamentals were articulated in *The Fundamentals: A Testimony to the Truth* as a series of 135 essays in 12 volumes essentially defending: the virgin birth, the vicarious atonement, the resurrection of Christ, the inerrancy of Scripture, and the miracles of Christ.[29] The World's Christian Fundamentals Association announced "a truceless war on the worst and most destructive forms of infidelity [in which] fundamentalists draw their weapon of their warfare from the arsenal of God's word; modernists draw theirs from evolutionary philosophy."[30] In May 1922, as the fundamentalists were preparing for the modernist yearly convention, a Baptist minister, Dr. Harry Fosdick preached a sermon in the pulpit of the First Presbyterian Church in New York City entitled "Shall the Fundamentalists Win?" His answer was No. Over the next couple of decades, the conservatives lost most of the major denominations and their schools. Conservative schools were founded to answer the need during the era of 1900–1940. In 1947, Carl Henry called evangelicals to answer the challenge of rigorous education and ethical engagement in *The Uneasy Conscience of Modern Fundamentalism*.[31] The Evangelical Theological Society was founded in 1949 to provide a forum for scholars of various Christian traditions to sharpen each other within a perspective that acknowledges the inspiration and inerrancy of the Scripture. The new evangelical vision of Kingdom follows George Eldon Ladd in affirming an "already/not yet" expression of inaugurated eschatology.[32] Billy Graham's evangelistic campaigns moved toward a respectable center after 1957, splitting with the hard line

28 Cf. Donald Dayton, *The Variety of American Evangelicalism* (Knoxville: The University of Tennessee Press, 1991); Kenneth Kantzer & Carl Henry, *Evangelical Affirmations* (Grand Rapids: Zondervan, 1990); Kenneth Kantzer and Stanley Gundry, *Perspectives on Evangelical Theology* (Grand Rapids: Baker, 1979); George Marsden, *Evangelicalism and Modern America; Understanding Fundamentalism and Evangelicalism; Fundamentalism and American Culture: The Shaping of Twentieth-Century Evangelicalism 1870–1925* (Oxford: Oxford University Press, 1980); David F. Wells & John Woodbridge, *The Evangelicals: What They Believe, Who they Are, Where They are Changing* (Grand Rapids: Baker, 1975).

29 William Jennings Bryan addressed these same questions in his volume: *Seven Questions in Dispute*.

30 Quoted by Martin Marty, *The Noise of Conflict 1919–1941*, pp. 188–89.

31 Carl Henry, *The Uneasy Conscience of Modern* Fundamentalism (Grand Rapids: Eerdmans, 1947).

32 George Eldon Ladd, *Crucial Questions about the Kingdom of God* (Grand Rapids: Eerdmans, 1952); *The Gospel and the Kingdom: Scriptural Studies in the Kingdom of God* (Grand Rapids: Eerdmans, 1959); *The Presence of the Future: The Eschatology of Biblical Realism* (Grand Rapids: Eerdmans, 1974).

fundamentalists.[33] *Christianity Today* under the leadership of Carl Henry supported a unified evangelical social and intellectual program which ushered in the World Congress on Evangelism in 1967.[34] In the 1970s Jerry Falwell led fundamentalism back into a coalition of engagement for social and political causes through the Moral Majority. After a century of evaluation, Martin Marty answered Fosdick's sermon, that numerically the evangelicals have won.[35] Marty indicates that evangelicals won "first by contributing to a new kind of ecumenism...that pays little attention to historical confessional definition. Second, evangelicals won by moving from what I used to call 'private Protestantism' to visibility and at-homeness in the genus 'public' and the species 'political' religion."[36] This coalition placed Southerners and Reagan conservatives into the White House (e.g., Carter, Reagan, Clinton, G. W. Bush). The exit polls placed the top issue for the 2004 campaign to be moral values of anti-gay marriage and pro-life (22% nationally).[37] Marty identifies that culturally evangelicalism has won with regard to religious culture.

> A glance at the covers of the publications peddled at airport newsstands, at the entertainment advertised in the free metropolitan weeklies, at most films and cable television, at most of what goes on in the market and the mall–all this would make a visitor wonder whether a hint of a tinge of a whisper of a reminiscence of a 'Jewish-Christian' culture exists...Globally, thanks to their missionary and humanitarian ventures, [evangelicals] are poised to 'go global' though here the other religious clusters do remain very much on the scene. Evangelicals produce and buy religious bestsellers whose sales totals have left all other religious camps far behind (e.g., Hal Lindsey's *The Late Great Planet Earth*[38] and Jerry Jenkins & Tim LaHay's *Left Behind* series popularized dispensational eschatology). Though many heard the rock music beat as demonic a score of years ago, they now are at home in their $1 billion-a-year Christian rock music business. They alone

33 Butler Farley Porter, Jr. "Billy Graham and the End of Evangelical Unity" (Ph.D. dissertation, University of Florida, 1976).

34 George Marsden, *Understanding Fundamentalism and Evangelicalism*, pp. 73–74.

35 Martin Marty, "At the Crossroads: Evangelicals have become major players in American culture, and that may be their biggest problem." *Christianity Today* 48:2(February 2004): 39.

36 Martin Marty, "At the Crossroads: Evangelicals have become major players in American culture, and that may be their biggest problem." *Christianity Today* 48:2(February 2004): 39.

37 Duane Gang, "Voters say Moral Major Concern," *Chattanooga Times Free Press* 135:326(Nov. 4, 2004): A-1 & 4; Steven Thomma, "Election Confirms US Moderate to Conservative," *Chattanooga Times Free Press* 135:329(Nov. 7, 2004): A-1 & 7.

38 Hal Lindsey, *The Late Great Planet Earth* (Grand Rapids: Zondervan, 1970).

command religious television, and they alone produce religious celebrities—unless we want to count the Pope as one.[39]

Have we become overconfident and begun to act from a position of power and "the haves"? Can evangelicalism retain its soul as it becomes aligned with power and wealth? In Barna studies of the mosaic generation (those born between 1984 and 2002) there is a backlash in reaction to evangelical self presentation during the decades before and after the millennium change. These mosaics consider that the previous generations of evangelicals often sold out the essence of Christianity for political activism placing nationalism, gay hatred and "right to life" over Christ and Kingdom.[40] Evangelical misguidedness can be seen in the reaction of 87% of mosaics outside evangelicalism consider that evangelicals are essentially hypocritical and judgmental.[41] For example, 91% of these non-evangelical mosaics consider that the most defining criterion of an evangelical is one of anti-homosexual.[42] Additionally, 75% of these mosaics consider that evangelicals are too defined by their politics and in that they are also out of touch.[43] These statistics are disconcerting because we may be presenting an ugly evangelicalism because we evangelicals may be living as hate dominated politicals rather than imitating Christ. Let's come back to Jesus and His narrow beatitude way unto Kingdom.

On other fronts, theology is driving the events of the world. This is evident among conservative America's commitment to Israel and dealing with the problems of the Middle East. However, the prominence of theology also is evident on the Islamic side as well. For example, Forensic theology surfaces which religious spokesman incites expressions of terrorism.[44] How will two religious theologies vie for the hearts of the people? Will it be by which one is more persistent in its use of force? Has it come down to a crusade?

The last few years, the Evangelical Theological Society has been trying to firm up what is meant by its doctrinal tenet of inerrancy, especially as some of its members concluded inerrancy and open theism were mutually exclusive. The November 2004 national meeting of ETS

39 Martin Marty, "At the Crossroads: Evangelicals have become major players in American culture, and that may be their biggest problem." *Christianity Today* 48:2(February 2004): 39.

40 David Kinnaman, *Unchristian: What a New Generation Really Thinks About Christianity...and Why it Matters* (Grand Rapids: Baker, 2007), pp. 28, 30, 34, 153–80.

41 David Kinnaman, *Unchristian*, pp. 26–29, 41–66, 181–204.

42 David Kinnaman, *Unchristian*, pp. 28–29, 91–120.

43 David Kinnaman, *Unchristian*, pp. 28, 30, 121–80; I tried to address this in my article, Douglas Kennard, "Evangelicalism is Healthy but Diverse," *Chattanooga Times Free Press* 139:191 (Sunday, June 22, 2008): G1–2: *Perspective*..

44 Stephen Grey, "Follow the Mullahs," *The Atlantic Monthly* 294:4(Nov. 2004): 44–47.

accepted an executive committee decision reiterating inerrancy, and in November 2006 passed it as a amendment defining a By-Law,[45] "the Society refers members to the Chicago Statement on Biblical Inerrancy (1978)" with two qualifications: 1) a positive qualification, "A proper understanding of inerrancy takes into account the language, genres, and intent of Scripture," and 2) a negative qualification excluding anti-realist options, "We reject approaches to Scripture that deny that biblical truth claims are grounded in reality."[46] This statement was clarified by Millard Erickson to be: 1) an exclusion of anti-realism, as well as, 2) interpretations like Gundry did in his Matthew commentary,[47] in claiming some things in Matthew were not historical,[48] and 3) interpretations like John Sanders' proposal that prophecy is merely God's intention to work toward a particular end, rather than guaranteeing real fulfillment.[49] Greg Beale agreed with Erickson's third claim above that this realist claim would stand against some open theist's claims that future hypotheticals are not real.[50] Such pressing of this issue may be having negative consequences for open theists, and the more mainstream community of Arminians were less in attendance at the 2004 meeting than in the previous years. However, this orientation was clarified to not exclude the post-modern evangelicals who are members of ETS,[51] but they were rather light in attendance at the 2004 and 2006 national meetings. The stated rationale for the whole statement is, "The case for biblical inerrancy rests on the absolute trustworthiness of God and Scripture's testimony to itself." This resolution passed the membership in 2006 by a 90% majority, or 172 votes. This amendment to the by-laws clarifies the doctrinal basis of the Evangelical Theological Society.[52]

These evangelical concerns have been mirrored by the upheavals within the Southern Baptist denomination, the numerically largest

45 78.5% favorable vote at Friday Nov. 17 Business Meeting, 2004 to advise executive committee (234 to 54) and a 90% vote in favor (172 to 17), Thursday Nov. 15, 2006 to define by-laws of ETS for advising members.

46 ETS letter from Greg Beale (President) and Jim Borland (secretary) to membership, Sept. 2004. Blaising clarified Nov. 17, 2004 Special Business Session that this meant only the 19 articles.

47 Robert Gundry who was asked to leave ETS in 1983 for genre claims that took Matthew at spots as not historical in *Matthew: A Commentary on His Literary and Theological Art* (Grand Rapids: Eerdmans, 1982).

48 Evangelical Theological Society Meeting, Nov. 17, 2004 Special Business Session.

49 Evangelical Theological Society Meeting, Nov. 15, 2006 Special Business Session.

50 Evangelical Theological Society Meeting, Nov. 17, 2004 Special Business Session. This shows that there is some concern to continue to prosecute Open Theisim among the ETS leadership, but I don't think that this statement gives them the leverage desired since John Sanders future hypotheticals (while not real) are analogically grounded in reality.

51 Millard Erickson's comments at the Evangelical Theological Society Meeting, Nov. 17, 2004 Special Business Session.

52 A further proposal to add to the doctrinal basis was attempted Nov. 19–21, 2008 by the UCCF statement of belief of the Tyndale Fellowship but it failed 47 to 130.

denomination in our region. The issues focused on inerrancy of Scripture and whether women had a possible pastoral role in ministry, though the issues range beyond these lightning rods. In the late 1970s fundamentalists began to gain control of the national denomination, seminaries, missions agencies, and publishing houses. Some state conventions supported this conservative move (namely, South Carolina, Florida, and Georgia). In Texas and Virginia there are two state conventions, the old controlled by the moderates and a new controlled by the fundamentalists. Other state conventions have negotiated a moderate route between these (namely: Kentucky, North Carolina, Alabama, and Mississippi). Some of the moderates have pulled churches out of the denomination and new Baptist societies have been founded (e.g., Alliance of Baptists, Cooperative Baptist Fellowship, and Texas Baptist Committee). In 1998 the Southern Baptist denomination posted its first decline in membership over thirty years.

Epistemologically, evangelicalism emerged with a commitment to Scottish common-sense realism but is now undergoing a transition to critical realism among progressive evangelical scholars. Theologians saw the Scriptures as the primary source for the facts of their discipline. Exampling common-sense realism, Charles Hodge defined theology as "the science of the facts of divine revelation so far as those facts concern the nature of God and our relation to him."[53] Many others join this perspective, such as Lewis Sperry Chafer, who defined theology as the "collecting, scientifically arranging, comparing, exhibiting, and defending of all facts from any and every source concerning God and His works."[54] William G. T. Shedd acknowledged progressiveness within the discipline of theology that would be characterized as a discipline-wide critical realism in his comments such as, "The first investigator is not so likely to strike upon the intrinsic constitution of a thing as the last one, because he has not the light of previous inquiries. Methods of investigation are continually undergoing correction and modification, and are thus brought closer to the organization of the object."[55] Among evangelicals of these earlier days perhaps only A. H. Strong opted for a more nuanced personal critical realist position. Strong affirms that "the laws of our thought are laws of God's thought and that the results are normally conducted thinking with regard to God correspond to the objective reality."[56] At the same time he conceded that "all knowledge

53 Charles Hodge, *Systematic Theology* (3 vols.; Grand Rapids: Eerdmans, 1929, 1977 reprint), 1:21; cf. John C. Vander Stelt, *Philosophy and Scripture: A Study in Old Princeton and Westminster Theology* (Marlton: Mack Publishing Co., 1978).

54 Lewis Sperry Chafer, *Systematic Theology* (8 vols.; Dallas: Dallas Theological Seminary, 1947), 1:5.

55 William G. T. Shedd, *Dogmatic Theology* (Grand Rapids: Zondervan, n.d.), vol. 1, p.4, Ch. 1, sect. 1.

56 A. H. Strong, *Systematic Theology* (3 vols.: Philadelphia: The Judson Press, 1907), 1:10.

is relative to the knowing agent; that is what we know, we know not as it is objectively but only as it is related to our senses and faculties."[57] Moving to the contemporary 2004 ETS proposal, that: "We reject approaches to Scripture that deny that biblical truth claims are grounded in reality,"[58] there is affirmation of epistemic dualism, that is, one's idea is distinct from the object which the idea approximates. While this is a feature in Descartes and Locke, it is the essential crux upon which critical realism stands. Upon this basis a more contemporary theologian, Alister McGrath often presents an empirically based pragmatic realism combined with mathematical derivation, which he calls critical realism.[59] He sees that empirically based pragmatism is the foundation for this realism in the natural sciences.[60] He then justifies this realism as against conventionalist approaches, which would be either anti-realist, theory dependent, or indebted to James pragmatism. He develops a critical realism that engages the world at a variety of levels, each evaluated for its clarity and predictability. He extends this scientific method to theology as an attempt to ground theology as a scientific discipline with a critical realist methodology. Likewise, this approach has been appropriated into contemporary hermeneutics by moderate evangelicals who wish to express critical realism's *hermeneutical spiral* with precision and find value in allowing epistemic categories to inform hermeneutical ones.[61] That is, the textual data is observed by interpreter, in such a way that they float a proposal for the meaning of a text that is then checked by comparing it to the details present in the text itself. Then the process is repeated drawing closer and closer to what the text actually says in itself.

Progresive evangelical exegetes focused on the historical Jesus have especially developed the appropriateness of critical realism to their studies as well. N. T. Wright identifies his form of critical realism.

> This is a way of describing the process of 'knowing' that acknowledges the *reality of the thing known, as other than the knower* (hence 'realism'), while also fully acknowledging that the only access we have to this reality lies along the spiraling

57 A. H. Strong, *Systematic Theology*, 1:10.

58 ETS letter from Greg Beale (President) and Jim Borland (secretary) to membership, Sept. 2004.

59 Alister McGrath, *A Scientific Theology: Reality,* vol. 2, pp. especially identifying himself as a critical realist xv-xvi, 123–244, and especially developing his view on p. 188. Bernard Lonergan presents a similar analysis in "Cognitional Structure," *Collection: Papers by Bernard Lonergan* (Toronto:University of Toronto, 1988), pp. 205–21 and *Method in Theology* (London: Darton, Longman and Todd, 1972), p. 238.

60 Alister McGrath, *A Scientific Theology: Reality,* vol. 2, pp. 257, 174–175.

61 Kennard, *The Relationship Between Epistemology, Hermeneutics, Biblical Theology and Contextualization*, pp.57–58, 124–25, 133–34; other examples regularly occur at the November AAR/SBL meeting.

> path of *appropriate of or conversation between the knower and the thing known* (hence 'critical').[62]

James Dunn affirms this approach preferring to call it a *dialog* with the text.[63] Dunn warns us about the parameters of this Critical Realist dialog with the text.

> The point is that without the interpreter's openness to being addressed by the text, the interpreter can scarcely hope to avoid abusing the text. Unless the text is at least in some sense, allowed to set its own agenda, it is questionable whether it is being heard at all.[64]

Dale Allison also approaches the historical Jesus through a Lakatos version of Critical Realism.

> Viewing Jesus as a millenarian figure has proven to be productive. In other words, this take on the tradition has become what Imre Lakatos called a "progressive research program," which has led to an ever-enlarging series of new questions and useful answers. I have found that once one approaches the early Christian sources with the idea that Jesus was an apocalyptic prophet, much that otherwise has no good explanation falls into place and indeed becomes almost self-evident.[65]

Such a critical realist epistemology is expressed in the coursework and research from Houston Graduate School of Theology.

Part of a critical realist contextualization strategy will take these features into account to sensitize the Biblically driven theologian so that he would sensitively speak the Word of God to his part of the people of God. To do otherwise would likely either repeat a static tradition or to syncretize theology to his context. To the extent that this theology becomes a voice for a church or ministry, then there needs to be

62 N. T. Wright, *The New Testament and the People of God* (Minneapolis: Fortress Press, 1992), pp. 31–46 and especially p. 35 here with Wright's emphasis. Robert Stewart ("N. T. Wright's Hermeneutic: An Exploration: Part 1 and 2," *Churchman,* 117[2003]: 153–175, 235–266, especially p. 154) wrongly identifies Wright as affirming, "one can never have knowledge of the thing-in-itself," which more Jamesian or Kuhnian critical realists do affirm. However, Wright's historical Jesus work identifies him as more Peircian in trying to obtain the real historical Jesus to which the evidence points, when approached with scientific enquiry.

63 James Dunn, *Jesus Remembered* (Grand Rapids: Eerdmans, 2003), pp. 110–111.

64 Dunn, *Jesus Remembered,* p. 124.

65 Dale C. Allison, *Constructing Jesus: Memory, Imagination, and History* (Grand Rapids: Baker, 2010), p. 87.

community building activity to cultivate understanding, peer review, and consensus of the community. The theologian in such a conversation needs to be honest in reflecting with emphasis where there is communal agreement and where there are instead a variety of options within the community. Through the midst of this sensitivity, the goal of the exegete is to allow the Biblical text to retain its authentic voice.

9. Creation and Fall

The Bible begins with God creating the heavens and the earth. Biblical theology and Biblical creation begin with God.

The term *'el/* , which means "god," suggests power and authority. Some suggest that *'el* derives from the root *'wl* (strong), others suggest *'eloah* (God), and others see the root *'lh* together with *'eloah* (implying fear).[1] Though there is disagreement in the etymology of the term, it is broadly recognized in its use *'el/* means "god." Here in Genesis it is used to describe a profoundly powerful God in contrast to the other cosmologies of the ancient Near East. So the effective power and authority to create swiftly and effortlessly helps to inform the grandeur of this God *'el*. Many suggest that the plural, *Elohim*, extends these conceptions of power, authority and majesty beyond which a singular name can do justice. For example, Eichrodt developed this as an overwhelming monotheism.

> A similar design led the writer of Genesis 1 to use the term *elohim* for the Creator God. By choosing this particular name, which as the epitome of all embracing divine power excludes all other divinity, he was able to protect his cosmology from any trace of polytheistic thought and at the same time describe the creator God as the absolute Ruler and the only Being whose will carries any weight.[2]

It has become popular in certain contexts to see *elohim* as God's court or angels. For example, Psalm 8:5 as understood by the LXX and Hebrews 2:7 takes *elohim* as angels. Additionally, Job 1:6 and 2:1 presents the sons of *elohim* to be angels in God's court. However, Job denies angels a role involved within the creation except that of worship while God creates the universe (Job 38:1–7–11). Furthermore, Isaiah in his development of the incomparability of Yahweh develops that He is the One Who creates the universe and its people as well; there is no other creator but God

1 An example of a brief discussion of this etymology can be found in Laird Harris, Gleason Archer and Bruce Waltke, *Theological Wordbook of the Old Testament* (Chicago: Moody Press, 1980).

2 Walter Eichrodt, *Old Testament Theology* (Philadelphia: Westminster Press, 1961), vol. 1, pp. 186–7. There is no development of trinity in these early chapters of Genesis for if plural is to be taken as a plural of person it would mean polytheism in this early context of revelation and that is clearly not correct in a Pentateuch context in which monotheism dominates.

(Isa. 42:5–9)[3] which brings us back to this context of Genesis in which no other than *elohim* is described as the creator. And the creation is singularly done so effectively by God's speech.

Such a God reference is better understood in this Mosaic context as a single monotheistic God (Deut. 6:4), Who as the creator creates so effectively that the plural is best taken as a plural of majesty. This plurality of majesty may be viewed as carrying over into the pronouns that are used in grammatical agreement with *Elohim* like the 'Us' and 'Our' of Genesis 1:26 and 3:22.[4] So no development of plurality of person is being developed by these texts, when they are easily explained by simple grammatical agreement. Perhaps the abundance of singular pronouns used throughout the creation account with the plural *Elohim* makes a case for monotheism affirming the Mosaic monotheistic perspective.

9.1. Creation

There is a broad based agreement that the Biblical creation account especially in Genesis 1:1–2:3 polemics the ancient Near Eastern cosmology accounts. Gerhard Hasel popularized five areas of polemic, which Gordon Wenham summarized as follows.

> First, in some Near Eastern cosmologies, dragons *tnn* are rivals whom the Canaanite gods conquer, whereas in Gen. 1:21 the great sea monsters are just one kind of the aquatic animals created by God. Second, these cosmologies describe struggle of the gods to separate the upper waters from the lower waters; but Gen. 1:6–10 describes the acts of separation by simple divine fiat. Third, the worship of the sun, moon, and stars was current throughout the ancient orient. Genesis pointedly avoids using the normal Hebrew words for sun and moon, lest they be taken as divine, and says instead God created the greater and lesser light. Fourth, Babylonian tradition sees the creation of man as an afterthought, a device to relieve the gods of work and provide them with food. For Genesis, the creation of man is the goal of creation and God provides man with food. Finally, Genesis shows God creating simply through his

---

3 Cf. Doug Kennard, *The Classical Christian God* (Lewiston: Edwin Mellen Press, 2002), pp. 121–34.

4 There does not seem to be any other creator involved in Genesis or crafting the image of God, man. The second pronominal referent is in Genesis 3:22. Nor is there any development in this pronoun to fund the doctrine of the Trinity as Augustine alludes in *On the Trinity* 12.6.6, *Fathers of the Church: A New Translation* (Washington D.C.: Catholic University of America Press, 1963), 45.348. Here the singular referent who is the judge is Yahweh Elohim. It is only after the judgment that a cherib appears on the scene. In other contexts, where the plural is clearly developing God and His court the variety of referents are clearly visible in the context before the plural pronoun is used, as in Isa. 6:8.

> spoken word, not through magical utterance as is attested in Egypt.[5]

In ancient Near Eastern cosmology the creation accounts often involve a long period of time with deep conflicts through which a born god who would be king battles and destroys rival gods and the forces of chaos in order to remake them into the new creation. An example is seen in the *Enuma Elish*. In stark polemical contrast, *Elohim* is not born or developing. Carroll Stuhmueller develops the unique theological entrance of this God, for He alone among all semitic creative gods undergoes no birth or metamorphosis.[6] God is complete in Himself and He stands transcendently apart from all that is created. This polemics both the Egyptian and Mesopotamian polytheisms, which both are populated by developing inferior gods. Our God is truly worthy of control because only our God truly created everything. God is presented as creating swiftly and effortlessly a whole creation with no threatening rivals within the creation. John McKenzie develops that there is no cosmic mortal combat with the risk of God being defeated by a monster of chaos, but rather God is in His shop as a carpenter with no risk of being devoured by His chair, the creation.

> Against this background, the Hebrew account of the origins can scarcely be anything else but a counter statement to the myth of creation...The Hebrew author enumerates all the natural forces in which deity was thought to reside, and of all of them he says simply that God made them. Consequently, he eliminates all elements of struggle on the cosmic level; the visible universe is not an uneasy balance of forces, but it is moderated by one supreme will, which imposes itself with effortless supremacy upon all that it has made. By preference the author speaks of the created work rather of the created act, because he wishes to emphasize the fact that the creative Deity, unlike *Marduk*, has not had to win supremacy by combat with an equal.[7]

---

5 Gordon Wenham, *Genesis 1–15* (Waco: Word Books, 1987), vol. 1, p. 9; Gerhard Hasel, "The Polemic Nature of the Genesis Cosmology," *Evangelical Quarterly* 46(1974): 81–102.

6 Carrol Stuhmueller, 'The Theology of Creation in Second Isaias' *CBQ* 21(1959): 429–67.

7 John McKenzie, *The Two Edged Sword* (New York: Image Books, 1966), pp. 101–2.

This chapter will especially draw together the parallel texts of Genesis 1 and 2, and Psalm 8 and 104 to develop a Biblical theology of creation from the O.T.[8]

The structure of Genesis develops literary units with the hinge of the word 'account' (*toledot/* ; Gen. 2:4; 5:1; 6:9; 10:1, 32; 11:10, 27; 25:12, 13, 19; 36:1, 9; 37:2).

By comparing the beginning of both Genesis creation accounts an interpreter can notice the same grammatical structure: a summary of the whole creation within the unit, followed by three circumstantial clauses (Gen. 1:1–2; 2:4–6). The summary is not a separate event from the whole of the creation account, so it could be viewed as a heading to the account that follows. This summary is followed by three circumstantial clauses exploring the attending circumstance of lack within which the creation makes sense. The fact that these circumstantial clauses of Genesis 1:2 and 2:5–6 depend on the main verb of the overview statement (Gen. 1:1 or 2:4) clarifies that grammatically there is no temporal gap or events between these textual statements. Therefore for grammatical reasons, no gap theory fits the Biblical text.

There is no existing creation before the summary statement of Genesis 1:1. This summary of event begins with the first two words connected together by the alliteration of *BRA* sound in the words 'In the beginning' and 'created.' Or as Young develops, "This is a beginning that is characterized by creation, and this is a creation that is characterized by the beginning. Here it means 'the absolute beginning!'"[9] There is no history or creation before Genesis 1:1.

The word created (*bārā'/*) is an activity of God alone; it is never used of man. The result is always a definitive creation, something new and fresh. Within the summary of the creation "the heavens and earth" is a merism of opposites presenting God as the creator of all (Gen. 1:1).

A number of chaos metaphors are developed in the conditional clauses that set a conceptual framework in order to bring out the creation order. For example, the concepts of formless (*tōhû/*) and void (*bōhû/*) signify chaos and lack of order, as in a desert waste (Deut. 32:10; Job 6:18) or after a devastating judgment (Jer. 4:23–26; Isa. 34:11).[10] Perhaps

---

8 Other Jewish texts join Ps. 104 in praising God through the creation, especially Ps. 19 and *Test. Adam*.

9 E. J. Young, *In the Beginning* (Edinburgh: The Banner of Truth Trust, 1976), p. 24; same point made by Gordon Wenham (*Genesis 1–15*.. vol. 1, pp. 13–14); John Walton, Victor Matthews & Mark Chavalas, *The IVP Bible Background Commentary: Old Testament* (Downers Grove: InterVarsity Press, 2000), p. 28, the ancient Thebian Egyptian of text *Dd Ee on Nuts right side* in *The Book of Nut* speaks of the god Amun with the same expression "in the beginning" with the same meaning-"Egyptologists interpret this not as an abstract idea but as a reference to a first-time event."

10 *Wisdom of Solomon* 11.17 follows Plato (*Sophist* 265c) in having the creation made from formless matter while the Biblical account is not so clearly aligned in this direction.

the form of God's creation is given through God's activity of the first four days[11] and then God fills the creation in days four through six, however here the two words operate as a hendiadys for amorphous chaos. Additionally, darkness is symbolic of evil and vulnerability throughout the Bible (e.g., Ex. 10:21–22; 14:20), however in this context darkness is merely part of the designed time of day without light (Gen. 1:4–5, 18). Furthermore, the watery deep (*thm/*) is not conducive to life and represents the abyss. This deep is what drowns Egypt, Tyre and everyone in the flood when it is released by God to fight sin with chaos flood (Gen. 7:11; 8:2; Ex. 15:5, 8; Ezek. 26:19). God's way of deliverance for Israel was to pass through this deep on dry ground in the midst of the exodus into kingdom (Ps. 106:9; Isa. 51:10; 63:13). God conquering over this chaos is a polemic against the Babylonian goddess *Tiamat* and other mythological conceptions of the sea of chaos (*yaym/*), which is occupied by the monsters of chaos (*Leviathan* and *Rahab*). None of the O.T. instances of *thm/* contain any hint of personification, so they are no rival to God.[12] Here God does not Himself sense any risk from the deep and later it can be seen as a creation sea out of which blessing may come (Gen. 49:25).

The *"ruh* of *Elohim"* ( ) could join the chaos metaphors as a chaotic *wind* from God (Isa. 11:4; 30:28) without the battle imagery of *Marduk*'s use of the chaos wind to defeat *Tiamat*,[13] but *Elohim* is presented in Genesis one as God involved in creation so it is best to take this reference as the monotheistic "Divine *Spirit*" involved in creation.[14] There is no life besides God so the Spirit of God hovers like a mother bird over her brood with such movements as to cause her brood, the creation, to take flight (Deut. 32:11); God has intimate contact with the creation to bring forth order. Waltke develops that there is no restrainer of the chaos as in the ancient Near Eastern myths and there is no threat or rival to God; the monotheistic God creates utilizing these chaos metaphors.

> The Spirit of God does not contend with a living hostile chaotic force but hovers over the primordial mass awaiting

11 In days one through four of the creation, God brings separation (*ybdl/*) to the creation (Gen. 1:4, 7, 14, 18). This first separation is brought about by God separating the light from the darkness (Gen. 1:4). The fourth day separation parallels this of the first day with a separation of day from night (*hbdyl/* ; Gen. 1:14, 18). The second separation (*ybdl/*) separates the waters within the creation (Gen. 1:7) parallel to firmament (*rāqîa'/* ; LXX:). The third instance shifts the word to gathering or collecting (*mqh/*) the seas as separate from the dry land that then appeared (Gen. 1:9–10).

12 Claus Westermann, *Genesis 1–11: A Commentary* (Minneapolis: Augsburg Publishing House, 1984), pp. 104–6.

13 *Enumah Elish* Table 1, lines 105–110.

14 Do not read this as the Holy Spirit as in a trinitarian understanding for in the Pentateuch of monotheism is emphasized as a foundational stage of progressive revelation. The trinity is not clearly taught in the Bible until the N.T.

> the appropriate time for history to begin. How can the chaos be hostile when it is not living but inanimate? It can only be shaped according to the will of the Creator.[15]

The pattern of creation in Genesis 1 follows regularly as: 1) an announcement (And God said), 2) command (let there be...), 3) report (and it was so), 4) evaluation (And God said that it was good) and 5) temporal framework (And there was evening and morning, the ... day). *Elohim*'s creating by word implies sovereignty and extends far beyond *Marduk*'s magic by word as he was unable even to quiet *Tiamat* by word.[16] God's creation by word spoken shows that when God speaks in the creation context that the creation and blessing is dependent upon God for realization. The fact that God creates only good reflects back on to Him as the Good God (e.g., Matt. 19:17; James 1:17) Who creates with wisdom (Prov. 3:19).

The evaluation of "good" (*tōb/*) can be an aesthetic judgment of beauty (perhaps in Gen. 6:2) but in this context it is an acknowledgment of purpose and order and blessing, thus the creation is fitting into God's sovereign design (Gen. 1:4, 10, 12, 18, 21, 25, 31; 2:9, 17–18; 3:5–6, 22). This goodness of design does not indicate static perfection, for though the created light was evaluated by God to be good, God further developed this light (Gen. 1:4, *h'wr/*) to be sourced and governed by lights (Gen. 1:14, *m'rt/*). God then pronounced again that these lights of the creation were good (Gen. 1:18). So the concept of good (*tōb/*) permits development within whatever is evaluated. In light of this development of good (*tōb/*) for light and lights, plants, animals and humans, which are created and affirmed as good (*tōb/*), have the possibility of further development after this creation account.

This evaluation that things are assessed by God as good (*tōb/*) comes sometimes in the middle of a creation day to structure levels of the creation. For example, the water, sky, and land are all separated into a structure on day two and three, the evaluation of 'good' (*tōb/*) coming after these and before vegetation separates these as a lower structure than that of vegetation (Gen. 1:10). Likewise, in the middle of day six after the land beasts were created, the evaluation occurs to identify man in the creation as a superior content of creation.

The days (*yōm/*) of Genesis can be taken as the light part of the day in contrast to darkness (Gen. 1:5), or as an age of creation (Gen. 2:4) but the term day used with a number and described in the Hebrew way as dark of night and then light of morning is best taken as a natural calendar day (Gen. 1:5, 8, 13, 19, 23, 31, 2:2–3). Once the sun is

15 Bruce Waltke, *Creation and Chaos* (Portland: Western Conservative Baptist Seminary, 1974), p. 48.

16 Compare tablet 2:117 or the sovereignty theme is developed by Nahum Sarna, *Understanding Genesis* (New York: McGraw Hill, 1966), p. 12.

attached to these days then they would be understood as solar days. The word *yōm/* appears in the O.T. 359 times with an ordinal number, in which at least 358 times it is a solar day.[17] Sometimes it is in the plural (as in a week is 7 solar days) but the majority of the instances are in the singular as here, meaning a solar day. Hugh Ross' claim that this instance is unique as divine activity instead of the majority of instances of the word being in contexts of human activity,[18] neither appreciates God's sovereign involvement throughout the Bible, nor the fact that the meaning of words is dependent upon their use. The use of *yōm/* is dominated throughout the O.T. in identifying solar days, especially when the additional corroborating features of ordinal and evening and morning are accompanying. The words "evening" and "morning" are used 38 times in the O.T. with some different connectors, and every Biblical instance, including these in Genesis one utilize "evening and morning" as referring to a solar day or parts of a solar day. Sometimes the words "evening" and "morning" do not have the word *yōm/* with them while they continue to mean solar day (e.g., Ex. 27:21).

While the seventh day does not specifically say it has an evening and morning, it should be understood as a solar day after the pattern through the literary unit and the appeal to a seven day creation week which informs the Sabbath mandate (Ex. 20:11).[19] This six calendar days

17 Zechariah 14:7 "day one" may refer to the day of the Lord or it may refer to a unique (solar?) day of battle. Hosea 6:2 "two days... on the third day He will raise us up" does not mean a long period of time as some claim (e.g., John Calvin, *Commentaries on the Twelve Minor Prophets: Hosea* [Edinburgh: Calvin Translation Society, 1846], 1:218-9) for if the third day resurrection of Christ is "according to the Scriptures," as 1 Corinthians 15:4 claims and this prophetic text of Hosea 6:2 is the only Biblical text that was understood to teach such a view, then Hosea must refer here to solar days. Thus the Jewish tradition and Paul understood Hosea to refer to solar days as in Jesus' resurrection on the third solar day. Jewish tradition embraced a third day resurrection of all believers into Kingdom and that the Messiah would lead the way (E.g., *1 En.* 58.3; 62.14–16; 91.10; 92.2; 108.11–14; *2 Bar.*[Syriac] 30.1–5; *2 Macc.* 7.9–14, 22–23; 14.43–46; *4 Macc.* 7.19; 16.25; *4 Ezra* 7.32; *Sib. Or.* 4.180; *T. Ben. 10.6–8*; *T. Levi* 18; *T. Jud.* 24; *Tq.* Hos. 6:2 interprets this text to be resurrection whereas the text speaks of the reviving of Israel on the third day; *Tg. Jon.* on Isa. 27:12f describes salvation as being accomplished on the third day; in *b. Sanh.* 90b Gamaliel claims that God would give the resurrected patriarchs land, not merely their descendants and Johanan claims Numbers 18:28 the portion of YHWH given to Aaron is taken that he will be alive again, likewise Num. 15:31 is claimed that the remaining guilt of the offender will be accountable in the world to come; 91b–92a; *B. Ta'an.* 2a; *B. Ket.* 111; *m. Sanh.* 10.1, 3; *T. Mos.* 10.8–10; *Gen. Rab.* 14.5; 28.3; *Lev. Rab.* 14.9; *Messianic Apocalypse* adds resurrection to a modification of Psalm 146:5–9 as a Messianic expectation to be done to others; *T. Jud.* 25.4 claims this Messianic resurrection would begin with Abraham, Isaac, and Jacob; *T. Benj.* claims that after these are raised the whole of Israel will be raised; *Pss. of Sol.* 3.11–12; 4Q521 frag. 2, col. 2.1–13; frags. 7 and 5, col. 2.1–7; 1QH 14.29–35; 19.10–14; *Targum Songs* 8.5; the benediction in the *Amidah,* the *Shemoneh Esre*).

18 Hugh Ross, *A Matter of Days* (Colorado Springs: Nav Press, 2004), p. 74.

19 Contrary to Meredith Kline ("Because it Had Not Rained," *Westminster Theological Journal* 20[1958]: 156) who maintains that the seventh day is unending.

of creation is specifically declared to be the length of time for creation in order to explain the rationale for the seventh solar day each week being designated as a Sabbath rest (Ex. 20:11).[20] Such a foundational connection of the creation week for Israel's Sabbath commemorations argues strongly for a historical creation of the universe by God in six calendar days, utilizing a pre-modern concept of real history as elsewhere in the Biblical narrative which is connected to Israel's life (Ex. 20:11). So in comparison to other ancient Near Eastern creation accounts the Biblical creation moves swiftly to its completion in six solar days. With this brief creation account of six days polemicing the ancient near Eastern accounts of months and years, no doubt this swift creation account would then also polemic modern evolutionary models of origins that take millions and billions of years. That is, our God is so able to dispatch creation so swiftly when compared to the gods of the ancient near East and modern science.

The framework interpretation partly resists this historical calendar week of creation for a literary appeal to patterns during the creation week.[21] I think that their literary patterns have some basis for organizing the week in parallel days: 1 and 4 for light and lights, 2 and 5 for water and separation and animals in both, and 3 and 6 for land with land animals. Though I will show that separation occurs through day four and contents occur from at least days three through six, so the parallel is not so nice in Hebrew as it is when viewed as a simple overview. I think that these parallels are part of the design reflected in that the creation is good. However, such a Framework Hypothesis should not overrule the textual evidence developed here for sequential historical days. Furthermore, the abundant use of the *waw* consecutive through the narrative account with a preterite indicates of sequence, which in this text would be best taken as a historical sequence (e.g., "then God said," Gen. 1:3–31; 2:3).[22] Whereas, the *waw* consecutive through Genesis two presents a

20 *Jubilees* 2.1, 17–22 also supports a seven day creation to justify Sabbath. *Jubilees* 2 follows the Biblical pattern of creation within this first week. It might be coincidental that the *Enuma Elish* is contained in seven tablets or in the midst of a journey *The Gilgamesh Epic* Tablet 11, column 5 has Gilgamesh sleep for seven nights, since Ex. 20:11 makes the claim for a historical creation by God in six solar days to source Sabbath mandate.

21 Arie Noordzij, *God's Word en der Eeuwen Getuigenis. Het Oude Testament in het Licht der Oostersche Opgravingen* (Kampen: University of Utrecht, 1924); summary and critique by Edward J. Young, *Studies in Genesis One* (Phillipsburg: Presbyterian & Reformed, 1964), pp. 43–105; N. H. Ridderbos, *Is There a Conflict Between Genesis 1 and Natural Science?* (Grand Rapids: Eerdmans, 1957); Meredith Kline, "Because it Had Not Rained," *Westminster Theological Journal* 20(1958): 145–57; "Space and Time in the Genesis Cosmogony," *Perspectives on Science and Christian Faith* 48(1996): 2–15; view critiqued by Robert McCabe, "A Critique of the Framework Interpretation of the Creation week," paper presented at Evangelical Theological Society, Nov. 2008.

22 Bill T. Arnold and John H. Choi, *A Guide to Biblical Hebrew Syntax* (Cambridge: Cambridge University Press, 2003), pp. 84–85; Robert McCabe, "A Critique of the

narrative description around the man without claiming chronology as Genesis one's use of consecutive days demands.[23] Historical sequence for Genesis one is also indicated by other repetitive elements, such as "God said" (Gen. 1:3,6, 9, 11, 14, 20, 24, 26, 28, 29), "let there be" (Gen. 1:3, 6, 9, 11, 14, 20, 24, 26), "and it was so" (Gen. 1:3, 7, 9, 11, 15, 24, 30), "and there was evening and morning" (Gen. 1:5, 8, 13, 19, 23, 31), and the ordinal sequence "one day...second day" (Gen. 1:5, 8, 13, 19, 23, 31).

The fact of creation implies that whatever is created will a moment later have the appearance of age. If the earth is created then there is the appearance that it has been there for a while. Rabbinic interpretation concluded that the sun and the moon were created with their contemporary characteristics.[24] Thus this account explains how they function as markers for days and seasons. If light is created there is the appearance that it has traveled from some source. If animals or humans are created then there is the appearance that they have matured to that point. For example, Rabbi Bar Kappora claimed in his interpretation that the humans were created as adults aged twenty years old.[25] If wine is created then there is the appearance that it has gone through fermentation. So if an observer were able to investigate the first evidences of creation, then empirically this evidence would indicate a longer age than creation would entail, by virtue that a creation has occurred. In light of this creation with the appearance of age, I conclude that there are six days of God creating, without a gap or a pre-existent creation. This very fact would argue for a relatively young earth.

Such a young earth view and the historicity of the creation accounts is further developed from the genealogies realistically describing historical generations from Adam to living Israelites during the exodus without too many gaps. This repeated use of genealogies through the book of Genesis into Exodus identifies the Genesis creation accounts as different than the ancient Near East mythological creation accounts which do not have genealogies to connect their proto-mythological human with those living in the later days in which their creation accounts are read. The connectedness of Biblical genealogies from Adam to figures of Israel's history argues strongly for the Biblical creation account to be historically real in a pre-modern manner. That is, real history of real humans who lived in time being selectively described with significant theological framing that contributes to a Biblical worldview. So this makes me a young earth advocate for Biblical textual reasons. However,

---

Framework Interpretation of the Creation week," paper presented at Evangelical Theological Society, Nov. 2008, pp. 5.

23 Robert McCabe, "A Critique of the Framework Interpretation of the Creation week," paper presented at Evangelical Theological Society, Nov. 2008, pp. 17–23.

24 *Num. Rab.* 12.8.

25 *Num. Rab.* 12.8.

the more important Biblical issue is to discern and frame one's life by the theological elements of a Biblical worldview, such as one's relationship and responsiveness to God.

Such a young earth interpretation has the ramification for science that non-death related evidence of the age of the geological strata or the universe could be theorized to be part of this initial creation with the appearance of age. So scientific theories that are proposed on the basis of this empirical evidence need to submit to the Biblical textual timeframe that takes revelational priority. Empirical evidence should not be utilized to overrule clear Biblical statement sensitively interpreted within context and genre. Furthermore, once evidence of death (such as fossils) is involved in this empirical evidence of age then this should be seen as in the wake of the fall (to be discussed later).

Genesis one's days of creation set up a loose textual parallel (separated environs [light, water, air, land], and climax) between the structure of days one through four and the contents of days three through six. Usually, the framework hypothesis notice these parallels from an English text on days one through three and four through six. However, if examined in the Hebrew text there are overlapping indications on days three and four. The first four days provide form or structure to answer formlessness (Gen. 1:2–13, *tōhû/*)and days three through six fill up the condition of void with contents (Gen. 1:2, 14–31, *bōhû/*). In days one through four of the creation, the structure or form is indicated by the use of separating terms. God brings *separation* (*ybdl/*) to the creation (Gen. 1:4, 7, 14, 18). This first *separation* is brought about by God separating the light from the darkness (Gen. 1:4). The fourth day *separation* parallels this of the first day with a separation of day from night (*hbdl/* ; Gen. 1:14, 18). The second *separation* (*ybdl/*) *separates* the waters within the creation (Gen. 1:7) parallel to spreading/firmament (*rāqîa'/* ; LXX:). The third instance shifts the separating word to *gathering or collecting* (*mqwh/*) the seas as separate from the dry land that then appeared (Gen. 1:9–10).

The creation of light does not occur prior to the creation as in other ancient Near Eastern myths where it is an attribute of their gods (e.g., *Apsu* and *Marduk*). In this case light is created by God to dispel the chaotic darkness effortlessly obtaining an immediate victory (Gen. 1:3–5). There is no account of the source of the light appearing (as from an object), for the creation account is theological in affirming God is the source of the light and it fits His design. The separation of light from darkness and the naming of them demonstrate *Elohim's* sovereignty, as von Rad develops.

> The ultimate enunciation of this orderly cosmic arrangement and wholesome stabilization is the divine naming of the present darkness as night and the present light as day. The

> name given by God, is an expression of the essence and a seal of the way it will look henceforth. Thus the accent lies, not on the verbal naming, but on the calling into and fixing of the existence of creation. The precise translation, therefore is 'And God *appointed* the light as day.....' But in the ancient Oriental view the act of giving a name meant, above all, the exercise of a sovereign right (cf. 2 Kings 23:34; 24:17). Thus the naming of this and all subsequent creation works once more expresses graphically God's claim of lordship over the creatures.[26]

Israel would remember the plagues (Ex. 10:21–24), how God brought thick darkness over the Egyptians but light among the Israelite huts. Light would represent good and salvation as darkness represents chaos, evil and judgment. Psalm 104:1 contemplates that in this creation God wraps Himself with a majestic garment of light. Israel would know that God was the way when they followed the light phenomena through the wanderings, day and night. They would also see here that this same God is sovereign over both light and darkness; goodness and evil were both present but in their proper place.

The parallel creation of lights on day four simply brings the word for lamps as visible from below as in the expanse of the creation (Gen. 1:14–19).[27] If any of these lights were named it would conjure up the names for pagan gods but here the word "light" is meant to be prosaic and degrading, as to exclude polytheism. These are created objects; sun and moon are not named for the words sun and moon are also names for pagan deities, namely *Shemesh* and *Yareach*. So every tempting association with paganism may be avoided in this account. Additionally, the stars are briefly stated as created lights showing no place for astrology. These lights are established as functionaries in the creation for signs, seasons, days and years. *Elohim* has created these real lights to fill His heavens showing again His sovereignty and that they function under His dominion.

The description of the shape of the earth from the Bible is not specific enough to identify it definitively. The earth might be a disk, a sphere or ellipsoid, or maybe not described. The available Biblical evidence is the following: Proverbs 8:27, indicates the boundary shape on the face of the seas to be either a ball or perhaps only that the earthly waters are bounded as will be discussed below. Additionally, Job 22:14 and Isaiah 40:22 either mean: 1) an earthen disk, a sphere or ellipsoid, if (circle of the earth) is in synthetic parallelism, whereas 2) if these verses are synonymous parallelism they contribute to the next paragraph, describing the firmament (as the vault

26 Gerhard von Rad, *Genesis* (Philadelphia: Westminster Press, 1972), p. 53.

27 Jewish tradition evident in *2 Baruch* 59:5–11 describes Moses as being shown these details of the cosmology while on the mountain with God.

of the earth). Synonymous parallelism is my literary preference when all else is exegetically equal. All these views are exegetically possible, so an interpreter should be tentative, and I would allow science to determine the shape of the earth to be an ellipsoid. Furthermore, the earth is poetically described as a building project with foundation and corner stone, in which God is the designer, surveyor, and builder (Job 38:4–6). However, this construction imagery does not require the earth to be a disk built on top of something with foundation pillars, though that is the poetic imagery of construction.

In days two and three of creation, God continues to bring separation to the creation (Gen. 1:6–10). This day two separation (*ybdl/*) was brought about by either 1) the *process* of figuratively hammering out a separation or 2) an actual stamped *barrier*, called firmament (*rāqîa'/* ; LXX:). Some take this firmament to be an extended surface (view 2), a solid expanse as if beaten out in a bowl. There are a variety of these substance views, sometimes hybridized as combinations:

a. Structural Dome made of snow.[28]
b. A Symbol of the division between the corporeal and the incorporeal.[29]
c. Clouds as these waters above.[30]
d. Mythological solid dome supporting an elevated ocean.[31]

28 Rabbinical teaching of fifth century A.D., *Num. Rab.* 12.8 built on a structural separation of the waters above from the waters below as in *Jubilees* 2.4, 7, and 5.24–25 where water goes through the flood gate in the firmament (second century B.C.).

29 Origen, *Homilies on Genesis* 1.2 in *Fathers of the Church: A New Translation* (Washington D.C.: Catholic University of America Press, 1947), 71:48–49; Augustine, *Two Books on Genesis Against the Manichaeans* 1.11.17 in *Fathers of the Church* 84.165; *On the Literal Interpretation of Genesis* 8.29, *Fathers of the Church* 84.165–66; Basil the Great counters this view *Hexaemeran* 3–9 in *A Select Library of the Nicene and Post-Nicene Fathers of the Christian Church* (Buffalo: Christian Literature, 1887-94), 2.8.70–71; cf. Andrew Louth, *Genesis 1-11. Ancient Christian Commentary on Scripture* (Downers Grove: InterVarsity, 2001), 1:10–11.

30 John Calvin, "Genesis," In *Calvin's Commentaries*. 8 vols. (Grand Rapids: Associated Publisher & Authors, n.d.) 1:5; Edwyn Bevan, "The Religious Value of Myths in the Old Testament" affirmingly quoted in Derek Kidner, *Genesis* (InterVarsity Press, 1967), pp. 47, 55; H. C. Leupold, *Exposition of Genesis* (Columbus: The Wartburg Press, 1942), pp. 59–60; Robert Newman, "The Biblical Teaching on the Firmament" (Unpublished Thesis, Biblical School of Theology, Hatfield, 1972), p. 59.

31 Rabbi Eliezer (*Pirqe R. El.* 4) says that the "firmament saves the earth from being engulfed by waters of heaven;" John Skinner, *A Critical and Exegetical Commentary on Genesis* (Edinburgh: T & T Clark, 1930), pp. 21–22; Gerhard von Rad, *Genesis: A Commentary* (Philadelphia: The Westminster Press, 1961, 1972), p. 53; Claus Westermann, *Genesis 1–11: A Commentary*, p. 117–8; Gordon Wenham, *Genesis 1–15. Word Biblical Commentary*. vol. 1, pp. 8, 20.

e. Watery shell beyond the universe.[32]
f. Canopy of water, vapor, or ice around the earth.[33]

Advocates of these "firmament" views argue that the firmament was created by God. Since view b serves as merely a division between the heavenly incorporeal and corporeal, this view conceives of no material creation above the firmament. The Biblical claim of heavenly waters above the firmament counters this view. All the other substance views consider that the firmament is holding up the heavenly waters, so that the birds can fly in an open environment under its expanse (Gen. 1:6–8, 20). In models a, c, d, and f, the sun, moon and stars are phenomenologically presented as seen in the firmament and as such the firmament declares God's glory through the created items seen through it (Gen. 1:14–15, 17; Ps. 19:2; Dan. 12:3). Whereas, in view e the firmament is at the edge of the universe so the sun and stars are contained within the firmament's contents.

There is no Biblical description as to the material content of the firmament, unless one allows Ezekiel 10:1 to describe this firmament then it would be something like sapphire stone. If these texts are describing the same firmament, then views a, c, e, and f are less likely. If Revelation 4:6 is relevant then views a and f might have some basis in Biblical description as "a crystal sea."

Sometimes these views argue that the "in" in Genesis 1:20 as within the firmament. The Hebrew does not support this confidence of location within space. For example, in verse 20 God permits the flying things to fly on or above (*'l* ;) the earth, on or above ( ) the face of the heaven's firmament (/LXX:). With the same preposition (*'l*) in Hebrew repeated so closely it probably should have a similar sense, the face of the firmament would probably be beneath the birds like the earth is beneath the birds in Genesis 1:20 and as the face of the earth is beneath the Spirit in Genesis 1:2 ( ). So the use of the preposition *'l* diminishes views c and d and maybe even view a, since clouds usually are above birds. This would also mean that especially in structural view d) that likely the birds would be surrounded by "the waters above," and they would not be able to survive immersed in this vapor canopy of water. Likewise, being at or above the "face" (the use of the phrase) would indicate

32 A. M. Rehwinkel, *The Flood* (St. Louis: Concordia, 1951), p. 97; Russell Humphreys, *Starlight and Time: Solving the Puzzle of Distant Starlight in a Young Universe* (Green Forest: Master Books, 1994); Charles Taylor, "Waters Above or Beyond?" *CEN Tech. J.* 10:2(1996): 211–13.

33 John Whitcomb and Henry Morris, *The Genesis Flood: The Biblical Record and Its Scientific Implications* (Grand Rapids: Baker, 1961), pp. 9, 77, 121; Jody Dillow, "Earth's Pre-Flood Vapor Canopy" Ph.D. dissertation Dallas Theological Seminary, 1978; *The Waters Above* (Chicago: Moody Bible Institute, 1981).

a proximity of closeness to the firmament[34] which would render view c completely unreasonable, since it would place the firmament millions of light years away from the birds. In the LXX different prepositions are used, so the communicates the birds flight is "according to," or "into" or "toward" the firmament, which would likely indicate some degree of closeness, excluding view c as well. Of these views only the view b with its mythological sense survives the near context analysis of the Hebrew, but it would be odd for a passage that so repeatedly polemics ancient Near Eastern mythology as Genesis 1 does, to embrace such myth here.[35] In such a mythological view the ancient Near Eastern context would still conceive of the dome as real, albeit maybe spiritual or other than physical some of the time.

Some propose that the firmament collapses with the flood water from the heavens. However, other defenders of substance views utilize the prophets and wisdom as a case for the *rāqîa'* ( ) being the pavement within the throne room in heaven.

This solid view is especially dependent upon wisdom and prophetic sources. In this view, other words describe a vaulted arch since Isaiah 40:22 and Job 22:14 might indicate God sits upon such a shape above the earth in the context of the clouds, but the point of these texts is not primarily shape of a firmament, but the incomparable sovereignty of God. Other metaphors of God creating communicate a structural element in more fabric ways as of a heavenly tent curtain or clothes, or with upper chambers with beams for support (Ps. 104:2–4). Using the firmament word (*rāqîa'/*) the structural expanse appears as a crystal roof with God's sapphire throne sitting upon it (Ezek. 1:22–26; 10:1). If these Ezekiel references were fused with those of Genesis, the divine throne room constructed upon the firmament (*rāqîa'/*) would be swamped with water or perhaps God's throne room would only be available for God after a vapor canopy vacated the area above the *rāqîa'* ( ).

Within such realist imagery, the use of *'arubat* (; windows or lattice in a literal building Eccl. 12:3; Isa. 6:8) is used for a window where the flood waters pour through these heavenly windows (Gen. 7:11; 8:2). Furthermore these heavenly windows may be either spiritually real or metaphorical in the instances where a more generic judgment of entrapment, or blessing of deliverance from enemies or food as coming from God (2 Kgs. 7:2, 19; Isa. 24:18; Mal. 3:10). However, taking this barrier as metaphorically or spiritually real would diminish

34 *pany/* conveys closeness or connection in the of account (Gen. 1:2, 20, 29; 2:6; 3:8) and throughout the Pentateuch. Likewise the phrase conveys closeness in the presence of, on, and toward (Gen. 1:2, 20, 29; 6:1; 7:3, 18, 23; 8:9; 11:4, 8, 9; 11:28; 18:16; 19:28 and throughout the O.T.

35 Bruce Waltke, *Creation and Chaos* (Portland: Western Conservative Baptist Seminary, 1974), pp. 13–15, 43–53; Gerhard Hasel, "The Polemical Nature of the Genesis Cosmology," *EQ* 46(1974): 81–102.

the applicability of the view that sees the firmament *rāqîa'* ( ) rather substantially. In such a substantial view, there is the additional problem of how would advocates explain why rockets have been able to pass through without hitting a solid object. As such if a substance view is maintained, then the strongest of these options is the mythical view.

There may be additional scientific problems with a water canopy either held up by *rāqîa'* ( ), [view d] or in a vapor canopy configuration [view f], in that the canopy's green house effect if it was thicker than 20 inches might kill the animals and humans before the ark was ever built.[36]

Cosmological genre, like Genesis 1–3 explains how things have come to be as they are at the time of writing (e.g., Moses day) so the readers can understand their heritage. Therefore, the "waters above" explains rain experienced in the flood, as coming from above, namely clouds or God (Gen. 1:7; 2:5; 7:11–12). This phrase does not require there to actually be a body of water suspended in early history. The phrase "waters above" also might function phenomenologically, as one looks at the sky, it appears blue like water.

Even better, firmament *rāqîa'* ( ) is better seen as the process of spreading (view 1 above). Victor Hamilton explains that such a verbal idea is the basic meaning of the term.[37] However, meaning is determined by use. This Genesis instance of *rāqîa'* ( ) would join with other Mosaic texts that take *rāqîa'* ( ) verbally (Ex. 39:3, ; Num. 16:39 in English [17:4 in MT and LXX,]) describing a spreading of something, like gold plating. So the nearer Mosaic context taking the word more as a spreading, thus would see *rāqîa'* ( ) as parallel to *ybdl/* (separation) in contributing to the structure of the creation. This would mean that Genesis 1:6 would join Job 37:18 ( ) indicating a spreading of the skies, separating earthly waters from the heavenly waters (those on reserve by God for judgment without any structure required to keep a vapor canopy aloft). This view better fits the LXX expression of as a spreading spanning from water below to water above because it places the "spreading in the middle of the waters" (Gen. 1:6–7 LXX: and), rather than holding up the heavenly water. Thus the LXX expression would include all occupants like humans to be within the spreading rather than conceiving of it as solid barrier. The separation allows for the heavenly

36 David E. Rush and Larry Vardiman, "Pre-Flood Vapor Canopy Radiative Temperature Profiles," in *Proceedings of the Second International Conference on Creationism* ed. Robert E. Walsh and Chris L. Brooks (Pittsburgh: Creation Science Fellowship, 1990), 2:238-45; Glen R. Morton, *Foundation, Fall and Flood* (Dallas: DMD, 1994), pp. 54–56.

37 Victor Hamilton, *The Book of Genesis Chapters 1–17. The International Commentary on the Old Testament* (Grand Rapids: Eerdmans, 1990), p. 122; also in conversations this is the view of John Walton, Paul Wegner, and Dave Fouts.

objects to be seen and to declare God's glory (Gen. 1:14–15, 17; Ps. 19:2; Dan. 12:3). The previous fabric and vault descriptions would largely be poetic texts and could be taken metaphorically placing the emphasis where the passage does on God's incomparable sovereignty (Job 22:14; Ps. 104:2–4; Isa. 40:22). This would allow throne room texts to be something else than what the creation account is describing (Ezek. 1:22–26; 10:1). The window lattice imagery (*'rubat/*) would be a metaphor of delivering blessings or judgment through the separation that the heavens have from the earth, the point being that these blessings and judgments come from God rather than through a specific structure (2 Kgs. 7:2, 19; Eccl. 12:3; Isa. 6:8; 24:18; Mal. 3:10). This would mean that the flood waters were also coming from the heavens (or God with no allusion to a vapor canopy), while the flood water also comes from the deep (Gen. 7:11; 8:2).

For all these reasons I prefer to see *rāqîa'* ( ) as describing the process of spreading rather than a real actual item of the creation. Either way, praise is appropriate anywhere in this created sanctuary of the earth (that is within the firmament dome or separation [my preference]) that God has made (Ps. 150:1).

This separation imagery is joined by God speaking to cause the rising of land that separates the land from the seas on the third day of creation (Gen. 1:9–10). Here the separation is expressed by gathering or collecting (*mqwh/*) the seas as separate from the dry land that then appeared (Gen. 1:9–10). Psalm 104:6–9 portrays the rising of the land and the fleeing of the waters as dramatically responding to God's thunderous rebuke which limits the earth's garment to its proper place. That is, in the psalm the water is more presented as an opponent (than the passive seas of Genesis) that flees in obedience since the word "shout" (*g'rt/* ; Ps. 104:7) which appears often in war as a battle cry (2 Sam. 22:14; Pss. 18:13; 76:6; 106:9; Isa. 66:15; Nah. 1:4) and "sound of thunder" (*ql r'md/* ; Ps. 104:7) which is related to the word which reveals God as a warrior (*r'm/* ; 1 Sam. 2:10; 7:10; 2 Sam. 22:14; Pss. 18:13; 29:3; Job 40:9). Thus in Genesis the polemic against the water and chaos is more acute since God merely speaks and the water separates to its place, whereas in the poetic texts of the Writings more violent imagery is used as in conquest cosmologies. The design statement in the psalm, that these waters might "not return to cover the earth" (Ps. 104:9) does not prevent the global flood judgment but does indicate a design pattern for which the psalmist praises God. In Proverbs 3:20 the chaotic deep (*thmt/*) is broken up in the separation of the waters below from the above that drips dew. Likewise, Job 26:5–14 presents God in conquest over the chaos power of Rahab, a multi-headed serpent, as He wraps the earth in waters including the spreading of its clouds. Similarly, Psalm 74:13–17 exults in God dividing the sea and breaking the heads of the multi-headed chaos monster Leviathan in a context in which the sea is bounded and the sun, day and seasons get established (also Ps. 89:9–12). Extending these polemical contrasts, Job 38:8–11 poetically describes God limiting the seas by boundaries and doors. Something like these descriptions occur again as the flood waters recede and the earth is once again brought up from the waters of chaos (Gen. 8). However, the Jobian limiting of the waters, also described as a poetic birthing and diapering of the sea with awesome clouds, draws this text to the describing of the initial creation's dependence upon God (Job 38:8–9). The simplicity in Genesis 1 of accomplishing these divisions by a word stands boldly as a claim for Elohim's sovereignty; He rules over the domains ruled by and threatening to the pagan gods. God as Sovereign separates and controls them. Once the passive waters are separated under God's sovereign control they become territorial markers and irrigation channels by God to do His bidding as tools which water the plants and animals (Gen. 2:6, 10–14; Ps. 104:10–13).

The first mention of contents within this structure is God's creation of vegetation. Plants are never said in the Biblical text to be alive; the Biblical words for 'life' (*nepeš hyh/*) are not capturing what biologists have in mind, but rather the idea of vibrancy, intentionality, wholeness, and movement. So vegetation is not alive but becomes food for those who are alive (Gen. 1:29–30). Only a vegetarian diet is indicated until the Noahic Covenant changes animal and human diet to possibly include meat from beasts, birds, crawlers, and fish (Gen. 1:29–30; 9:2–5). This would likely indicate that animals and humans were created with resources (like claws and teeth) that were used in vegetarian ways, and thus had a sufficient reserve to later be developed or utilized carnivorously. There is no time of change spelled out for animals to undergo such a change from vegetarian to carnivorous ability. However, in the creation account these animals are named with their later carnivorous names, probably implying that the animals Israel and we know by these names probably already have their abilities latent in their creation by God. Additionally, in the Fall, a venomous serpent biting humans (a familiar experience for Israel; Num. 21:6–9; Deut. 8:15) is part of the oracle of the curse (Gen. 3:15), probably implying that such serpents have the potential of a venomous bite in their creation by God. Furthermore, carnivores are operative by the time of the Noahic covenant, where man is permitted to eat of animals and protected from being animals' prey. As the psalmist praises God for the creation, he identifies that in his day the lions "roar after their prey, and seek their food from God" (Ps. 104:21). This comment does not bring animal death into the creating process.

God brings vegetation from the inanimate earth identifying it with the earth in contrast to the ancient Near Eastern gods, who have been sidelined again. The speed (within part of a day) at which Elohim creates the plants demonstrates God's sovereign power, as well as continues to polemic evolutionary views. This vegetation is primarily developed in these creation accounts to show God's generosity in blessing animals and man with food as a loving Father who crafts the environment for those who are His (Gen. 1:11–12, 29–30; 2:16; Ps. 104:14–17).

The word *mîn* ( ) means a generic "kind;" it is not a technical term. With regard to plants, this "kind" (/*mîn*) indicates a category of plant reproduction by the seed which the plant produces (Gen. 1:11–12). It is described with an emphasis on its kind maintaining the God given order and its fruit sustaining this God given order. With regard to animals, "kind" (/*mîn*) can indicate broad categories of reproduction lineage like fish (Gen. 1:21; Ezek. 47:10), birds (Gen. 1:21; 6:20; 7:14), live stock, creeping things (lizards and insects), and wild animals (Gen. 1:24–25; 6:20; 7:14). It is possible that the word is used in a collective or distributive sense, since it is a singular word with plural referent.[38] As a collective (like flock of sheep), "kind" would refer to more than one within a reproduction lineage. In a distributive sense (like the men wore a suit), "kind" would refer to a quality of reproduction lineages by which the group is described. Pete Williams argues for a distributive sense from references that have a large scale category that would likely include several "kinds" within it (like "winged fowl" in Gen 1:21b; "fish" in Ezek. 47:10).[39] Additionally, the use of "every" (/*kl*) before certain groups (such as "every creeping thing on the ground according to its kind") indicates several "kinds" (Gen. 1:25c; 6:20c; 7:14c). There is no Biblical indication how many "kinds" there are unlike Jubilees 2.13–15 which claims that there are 22 animal "kinds." The word can also mean specific categories within these broader categories to fund kosher lists and even more specific as well, like kite, red kite, falcon, raven, ostrich, owl (additionally: little owl, great owl, and white owl), sea gull, hawk, pelican, cormorant, carrion vulture, stork, heron, hoopoe, locust, devastating locust, cricket, grasshopper, mole, mouse, great lizard, gecko, crocodile, sand reptile and chameleon (Lev. 11:14–19, 22, 29; Deut. 14:13–18). This indicates that "kinds" are recognizable by distinct traits, which are reproducible multigenerationally.

38 Kenneth Turner, "The Kind-ness of God: A Theological Reflection of *Mîn,* "Kind," *CORE Issues in Creation*, 2008; Collective: Walter Kaiser, " " *Theological Wordbook of the Old Testament* (Chicago: Moody Press, 1980), 1:503; Westerman, *Genesis 1–11,* p. 140; Distributive: Paul Beaucamp, *Création et separation* (Paris: Descalée de Bouwer, 1969), Pete J. Williams, "What Does *min* Mean?" *Creation Ex Nihilo Technical Journal* 11/3(1997): 345–52.

39 Pete Williams, "What Does *min* Mean?" *Creation Ex Nihilo Technical Journal* 11/3(1997): 345–6 lists Gen. 1:21a, 21b, 25c; 6:20c; 7:14 (4x) but Kenneth Turner correctly excludes 1:21a because it is plural and if included would make Lev. 11:15; Deut. 14:14 indicate more than one "kind" of raven, which is unlikely ("The Kind-ness of God: A Theological Reflection of *Mîn,* "Kind," *CORE Issues in Creation*, 2008, p. 5–6). The plural also appears in the *Samaritan Pentateuch* Gen. 6:20; *Damascus Document* 4.14–18; *Community Rule* 3:13–14; Williams also identifies plural instances in the *Mishnah* ("What Does *min* Mean?" pp. 347–48).

When it comes to humans, there is no use of "kind" (/*mîn*), for all humans are combined without reference to race, ethnicity, or color. Humanity is not to be divided into "kinds."

Then God created the animals. The creation of the animals involves both the spoken word and the intimacy of personal creation, which indicates a higher form of existence. These animals are created as "living creatures" or more appropriately as "living souls" (*nepeš hayāh/* , Gen. 1:20, 24, 30; 9:10, 12, 15). In Hebrew, the word "soul" is not a special human psychological or spiritual quality, but nephesh refers to a holistic living, willing, moving being. These souls are enumerated as the swimming things, flying things (e.g., birds and insects), livestock, crawling things (e.g., insects, reptiles, and rodents), and wild animals (Gen. 1:20, 24, 30). The animals pre-modernly described as souls are non-microbial animals (fish, foul, insect, reptile, amphibian, and mammal). It is this animal pattern of holistically being a soul that is then applied to man as well in creation (Gen. 2:7). As such souls, these animals and man experience the blessing of God in fertility. Once again the pagan myths are polemicized, for fertility comes from the Creator, Who designed them to be fruitful, multiplying and filling the earth (Gen. 1:22–25). The fact that animals are souls identifies them to be responsible agents, who should and do receive consequences for their sins. For example, the serpent involved in the temptation is judged (Gen. 3:1, 14–15). Additionally in the Noahic covenant animals and humans alike who kill a human are to suffer capital punishment (Gen. 9:5–6). Likewise in the Law, the ox that gores a man to death is to be killed as the owner of the ox is also to be killed if the ox had a propensity to gore people (Ex. 21:28–29). The fact that animals are souls also means that they have limited rights as well, such as eating while they work and being rescued if they fall into a pit even on a Sabbath day (Deut. 25:4; Matt. 12:11–12).[40]

The greatest polemic of the false gods with regard to the animals is the way *tannînim* ( ) or sea monsters occur in the account (Gen. 1:21). Psalm 104:26 mentions them by name as the Leviathan. In Ugarit texts, the tannînim, called Leviathan, are ominous chaos rivals that have preceded Baal, which he must confront in warfare at the beginning; Baal must conquer these with much effort to bring order to the creation.[41]

40 CD 10:15–11:18 and especially 11:13–14 argue that one should not lift an animal out of a pit on the Sabbath; cf. 4Q265; *Miscellaneous Roles* fragment 7, 1.6–9; *m. Besa* 3.4. However, Jesus obviously takes issue with this view when He asks the question, "What man shall there be among you, who shall have one sheep, and it falls into a pit on the Sabbath, will not take hold of it, and lift it out? Of how much more value then is a man than a sheep! So then it is lawful to do good on the Sabbath." (Matt. 12:11–12; Luke 14:5).

41 *Die keilaphabetischen Texte aus Ugarit: Alter Orient und Altes Testament 24/1.* edited by M. Dietrich, O. Loretz, and J. Sanmartin (Münster: Neukirchen-Vluyn, 1976) and enlarged edition: *The Cuneiform Alphabetic Texts from Ugarit, Ras Ibn Hani, and Other Places* (Münster: Ugarit-Verlag, 1995), 1.3.3.37–44.

However, in the Biblical account, the tannînim or Leviathan are God's bath toys; thus no rival at all and the order of the creation is well under way before they are briefly mentioned in passing as created by Elohim. When compared to God, these puny creatures are created by God to play in God's seas. The tannînim experience the blessing of God's fertility along with the rest of the animals. In response to this polemical quality, much of the creation account in Psalm 104 breaks forth in petition and song for the glory of the Lord and the destruction of the enemies of God (Ps. 104:31–35).

An ontological creation hierarchy (or chain of being elevating land animals over those of air and water) might be indicated in Genesis 1, if humans are seen as the climax of creation contents. Such a hierarchy (or chain of being elevating land animals over those of air and water) is retained among the kosher lists. For example, the animals created on day six that are not to be eaten are merely "unclean," whereas the animals created on day five not to be eaten are lower than unclean, they are "detestable" (Lev. 11:4–43).

God is seen as the definitive Creator. In contrast to other ancient Near Eastern cosmologies God is seen in these Biblical accounts of creation as more powerful than any other being in His accomplishment of the creation. The Biblical text portrays God as a greater sovereign than the other cosmologies that require their gods to express huge effort in order to accomplish their attempts to rule. Perhaps the repeated reminders of the creation being good reflect on God as good or the source of goodness. These features in which God demonstrates Himself in Genesis one are then reflected in minute form through the image of God, which pictures God.

Man is the climax of God's creation. This is evident by the parallel structure to vegetation as after the pronouncement of good on their respective days (Gen. 1:10, 25). Additionally, the divine announcement of resolution preceding man's creation shows unique handling of this creation. Furthermore, the repetition of *bārā* ( ) in Genesis 1:27 indicates the highpoint of the creation. Cassuto also makes the case that the change from narrative to poetry ("God created him, male and female, He created them") accentuates man as the noblest of God's creatures.[42] Certainly the image of God and the intimacy with which God creates indicates that man is the superior creation by God.

Image (*selem/* and) and likeness (*demût/* and) are synonyms which convey a copy or a duplicate. Such a concept would not be thought of in this ancient Near Eastern context without accentuating the physical representation. Humans are statues or representations of God. In the ancient Near East the setting up of the

42 U. Cassuto, *A Commentary on the Book of Genesis1–11*, trans. I. Abrahams (Jerusalem: Magnes, 1961), p. 57.

king's statue was equivalent to proclaiming that his domain was over that sphere in which the statue was erected (e.g., Dan. 3:1ff).[43] For example, when in the thirteenth century B.C., pharaoh Ramesses II had his image carved out of rock at the mouth of the river *el-Kelb,* on the Mediterranean north of Beirut, the image meant that he was ruler of this area. The fact that God has set man up as His statues and man has dispersed around the globe in obeying God shows that *Elohim* is sovereign over the whole earth. Wherever we meet a fellow human, God is sovereign there as well.

Both male and female[44] are created in the image of God, thus both picture God as Creator and Sovereign.

One obvious implication in recognizing that we are images of God is likewise to recognize the utter foolishness of crafting an idol, because such lifeless things as idols do not represent the living God nearly so well as the living image does.

As representations of God we humans have the task of being His representatives, to do his will. *Elohim* has been strongly developed in this context as the creative and sovereign One. So humans are to reflect this design parameter of ruling the creation as miniature sovereign (Gen. 1:26–27).

To facilitate the image of God's rule of the creation, God provides blessings of: fruitfulness, to fill the earth, to subdue the earth, and to rule the earth (Gen. 1:26–30; 8:20–9:17).[45] Ruling the earth is both the design goal for we humans[46] and a blessing from God (Gen. 1:26, 28). These elements of blessing are softer than commands because they are within the genre of blessing, which the Blesser, God, grounds (Gen. 2:3; 5:2; 9:1; 12:2–3). *Blessing entails a relationship of privilege, mostly guaranteed by the blesser in relationship, which in this case is God.* In this creation context God's statement accomplishes what it says, so

---

43 Wolff, *Anthropology of the Old Testament* (Philadelphia: Fortress Press, 1974), pp. 160–1; additional support comes from other inscriptions of statuary, like the Tell Fekheriye inscription 1, 12, 15–16 which also use image and likeness words; also 4Q504 frag. 8, lines 4–6. These ancient Near Eastern views are very different than the Patristic options for image, which allow Greco-Roman or Christian context to overrule this ancient Near Eastern context, namely: 1) spiritual- Origen, *Homilies on Genesis* 1.13 in *Fathers of the Church* vol. 71, 2) Power of the Mind- Ambrose, *Hexaemeron* 6.8.44-45 in *Fathers of the Church* 42:256–58, 3) Freewill- Gregory of Nyssa, *On the Origin of Man* in *Gregorii Nysseni Opera Supplementum.* edited by Hadwiga Hörner (Leiden: E. J. Brill, 1972) vol. 10, and 4) Relationality and Trinity- Augustine, On the Trinity 7.6.12 in *Fathers of the Church*, 45:241.

44 There is no hint of seminalism with woman seminally inside Adam as Ephrem the Syrian maintained (*Commentary on Genesis* 1.29.2 in *Fathers of the Church: A New Translation* (Washington D.C.: Catholic University of America Press, 1947), 91:94.

45 The construction in Gen. 1:28 "God blessed them and said ..." identifies the content of the blessing using a narrative connecter waw consecutive as the author repeatedly uses throughout the chapter.

46 This design goal is recognized by Jewish writings (e.g., Ps. 8:4–6; *Jub.* 2.14; *2 En.* 58).

these blessings are guaranteed. God's speech in the first literary unit (Gen. 1–2:4) accomplishes His statement to make it so, even though He uses imperatives in these statements to render in reality the light, separation, waters, lights and swarms (Gen. 1:3, 6, 9, 14, 20). Few would conjecture that the imperative in each of these Divine statements renders light or water culpable for their existence, so God incorporates Divine statements using imperatives in this creation account as statements of His guaranteeing the creation order. However, that does not guarantee that these spoken creations (light, vegetation, and animals) are everywhere, nor does it guarantee all humans will be procreatively fruitful. Blessing makes it generically realizable for the human race, but not necessarily specifically realizable for everyone (Gen. 1:22, 28); some may be infertile without being culpable for sin concerning this. God makes us fruitful, and so corporately we fill the earth. God enables us to subdue, so we can rule.

Though these are God-grounded corporate blessings there is corporate culpability for involvement indicated through the use of imperatives to moral beings. The use of plural Hebrew Qal imperatives for all five blessings "Be fruitful, multiply, fill, subdue, and rule," and the LXX having "be fruitful and multiply" as present imperatives shows the group of humans should as a group participate within the corporate blessing which God provides.[47] However, the LXX use of "fill, subdue and rule" as aorist indicatives softens involvement with these to God's guaranteeing the design plan in this text.

No one is personally culpable if he does not avail himself of all blessings. For example, Jesus had the blessing of having angel protection (Matt. 4:6), but that is no cause for foolish choices. Likewise, the Sabbath blessing only becomes a culpable command when it is rendered into a stipulation within God's Mosaic Covenant for God's elect people Israel (Gen. 2:3; Ex. 20:8–11).

Blessing makes it generically realizable for the human race, but not necessarily specifically realizable for everyone (Gen. 1:22, 28); some may be infertile without being culpable for sin concerning this. God makes us fruitful, and so corporately we fill the earth. God enables us to subdue, so we can rule. There is no surprise that the blessings for the image of God reflect these attributes of God through humans being fruitful, multiplying, filling the earth so that they can subdue and rule the earth (Gen. 1:26–28; 9:1–7). Of course, each of the persons involved in the procreative task is evidencing a minute picture of God's creative blessing.

---

47 Rabbinics took these imperatives as commands and thus considered an individual as culpable if they did not marry and beget children (*m. Yebam.* 6.6; *Pesiq. Rab Kah* 22.2; *m. Git* 4.5; *Gen. Rab.* 23.4; 34.14; *Ex. Rab.* 1.13; Josephus, *Ant.* 4.8.40 #290; *'Abot R. Nat.* 31A; *b. Ber.* 10a; *b. Yebam.* 62b; *b. Qidd.* 29b–30a).

In fact, the concept of image in this context also can be seen as sonship (Gen. 5:1, 3; Luke 3:38). The concept of son of God in the ancient Near East is used of kings. Furthermore, the terms "subdue" and "rule" (*rādâ/* and *kābaš/* , Gen. 1:26, 28) are forceful terms that speak of trampling on others in conquest or vine press to force these others to serve. The naming of the animals and woman by Adam argues that man is in fact operating as an ancient Near Eastern sovereign, for kings have the right to name others and thereby demonstrate that these others are under the dominion of God's image, us (Gen. 2:19, 23; Dan. 1:7).[48] After the Fall the terms subdue and rule are never undone, but as humans become contorted by the lure of sin, so restrictions that limit man's excesses in these areas are seen instead (e.g., Gen. 9:2–6). Man remains viewed in contrast to the creation as a little lower than God with glory and majesty so that he can rule over the works and creatures of God's hands (Ps. 8:4–8).

The creation account in Genesis two emphasizes God in the role as Father creating the environment for His son Adam with the provision for place, resources, occupation, blessings and an arranged marriage. Man should recognize that the resources lovingly enable the vocation, which God has for man. The vocation itself has man expressing his care for the orchard (which is what an ancient Near Eastern garden is). Normally an ancient Near Eastern garden is surrounded by a hedge or a wall to set it off from the outside world (Gen. 2:8; 3:23). The fact that God is met in the garden hints that the garden is sacred space (Gen. 2:8; 3:8–9).[49] In the ancient Near East the meeting place of heaven and earth was on a mountain where a sacred stream ushers forth, which similar description further hints that the garden is sacred space (Gen. 2:10). When humans are finally excluded from the garden, the garden is then seen as holy in comparison to the surrounding area. At that point they are met by *cherubim* at the gate back to the garden, which creatures are associated in the ancient Near East with royalty and temples, thus further hinting that the garden is sacred space (Gen. 3:24).

48 *2 En.* 58 identifies that Adam's inspection and naming of animals is part of his ruling creation. *Jubilees* 3.1–3 contemplates this sovereign naming taking five days for Adam to work through the whole animal kingdom, however the Biblical text give no indication of how long that human activity took to be accomplished.

49 *Jubilees* 3.9–14 develops the garden as sacred space and elaborates on the delay of placing the woman in the garden as a foundation for the instruction of the female issues in the purity code. For development of this Garden of Eden as sacred space see Gordon Wenham, "Sanctuary Symbolism in the Garden of Eden Story" in *Proceedings of the Ninth World Congress of Jewish Studies* (Jerusalem: World Union of Jewish Studies, 1986). Additionally Jon D. Levenson, "The Temple and the World," *Journal of Religion* 64(1984): 275–98 develops the creation narratives as viewing the cosmos as a temple. Furthermore, Kathryn Gleason, "Gardens in Preclassical Times" *Oxford Encyclopedia of Archaeology in the Near East,* ed. E. Meyers (New York: Oxford, 1997), 2:383 develops the close relationship that temples tend to have with gardens in the ancient Near East.

The words of the care of the garden focus humanity toward the sacredness of his task as serving God. For example, "cultivate" (*'ābdāh/*) elsewhere in the Pentateuch expresses the idea of servant to God, which is the highest role a man can have (Gen. 2:15; Ex. 3:12; 10:3, 8, 11, 24, 26). Likewise, the word "keep" (*šāmrāh/*)is used elsewhere in the Pentateuch as obeying God's commands (Gen. 2:15; Ex. 15:26; 16:28; 19:5; 20:6, 8). These words hint that man's responsibility in chapter two may be priestly to balance the creative and regal thrust of chapter one, but all these roles can be subsumed within the role of man being the son of God. Humans have relationship to God accessing this relationship as priests and sons.

Humans reflect God in miniature as creative and ruling sons, including the privilege of availing oneself of the benefits of their situation. Using an infinitive absolute, God emphasized the freedom that humans have in eating any fruit from the garden, except one (Gen. 2:16–17). Such a role as son is however a role of stewardship under the sovereign. The verbs here are masculine singular. Is the singular used because there is only one human, or he alone has this freedom and restriction, or that each faces accountability for their actions? Within this profound generosity, there is one restriction that Adam should not eat from the fruit of the tree of the knowledge of good and evil. There is no evidence that this is an apple tree, and it may have unique fruit to match its unique description. Somehow in the eating of this fruit, there will be a change from the experience of good to an experience of evil or detriment among the good (Gen. 1:4, 10, 12, 18, 21, 25, 31; 2:9, 17–18; 3:5–6, 22). God specifically points out what that detriment is, using an infinitive absolute for emphasis, that on that day you eat of it you shall surely die (Gen. 2:17).

To enable this sonship role, God arranges a marriage for Adam. In fact, the only thing of the two creation accounts that is declared to not be good is that man is alone (Gen. 2:18). The Hebrew for alone (*lbado/*) means without aid or helpless; it does not mean psychologically lonely. The point is not man's need for a companion but that without the women's aid, the male can't do the tasks like: 1) serve/cultivate (perhaps *lbadô* [ ] in Gen. 2:18 is a word play with Gen. 2:15 *'ābdāh* [ ]), and 2) procreate (Gen. 1:28). So the female enables humanity not just in procreation but also in other service to God. Both males and females are needed to accomplish the purposes God has designated for the human race. The woman becomes a helper (*'ezer/*) to her husband, like God who assists in these tasks is also Helper (Gen. 2:18, 20; Ps. 121:1–2). Because she is a helper corresponding (*kenegdô/*) to man, she is seen as a duplicate or corresponding copy of himself. The descriptions of the woman further develop this similarity. The 'rib' (*misal'ḥāyw/*) actually means a 'side portion' as in barbequed ribs that have meat and bone together. Adam recognizes that they are made of the same flesh and bone, so that he poetically names her woman (*'îšāh/*), which contains the name man (*'îš/*) within it (Gen. 2:23). The use of poetry at this point emphasizes the value and joy of the marriage relationship as it is designed by God. In the commentary for Israelite readers, arranged marriages enable the man to leave or forsake a oneness with one's parents in order to cleave or physically join to each other in loyal love, ushering in sexual intercourse and progeny. This drive for marriage can be seen as an outworking of the original union of one flesh of man and woman in the creation.

God "ceased" (*yklw/*) creating the heavens and the earth, and all their hosts that He had created (Gen. 2:1–2). *Yklw/* is best seen as the ending of a phase of creation, which then permits further development within nature. Such a view challenges what some creationists have taught as grounded in this word. For example, George McCready Price writes, "*Creation is a completed work and is not now going on.*"[50] He argues that this statement is clearly taught in Genesis 1–2 and further supported by the institution of the Sabbath.

> This aspect of the case [is] very clearly stated in the first and second chapters of Genesis, but in addition we have the record of the institution of the Sabbath which was primarily designed as a memorial of a *completed* creation.[51]

While *yklw/* can mean a complete finish, within the Pentateuch in the piel imperfect as here (e.g., Gen. 2:1–2; 49:33; Ex. 40:33), however, it usually means a *finishing of the preceding narrative* or *finishing a phase* of which there is more to come.[52] William Domeris and Cornelis Van Dam define the word "in a positive sense to denote the end of a period of time."[53] For example, the word is used of God *finishing* talking at that time with a person, but God returned to talk with that individual again (Gen. 17:22 with 22:1–2; similar in Gen. 24:45 with 34–49; Ex. 34:33 with 34; Deut. 32:45 with 33:1–29). Similar to this is when camels have *finished* drinking at that occasion but will drink again (Gen. 24:19), or when the Israelite is finished gathering his tithe, so that he can give it and then do so again the next year or when appropriate (Deut. 26:12). Likewise, Moses *finished* setting up the Tabernacle several times in

50 George McCready Price, *Q.E.D. or New Light on the Doctrine of Creation* (New York: Fleming H. Revell Co., 1917), p. 42 in *Selected Works of George McCready Price,* edited by Ronald Numbers (New York: Garland Publishing, 1995), p. 136.

51 George McCready Price, "Can Revelation and Evolution be Harmonized?" *Signs of the Times* 53:4 (1926): 11.

52 E. Kautzsch and A. E. Cowley, *Gesenius' Hebrew Grammar* (Oxford: Clarendon Press, 1976), p. 328 calls this instance an imperfect and describes it as finishing the preceding narrative.

53 "3983" in *New International Dictionary of Old Testament Theology & Exegesis.* edited by Willem VanGemeren (Grand Rapids: Zondervan, 1997), v. 2, p. 641.

series at different locations (e.g., Ex. 40:33; Num. 7:1). In fact Moses' statement of this *completion* of the Tabernacle (Ex. 40:33) may be parallel and occurring at about the same time as Moses' description that God *completes* His creation as sacred space and establishes sacred time (Gen. 2:1 and more on this below and in reaction to the Fall). So the choice of *yklw/* in this creation account indicates that this phase of divine creation is complete, not that all divine creation is complete.

If this word *yklw/* is used to indicate a complete finishing with no further development by that creator, then an additional adverb would be added to indicate the finality of the creation project. For example, in Deuteronomy 31:24 Moses *finishing* the writing of the Torah is further modified by *tmm/* which indicates that it is composed "until it was complete." Without this additional modifier, the word *yklw/* does not require a finality of completion.

So the choice of *yklw/* in this of account (Gen. 2:1–2) indicates that this phase of divine creation is complete, not that all divine creation is complete. For example, in Kingdom, God creates (*bārā/*) a new heaven and new earth and within them He creates (*bārā/*) a new Jerusalem (Isa. 65:17–18; also Jer. 31:22). In forgiveness God creates (*bārā/*) a new heart (Ps. 51:10[12]). Furthermore, in miracles God creates manna, wine, fish and bread that had not been there before (Ex. 16:4, 15; Matt. 14:14–21; 15:32–39; Mark 6:34–44; 8:1–9; Luke 9:12–17; John 2:7–10; 6:5–13). That is, God miraculously provided manna (meaning "what's it?") in the wilderness for Israel's journey, where it hadn't been before or since. Jesus' changing water to wine does not merely exchange Jesus' water with wine from some winery, and Jesus' multiplying bread to the 5000 and 4000 does not reduce some baker's supply somewhere, and wild living fish were not lifted out of the Sea of Galilee without nets to appear in Jesus' baskets as He multiplied them. These are actual creation miracles because God can continue to create today, and God and Jesus have continued to create whenever miracles occur. However, this initial phase of the creation was finished in six days. The choice of *yklw/* permits continued development produced by the Creator God, though this six day phase of creation is complete.

With the close of the creation account in Genesis one there is the development of sacred time, which serves as the temporal climax for this first creation account, structured as it is by the repeated temporal framework (Gen. 2:1–3).[54] God set this day apart as a day in the calendar, which reflects God's stopping (*ykl/* , *yšbt/*) the creation process, not that he needed to rest. Later as the sign of the Mosaic covenant for Israel this sacred seventh day of creation is incorporated as the rationale for the Sabbath (*šbt/*) day (Ex. 20:8–11; 31:12–17).

54 To preserve the Sabbath as completely work free in Genesis 2:2 LXX, Samaritan Pentateuch, *Peshitta*, *Jubilees* 2.1.16a and Genesis Midrash *Bereshith Rabbah* reads "On the sixth day God ended His work."

The second Genesis creation account continues to explain the origin of temptation, sin and judgment (Gen. 3). This account provides a narrative that reflects the historical account of the fall of humanity into sin but also is selective in recounting the process of how temptation works so that Israelite readers and now Christian readers might not follow into the way of temptation. The account also provides a view of God as He responds to this temptation and sin that is instructive about human relationship with Him. The fact that man and woman are both naked and not ashamed shows that they are at ease with one another without any fear of exploitation and potential for evil in contrast to the tensions that will come as will be spelled out in the wake of the fall. There is however a word play which shows that in their naked (*'ărûmmîm/*) innocence, the snake was particularly shrewd (*'ărûm/*) to take advantage of them (Gen. 2:25–3:1).

9.2. Excursis: The Serpent in Genesis 3 is a Snake

The tempter serpent (*nahaš/*) in Genesis 3 is a *snake*, which will crawl on its belly, not a satan which is rarely developed in the O.T.

The serpent (*nahaš/*) within the ancient Near Eastern imagery could be a mythologically flying serpent within limits. For example winged serpents in Egyptian iconography are portrayed in a funerary papyrus of the twenty-first dynasty *Papyrus of Henuttawy* containing "a winged snake with two pairs of legs...A caption tell us 'death the great god, who made gods and men' a personification of death."[55] Likewise, the second Temple Jewish source *The Books of the Secrets of Enoch* identifies winged serpents with Seraphim "I looked and saw other flying creatures, their names...Chalkadri wonderful and strange," creatures Morfill identified with the Seraphim of Isaiah 6.[56] However, the Prophets and the Rabbinics universally identified the mythological serpent with Egypt and Pharaoh under God's curse from the exodus (Isa. 27:1).[57]

Serpents (*nahaš/*) in Mosaic theology of the Pentateuch are either: a) affirmed as good channels of the work of God (like a blessing to Dan, Moses rod, and the healing bronze snake), or b) threatening crawling animals (Gen. 3:1, 14; 49:17; Ex. 4:3; 7:15; Num. 21:6–9; Deut. 8:15; 2 Kgs. 18:4; 1 Cor. 10:9). In only one Isaiah text is *nahaš/* used of a mythological *serpent*, Leviathan, which is in that text described as an animal living in the sea, destroyed by God (Isa. 27:1). In 11 of the 14 Mosaic instances (or 79%) *nahaš/* refers to a crawling animal. The other Mosaic texts take *nahaš/* as a metaphor of blessing based on such a *snake* and a bronze reproduction of such a *snake* (Gen. 49:17;

55 Erik Hornung, *Conceptions of God in Ancient Egypt* (Ithaca: Cornell University Press, 1982), p. 81.

56 W. R. Morfill, *The Book of the Secrets of Enoch* (Oxford: Clarendon Press, 1896), pp. xxx, 12, 14.

57 *Ex. Rab.* 3.12.

Num. 21:9). So in Mosaic theology *nahaš/* should be seen as a *snake*. Evil is not invading on the back of one greater than man, but rather a subordinate snake as an expression of the creation is seen as rebelling against man who is the miniature sovereign, as the image of God. That is, there is no pre-existing evil, rather free-will snake choice to rebel becomes evil in the choice to rebel. So the humans and a snake choose to rebel in the same event, and God places them under the oracle of curse in response to their rebellious free choice.

Many in Christendom see an age old struggle with Satan and humans heavily developed out of the O.T.[58] However, there is no mention of Satan (*śāṭān/*) in this Genesis text.

The term *śāṭān/* is used as a descriptive for "adversary" in the O.T. in the following ways: a) of the angel of the LORD (which is likely God Himself) as the adversary to Balaam (Num. 22:22, 32), b) an ambiguous motivator of David to number Israel in 1 Chronicles 21:1, which may be the LORD since it is the LORD in 2 Samuel 24:1 who motivates David to this decision, c) an ambiguous accuser of Joshua the high priest (Zech. 3:1–2), d) some sort of heavenly being among the Sons of God who accuses God and Job (Job 1:6–2:7), e) Human adversaries (including: David, sons of Zeruiah, wicked men, Hadad, and Rezan; 1 Sam. 29:4; 2 Sam. 19:22 [MT 23], 1 Kgs. 4:4 [18]; 11:14, 23, 25; Pss. 38:20 [21]; 109:6, 20, 29). Throughout the whole O.T., 40% of the instances of the word *śāṭān/* are of humans as adversaries and a similar 40% (exclusively in the book of Job) are of a heavenly being among the sons of God. Possibly in Job alone the descriptive *śāṭān/* mentioned ten times in quick succession may take on a quality of a name, which displays his adversarial character in that context. The only Mosaic instance of *śāṭān/* is of the angel of the LORD or possibly God Himself. No Biblical text places a named angel Satan in the Genesis 3 account. So to claim that Satan is in the Genesis temptation is to assume something which the Biblical text no where claims to be the case.

Genesis 3 presents the tempter as an animal. The in Genesis 3:1 is best seen as a superlative "*more clever than* all the other animals" and thus indicating that the serpent is an animal.[59] The Rabbinics (that is mainstream Jewish interpretation) universally and many Essene sources identify this serpent of Genesis 3 as an animal, a snake, whose descendants bite Israelites in Numbers 21:6.[60] Many of the patristics also

58 Greg Boyd, *God at War* (Downers Grove: InterVarsity Press, 1998).

59 This argument is presented by Rabbi Eleazar in *Gen. Rab.* 20.3.

60 *Jub.* 3.17–19, 23; *Sib. Or.* 1.40–45, 59–61; *Greek Apocalypse of Ezra* 2.17; *Gen. Rab.* 19.1; 20.3–4; 21.4; *Ex. Rab.* 3.12; *Num. Rab.* 14.12; 19.22; *Koheleth Rab.* 10.1; Rabbi Yose in *The Fathers According to Rabbi Nathan* 1.17.1.E. It is coincidental in *The Gilgamesh Epic* tablet 11, column 8 that a snake ate the thorny bush "reborn man" collected from under the sea by Gilgamesh and thus robs him of immortality and enables the snake in the story to molt his skin every month.

follow this view that the serpent is merely an animal,[61] while others under the influence of neoplatonism allegorize the serpent to be identified with Satan.[62] Gerhard von Rad develops that the serpent is a snake.

> The serpent which now enters the narrative as one of God's created animals (ch. 2.19). In the narrator's mind, therefore, it is not the symbol of a "demonic" power and certainly not a Satan. What distinguishes it a little from the rest of the animals is exclusively its cleverness.[63]

Claus Westermann,[64] John Skinner,[65] E. A. Speiser,[66] and Gordon Wenham[67] agree that Satan is nowhere in Genesis 3, rather it is a conflict between a *serpent*, humans, and God Who judges them all. Obviously some other commentaries disagree,[68] but that is the essence of the word study before us.

The big picture sees the Genesis creation account explaining the origin of temptation, sin and judgment (Gen. 3). This account provides a narrative that reflects the historical account but also is selective in recounting the process of how temptation works so that Israelite readers and now Christian readers might not follow into the way of temptation. The account also provides a view of God as He responds to this temptation and sin that is instructive about human relationship with Him. The fact that man and woman are both naked and not ashamed shows that they are at ease with one another without any fear of exploitation and potential for evil in contrast to the tensions that will come as will be spelled out in the wake of the fall (Gen. 2:25). There is however a word play which shows that in their *naked* (*'ărûmmîm/*) innocence which the serpent was particularly *shrewd* (*'ārûm/*) to take advantage of them (Gen. 2:25–3:1). For example, this particular serpent is described as a beast with unusual craftiness like being able to talk, and there is no mention

61 E.g., *Theophilus to Autolycus* 2.21 in *The Ante-Nicene Fathers,* edited by Alexander Roberts and James Donaldson (Edinburgh: T & T Clark, 1989) 2:102; an anonymous author of *Genesis* 130–4 in *The Ante-Nicene Fathers* 4:134; Ephrem the Syrian, *Commentary on Genesis* 2.15.1 in *Fathers of the Church* 91:107.

62 E.g., Augustine, *Two Books on Genesis Against the Manicaeans* 2.14.20 in *Fathers of the Church* 84:116.

63 Gerhard von Rad, *Genesis: A Commentary* (Philadelphia: The Westminster Press, 1972), p. 87.

64 Claus Westermann, *Genesis 1–11: A Commentary* (Minneapolis: Augsburg Publishing House, 1974), pp. 237–8.

65 John Skinner, *A Critical and Exegetical Commentary on Genesis* (Edinburgh: T & T Clark, 1930), pp. 71–4, 79–82.

66 E. A. Speiser, *Genesis. The Anchor Bible* (Garden City: Doubleday, 1986), pp. 25–28.

67 Gordon Wenham, *Genesis 1–15*, pp. 72–3, 78–9.

68 E.g., Augustine, *Two Books on Genesis Against the Manicaeans* 2.14.20 in *Fathers of the Church* 84:116; John Calvin, *Genesis*, 1:140-50; Derek Kidner, *Genesis*, pp. 70–71.

that Eve was surprised nor that other snakes need to have these abilities. However, Jesus alludes to serpents as having a shrewd character in order for Him to instruct His disciples in their being prudent ambassadors for the Kingdom (Matt. 10:16). Jesus' allusion increases the likelihood that we should think of a serpent as the deceiver in this Genesis 3 account, since Jesus likely does; what else would Matthew 10:16 likely refer.

Genesis does not develop other animals talking like is done within the Pseudepigraphical *Jubilee* 3.28 (where animals lose this ability in the Fall of the Creation)[69] or C. S. Lewis in *The Narnia Chronicles: The Last Battle* (where some animals lose this ability in individual non-alliance with Aslan). The only other talking animal in the O.T. is mentioned in Numbers 22:21–34, where Balaam is berated for his spiritual blindness by his ass. However, that instance of animal conversation could be supernaturally unique because there are other miracles such as a threatening angel with a sword in the account. It is possible that other animals might have some of these conversational abilities, but the Biblical text just does not say how extensive animal reasoning and communication happens to be. However, there had been some hint in the creation account that humankind's miniature sovereign role would be resisted by the choice of such forceful terminology as *rādâ/* and *kābaš/* (Gen. 1:26, 28). Evil emerges in the human rebellion of disobedience.

A closer look at God's oracle of judgment against the serpent in Genesis 3:13–15, would include first that he is an animal; to the serpent, God says, "Cursed are you more than all cattle, and more than every beast of the field." Notice the direct address is to the serpent ( ) and the singular second person address as suffix pronouns "you" (, , , ,), and the singular address verbs "cursed are you" ( ) and "you shall eat" ( ) all refer back to the nearest referent, the serpent being addressed. There is no allusion to another beyond or behind the serpent with the singular "you" statements referring to the serpent. Next the description presents that the curse is appropriate of the serpents as snakes elsewhere in the Mosaic context, for these snakes crawl on their belly[70] in the dust with their heads close to the ground so that they could be described metaphorically as eating dust. Elsewhere *serpents* (*nahaš/*) are described as eating the dust due the position of its head so close to the ground (Isa. 65:25; Mic. 7:17). This curse could also extend figuratively to stand for abject humiliation of subjection and defeat, especially before enemies (Ps. 72:9; Isa. 49:23; Mic. 7:17).

Part of the curse now extends to the progeny of this serpent and humans (Gen. 3:15). Addressing the serpent, God refers that there will be enmity between the woman Eve and this very serpent. This enmity would then extend multigenerationally between her seed and "your

69 Also *Apocalypse of Moses* 10–12 and *Life of Adam and Eve* 37–39.

70 The description of crawling on its belly identifies snakes as unclean in Leviticus 12:42.

seed" (*zer'ak/*), using the same phrase that God uses to address Abram with "your seed" ( ). The word for "seed" (*zer'ak/*) is a collective referring to plural descendents of snakes, and humans (compare with other Genesis *zer'ak/* texts like Gen. 15:3–5, 13, 18; 16:10; 17:7–19). So there is no allusion behind the serpent by the word "seed" (*zer'ak/*); there is only the continuing multigenerational progeny and their hostility between humans and serpents, which prefigures the Israelite experience with the snake attacks of Numbers 21:6. However, this hostility is not a collective biting and crushing but one of an individual on individual, "He will bruise you on the head, and you will bruise him on the heel" (Gen. 3:15). In the Hebrew the pronouns are all masculine since "serpent" (*nahaš/*) and "seed" (*zer'ak/*) are both masculine. However, the LXX merely copies this phrase "He will bruise you on the head, and you will bruise him on the heel" using masculine Greek pronouns to follow the Hebrew masculine pronouns, in spite of the word for seed in the Greek ( ) shifting to the neuter, which was suggested by Ken Turner to possibly be what Gordon Wenham might mean by referencing the Satan view as clear in the Septuagint.[71] However, I think Wenham means that the Apocryphal book *The Wisdom of Solomon* which does mention the devil clearly since he is listing clear textual references and by the fifth century A.D. is being bound into the Christian Bible as part of the Apocrypha, but never was embraced by mainstream Judaism as canonical in the LXX pre-bound condition. Remember the LXX in Gen. 3:15 simply copies the MT with the masculine pronouns, so it is trying to be faithful to the MT text. Additionally, the neuter word for "seed" ( ) in LXX always takes *masculine* pronouns with it in all other Genesis verses where they occur, following the MT and making no new novel theological point (e.g., Gen. 15:13; 17:7, 9; 22:17; 24:60). Additionally, as in personal address, this *singular* verbal address is retained in MT and LXX when it includes the seed as well (Gen. 3:15; 28:14 "*you* [singular] shall spread out to the west, east, north, and south;" 48:19 "his seed *will become* [singular]"). So, the shift in Genesis 3:15 from addressing the serpent as "you" to the seed as "he" and "him" is the normal manner in which the Hebrew and Greek pronouns function in the MT and LXX with reference to "seed" (*zer'ak/* ;). Thus no new theological point of an empowering agent is being implied by the singular in MT and LXX, or by the LXX grammatical non-agreement of neuter "seed" ( ) and masculine pronouns and verbs, as the LXX follows the MT.

In the cursed hostility between humans and serpents, both humans and serpents will kill the other. The word for bruise (*šwp/*) is the same for the serpents as for the humans and elsewhere it is used of a dominating covering (Job 9:17; Ps. 139:11). Such a dominating bruise

71 Gordon Wenham, *Genesis 1–15*, p. 80.

on the head is a deadly crushing blow that kills, such as the millstone that crushed Abimelech's head (Judg. 9:53). This crushing of the head is accomplished singularly by a human on a snake, based on the singular pronominal suffixes of the oracle of curse ( ).

Elsewhere in the Mosaic context a serpent biting on the heel kills the humans, unless God supernaturally stays the effect of the venom (e.g., Num. 21:6–9). This oracle of curse prefigures the Israelite experience with the snake attacks of Numbers 21:6 (also Deut. 8:15; 1 Cor. 10:9). Thus Genesis 3:15 is not a first statement of the gospel, for snakes and humans continue with such hostility. The term *nahaš/* continues to be used throughout the O.T. for venomous serpents biting and destroying humans (Num. 21:6–7; Deut. 8:15; Pss. 58:4(5); 140:3(4); Prov. 23:32; Ecc. 10:8, 11; Jer. 8:17; Amos 5:19; 9:3). Thus based on this Genesis text, there are some instances of God creating venomous serpents as a normal feature of the creation, only to be utilized as a feature of God's curse of sin, a view affirmed by Josephus.[72]

Psalm 91:13 promises that with God's help, the chosen in Israel will trample under foot dangerous serpents and wild beasts.[73] This sentiment is extended by the *Testament of Levi* 18.12 which promises that after the apocalyptic battle, the Lord will grant his children to trample on spirits.

With reference to the Genesis 3 event, 1 Timothy 2:14 identifies that Adam was not deceived but that Eve was deceived ( ), as they fell into transgression. No comments are made in this context about the identity of the deceiver. Whereas, in 2 Corinthians 11:3 Eve is described as being deceived ( ) by the serpent ( ), which serves as a historical grounding for the exhortation that the church should not be led astray from the simplicity and purity to Christ. Notice that in 2 Corinthians 11:3 the deceiver at the Fall is said to be a serpent, not Satan. This N.T. serpent reference identifies the serpent with craftiness ( ), which takes his ability in a unfavorable crafty direction than the LXX Genesis 3:1 development for the serpent being crafty in a more wise direction ( ),[74] and subsequent Jesus' disciple/ serpent prudence (; Matt. 10:16).

Without referring to Genesis 3 or the creation-fall account, Romans 16:20 encourages the plural church that "the God of peace will soon crush Satan under your-all feet." The term for crush ( ) is forceful requiring Satan to be utterly defeated before the church, in the same manner as Judas Maccabeus reassured his followers that they would crush the numerically superior foe before them.[75] Robert Jewett argues

72 Josephus, *Ant.* 1.45–50.4.

73 Robert Jewett, *Romans* (Minneapolis: Fortress Press, 2007), p. 994.

74 Walter Bauer; William Arndt; and F. W. Gingrich, *A Greek-English Lexicon of the New Testament and Other Early Christian Literature*. Chicago: the University of Chicago Press, 1957), pp. 612–13.

75 *1 Macc.* 3.22.

that in *1 Maccabees* that this term of crushing is a technical expression for "violent, military triumph."[76] The metaphor does not refer to Genesis 3:15 in any clear way in the Romans context but to the broadly depicted metaphor of a completely defeated person under the conqueror's feet, as developed in Jewish second Temple literature,[77] and from Greco-Roman Temples and history.[78] Thus blessing the church with such a final victory over Satan is praying for the eschatological conquest of Christ and Kingdom, in which the church will rule with Him.[79]

John 8 develops Satan as a "murderer from the beginning" ( ), in which "beginning" ( ) is used in the near context as the beginning of Jesus' ministry (John 8:25, 44). In fact, apart from the introduction uses of in the gospel of John (John 1:1–2), the other instances or 75% of the use of in the gospel are of the beginning of Jesus' ministry (John 2:11; 6:64; 8:25, and likely 44; 15:27; 16:4). There is no mention of the creation or Fall of humanity in this John 8 context. It is best to interpret the word "beginning" ( ) by how it is used in this same context, and the Johannine emphasis, which then means that refers to the *beginning of Jesus' ministry*, rather than assuming it to refer to Genesis 3. At the beginning of Jesus' ministry Satan tempts Jesus to try to kill Him by having Him throw Himself off the horn of the Temple (Matt. 4:5–6; Luke 4:9). When Jesus announces His ministry in the Nazareth synagogue those in attendance try to kill Him (Luke 4:28–30). The religious leaders have a lineage of being those who murdered the prophets (e.g., Matt. 23:31). The subject of Satan murdering through the Jewish leadership (which has aligned with Satan) is the immediately preceding context to the statement for how Satan is a murderer from the beginning. The religious leaders have been seeking Jesus' life (John 8:40, 42–47, 59).

In 1 John 3:8, "the devil has sinned from the beginning." Once again notice that creation and the Fall are not in the context of this passage. Like in the gospel of John, so here in his epistle the strong emphasis of the use of is of the *beginning of Jesus' ministry* which then makes Jesus able to be seen, handled, proclaimed, and then heard by which they obtained everlasting life (1 John 1:1, 2:7, 24 [2x]; 3:11). While some commentators wish to see 1 John 1:1 as in the pattern of a pre-creation "beginning" as occurred in John 1:1–3 the emphasis in 1 John 1:1 is that which is present which can be heard, seen, and handled for John to say

---

76 Robert Jewett, *Romans*, p. 994; *1 Macc*. 3.23; 4.10, 30, 36; 5.7, 21, 43; 7.42–43; 8.4–6; 9.7, 15–16, 68; 10.52–53, 82; 13.51; 14.13.

77 *1 Macc*. 3.22–3; 4.10, 30, 36; 5.7, 21, 43; 7.42–43; 8.4–6; 9.7, 15–16, 68; 10.52–53, 82; 13.51; 14.13; *T. Levi* 18.12.

78 A. Gotsmich, "Die 'grausame' Aphrodite am Gigantenfries des Pergamener Altars," *AA* 56(1941): 844–79; Michael Malaise, *Les conditions de penetration et de diffusion des cultes Égyptiens en Italie, EPRO 22* (Leiden: Brill, 1972), pp. 179–80; Diodorus Siculus, sect. 17.100.8.

79 Robert Jewett, *Romans*, p. 994–5.

that the apostles saw him and witness concerning Him. This empirical viewing and handling emphasis strongly refers to the humanity of Jesus. Such humanity of Jesus was there in the beginning of Jesus' ministry when the apostles heard, saw and handled Him but His humanity was not there before creation. So based on the empirical emphasis of 1 John 1:1–3 context, Raymond Brown concludes that the most plausible way to understand in 1 John 1:1 is with the emphasis of the context, namely the beginning of Jesus' ministry when the apostles observed Jesus, thus consistent with the emphasis of this term ( ) in the Gospel of John.[80] In 1 John 2:13–14, the one who has been from the beginning is probably Jesus, since: 1) Jesus has been the empirically handled Word of life which witnesses to brings eternal life (1 John 1:1–2), and 2) the Father is other than He and we are in a context in which the believers are confessing the Father and the Son (1 John 2:22–24). However, the term is ambiguous in 1 John 2:13–14 as to which beginning is being referred to, but I am more inclined to understand it in light of its use in the near context (1 John 2:7, 24 [2x]) and the majority use in the epistle, so I take these references of in 1 John 2:13–14 as referring to the beginning of Jesus' ministry. With clearly six of the nine references (65%) of and likely eight of these (89%) best taken as referring to the beginning of Jesus' ministry, then 1 John 3:8 is best taken in that manner as well. Likewise, with the references of just before and after this text (1 John 2:24; 3:11) referring to the beginning of Jesus' ministry, it is better to take 1 John 3:8 as making reference to the beginning of Jesus' ministry as well. This means that the devil was sinning at the beginning of Jesus' ministry. Remember, at the beginning of Jesus' ministry Satan tempts Jesus to worship him and try for a shortcut to Kingdom (Matt. 4:1–11; Mark 1:13; Lk. 4:2–13).

Revelation 12:9 and 20:2 develops that Satan has a long standing conflict with the woman (Israel) and her son (Christ). The woman is not named, though she births a son, Who is described in Revelation 12:5 as a Son Who will rule the nations with a rod of iron, and is caught up into the heavenly throne room by the Christian's monotheistic God. This imagery already in the Revelation context identifies the Son as Jesus Christ (Rev. 1:12–20; 2:26–27). The previous paragraphs show that John is concerned with Satan opposing Christ throughout His earthly ministry (John 6:70; 8:44; 13:2, 27; 1 John 3:8). With the son being Christ, the views that propose the woman to be a pagan deity or mythological character are clearly excluded. This leaves Jewish-Christian views that conjecture the mother as Eve, Israel or Mary. No texts fit the woman's description as closely as those of Israel. Of these options, only Israel is described by the sun, moon and 12 stars prior to the composition of Revelation (Gen. 37:9). Second Temple literature multi-generationally extend this

80 Raymond Brown, *The Epistles of John* (Garden city: Doubleday, 1982), pp.157–8

description of sun, moon and stars upon the people of Abraham, Isaac, Jacob and the twelve tribes.[81] Only Israel and Mary have undergone an exodus into the wilderness, but of these only Israel is described Biblically and by second Temple sources to undertake an exodus eschatologically as Revelation seems to be describing (Deut. 30:4–5; Isa. 32:15; 35:1; 40:3; 41:18; 43:19-20; 51:3; Jer. 31:2; Ezek. 34:25; Rev. 12:6).[82] So it is best to see the woman in Revelation 12 as Israel birthing the Messiah in this context.

Second Temple literature presents Satan as the accuser of Israel[83] and Michael as the defender of Israel in the heavenly court.[84] This Jewish tradition prefigures Revelation 12:7–10 and shows a long standing conflict between Satan and Israel (with Michael) that can be described as ancient. The description of "serpent of old" could refer to Satan as the adversary who has such a long standing conflict with Israel.

There is no direct comment or description of the creation or the Fall of humanity in this context, so it should not be read on to the Genesis 3 text. However, there is the possibility that such an apocalyptic text is framing things in a grand mythological manner common among the ancient near-East and Greek context.[85] However, Jewish use of combat myths polemics in destruction, rather than embracing the chaos serpent Rahab and Leviathan as an ongoing threatening agent (Job 41:1; Pss. 74:14; 87:4; 89:10; 104:26; Isa. 27:1; 51:9). If combat myths are used in Revelation 12 it does not seem to be in the Biblical use of polemic, and the myths would have been altered to a Christianized version to include Messiah Jesus.

The primary description of Satan in this Revelation 12 context is as a dragon (; 7 times in the context), though he is mentioned in

81 *T. Abr.* B 7.4-16; *Ex. Rab.* 15:6; *Lev. Rab.* 30:2; *Num. Rab.* 2:4, 13 and 9:14; *Deut. Rab.* 1:14; *Midr. Pss.* 22:11-12; *Sifre* Deut. 10:47; *Pirke de Rabbi Eliezer* 42; *Tanna debe Eliyyahu,* Pirke Hay-Yeridot, S, p. 56; *Pesikta de Rab Kahana*, Piska 22; Greg Beale, *The Book of Revelation* (Grand Rapids: Eerdmans, 1999), pp. 625–6.

82 1QH 3.7-12; 1QM 1.2-3; 1QS 8.12-15; 9:18-21; 4QpPs a; *Ex. Rab.* 2:4; *Sifre* Deut. 31:3; *Midr.* Ruth 5.6; *Midr.* Cant. 2.9.3; *Pesikta Rabbati* 15.10; *Pesikta de Rab Kahoma* 5.9.

83 *Jub.* 1.20; 17.15–16; 18.9–12; 48.15–18; *1 En.* 40.7; *T. Levi* 5.6; *T. Dan* 6.2.

84 1QM 13.10–13; 1QS 3.18–25; *Test. Levi* 5.6; *Test. Dan* 6.1–6; *Midr. Rab.* Ex. 18:5; *b. Yoma* 77a; *Pesikta Rabbati* 44; Greg Beale, *The Book of Revelation* (Grand Rapids: Eerdmans, 1999), pp. 661–2.

85 Ancient Near East: H. Gunkel, *Schöpfung und Chaos in Urzeit und Endzeit: Eine religionsgeschichtliche Untersuchung über Gen 1 und Ap. Joh. 12* (Göttingen: Vandenhoeck & Ruprecht, 1895), pp. 171–398, esp. 379–98; and Greek: A. Deiterich, *Abraxas: Studien zur Religionsgeschichte des späteren Altertums.* Leipzig: Teubner, 1891), pp. 117–22; W. Bousset, *Textkritische Studien zum Neuen Testament. TU 11/4* (Leipzig: Hinrichs.1894, 1906), pp. 350–56; J. Fontenrose; W. K. Hendrick; and A. Yarbro Collins, (1959). *Python: A Study in Delphic Myth.* Berkeley: University of California, 1959), p. 210; David Aune, *Revelation 6–16. Word Biblical Commentary.* Nashville: Thomas Nelson Publishing, 1998), pp. 670–93; Lucan, 1685, sect. 60.5.79–81; Lucian, 1882, sect. 300.9.

passing (2 times in the context) as a serpent utilizing the same word as the LXX does of the snakes. This description of Satan as a "serpent of old" ( ) in this context would likely indicate: 1) the long standing conflict that Satan has with Israel, the Messiah Jesus, or the people that surround Christ, as the context of Revelation 12:1-6 develops (also Rev. 2:9–10, 13, 24; 3:9). Thus this conflict would likely be over a millennium long by the time of John's writing and is a couple more millennium to our day. Eschatologically, Satan continues the conflict when he is released after the future millennium by then deceiving some on the field of battle to try to destroy the saints, but Satan and his allies are destroyed (Rev. 20:2, 7–10). Other options include: 2) Satan's involvement near creation and the Fall, or 3) the mythological, longstanding conflict in the heavenlies, but I have already discussed some reasons why these options are less likely.

To help further decide between these options a word study of (of old) is in order. Some take umbrage in the root of being that of "beginning" ( ), and Liddell and Scott defining the term "from beginning or origin."[86] This option might support view two or three above. However, with no mention of creation or Fall in the context, there would actually be more evidence between these options in favor of the mythological serpent view. However, no evidence is marshaled for this basic definition by Liddell and Scott for this meaning, only an allusion to the root . Remember that in Johannine writing refers to the *beginning of Jesus' ministry* 81% of the time (John 2:11; 6:64; 8:25, 44; 15:27; 16:4; 1 John 1:1; 2:7 [2x], 13–14, 24 [2x]; 3:8, 11; 2 Jn. 5–6). Furthermore, Liddell and Scott's top three definitions with evidence are: "ancient," "old fashioned" and "former." Here we need to be careful that we do not define the meaning of a term by its root (the root fallacy),[87] for the meaning of terms is defined by their use. So the meaning of is best understood as "a former time" based on Jewish-Christian use of and before the time John writes Revelation (i.e., LXX, N.T. and Josephus). These meanings based on use can be separated as follows: before the flood (3 millennium years; 2 Pet. 2:5); the era of Moses and the conquest (400–700 years; Pss. 44:1[43:2]; 76:5[6]; 78[79]:8; Isa. 25:1; 37:26);[88] post-Mosaic torah teaching which the listeners have heard (1400 to 1 years; Matt. 5:21, 27, 33; Acts 15:21); Jesus was viewed by some as a resurrected prophet (800–600 years; Luke 9:8, 19); ambiguous former judgment or wisdom (Judg. 5:21; 1 Sam. 24:13[14]; 1 Kgs. 5:10; Isa. 22:9, 11);[89] three to six decades (Ps. 142:5; Isa. 43:18; Lam. 1:7; 2:17;

86 Henry George Liddell and Robert Scott, *A Greek-English Lexicon* (Oxford: Clarendon Press, 1996), p. 251.

87 D. A. Carson, *Exegetical Fallacies* (Grand Rapids: Baker, 1996), pp. 28–33.

88 Josephus, *Ant.* 7.171.

89 *Sir.* 39:1; *Wis. Sol.* 8:8; 13:10; Josephus, *Ant.* 9.264.

Acts 21:16);[90] about sixteen years before, around the founding of Christianity (Acts 15:7), within the last few years when the old character was disposed of and we were made new in Christ (2 Cor. 5:17); and in the surrounding context (Ps. 138:5). None of these texts takes this term as referring to the creation or Fall of humanity. Only one of these texts (2 Pet. 2:5) or 3% places the term as ancient in the early pre-flood stage of humanity. Seven of these texts or 22% describes events of 400 to 700 years before the writing. Seven of these texts or 22% describe as within the last few decades before writing. Eight of these texts or 25% present as an ambiguous former era. A couple of instances indicate merely a few years. The emphasis of the N.T. use of is that of since the torah and prophet era, or hundreds of years. Such a length of time would easily fit the longevity of conflict which Satan has with Israel. There is no need to conjecture about more time than this to require either the mythological serpent view (view 3 above) or involvement with the creation and Fall (view 2 above). The nearer context of Revelation 12 develops the hundreds of years hostility of Satan with Israel and that parameter of time easily accounts for the serpent "of old" ( ) reference and fits within 66% of the terms (LXX, N.T. and Josephus') use. The main alternative to this use of would be the last few decades, which also views Satan as antagonistic to Israel and to Christ. So over 99% of the early Jewish-Christian use of fits with the context emphasis that Satan as the "serpent of old" is probably an allusion to the longstanding conflict between Israel and Satan.

Luke 10:18–19 identifies that while Jesus' disciples were proclaiming Kingdom Satan fell from heaven like lightning with Jesus stated rationale, "Behold I have given you authority to tread upon serpents and scorpions, and over all the power of the enemy, and nothing will injure you." Notice there is no direct connection with the Fall in Genesis 3. Luke 10:19 is describing a present benefit for Jesus' disciples as it extends into a future benefit.

In the Kingdom parable of Matthew 13:27–28 the enemy, Satan, attempts to thwart Jesus' Kingdom program, but there is no clear statement that this sowing of the tares of the world occurs in Genesis 3. In fact, in context, the tares would be presently sowed and growing in opposition to Jesus' Kingdom ministry as it develops before eschatological judgment (Matt. 13:38–41). Namely, the tares are like the Pharisees of Matthew 12 in contrast to the sons of the Kingdom (disciples).

Ezekiel 28:11–19 does not mention "Satan" nor describe what relation the described event has to Genesis 3. However, it does describe a cherub in the garden of Eden in a beautiful non-fallen condition and there is one cherub on the way to the tree of Life in the Genesis 3 account but no mention of one behind the snake (Gen. 3:23–24; Ezek. 28:12–14).

90 *Sir.* 9:10; *2 Macc.* 6:22.

So if Satan is being described in Ezekiel 28, then I have more Biblical evidence for humanity falling before this cherub does as it remains in a nonfallen condition to defend the way to the tree of life.

So where does this resilient tradition of Satan as behind the snake come from? Jeffrey Russell claims that the first century pseudepigraphal works *The Books of Adam and Eve* and the *Apocalypse of Moses* are the first to identify Satan as tempting Adam and Eve in the garden.[91] Russell explains that there is a consensus among historians that this is the effect of Iranian Zoroastrianism on these texts. Under this influence, Judaism identified the *Ahriman* myth (a dualistic god of evil which takes the form of a snake to destroy happiness by the two men eating some fruit)[92] and conflated it with a chief angel Sammael and the apocryphal text *Wisdom of Solomon* 2:24 "by the envy of the devil death entered into the world."[93] *The Life of Adam and Eve* 33 speaks of "the adversary, the devil...[who] deceived Eve." However, in *1 Enoch* 69:6 one of the lesser angels, Gadreel, is identified as leading Eve astray through the guise of a serpent. So in sectarian second Temple Judaism, the tempter in the Fall is an angel but there is disagreement about the name (devil, Sammael, Gadreel) of who it is who tempts Eve. None of these fringe writings were accepted as canonical by mainstream Judaism, for rabbinics continued to maintain that the tempter in Genesis 3 was an animal, a snake.[94] Furthermore, I don't think that we want to identify with a view that has Zoroastrian myth as its root as seen through the lens of rejected Jewish sectarian writings. I think that interpreters see Satan in Genesis 3 because they assume one of the less contextualized options for the Biblical text, inclined by this second Temple Jewish tradition because the majority of Christianity follows it. However, I see no clear Biblical text that places Satan as involved with the temptation and fall of humans. Furthermore, remember that mainstream Pharisaic Judaism as evident in Rabbinic Judaism unanimously identifies the Genesis serpent with a snake, not Satan, and even some from sectarian Judaism join with them.[95]

How much do we let later texts govern our reading of earlier texts like Genesis 3? I am of the opinion that earlier texts should be read in their context. Later texts that are clear can further inform about the activities and characters that an earlier text discusses. However, the

91 Jeffrey Russell, *The Devil: Perceptions of Evil from Antiquity to Primitive Christianity* (Ithaca: Cornell University Press, 1977), pp. 207–9.

92 *Zendavesta, Th.* 3, N. L. Westergaard, translator and commentator. *Zendavesta or the Religious Book of the Zoroastrians* (Wiesbaden: Ludwig Reichert Verlag, 1993), pp. 54–55, 62.

93 This is echoed in *2 En*. 31.3–6.

94 *Gen. Rab.* 19.1; 20.3–4; 21.4; *Ex. Rab.* 3.12; *Num. Rab.* 14.12; 19.22; *Koheleth Rab.* 10.1.

95 *Jub.* 3.17–19, 23; *Sib. Or.* 1.40–45, 59–61; *Greek Apocalypse of Ezra* 2.17; *Gen. Rab.* 19.1; 20.3–4; 21.4; *Ex. Rab.* 3.12; *Num. Rab.* 14.12; 19.22; *Koheleth Rab.* 10.1; Rabbi Yose in *The Fathers According to Rabbi Nathan* 1.17.1.E.

meaning of an earlier text should not be changed by texts that enter on the scene a millennium later. Furthermore, the Biblical canon is that which has the authority. If the Biblical texts are at best ambiguous about placing Satan in the Fall event, then I think we should resist reading them through the bias of the Jewish sectarian sources that are clear about placing Satan in the Fall event. This is especially the case because to read Genesis 3 with Satan's involvement turns the event into a quasi-dualism like Zoroastrianism proposed with humans being overpowered by a greater force ("the devil made us do it"), rather than reading the text as humans (the co-regents with God) throwing away their privilege when confronted by an animal that we had the power to resist.

Thus, the serpent (*nahaš/*) in Genesis 3 is a venomous snake, created by God with this venomous capacity within the good creation. The venomous capacity was likely already within God's good creation. However, there does not seem to be any use of the venomous snake bite until after the Fall in Genesis 3 (e.g., Gen. 3:15; Num. 21:6–9). This use of venom in snake bite is never said to be removed either, only that in the Kingdom, the hostility between snakes and humans will be removed, such that children in the Kingdom are not at risk playing in the viper's den (Isa. 11:8–9). "They will not hurt or destroy" in that day (Isa. 11:9).

9.3. The Fall

The temptation is a pre-modern event. So as an event it needs to be taken together without dividing it up into seconds or its parts as if they could stand alone. The whole narrative recounts our fall into sin.

The Creation and Fall is presented as a historical event in a contiguous narrative that continues through genealogies into the lives of the earliest readers and extra-Biblically recorded history. We do not have any indication of how long after creation the Fall occurred.[96] As a specific historical event there are devastating consequences, as this section will indicate. However, the narrative of the Fall includes specifics that identify that it is written to teach aspects of the temptation process, so that Jews and subsequently Christians may learn the process of temptation so that they do not follow in Adam and Eve's footsteps. As a narrative teaching tool to warn of steps toward personal sin, the narrative becomes a warning to not pile further consequence on oneself and others within the way of sin.

The Rabbinics understand the Fall through a Two-Ways framework. For example, *Song of Songs Rabbah* 1.9.2 claims "God set before him two ways, the way of life and the way of death, and he chose the way of death and rejected the way of life."

96 Jewish tradition rarely conjectures on how long after creation the Fall occurs but *2 Enoch* 32.1 identifies it as five and one half hours after the creation is complete, while *Jubilees* 3.17 identifies it as occurring on the seventh year, second month and seventeenth day after creation.

The temptation begins with a subtle distortion questioning God's generous freedom given to them to eat freely from the trees of the garden (Gen. 2:15; 3:1). Eve betrays her lack of knowledge[97] of God's word by overemphasizing God's strictness ("nor touch it"), minimizing the freedom (the infinitive absolute "eat freely" is reduced to "you may eat"), and weakening the penalty (the infinitive absolute "surely die" is reduced to "lest you die" Gen. 2:15–16; 3:3). In such a vulnerable condition of inaccurate knowledge of God's word, the serpent responds by denying God's word, especially with regard to denying judgment. Such comments judge God's nature with a bias toward disobedience, and in God's place the serpent promises good things that are half true with a horrible double meaning (Gen. 3:4–5). As the serpent moves from the focus of the narrative, the temptation continues with the woman (Gen. 3:6). It is the lure of the world that thrusts the temptation home. There is a progression from the external description of physical practicality and beauty to internal desire (a longing for wisdom perceived to be helpful from a twisting independent mindset). Once in the act of sin, sin involved others with it, so she gave to her husband with her and he ate. Their eyes were opened as the serpent had said but with a twisted perception that was ashamed of their nakedness and pathetically tried to cover it up (Gen. 2:25; 3:7). For example, fig leaves look like they will cover more than they actually do; they dry quickly; and they have fuzz on them that itches. They also hid themselves from God (Gen. 3:8).

In the setting of the sacred space of the garden, God manifested Himself to man intimately by walking and talking with man face to face (Gen. 3:8–9). However, with this sin man forfeits this privilege of intimacy by fleeing in fear and is expelled from the holy garden to common soil (Gen. 3:8–10, 23–24). However, humans are able to maintain some relationship with God but so few do so. It takes until Enosh is born before men begin to call upon the Lord in prayer (Gen. 4:26).[98] Additionally, Enoch and Noah are unique in recovering this intimacy of walking with God (Gen. 5:22; 6:9). The choice of relationship seems to be available but the record shows that we humans chose sin or distraction with other things.[99]

Unfortunately, the record shows that humans increasingly gave themselves over to sin. With the taking of the forbidden fruit, it was shared with others (Gen. 3:6). This act of sin is extended by Cain in his submitting to the dominance of the beast of sin (Gen. 4:7). However,

97 The text does not explain whether she had been told correctly or whether it is a lapse in her memory. The text merely points out the proper point of view and by contrast her slightly askew view of it reflected here. However this lack occurs, she reflects an incorrect knowledge of the tree and its fruit.

98 When the Qal infinitive takes the Lord as the object of the call, prayer is the action described (e.g., Pss. 4:1, 3; 20:9; 69:3; 141:1).

99 Compare the successes of the two genealogies of Genesis 4:17–26. Seth obtains prayer while Cain's line obtains city making, metalurgy, and other distractions.

Adam and Eve had shame in their sin (Gen. 3:10–13), but Cain had shame in his punishment (Gen. 4:13–14). In bragging about his double murders, Lamech is a harbinger of our era with the loss of shame even when the crime is found out (Gen. 4:23–24). In such a condition as this, sin eventually dominated the earth. The description of man's sin prior to the flood is one of the most pungent statements of total depravity, "the wickedness of man was great on the earth, and that every intent of the thoughts of his heart was only evil continually" (Gen. 6:5).

The sovereign God fights chaos with chaos within the created order, as evident in divine oracles of judgment (e.g., Gen. 3:14–19; Rom. 8:20–21). Chaos becomes both active and passive as a weapon in God's use.

> God's actions burst all human scales of measurement as do those terrifying pictures of judgment in which the insane fury of Chaos is allowed to return for the purpose of destroying Yahweh's enemies.[100]

God's active use of chaos powers is apparent in more distant judgments, as God takes: 1) the waters (*yaym/*) of the deep (*thm/*) to destroy all with flood, and again destroying the Egyptian army at the Red Sea (Gen. 7:11; 8:2; Ex. 15:5, 8; Ezek. 26:19), 2) the darkness to destroy the Egyptians (Ex. 10:21–22; 14:20), 3) the formless (*tōhû/*) and void (*bōhû/*) returning as the desert during the exodus traverse, and the remains of destroyed nations (Deut. 32:10; Job 6:18; 12:24; Ps. 107:40; Isa. 34:11; Jer. 4:23), 4) the spirit/breath of Yahweh destroying Assyria (Isa. 30:28),[101] and 5) sin progressively dominating like a beast (Gen. 3:6; 4:7, 23–24; 6:5). Additionally, darkness and the deep house many of these chaos actors, like Leviathan (Gen. 1:21; Ex. 7:9–12; Deut. 32:33; Neh. 2:13; Job 7:12; Pss. 74:13; 91:13; 148:7; Isa 27:1; 51:9; Jer. 51:9; Lam. 4:3).[102] Such animals are among those who shed blood of humans (Gen. 9:5–6; Ex. 21:28–29; Num. 21:6–9; Deut. 32:24; Isa. 18:6; Jer. 15:3; 16:4; 19:7; 30:6; 34:20; Ezek. 14:21; Micah 5:7).

Chaos as the futile frustration of God's creative order against itself is instituted by God in His Oracle of Judgment in the Fall, as indicated

100 Walter Eichrodt, *Theology of the Old Testament*, pp. 499–500.

101 *Enumah Elish* Table 1, lines 105–110, though not taken this way in Genesis 1:2.

102 H. Gunkel, *Schöpfung und Chaos in Urzeit und Endzeit: Eine religionsgeschichtliche Untersuchung über Gen 1 und Ap. Joh. 12,* pp. 171-398, esp. 379-98; W. G. Lambert, and S. B. Parker, *Enuma Elish: The Babylonian Epic of Creation*; T. Jacobsen, *Treasures of Darkness*. (Yale University Press, New Haven, 1976), pp. 167–91; A. Deiterich, *Abraxas: Studien zur Religionsgeschichte des späteren Altertums*; W. Bousset, *Textkritische Studien zum Neuen Testament,* pp. 350–56; J. Fontenrose, W. K. Hendrick and A. Collins. *Python: A Study in Delphic*, p. 210; David Aune, *Revelation 6-16*, pp. 670–93; Lucan, *La Phassale de Lucain, ou Les guerres civiles de Cesar & de Pompée* 60.5.79–81; Lucian, *Dialogi. mortuorum*, 300.9.

by the following six points (Gen. 3:14–19). 1) Futility permeates all relationships as intimacy with God breaks down (Gen. 3:8, 23–24). In the setting of the sacred space of the garden, God manifested Himself to man intimately by walking and talking with man face to face (Gen. 3:8–9). Their eyes were opened as the serpent promised, only with a twisted perception that was ashamed of their nakedness and pathetically tried to cover it up (Gen. 2:25; 3:7). They also hid themselves from God (Gen. 3:8) as intimacy fled before fear (Gen. 3:8–10). Then God expelled them from the holy garden to common soil (Gen. 3:23–24). However, humans are able to maintain some relationship with God, but so few do so. It took generations until Enosh was born before men begin to call upon the Lord in prayer (Gen. 4:26).[103] Additionally, Enoch and Noah are unique in recovering this intimacy of walking with God (Gen. 5:22; 6:9). The choice of relationship with God seems to be available but the record shows that we humans chose sin or distraction with other things, rather than prayer and walking with God.[104]

2) Humans are exhausted in their work now that the ground is cursed (Gen. 3:17–19). In cursing the ground, Yahweh transforms Adam's cultivation of the ground to become hindered by thorns and thistles, so that cultivating the ground takes repeated toil and sweat. John Calvin resists labor being part of the curse but includes within the curse "hard labor and full of fatigue and weariness, which, by its difficulty, produces sweat."[105] Even in the midst of God cursing the ground, it still yields its grain for bread, though it takes much effort.

Rabbai Isaac of Magdala extends these pests of curse from thorns and thistles to include insects, such as "gnats, midges, and fleas."[106] The Biblical text likely included these insects as created on the fifth day rather than imposed as pests in reaction to the Fall of humanity (Gen. 1:21). No Biblical text identifies when these pests began to annoy and hinder, but they certainly were effective at causing difficulty by the time God was cursing Egypt to free Israel (Ex. 8:21–24; 10:4–15).

Humans will be eventually rescued from this frustration of life by dying and returning to dust, the constituents of our original creation (Gen. 2:7). Most commentaries consider that death is indicated in the oracle as a realization of God's warning in Genesis 2:17, and thus resulting in all creation being subjected to futility.[107] While Qoheleth considers this decomposition of our bodies to be an expression of futility (Eccl. 3:14,

---

103 When the Qal infinitive takes the Lord as the object of the call, prayer is the action described (e.g., Pss. 4:1, 3; 20:9; 69:3; 141:1).

104 Compare the successes of the two genealogies of Genesis 4:17–26. Seth obtains prayer while Cain's line obtains city making, metalurgy, and other distractions.

105 John Calvin, *Genesis*, 1:175.

106 *Gen. Rab.* 20.8.

107 E.g., C. F. Keil and F. Delitzsch, *Commentary on the Old Testament in Ten Volumes: Pentateuch* (Grand Rapids: Eerdmans, 1976), 1:103– 5; Gordon Wenham, *Genesis 1–15*, p. 83.

19–20), Rabbai Simeon ben Yo*h*ai considers the expression of "thou shalt return" to be that of resurrection.[108] Adam named his wife Eve, "mother of all living" in response to this divine statement, either indicating surprise that he didn't die immediately (contrary to Gen. 2:17), or in hope that they will be eventually rescued from such futility by death and decay, or if rabbinic resurrection hopes are in view (which I doubt) then their rescue is through God resurrecting them. Claus Westermann does not consider death to be part of the oracle of the curse here since Adam responds with hope in naming his wife Eve, "mother of all living."[109]

3) The marital relationship will have tension between woman's quest for liberation[110] and male dominance (Gen. 3:10, 16). For example, the word "desire" (*tšwqt/*   ) in Genesis 3:16 should be taken as the near context takes it in Genesis 4:7 *"desire" to dominate and conquer* rather than the distant context of Song of Songs 7:10 "desire" of that husband for his wife. However, God's oracle indicates that the husband will rule over his wife (Gen. 3:16).[111] Another feature of the male dominance and female submission is that she will have increased pain in childbirth.

4) There is increased pain in child bearing (Gen. 3:16). The repetition of the term (*rbh/*   ) and use of the infinitive absolute (   ) presupposes there would already be some pain with the birthing experience but that it will now be significantly increased. For example, the same expression is used later after Abram obtains Ishmael and then Isaac as an heir, when God says "I will greatly multiply" your descendants (Gen. 16:10; 22:17). The rabbinics understand this increase in pain to especially include an increase of the gestation period as a way of increasing this pain, by comparison to animals.[112] However, Skinner conjectures that the frequency of childbirth is now being contemplated for humans as they try to retain domination over creation, now being faced with their inevitable death.[113] Extending this, Skinner goes on to conclude that the pain of childbirth is proverbial for merely the extremity of human anguish.[114] That is, maybe the pain is not just in the biological birthing process for this curse needs to contextually make sense sandwiched between her offspring and her relationship with her husband. That is, in the areas of fulfillment for wife and mother, there will be pain.

108 *Gen. Rab.* 20.10.

109 Westermann, *Genesis 1–11*, p. 267 does not consider death here to be a punishment but an encouraging rescue.

110 The word 'desire' in Genesis 3:16 should be taken as the near context takes it in Genesis 4:7 desire to dominate and conquer rather than the distant context of Song of Songs 7:10 desire of that husband for his wife.

111 *Gen. Rab.* 20.7; Allen Ross, *Creation and Blessing: A Guide to the Study and Exposition of the Book of Genesis* (Grand Rapids: Baker, 1988), p. 146.

112 *Gen. Rab.* 20.6.

113 John Skinner, *Genesis*, p. 82.

114 John Skinner, *Genesis*, pp. 82–3.

5) There is enmity in human and snake relationships (Gen. 3:15). This enmity (*'ybh/*) prefigures the Israelite experience with the snake attacks of Numbers 21:6. The term enmity (*'ybh/*) is used elsewhere only of enemies (Num. 35:21–22; Ezek. 25:15; 35:5). Thus Genesis 3:15 is not a first statement of the gospel, for snakes and humans are described here in a hostile relationship. The word for seed (*zer'ak/*) is a collective referring to plural descendents of snakes, and humans (compare with other Genesis *zer'ak/* texts like Gen. 15:3–5). Thus there are some instances of God creating venomous serpents as a normal feature of the creation, only to be utilized as a feature of God's curse of sin (a view affirmed by Josephus).[115] The Rabbinics (that is mainstream Jewish interpretation) universally and many Essenes identify this serpent of Genesis 3 as an animal, a snake, whose ancestors bite Israelites in Numbers 21:6.[116] Many of the patristics also follow this view that the serpent is merely an animal.[117] Calvin weds three statements of serpent curse together; serpents are cursed more than other animals for this feature of enmity and because they are so uppity God has plunged their head into the dust to crawl.[118] Claus Westermann follows this rationale and proposes that the curse "from" (*m/* , Gen. 3:14) the animals is best understood as banishment "from" ( ) after the pattern in Genesis 4:11, since both expressions are both within statements of curse.[119] So Genesis 4:11 and 3:14 use of "from" (*mn/*) is a closer contextual idea than the instance of the word in Genesis 3:1. This view is reflected in the LXX choice that announces that serpents are cursed "from" ( ) cattle and the beasts of the field (Gen. 3:14 LXX). Keil and Delitzsch prefer this view of banishment from the animals in the curse mentioned here and resist tying the truth of creation being subjected to futility (Rom. 8:20–21) to this statement of oracle of curse (Gen. 3:14).[120]

If an interpreter does not follow Calvin, Keil, Delitzsch, and Westermann, as I am inclined to follow them, then there is the tendency to view all beasts of the field as also cursed in this curse oracle but not as much as snakes (Gen. 3:14). Gordon Wenham holds this view as

115 Josephus, *Ant.* 1.45.1–50.4.

116 *Jub.* 3.17–19, 23; *Sib. Or.* 1.40–45, 59–61; *Greek Apocalypse of Ezra* 2.17; *Gen. Rab.* 19.1; 20.3–4; 21.4; *Ex. Rab.* 3.12; *Num. Rab.* 14.12; 19.22; *Koheleth Rab.* 10.1; Rabbi Yose in *The Fathers According to Rabbi Nathan* 1.17.1.E. It is coincidental in *The Gilgamesh Epic* tablet 11, column 8 that a snake ate the thorny bush "reborn man" collected from under the sea by Gilgamesh and thus robs him of immortality and enables the snake in the story to molt his skin every month.

117 E.g., *Theophilus to Autolycus* 2.21 in *The Ante-Nicene Fathers,* edited by Alexander Roberts and James Donaldson (Edinburgh: T & T Clark, 1989) 2:102; an anonymous author of *Genesis* 130–4 in *The Ante-Nicene Fathers* 4:134; Ephrem the Syrian, *Commentary on Genesis* 2.15.1 in *Fathers of the Church* 91:107.

118 John Calvin, Genesis, 1:166–7.

119 Claus Westermann, *Genesis 1–11,* pp. 258–9; A. E. Cowley, ed. *Gesenius' Hebrew Grammar,* 119w, p. 382.

120 C. F. Keil and F. Delitzsch, *Pentateuch,* 1:98.

he proposes a superlative in Genesis 3:14 (similar to Genesis 3:1) to indicate that all the other cattle and beasts of the field are also cursed, even though the serpent is cursed "more than" they are.[121] This view would indicate that God has subjected major groups of the beasts of the field of the whole of creation to futility in this curse statement concerning the serpent (e.g., Rom. 8:20). There is no development in Genesis 3 oracle of curse for how the animals would then be cursed as there is for the serpents. Claus Westermann correctly points out that being the recipient of such a curse treats animals as moral and thus culpable beings akin to persons (similar to Gen. 9:5).[122] This feature of the oracle that includes all animals as divinely cursed is not preserved within the LXX since this statement instead announces that serpents are cursed from ( ) cattle and the beasts of the field. That is, the serpent bears the curse, rather than the other animals it is separated from ( ). However, the LXX includes animals as culpable souls in the capital punishment judgment of Genesis 9:5. So while the LXX considers animals to be culpable morally it simply does not include them in this oracle of curse in Genesis 3:14.

However, *Genesis Rabbah* and the rabbinics preserve the condition of the serpent being cursed among the other beasts, but the serpent is cursed more especially in the serpent's crawling posture.[123] Rabbi Levi concludes that in the Messianic Kingdom all other animals will be healed from their disabilities after the pattern of human Kingdom healing (Isa. 26:19; 35:5–6; 61:1–2)[124] but that the serpent is not healed as it continues to crawl in its den (Isa. 11:8; 65:25).[125]

Another manner that serpents are conjectured to be cursed more than other animals is that the prolonged hostility that snakes and humans maintain when compared to other animals that might risk human life.[126] There is no development of this other animal hostility to humans included in the Genesis 3 context.

Part of this animal curse was considered by some rabbinics to be the age it took for an animal to bear offspring, placing serpents at seven years and adders at seventy years.[127] Within this list of animals, the domesticated (such as cattle around one year) are accurate with regard to the animal sexual maturity but those animals that are wild do not fit the empirical data (some significantly low such as the claim for wild dogs puberty of two months and some too high such as that of serpents and

---

121 Gordon Wenham, *Genesis 1–15*, pp. 78–9; John Piper Lange, *Commentary on the Holy Scriptures: Critical, Doctrinal and Homiletical: Genesis-Leviticus* (Grand Rapids: Zondervan, 1978), 1:232 claims Rosenmüller wrongly holds this view.

122 Claus Westermann, *Genesis 1–11*, pp. 257–8.

123 *Gen. Rab.* 20.4–5; *Bek.* 8a.

124 4Q521 7–8, 11–12.

125 *Gen. Rab.* 20.5.

126 Westermann, *Genesis 1–11*, p. 259.

127 *Gen. Rab.* 20.4.

adders). Their opinion of serpent sexual maturity does not hold up under contemporary biological observations which recognizes reproductive maturity (depending upon species) to be between nine months and three and a half years.[128]

However, there is more to this curse in the rabbinics, for Rabbai Gamaliel considered "the serpent seven times more accursed than cattle."[129] He didn't explain the manner of the extent of such serpent curse though it funds this comparison with animals.

It is better to see this *animals as cursed* view as not sourced in the curse oracle of Genesis 3. Instead of taking the Genesis 3:14 as a superlative (as in Gen. 3:1) it is better to understand the *mn/* as indicating banishment from animals (through comparison with Gen. 4:11). Thus on the closer parallel between of *mn/* in Genesis 3:14 and 4:11 as both oracles of curse it is better to see Genesis 3:14 leaving the animals not cursed in this oracle statement.

6) Snakes are cursed to crawl in the dust (Gen. 3:14). *Genesis Rabbah* indicates that angels descended and cut off the hands and feet of the serpent in order for it to be reduced from an upright stance to that of crawling.[130] This curse also retains a multiple generation reproduction with the reduced crawling condition. John Skinner identifies that this crawling fits within Akkadian humiliation metaphors.[131] While many exegetes consider the eating of dust to be pictorial poetry of the serpent's posture, Rabbi Hilpi identifies that the serpent actually eats dust in its burrowing and crawling posture.[132] Rabbi Levi concludes that in the Messianic Kingdom all other animals will be healed from their disabilities after the pattern of human Kingdom healing (Isa. 26:19; 35:5–6; 61:1–2)[133] but that the serpent is not healed as it continues to eat dust in Kingdom (Isa. 65:25).[134]

Beyond the oracle of the curse (Gen. 3:14–19), such futility leaves the blessings (be fruitful, multiply, fill the earth, subdue, and rule) intact,

---

128 Roland Bauchot, *Snakes: A Natural History* (New York: Sterling Publishing Co., 2006), p. 104 identifies reproductive maturity from 9 mo. to 2.5 years; Richard Shine, "Ecology of the Austrian Death Adder *Acanthophis antarcticus* (Elapidae)", *Herpetologica* 36:4(1980): 281–9 identifies for this species reproductive maturity occurs between 2 and 3.5 years.

129 *Gen. Rab.* 20.4.

130 *Gen. Rab.* 20.5.

131 John Skinner, *Genesis*, p. 79; von Eberhard Schrader, ed. *Keilinschriftliche Bibiothek: Sammlung von assyrischen und babylonischen Texten in Umschrift und Übersetzung* (Berlin: Reuther, 1889), 5:232–3.

132 *Gen. Rab.* 20.5; cf. Samuel Bochartus, and David Clodius, *Hierozoicon, sive bipertitum opus de animalibus Sacrae Scripturae* (Zunner: Francofurti ad Moenum, 1675), 3:245; Arabian notion that the *ğinn* eat dirt J. Welhausen, *Rest arabischen Heidentums* (Berlin: G. Reimer, 1897), p. 150; Skinner, *Genesis*, p. 79.

133 4Q521 7–8, 11–12.

134 *Gen. Rab.* 20.5.

but now mingles them with the experiential knowledge[135] of evil, such as increased pain[136] in childbirth and increased effort in accomplishing labor (Gen. 1:28; 3:5; 9:1–7). Likewise, humans still retain the initial tasks like cultivating the ground but now in a manner that subjects them to futility with thorns and thistles and much labor (Gen. 3:17–19, 23). Even in the extreme measures of God utilizing the waters of chaos to attack the sin-dominated condition of the earth, God provides the remnant preservation in blessing and work (Gen. 9:1–7, 20).

One of the most devastating features of this chaos futility is that of death. Soul (*nephesh*) is a synonym to life,[137] so it is chaotic that souls die. God warned Adam that in the day that he would eat from the forbidden fruit that he would surely die (Gen. 2:17). God's oracle of judgment speaks of Adam eventually dying and returning to dust (Gen. 3:19).[138] The second Temple Jewish apocalypse *The Life of Adam and Eve* conjectures that God placed the cherubim to protect humans from the tree of life (in Genesis 3:22–24) so that they would not be fixed in our corrupted condition without any hope of change.[139] Paul identified that death began and reigned from Adam on, and when the Law came in with Moses, this Adamic sin was also imputed to humans as well, further dominating man by death (Rom. 5:12–21; Eph. 2:2–3). In this context, "death reigning" indicates a condition of the walking dead, under sentence for condemnation of everlasting death. Adam responded to God's oracle of judgment in Genesis 3 with a ray of hope, naming his wife Eve (the mother of all living),[140] either Adam took God's judgment to mean that he would not die in that day, or that there will be release from futility eventually (Gen. 3:20). God further barred their way to

135 The tree of the knowledge of good and evil was the test portal through which humans could enter into the experience of curse among the blessing. The second literary unit has three mentions of curse (Gen. 3:14, 17; 4:11) to mirror the three statements of blessing mentioned in the first literary unit (Gen. 1:22, 28; 2:3).

136 The use of the infinitive absolute presupposes there is some pain with the birthing experience but that it will now be significantly increased. For example the same expression is used later after Abraham obtains Ishmael and then Isaac as an heir, when God says "I will greatly multiply" your descendants (Gen. 16:10; 22:17). Cf. Francis Brown, S. R. Driver and Charles Briggs, *A Hebrew and English Lexicon of the Old Testament* (Oxford: Clarendon Press, 1977), p. 915, 3e.

137 Gen. 1:20, 24, 30; 2:7; 9:4-5, 10; Ps. 54:4; Acts 2:41; Hans Wolff, *Anthropology of the Old Testament* (Philadelphia: Fortress Press, 1974), pp. 24–25; F. Brown, S. R. Driver and Charles Briggs, *A Hebrew and English Lexicon of the Old Testament*, p. 659.

138 There is no justification in Genesis, as in the Rabbinics (e.g., *Num. Rab.* 5.4; 10.8) that a death sacrifice was actually carried out by forty stripes or penalties, ten for each participant: Adam, Eve, serpent and earth. For example, part of the curse of the ground in the rabbinics is the claim that part of the curse of the ground is that one third of humanity is cursed in Genesis 9:24 (*Num. Rab.* 10.8).

139 *The Life of Adam and Eve*-apocalypse 16.28.

140 *Jub.* 3.32 conjectures that Adam naming Eve occurred on the first day of the fourth month.

the tree of life, which had been available before, but now is beyond their reach so that humans will die, and probably so that they will not be caught in the teeth of sin perpetually (Gen. 3:24). Without Adam dying physically in that day, this life we live becomes a kind of walking death. However, when sin begins to dominate murder ensues (Gen. 4:8, 23). Reflecting this death, the repeated death bell rings out through the historical genealogy of Adam with the phrase "and he died" (Gen. 5:5, 8, 11, 14, 17, 27, 31). With sin burgeoning to total depravity all souls are killed in the global flood except those in the ark (Gen. 7:21–23).

Prior to the Law being given, this epidemic of condemnation and death from Adam was realized because humans joined Adam in his deed of sinning, even if we before the Law came did not violate its standard in transgression (Rom. 5:12–14), but now that the Mosaic Law has been given there is a more direct transaction of Adam's sin deed to our ledger in imputation, leaving us with the epidemic of death through a direct commercial means (Rom. 5:13, 15–16). Thus all humans get the resultant consequences of Adam's sin, condemnation and death (Rom. 5:16, 18).

However, "death reigning" is more than a commercial or legal transaction, it is a controlling domination by the power and consequences of death (Rom. 5:14, 17, parallel to the same verb where "grace reigns," Rom. 5:21 or "the Lord reigns," Rev. 19:6).[141] Such *reign of death* dominated and controlled over ( ) humans held guilty for Adams's offense (Rom. 5:14 parallel to Judg. 9:8, 10; 1 Kgs. 8:7; Rev. 5:10; 17:18) beginning through Adam. This rule of death is what Placeus describes concerning Adam's sin deed affecting and dominating human sin nature.[142] No discussion extends this human curse expression to animals, though animals also die.

141 In the LXX usually means rule as a human king over his realm (e.g., Gen. 36:32–39; Josh. 13:10–12), though in the psalms it indicates that God reigns over creation (Pss. 46:9; 92:1; 95:10; 96:1; 98:1); cf. Peter Lampe in *Exegetical Dictionary of the New Testament*. Ed. H. Balz and G. Schneider (Grand Rapids: Eerdmans, 1990), 1:208.

142 Placeus or La Place of Saumur, *De Imputatione Primi Peccati Adami,* (1655) in *Opera Omnia* (Franequerae: Johannis Gyzelaar, 1699 & 1702) not so much for the exclusion of federal transmission of sin in response to the Synod of Charenton (1645), but for the argument in chapter 8 which explores the addition of a lived quality of sin reigning, which can be hybridized with federalism as done by James Leo Garret, *Systematic Theology: Biblical, Historical, and Evangelical* (Grand Rapids: Eerdmans, 1990), vol. 1, pp. 493 and also 488–9; Albert Schweitzer, *The Mysticism of Paul the Apostle,* (New York: Seabury Press, 1968), pp. 115–27, 144, 166–67, 219; E. P. Sanders, *Paul and Palestinian Judaism* (Minneapolis: Fortress Press, 1977), pp. 474–523, 549; Axel von Dobbeler, *Glaube als Teilhabe: Historische und semantische Grundlagen der paulinischen Theologie und Ekklesiologie des Glaubens. WUNT 22* (Tübigen: Mohr Siebeck, 1987), pp. 166–70, 239–80.

Animal death begins with human death at the fall.[143] The oracle of judgment indicates that within the hostility between serpents and humans that both shall kill the other (Gen. 3:15). For example, the bite of the Egyptian adder kills Israelites in the wilderness until God treated it by the bronze serpent and faith (Num. 21:6–9). Likewise, humans will crush the heads of such serpents, killing them (Gen. 3:15; Rom. 8:20).[144]

Other animals experience the curse of death in the wake of the Fall. Ecclesiastes compares human and animal death to be alike in bringing a release of their spirit (*ruh/*) and bringing a vain end to their body to return to dust in the decaying process (Eccl. 3:18–22). So with human and animal death being of the same sort of futility it might be reasonable to assume animal death is also an implication in the Fall. The historical evidence is that the first animals die before humans, for some animals died for God to make clothes from animal skins to better cover the humans than the leaves provided, though nothing is said about this being a sacrifice (Gen. 3:21).[145] With the global flood all souls, including animals, are killed in the global flood except those in the ark (Gen. 7:21–23). This would indicate that the geological fossil record should be considered to be recording this animal death since the Fall.

Ecclesiastes compares human and animal death to be alike in bringing a release of their spirit (*ruh/*) and bringing a vain end to their body to return to dust in the decaying process (Eccl. 3:18–22). Michael Fox identifies that the concept of vanity in Ecclesiastes especially focuses upon ephemerality, nothingness, and senselessness, because it comes to nothing and doesn't last.[146] So the fact of human and animal death occurs with life being so brief and leaving so little affect centers in vanity. Likewise, not being able to tell of a lasting outcome for animal or human spirit likewise fits such vanity.

143 There are nice discussions of this issue Biblically, theologically, and historically by Marco T. Terreros, "Death Before the Sin of Adam: A Fundamental Concept in Theistic Evolution and its Implications for Evangelical Theology," Ph.D. dissertation Andrews University, 1994; "Is All Death a Consequence of Sin?: Theological Implications of Alternative Models," *Journal of the Adventist Theological Society* 14/1(Spring 2003): 150–75.

144 The superlative in Genesis 3:14 (similar to Genesis 3:1) indicates that all the other cattle and beasts of the field are also cursed, even though the serpent is cursed "more than" they are. This indicates that God has subjected major groups of the beasts of the field of the whole of creation to futility in this curse statement concerning the serpent (e.g., Rom. 8:20).

145 There is no discussion in Genesis about these animals that die for skins to clothe the humans being the pattern and first sacrifice like the Rabbinics propose (*Num. Rab.* 4.8). This Rabbinic pattern might be a conflation of *Jubilees* 3, where God kills animals for the human's clothes (*Jub.* 3.26, 30) and Adam responds with killing additional animals in sacrifice to God (*Jub.* 3.27). Perhaps the sacrifice view also reflects *The Life of Adam and Eve*-Apocalypse 27 which conjectures that Adam begged for forgiveness but was expelled from the garden anyway.

146 Michael Fox, *A Time to Tear Down and a Time to Build Up: A Rereading of Ecclesiastes* (Grand Rapids: Eerdmans, 1999), pp. 28–29.

Death and hostility continues; many of the creation animals become carnivorous with no described modification process. For example, the beasts of the earth (*bhmh/* ; Gen. 1:24-26), which is a generic term for animals, includes within it carnivorous animals like lions destroying flocks (Micah 5:7; Isa. 30:6; Pr. 30:30) and eating the dead Israelites under covenant curse (Deut. 32:24; Isa. 18:6; Jer. 15:3; 16:4; 19:7; 34:20). Ezekiel calls these beasts which God uses in judgment *evil* or *destroyers* (*hārā'îm/*) along with sword, famine, and plague (Ezek. 14:21). That is, the Biblical concept of evil (*rā'/*) is contextually *detriment* to another, not a Platonic philosophical lack within metaphysical Being, nor something ultimate. Additionally, as a term beasts (*bhmh/*) even includes poisonous and fiery serpents (Isa. 30:6; Num. 21:6–9). Additionally, some of the birds are also carnivorous in eating Jewish bodies from the battle field of God's Babylonian captivity (Isa. 18:6; Jer. 15:3; 16:4; 19:7; 34:20). So from the perspective of the animals or humans who are killed or eaten on the battlefield, these carnivorous beasts are evil. However, from the vantage point of God's design for providing food for the carnivorous animals after the flood in the psalmist's context, the prey eaten in carnivorous activity is a good (*tōb/*) which God provides and for which He is praised (Ps. 104:21, 24–28 echoes post creation and flood perspective and praise; also Job 38:39–40 shows animals depend on God for prey). That is, the Biblical concept of good (*tōb/*) is *benefit* in context, not a Platonic or ultimate philosophical concept.

These animals may have had this carnivorous quality (strength, teeth, claws) in the original creation.[147] There is no instance in the Bible where they are described as changed. They are simply called by the names and categories by which they are identified later in their carnivorous condition. Biblically by the time of the post flood, restrictions are placed on animals from killing humans on pain of capital punishment of the animal murderer (Gen. 9:5–6; Ex. 21:28–29). Thus some degree of carnivorous condition has at least developed by then. Ultimately, some of these same animals with no described modification (except an exclusion of carnivorous activity) are incorporated within Kingdom as a return to Paradise before the Fall (Isa. 11:6–9). Isaiah describes a healing in the Kingdom of the animal hostility which the Fall brought in, and a return to Edenic conditions.

A special case of this animal chaos includes the threatening Great Sea Monsters (*tannînm/*) within this carnivorous activity, and at times mythological chaos rebellion against God (Gen. 1:21; Ex. 7:9–12; Deut. 32:33; Neh. 2:13; Job 7:12; Pss. 74:13; 91:13; 148:7; Isa. 27:1; 51:9; Jer. 51:9; Lam. 4:3). However, as chaos monsters the *tannînm* are presented in a Jewish polemic as Rahab and Leviathan, whom God destroys (Job

147 Parallel to Josephus, *Ant.* 1.45.1–50.4 claim that God created venomous serpents.

41:1; Pss. 74:14; 87:4; 89:10; 104:26; Isa. 27:1; 51:9).[148] The Great Sea Monsters (*tannînm/*) being destroyed by God do not remain as an ongoing threatening agent in the Kingdom.

Suffering, corruption and mortality is part of the futility to which God has subjected the creation in hope of producing in time resurrected, immortal bodies for His human children (Rom. 8:18–23). Those who have the Spirit of God within them groan amid this futility of suffering, eagerly awaiting the redemption of their bodies (Rom. 8:23). The rest of the creation also groans under this futile suffering, awaiting the revealing of these sons of God in this way, for at that time creation will be set free from its slavery to corruption (Rom. 8:21–22). This redemption is to be expected in the Kingdom with Christian glorification and the redemption of the creation.

Meanwhile, within the increase of chaos, Elohim still provides hope. For example, God's questioning Adam and Eve shockingly reveals sin. Such divine questioning also limits the swift plunge toward total depravity as conscience might later.[149] Additionally, Adam took the oracles of judgment to still provide hope in naming his wife Eve (Gen. 3:20). Furthermore, God provided clothes to take care of human nakedness in a manner that did it better than the pathetic cover-up of fig leaves (Gen. 3:21).[150] However as sin increases, hope is primarily available for those who have a relationship with this living God. Enoch walking with God, found himself removed from this sinful earth to be translated to be with God (Gen. 5:24). Likewise righteous Noah in his walking with God obtained God's favor to continue God's created souls (human and animals) through God's deliverance through the ark (Gen. 6:9; 8:1). God's covenant with Noah and all life provides hope that no use of the waters of chaos in a global flood will ever come again; God has put this weapon of war down with a promise (Gen. 9:8–17).

Elohim has defined Himself intimately through His power to create and rule His creation. Thus God is intimately involved in the narrative of His creation. However, this narrative is an open one in which God

148 Bruce Waltke, *Creation and Chaos*, pp. 13–15, 43–53; Gerhard Hasel, "The Polemical Nature of the Genesis Cosmology," *Evangelical* Quarterly, pp. 81–102.

149 The concept of conscience is not present in Hebrew though it is developed in Greek; cf. discussion in the next chapter "Biblical Anthropology as a Creation and revelation Framework for Doing Bio-Ethics."

150 There is no development or teaching evident in this verse about sacrifice or atonement, like the Rabbinics propose (*Num. Rab.* 4.8). This Rabbinic pattern might be a conflation of *Jubilees* 3, where God just kills the animals for the human's clothes (*Jub.* 3.26, 30) and Adam responds with killing additional animals in sacrifice to God (*Jub.* 3.27). Perhaps the sacrifice view also reflects *The Life of Adam and Eve*-Apocalypse 27 which conjectures that Adam begged for forgiveness but was expelled from the garden anyway. Therefore, it is inappropriate to see gospel in a sacrifice here. Some of the ways God helps are just very practical and "clothes that last" are a generous gift from God.

continues to foster life, struggle, death, and hope. Ultimately, God is victorious and will exclude the forces of chaos in Kingdom.

10. Biblical Anthropology as a Creation and Revelation Framework for Doing Bio-ethics

Psalm 8:4 asks God the question in prayer, "What is Man, that Thou dost take thought of him?" and then answers this question in praise to the majestic God Who made humans for majesty and rule (Ps. 8:5–6, 9).

> God made him a little lower than God,
> and dost crown him with glory and majesty!
> Thou hast made him to rule over the works of Thy hands;
> Thou hast put all things under his feet.

This psalm orients the reader and prayer to focus on understanding humans in light of God's creation design and the revelational framework that describes us. Painting on this canvas invites a descriptive Biblical theology's assessment of humans, to which this text is itself contributing.

Bio-ethics as a field is dominated by philosophers and biologists using philosophical assumptions and categories. Since God created humans and provided a revelational description of us, this Biblicism should reframe our conceptuality of humanity so as to fund bio-ethics from Biblical thought forms, from start to finish. I propose to present an analysis of the words and concepts articulated in Old and New Testament literature that address the nature of a human. The conclusions presented from this analysis will be used to make a presentation of an integrated model of a human. I propose to then extend these Biblical theology categories into the field of bio-ethics to unpack their bio-ethical implications.

Following this approach results in a *functionalism* (because of the redundant descriptions of holistic humanity in the model), which I call a *multi-faceted unity* (of: image of God, soul, spirit, body, heart, mind, will, and conscience). However, the concreteness of especially Hebrew descriptive words could also be appealed to in claiming this model as an ontological model because it is describing the way we are from the Biblical perspective, and so we should think about ourselves in this manner.[1] Thus, this view should be thought as ontological and

1 I suspect if an ancient considered this model he would probably consider it to be essential metaphysics, especially as it is dependent upon concrete Hebrew

functionalist both, even though this is a novel way for philosophy to conceive of humanity. However, part of the point of this paper is to call philosophy and other human disciplines back to being reconfigured by the Word of God and Biblical theology.

For example, within Christendom there are many views of the nature of the human being. Among the most prominent are two views rooted in Platonism which have had long-standing traditions in Christianity. Dichotomists, following the *Epistle to Diognetus*, make a distinction between the material and immaterial parts of a human, reflective of Plato's soul and body concepts.[2] Theologians adhering to this view argue that soul and spirit are used interchangeably, whereas trichotomists, following Justin Martyr, point out that soul and spirit are distinct.[3] Such a trichotomy view is reflective of the neo-platonic trichotomy view of spirit, soul, and body. In the twentieth century, additional views of humanity emerged including advocates of a holistic model. For example, one holistic model in the wake of Gestalt psychology maintains that the person is greater than the sum of his parts.

In contrast to this, biologists define humans either by comparison to animal properties and traits, or if they are Christians, through a devotional lens of Jesus' disciples. For example, Institute for Creation Research biologist Daniel Criswell defined humans and proposed an ethic that identified that the core trait of humanity was to be a servant in the pattern of: 1) a non alpha male from a herd or pack and 2) Jesus' disciple.[4] With the proliferation of widely divergent views there is a real danger of the disciplines of ethics and theology fragmenting into different Wittgensteinian language games unable to meaningfully communicate between them. Is such a postmodern option a way to leave this discipline? How should a wise Christian choose among all these views of humanness? To be sure, whatever model one chooses, it brings with it a worldview which is indebted to the philosophy upon which it is built. The author rejects bio-ethics built within these alternative world views as significantly flawed, for they will insulate the advocate from arriving at a consistent Biblicism.

---

expression. He would probably add concepts like clean/unclean, holy/common, and life/death to this metaphysic (cf. Doug Kennard, "Life, Holy, and Clean" a paper presented to the Evangelical Theological Society, Nov. 1992).

2 *Epistle to Diognetus*. (Leiden: E. J. Brill, 1964).

3 Justin Martyr, *Apology* 1.29 in *Saint Justin Martyr: The First Apology, The Second Apology, Dialogue with Trypho, Exhortation to the Greeks, Discourse to the Greeks, The Monarchy; or the Rule of God.* Edited by Thomas B. Falls (New York: Christian Heritage, 1949); cf. George van Kooten, *Paul's Anthropology in Context: The Image of God, and Tripartite Man in Ancient Judaism, Ancient Philosophy and Early Christianity* (Tübigen: Mohr Siebeck, 2008),which presents a tripartite model especially philosophically, however on pp 376–7 the Pauline model is presented as more complex akin to the development in this chapter.

4 Daniel Criswell, "What Makes Us Human?" *Impact: Vital Articles on Science/ Creation,* Institute for Creation Research, Jan. 2006, pp. 1–4.

My approach is in contrast to the perspectives provided by philosophy, psychology, sociology, anthropology, and biology. Those disciplines give answers consistent with their worldviews and the methodologies dominant in these approaches. If an evangelical is working in these disciplines, often the extent of Christian integration is hanging a few Biblical proof texts on the rafters. When Christians extend their bilingual beliefs from these disciplines into the field of bio-ethics then they become a parody of Star Trek: timidly going where everyone has gone before.

The author suggests instead using the approach of the Biblical theology movement, that a Christian model of humanity start first with the Biblical text and then work out the implications for bio-ethics. In the second half of the twentieth century within the descriptive Biblical theology movement a model of the human being as a multifaceted unity gained dominance in the discipline. The near unanimity of Biblical theologians embracing this model can be seen by the treatment in the theological wordbooks[5] and by the scholarly descriptions of humanity from specialized Biblical theologies,[6] which corroborate the word studies of this paper. This near unanimity was bemoaned in the open question time and in the paper by Jeffrey Boyd at the Wheaton Theology Conference in 1997 focusing on the integration of psychology and theology. At this conference, Kennard and Holmes championed this near unanimous view as a framework for integrating psychology and theology.[7] Boyd's concern was the loss of spirituality as behaviorists

5 E.g., Gerhard Kittel and Gerhard Friedrich, *Theological Dictionary of the New Testament* (Grand Rapids: Eerdmans, 1964–76); Johannes Botterweck and Helmer Ringgren, *Theological Dictionary of the Old Testament* (Grand Rapids: Eerdmans, 1974–present); Colin Brown, *The New International Dictionary of New Testament Theology* (Grand Rapids: Zondervan, 1975); Laird Harris, Gleason Archer, and Bruce Waltke, *Theological Wordbook of the Old Testament* (Chicago: Moody Press, 1980); Willem VanGemeren, *New International Dictionary of Old Testament Theology & Exegesis* (Grand Rapids: Zondervan, 1997).

6 James Dunn, *The Theology of Paul the Apostle* (Grand Rapids: Eerdmans, 1998), pp. 51–78; Hans Walter Wolff, *Anthropology of the Old Testament* (Philadelphia: Fortress Press, 1974).

7 Douglas Kennard and Paul Holmes, "The Nature of Humanity: A Biblical Theology Approach" a paper presented at the Wheaton Theology Conference, 1997 on The Integration of Psychology and Theology is now two chapters in the Kennard, *A Critical Realist Theological Method,* this chapter on Bio-ethics is significantly redone by Kennard, and the next is largely intact as "A Transactional Model of Human Based on Biblical Theology" through which Paul Holmes was lead writer. Earlier versions of the Image and Soul sections of this paper include: "The Nature of Man: A Biblical Anthropology" presented at the Evangelical Theological Society, Nov. 1990; "Biblical Anthropology as a Creation and Revelation Framework for Doing Bio-ethics: With a Focus on Image of God, Soul, Life and Person" presented at: Baraminology Study Group, May 2006; the Bryan Center, Sept. 2006; Evangelical Philosophical Society on Image Mar. 2006, on Soul Mar. 2007; Society of Christian Philosophers April 2007; International Creation Conference Aug. 2008 "Bio-Ethics from God and Soul" which as also published in *Proceedings of the Sixth International*

reduce humans to programmed matter in appeals to a holistic view of soul. These descriptive Biblical theologians are not arguing for what some behaviorists claim, for the behaviorists selectively appeal to a small part of Biblical theology research to support their behaviorist agenda. So, Boyd's concern should be alleviated by the profound degree of spirituality retained within the view presented here.

Faced with a variety of psychological, philosophical and theological models, and the near unanimity of Biblical anthropology among descriptive Biblical theology, how is the Christian to understand the nature of humanness? I propose to follow the Biblical theologians through an analysis of the words and concepts articulated in O.T. and N.T. literature that address the nature of a human. The conclusions presented from this analysis will be used to make a presentation of an integrated model of a human. I propose to then extend these Biblical theology categories into the field of bio-ethics to unpack their bio-ethical implications.

This method provides Biblical grounding and thought forms to warrant the design and revealed framework for bio-ethics. From this approach we can with real warrant, boldly go where few have gone before, because God leads the narrow route through the galaxy of bio-ethical issues.

10.1. Image of God

A range of traditional options identify how several theologies understand humans to be made *in* the image of God. For example, Irenaeus proposed "image of God" to describe reason and free will, while "likeness" he identified as the supernatural endowment through the Spirit.[8] Aquinas follows Irenaeus' view identifying the *imago dei* as retained at the Fall, but the likeness is lost at the Fall.[9] In contrast, Martin Luther and John Calvin identified 'image of God' as identical to "likeness" in that both affirm the ability to reason and original righteousness.[10] Both Reformers saw these qualities as significantly marred in the Fall. Emil Brunner took "image of God" as a symbol for "moral uprightness or righteousness of God."[11] In contrast, Karl Barth identified "image of God" is essentially the relationality of humans that permits relationship with God and fellow humans after the pattern of the divine relationships

---

Conference on Creationism: Technical Symposium Sessions (Pittsburgh: Creation Science Fellowship, 2008), pp. 43–54.

8 Irenaeus, *Against Heresies* 3.23.5 and 5.6.1 in *The Ante-Nicene Fathers,* ed. A. Roberts and J. Donaldson (Grand Rapids: Eerdmans, 1995), vol 3.

9 Thomas Aquinas, *Summa Theologica* 1.93.4 in *Great Books of the Western World* (Chicago: Encyclopaedia Britannica, 1952), vol. 19.

10 Martin Luther, *Genesis* in *Luther's Works* ed. Jaroslav Pelikan (St. Louis: Concordia, 1958), 1:60–62; John Calvin, *The Institutes of the Christian Religion* (Grand Rapids: Associated Publishers and Authors, n.d.) 1:1.

11 Emil Brunner, *Man in Revolt* (Philadelphia: Westminster, 1947), p. 388.

within the Trinity.[12] Additionally, Thomas Torrance and G. C. Berkouwer identify "image of God" as "the focal point in the interrelationships between God and the universe."[13] None of these traditional views are how the Bible or the descriptive Biblical theology movement uses the term of "image of God."

The concept of humankind as the "image of God" is first introduced in the creation account in Genesis. As God creates humans, He formulates an image of Himself (Gen. 1:26–28). The words for "image" (*ṣlm*/צַלְמֵנוּ,) and "likeness" (*dmt*/דְּמוּתֵנוּ,) state that characteristics attributed to God in this passage are reflected in humanity. There is no distinction between the two words; they are totally interchangeable.[14] In this Genesis 1 instance, Eugene Merrill clarifies that the ("in") is best understood as the "*beth* of identity" and parallel to the ("according to") in indicating functionality.[15] That is, "image and likeness of God" means that humans function in the role as *representation* and *representative* of God.

This account introduces humans as a *representation of God* on earth. In the ancient Near East, kings would erect images of themselves indicating regions that were appropriately within their domain. For example, Ramesses II had his image hewn out of rock at the mouth of the *nahr el-kelb* on the Mediterranean north of Beirut, indicating he ruled this area.[16] Therefore, as God's image, man indicates by his very presence that God rules the earth. This emphasis of the greatness of God's creative and sovereign power reflects the emphasis of the first literary unit (Gen. 1:1–2:3) as it polemics other ancient Near East cosmologies. "Image of God " contributes to this polemic because we are living images that can accomplish something instead of the lifeless idols (*ṣlm*/צַלְמֵנוּ,)

---

12 Karl Barth, *Church Dogmatics,* ed. G. W. Bromiley and T. F. Torrance (Edinburg: T. & T. Clark, 1936–69), 3/2:196.

13 Thomas Torrance, *Divine and Contingent Order* (Oxford: Oxford University Press, 1981), p. 129; J. C. Berkouwer, *Man the Image of God* (Grand Rapids: Eerdmans, 1962), pp. 87–9, 179, 197–8.

14 Victor Hamilton in *Theological Wordbook of the Old Testament,* edited by Harris, Archer, and Waltke, 1:192; *Lev. Rab.* 34.3 R. Hillel emphasized wholeness of "image" and "likeness" as synonyms; Nissan Rubin, "Body and Soul in Talmudic and Mishnaic Sources," *Koroth* 9: special issue: Third International Symposium on Medicine in Bible and Talmud, Dec. 7–9, 1987 (1988): 153–4.

15 Eugene Merrill, in *Dictionary of the Old Testament: Pentateuch,* edited by T. Desmond Alexander and David Baker (Downers Grove: InterVarsity Press, 2003), pp. 443–44.

16 Hans Walter Wolff, *Anthropology of the Old Testament,* pp. 160–1; additional support comes from other inscriptions of statuary, like the *Tell Fekheriye inscription* 1, 12, 15–16 which also use image and likeness words, translated in A. R. Millard and P. Bordreuil, "A Statue from Syria with Assyrian and Aramaic Inscriptions," *Biblical Archaeologist* 45.3(1982): 137; also 4Q504 frag. 8, lines 4–6; A. H. Konkel in *New International Dictionary of Old Testament Theology & Exegesis,* edited by Willem VanGemeren, 1:969–70.

prohibited throughout the Biblical text (Num. 33:52; 2 Kgs. 11:18; 2 Chr. 23:17; Ezek. 7:20; Dan. 3:1–15).[17]

As God's representative on earth, man pictures God as both sovereign ruler and creator.[18] Thus, images of God are designed by God to rule the creation (Gen. 1:26). To help facilitate this ruling, the images of God are blessed to both reproduce themselves and thereby facilitate this ruling of the created order (Gen. 1:28). "Filling the earth" connects these two themes, showing the extent of man's procreative power and making it possible for him to rule. Creation and rule require a male and a female in the human realm. Persons are individually God's image and as a married pair the couple is God's image. Not that relationality is meant by image but that individually we humans contribute toward ruling and that married pairs also contribute toward ruling (being fruitful, multiplying to fill the earth so subduing and ruling can occur). God's image as one, yet plural, hints at the majestic creator character of *Elohim*.[19] From the chaotic images of formlessness that begin the passage, God shows his goodness through purposefully designing creation and then man in His image. Humans are to bring this creation under our control, which would include remaking it purposefully for the ends we think are best under our stewardship to God.

Genesis goes on to develop the idea that God's image included being His son, fitted by a loving Father with an appropriate situation, work, life and marriage (Gen. 2:23–24; 5:1–3; Luke 3:38).[20] The few additional references to man as God's image indicate that this image continues beyond the fall (Gen. 5:1, 3; 9:6; James 3:9) though dragged through futility and death as a result of sin.

In contrast to a creation-based view of man as image of God, the image of Christ is a future representation of humanity in their glorification. Jesus Christ in His incarnation comes in the image of God, but upon completing His work was highly exalted (2 Cor. 4:4; Col. 1:15; Phil.

---

17 Bruce Vawter, *On Genesis: A New Reading* (Garden City: Doubleday, 1977), p. 55.

18 Eugene Merrill, in *Dictionary of the Old Testament: Pentateuch*, edited by T. Desmond Alexander and David Baker, pp. 442, 444–5; *Gen. Rab.* 8.10; *b. Sanh.* 38b; *Wis.* 2.23; *Sir.* 17.3–4; *m 'Abot* 3.14; *b. Meg.* 9a; 28a; Gerhard von Rad, *Old Testament Theology* (New York: Harper and Row, 1962) 1:146; also in *Theological Dictionary of the New Testament*, edited by Gerhard Kittel, 2:392; O. Flender in *The New International Dictionary of New Testament Theology*, edited by Colin Brown, 2:287; A. H. Kookel in *New International Dictionary of Old Testament Theology & Exegesis*, edited by Willem VanGemeren, 1:969; Hans Walter Wolff, *Anthropology of the Old Testament*, pp. 159–65; John Hartley in *Theological Wordbook of the Old Testament*, edited by Harris, Archer, and Waltke, 2:768.

19 Douglas Kennard, *The Classical Christian God* (Lewiston: The Mellen Press, 2002), pp. 87–89.

20 Also the Egyptian sense of "Image of God" in *Instruction of Merikare* 1.106; Eugene Merrill, in *Dictionary of the Old Testament: Pentateuch*, edited by T. Desmond Alexander and David Baker, pp. 442.

2:6–11). As a result, the Christian is not merely having his damaged image of God repaired but is also being made into a more exalted image of God's Son (Rom. 8:29–30; 1 Cor. 15:49; 2 Cor. 3:18; 4:4; Phil. 3:21). In fact, the Christian's fallen condition will be transformed into a higher state than that of Adam before the fall.

The concept of "image of God" has implications for the individual as he lives out life. Terms such as sovereignty are associated with the concept and indicate the responsibility the first human inhabitants were given for the world in which they lived. The terms for subdue and rule ( ) are very forceful, encouraging utilization and dominance of the creation by humans (Gen.1:26, 28). Such forceful words are used elsewhere in instances of conquest and rape, implying that the created world will resist some of our rule (Lev. 26:17; Num. 32:22, 29; Neh. 5:5; Jer. 34:11, 16; Gen. 3:1–5 shows first resistance). This is especially the case once the creation is subjected to futility by the oracle of judgment in response to the fall of humans (Gen. 3:14–19; Rom. 8:20). However, humans are to provide the structures and guidelines for co-existing and engaging with their natural environment. In this sense, our responsibility to nature included those encompassed by that of a fiduciary or curator (Gen. 2:15–19). Humans are to nurture nature. Both before the Fall and after the Fall the original inhabitants provided organization to diminish chaos and promote an environment in which the needs of all are observed. This is evident in the naming, organizing and agricultural work humans were to accomplish. This structure provided an atmosphere in which the inherent potential of both human beings and nature itself could be actualized. As images and sons of God, humans are to play god in bio-ethics, not be God (the Sovereign), but do miniature acts of sovereignty within the stewardship which has been delegated to us by the Sovereign God. In the same way as our kids play house and army men, so in our stewardship we are to play god in bringing control to the area of biology.

Anything that is not Biblically excluded, we have free range to conceptually plan and explore for the potential gain that we can bring to the creation. This is especially the case because the command "rule" encourages aggressive engagement over the creation.

Such subduing control does not control all factors, for God remains sovereign over our stewardship under Him. The causalities are best understood as a divine-human compatibilism in which both God and humans choose and implement everything that comes to pass (Gen. 4:1; Acts 2:23).[21] Thus we do not violate God's sovereignty by our humanly responsible attempts to subdue and rule the creation. This legitimates humans attempting prevention and recovery means, such as ways of controlling pests (e.g., serpents), aids to diminish pain in child birth,

21 Douglas Kennard, *The Classical Christian God*, pp. 135–166, 185–204.

pesticides and herbicides, fertilization of crops, genetically modified food, inoculations, drug and surgery treatment, AID, *in vitro*-fertilization (especially if all fertilized eggs are used to try to implant), stem cell treatment, gene therapy, and reproductive cloning.[22] Such an image of God concept identifies the theoretically permissible even though I recognize methodologically ethical principles raised elsewhere in the paper bring certain restrictions. For example, I recognize that embryonic stem cell research should not destroy the embryo (because it is life) but may be possible without such destruction, however pragmatically may not be therapeutically productive unless the problem of tumor production is significantly diminished. Possibly these stem cells could be provided by umbilical cords, placenta or the blood contained within them. Furthermore, a clone does not become a substitute for a person, nor should be insurance for a person (as was done in the movie, "The Island"), but such a clone is a whole new image of God. That is, cloning only provides a biological duplicate to progress through a developmental process that will at least in some respect be different from the original. Nature provides possibilities, whereas nurture realizes some of those possibilities.

Thus genetic determinism is too limited an idea to reflect what Biblical divine-human compatibilism entails. In fact, with only 20,000-25,000 protein-coding genes[23] this is probably too few to determine all aspects of our life and destiny. Furthermore, if one could methodologically develop filtering to recognize cystic fibrosis or Down syndrome, genetic therapy of the zygote would not be forcing genes upon the new individual (albeit, with parental consent) for these genes would be utilized in the early creation process making the new individual who he is in creation. Nurture, of course, would then develop the given of these genetic possibilities. Likewise, a clone and a genetically manipulated fertilized egg is a new image of God in a different situation than that of the original. This is evident in recognizing observable differences among identical twins who occupy the same womb.[24] The nurturing environment will significantly affect the development of this new image of God. The cloned or genetically aided image of God will live life within the same stewardship as other images of God: responsible, accountable, answerable, praised or judged.

Of course, the fact that we can and should explore ways of controlling the creation does not guarantee funding or ease in obtaining resources. The utility of greater gain for the greater good would argue

---

22 My statements are similar to those in "'Statement on Cloning' by the United Church of Christ Committee on Genetics," in *Human Cloning: Religious Responses*. ed. Ronald Cole-Turner (Louisville: Westminster John Knox, 1997), pp. 149–51.

23 International Human Genome Sequencing Consortium, "Finishing the Euchromatic Sequence of the Human Genome," *Nature* 431:21(21 Oct. 2004): 931–945.

24 Conversation with Bryan College biologist Dr. Todd Wood, 12/15/05.

for the public funding to pursue those health needs which would accomplish the most societal good. Communal oversight helps to: 1) alleviate potential problems, 2) limit violating societal conscience, and 3) rule of responsibly. For example, in the United States genetically modified food is not much of an issue probably because of the oversight brought about by the Food and Drug Administration.[25] This was aided by the FDA defining genetically modified food as "essentially equivalent" to the natural. Perhaps something like the FDA could help relieve the international fears as well. Furthermore, personal funding could be utilized to support those concerns which an individual is passionate about. Provided resources and means were available, such expressions of control are to be encouraged. As images of God, we each have responsibility to reason and obtain consent of the responsible parties in pursuing our control of part of the creation. Of course, obtaining of resources does not provide license to violate ethics (e.g., abortion to obtain stem cells will be shown to be a violation of Biblical ethics).

To facilitate this control of the creation, human beings possess cognitive abilities that enable self-reflective thought and the ability to assess, learn from past experience, anticipate future contingencies, and to choose purposefully to accomplish desired ends.[26] These capacities make him uniquely qualified for the task of stewardship. For example, Adam was given the responsibility of naming the creatures in the garden and identifying a partner for himself (Gen. 2:20). The roles and responsibilities inherent within humanness, such as cultivation and care, suggest that the truly human individual comprehends the ecological balance of nature and interacts with it in a manner that respects the place of all things created. This individual understands that the project of true humanness is increased when the potential of all nature is encouraged. Thus to thwart the actualization of the least of created things hinders the peace (*shalom*) intended for all.

In ruling the creation, anything is permitted provided it is: 1) Not excluded by God's command, like judging someone with a different opinion or practice (Rom. 14:3–10, 13). That is, don't disobey God or He could judge you (Gen. 3:17–19; Rom. 14:10–12). 2) Anything is permitted provided it fits within the priority of the design parameters and is 3) actively engaged in for the Lord's glory (Rom. 14:6–12). 4) Anything wise is permitted, in that it helps and does not hinder (Rom. 14:13–15:6). 5) Anything is permitted that fits within an affirming conscience, rather than violating one's conscience (a New Covenant thing; Rom. 14:5, 22–23).

To facilitate the image of God's rule of the creation God provides blessings of: fruitfulness, to fill the earth, to subdue the earth, and to

25 "Talk of the Nation: Science Friday" National Public Radio, 12/16/05.

26 Douglas Kennard, *The Relationship Between Epistemology, Hermeneutics, Biblical Theology and Contextualization* (Lewiston: Edwin Mellen Press, 1999), pp. 35–70.

rule the earth (Gen. 1:26–30; 8:20–9:17).[27] Ruling the earth is both the design goal for we humans and a blessing from God (Gen. 1:26, 28). These elements of blessing are softer than commands because they are within the genre of blessing, which the Blesser, God grounds (Gen. 2:3; 5:2; 9:1; 12:2–3). *Blessing entails a relationship of privilege, mostly guaranteed by the blesser in relationship, which in this case is God.* In this creation context God's statement accomplishes what it says, so these blessings are guaranteed. God's speech in the first literary unit (Gen. 1–2:3) accomplishes His statement to make it so, even though He uses imperatives in these statements to render in reality light, separation, waters, lights and swarms (Gen. 1:3, 6, 9, 14, 20). Few would conjecture that the imperative in each of these Divine statements renders light or water culpable for their existence, so God incorporates Divine statements using imperatives in this creation account as statements of His guaranteeing the creation order. However, that does not guarantee that these spoken creations (light, vegetation, and animals) are everywhere, nor does it guarantee all humans will be procreatively fruitful. Blessing makes it generically realizable for the human race, but not necessarily specifically realizable for everyone (Gen. 1:22, 28); some may be infertile without being culpable for sin concerning this. God makes us fruitful, and so corporately we fill the earth. God enables us to subdue, so we can rule.

Though these are God-grounded corporate blessings there is corporate culpability for involvement indicated through the use of imperatives to moral beings. The use of plural Hebrew Qal imperatives for all five blessings "Be fruitful, multiply, fill, subdue, and rule," and the LXX having "be fruitful and multiply" as present imperatives shows the group of humans should as a group participate within the corporate blessing which God provides. [28] However, the LXX use of "fill, subdue and rule" as aorist indicatives softens involvement with these statements of God's guaranteeing the design plan in this text.

No one is personally culpable if he does not avail himself to all blessings. For example, Jesus had the blessing of having angel protection (Matt. 4:6), but that is no cause for foolish choices. Jesus was not culpable for not availing himself with all these potential blessings.

God's blessings can change. For example, the blessing of a vegetarian diet changed to include meat at the Noahic Covenant (Gen. 1:29–30; 9:2–4).

---

27 The construction in Gen. 1:28 "God blessed them and said ..." identifies the content of the blessing using a narrative connecter waw consecutive as the author repeatedly uses throughout the chapter.

28 Rabbinics took these imperatives as commands and thus considered an individual as culpable if they did not marry and beget children (*m. Yebam.* 6.6; *Pesiq. Rab Kah* 22.2; *m. Giṭ* 4.5; *Gen. Rab.* 23.4; 34.14; *Ex. Rab.* 1.13; Josephus, *Ant.* 4.8.40 #290; *'Abot R. Nat.* 31A; *b. Ber.* 10a; *b. Yebam.* 62b; *b. Qidd.* 29b–30a).

While God's corporate blessings in themselves are not themselves ethically binding for individuals. However, they can have restrictions within them, so there may be aspects of responsibility. When there is individual culpability, it is usually spelled out with its gain or consequences. For example, gain is apparent in that the male and female within image of God fosters fruitfulness (Gen. 1:27–28). This would have obvious ethical implications for heterosexual marriage. Likewise, the Noahic Covenant stipulation against murder is immersed within an *inclusio* of blessing, and provided with the teeth of capital punishment to enforce its mandate (Gen. 9:1–7). As a blessing, fruitfulness to fill is only reiterated when the population is small, showing God's insistence on individuals' participation in procreation is only essential when the population is small (Gen. 1:28; 9:1, 7).

So blessing is contextually dependent. Within the specific context of family protection and gain from labor, children are a blessing from the Lord (Ps. 127:1–5). This psalm does not declare kids to be a blessing in all contexts. For example, a destructive, foolish son is not a blessing (Prov. 10:1; 30:11–14). So the context of one's child's life virtues and vices indicates whether a specific child is a blessing for his parents or not.

This creation pattern does not legitimate natural rights or natural law, but rather God provides the privilege of *blessings in responsible relationship*. We as images of God can not insist on a right of the status of what we are. That is, an infertile lady can't insist that God make her fruitful. The whole ethical approach that defends natural rights or natural law is far more indebted to Stoicism, Aristotle, Aquinas and Jefferson than to the Biblical text. Now don't misunderstand me, there may be truth through natural rights and it may be helpful in bilingual communication to other worldviews to use natural rights arguments, but natural rights and law are not the Biblical theology framework within which God creates, elects, and provides. That is, we images of God must frame our ethic by God's fiat and thus fit into His Biblically revealed framework for our stewardship. These creation frameworks especially develop blessings of fruitfulness, to fill the earth, to subdue the earth, and to rule the earth (Gen. 1:26–30; 8:20–9:17). Amid these blessings is the stewardship with ethical admonitions of: 1) cultivating and keeping the garden and then the earth (which has ramifications for development, recycling, and retention of resources), 2) enjoying the freedom and abundant resources, and 3) don't disobey God or He can judge (Gen 2:15–17; 3:17–19; 8:20–9:17). These ethical frameworks have huge ethical ramifications.

Let us briefly explore fruitfulness to fill the earth. This blessing is affirmed whenever the population is low, so it is a critical admonition in those instances (Gen. 1:28; 9:1, 7). Obviously, on an individual level fertility can be foregone as a human wishes to pursue a noble goal, like a single life of ministry to Christ (e.g., 1 Cor. 7). Presumably, this would also legitimate family planning so that ministry and the quality of child rearing could also be facilitated. This is because sexuality is not just for procreation but also includes pleasure and cultivating a marriage relationship within its purposes (Gen. 2:23–24; 26:8; Prov. 30:18–19; Song 5:1). The spilling of Onan's seed is wrong because he did not fulfill his obligation to his sister-in-law/wife in levirate marriage (which is designed to raise up a family heir for the land [a quality of life concern]); it is not a judgment on birth control (Gen. 38:8–10; Deut. 25:5–10).[29] However, as a blessing, fertility can not be insisted upon as a right. Unfortunately, some will be infertile, and there is no sin in this, even if it is repeatedly a condition of pain throughout the Bible and life. Likewise, there is no sin in attempting to comply with God's broad blessing to become fertile, provided it is through ethical means. Fertility can be accomplished by a range of enablements of each spouse (medication, surgery, AID, invitro-fertilization, egg donation, cloning) and by adoption from another, as well. Additionally, surrogacy is theoretically moral but may be practically difficult to facilitate but it might be possible to find a person so generous and giving of themselves as to carry a baby to term for the purpose of the intended couple to adopt and raise him as their own, but it has been done in this generous manner. Of course, in a polygamous situation fertility through one wife can diminish some felt need of infertility of the other, but it rarely meets the psychological need of the infertile wife and will likely raise other problems since monogamy is God's design and humans are sinful, and of course in many nations polygamy is illegal (e.g., Gen. 2:24; 16:1–16; 21:8–21; 29:15–30:24; 1 Sam. 1:2–28). Sometimes God will even please the infertile couple with fertility in spite of their fertility treatment (e.g., Gen. 30). On this issue, like other infirmed conditions, God promises to heal the infertile condition in the everlasting Kingdom (Isa. 54:1–3).

On the other side of the fertility issue, it would be permitted for a society commitment to mutually and voluntarily limit population because they corporately consider that they have "filled" that region of the globe. That is, then fruitfulness enables multiplying to a full condition through which subduing and ruling can be accomplished. Such control that an image of God can bring subdues the creation to comply with the blessings of God. However, if procreative activity hinders human attempts to rule the creation, procreation as a blessing can be limited to facilitate the greater purpose and blessing designed for the image of God, that of ruling the creation (Gen. 1:26 purpose over blessing in 1:28 to facilitate purpose).

29 This is corroborated by *Coitus interuptus* being permitted by second Temple rabbi Eliezer, *b. Yebam.* 34b; *t. Nid.* 2.6; cf. David Feldman, *Birth Control in Jewish Law* (Westport: Greenwood, 1968), p. 187.

10.2. Soul

While "image of God" wonderfully elevates humanity above the rest of creation, "soul" connects a human with the rest of the creation. That is, the language of the Genesis account identifies that animals and humans *are* "living souls" (Gen. 1:20, 24, 30; 2:7; 9:4–5, 10).[30] The animals pre-modernly described as souls are non-microbial animals (fish, foul, insect, reptile, amphibian, and mammal). No Biblical text discusses the microbial. Soul has a holistic connotation in that it signifies a *complete living being*.[31] The words for "soul", *nephesh* (*npš*/נֶפֶשׁ) in the Hebrew and *psyche* ( ) in the Greek, have developed from the idea of breath to mean the whole person who both breathes and desires, lives and moves (Ex. 23:12; Deut. 12:12).[32] Very few Biblical references develop "soul" as a part of a human,[33] and in those cases it refers to the throat or neck, the organ of breathing (Isa. 51:23; Jer. 15:9; Luke 2:35).[34]

30 H. Seebass in *Theological Dictionary of the Old Testament,* edited by Johannes Botterweck, Helmer Ringgren, and Heinz-Josef Fabry, 9:510–16; Edmund Jacob in *Theological Dictionary of the New Testament* edited by Kittel and Friedrich, 9:620, 639–40, 648–9, 653; D. C. Fredericks in *New International Dictionary of Old Testament Theology & Exegesis,* edited by Willem VanGemeren, 3:133; Bruce Waltke in *Theological Wordbook of the Old Testament,* edited by Harris, Archer, and Waltke, 2:589–91.

31 Hans Walter Wolff, *Anthropology of the Old Testament*, pp. 24–25; H. Seebass in *Theological Dictionary of the Old Testament,* edited by Johannes Botterweck, Helmer Ringgren, and Heinz-Josef Fabry, 9:510–16; Edmund Jacob in *Theological Dictionary of the New Testament* edited by Kittel and Friedrich, 9:620, 639–40, 648–9, 653; D. C. Fredericks in *New International Dictionary of Old Testament Theology & Exegesis,* edited by Willem VanGemeren, 3:133; Bruce Waltke in *Theological Wordbook of the Old Testament,* edited by Harris, Archer, and Waltke, 2:589–91; James Dunn, *The Theology of Paul the Apostle,* pp. 76–78; John A. McKenzie, *Dictionary of the Bible* (New York: Macmillan, 1965), p. 839; Karl Rahner and Herbert Vorgrimler, *Theological Dictionary* (New York: Herder and Herder, 1965), pp. 442–43; John Cooper, *Body Soul & Life Everlasting* (Grand Rapids: Eerdmans, 1989), pp. 42–43; Nancey Murphy, "Human Nature: Historical, Scientific, and Religious Issues" and Ray Anderson, "On Being Human: The Spiritual Saga of a Creaturely Soul" in *Whatever Happened to the Soul?: Scientific and Theological Portraits of Human Nature,* edited by Warren Brown, Nancey Murphy and H. Newton Malony (Minneapolis: Fortress Press, 1998), pp. 22, 178, 186; 11QTemple 51.19; 54.20;61.12; 1QS 11.13; CD 12.11–12; 1QH 2.2, 24; 3.6; 5.17–18; 9.18; 15.16.

32 Colin Brown, *The New International Dictionary of New Testament Theology,* vol. 3, pp. 676 and 679.

33 Hans Walter Wolff, *Anthropology of the Old Testament,* pp. 24–25; Edmund Jacob in *Theological Dictionary of the New Testament* edited by Kittel and Friedrich, 9:620, 639–40, 648–49, 653; D. C. Fredericks in *New International Dictionary of Old Testament Theology & Exegesis,* edited by Willem VanGemeren, 3:133; Bruce Waltke in *Theological Wordbook of the Old Testament,* edited by Harris, Archer, and Waltke, 2:589–91; James Dunn, *The Theology of Paul the Apostle,* pp. 76–78; Wolfhart Pannenberg, *Anthropology in Theological Perspective* (Philadelphia: Westminster, 1985), p. 523.

34 Albert Dihle and Edmund Jacob in *Theological Dictionary of the New Testament* edited by Kittel and Friedrich, 9:609 and 618.

In other places, soul stands in the place of a pronoun, indicating living persons (Ps. 54:4; Acts 2:41). At times, especially in the Psalms, soul in Hebrew has a pronominal suffix "his soul" or "my soul," which in these instances is not a part of a person but akin to "my life" (Pss. 3:2; 6:3). At times soul is combined in a list with other descriptors of human to communicate that all of a person must be involved in a task such as loving God (Deut. 6:4–5; Matt. 22:32; Acts 4:32; 1 Thess. 5:23).

Only rarely is there a verse like Hebrews 4:12, which indicates that the Word of God can separate between soul and spirit, suggesting the two concepts are not identical.

This Biblical concept of soul is very different from the philosophical and traditional theological alternatives. For example, Tertullian followed the Stoics in conceiving of the human soul as corporeal, generated with the body, but departs from them in considering the soul to be depraved by sin and renewed by regeneration.[35] Plato reasons that the soul is an eternal form for each human, which as eternal continues from a pre-incarnate existence to a post-incarnate afterlife, while our shadowy bodies are birthed and then decay.[36] While Origen followed Plato's view of soul,[37] Augustine modified the concept in the direction of neo-platonism, denying eternal pre-existence and affirming a created tripartite quality of each human soul to reflect the Trinity.[38] In contrast, Aristotle and Aquinas proposed a hylomorphic view in which the material human is formed as soul.[39] René Descartes proposed a radical form of substance dualism in which the soul is akin to a thinking substance that is the real person within the extended substance of body.[40] Karl Barth identifies that body and soul are a "concrete monism," both terms describing the unique

35 Tertullian, *A Treatise on the Soul* 4–5, 10–11, 24, 27, 38, 41, 51 in *The Ante-Nicene Fathers*, edited by Alexander Robert and James Donaldson (Edinburgh: T & T Clark, 1989), 3:183–229; *De* an. 9 in *Against Praxeas*. In *The Writings of Quintus Sept. Flor. Tertullianus*. Edited by Richard Ellmann (Kila: Kessinger, 1869–70).

36 Plato, *Cratylus, Phaedrus, Phaedo, Laws* bk. 10 in *Great Books of the Western World, #7 Plato*. (Chicago: Encyclopaedia Britannica, 1952), pp. 93, 124, 244–46, 763–4 respectively.

37 Origen, De Princ. 2.9.6 in *On First Principles. Ante-Nicene Fathers* vol. 4 (Grand Rapids: Eerdmans, 1976).

38 Augustine, *City of God* 7.23, 11.23, 13.2, 19.3, 21.3, 22.4 and *Ep.* 166.27 in the *Great Books of the Western World,* vol. 18, edited by William Benton (Chicago: Encyclopaedia Britannica, 1952), pp. 265, 360–1, 510, 561, 588.

39 Aristotle, *Topics* 4.6; *Metaphysics* 5.8; 7.10; 8.3; 12.5; 13.2 and *Soul* 2.1–3 in *Great Books of the Western World*. Vol. 8, pp. 177, 538, 559, 567, 600, 631, 642–5 respectively; Thomas Aquinas, *Summa Theologica* 1.3.1; 1.18.3 ans and rep 1; 1.51.1 rep. 3; 1.70.3 ans and rep 2; 1.72.A 1, rep 1; 1.75–76; 1.97, A 3 ans in *Great Books of the Western World*. Vol. 19, pp. 14–15, 275–6365–7, 368–9, 378–9, 515.

40 René Descartes, *Meditations on First Philosophy*. *Great Books of the Western World,* vol. 31. *Descartes, Spinoza*. (Chicago: Encyclopaedia Britannica, 1952), pp. 20, 135–6, 208–9.

and singular experience of the person.[41] None of these philosophical or traditional theological views captures the sense of the Biblical text and the Biblical theology movement on the holistic human concept of soul as life or person.

A special contemporary challenge excludes the concept of soul from theological discussion by advocating humans as nonreductive physicalism. Nancey Murphy, Warren Brown, Elving Anderson, and Robert Van Gulick advocate a nonreductive physicalism that considers humans as a "whole complex function, both in society and in relation to God, which gives rise to 'higher' human capacities such as morality and spirituality."[42] Their view is better analyzed as affirming a full concept of body (which I agree with and develop in that section) because it actually explores the cognitive and religious capacities rooted in embodiment and genes, rather than the absence of the presence of soul. Their case for this view excluding soul is merely to join Murphy in *assuming* that their case for embodiment excludes soul (perhaps on the basis of Ockham's razor, though this is never mentioned), but they marshal no evidence for that assumption. So nonreductive physicalism is no defeater of soul, merely an affirmation of body. Such an *assumption that redundant analysis and causalities exclude each other* counters Murphy's own assumption and practice of granting "multiple causation" analyses.[43] Such a commitment to "multiple causation" analysis is a commitment that Biblical theology's multifaceted-unity hypothesis of humanity here and Murphy elsewhere share in common. Additionally, for purposes of informing bio-ethics (which is what this chapter is about), Murphy's nonreductive physicalism is a degenerative hypothesis, because she nowhere develops the concept when she discusses her broadly Christian ethic.[44] So if Murphy ignores nonreductive physicalism for discussions

---

41 Karl Barth, *Church Dogmatics*, 3/2:393.

42 Warren Brown, Nancey Murphy, and H. Newton Malony, *Whatever Happened to the Soul?: Scientific and Theological Portraits of Human Nature* (Minneapolis: Fortress Press, 1998), p. 2, 25, 49–72, 99–148; Nancey Murphy, *Bodies and Souls, or Spiritual Bodies?* (Cambridge: Cambridge University Press, 2006); Nancey Murphy "Reductionism: How Did We Fall Into It and Can We Emerge From It?" and Robert Van Gulick "Reduction, Emergence, and the Mind/Body Problem: A Philosophic Overview" in *Evolution and Emergence: Systems, Organisms, Persons* edited by Nancey Murphy and William Stoeger (Oxford: Oxford University Press, 2007), pp. 19–73. A reverse reductionism to see all through the lens of soul is accomplished by Richard Swinburne in *The Evolution of the Soul* (Oxford: Clarendon Press, 1986). The Biblical theology movement does neither.

43 Nancey Murphy and George Ellis, *On the Moral Nature of the Universe: Theology, Cosmology, and Ethics* (Minneapolis: Fortress Press, 1996), pp. 195–228; throughout Nancey Murphy, *Religion and Science: God, Evolution, and the Soul* (Herald Press, Scotdale, 2002).

44 Nancey Murphy and George Ellis, *On the Moral Nature of the Universe: Theology, Cosmology, and Ethics* (Minneapolis: Fortress Press, 1996); Nancey Murphy, Brad Kallenberg & Mark Thiessen Nation, *Virtues & Practices in the Christian Tradition: Christian Ethics after MacIntyre* (Harrisburg: Trinity Press International, 1997).

in bio-ethics, I will do the same. Furthermore, the Bible and the Biblical theology movement develop "soul" as a meaningful concept, showing Murphy has different allegiances than inform this chapter.

Biblically, soul can be likened to the self or person. This concept refers to the most basic or elemental aspect of the person. Thus, soul is the relationship of the person to himself and others on an ontological level. We should not define 'preson' in a Descartian or Lockian manner as a *self-aware individual* or in an Aristotelian manner as *having the capacity of self-assertion and self-manipulation*. This is most important in discussions of Trinity and Christology where the concept of person and nature must be clarified precisely. If nature is defined by the attributes of a being, cognition would be an attribute related to nature. With such a definition of nature, Lockian, Cartesian or Aristotelian definitions for 'person' would render the Trinity into a contradictory concept, affirming three and one mental Beings simultaneously.[45] In the orthodox Trinitarian model,[46] then person is defined by the following coherent manner: *an instance of a spiritual being as a moral end in itself, in relation to others*. In Trinity there are three persons ontologically and one Divine nature. It is the Divine nature that is omniscient. In Christology there are two natures (Divinity and humanity) and one person Jesus Christ. Chalcedon's decision identified Christ's Deity as omniscient, and humanity as limited and growing in knowledge. Thus person and nature are not the same thing, nor should they be confused. The Divine persons are to be worshipped, whereas, human, angelic and animal persons are to be respected to the level of their respective natures. That is, while both humans and animals are souls, only humans are images of God, thus humans are of a higher level of being than other animals.

Thus on the authority of stipulations and blessings of the Noahic covenant: 1) no one should murder (or euthanize) a human person, 2) humans and animals who do murder (or euthanize) humans should forfeit their lives by societal fostered capital punishment, 3) humans can eat animals, but not while they are alive, and 4) humans should not eat the emblem of soul, the blood of the animal (Gen. 9:2–6; Acts 15:20, 29; Rom. 13:4, 7). No governmental response should over-rule the divinely designated stewardship and blessings that are set by God in relationship with humans. Therefore, it would be unethical to argue that humans have a moral right to die with dignity in either natural law or from constitutional rights, such as the right to privacy. Furthermore, there is no right to limit suffering, but as responsible agents in our stewardship under God, we can make attempts to diminish pain within suffering, especially when it is requested by the responsible agent or the sufferer. Quality of life concerns should not be used to over-rule the Divinely

45 Doug Kennard, *The Classical Christian God*, pp. 75–78.

46 Orthodox in that it is defined by the seven patristic universal councils.

sourced stewardship pressed upon the human race *in toto* requiring the communal obligation to the right to life.

Likewise, there should be a concern for animal privilege in a Biblical view of soul. Animals are responsible agents and should be rewarded or punished appropriately to their level of personhood (Gen. 3:1, 13–15; 9:5–6; Ex. 21:28–29; Deut. 25:4; Matt. 12:11–12).[47] Animals, like other souls, were to keep Sabbath within the Mosaic Covenant (Ex. 20:10; Deut. 5:14). However, animals are to be subdued and ruled by humans, and even eaten (Gen. 1:26–28; 9:2–4). Specifically, animals are available for bio-ethical experimentation and attempts to improve human conditions. Furthermore, it is ethical to use eggs to cultivate human vaccines. Drug, cloning and surgery experiments on animals are appropriate to develop treatments for humans. The bio-ethical concerns would urge against frivolous or needlessly painful or wasteful use of these animals, because they are souls and thus persons. To concretize this, animal tests are permitted to guarantee humans will not be accidentally injured.

Furthermore, in bio-ethics the origin of life is the origin of the soul and person. David considers that his inward parts[48] and bones were made by God in the womb of his mother (Ps. 139:13–15; likewise Jeremiah, Jer. 1:4–5). The continuity before birth to growing up to adulthood is considered by David to continue to be himself. David considers that God has completely planned out his life before he had experienced any days of it. Eve recognizes that procreation includes the human intimate sexual activity *and* the divine aid to produce a human life (Gen. 4:1, 25). So no procreation is without divine and human effort to bring it about. David actually considers that he and his continuing personal identity began in the heat of intimate sexual passion and knowledge (*'d'l* , *tmd/*), or more precisely conception begins soul and personal life (Ps. 51:5).[49] Thus David views himself as in the condition of sin from

47 CD 10:15–11:18 and especially 11:13–14 argue that one should not lift an animal out of a pit on the Sabbath; cf. 4Q 265; *Miscellaneous Roles* fragment 7, 1.6–9; *m. Besa* 3.4. However, Jesus obviously takes issue with this view when He asks the question, "What man shall there be among you, who shall have one sheep, and it falls into a pit on the Sabbath, will not take hold of it, and lift it out? Of how much more value then is a man than a sheep! So then it is lawful to do good on the Sabbath." (Matt. 12:11–12; Luke 14:5). Furthermore, the fact that plants or the ground get cursed does not mean that they are culpable because their being cursed reflects the culpability of the human agents who oversee the plants well being (e.g., Gen. 3:17–18; Matt. 21:12–19–46; Mark 11:12–14–33). So their being cursed evidences the precariousness of the culpable humans in the context.

48 Technically *klyty/* means "kidneys" or the cognitive center of his being; Hans Wolff, *Anthropology of the Old Testament*, pp. 63–66.

49 This position of right to life, which begins at conception is strongly supported by Roman Catholic Pope John Paul II, *Evangelium Vitae (The Gospel of Life)* (New York: Random House, 1995), p. 41, and Congregation for the Doctrine of Faith, "DonumVitae (Instruction for Human Life in its Origin and the Dignity of Procreation): Replies to Certain Questions of the Day," (online: www.vatican.va/roman_curia/congregations/cfaith/index.htm (Feb. 22, 1987), sect. II, A, 2. Such a position strongly

his parent's sexual deed on into his adulthood. David as fetal soul is already immersed in the depravity of sin in the wake of the Fall. Thus, the biblical text describes a continuity of human personal identity of the fetal condition in a pre-modern event-oriented description as from the sex of conception through birth as a continuity of the person after birth, and attribute to the unborn personal characteristics (such as a sin condition) from the parental sexual intercourse on. Likewise, the unborn are even called by God before birth (Gen. 25:22–23; Judg. 13:2–7; Isa. 49:1, 5; Jer. 1:4–5; Gal. 1:15). Even John the Baptist lept in his mother's womb before birth when Mary showed up at Elizabeth's home (Luke 1:41, 57). Likewise, Qumran considered the fetus to be a separate living creature.[50] Thus, this awareness would commend Dr. Joseph Bruner, of Vanderbilt University Medical Center for his 2007 operation on Samuel Armas as a 21 week old fetus by c-section to correct Samuel's spina bifida, returning this now healthy baby back into the womb to be carried by his mother (Julie Armas) and be birthed a healthy baby. Both mother and son are doing fine, with no indication of continuing medical problem.

Thus abortion is wrong either intentionally or unintentionally. Exodus 21:22–24 discusses a relevant legal case concerning the unintended consequences of striking a pregnant lady.[51] In the striking,

---

undercuts the Greek practice of considering soul only to exist after the father affirms its place in the family after birth in the "run around" ceremony at the hearth, which sets up the exposing of children. These exposed children were often made slaves, or raised by Christians as their own, or died. Cf. S. M. Baugh, "Marriage and Family in Ancient Greek Society" and Susan Treggiari, "Marriage and Family in Roman Society" in *Marriage and Family in the Biblical World.* edited by Ken Campbell (Downers Grove: InterVarsity Press, 2003), pp. 122–4, 175–7. Likewise, this Biblical origin of identity predates Jewish traditional ideas of human person beginning on the fortieth day of gestation (*Babylonian Talmud, Yevamot* 69b embryos are "mere water until the fortieth day") and implantation ("Testimony of Rabbi Elliot Dorff for National Bioethics Advisory Commission" in *The Stem Cell Controversy: Debating the Issues.* Michael Ruse and Christopher Pynes eds. [Amherst: Prometheus Books, 2003], pp. 195–200). In contrast, the silence of the Quran on when ensoulment occurs allows for some Muslims to separate the biological and moral status, placing the latter after the first trimester of pregnancy ("Testimony of Abdulaziz Sachedina for National Bioethics Advisory Commission." in *The Stem Cell Controversy.* Michael Ruse and Christopher Pynes eds., p. 206.

50 4Q270 frag. 2 and *Temple* Scroll 64. 6–9 identify that killing a pregnant animal for food is wrong because one kills both the mother and the living fetal offspring at the same time. Additionally, 11QTemple 50.10–19 treat a fetal corpse in the womb as a separate entity that had been alive, thus the fetal corpse causes corpse impurity to his mother. Cf. Joseph Baumgarten, "A Fragment on Fetal Life and Pregnancy in 4Q270" in *Pomegranates Golden Bells: Studies in Biblical, Jewish, and Near Eastern Ritual, Law, and Literature in Honor of Jacob Milgrom,* ed. David Wright, David Noel Freedman, and Avi Hurvitz (Winona Lake: Eisenbrauns, 1995), pp. 445–8, especially p. 446.

51 This compares with other ancient Near Eastern law forbidding abortion on pain of death (Mesopotamian Law: *Middle Assyrian Laws* A 51-53; *Laws Lipit-Ishtar,* Laws d-f; cf. David Chapman, "Marriage and Family in Second Temple Judaism," in *Marriage and Family in the Biblical World,* pp. 226–7. Abortion and infanticide are

"her child" (*yldyh/*) is made to "come out" (*yṣ'/*) in a live birth. That is, *yṣ'/* always refers to a live birth (Gen. 25:25–26; 38:28–30; Jer. 1:5; 26:18), unless it is accompanied by the word 'death' (*mt/* , Num. 12:12; Job 3:11). So, in this instance *yld/* refers to a live child, not a miscarriage. There is another word for "still birth" in the context, but it is not used in this instance (*škl/* , Ex. 23:26; Hos. 9:14). Therefore, the baby born in Exodus 21:22 is a soul/life put at risk through her premature birth, so the judges need to decide on a fine for the striker, since he put the baby at risk in her pre-maturity. That is, if there is no further injury to baby or mother then the assessed fine is the extent of the punishment. However, if the mother or the baby have further injuries, then whatever that injury is will be legally meted out against the striker. If either the baby or the mother dies the abuser forfeits his life (Ex. 21:23). Both mother and fetus are treated in this passage as persons with legal rights. Therefore, it is bio-ethically wrong to abort a fetus for quality of life concerns and to intentionally use means that prevent fertilized eggs from being implanted (e.g., use of Intra-Uterine Device or RU486) and birthed.

This would mean that *in vitro* fertilization would best be done without producing any more fertilized eggs than are used to implant and extra fertilized eggs should be utilized with parental consent to help others attempt procreation. There are over 400,000 ova stored in fertility clinics. Christians should be outraged at the discarding of surplus embryos from fertility clinics, causing thousands of murders each year. The fertilized eggs are not property but persons and should not be treated as property. This would argue that *in vitro* fertilization extraction of ova should be taken in multiple cycles, collecting only what number can be reasonably used in the implantation process. This would likely increase the costs of *in vitro* fertilization but would render it more ethical. If the biological parents consider that they do not wish to make further attempts of implantation of eggs, then these fertilized eggs should not be discarded nor made available for stem cell research in a manner that destroys them, but they could be made available for infertile couples who could benefit by such adoptive egg donation. Such a process is similar to that of egg donation, which is already available. Furthermore, the fact that half of the

---

repudiated by these texts with fines of 10-20 shekels of silver for abortion in these texts: *Sumerian Laws Exercise Tablet*, 1′ and 2′; LXX translators; *Ps.-Phoc.* 184–5; *Sib. Or.* 3.765–766; Philo, *Spec. Laws* 3.110–9; *Virtues* 131–3; *Hypothetica* 7.7; Eusebius, *Praep ev.* 8.7.7; Josephus, *Ag. Ap.* 2.202; *b. Nid.*30b; Basil letter #188, section 2 requiring a 10 year punishment, *The Nicene and Post-Nicene Fathers* ed. Philip Schaff and Henry Wace (Edinburgh: T & T Clark, 1991), series 2, vol. 8, p. 225; cf. Menachem Elon, "Abortion," *Encyclopaedia Judaica* (New York: Macmillan Company, 1972–1994), 2:99. Josephus, *Ant.* 4.278 applies this Exodus law only to the death of the mother (cf. Louis H. Feldman, *Judean Antiquities 1–4,* vol. 3 of *Flavius Joseph: Translation and Commentary,* ed. Steve Mason [Leiden: Brill, 2001], pp. 448–89), which approach is followed by *Neziqin* 8.

normally fertilized eggs in the normal biological process do not implant, neither legitimizes abortion, nor frees humans from the responsibility to do what is reasonable to facilitate fertilized eggs developing into fully functioning humans to the extent that we can. A simpler ethical strategy for *in vitro* fertilization would be to only fertilize one egg per attempt at implantation, because it can side step this problem of actual human lives cut short by the choice of not trying for implantation.

It has been suggested that therapeutic use of skin cells converted to stem cells could side step the problem of killing an ovum, because it is claimed that they can't be implanted and become viable.[52] This research has been accomplished in mice. However, these same skin cells converted to stem cells have been implanted and birthed as cloned mice by Jinsong Li of Rockefeller University.[53] So once they are cloned stem cells even from skin, they are souls and it would be wrong to destroy them for therapeutic use of another.

Furthermore, a person as soul (*npš*/נֶפֶשׁ) wills and feels hate, love, grief, joy, patience, fear, despair, bitterness and sympathy (Isa. 1:14; Jer. 12:7; 13:17; Job 6:4; 30:25; Pss. 6:3; 35:9; 42:5; Prov. 31:6). The continuing legacy of the living self is the soul. A person's emotions and cognitive ability may change as she digresses through illnesses like Alzheimer's or dementia or stroke or MS or brain injury, however there is continuity of soul/person there. Finally, Revelation 6:9 identifies that the person as soul retains life beyond death. Further, in this afterlife, such debilitating illnesses are remedied, so that the afterlife gets beyond these diminishments.

In an attempt to be bilingual and communicate philosophically to other worldviews, human personal life may be noticed biologically, to evidence this Biblical model. 1) Humanness is noticed by the range of human DNA in an after conceived and before death condition (while normally 46 chromosomes, this permits the 45 chromosome condition of Turner's syndrome and the 47 chromosome condition of Down's syndrome to also be human). 2) Personal and 3) Life can be noticed by the fusion of soul/life that Biblically begins at conception. This personal life may be evidenced by noticing the congruence of the properties of growth (proceeding through a life cycle including effecting the change permitting only one sperm to penetrate the fertilized egg, fusion of DNA with forty-six chromosomes, and at least in some fertilized eggs the addition of a Y chromosome where it had not been there in the

52 Rick Weiss, "Skin Cells Converted to Stem Cells: Scientist's Work Could Clear Moral Hurdle to Embryonic Research" *Washington Post* (Mon., Aug. 22, 2005): A01 and http://www.washingtonpost.com/wp-dyn/content/article/2005/08/21/AR2005082101180.html; also National Public Radio, Talk of the Nation: Science Friday April 27, 2007.

53 Rockefeller University, *Science Daily* (Feb. 12, 2007) or http://www.sciencedaily.com/releases/2007/02/070212173432.htm

egg before fertilization), and perhaps self-replication on a cellular level. The condition of identical twins would also argue for life beginning at conception, when the twins are fertilized and the ovum split in two.[54] Prior to implantation, I consider ovums to be souls (personal human life) as evident by this prior criteria, even though 50% infant mortality is due to some of these fertilized eggs being lost in natural pregnancy. Of course with implantation, there are further changes (stopping the woman's period) and metabolism (cellular and fetal) through the mother's blood stream. In this condition the fetus is not like an organ, because bodily organs do not eventually have a somewhat independent life like children can have. As the fetus goes through the life cycle it adds additional qualities which continue to increase until puberty (when the person can reproduce them-self as a full person). So there is more evidence biologically for the ontological condition of life, as the fetus develops, is birthed and becomes fully functioning. Eventually, through menopause (self-replication) and dementia (irritability and dynamic equilibrium), qualities that indicate life may be lost, but the ontological person/soul remains. However, this biological argument is only an empirical way of noticing the deeper Biblical ontological reality of the continuing soul/life. That is, the observable congruence samples some evidence of the deeper issue of the consilience of human personal life.

Within a person there is the cultivation of his awareness of himself as the agent of his own thought and behavior.[55] In other words, the self relates to the person's experience of himself, without the trappings of social facade or presentation, the individual as he stands before himself, as it were, psychologically naked. Thus, self as context or perspective is the primary personal experience.

The blessing of language acquisition is that humans develop a more sophisticated way of conceptualizing and having their experience,[56] and within validating environments, a sense-of-self becomes increasingly under private control. Language allows for a temporal perspective on experience and for the ability to transcend immediacy - the remembered present.[57] Thus ethically, we should make our decisions reflect a gradation which prefers fostering meaningful personhood, especially in the case of conflicting ethical options.[58] That is, in conflicting absolutes (which are rare), maximizing personhood (spirituality, relationship, and

---

54 This does not mean that twins share a soul momentarily, but that they are separate living, willing entities after birth would indicate that there are two souls prior to birth.

55 Sören Kierkegaard, *Sickness Unto Death*, translated by Lowrie Walter (Princeton: Princeton University Press, 1941).

56 Ludwig Wittgenstein, *Philosophical Investigations* (New York: Macmillian Publishing Co., 1953).

57 Thomas Nagel, *The View from Nowhere* (New York: Oxford Press, 1986).

58 Sören Kierkegaard, *Stages in Life's Way* (New York: Shocken Books, 1967); or more popularly: Norman Geisler, *Ethics: Alternatives and Issues* (Grand Rapids:

respect) could provide a guide for identifying higher norms from lower norms. Namely, love and affirm God (the greatest person) as primary. Love and affirm those with whom you have a more intimate relationship, for it reflects the degree of trust in the covenant (as in marriage) or relationship that you have with them. Prefer the household of faith and those who foster respect. This sort of orientation could even drive a utilitarianism which prefers more persons and complete persons over potential persons (sperm and non-fertilized egg are potential persons and not mere possessions). However, rarely do we have to choose one to the exclusion of the other, because often ethical absolutes do not in fact conflict and with some creativity and faithfulness a way of resolution through apparent conflicts can often be found. Of course, such gradation does not censure self-sacrificing choices, for the others benefit.

However, humans also have the unique ability to over identify with the categories of language (e.g., husband, lawyer, father) and become trapped in contrived experiences that occur only in their "mind." When the contrived experiences are associated with dreaded pasts that will not change or futures that have not happened, the individual is the author of their own distress.

The self or soul, in the context of living, is an individual capable of considering his own private and public behaviors before, during and after an event. He is capable of being mindful of the moment in which he is living - his environment, his thoughts and emotions, and his potential responses to them. This self-reflective being develops public and private behaviors both in response to the content of mindfulness and toward mindfulness itself. He can train himself to be either mindful or mindless in the moment with predictable outcomes. Mindlessness or the lack of self-reflective behavior leads to impulsive, habitual behaviors on the one hand and on the other, via the function of verbal behavior, be obsessively "stuck" in catastrophic pasts and futures that do not exist at the moment, either of which can result in ineffective living. Such mindless behavior diminishes consistent ethical thought and praxis.

Implicit in the Biblical discussion of the soul or self is the suggestion that the person can only have a self-reflective relationship to himself in context. For example, when attempting to empathize with another person, an individual will experience increasing levels of understanding as he gains more information about the context in which the other lives. Thus, the self is understood in relationship to one's awareness of one's thoughts, feelings and behaviors in response to one's environment, both physical and spiritual. This has significant implications for the person in terms of purpose, meaning and definition.

Zondervan, 1971), pp. 114–138; *Christian Ethics: Options and Issues* (Grand Rapids: Baker, 1989), pp. 113–133.

10.3. Spirit

In contrast to image of God and soul, spirit does not refer to the person as a whole but rather indicates a facet of her being (Isa. 19:3; Dan. 7:15; Zech. 12:1). It is that aspect of the person relationally oriented to God and other spirit beings.[59] For example, Isaiah 19:3 indicates that the Lord in his judgment "demoralizes the spirit" of the Egyptians "within them."

Several philosophers and theologians conceive of the traditional concept of spirit to be identical to that of soul, often in a dichotomy of spirit or soul and body. For example, Tertullian followed the Stoics in conceiving of the human of as corporeal, generated with the body.[60] Plato reasons that the spirit is an eternal form for each human, which as eternal continues from a pre-incarnate existence to a post-incarnate afterlife, while our shadowy bodies are birthed and then decay.[61] While Origen followed Plato's view of spirit,[62] Augustine modified the concept in the direction of neo-platonism, denying eternal pre-existence and affirming a created tripartite quality of each human spirit or mind to reflect the Trinity.[63] In contrast, Aquinas proposed a hylomorphic view in which the material human is formed as soul which constitutes a spiritual and immortal aspect of life.[64] René Descartes proposed a radical form of substance dualism in which the spirit is akin to a thinking substance that is the real person within the extended substance of body.[65] Paul Tillich conceives of human spirit as an existential dimension extending an Einstinian relativistic metaphysic, which human existence participates along with God.[66] Wolfhart Pannenberg metaphorically illustrates the

---

59 Hans Walter Wolff, *Anthropology of the Old Testament*, p. 36; Friedrich Baumgärtel, Werner Bieder, Erik Sjberg, and Edward Schweizer in *Theological Dictionary of the New Testament* edited by Kittel and Friedrich, 6:362–3, 367, 370, 375–6, 396–401; M. V. VanPelt, W. C. Kaiser, and D. Block in *New International Dictionary of Old Testament Theology & Exegesis*, edited by Willem VanGemeren, 3:1075–7; Barton Payne in *Theological Wordbook of the Old Testament*, edited by Harris, Archer, and Waltke, 2:837; James Dunn, *The Theology of Paul the Apostle*, p. 77; Colin Brown, *The New International Dictionary of New Testament Theology* 3:693–4.

60 Tertullian, De an. 9 in *Against Praxeas*. In *The Writings of Quintus Sept. Flor. Tertullianus*. Edited by Richard Ellmann.

61 Plato, *Cratylus, Phaedrus, Meno, Phaedo, Timaeus* in *Great Books of the Western World*, vol. 7 *Plato*, pp. 93, 124–6, 179–80, 250, 452–4 respectively.

62 Origen, De Princ. 2.9.6 in *On First Principles. Ante-Nicene Fathers* vol. 4.

63 Augustine, *City of God* 8.16; 19 in the *Great Books of the Western World*, vol. 18, *Augustine*, pp. 267, 369–70.

64 Thomas Aquinas, *Summa Theologica* 1.29.A 1, rep 5; 1.75.A 4; 1.76.A 1, Ans.; 1.118.A 3 Ans.; 3. Suppl.79. A 1 Ans and Rep 4 in *Great Books of the Western World*, 19:162–3; 381–2; 385–8; 393–4; 396–7; 603–4; 20: 951–3.

65 René Descartes, *Meditations on First Philosophy*. *Great Books of the Western World*, vol. 31. *Descartes, Spinoza*, pp. 51–2; 60; 77–81; 98; 119–20; 130; 135–6; 152; 155–6; 207–8.

66 Paul Tillich, *Systematic Theology, volume 3, Life and the Spirit History and the Kingdom of God* (Chicago:University of Chicago Press, 1963), pp. 15–30, 111–161, 297–423.

relationship of spirit in God and in humanity through Michael Faraday's universal force field which relate the effect of electricity on another dimension, that of magnetism.[67] Many of these views are foreign to the Biblical text, though Tillich's and Pannenberg's metaphors may have some relevance if corralled back in ontological and functional directions to reflect the Biblical ideas, though complex scientific metaphors may put most people off rather than be an aid to relate significance.

The Hebrew and Greek words for "spirit" (*ruh*/רוּחַ and) refers to air in motion (Ex. 14.21).[68] By extension, it can refer to the breath of man or animals (Gen. 7:15; Eccl. 3:21, 12:7) and to God's life-giving breath (Gen. 45:27; Job. 17:1, 27:3).[69] However, well over two-thirds of the uses of *ruh*/רוּחַ and are used of God and His angels (John 4:24; Zech. 1:9). This preponderance of uses emphasizes *a dimension of existence that is not normally taken into account*, for clearly God and the angels act within the visible world (2 Kgs. 6:16–17; Dan. 10:20–21).[70] At times, this spirit ontological dimension appears in the visible world somewhat like a three-dimensional sphere penetrating a two-dimensional flatland.[71] This actual dimensionalism of spirit goes deeper than the existential dimensionalism by which Tillich described the realm of the spirit. The uninitiated may not be sensitive to spirit presence or be able to explain spirit nature while those who lift their eyes from the

67 Wolfhart Pannenberg, *Systematic Theology* (Grand Rapids: Eerdmanns, 1988) 1:382–4; I think the universal ambiguity of Faraday works in Pannenberg's favor of this metaphor rather than extending it to the specificity of Maxwell's equations.

68 Hans Walter Wolff, *Anthropology of the Old Testament*, p. 32–33; Hermann Kleinknecht, Friedrich Baumgärtel, and Werner Bieder in *Theological Dictionary of the New Testament* edited by Kittel and Friedrich, 6:334–5, 360, 368; Barton Payne in *Theological Wordbook of the Old Testament,* edited by Harris, Archer, and Waltke, 2:831; E. Kamlah in *The New International Dictionary of New Testament Theology* edited by Colin Brown, 3:690–1.

69 Hans Walter Wolff, *Anthropology of the Old Testament*, p. 33–35; Hans Friedrich Baumgärtel, and Werner Bieder in *Theological Dictionary of the New Testament* edited by Kittel and Friedrich, 6:360–1, 368; E. Kamlah in *The New International Dictionary of New Testament Theology* edited by Colin Brown, 3:690–1; M. V. VanPelt, W. C. Kaiser, and D. Block in *New International Dictionary of Old Testament Theology & Exegesis,* edited by Willem VanGemeren, 3:1073–4; Barton Payne in *Theological Wordbook of the Old Testament,* edited by Harris, Archer, and Waltke, 2:836; James Dunn, *The Theology of Paul the Apostle,* p. 77.

70 Hans Walter Wolff, *Anthropology of the Old Testament*, p. 36; Friedrich Baumgärtel, Werner Bieder, Erik Sjöberg, and Edward Schweizer in *Theological Dictionary of the New Testament* edited by Kittel and Friedrich, 6:362–3, 367, 370, 375–6, 396–401; M. V. VanPelt, W. C. Kaiser, and D. Block in *New International Dictionary of Old Testament Theology & Exegesis,* edited by Willem VanGemeren, 3:1075–7; Barton Payne in *Theological Wordbook of the Old Testament,* edited by Harris, Archer, and Waltke, 2:837; James Dunn, *The Theology of Paul the Apostle,* p. 77; Colin Brown, *The New International Dictionary of New Testament Theology* 3:693–4.

71 Edwin Abbot, *Flatland: A Romance of Many Dimensions* (London: Seeley & Co., 1884), pp. v, 68–78, 93–94, 97–100; cf. Paul Tillich, *Systematic Theology, volume 3, Life and the Spirit History and the Kingdom of God*, pp. 15–30, 111–161, 297–423.

four-dimensional world of space and time will find a whole realm racing with activity that affects human existence at every turn. No one can grasp the spirit with his hands just as no one is able to catch the wind, but the effects of the spirit are evident in our environment (John 3:8). Therefore, since God is spirit, an individual must be spiritually alive to relate to him. Thus, *spirit is that avenue through which God encounters the person* (Rom. 8:16; Gal. 6:18; Phil. 4:23; 2 Tim. 4:22; Philemon 25) *and through which the individual is most open and responsive to God* (Matt. 5:3; Luke 1:45; Rom. 1:9; 1 Cor. 7:34; 1 Pet. 3:4). James Dunn further delineates the relational aspect of spirit in contrast to philosophical and theological misconceptions.

> The New Testament writers can speak of the (human) spirit as though it was a something possessed by the individual; but this does not mean that they envisioned the spirit of man as a divine spark (the real "I") incarcerated in the physical, 'the ghost in the machine' (an anthropology more typical of Greek philosophy). This language is more likely to be simply a natural and easy way of speaking about man in his belongingness to the spiritual realm, the power he experiences in him which relates him to beyond, "the dimension of the beyond in the midst."[72]

While the human spirit includes intellect (1 Cor. 2:14), emotions (Ex. 7:8; Num. 5:14; 1 Kgs. 10:5; 21:5; Isa. 25:4) and will (Num. 14:24; Ezra 1:15; Pss. 32:2; 51:10, 12), it extends beyond these human facets to include an orientation to the spiritual dimension. For example, spirit lives beyond this life (Luke 24:37, 39; 1 Tim. 3:16; 1 Pet. 4:6), so death is referred to as giving up the spirit (Matt. 22:50; Luke 23:46; Acts 7:59).[73]

With reference to death, animals are also said to have spirit (*ruḥ*/רוּחַ), and thus it is beyond our wisdom awareness whether their spirits ascend or descend in the common experience of death and the decay to dust that animals have with humans (Eccl. 3:19–21). However, some animals get into the everlasting Kingdom, for Isaiah 11:6–8 presents their presence as part of the undoing of the Fall and divine oracle of judgment. Then animals will live in peace with their predators, including peace among the seed of woman (children) and serpents.

Since the spiritual dimension is active, it is clear that two or more causes may determine an event simultaneously even when they involve heinous sins (Acts 2:23). On the one hand, God chooses regardless of an individual's works, who will rule or serve, who will be softened or

72 James Dunn in *The New International Dictionary of New Testament Theology*, edited by Colin Brown, vol. 3, p. 694.

73 M. V. VanPelt, W. C. Kaiser, and D. Block in *New International Dictionary of Old Testament Theology & Exegesis*, edited by Willem VanGemeren, 3:1074–5.

hardened and who will be saved or condemned (Rom. 9:6–29). On the other hand, each individual is responsible for diligence in utilizing the knowledge and faith God has given him (John 3:16–18; 2 Pet. 1:1, 3–5). The combined effect of the Holy Spirit's agency and the individual's responsibility brings about new birth (John 3:3–8; 1 Pet. 1:10–12, 22–25). If a person is a knower and believer of some salvific truth, he must work diligently to increase his knowledge and faith, along with other qualities such as goodness, self-control and perseverance, in order to provide assurance of his eschatological salvation (2 Pet. 1:5–11). However, if such a person does not diligently increase these qualities, then he is doubly blind and may be condemned (2 Pet. 1:9, 2:1, 18–22; Acts 1:16–20; 8:12, 24). All those actually chosen by God will not only continue within God's protecting power, but already have their eschatological salvation prepared for them (1 Pet. 1:2–5). Emphasizing the process of growth in the Christian life, the Apostle Paul sees the indwelling Holy Spirit prompting the Christian to think and act righteously according to of (Rom. 8:3–13). Those who undergo this leading of the Spirit in their lives will see His fruit manifested, and they will cry out intimately to God, "Dada, Father" (Rom. 8:14–15; Gal. 5:22–23). Furthermore, as the Spirit cultivates these traits in them, the believers experience a testimony from the Holy Spirit to their human spirits that they are children of God, therefore, inheriting Christ's salvation benefits (Rom. 8:16–17). However, the Holy Spirit's prompting entails authentic human choices as well. For example, instead of corporately choosing drunkenness, the Church should depend upon the Holy Spirit to fill them with the fullness of worship (Eph. 5:18–21). As such, Paul calls his readers to live not as they once did because they are no longer the same people they were (Rom. 6:1–14). In this, he asks Christians to do acts of righteousness consistent with their status as new creatures and to avoid behaviors that are inconsistent with their new life (Rom. 6:15–23). So through the avenue of spirit, both the divine and the human can make authentic choices. Without these choices, any event might well have occurred differently or not at all, evidencing the authenticity of human choice and the real responsibility human beings therefore hold.

In the psychological frame, spirit in the human being refers to the sense that his existence is more than a bodily one. Humans live with this haunting notion that they are more than the sum of their biology. They tend to pursue various ways of reaching for and expressing this aspect of their being through religious and non-religious means. Human history is replete with examples of human efforts to tap into that part of the person's existence that is beyond the grasp of his physical senses. Common examples include religious and secular rituals, mind-altering drugs, and asceticism.

The individual becomes oriented to a spiritual dimension of existence by means of spirit. Without this orientation, the body dominates "being."

Spirit provides a dialectical balance with body which brings fullness to a person's existence. Thus, fullness of the self is determined both within its relationship to the material and spiritual spheres. Implications for completeness of self are apparent for persons who do not adhere to a worldview that includes God or the spiritual realm. While they are persons, they are incomplete spiritually and since spirit is an aspect of personhood, they are incomplete personally. This could also fund gradation in ethical absolutes and explain why ethical choices prefer the benefit done first to the household of faith, if one must choose between them and others (Gal. 6:10).

10.4. Body

The body describes a human in the *physical dimension and in relationship to others*. Plato considers that humans are pure of utilizing a body for their existence in world of shadows.[74] Origen and Augustine followed Plato's view of spirit, but they modified the concept of body and things in the direction of affirming creation of bodies as a good, accomplished by the creative act of God.[75] Reflective of his Aristotelianism, Aquinas proposed a hylomorphic view in which the material human is formed as soul, utilizing a body for the person's connectiveness to the world.[76] René Descartes proposed a radical form of substance dualism in which the spirit is akin to a thinking substance that is the real person within the extended substance of body.[77] In contrast, Nancey Murphy, Warren Brown and Elving Anderson advocate a nonreductive physicalism that considers humans as a "whole complex function, both in society and in relation to God, which gives rise to 'higher' human capacities such as morality and spirituality."[78] Their concept supports a full conceptuality of embodiment that may be helpful here. However, Biblical literature presents a balance between the extreme views which

74 Plato, *Cratylus, Phaedrus, Meno, Phaedo, Timaeus* in *Great Books of the Western World,* vol. 7 *Plato,* pp. 124–6, 179–80, 231, 250, 452–4 respectively.

75 Origen, De Princ. 2.9.6 in *On First Principles. Ante-Nicene Fathers* vol. 4; Augustine, *City of God* 8.16; 19 in the *Great Books of the Western World,* vol. 18, *Augustine,* pp. 267, 369–70.

76 Thomas Aquinas, *Summa Theologica* 1.29.A 1, rep 5; 1.75.A 4; 1.76.A 1, Ans.; 1.118.A 3 Ans.; 3. Suppl.79. A 1 Ans and Rep 4 in *Great Books of the Western World,* 19:162–3; 381–2; 385–8; 393–4; 396–7; 603–4; 20: 951–3.

77 René Descartes, *Meditations on First Philosophy. Great Books of the Western World,* vol. 31. *Descartes, Spinoza,* pp. 60; 77–81; 98; 119–20; 130; 135–6; 152; 155–6; 207–8.

78 Warren Brown, Nancey Murphy, and H. Newton Malony, *Whatever Happened to the Soul?: Scientific and Theological Portraits of Human Nature,* p. 2, 25, 49–72, 99–148; Nancey Murphy, *Bodies and Souls, or Spiritual Bodies?.*

see body as either "the totality of man from every aspect,"[79] or reduce it to solely the material.[80]

The Biblical words for body used in the O.T. and N.T. reflect that "body" describes a human in the *physical dimension and in relationship to others*. For example, Rudolf Bultmann and the descriptive Biblical theology movement emphasize that the concept of "body" is holistic of the human person; "man does not have a *sōma*; he is *sōma*."[81] The Hebrew *gwytynu*/גְּוִיָּתֵנוּ, a minor word for bodies, describes the whole human as either possessed by himself along with lands and cattle or as a dead corpse (Gen. 47:18; Neh. 9:37; Ps. 110:6).[82] This word is also used to describe a visible body (Ezek. 1:11, 23; Dan. 10:6). The other words for body, *bśr*/בָּשָׂר in the Hebrew and and in the Greek, are typically defined as corpse, flesh or meat (Lev. 4:11; Deut. 21:23; Matt. 26:26; 27:52; Luke 24:39). In addition, usage of these words indicate that the body contacts its environment and others through various members (i.e., reaching with the hand, walking with the feet, speaking with the mouth and tongue, seeing with the eye and hearing with the ears). In other contexts, the words emphasize ownership of servants and possessions (Num. 8:7; Job 4:15; Mark 5:29; John 2:16, Eph. 2:15; Rev. 18:13). However, the words *bśr*/בָּשָׂר, and also refer to the whole body. In this sense, for example, *bśr*/בָּשָׂר is used as a personal pronoun indicating the individual as a whole (Ps. 119:120). Further, body is not merely something a man has but something he is. Matthew 5:29, 6:22 and 25 illustrate that the actions of particular members of the body lead to consequences that affect the whole person. Christ provides another example. Ephesians 2:15 (some Greek manuscripts identify it in 2:14) and other passages state that He bore our sins in His whole person ( ) rather than only in his physical body (Heb.

---

79 M. E. Dahl, *The Resurrection of the Body* (London: SCM, 1962), pp. 121–6.

80 Robert Gundry, *Soma in Biblical Theology: With Emphasis on Anthropology* (Grand Rapids: Zondervan, 1987), p. 156.

81 Rudolf Bultmann, *Theology of the New Testament* (New York: Scribner, 1951), vol. 1:194; Hans Walter Wolff, *Anthropology of the Old Testament*, pp. 28–29; N. P. Bratsiotis in *Theological Dictionary of the Old Testament* edited by Johannes Botterweck and Helmer Ringgren, 2:318, 323–331, especially pp. 325–28;Friedrich Baumgärtel, Edward Schweizer, and Rudolf Meyer in *Theological Dictionary of the New Testament* edited by Kittel and Friedrich, 7:1056, 1058, 1111; John Oswalt in *Theological Wordbook of the Old Testament,* edited by Harris, Archer, and Waltke, 1:136; R. Chisholm in *New International Dictionary of Old Testament Theology & Exegesis,* edited by Willem VanGemeren, 1:777–8; James Dunn, *The Theology of Paul the Apostle,* pp. 56–61; J. A. Motyer in *The New International Dictionary of New Testament Theology* edited by Colin Brown, 1:233–8; H. Conzelmann in *Die Kleineren Briefe des Apostels Paulus,* edited by H. W. Beyer, Paul Althaus, Hans Conzelmann, Gerhard Friedrich, and Albrecht Oepke (G□ttingen, Vandenhoeck & Ruprecht, 1962) 8:137; John A. T. Robinson, *The Body: A Study in Pauline Theology* (London: SCM, 1952).

82 Johannes Botterweck and Helmer Ringgren, *Theological Dictionary of the Old Testament*, p. 435.

10:5; 1 Pet. 2:24). In addition, while living in a physical body ( ), Christians are commanded to put away sins they used to commit and live a life of worshipful service (Rom. 6:6, 12, 13; 12:1). Although the body dies (, Rom. 7:24), it extends beyond death with the promise of transformation into immortal spiritual bodies (, 1 Cor. 15:38–54).

The O.T. and N.T. literature describe an intermediate state between a person's present bodily existence and his future spiritual body. The O.T. concept of the intermediate state is *sheol*, a shadowy and weakened existence. The word *sheol* refers to the grave in several passages and thus contains the body. As the shadowy and weakened intermediate state, it contains relational and physical body imagery such as spirits of dead kings sitting on thrones and rising to meet the king of Babylon in his death (Isa. 14:9). Additionally, upon conjuring up Samuel, both the medium and Saul became terrified at the real presence of the prophet (1 Sam. 28:12–21). The N.T. expands the concept of *sheol* into two distinct yet real physical realms, Paradise and Hades. On the one hand, Paradise, includes imagery like the tree of life (Rev. 2:7), is patterned after the Garden of Eden and is accessed on the very day that a believer dies (Luke 23:43). Likewise, Hades exhibits spatial and physical imagery. For example, in the story about the rich man and Lazarus, both are in Hades separated by a great distance (Luke 16:23). In the verse which follows (Luke 16:24), the writer makes the point that Lazarus is in Abraham's bosom or on his lap, communicating relational blessing, if not physical privilege. The Pauline corpus also describes an intermediate state, having a deficient bodily existence between the earthly soulish body ( ) and the resurrection spiritual body (; 1 Cor. 15:40, 44; 2 Cor. 3:1–10). Our present physical state, referred to as a "clothed" entity or "tent," and the future bodily condition, called "everlasting house," are preferred over the intermediate state. However, even in this intermediate state, images are used that are appropriate only for a body (i.e., "naked" and "unclothed," 2 Cor. 5:3–4). Obviously, the transition from an earthly body to that of the intermediate state entails the presence of both a decaying corpse in the grave[83] and a continuing spatial and relational existence in Hades.

Body extends beyond the physical in relational ways as well.[84] Clearly some relational uses are more physically dependent like

83 For the honor or dishonor of corpse and the effect on the afterlife, see: Saul Olyan, "Some Neglected Aspects of Israelite Interment Idealogy," *JBL* 124:4(2005): 601–16 and Hanan Brchto, "Kin, Cult, Land and Afterlife-A Biblical Complex," *HUCA* (1973): 36–37.

84 Hans Walter Wolff, *Anthropology of the Old Testament*, p. 29; N. P. Bratsiotis in *Theological Dictionary of the Old Testament* edited by Johannes Botterweck and Helmer Ringgren, 2:319;Friedrich Baumgärtel, Edward Schweizer, and Rudolf Meyer in *Theological Dictionary of the New Testament* edited by Kittel and Friedrich, 7:1066–80, 1111; R. Chisholm in *New International Dictionary of Old Testament Theology & Exegesis*, edited by Willem VanGemeren, 1:778; James Dunn, *The*

the body in the sexual relationship and the resulting offspring (Gen. 2:24; Matt. 19:5–6). Such singleness of body in marriage argues for lifelong monogamous marriage as the design, and therefore identifies that divorce is less than the best that God has for us. Furthermore, the physical relationship a person has to blood relatives, all human, and all life involves this physical component (Gen. 6:12, 17; 29:14; Ps. 145:21; Rom. 1:3, 13:20). While Paul's reference to the body of Christ employs images of physical members, these are metaphors for the spiritual nature of each member, authored and unified by the Holy Spirit (1 Cor. 12:3–27). The body of Christ expresses this relational tie and the interdependency which we have in the assembled church. Such relationality should be encouraged by the ethical choices we make.

The words used for "body" also describe a mind set or way of being. In the O.T., a fleshy (*bśr*/בָּשָׂר) heart, one that is responsive and obedient, contrasts with a heart of stone, describing a rebellious and unrepentant attitude. For example, in Ezekiel 11:19; 36:26, God tells the prophet that he promises to take the heart of stone from the people of Israel and give them a heart of flesh. This transformation makes them responsive and obedient to God, the new covenant way of being. In the N.T., particularly develops the sensual side of body. The non-Christian lives in the realm of flesh and according to the flesh, a perspective characterized by sensuality (Rom. 7:5; 8:4–7). This flesh is the life which pursues sensual lusts within Satan's world system, opposed to God and His grace (Rom. 8:7; 2 Cor. 1:12; Gal. 5:17, 19; Eph. 2:3; Col. 2:18, 23; 2 Pet. 2:10, 18; 1 John 2:16). This results in many sinful acts, such as jealousy, dissension, arguing, anger, drunkenness and sensuality (Gal. 5:19–21; Jude 7). This fleshly lifestyle cannot please God; it is under condemnation of death (Rom. 8:8, 13). Christ, who lived in the flesh, condemned sin in the flesh thereby justifying the believer. Having been freed from the bonds of sensual desires, he is able to please God (Rom. 8:1–4).

The epistles repeatedly admonish the Christian who lives in the flesh (bodily) not to live according to it (sensually) (Rom. 8:9; 1 Cor. 10:2–3). He is no longer alive to the realm of sensual desires; he is now alive to the spiritual realm (Rom. 8:6, 9–12; Gal. 5:16, 24). However, the Christian is not separated from flesh, merely the realm and authority of flesh. Thus, flesh is peripheral to the regenerated inner man or mind (Rom. 7:18–20, 25). As a result, there is a continual antagonism between the regenerated mind that desires to do good and the believer's flesh, which has a propensity for the sensual (Rom. 7:18). Within this struggle, Paul presents indwelling sin in the flesh as that power within the person prompting him to do sins (Rom. 7:17, 20, 23). Flesh remains a non-central part of the believer resulting in occasional sins of the flesh,

---

Theology of Paul the Apostle, p. 56–57, 59–61; John Cooper, *Body Soul & Life Everlasting*, pp. 44–45.

causing the believer to yearn for release from the body (Rom. 6:14; 7:14, 25; 8:3; 13:14; Gal. 3:3; 5:13). Its influence can be seen in the Christian father who purposes to spend time with his family but wastes the time watching the game on television, or the Christian woman who has purposed to diet and finds herself snacking again between meals. Or again the Christian boy who purposes to not masturbate but finds himself doing so again, or the girl who wishes to live for Jesus but continues to check herself out every time she is before a storefront window. Though intending to do otherwise, they have given into the urges of the flesh. The flesh mindset that would pursue internet porn is also ethically sin. Many of our addictions have a flesh component: alcoholism, drugs, sensuality. The Christian is commanded to abstain from "fleshly desires" ( ) though often in times of strife, their behavior may appear willfully sensual in nature (1 Cor. 3:3; 1 Pet. 2:11). "Weak flesh" ( ) can also refer to spiritual immaturity. Although Paul entreats Christians to grow beyond the weakness of their flesh, he acknowledges that an element of this weakness extends throughout life in the physical body of all believers (Rom. 7:14, 25; 1 Cor. 3:1).

The physical body is the organ through which the soul or self touches and is touched by its environment. It is the means by which the soul is mobilized; it allows for active engagement with the world rather than passive observation of it. As it engages with the world, the body experiences a myriad of feelings including pleasure and pain. These responses are not intended to be ends in and of themselves. Physical pain and emotions (physiological sensations with cognitive attributions) are the culmination of an intricate process designed to provide an individual with feedback about his behavior. Pain, a warning that the body is under assault, and pleasure, a primary reinforcement for effective behavior, are important but not sufficient factors for governing a person's interactions with the physical world or other people.

It is by means of this intricate biological process that one individual interacts with another; by means of the body, one self "touches" another self. The body houses the apparatus (biologically the brain but Biblically the heart) for estimating the meanings and purposes expressed via the body of another self. Thus, certainty about the intentions expressed by another self is tenuous. The role of communication as the foundation and task of two or more selves is fundamental to their efforts to develop successive approximations of comprehension. The presence of cognitive capacities (such as abstraction, verbal and non-verbal comprehension, flexibility, discrimination, concentration, and affect regulation) enable a person to gain increasing degrees of understanding. To that end, listening is the cornerstone to successful communal living. Without comprehension, a community of individuals remains isolated and empty in the midst of superficial interaction.

Many of the medical treatments using drugs or surgery are effecting a bodily change with the intention that such bodily change goes beyond mere body to include mental, emotional and perhaps spiritual issues as well. For example, Huntington's disease is to some extent rooted in genetic causation, the mutation of the Huntington's gene. Yet in this condition there is an increasing diminishment of one's mental ability, which progressively destroys the mind and personality. If gene therapy could provide a filter to recognize the problem early enough and treatment to correct the Huntington gene for a potential patent, then such a bodily change could have profound affects for their health and well being. Such medical actions should be encouraged. These genetic treatments should be engaged with parental consent, but they should be seen as creatively making the new person what she is, so that nurture can cultivate what God through nature and genetic engineering provided among the possible.

A more realistic genetic therapy would be that of treating the genes of an adult as in alcoholism and drug addition. There is ample evidence that alcoholism is partly a genetic problem. For example, doctors Oronzi and Goldman summarize their genetic study of alcoholism as follows:

> The strong heritability of alcoholism suggests the existence of inherited functional variants of genes that alter the metabolism of alcohol and variants of other genes that alter the neurobiologies of reward, executive cognitive function, anxiety/dysphoria, and neuronal plasticity. Each of these neurobiologies has been identified as a critical domain in the addictions.[85]

Furthermore, addressing the larger issue of illicit drug addiction, the Harvard Twin study of Substance Abuse concluded for a genetic factor, among others.

> Our research has demonstrated significant factors on the abuse of illicit substances. Multivariate analysis have indicated that the co-occurrence of abuse of various types of illicit drugs reflects a common vulnerability, influenced by both genetic and environmental factors, that cuts across all categories of illicit drugs.[86]

85 G. Oroszi and D. Goldman, "Alcoholism: Genes and Mechanisms." *Pharmacogenomics* 5:8(Dec. 2004): 1037–48.

86 M. T. Tsuang, J. L. Bar, R. M. Harley, M. J. Lyons, "The Harvard Twin Study of Substance Abuse: What We Have Learned." *Harvard Review of Psychiatry* 9:6(Nov-Dec, 2001): 267–79.

Oronzi and Goldman summarize their attempts to understand genes related to alcoholism and to influence them genetically with pharmacological aid:

> Functional alleles that alter alcoholism-related intermediate phenotypes include common alcohol dehydrogenase 1B and aldehyde dehydrogenase 2 variants that cause the aversive flushing reaction; catechol-O-methyltransferase (COMT) Val158Met leading to differences in three aspects of neurobiology: executive cognitive function, stress/anxiety response, and opioid function; opioid receptor microl (OPRM1) Asn40Asp, which may serve as a gatekeeper molecule in the action of naltrexone, a drug used in alcoholism treatment; and HTTLPR, which alters serotonin transporter function and appears to affect stress response and anxiety/dysphoria, which are factors relevant to initial vulnerability, the process of addiction, and relapse.[87]

This genetic component in addiction and in treatment does not remove the issue that wills are involved and that drunkenness is sin.

Likewise, gene therapy would be encouraged to address other genetically caused conditions such as diabetes and sickle cell. In such adult conditions, it may be possible to engineer a virus to carry and transmit the corrected gene.[88] In fact, such a viral carrier has been used in gene therapy but to date the bugs aren't worked out of this procedure, because viruses are dangerous and need to have their negative effects significantly diminished before they should be used in this manner.

Furthermore, body cultivation and re-habilitation provides significant concerns for self definition. While body should not dominate one's self definition, it is a factor. If the opportunity avails itself with available resources, it is appropriate to heal cleft palates and facilitate reconstructive plastic surgery. Such corrections can be an aid to a person's sense of self and relationship with others. In instances of frivolous plastic surgery, I consider that it would be appropriate to charge more than the cost so as to support the poor in undergoing more justifiable re-habilitation. However, if the resources or medical means are not available, then a person should cultivate contentment, knowing that they are far more than their bodies. In such a context, handicaps can be used to motivate the more important aspects of the person, those things that foster spirituality, relationship and ethical choices. Furthermore, brain damage reduces culpability for the sufferer.

---

87 G. Oroszi and D. Goldman, "Alcoholism: Genes and Mechanisms." *Pharmacogenomics* 5:8(Dec. 2004): 1037–48.

88 In conversations with Bryan College biologist Todd Wood, 12/15/05.

Additionally, organ donation and blood donation would be encouraged as a Judeo-Christian ethic of loving your neighbor as you love yourself (Lev. 19:18; Matt. 5:43; 19:19; 22:39; Mark 12:31–33; Luke 10:27–36). Significant therapeutic gain is made available to patients in having blood and organs available to replace those that are failing within the patient's body. Of course, to give up an extra organ or to give blood at a rate of replacement is generous as a neighbor who loves. Furthermore, to donate organs upon death would be generously loving as a neighbor as well, because in the continued expression of after death personal identity being embodied, these organs of our physical body are not needed, since they would merely decay.

However, issues arise with the overlap soul and body that show donation to ethically be done only when the person has died and the donation is voluntarily being initiated by the responsible agent. For example, organs being surgically removed from a prisoner for donation or experimental testing without the responsible agent's permission should not happen as occurred in the holocaust or was explored in the movie *The Island*. Closer to the line is the 1987 situation of Karen Schouten's anencephalic daughter being used for organ donation. Since children born with anencphaly only survive a few days outside of the womb, Karen continued to carry the baby to term for the purpose of birthing her daughter for harvesting of organs, to let her life have some meaning.[89] The physicians at Loma Linda University Hospital removed the baby's heart before Karen's daughter had been declared brain dead under the *Uniform Determination of Death Act* and placed her heart in a baby boy who was likely to die without this treatment. The rationale for harvesting organs before death was that such organs rapidly deteriorate. However, couldn't they be harvested by a team standing by upon pronouncement of death? The concept of "body" permits organ donation. However, the concept of "soul" would include Karen's daughter as alive thus precluding such donation.

10.5 Heart

The most emphasized concept of Biblical anthropology is "heart" (*lb/* לֵב and), which stands *wholistically for a person thinking and feeling.*[90] Rarely do philosophers and theologians develop a meaningful

89 Brenda Winner, *Ten Perfect Fingers* (Monrovia: Jarren Press Books, 1999), pp. 24–25; Sabra Chartrand, "Legal Definition of Death is Questioned in Florida Infant Case," http://query.nytimes.com/gst/fullpage.html?sec=health&res=9E0CE0DE163AF93AA15750C0A964958260; Bertha Alvarez Manninen, "The Human Embryo as Neighbor: A Christian Argument in Favor of Embryonic Stem Cell Research" paper presented at the Society of Christian Philosophers, April 21, 2007.

90 Hans Walter Wolff, *Anthropology of the Old Testament*, pp. 40, 44–55; Friedrich Baumgärtel, Johannes Behm, and Edmund Jacob in *Theological Dictionary of the New Testament* edited by Kittel and Friedrich, 3:607, 611–3; 9:626–7; Andrew Bowling in *Theological Wordbook of the Old Testament,* edited by Harris, Archer,

description of humanity with the concept of heart, though John Calvin does.[91] This is only a slight surprise, since the Biblical orientation of the Reformation can be understood to lead toward the descriptive Biblical theology movement which expounds the concept here. Within this Biblical perspective, only rarely does the Biblical term for heart identify the biological pumping organ in the chest, enabling life and movement (Ex. 28:29; 1 Sam. 25:37; Luke 21:34).

In the Bible the concept is usually *holistic for a person thinking and feeling*. For example, T. Song identifies "*Leb* means less an isolated function than the man with all his urges, in short, the person in its totality (Ps. 22:26; 73:26; 84:2)."[92] Walter Eichrodt echoes this sentiment that the heart is "a comprehensive term for the personality, its inner life, its character. It is the conscious and deliberate spiritual activity of the self-contained human ego."[93] Thus, the exhausted traveler needs to eat, strengthening his heart as the whole person may be revived (Gen. 18:5; Judg. 19:5, 8; 1 Kgs. 21:7). However, these words also provide a metaphor for the person with all her abilities. In the O.T., *lb*/לֵב conveys the idea of *a person in his totality* (Pss. 22:26; 73:26; 84:2). It also suggests that action done to someone's heart is action done to a person (Ex. 9:4; 28:29).

From a different perspective, of encompasses the emotional disposition of the person.[94] The status of the heart dominates all the manifestations of life: "A joyful heart makes a good face, but when the heart is sad, the spirit is broken" (Prov. 15: 13). In many passages the heart is depicted as suffering, constricted, evil, grieved, broken, and sad (Neh. 2:2; Deut. 15:10; Ps. 34:18; 1 Sam. 1:8; John 16:6). Comforting words enlarge the heart of a suffering person (Gen. 34:3; Ps. 119:32; Isa. 40:2). On the other hand, traumatic events can stun or numb the heart (Gen. 45:26), while fear can cause it to sink (Gen. 42:28; 1 Sam.17:32; Ps. 40:12). The heart experiences positive emotions such as love, joy, peace, generosity, faith and courage (Judg. 16:15; 2 Sam. 15:6; 2 Cor. 7:3; 1 Sam. 2:1, 8; Acts 2:26; Deut. 28:47; Ex. 35:5; Ps.

---

and Waltke, 1:466–7; Alex Lac in *New International Dictionary of Old Testament Theology & Exegesis,* edited by Willem VanGemeren, 2:749;T. Song in *The New International Dictionary of New Testament Theology* edited by Colin Brown, 2:181–2; H. D. McDonald, *The Christian View of Man* (Westchester: Crossway Books, 1981), pp. 24–25.

91 I am aware that "heart" did not make it into *The Institutes* as a subsection, like in bk. 1, ch. 15 but it is a concern there and Calvin is faithful to exposit it in the commentaries and sermons. Cf. John Calvin, *Commentaries* (Grand Rapids: Baker, 1979), Deut. 29:4; Isa. 51:7; Matt. 14:24; John 12:40; Rom. 2:15; Eph. 1:16; 1 Thess. 3:13; and Sermon No. 45 on Deut. 4:22.

92 T. Song in *The New International Dictionary of New Testament Theology* edited by Colin Brown, 2:181.

93 Walter Eichrodt, *Theology of the Old Testament* (Philadelphia: Westminster, 1967), vol. 2, p. 143.

94 E.g., James Dunn, *The Theology of Paul, the Apostle,* 74–75.

78:8; 27:14). Likewise, it can experience negative emotions including pride, envy, anger, contempt, worry and fear (1 Sam. 4:13; 2 Chr. 26:16; Prov. 10:3; 23: 17; Isa. 7:2; John 14:1, 27; 16:6). Heart also represents human mentality as a process involving the whole person in contrast to concepts such as mind, conscience and will which are faculties of heart. For example, heart in both O.T. and N.T., expresses the idea of a person who is thinking (1 Kgs. 3:12; 4:29; Dan. 2:30; Luke 1:51; 2:35; Rom. 8:27; 2 Cor. 3:14–15; Phil. 4:7; Heb. 4:12). As such, heart reflects one's worldview. Therefore, a person considering which movie to select or deciding whether to shoplift a chocolate bar is engaging the faculties of conscience and will in the heart (Ex. 36:2; 1 Kgs. 8:17; Acts 8:22; 1 Cor. 4:5; Acts 11:23; 2 Cor. 9:7).

When sin affects the heart, it affects ones' whole being. Evil thoughts come from the heart (Mark 7:21). Shameful desires dwell in the heart (Rom. 1:24). The heart is disobedient, faithless and unresponsive (Mark 7:6; Rom. 1:21; 2:5; 2 Cor. 3:14–15; Eph. 4:18; Heb. 3:12). Hard heartedness expresses unbelief (Mark 16:14). Finally, the heart can be extremely deceitful. For example, in the midst of sin, Jeremiah's voice rings out, "The heart is deceitful above all things and beyond cure. Who can understand it?" (Jer. 17:9).

God's remedy for a sinful heart is a divine infusion. The Scripture describes this infusion in various ways. For example, the gospel message pierces the heart (Acts 2:37, 5:33, 7:54); God opens the heart (Acts 16:14); and faith begins in and brings Christ into the heart (Rom. 10:6-10; Eph. 3:17). Further, the Spirit infuses it as a pledge and prompt to intimate Christian prayer, "Dada, Father" (2 Cor. 1:22; Gal. 4:6). Finally, through His Holy Spirit, God pours His love into the believer's heart (Rom. 5:5).

Purity of heart is another expression used to depict God's divine remedy. This purity is established by God (1 Thes. 3:11–13), and believers are commanded to submit to Him for this cleansing (Heb. 10:22; Jas. 4:8). As a result, Paul instructs the believer to respond from a pure heart (1 Tim. 1:5). In addition, Christ's great promise of blessing for those of a pure heart is that they will see God in the kingdom (Matt. 5:8).

Clearly, heart is the human as he processes and responds to his experience. It is the private behaviors of the person - his thoughts, feelings, images and impetus for actions. The heart can be compared to contemporary concepts such as the "ego" or ego functions as articulated in psychoanalytic or constructivist literature. Other Biblical concepts such as mind, will, and conscience (see below) can be understood to be aspects of heart. Heart comprises those capacities involved in regulating interaction with the environment in the broadest sense of the word. Said differently, heart manages the interactions of self with the physical world, other persons and God. Engaging with the world or another individual allows for the process of influence. Thus heart is impacted by experience, both the present as well as the past, and relies on these experiences as a guide for shaping responses in the future. Typically, operations of assimilation and accommodation play a significant role in the processing of experience.[95] The degree of dissonance created by the disparity between one's self-image and his present behavior determines the extent to which the self assimilates or accommodates current experience. Heart is manifest in numerous capacities including introspection, initiative, striving, awareness of need, anticipation of consequences, and judgment. Heart conveys not only the notion of process but also content and therefore includes beliefs and assumptions about the world, self and others.

Bio-ethically, heart surgery and treatment are permitted. The pumper is exploring heart on a physical level rather than the relational, worldview, and functional levels of Biblical theology.

10.6. Mind

The philosophical and theological discussions about mind primarily discuss two concerns: 1) the relationship of mind to body and 2) the effect of sin on the mind. The second question is discussed by the Biblical text and is thus included in this section.

A survey of the Mind-Body relationship between the extremes of Hobbes' materialism[96] and Berkeley's idealism[97] would include those who try to relate mind and body. Plato advocates a noninteractive parallelism between mind and body[98] that is modified by some others, such as Augustine into a Divine illuminational occasionalism.[99] Descartes considers that the mind and body interact on each other.[100] In contemporary Christianity, Nancey Murphy, Warren Brown, Elving Anderson, and Robert Van Gulick advocate a nonreductive physicalism that considers humans as a "whole complex function, both in society and

95 Mary Ann Spencer Pulaski, *Understanding Piaget* (New York: Harper & Row, 1980).

96 Hobbes, *Leviathan* in the *Great Books of the Western World,* vol. 23, (Chicago: Encyclopaedia Britannica, 1952), pp. 49, 52, 162.

97 Berkeley, *Human Knowledge* sect 18–20, 50 in the *Great Books of the Western World,* vol. 35, (Chicago:Encyclopaedia Britannica, 1952), pp. 416–7, 422.

98 Plato, *Timaeus* in the *Great Books of the Western World,* vol. 7, *Plato,* pp. 452–3, 474–6.

99 Augustine, *Enarrations on the Psalms,* 118 in *A Select Library of the Nicene and Post-Nicene Fathers of the Christian Church,* vol. 8. Edited by Philip Schaff (Edinburgh/Grand Rapids: T & T Clark/Eerdmans, 1994); *De peccatorum meritis et remissione et de baptismo parvulorum* 1.25.38 in *Sanct Aureli Augustini De peccatorum meritis et remissione et de baptismo parvulorum ad Marcellinum libri tres.* Edited by Carl Franz Vrba and Joseph Zycha (Vindobonae, F. Tempsky, 1913); *De civitate Dei* 10.2 or *The City of God* in the *Great Books of the Western World,* vol. 18, *Augustine.* The medieval church tends to appreciate platonic illuminationism following Augustine until Aristotelian sensibility wins out in the wake of Aquinas.

100 Descartes, *Discourse* 5 and 6, *Meditations* 6, and *Objections and Replies* in the *Great Books of the Western World,* vol. 31, pp. 60–61, 99, 207–9.

in relation to God, which gives rise to "higher" human capacities such as morality and spirituality."[101] Other forms of materialism propose different mechanisms. In contrast, Kennard aligns with Tillich in identifying that the mind can follow the spirit into being conceived of as a different dimension that overlappingly interacts with the body.[102] Additionally, there are a wide variety of functionalisms (and this chapter is one form), where different kinds of constructs yield the same mental event.

Biblically, Mind, more than any other concept is referred to by a number of words which carry approximately the same meaning, including the Hebrew *yd'*/יָדַע and *nkr*/נָכַר, and the Greek , , , and .[103] They are usually used as descriptions of how people *think* or commands about how they should think. The scope includes thought, understanding, assessment, intent and purpose (Luke 1:51; Acts 20:3; 28:22; 1 Cor. 1:10; 7:25, 40; 13:11; Eph. 1:18; Heb. 4:12; 1 John 5:20; Rev. 17:13, 17). O.T. references to liver, kidneys and bowels convey that an individual's mental, spiritual and ethical impulses proceed from the center of his being (1 Sam. 25:37; Job 19:27; Ps. 16:7; Prov. 13:25; 14:33; 23:16; Lam. 2:11). The mind is occasionally contrasted with external acts or behaviors (Rom. 7:23, 25; 1 Cor. 14:14, 15, 19; Col. 2:3). The unregenerate mind is described as depraved, carnal, earthly, proud or factious and darkened by a futile lifestyle which does not seek God (Rom. 1:28; 8:6, 7; 12:3; 1 Cor. 4:6; Phil. 3:19; Col. 1:21). Instead, the believer is commanded to set his mind on things above and love God with all his soul, strength and mind (Matt. 22:37; Mark 12:30; Luke 10:27; Col. 3:2). This mental control is both developed and maintained through the Holy Spirit's indwelling ministry and results in spiritually minded believers (Rom. 8:6–7). They are encouraged to resist being squeezed in to the world's mold and to renew their minds through God's Word (Rom. 12:2). For example, the Christian is to be unified in mind with other believers (Rom. 12:3, 16; 1 Cor. 1:10; 4:6; 2 Cor. 13:11; Phil. 2:2, 5; 4:2).

Mind as described in Biblical literature is the self involved in logical, sequential analysis of information perceived via the person's

---

101 Warren Brown, Nancey Murphy, and H. Newton Malony, *Whatever Happened to the Soul?: Scientific and Theological Portraits of Human Nature*, p. 2, 25, 49–72, 99–148; Nancey Murphy, *Bodies and Souls, or Spiritual Bodies?*; Nancey Murphy "Reductionism: How Did We Fall Into It and Can We Emerge From It?" and Robert Van Gulick "Reduction, Emergence, and the Mind/Body Problem: A Philosophic Overview" in *Evolution and Emergence: Systems, Organisms, Persons* edited by Nancey Murphy and William Stoeger, pp. 19–73.

102 Paul Tillich, *Systematic Theology, volume 3, Life and the Spirit History and the Kingdom of God*, pp. 15–30, 111–161, 297–423.

103 Paul Gilchrist and Marvin Wilson in *Theological Wordbook of the Old Testament*, edited by Harris, Archer, and Waltke, 1:366, 2:580; James Dunn, *The Theology of Paul the Apostle*, pp. 73–4; J. Goetzmann in *The New International Dictionary of New Testament Theology* edited by Colin Brown, 2:616–20; H. D. McDonald, *The Christian View of Man*, pp. 24–25.

senses and spirit. It is the self engaged in processes such as perceiving, attending, analyzing and remembering. The process of comprehension and development of a response to incoming information is influenced by numerous factors including neurological impairment, acute psychological states, and affectively laden memories.

Biblical literature depicts the mind as an active organizer of experience. Rather than being a blank slate that passively registers external experience, mind actively organizes it in *a priori* meaningful ways. Self as mind is capable of abstracting from thought; that is, it can imagine that which it has not been exposed to through experience. It can automatically assume not-A when A is presented. In other words, while capable of demonstrative (linear) thinking, of processes dialectically. Rather than unipolar thought, the human being tends to engage in multi-polar thinking. For example, having no experience with a piece of information, an individual may experience doubt or skepticism that may lead to other possible ways of considering it - an indication of dialectical thought.

The ability for dialectical reasoning has significant implications for the nature of man, including the possibility of free will as a form of determinism and the capacity to love. Further, suspension of this type of reasoning may contribute to problems related to ineffective living or pathology.

The extensive, legitimating Son of God notion for progressive engagement in bio-ethics should be balanced by the use of one's mind to weigh a cost/risk analysis against the potential gain. Because something is possible should not mean that it should be viewed as the option to take. It would be more advisable to take less risky and costly options that have the promise of providing equal or greater gain than to opt for the novel that has greater risk. Initially the French face transplant is criticized on this count.[104] Additionally, the physicians in charge of treatment should include the patient within the loop of informed options, so that her consent could be informed by the facts and the options. Such an epistemic framework to evaluate such treatment could be thought of as in lines with Gary Friesen's *Decision Making and the Will of God* or William James' pragmatism.[105] Certainly, treatments should be preferred that are less intrusive with a higher likelihood of recovery performed by those doctors with a repeated track record of success. Such decisions need to take into account secondary consequences that were not intended. The patient should be amply informed and active to decide which option she wishes her doctors to attempt.

104 National Public Radio: *Talk of the Nation, Science Friday* Dec. 9, 2005.

105 William James, *The Will to Believe and Other Essays in Popular Philosophy* (New York: Longmans, Green & Co., 1897), ch. 1; Gary Friesen, *Decision Making and the Will of God: A Biblical Alternative to the Traditional View* (Portland: Multnomah Press, 1980).

Bio-ethically the Bible does not contemplate issues of euthanizing individuals with limited mental functioning (like occurs when the brain-stem is the only functioning aspect of the brain) because in its pre-modern perspective if a person could not function well enough to think and feed themselves they would probably shortly die. So euthanasia issues with limited brain functioning should be handled under the previous pattern laid down under soul/life.

10.7. Will

One of the subcategories of mind is will. The human will is a mental capacity involved in *choice*.[106] Several words in O.T. and N.T. literature including the Hebrew (*ḥps/* , *'bh/* , and *m'n/*) and the Greek ( ) suggest *desire, purpose and choice* (Mark 15:14; Acts 12:4; 1 Tim. 2:8; Jas. 4:4; 2 Pet. 1:21). Often these words are used in the context of God's choosing. This suggests that choices made by God or man are authentic in nature and cause events to occur (Acts 2:23).

Lived out in daily activity, will is the self's awareness of his responsibility for actions. Self as will plans and initiates responses to her environment. As a faculty of mind, "will" can choose to respond for reasons that may appear contrary to external contingencies, hence, Victor Frankel's statement that an individual always has the freedom to choose how he will react even when all other freedoms have been denied.[107]

For bio-ethical purposes it is always right to get the responsible person's informed consent before action is taken on her behalf. Furthermore, a living will can clarify issues for such a responsible agent to express her intentions in case an instance arises in which she can't later provide her consent at that time. The patient's agent should follow the prior consent to the extent that it urges moral activities and means, and to the extent that resources are available to do so.

10.8. Conscience

Conscience refers to a second subcategory of mind, entailing a *person's fallible personal self-assessment*. The Old Testament does not develop a word for self-judgment; God's judgment of human actions through His word comes closest to the N.T. concept of conscience (Pss. 51:10; 119). The Greek word for conscience ( ) conveys awareness of personal thought and behavior.[108] In contrast to the external standard or law, conscience is subjective in its assessment of self's attitudes

106 Colin Brown, *The New International Dictionary of New Testament Theology,* vo1. 3:1015; Gottlob Schrenk in *Theological Dictionary of the New Testament* edited by Kittel and Friedrich, 3:44–47; Leonard Coppes in *Theological Wordbook of the Old Testament,* edited by Harris, Archer, and Waltke, 1:4.

107 Victor Frankel, *Man's Search for Meaning* (New York: Pocket Books, 1959).

108 Colin Brown, *The New International Dictionary of New Testament Theology,* vol. 1:349; Gerhard Friedrich, *Theological Dictionary of the New Testament,* vol. 7:904–5; H. D. McDonald, *The Christian View of Man,* 16–19.

and behaviors (Acts 5:2; 12:12; 14:16; 23:1; Rom. 2:15; 2 Cor. 4:2). Conscience is not the ultimate standard; God is. Therefore, conscience should not be equated with divine assessment. Nevertheless, the believer described as having a weak conscience is encouraged not to act against it, for to do so is sin (Rom. 14:22–23; 1 Cor. 8:4, 7). The strong brother is to avoid behavior that will lure the weak brother to stumble (1 Cor. 8:12; 10:25–39). Due to the human condition, conscience can accuse falsely and result in unfounded psychological guilt. This occurs because conscience can be shaped to be more restrictive or permissive. As the believer re-educates the conscience, it can affirm his godly living. The New Testament concept includes the idea of having a good conscience, in contrast to the classical Greek concept which only condemns (Acts 23:1; 1 Tim. 1:4, 19; 1 Pet. 3:16, 21). The death of Christ and the cleansing of the Spirit change the focus of the conscience from dead works to the living God (Heb. 9:9, 14; 10:2, 22). In fact, an aspect of baptism is a pledge to pursue a good conscience (1 Pet. 3:21), that is, a commitment to live obediently, serving God because Christ has been raised. As the commitment to right living finds fruition in one's life, conscience ceases to condemn. Therefore, a good conscience is important for all believers but is essential for Christian leaders (1 Tim. 1:19, 3:9). I strongly advise the maintenance of a good conscience in bio-ethics.

Conscience manifest in life is the self's subjective response to his evaluation of the congruence between his self-perception and current behaviors. Thus, when they are synchronous, the self is at peace, whereas, when lacking congruence, the self experiences dissonance. The self alleviates this dissonance by reframing the lack of congruence in a way that provides a semblance of agreement between behavior and self-image, or it undergoes the painful task of re-organizing its self-perception to accommodate current behaviors. For example, on the one hand, the believer who does not acknowledge anger as a possible response of spirit-filled person, may reframe his angry outburst as righteous indignation. On the other hand, a person with a history of substance dependence who consumes three beers after eighteen months of sobriety, may respond by choosing to drink another ten beers because "I must be an alcoholic. I can stay sober for a while but in the end I slip." Here drunkenness is the sin for which his conscience should make him feel guilty, not the vulnerability to temptation. However, conscience can remind an individual of his vulnerability to temptation such that he would hopefully abstain from the temptations.

10.9. Biblical Theology Bio-ethical Conclusion

Biblical theology yields a multifaceted unity of an ontological and functional nature of human. As such we are privileged in relationship with a stewardship to invent, implement, and control treatment and rehabilitation of the created order. In so doing, we should preserve life as responsible agents. This includes maximizing the gain with the available means and resources. This also includes being faithful within the relationships that we have, and allowing the effected to consent to those actions that will affect them. In all this it is important to maintain an affirming conscience.

THE NATURE OF HUMANS

As Developed from the Biblical Emphasis

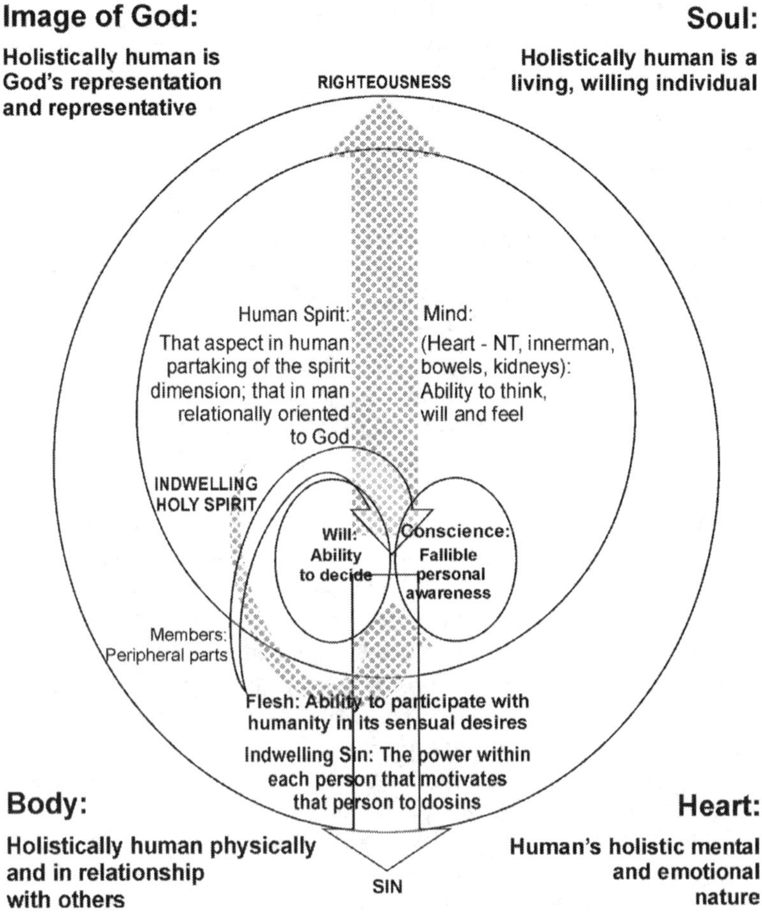

11. A Transactional Model of Human Based on Biblical Theology

BY E. PAUL HOLMES AND DOUGLAS W. KENNARD

Initially this was the second half of a paper entitled: "The Nature of Man: A Biblical Theology Justification of Trans-Therapeutic Strategies" and presented at the 1997 Wheaton Conference on the Integration of Psychology and Theology. This half of the original paper, the University of Chicago Psychologist E. Paul Holmes lead to mirror the Biblical and psychological insights of the previous chapter. Since the time of the paper's presentation, Dr. Holmes has become affiliated with Heritage Professional Associates of Chicago. Because the previous chapter was reworked to extend it to the issue of ethics, it was important to separate this chapter from the previous to express here an attempt to integrate psychology with theology for practical therapeutic benefit. Furthermore, if the previous chapter had insightful psychological comments then the reader can credit Dr. Paul Holmes with those suggestions and if the previous chapter troubled the reader then Doug Kennard takes full responsibility for what that chapter has become.

An examination of a single cell of liver tissue gives no indication of the overall function the liver serves in the biological processes of the human being. In the same vein, the individual components or facets of the human being as articulated in O.T. and N.T. literature cannot provide a living, dynamic picture of the process or function of human "being." These concepts can be understood as aspects or spheres of the person's existence. That is, only an integration of all the components of the person, influencing and being influenced, can present a viable delineation of living out human existence. Therefore, a picture of the person as outlined in Biblical literature is best understood as a transactional model. This type of model suggests that each component (soul, spirit, body, etc.) continually interacts with every other component in an interdependent way. In this sense, soul, spirit, and body have a mutually deterministic influence.

Being in relationship is an essential characteristic of humanness. That is, from the perspective of Biblical theology true humanness is an emergent quality of persons in a growing dynamic relationship with God, oneself and the natural world. Humans have purpose and relating in this way bring fulfillment of purpose and therefore, justification for being. To not include God in one's relationships is to not fulfill one's purpose, hence to not justify one's existence. "Sin" separates human beings from God and sin at its most basic level is the conviction that one can justify his existence in and of himself. Thus, the most basic drive or motivation for a human being is to justify or validate his existence. This is not a task humans are capable of and the message of Biblical literature is that one does not have to attempt to justify his existence, one has a just reason for being in relation to God.

The essence of the human is the self or soul, the person aware of his relation to himself. This awareness occurs through interaction with his environment in general. The conduit or means of relating the self to others is the body and the spirit. Spirit is the self as it relates itself to God. In other words, spirit is the interface between self and those aspects of existence that are not subject to empirical analysis. Just as spirit is the interface between God and soul or self, the body is the intersection of self and the physical world. The body is the public display of the self as it relates to its environment via the five senses. Heart is the private experience of the self as it attempts to make sense of its relation to physical and spiritual realms. The relationship of soul and heart can be likened to that of the self and ego functions or verbal behavior in various contemporary theories (i.e., constructivist theory). Further, concepts such as mind, conscience, and will describe more discrete delineations of heart.

Heart is the soul or self, perceiving, comprehending, planning and responding to its experience via spirit and body. Heart is the context of self, that is, the self's capacity to attribute meaning to its experience. The creation of meaning is significantly influenced by external stimuli, physiological sensations, and past experience. Thus, the self can create a biased context for relating to itself. In other words, via the heart, self can falsely relate to itself and its environment (see earlier discussion of the role of language in experience).

The complexity of living in a particular place and time in history with its influence on the individual suggests a homeodynamic rather than a homeostatic model. This fluidity of influence among the various aspects of the person and his environment changes over time. This is an important consideration for any model that attempts to provide explanatory power for the potential transition from humanness under the influence of the principles of a closed-system world-view (flesh) to humanness as it is lived from an open-system world-view (spirit).

11.1. Of What Mind

A worldview is a set of assumptions about existence (including: how a person comes to be, how he knows). Every person has basic beliefs about life - a personal worldview. Humanness as outlined in Biblical literature suggests two orientations of the human being to existence, a closed-system worldview and an open-system worldview. Each of these orientations to life has direct implications for issues such as hope, meaning, and relatedness. Several N.T. epistles delineate the differences between the two worldviews in terms of flesh-mindedness and Spirit-mindedness (e.g., Rom. 8:5–17).

A closed-system world-view holds that existence consists of those things that can be empirically derived. Reality is simply what can be observed or measured (i.e., length, frequency, intensity). There is no God who creates or influences the process of existence from outside the realm of time and space, and humankind must rely on reductionistic explanations of existence. Further, nature is the result of material evolution, which lends to the illusion that the forces of natural laws govern the history of the human race and the cosmos.

This perspective leads to inevitable consequences for man's view of himself, how he relates to other persons and his stance toward nature. First, the individual assumes that he does not possess qualities or purposes that make his existence important. Like the rest of nature, he exists purely by chance. This robs him of meaning and any sense that he is a unique form of life distinct from the rest of nature. He is left with little hope beyond his own capacity to survive, and he must rely entirely on his own devices. He shuns that aspect of existence expressed in spirit, which inevitably diminishes him. In spite of this, his emphasis on spirituality often reflects his attempt to reach out to something beyond himself and address his sense of being more than a bodily existence. In cultures where basic needs for shelter, safety and stability are easily attained, the individual is motivated by a need to justify or validate his existence, typically via possessions, power, and prestige. The body dominates self and the person's self-definition is increasingly related to physiological needs and temporal matters.

In addition, the basic assumption of the flesh-minded person is that he is capable of being in-and-of himself, which inevitably distorts humanness. A sense of vulnerability and alienation pervades his existence. People and nature becomes the vehicle for coping with existential concerns such as isolation and validation. He pursues freedom on the one hand though shunning alienation on the other. He lives in a tension between adhering to social norms for a sense of connectedness and safety while deviating from social constraints in order to experience a sense of validation beyond an identity smothered in group participation. Therefore, nature and other individuals become means-to-an-end rather than ends in themselves, and the self becomes meaningfully related to nothing.

The image of God in man also becomes distorted. Man becomes a despot who exploits and abuses nature for personal gain and validation. Rather than structuring and enhancing constructive engagement with nature, he conquers it. He walls himself off from nature and creates an artificial environment that alienates him from a vital part of his humanness. Ultimately, this distorted equilibrium destroys the self and its relationship to its environment. As a result, the flesh-minded person looks for temporal satisfaction, and ultimately, is left to himself with no means of communion with God or others - a hell in itself.

An open-system world-view assumes that the process of existence is impacted by an influence outside of the realm of time and space. The O.T. and N.T. state that the Judeo-Christian God is directly and intimately involved in the lives of human beings. This perspective suggests that the human being is a unique creation with a reason for being. While having this privileged status, he shares a common animating force with the rest of creation, placing him in a unique relationship to both God and nature. Humans are fashioned with the faculties to comprehend truth and to order life accordingly. In his relatedness to God, he has both the hope of fulfillment and the responsibility to soberly work out true humanness. Ultimately, Spirit-mindedness or true humanness manifests itself in the behaviors of the body.

The Spirit-minded individual is said to have purity of heart. He is characterized by seeking true humanness in the moment rather than attempting to live righteously for other ends (i.e. fear of damnation, hope of gaining paradise, pleasing the crowd). Thus, this individual has vitality in God that transcends a finite temporal existence. Mindful of all of reality, he experiences a freedom to choose for the sake of contingencies not determined by factors empirically understood.

In addition, rather than using other persons to enhance his own life, Spirit-minded humans are redemptive in their discourse, looks for true fellowship, values the importance of accountability and is open to the wise counsel of like-minded persons. In every interaction, they are both humble and respectful. Furthermore, man in this state recognizes the inherent value of all creation and actively participates in nature in the role of steward.

The implications for living in the particular are significant when considering the pursuit of true humanness. True humanness may be understood as the actualization of the inherent potential residing in the self. Biblical literature states that true humanness is seeking God and his rightness. He does this by developing growing dynamic relationships with God and his neighbor. Therefore, he is characterized by his willingness to use his life to enhance or redeem the lives of those with whom he has contact. That is, he acts like God. God is, in the end, servant to all. He provides everything to sustain man's life, to the point of giving His own - the ultimate expression of love and servanthood (1 John 3:16).

Repeated throughout the N.T. is the admonition to those who articulate a commitment to spirit-mindedness to cease from living out a life that displays flesh-mindedness (Col. 2:20). Most of the apostles focused considerable time to addressing believers who live in the flesh. They defined a flesh-minded believer as an individual who attempts to live truly human according to the principles of this world or a closed-system worldview (2 Pet. 1:5–11). James characterized believers in his state as double-minded. Thus, the double-minded person articulates an open-system worldview but makes daily decisions based on a closed-system worldview. He makes decisions on the potential costs and/or benefits rather than being righteous in the moment.

Human beings can be characterized as living in one of three spheres of existence, flesh-mindedness, double-mindedness or spirit-mindedness. These states of mindedness provide a heuristic from evaluating existential issues associated with ineffective living.

11.2. Mindedness: Implications for Ineffective Living

The etiology of ineffective living is multifaceted and transactional in nature. Individual factors (i.e., biology, social learning history, current behavior repertoire and free will) interact with environmental factors (i.e., environmental contingencies and social context) to influence personal existence in time and space. Although these factors are necessary to place current "being" in context, they do not completely determine individual behavior. The interplay of these factors may be conceptualized by using a three-phase compensation model. This model suggests that ineffective living is a result of the interaction of vulnerability, precipitating and perpetuating factors. Vulnerability factors, as outlined above, limit an individual when confronted with a precipitating event such as chronic stress or acute trauma. Mindful choices or effective coping leads to alleviation of transitory signs and symptoms and cessation of mental and/or physical distress. Habitual or impulsive coping tends to lead to avoidant behaviors with the goal of immediate relief from negative affect states. This style of coping tends to perpetuate symptoms by establishing a lifestyle that maintains mental and/or physical distress. For example, as a result of a demotion (precipitating factor) an individual may suffer a major depressive episode. While it may be rational that this person resigns himself to his bed due to a biological process (vulnerability factor), it is not a rational response in his current context as a husband, father, and corporate executive. Nor is it sound in terms of his stated long-term goals. While a precipitating event (demotion) may have triggered a biological process that led to the resignation to bed behavior, continuation of this behavior will very likely perpetuate a set of beliefs and biological processes that maintain the depressed mood, lack of interest in activity, and hopelessness.

Unfortunately, a lack of differentiation between challenged living due to biological processes and social learning history and ineffective living due to mindedness has been the impetus for much of the debate regarding the place of psychology in the church. It is imperative when evaluating ineffective living to differentiate causes due to biological process and mindedness. By now, it is well established that major mental illnesses such as schizophrenia spectrum disorders, many forms of major depression, anxiety disorders, substance abuse, and even some personality disorders such as borderline personality disorder have a biological component. Typically, these disorders are conceptualized from a transactional or stress-diathesis model. An individual with a biological vulnerability to a particular disorder (of disease, schizophrenia) and lacking effective coping skills, will develop symptoms when exposed to significant and/or chronic environmental stressors. Based on a significant body of literature now available, practice guidelines are currently being developed for numerous disorders. For example, the use of exposure and response prevention for the treatment of many anxiety disorders has been show to be so effective that to use other types of therapy could be construed as misguided.

A person living in any of the three spheres of humanness may as readily suffer with a biologically based mental illness as with a chronic medical condition. Mental illness, like medical illness, is not an indication of a person's true humanness. In fact, his of set toward the illness may be more of an indication of his true humanness than the presence of the illness itself.

Further, skills acquisition may also influence a person's ability to live effectively despite his level of mindedness. For example, a spirit-minded individual with a learning history associated with an alcoholic parent may not possess effective conflict resolution skills because of a lack of modeling and validation. Should this person genuinely desire to cope more effectively in conflicts, no amount of insight or reflective listening will provide him with the skills he requires. In fact, to remain non-directive and not provide specific training would be a recapitulation of the invalidation he has experienced in the past. Therefore, the truly human of may lack skills or suffer from medical or mental illness; what actually distinguishes him from flesh-minded and double-minded individual is the consistent (but not perfect) congruence between his mindedness and his behavior.

Ultimately, ineffective living is missing the mark of true humanness in a given moment. If purity of heart or one-mindedness is understood as living rightly in the moment, being ineffective is living the moment for ulterior motives, motives other than being truly human. This tends to characterize the ineffectiveness experienced by flesh-minded and double-minded persons. Nonetheless, ineffective living tends to manifest itself differently for each of these spheres.

Being "of the flesh-minded" has obvious implications for an individual's quest for hope, meaning, and relatedness. Certainly, not all persons who operate from a closed-system world-view live ineffectively. Nevertheless, as outlined in the previous section, the ramifications of living in this way are significant. The "troubled person" typically has been unsuccessful in justifying his existence via his own abilities. He feels hopeless, ineffectual, and alienated. Thus, many of his difficulties are a result of his lack of sophistication in managing his environment in a way that provides possessions, influence, or recognition. Typically, after numerous attempts to cope with the concerns of life, he has lost his ability to reason dialectically and is caught in a self-deprecating thought pattern. This may involve prescribed areas of life (i.e., fear of elevators) or pervade his whole lifestyle (i.e., depressed mood, loss of appetite, inability to sleep, lack interest in work, and no energy). The more pervasive the problem, the more this becomes an existential crisis. Typically, this increases the probability that a flesh-minded person will present at a religious institution. With appropriate support, direction, and provision of resources, he may become more likely to be open to the re-evaluation of his world view.

For the double-minded, ineffective living is typically the result of articulating one worldview but reflecting a contradictory worldview in one's behavior. The person in this mind-set sincerely confesses belief in Christ, but is not mindful of his choices in the moment or the pursuits of his heart. He attempts to justify his existence via his own abilities (i.e., gifts, talents). He pursues possessions, status and influence which reflect values that are meaningless in light of eternal matters (John 3:19–21). He relies on the behaviors of religion to justify his existence and is vulnerable to external or intellectual legalism. For example, he may scoff at those who suggest that external appearance or behaviors indicate righteousness, yet he measures his own righteousness by his ability to debate fellow believers at the weekly Bible study. Although intending to live out the fruits of the Spirit, the double-minded person tends to become egocentric and rights-oriented in choices of the moment. Because of sincerely perceiving himself as Christian, this person tends to reframe his behaviors to justify them. Due to group pressure to appear that he is experiencing the benefits of his belief, the double-minded person may be less apt to seek help. Ambivalence tends to be characteristic of the double-minded individual (Jas. 1:2–8). On the one hand, he may participate in church functions (Bible study, prayer meeting) yet avoid activities that require a person to be vulnerable and accountable.

Like the flesh-minded individual, the "troubled" double-minded person does not possess the resources or skills to successfully work his environment to gain the possessions, influence, or prestige that provide comfort, safety, and stability. Typically, he has alienated himself (i.e., from spouse, peers, co-workers), feels frustrated and angry, and sees little hope. At this point, he presents in much the same way as a flesh-minded person.

11.3. Ineffective Living Mindedness Implications for Change

Mindfulness is a key element in the process of change. Human beings process information at conscious and unconscious levels. Effortful processing is more or less sequential in nature, has a very limited capacity and occurs in awareness. Automatic processing occurs out of awareness and involves the simultaneous processing of large amounts of information. Most people's behaviors are over learned and occur automatically. They rarely consider the basis of their decisions or behaviors in the moment. The "troubled person" tends to suffer from a lack of awareness of the habitual ways of thinking and behaving that have led to his distress. While he seeks help for relief from his emotional pain, he is often less committed to significant changes in lifestyle. In many cases, the ineffective thinking and behaviors that other people may consider the problem are actually the individual's best effort to cope; they are his solutions to other problems. As a result, he finds change a difficult consideration despite his emotional distress.

Prochaska and Declemente suggest that change is a process that occurs over time.[1] Based on studies of self-changers, they delineated six stages through which individual advance. The most prevalent characteristic of persons involved in this process is ambivalence. In fact, a major portion of the therapeutic dialogue focuses on ambivalence and commitment to change. Thus, the goal of the counselor is to create an atmosphere in which he can empathically highlight the discrepancies between a person's current lifestyle (i.e., attitudes and behaviors) and his stated goals and values. Confrontation and directives tend to interfere with a person's ability to grapple with these discrepancies. Thus, while confrontation may not be an effective strategy, it remains the goal.[2]

The role of the Spirit is essential for the counselor who works from an open-system worldview. Trusting in the influence of the Spirit, the counselor facilitates a process in which an individual comes to the realization that he must make an informed decision about his current behaviors in light of what he states are his goals and values in life. Several basic principles enable the counselor to maintain a collaborative relationship with persons considering change.[3] First, the counselor must communicate through his verbal and non-verbal behavior that the person he is sitting with is worth listening to. Using reflective listening, he conveys an understanding of the other person's psychological state and that, at some level, his behavior and thoughts make sense. Since acceptance and validation are prerequisites to considering change, this stance is

1 James Prochaska, John Norcross and Carlo Diclemente, *Changing for Good* (New York: Avon Books, 1994), pp. 3–27.

2 Neal & Heather Miller (Eds.), *Treating Addictive Behaviors: Processes of Change* (New York: Plenum Press, 1986), p. 13.

3 Neal & Heather Miller (Eds.), *Treating Addictive Behaviors: Processes of Change*, pp. 55–63.

necessary for assisting an individuals contemplating change. Second, active listening enables the counselor to highlight the discrepancies in the person's life. He brings together meanings that the individual had not previously connected in awareness. Third, he conveys the attitude that he is in no position to decide if his client's behavior is a problem, but he is willing to help him examine his lifestyle and move to an informed decision about it. Fourth, the counselor understands that if the person with whom he is working disagrees, argues, or withdraws, this is an indication that he is taking responsibility for change at that moment. Thus, as facilitator, the counselor is always following the individual's lead.

The ultimate goal of the interaction is for the counselor to facilitate an experience during which the individual confronts the discrepancies between his stated goals and value and his daily choices, makes an informed decision about his current lifestyle and a commitment to either maintain his current stance toward life or make lifestyle change. Prochaska, Norcross and Declemente outline several factors often present that lead to this type of commitment.[4] The counselor creates an atmosphere in which, via the functions of verbal behavior, the person comes in contact with cues associated with contingencies related to his learning history. When verbalization is associated with contingencies of past learning and not those in the room, a counselee tends to develop consciousness of self in context, experiences emotion arousal, again indicating contact with past experiences of ineffective living. Only as the counselee is in emotional contact with the consequences of his past is he in contact in the present with incentives to self re-evaluation and commitment to lifestyle change. Should an individual make a commitment to change, the counselor's role changes to that of a cheerleader and consultant. At this stage, the individual may require specific resource to bring change to fruition. Ultimately, commitment to a lifestyle is the choice of the individual. As a result, the counselor is open to and accepting of the fact that the individual may choose to maintain his current lifestyle even in the face of his awareness of the discrepancies in his life and the potential consequences.

This approach may be utilized with persons in any of the three realms of mindedness. For flesh-minded, the counselor highlights the inevitable consequences of living according to the principles of the world and the discrepancies between his goals and the values from which he operates. The double-minded person is involved in a process in which he becomes aware of the divergence between his stated values and the values expressed in his behaviors. His goal is to become increasingly aware of his values in the moment and choose mindfully. This approach

4 James Prochaska, John Norcross and Carlo Diclemente, *Changing for Good.*

to the human in distress acknowledges the role of spirit, personal autonomy, and individual responsibility for change.

12. A Theology of Work

God created humans to rule the creation for God, under God's authority. Biblically, humans have vocation before the Fall.[1] In Genesis 1:26, 28 and 2:7–25 humans (male and female) are treated as God's sons. The "image of God" concept develops this sonship by comparing it with the way image is used in the context (Gen. 1:26, 28; 5:1, 3). In the ancient Near East such a concept of sonship to God is used for kings. Furthermore, God's design and blessing identifies the image to "subdue" and "rule" (Gen. 1:26, 28 *kbšh/* and *rd/*). These are forceful terms that speak of trampling on others in conquest and to force others to serve the purposes of the king. In this context, Adam begins to implement this strategy as a co-regent, under God, by his naming the animals and his wife, for naming is the prerogative of ancient Near Eastern kings (Gen. 2:19, 23; Dan. 1:7). Thus work which brings order and control over part of the creation is a valuable end in itself. That is, part of the creation blessing from God is that we continue to represent Him through our miniature sovereignty on the earth. After the fall, the terms, "subdue" and "rule," are never undone, but as humans are contorted by the lure of sin, restrictions are put in place to limit the excesses (eg. Gen. 9:2–6). Such limitations would be a significant part of the role performed by governments. However, the ordering accomplished in this ruling will reflect the concerns of our cultures, including religion and ethics, availability of resources and technology, and the population density.[2] This chapter is an attempt to sensitize the reader to a Biblical perspective, which is an oriental Judeo-Christian perspective as seen through my Western modern context.

This concept of sonship has an immediate implication toward continuing and extending God's reign on earth through human procreation and co-regency with Him. Because humans, in our finite embodiment, do not live forever, we need to be fruitful in procreation

1 Unlike *Sib. Or.* 1.55–59 which presents this as after the Fall.

2 Cf. Joseph Pelikan, Joseph Kitagawa, Seyyed Hossein Nasr. *Comparative Work Ethics: Judeo-Christian, Islamic, and Eastern* (Washington, Library of Congress, 1985). Additionally, the concerns from a technological society might be represented by Michael Novak, *Toward a Theology of the Corporation* (Washington: American Enterprise Institute, 1981), while a society that is dominated by high population density might be better reflected by F. F. Schumacher, *Small is Beautiful: Economics as if People Mattered* (New York: Harper & Row Publishers, 1973) and M. K. Gandhi, *Bread Labor [The Gospel of Work]* (Ahmedabad-14, Navajivan Publishing House, 1960).

so that we might fill the earth with sufficient co-regents, so that this task of creation oversight and development is accomplished. The labor of birthing and raising kids is an integral vocational role to accomplish this divine oversight (Gen. 1:28; 1 Tim. 2:15). Human oversight of the creation is put at risk, unless the next generation is raised with faith, love, and sanctity. Inherent in this task is the education of subsequent generations through personal quality means that reproduce in them our worldview, commitment and affections. Humankind continues multi-generational as a little lower than God, with glory and majesty, so that we can rule over the works and creatures of God's hands (Ps. 8:4–8).

Within this orientation for work, God creates sacred time to stop work. In the process of creating, God stopped His work, making the seventh day a work stoppage (Gen. 2:1–3). For Israel in the Mosaic covenant, this Sabbath[3] likewise was to be a day of rest, from which all work was to stop so that this covenant community could reflect the sacredness of this time (Ex. 20:8–11). This limitation of excess work reflects a stewardship imposed upon Israel by their Sovereign. With His generosity, Sabbath also took on the meaning of a freedom from bondage (Deut. 5:15) and by extension served as a model for festivals of release.[4] Additionally, every seventh year is a sabbatical year freeing people from servitude and need, as well as giving the land rest (Ex. 21:2–4; Lev. 25:2–7; Deut. 15:1–18). After seven sevens of years there was a super-sabbatical year, the year of Jubilee which again freed people from servitude, debt, prior sale, and gave the land rest (Lev. 25:8–55).[5] All the land and houses (outside of cities) were to be redeemed to the rightful tenant, since "the land is Mine, for you are but aliens and sojourners with Me" (Lev. 25:23). This is a generous way of limiting debt, bankruptcy, servitude, while providing for land redistribution and earning ability. Such a framework shows that God owns all the land (not just Israel) and that all humans operate as stewards under His sovereignty (Ps. 24:1). So the dominant issues of work become how responsible we are to the stewardship which God places us within. This periodical redistribution was designed to elevate the poorest[6] and draw down the stratospherically rich.[7] Unfortunately, there is no evidence that Israel celebrated these Sabbatical years or

3 In the Jewish construct this is Friday night sundown to Saturday night sundown (ie. evening and morning of a day).

4 Passover commemorating release from Egypt occurs on the Abib 14th (two 7's into the month), Unleavened bread lasts 7 days (from the 15th to 21st), Weeks occurs day after 7th Sabbath after Passover, then a number of festivals occur in the seventh month (trumpets, day of atonement, and the 7 day long tabernacles).

5 Robert North, *Sociology of the Biblical Jubilee* (Rome: Pontifical Biblical Institute, 1954).

6 The opportunity to glean from fields of material left and especially the corners provided a welfare system for the needy and traveler (eg. Lev. 19:9–10).

7 The idle rich, who lavished their wealth upon themselves helped to bring on the Babylonian captivity (Amos 6:3–7).

Jubilee until Jews returned from the Babylonian captivity during the second Temple Jewish era.[8] In fact, one of the reasons Israel goes into captivity for 70 years is to pay God back for these years lost in Israel's stewardship (Jer. 25:11–12; 29:10; Dan. 9:2). In the wake of impending captivity, Jubilee becomes a metaphor for the eschatological Kingdom release (Isa. 61:1–3). It is this evidence of eschatological Kingdom that Jesus identifies as indicating His New Covenant ministry (Luke 4:18–21 quoting Isa. 61:1–2). As we in the New Covenant long for the Kingdom, we should remind ourselves that we should forgive other's debts against us, because our forgiveness of others becomes the pattern by which our Lord Jesus instructed us to pray for forgiveness of debts before our Father (Matt. 6:12, notice the in this text). This approach to stewardship helps to foster generosity toward others, so that we meet real needs (e.g., Matt. 5:40–48). Practically, we should make it easier to forgive debts and bankruptcies of the poor brought on by medical expenditures to save and preserve life within health conditions not resulting from destructive lifestyle choices, especially for the aged. Instead of giving the wealthiest people tax cuts, we should make sure that benefits go to the poor. Likewise, the World Bank and International Monetary Fund (IMF) should forgive the debts of the poorest nations and take advantage of providing more grants.

Likewise, in a context where Adam is developed as God's son[9] the agricultural tasks of "cultivate" and "keep" the garden[10] are specifically commanded by God (Gen. 2:15). This particular garden with its rivers and precious stones is developed as a sacred space, much like those gardens attached to ancient Near Eastern temples.[11] No temple is mentioned, but God Himself occupies the place so that the garden functions like a temple providing access to God. These words developing the care of the garden refer to agricultural activity of a steward involved in irrigation, fertilizing, pruning and picking for the orchard of trees. However, these specific terms in the Mosaic context also focus humans toward the

---

8 Josephus, *War* 1.157-60; Jews compliance with Sabbath law was well known in the ancient Near East (Josephus, *Ant.* 14.10.12; *Ag. Ap.* 2.2, 39; Philo, *Vit. Mos.* 2.21; and even more so in sectarian Judaism [*CD* 10.14–11.18; *Songs of the Sabbath Sacrifice*; *Temple Scroll* = 11Q19]).

9 In Genesis 2 Adam is treated as God's son in that God as an ancient Near Eastern father gets him in the first place and then crafts the environment around him with expression of home, wealth, vocation, and arranged marriage. Luke 3:38 also hints at this.

10 Such a garden in the ancient Near East, is an orchard of fruit trees.

11 For development of this theme see Gordon Wenham, "Sanctuary Symbolism in the Garden of Eden Story" in *Proceedings of the Ninth World Congress of Jewish Studies* (Jerusalem World Union of Jewish Studies, 1986). This point is made even clearer by the expulsion from the garden once the humans have become sinners; they as sinners can not remain or return to such a sacred place (Gen. 3:23–24). Cf. Kathryn Gleason, "Gardens in Preclassical Times" *Oxford Encyclopedia of Archaeology in the Near East*, ed. E. Meyers (New York: Oxford, 1997), 2:383.

sacredness of their task as *serving* God. For example, "cultivate" (*'bdh/*עָבַד) elsewhere in the Pentateuch expresses the idea of servant to God, which is the highest role a human can have (Gen. 2:15; Ex. 3:12; 10:3, 8, 11, 24, 26; etc.). Likewise, the word "keep" (*šmr/*שָׁמַר) is used elsewhere in the Pentateuch as *obeying* God's commands (Gen. 2:15; Ex. 15:26; 16:28; 19:5; 20:6, 8; etc.). These words hint that human responsibility in work may be obedient priestly service within the role of man being that of the son of God. Such work is also what God would have done as obedience keeps the commands of God. In such a stewardship, we are the Lord's and so we should work for God, in His name and for His glory as outstanding workers (Rom. 14:4; 1 Cor. 10:31; Col. 3:17, 23; 1 Pet. 4:11). Work accomplished is a service for God and should be viewed as such. This recognition that all forms of work are a service unto God was especially developed in the Lutheran idea of work as vocation, overthrowing the medieval construct of the higher standing of religious service over lay work.[12] The Reformation re-infused all work as a stewardship under God. Among these, Calvin and the Puritans splice church with work more closely than did the two kingdoms perspective of Lutheranism.[13]

In the modern context, the choice of work is open for an individual to cultivate as they see fitting with their own desires and abilities. In pre-modern societies it is often not this way, as each generation largely replaces their parents in the family business. However, even in a pre-modern society, an individual can craft work suited to himself, provided that there is a market for it,[14] society values such work,[15] and people benefit from the work.[16] For example, coming from the creation, early humans pursued agriculture, city building, music, metalworking and a range of other entrepreneurial professions (Gen. 4:2, 17, 21–22). All these are developed in the narrative as accomplishments within acceptable professions to pursue. Such occupations increase productivity

12 *Luther's Works,* 34.II.306; 10.I.308; and especially *Kirchenpostille*, p. 1522 where he first uses the term vocation for a secular activity. This Reformation view echoes that of the 14th-15th century mystics Eckhardt and Tahler, Alan Richardson, *The Biblical Doctrine of Work* (London: SCM Press, 1952), p. 36; the continuing legacy of the medieval Catholic perspective is explored in Lother Roos, "On a Theology and Ethics of Work," *Communio* 11(1984): 100–119. Cf. Miroslav Volf, *Work in the Spirit: Toward a Theology of Work* (Oxford: Oxford University Press, 1991), p. 106; Ronald Preston, "Vocation" in *The Westminster Dictionary of Christian Ethics* (Philadelphia: The Westminster Press, 1986), pp. 650–651.

13 John Calvin, *The Institutes of the Christian Religion,* Bk. 4, ch. 20; Max Weber, *The Protestant Ethic and the Spirit of Capitalism* (New York: Charles Scribner's Sons, 1958); Paul Johnson, *Grace: God's Work Ethic* (Valley Forge: Judson Press, 1985), p. 20.

14 Michael Novak, *Toward a Theology of the Corporation* (Washington: American Enterprise Institute for Public Policy Research, 1981).

15 Lother Roos, "On a Theology and Ethics of Work," *Communio* 11(1984): 100–119.

16 Gandhi, *Bread Labor,* pp. 12–16.

if ingenuity and technology are applied to their concerns.[17] However, it is unfortunate if such work distracts a person from the spirituality of prayer and giving the first and the best of their gifts to God (Gen. 4:3–4, 26). So that with the variety of work available, we are warned not to secularize whatever work we decide to do.

Our work often defines us and we derive some definition of ourselves by what we do. For example, Jesus worked as a carpenter, and others thought of him in that way (Mark 6:3). However, Jesus became more defined by His doing the work given Him to do by His Father (John 4:34; 5:17; 6:28; 9:3; 17:4). This work involved Jesus in many ministry roles including rabbi, sage, carpenter-day laborer, healer, prophet, priest, judge, and ultimately King.[18] The fact that Jesus did these tasks is one reminder of their value. However, any job can be valuable in a person's choice to define oneself, especially if a person has the sense of a vocation, which becomes a long term pursuit in life. With a sense of vocation, the worker often moves to a higher level of commitment and satisfaction in their workplace.[19] However, younger audiences or those going through a mid-life crisis may find it difficult to cultivate a long term satisfaction having shorter job arrangements with whatever is available. Additionally, if a situation forces an individual into unemployment or underemployment this often results in alienation; as an unemployed worker exclaimed, "those who don't have a job don't fit anywhere."[20]

Labor is not a result of sin and the Fall, but work is made more difficult and frustrating because of sin and the effects of sin. For example, in the Fall of humanity's work is infused with an element of futility, such as the increased pain in child birth, and now agriculture requires hard labor to keep down the weeds (Gen. 3:16, 18–19). The continuing of sin fosters work crises with varieties of abuse: endless slavery,[21] child

---

17 Western technological society is built upon this recognition, but it is noticed as early as John Locke, *Second Treatise of Civil Government* (New York: Macmillan Co., 1947), p. 20; contrary to Frederick Winslow Taylor's, *Principles of Scientific Management* (New York: Harper & Row Publishers, 1911) who programmed workers as a part of the machine, Douglas McGregor (*The Human Side of Enterprise* [New York: McGraw Hill, 1960], p. 113) advocates each worker should use her creativity.

18 cf. Douglas Kennard, *Messiah Jesus: Christology in His Day and Ours* (New York: Peter Lang, 2008).

19 Abraham Maslow, "A Theory of Human Motivation," *Psychological Review* 50(July, 1943): 370–396.

20 Miroslav Volf, *Work in Spirit*, pp. 37–38; cf. Richard Gillett, *The Human Enterprise: A Christian Perspective on Work* (Kansas City: Leaven Press, 1985), pp. 1–6, 11–22; F. F. Schumacher, *Small is Beautiful: Economics as if People Mattered*, pp. 172–190, 206–220.

21 Andrew Cockburn, with photographs by Jodi Cobb, "21st Century Slaves," *National Geographic*, 204:3(Sept. 2003): 2–29.

labor and exploitation,[22] discrimination,[23] and dehumanization.[24] The proclaimer in the book of Ecclesiastes decries these scenarios of oppression, indicating that better are the dead and those who have never been born than these who suffer in this manner (Eccl. 4:1–3). Each of these abuses treat the worker merely as a means only and not as an end in itself. Kant urged his readers to "Act so that you treat humanity, whether in your own person or in that of another, always as an end and never as a means only."[25] Likewise, Marx speaks of the devastating consequences to physical and mental health from the kind of labor that makes the worker merely part of the industrial machine.

> The worker is related to the product of his labor as to an alien object. The object he produces does not belong to him, dominates him, and only serves in the long run to increase his poverty. Alienation appears not only in the result, but also in the process of production and productive activity itself. The worker is not home in his work which he views only as a means of satisfying other needs. It is an activity directed against himself, that is independent of him and does not belong to him. Thirdly, alienated labor succeeds in alienating man from his species. Species life, productive life, life creating life, turns into a mere means of sustaining the worker's individual existence, and man is alienated from his fellow men. Finally, nature itself is alienated from man, who thus loses his own inorganic body[26]

Such a condition of sin, alienation and abuse destroys the value and motivation for work. This kind of sin and abuse is often more than a volitional problem, stemming from the deep structures of society. Neither the Biblical nor the rabbinic economic system was a market driven economy but rather a distributive economy of barter and trade where the price of items and labor must be within 20% of fair market cost or it is an

---

22 E.g., Charles Dickens, *Hard Times* (New York: Norton, 1966).

23 The world is still full of racism, gender inequality and nationalism that ostracize and exclude workers. Cf. Richard Gillett, *The Human Enterprise*, pp. 6–9, 23–53, 71–83.

24 E.g., Karl Marx, The Early Texts, ed. D. McLellan (Oxford: Blackwell Publishers, 1971), p. 133, 137–38, 202.

25 Immanuel Kant, *Foundations of the Metaphysics of Morals* (New York: Bobbs-Merrill, 1969), A.428–429.

26 Karl Marx, Paris Manuscripts in The Early Texts, ed. D. McLellan (Oxford: Blackwell Publishers, 1971), pp. 137–38 these conditions were accentuated under Taylorism (cf. Principles); cf. Melvin Kohn, "Occupational Structure and Alienation," in Work and Personality: An Inquiry into the Impact of Social Stratification (Norwood: Ablex Publishing Co., 1983), pp. 82–97 for a further analysis of capitalism and bureaucracy and the detrimental psychological affect. Charlie Chaplin's film Modern Times dramatizes this alienation.

abuse of usury which the community would insist need be remunerated to keep the community fair for all.[27] Does stewardship to God, fair market pricing, and generosity toward others drive our society? Or are we framed and passionate about our capitalistic freedom, or socialistic justice, or personal honor? However, it does not have to be this way if the worker and employer know how they fit into the stewardship of creation order and structure a workplace sensitive to this divine design.

The creation order provides a framework for wisdom in the book of Ecclesiastes on how work and pleasure are to be viewed. In contrast to the abundance of things that do not satisfy, a repeated chorus throughout the book of Ecclesiastes highlight that pleasure and work can satisfy if you recognize that they are a gift from God. For example, there is nothing better than to enjoy and be content in one's pleasure and work, for that is what God gives (Eccl. 2:24–26; 5:10–20; Ps. 128:2). This is a very foreign sentiment to that of Aristotle who saw that the only purpose for work was to obtain leisure.[28] Of course, God is concerned that we are remunerated appropriately for work rendered (1 Cor. 9:9–11; 1 Tim. 5:18). This provides a motivation to work, for the lazy might not get paid, thus destroying himself (Eccl. 4:5; 2 Thess. 3:10). Additionally, there is a need to be content with one's pay (Matt. 20:1–16; Phil. 4:11). However, Ecclesiastes reminds us that we should not just live for our remuneration or our recreation, but that there is real satisfaction to be had in the workplace as well. There is nothing better than to enjoy and do good within your abilities in harmony with God's timing, because we do not know the future quality and length of life (Eccl. 3:12–15, 22; 9:1–12). A person's deeds will abound back upon him, therefore be wise, gracious and put work before pleasure (Eccl. 10:8–20). In this you prepare for the uncertainties of life by diversifying your industry, for we do not know the activity of God or when misfortune will occur. Also, cultivate contentment in one's work, since being a workaholic to satisfy greed of experience or possessions, does not ultimately satisfy (Eccl. 2:1–16; 4:8; 5:10–20). This is similar to President Franklin D. Roosevelt's address in 1935 to the Young Democratic Clubs, describing the American hope for the workplace.

> You place emphasis on sufficiency of life, rather than on a plethora of riches. You think of the security for yourself and your family that will give you good health, good food, good

27 Jacob Neusner, *Handbook of Rabbinic Theology: Language, System, Structure* (Boston: Brill Academic Publishers, 2002), pp. 198–209 especially 200–201, 204; e.g. *Mishnah Baba Batra* 5.1; *Baba Mesi'a* 4.1–2; 5.1.

28 Aristotle, *Politics*, 1334a, in *The Great Books of the Western World: Aristotle: II* (Chicago: Encyclopaedia Britannica, 1952), pp. 538–539.

> education, good working conditions, and the opportunity for normal recreation and occasional travel.[29]

Jesus has much to say about wealth and Kingdom, and some of it has to do with vocation. For example, after the rich ruler refused to follow Christ by refusing to give his wealth away in love to those who needed aid, Jesus told a Kingdom parable in response to Peter and the disciples' claim that they have left everything to follow Him (Matt. 19:27).[30] Jesus reassures them that their chosen vocation of following Christ will be truly rewarded with responsibilities and benefits in Kingdom. When the regeneration phase of Kingdom has the Son of Man sitting on His throne, then the disciples will also sit upon twelve thrones, judging the twelve tribes of Israel, which seems to be an extreme privilege for them (Matt. 19:24, 28). The Kingdom is described as of heaven and of God and salvation and where Christ reigns (Matt. 19:23–25, 28); when Jesus is involved there is no distinction between sovereign and Davidic Kingdom. Within this Kingdom, the disciples also have the benefits of everlasting life and many times more reward than the cost of those things and family, which they left to follow Him. Jesus then said a phrase which He says again in reverse order after the parable, "the first will be last; and the last first" (Matt. 19:30; 20:16). Obviously the disciples are one or the other of these groups. One needs to resist importing Jew and Gentile issues into this parable and phrase, since everything in the near context is presented without any Gentile allusion. Additionally, there is no extended Kingdom ministry of the prophets in the context so that this phrase might grow out of the preceding issue and events, meaning: that the wealthy (first) will be last place in the Kingdom and those who have given up everything (last) will be first place in the Kingdom with responsibilities and benefits; which further encourages the disciples. However, there is no evidence that the rich young man enters Kingdom, for he does not follow Jesus but instead leaves grieving (Matt. 19:22). Jesus responds that it is hard for a rich man to enter into the Kingdom of heaven, illustrating it by the idea of a camel going through the eye of a needle as being easier than for a rich man to enter the Kingdom. The disciples recognize the impossibility of this.[31] Jesus corrects them by saying that with man it is impossible, but with God all things are possible. So that the impression the context brings is not that the rich will necessarily be in a low position in the Kingdom, but that they tend to not

29 Franklin D. Roosevelt, Address to the Young Democratic Clubs (1935), contained in *American Poletical Rhetoric: A Reader,* edited by Peter Lawler and Robert Schaefer (Lanham: Rowan & Littlefield, 2001), p. 184.

30 Douglas Kennard, *Messiah Jesus*, pp. 229–31.

31 Exegetes who reduce the extravagance of Jesus' simile fail to appreciate the authenticity of Jesus' idioms within rabbinic parallels: *b. Ber.* 55b and *b. B. Mes.* 38b which portray the impossible by describing an elephant going through a needle, and *b. Yebam.* 45a which describes a camel dancing in a tiny area.

even make it into the Kingdom in the first place. Such an orientation to wealth would be very telling in the work place, and place one at grave risk with regard to Kingdom. Mark 10:29 and Luke 13:30 do not have a subsequent parable and reiteration of the idea of the last being first, so they tend to reinforce that this text is emphasizing that the disciples shall gain great place and the rich will be last. The word "last" ( ) in Luke 13:30 is best seen in that context as those Jesus casts away as evildoers who weep and gnash their teeth (Luke 13:23–30). Only those who enter by the narrow door gain entrance into the Kingdom, though others may try and be damned.

In this context in Matthew, Jesus tells a parable likening the Kingdom to be like a land owner who hired laborers for his vineyard at the wage of a denarius[32] for the day (Matt. 20:1–16). He then hired laborers at noon, three and five p.m. for "whatever is right." They trust the integrity of the landowner. The pay time fits within the Jewish pattern of eschatological judgment in which what one does in life matters.[33] The last group chronologically hired, got paid first, on to the first hired. They all received the same wage regardless of when they commenced their work. When the first group hired (which might stand for those such as the disciples) noticed that the wage was the same, they protested about the excessive burden they bore. The landowner clarifies that he has done no wrong and that they have the contracted amount, and the landowner is within his rights to pay others as generous as he desires. This landowner justifies such generosity which probably has the implication that wealthy Kingdom bound who hire others should demonstrate such generosity toward those they hire. Such owners should not just be known for fairness but evidence their Kingdom bound orientation by their generosity when able. Other parallel Jewish parables also make the point that a landowner may be as generous with his pay as he desires.[34] Presumably, Jesus is telling the disciples this parable to keep them from envy over His generosity or that they should cultivate contentment with their wages in their work before Kingdom.[35] Blomberg claims that this parable informs the reader about Kingdom benefits from God as landowner with more than two groups involved develops three points to be obtained as follows:

> (1) From the earlier groups of workers, one learns that none of God's people will be treated unfairly...(2) From the last

32 The common price for a day laborer; *Tob.* 5.14; Pliny, *N.H.* 33.3; Tacitus, *Ann.* 1.17; cf. Davies and Allison, *Matthew*, 3:72.

33 *4 Ezra* 8.33; *T. Abr. A* 12–13; Gk. *Apoc. Ezra* 1.14; *m. 'Abot* 3.15; *t, Qidd.* 1.14; *b. Qidd.* 39b.

34 E.g., *Sifra* on Lev. 26.9 and *Eccl. R.* 5.11.5 tell of a generous employer who paid an exceptional amount in response to an exceptionally able laborer.

35 Such envy was understood in Israel as having an evil eye (Prov. 23:1–6; 28:22; Matt. 20:15).

> group of workers comes the principle that many seemingly less deserving people will be treated generously, due to the sovereign, free choice of God. (3) From the unifying role of the master stems the precious truth that all true disciples are equal in God's eyes.[36]

Whereas, Amy-Jill Levine develops this parable as instruction for how Kingdom bound disciples should function in the work place as owners and workers. If Jesus' disciples have means then they should be known for generosity to their workers. If Jesus' disciples are employed then they should be known for contentment with their wages and work assignments.[37] Both meanings fit the context which develops wealth, Kingdom, generosity and contentment. Here the last (; Matt. 20:12, 14, 16) are chronologically the last group into the labor force who gain a generous payment and may be paid first. Whereas, the first labored earlier and are paid chronologically last. This group (perhaps the disciples) need to watch out and excise envy from their lives. In their envying the last ( ) position they might be warned of the risk of damnation, keeping all statements of "the first will be last and the last will be first" with the same meaning (Matt. 19:30; 20:16; Mark 10:31; Luke 13:23–30). At any rate, it is a warning to the disciples not to envy.

Returning to the wisdom context of Ecclesiastes, it is best to work in partnership with others (Eccl. 4:4, 9–12). That is, skilled workers are spurred to workaholicism or alienation by rivalry, which is not the answer. However, in a partnership, the strengths of each make the team stronger by bringing assistance, warmth, and protection. Here the golden rule provides generosity in the work place.[38]

Complimenting this generosity is the wisdom adage of "Iron sharpens iron, so one man sharpens another" (Prov. 27:17). The precision, awareness, skills, and competence that a specialist brings to a team can sharpen the whole team if the community and individuals welcome and encourage these contributions. When this is done everybody in the team is made stronger. For example, peer review enables whittling tools to be sharpened to the precision of expert surgery. However, peer review can also be undertaken by those in related fields. When that happens, peer review fosters clear communication into these other contexts than that of the expert, thus increasing the usability of the specialist's contribution to the team. Within such a loving community, such peer review presses everyone on the team to give their best, which results in both depth and

---

36 Craig Blomberg, *Interpreting the Parables* (Downers Grove: InterVarsity Press, 1990), p. 224.

37 Amy-Jill Levine presented this view in her paper "Standard and Poor: The Economic Index of Parables" at the Greer-Heard Point-Counterpoint Forum: The Message of Jesus, New Orleans Baptist Seminary, Feb. 27, 2010

38 Johnson, *Grace*, p. 83.

breadth of all the members of the team. In fact, such tough love removes dullness and presses beyond the theoretical into that of consistent thought, communication and living.

Cooperate with God in your work.[39] Eve acknowledged that in the getting of kids she was cooperating with God (Gen. 4:1). Paul's fellow-worker, Epaphroditus risked his life in doing the work of Christ, thus cooperating with Him (Phil. 2:25, 30). The fact of doing work according to God's design framework is a part of cooperating with God. Additionally, the practice of generously giving back to God reflects that same sentiment (e.g., Gen. 4:4). Furthermore, God as Spirit can source and enable our work (e.g., Ex. 31:3–5; Judg. 3:10; 1 Sam. 16:13; 23:2). Everything in the New Covenant is grounded in the Spirit's gifts (Rom. 8:5–27; 12:3-8; 1 Cor. 12–14; Eph. 4:11–13; 1 Pet. 4:7–11).[40] One of the primary issues in "giftedness" is the recognition that God sources this ability and so we work with gratitude to Him for whatever we can do. Such work fostered by the Spirit is cooperating with God. Of course, this giftedness has the direct implication that we do our work with the virtues that the Spirit also fosters and in obedience to His commands (e.g., Gal. 5:22–26). Additionally, in the work force it makes great sense if at all possible to employ people where their strengths reside.[41] Likewise, we should hire a team whose strengths provide a complimentary fit, rather than duplicate each other.

Our work ( ) should be full of good works ( )[42] (1 Cor. 15:58; Eph. 2:10; Col. 1:10; 2 Thess. 2:17; 1 Tim. 6:18; 2 Tim. 2:21; Tit. 3:8, 14; Heb. 13:21; Jas. 2:14–26). We should work with generous intentional labor to help others because it identifies us as being Christ's kingdom people, and this is taken into consideration as part of God's gracious eschatological assessment of our destiny (Matt. 10:40–42; 25:34–46; 2 Tim. 4:14; Rev. 20:12–13). That is, our 'good works' shows us to be an expression of His good work in us, which people God blesses everlastingly.[43]

The everlasting Kingdom is presented with a continuity of work. Isaiah describes the kingdom as including an abundance of agricultural and commercial produce (Isa. 2:4; 25:6; 32:20; 60:5–11; 62:8–9;

---

39 Doug Kennard, *The Classical Christian God* (Lewiston: The Edwin Mellon Press, 2002), pp. 135–166, but also developed in pp. 185–204.

40 Volf, *Work in the Spirit*, pp. 111–120; Ernest Kaseman, "Amt und Gemeinde im Neuen Testament," and "Gottesdienstim Alltag der Welt." in *Exegetische Versuche und Beswnungen* (Göttingen: Vanderhoeck & Ruprecht, 1970), vol. 1, pp. 109–134 and vol. 2, pp. 198–204, especially p. 204.

41 Cf. Marcus Buckingham, *First, Break all the Rules: What the World's Greatest Managers do Differently* (New York: Simon & Schuster, 1999); *Now, Discover Your Strengths* (New York: Free Press, 2001).

42 This is a fitting reminder since our occupational work ( ) is the same word for good works of these passages.

43 Weber, *The Protestant Ethic and the Spirit of Capitalism*, p. 238 points out that work demonstrates reassurance of salvation.

65:22). Presumably, those in Kingdom will do the work to handle this abundance. Additionally, Jesus tells the parable of the talents to postpone some kingdom expectations and to remind the disciples of their need for faithful stewardship now (Matt. 25:14–30; Luke 19:11–27). For those who hear the "well done good and faithful servant" will also have increased responsibility in Kingdom; "because you have been faithful in a very little thing, I will put you in charge of ten cities." Such reward with increased responsibility is a very Jewish perspective.[44] Likewise, Paul reflects this everlasting life responsibility with the metaphor of co-reigning with Christ (Rom. 8:17). Therefore our final destiny is continuing to work in meaningful stewardship under God's sovereignty forever.

44 *m.'Abot* 4.2; *b. Ber.* 11b.

13. Putting the Method Together

Community in Christ is too great and precious to put at risk. We live in community and should think within community, which means that in expressing ideas, we should float them for peer review within the community. If we disagree with another we should give the other the honor of meeting with them in private for dialog and understanding. Hopefully, the subjectivity of one perspective is aided by the subjectivity of another perspective so that both partners are aided by the joint adventure. It is only appropriate to publicize critique when the other acknowledges that you have understood them correctly. To do otherwise destroys dialog. The goal is not to win a battle about facts. The goal is to woo the whole of the body of Christ to the unity and full maturity of Christ. To do otherwise is to destroy love and community for truth, and that is too costly, we do not have to choose between them. We can love God and the other, while committed to truth. But this requires humility and respect toward others rather than hubris in thinking that I have a corner on the truth.

Critical Realism identifies that I wish my theology to operate with precision. With regard to how epistemology works, a critical realist approach is more nuanced and informed about the contributions which philosophy has made. With regards to source material, critical realism more precisely represents what texts say in their context and encourages warranting our conclusions by the details of the text. For these reasons this approach is gaining adherents, like N. T. Wright and James Dunn, among those working within historical Jesus studies. With regard to the Biblical text, it is an attempt to represent the best of the scholarship available as it tries to represent the Biblical text within its context. With regard to theology, critical realism recognizes and reflects that every theological statement is in time and context. Thus a critical realist theology should utilize the best scholarship of the time and be connected to the theologian's communal context. That is, the divinely authoritative message of the Bible is brought sensitively to the theological context of application. Science would then use an appropriate method that likewise reflects the current status of the field as permitted within the grid established by the Bible and such critical realist theology.

The particular approach which I prefer within critical realism is that put forth by Lakatos because his view is more nuanced and accurate with rival traditions that continue to challenge each other, each being embraced by their respective communities. This approach also argues against static and dated traditions which Biblical scholarship moves beyond. Such traditions are degenerative in that they do not keep pace with scholarship broadly or even evangelically accepted scholarship. The Lakatos approach encourages perpetually trying to improve and work for the most accurate and comprehensive understanding of a theological idea as connected to its sources of support. Such progressive research programs that accurately and comprehensively represent the Biblical and historical sources will advance the discipline for our era and context. Such progressive models are the theological views that should be embraced, taught and refined for further progressive contributions to the discipline of theology.

The increased nuance and sensitivity present in a Thiselton-Ricoeur hermeneutic reflects this continued development within a progressive program of being faithful to the Biblical text in its context and faithfulness within a context of the scholarly communities of specialists such as in O.T., N.T. and historians of the ancient near East. As an approach it also is reflective of how literature works within us prompting a variety of affects. This level of engagement is important to stem the tide of theological hermeneutics which can be severely questioned as to whether it lets the text speak with its own voice; they sacrifice the voice of God for a tradition. We need to let the Bible speak with its own voice.

I edited a volume entitled, *The Relationship Between Epistemology, Hermeneutics, Biblical Theology and Contextualization*[1] reflecting an earlier form of this method. Grant Osborne peer reviewed this earlier volume and proposed method, affirming its purpose.

> The purpose of this book is to forge a way through the morass of options to develop a positive theory for both understanding and living truth. Epistemology deals with the possibility of discovering meaning or truth by examining both what it is and how to get there. Critical realism assumes there is a final truth to be discovered and that it is possible to understand and attain it. Hermeneutics provides the methodology for interpreting texts, for working with the process of coming-to-understanding via the statements of the text filtered through tradition, community and experience. Its goal is to develop an ethics of reading that moves from the claims of the author in a text to the needs of the readers as they study the text. This last is the task of contextualization, which brings together the three elements of J. L. Austin and John Searle in discovering the action side of hermeneutics - the locutionary (the propositional side), the illocutionary (what the text accomplishes-assertion,

1 Douglas Kennard, *The Relationship Between Epistemology, Hermeneutics, Biblical Theology and Contextualization* (Lewiston: Edwin Mellen Press, 1999).

> etc.), and the perlocutionary (the effect it produces). The task of this volume is to combine these areas from the standpoint of theology, philosophy and missiology so as to develop a working hermeneutic for the next millennium.[2]

This summary and review could summarize the present volume as well.

Biblical theology, sensitively reflective and framed by the Biblical text, becomes the major focus in this approach. This is because the Biblical text must speak with its own voice. Furthermore, even in interacting with our context, traditions and disciplines, the most valuable contributor to a theological view is that which comes with divine authority, the Biblical text. Likewise, the genre, passion and trajectory of the Biblical text should be allowed to speak so that our Biblical theology and systematics reflect this deep Biblicism and draw us in affectively with God and His Word.

Such a Biblical theology emphasis poises theology for sensitive contextualization either into our personal academic context or provides the foundation for students heading to a different mission field to have the resources to contextualize their theology there. In class, I (and other faculty members) give examples to help the student think through some of the possibilities of contextualization in alternative settings.

Concluding the prolegomena is only framing the method. Now, get along with the task of doing theology. In this volume, I provided chapters on creation, humanity and work, where Biblical theology dominated the areas of discussion, while I interacted with some of the traditional and contemporary thinkers in these fields. The message and authority was essentially Biblical, while our own context is incorporated for communications sake.

In my volume on theology proper, *The Classical Christian God,* I attempted to draw upon the resources of philosophy, physics and especially Biblical theology to elucidate how the Christian God should be conceived. So as an example of integration I would recommend that volume for its attempt to fuse a variety of sources into a unified theological statement. In the volume I argue 1) against process, and open theism, and 2) for a classical Christian God with nuance of the contemporary context. Millard Erickson peer reviewed the work and gave this brief endorsement.

> I am glad to write a brief endorsement. I think Doug Kennard has made a contribution in his book *The Classical Christian God* that needs to be heard. Doug has undertaken quite a project, of uniting both philosophical and biblical considerations, and has demonstrated the competence in both areas necessary to

2 Douglas Kennard, *The Relationship Between Epistemology, Hermeneutics, Biblical Theology and Contextualization*, pp. i–ii. There was also a positive extended review in *Andrews University Seminary Studies* 41:2(2003):322–27.

> do this. My impression is that this is an attempt to show how the two areas of consideration fit well together when discussing the nature of God. Doug has obvious familiarity, not only with the classical but also with contemporary authorities in philosophy, and has also developed well the biblical materials. The chapter on freedom and sovereignty seems to me to be especially strong. Such a combination of knowledge of the philosophical literature and biblical exegesis is not common these days.[3]

However, I believe theologians need to develop these kinds of expertise, for it is in the integration between Biblical theology, philosophy, tradition and context that systematics best delivers its gems. This present volume has made a prolonged argument and demonstration of this kind of critical realist integration.

However, beyond methodology issues, the content of theology begins with God. As an expression of a model of God, my *Classical Christian God* tries to frame the beginning of a love relationship that includes communal growth with the Love of our lives.

With the explosion of availability of second Temple sources in recent decades, a theologian also needs to at least follow the experts into this additional resource as it shines light on the Biblical text. For example, when Marv Pate and I were writing our eschatology volume, *Deliverance Now and Not Yet*, the issue was less the philosophical and more the critical realist use of Biblical theology and extra-Biblical sources.[4] We follow Albert Schweitzer's view of mystically dying with Christ and Merkabah mysticism at Qumran to propose that the New Testament pictures Christ's atonement with mystical implications for how the Christian relates to tribulation. These pictures set up three forms of the New Testament eschatology: consistent, inaugurated, and realized. We approach each of these from a Biblical theology point of view to unpack the unique thrusts of the Biblical authors. With regard to the relationship of the Church and the Great Tribulation: 1) Paul and John present deliverance now (realized eschatology), and 2) the rest of the New Testament presents deliverance not yet in two categories-2a) Mark, James, Peter, and Jude present deliverance not yet (consistent eschatology), and 2b) Matthew, Luke-Acts, Hebrews, and Revelation portray deliverance as now and not yet (inaugurated eschatology). This Biblical theology sensitivity of letting each author's voice speak is reflective of our critical realist methodology. Taken together, the

3 Millard Erickson, "Preface" in Douglas Kennard, *The Classical Christian God. Toronto Studies in Theology Volume 86* (Lewiston: Mellen Press, 2002).

4 C. Marvin Pate & Douglas W. Kennard *Deliverance Now and Not Yet: The New Testament and the Great Tribulation. Studies in Biblical Literature vol. 54* (New York: Peter Lang, 2003, 2005).

Christian's experience of the Messianic woes and mystical expression of the Kingdom prompts us to long deeply for the climactic expression of the Kingdom of God. Such an orientation toward Kingdom draws theology out toward the affective, hoped for goal. Thus this volume is not merely a book end on the other side of theology from God; rather, it provides an open-ended hope and journey with the God we love. Brant Pitre peer reviewed this volume for three pages and positioned his own work in its wake, concluding that *Deliverance Now and Not Yet* "is by far the most detailed, extensive, and illuminating treatment of the entire topic of the eschatological tribulation penned to date."[5] Additionally, Christopher McMahon carefully peer reviewed the book for three pages in the *Review of Biblical Literature* for the Society of Biblical Literature, and then concluded that we were careful, historically accurate, contextual in analysis, consistent, interacting with the current and traditional views, thorough and provocative. His concluding paragraph summarized his evaluation.

> Pate and Kennard argue consistently and boldly for their thesis, and they offer a detailed study that does a great service for those interested in the question of apocalyptic eschatology in the New Testament. While some readers will find aspects of their argument difficult to accept, the thoroughness of their argument demands attention. The most pleasing aspect of the work may be its retrieval of Schweitzer's account of the connection between Paul's eschatology and his mysticism. The work's thorough engagement with contemporary New Testament scholarship will make the book an important contribution to the field.[6]

These appraisals summarize the values that critical realism seeks to provide as a method for doing scholarly work in theology and in New Testament studies.

I continue in this same method to fill in the means toward the Kingdom by focusing on the King. In my book, *Messiah Jesus: Christology in His Day and Ours*,[7] a Christology from below shows what the O.T. predicted, what second Temple Jewish expectations hoped for, and how Jesus fleshed out these expectations and modified them to more clearly show who He is. This is melded with a Christology from above

5 Brant Pitre, *Jesus, the Tribulation and the End of the Exile* (Tübingen/Grand Rapids: Mohr Siebeck/Baker, 2005), p. 21, with discussion on pp. 20–23.

6 Christopher McMahon review of Pate and Kennard, *Deliverance Now and Not Yet: The New Testament and the Great Tribulation* available throughhttp://www.sblonline.org/bookdetail.asp?TitleID=3825 published 6/6/04; cf. *New Testament Abstracts* 48(1,'04): 190–1 for another peer review.

7 Douglas Kennard, *Messiah Jesus: Christology in His Day and Ours* (New York: Peter Lang, 2008).

presented by a few of the Biblical authors as they unpack the Deity and incarnational life of Jesus. Thus, again this work is especially unpacking a Biblical theology of Jesus sensitive to each author and context. Craig Blomberg has reviewed *Messiah Jesus* on the Denver Seminary web page[8] including the following comments which support that I am a practitioner of critical realism and Biblical theology:

> If there is both a unifying theme as well as a distinctive to Kennard's numerous self-contained chapters, it involves his copious references to Jewish backgrounds. The most relevant of these are discussed in the text itself, but the endnotes after each chapter are a gold mine of additional information with countless references to both Second Temple Jewish and post-Christian rabbinic literature.
>
> Some of the stronger treatments in the book include Kennard's studies on faith in the Synoptic Gospels, the ways in which Jesus made clean the unclean rather than contracting impurity from them, the distinctively Hebraic style and form of numerous teachings of Christ (especially his ethical injunctions), the intentional devices by which Jesus trained his disciples, the interpenetration of the various persons of the Trinity in the Johannine Farewell Discourse and Jesus' final prayer and their implications for believers' relationship with the Godhead, a *via media* in interpreting the parables (between detailed allegorizing and none at all) based on what the original audiences would have most likely understood, Jesus' emphasis on the relationship between God forgiving us and our forgiving others, a preterist-futurist approach to the eschatological discourse, the intertestamental developments of the concept of sacrifice, the centrality of Jesus' role as King in the Passion narratives, the impossibility of fairly excising final judgment from the message and mission of Jesus, the unity and diversity in Acts in the various speeches that present Jesus himself as the Gospel, and the evidence for Jesus as the God-man (still within a fully Jewish context) that would prepare the way for expanded Christological affirmations among the Patristic writers without distorting earlier generations' less elaborate beliefs.

The blind peer review of *Messiah Jesus* also affirmed the critical realist use of sources.

---

8 Craig Blomberg, Review: www.denverseminary.edu/article/messiah-jesus-christology-in-his-day-and-ours

> The author's discussion throughout is anchored in original sources and shows impressive facility with scholarly primary and secondary works. In fact, these form the backbone of the discussion, giving it both depth and breadth in the topics raised by the author.[9]

To illustrate the theological expression of each chapter into the Houston Graduate School of Theology context, I complete each chapter in an electronic form for the students by discussing art, literature and song as they complement or contrast with these Biblical images of Christ.[10]

So a critical realist theology done well is precise, coherent, grounded in epistemic foundations and corroborative historical sources, Biblical, current, contextualized, integrative, clear communication and sensitive to affective impact. That is what I am trying to do in this volume and my other books as well.

Science should mirror this task with the appropriate methods of their respective discipline. So my hope for this volume is that science can be seen as nested within the epistemic warrant and Biblically informed theological method that I have set out here.

9 Blind Peer Review Reader's Report for Peter Lang Publishing.

10 http://www.hgst.edu/academics/faculty/douglas-kennard/kennard/

Index

CORE Issues in Creation

Established in 2005, the *CORE Issues* monograph series presents high quality scholarly work from or related to a young-age creation perspective. This monograph series is not for the publication of scholarly critiques of alternative positions (other venues exist for that kind of publication). Rather, *CORE Issues* has been created to publish any monograph in any discipline (philosophy, theology, physics, geology, biology, archaeology, linguistics, etc., etc.) which substantially contributes to the systematic development of a positive, young-age creation model. Original monographs will thoroughly review the conventional and creationist literature on the subject, offer a constructive interpretation of the subject's data, integrate well with other disciplines as the model is constructed, and advance creation model development. Other monographs offer reprints, compendia, or translations of significant historical works that are currently unavailable. *CORE Issues* is peer-reviewed and will strive for the very highest scholarship standards. *CORE Issues* is a joint publication of the Center for Origins Research at Bryan College and Wipf & Stock Publishers.

CORE Issues does not publish works written only by Bryan College faculty but encourages outside submissions. Researchers may submit monograph proposals (full manuscripts are not accepted) to CORE either electronically at core@bryancore.org or by regular mail:

CORE Issues editor
Bryan College 7802
721 Bryan Drive
Dayton, TN 37321

CHRIST ABOVE ALL
BRYAN COLLEGE

CORE
CENTER FOR ORIGINS RESEARCH

Previous Volumes in the *CORE Issues* Series

1. A Creationist Review and Preliminary Analysis of the History, Geology, Climate, and Biology of the Galápagos Islands, by Wood (2005)
2. Johannes Buteo's The Shape and Capacity of Noah's Ark, trans. by Griffith & Monette (2008)
3. Animal and Plant Baramins, by Wood (2008)
4. Christian Perspectives on the Origin of Species, edited by Garner (2009)
5. Genesis Kinds: Creationism and the Orign of Species, edited by Wood & Garner (2009)